Managing Recreation, Parks, and Leisure Services:

An Introduction

Christopher R. Edginton
University of Northern Iowa

Susan D. Hudson
University of Northern Iowa

Samuel V. Lankford
University of Hawaii

Sagamore Publishing
Champaign, Illinois

Production Coordinator: Janet Wahlfeldt
Cover Design: Charles L. Peters

Library of Congress Catalog Card Number: 00-107165
ISBN: 1-57167-478-0

Printed in the United States

9 8 7 6 5 4 3 2

*To the future managers of the recreation,
parks and leisure services profession.*

Contents

Preface

The management of leisure service organizations is sophisticated, challenging, and at times complex, requiring a high order of ability. Leisure service managers are sought in a variety of venues for their ability to enhance and improve the quality of life for individuals. Promoting greater community livability through leisure services and programs, natural resource development, and tourism activities, leisure service managers have created a host of social innovations and institutions that have enhanced the well-being of humankind. With a focus on life satisfaction, leisure service managers have played a major role in transforming North American society.

We can think of the management of leisure service organizations as being both an art and a science. It is an art because it involves crafting environments to sustain, nourish, and support the best efforts of people. Relationships between and among people are fluid by nature. No management system can fully account for the wide variability that comes from the complexity of interaction that arises between individuals and their environment. Thus, management often involves the use of one's intuition, wisdom, emotional intelligence, and ability to assist people to learn and grow in new and different ways. The management of leisure service organizations can also be thought of as a science. It is a science in that methods, strategies, and procedures can be drawn on to assist in planning, decision making, and other elements involved in managing leisure service organizations. Mathematical modeling, simulations, and computer analysis all provide examples of the scientific nature of management. Successful leisure service managers are those who understand what works and how, and when to act in order to move an organization forward in a productive fashion.

It has been suggested that the half-life of management knowledge is about seven years. In other words, half of the knowledge and information that we use to practice our profession will become obsolete in a relative short span of time. In other areas, the half-life of knowledge is projected to change even more rapidly. It has been over 20 years since the first edition of this book (originally titled *Productive Management of Leisure Service Organizations*) was conceptualized, written, and published. Much has changed in the last 20 years in the way in which we conduct business in the field. Consider three critical changes in our environment. First, 20 years ago the technological and information revolution had just begun and was incredibly accelerated by the advent of personal computers. Today, we access and move information via the Internet at lightning speed. We have more and more information accessible to us instantaneously. Second, the nature of the workforce is changing dramatically. Not only is it more diverse, but also it is better educated and more focused on finding meaningful, worthwhile, and satisfying work opportunities. In fact, there has been a basic shift in our thinking, in which we have recognized the importance of human resources in our organizations. Last, we have seen a basic revision of our economy. Based on a new set of assumptions, our economy is now a knowledge-based one. It is focused on a new set of products, services, and ways of producing these benefits for those we serve.

In the past several decades, we have seen a revolution in business and government, and in the growth of nonprofit, nongovernmental organizations. Beginning with the passage of Proposition 13 in California in 1978, government organizations have been challenged to reinvent themselves to find new and different ways to effectively meet the needs of the citizens of any given community. After slow economic growth rates and high inflation in the 1960s and 1970s, the 1980s and 1990s were decades of stellar growth. Commercial and private leisure service organizations have been challenged to rethink and reengineer dramatically their methods of management. Greater emphasis has been placed on providing services of higher quality and value that are customized to meet the individual needs of patrons. The emphasis is no longer on providing standardized services, but on offering premium services that can be customized to meet individual interests. The explosive growth of nonprofit, nongovernmental organizations has emerged as a result of the desire to enhance community life. These types of organizations have become important not only in promoting the welfare of communities, but also in improving their livability. Increasingly, we seek higher-quality life experiences, and nonprofit, nongovernmental organizations have supported the quest of North Americans in their search for meaning and enhanced well-being.

As indicated, one of the most important developments of the latter part of the 21st century was the stunning growth in the number of knowledge-based workers. Knowledge and information have now become the currency of contemporary organizations. This fact has made the human resources of any organization its most important capital. The nourishment and encouragement of any organization's human resources will be paramount to its productivity and success. In the first edition of this book, we made a conscious effort to emphasize the management of human resources. That theme is also a feature of this current edition.

Acknowledgments

As is the case with any project, *Managing Recreation, Parks, and Leisure Services* is the result of the effort and creative endeavors of numerous individuals. Perhaps most important when viewed in the long term have been the contributions of John G. Williams. John served as the co-author of the first edition of the textbook. His conceptual influence—indeed his words—remain a part of this current effort. A distinguished professional with service in Sunnyvale, California; Miami–Dade County, Florida; Baltimore, Maryland; and Decatur, Georgia; We thank John for his commitment to the profession and for his contributions to this book and to the original publication.

The second edition of *Managing Recreation, Parks, and Leisure Services* would not have been possible without the persistence of Joe Bannon. Once Joe has decided that a project is to be developed, he approaches the effort with great élan and tenacity, with an almost single-minded determination. Pushing, pulling, and cajoling, his enthusiasm for this project literally willed the book to its completion. Joe was always available, always ready to assist, and always prepared to provide his wisdom, counsel, and positive advice. We thank Joe for his constant support and attention to our careers and to the projects that give meaning to our professional endeavors.

Numerous professionals in the park and recreation field responded to our call for documentation and examples from their organizations. We greatly appreciate the time that they took to provide us with information, and we thank them for their contributions. Those providing support include: Ken Winslade, Corporation of the City of New Westminster, British Columbia; Patrick J. O'Brien, East Bay Regional Park District, Oakland, California; Sue Occhowy, Parks and Recreation Cultural Services Department, Burnaby, British Columbia; Alekxos Stater, Parks and Recreation Cultural Services Department, Burnaby, British Columbia; Steve Wurm, Boys & Girls Club of Waterloo, Iowa; Ward Stubbs, Department of Human and Leisure Services, Cedar Falls, Iowa; Steve Wallace, Black Hawk County Conservation Board, Waterloo, Iowa; Ron Dodd, Joliet Park District, Joliet, Illinois; Dan Plaza, Willamalane Park and Recreation District, Springfield, Oregon; Jim Colley, Parks, Recreation, and Library Department, Phoenix, Arizona; Tom Reardon, Waterloo Leisure Services Commission, Waterloo, Iowa; Jon Westhoff, Family YMCA of Black Hawk County, Iowa; Barbara Heller, Elk Grove Park District, Elk Grove, Illinois; Jeff Hovarter, City of Battle Creek Parks & Recreation Department, Battle Creek, Michigan; Bill Clevenger, Decatur Park District, Decatur, Illinois; Don Cochran, Maryland Capital Park and Planning Commission, Silver Spring, Maryland; Harvey Faust, Parks and Recreation, Germantown, Tennessee; Dale Larsen, City of Phoenix Parks, Recreation and Library Department, Phoenix, Arizona; Nancy MacCartney, Parks, Recreation, and Community Services Department, Reno, Nevada; Graham Skea, Department of Parks, Recreation, and Conservation, Orange City, New York; and Sandra Whitmore, Recreation and Parks, Alexandria, Virginia; We would also like to thank Joyce Spoehr, Willy Ching, Arthur Wong, Ellen Katoda, and Toni Robinson, Department of Parks and Recreation, Honolulu, Hawaii; Mariane Feenstra, Val Morgan, John Buck, Tamara Horajo, and Bob Straub, Department of Parks and Recreation, Maui County, Hawaii; Bernard Carvalho, Department of Recreation, Kauai County, Hawaii; Edward Yokoyama, Hawaii County Parks and Recreation, Hawaii; Bobby Stivers, Honolulu YMCA, Hawaii; Wally Iaea, U. S. Army, Hawaii.

To complete a writing project of this magnitude, one needs the support of individuals willing to assist in the actual compiling of the information as well as in the writing of the document. Throughout the project, Lynda Moore has been a steady organizational force in the project. Lynda was particularly adept at managing the clerical and other support functions of this project in a low-key, calm, relaxed fashion. When juxtaposed against the fanatic pace at which the authors work, this enabled the project to flow smoothly. We thank Lynda for being a great support, a good-hearted person, and one who is also dedicated to our success. Other staff members assisting in the project included Sharon Graber, Karen Peterson, Nicki Pals, Konni Haverman, Brooke Johnson, and Eugene McClelland.

Also, we would like to thank the support staff at Sagamore Publishing. These included: Susan Krusemark, Editor; Janet Wahlfeldt, Production Coordinator; Charles L. Peters, Graphic Designer; Doug Sanders, Director of Educational Sales, and Joseph J. Bannon, Publisher. We appreciate their efforts and value their creative contributions in the development and marketing of the book.

Last, we would like to extend our warmest appreciation to our family members. Susan Edginton, David Edginton, Carole Flack, Tom Flack, and granddaughter Hanna Michelle Flack have all been an inspiration and provided strong support to the senior author's creative endeavors. They have provided a bubble of time and opportunity to enable me to pursue my writing and other academic efforts. Gloria Hudson, "mom" to all of us, is a grand person. She has given unconditional support to her daughter and imbued in her the qualities of hard work, integrity, and a strong commitment and caring for others. Jill, Jordan, and Jessie Lankford have provided great support for this and other professional activities. We thank all of these individuals and value their love and commitment to our well-being and success.

Christopher R. Edginton
Susan D. Hudson
Samuel V. Lankford

Chapter

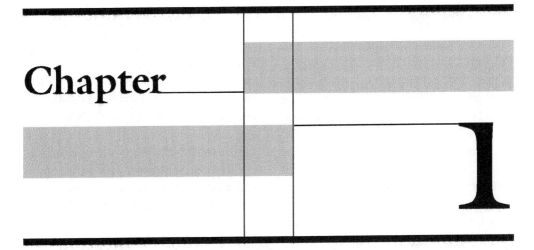

The Leisure Service Manager and the Management System
A 21st Century Perspective

The University of Northern Iowa's national award-winning Wellness/Recreation Center reflects a bold, 21st century approach to the management of campus recreation and wellness services.

Introduction

Over the past 150 years, a number of social movements and institutions have emerged. One of the concepts to emerge that has been most beneficial to humankind has been the rise of management. Rarely has there been an institution emerging so rapidly that has had such an impact on our society as the spread of manage- ment ideas, concepts, and practices. In less than two centuries, the application of management theories and practices has literally transformed the way that we think, live, and play. The basic social, cultural, economic, and environmental fabric of our society has been dramatically trans- formed.

Another of the most significant changes that has occurred in the last 150 years has been the way we view and conceptualize work. At the beginning of the 20th century, most individuals worked as domestic servants, farmers, or in factories as laborers. In such occupations, individuals often worked 60 to 70 hours per week with little time for leisure. Today, the workforce is far different than it was in the early 1900s in North America. Individuals involved in agriculture represent approximately 3 percent of our workforce, those involved in manufacturing are about 18 percent of the workforce, and the remaining individuals are involved in what could be defined as information-based or service-related activities (Drucker, 1994). What has accomplished this great transformation of the workforce? That transformation and its resulting contributions to improving the quality of life North Americans have, without question, due to the rise of management. As Peter Drucker (1994:54) reminds us, "the main ingredient in the transformation of society has been of the rise of management." He maintains that "for the first time in history we have been able to focus the efforts of a large number of knowledgeable and skilled individuals on improving the well being and welfare of society as a whole."

A third significant change in the lives of North Americans has been the substantial improvement to the population in improving its basic quality of life. Today individuals live longer, are healthier, have more discretionary time and money, and in general achieve higher levels of self-actualization than were available 150 years ago. In the late 1800s and early 1900s, industrial society produced urban crowding, child labor, squalor and poverty, and un-

healthy and often unsanitary living conditions for individuals. These conditions were met with a host of social reforms that led to improved conditions involving the creation of "a host of innovative social institutions including parks, open spaces, and other amenities such as recreation centers, public baths, settlement houses, playgrounds, child care programs, and services for older persons in response to the conditions of a new social era" (Edginton, 1998:2).

Leisure Service Managers and Social Transformation

Daniel Bell (1968), Alvin Toffler (1980), and John Naisbitt (1982) have all pointed to the significant transformation that society is undergoing as we move to the 21st century. Writing in *Toward the Year 2000*, Bell (1968) initially introduced the idea that we were dramatically changing, moving from an industrial-oriented society to what he called post-industrial society. Toffler suggested in the book, *The Third Wave*, that history can be divided into three eras—the agricultural era, the industrial era, and the technological era. Naisbitt, author of *Megatrends*, wrote that we are amidst a major paradigm shift and that we are evolving into an information-based society. These transformations are changing the very nature of the way that we live our lives.

As professionals, leisure service managers are involved in the process of creating social transformations. This process involves creating or reinventing social institutions that promote some social interest. Another term for this effort is the notion of "social reconstruction." As leisure service managers, our work is focused on transforming behavior internally within organizations and externally within society as a whole. The role of the manager becomes that of helping an organization and society to mobilize its resources and to focus these in such a way as to promote social reform. Often the role of the leisure service manager is one of being a social critic. The leisure service manager establishs, (with others) a vision for social change, not merely the establishment of organizational goals. In this sense, leisure service managers work toward helping to change not only an organization, but also to change community structures. Social transformation, in the sense of promoting community life, helps to empower individuals so that their lives are enriched, their well-being enhanced, and in general, the quality of their lives is improved.

As indicated, a key component in the social transformation from the agricultural era to the industrial era and now to the information age has been an increased focus on improving the quality of life. At the heart of this social transformation in improving the quality of life for North Americans has been the work of leisure service managers. As Edginton (1998:2) has noted, "we are a profession of developers, builders, and creators of hope." Further, he states (1998:2) that leisure service managers

> "have transformed American society in the last 150 years with a minimum of attention, friction, or even public acknowledgment for our efforts...We have created a degree of social equity by offering programs and services for the masses that were formerly available only to a few. We have encouraged a conservation and preservation ethic that has increased the likelihood

that tomorrow's children will have access to our precious environmental resources."

Without question, the work of leisure service managers has been instrumental in the process of social change in America in the past 150 years. The efforts of individuals such as Frederick Law Olmsted , Jane Addams, Joseph Lee, Mabel Peters, Luther and Charlotte Gulick, Henry Curtis, Aldo Leopold, and others were not only works of great social vision, but also constituted great management efforts. Again, as Edginton et al. (1998:3) note:

> "Olmsted directed what at that time was the largest public works project in the history of the United States: the development of Central Park in New York City. He supervised and directed the work of 3600 employees (Hall, 1995:69). Jane Addams directed a social enterprise—Hull House—founded in 1898 in an old mansion on Chicago's South Halstead Street. "By 1910, Hull House had grown into an imposing complex of 13 buildings that covered nearly a city block and served more than 9000 people weekly. By the 1920s, Hull House had expanded into fully developed complex programs, each with its own staff of experienced leaders" (Johnson, 1989:1). Ten years after beginning his career with the U.S. Forest Service, Leopold was appointed as Assistant District Forester in Charge of Operations. He was responsible for overseeing and evaluating the day-to-day functions—personnel, construction, fire control, roads and trails, other permanent improvements, public re-

lations, recreation, timber management, land acquisition and exchange, supplies and equipment, grazing, and watershed maintenance—on 20 million acres of Forest Service land. (Meine, 1988:175). It was in the context of his professional work as a manager that "Leopold saw in the eyes of the wolf what he would describe years later as 'a fierce green fire'" (1988:94). This was the transformational moment in his life that seared Leopold's commitment to ecology and his distillation of a strong land ethic."

It is evident that we have a rich tradition and historical foundation on which to draw. The historical work of previous leisure service managers has enabled the movement toward an idea of social reform to became a broadly integrated institutionalized set of programs, services, areas, facilities, and structures dedicated to meeting the leisure needs of North Americans. Knowledge of the experiences of these early leisure service managers can help provide an understanding of the management challenges and strategies used to advance concepts related to parks, recreation, and leisure in North America.

21st Century Management: A New Paradigm

The coming of the 21st century provides an opportunity to gain a new perspective on the work of individuals serving as managers of leisure service organizations. As we move from one era to the next—the agricultural to the industrial to the knowledge-based—the basic assumptions of how we live our lives, work and play change. The same case could be made for the way we manage the work of people in organizations.

A paradigm can be thought of as a conceptual framework or a way of thinking. Thomas Kuhn (1970) introduced the idea of a paradigm, suggesting that the term may be defined as a model, a framework, a way of thinking, or a scheme for understanding reality. It is a way of explaining a complex process, idea, or pattern of behavior. Drucker (1999:3) suggests that a paradigm helps us understand the basic assumptions about reality. They are basic assumptions about reality that help determine what a discipline or area focuses on. Drucker concludes that management has undergone a basic paradigm shift in recent years. Table 1.1 identifies his

Table 1.1
Past and Current Management Assumptions

Past Management Assumptions	Current Management Assumptions
Management is business management.	Management is the specific and distinguished organ of any and all organizations.
There is—or there must be—one right organization.	The organization used is the one that fits the task.
There is—or must be—one right way to manage people.	One does not "manage" people. The task is to lead people, and the goal is to make productive the specific strengths and knowledge of each individual.

ideas regarding management assumptions about the past when compared with current thinking. As he points out, management is universal. Also, there is no one best organizational structure or design, and there is no one right way to manage individuals.

Another way of looking at the paradigm shift in management is through the roles and expectations of managers. Table 1.2 presents managerial roles of

trends in internationalization, information technology, diversity, and issues related to quality have led to new rules and new ways of thinking in order to ensure that organizations are successful. Increasingly, we see the call for leisure service organizations to become more flexible, agile, fluid, and customer-focused. Further, new technology and the flow and spread of information have had a dramatic impact on the manage-

Table 1.2
Past and Current Management Roles

Past Management Roles	Current Management Roles
Overseer	Cheerleader
Police person	Encourager
Controller	Facilitator
Authority figure	Coach
Order issuer	Teacher
Policy enforcer	Humanizer of policies
Punisher	Promoter of values
Manipulator	Developer of people
Dictator	Communicator
	A symbol of integrity

the past and the present. In managerial roles of the past, negative connotations were associated with control, exercise of authority, manipulation, and enforcement of obedience to policies, procedures, rules, and regulations. Contemporary management roles require a different set of expectations for leisure service managers. These roles identify the leisure service manager as an encourager, facilitator, teacher, coach, and an individual who helps clarify values and provides meaning to the work efforts of others. The contemporary manager is an individual who is committed to the development of people and assists them in their growth.

Fred Luthans (1998) supports the idea that management is undergoing a major paradigm shift. He notes that

ment of leisure service organizations. Coupled with a new perspective on what motivates people to work within organizations, especially the greater emphasis placed on engaging employees in worthwhile and meaningful work, is a new paradigm to guide the work of individuals within the leisure service organization.

We can use the model of historic social transformation established by Bell, Toffler, and Naisbitt to better understand assumptions of the agricultural, industrial, and knowledge-based eras that may have influenced or will influence the management of individuals. During the agricultural era, there were great feats of management that involved organizing the work of thousands of individuals. The building of the pyramids, the Great Wall of China, the Temples of the Mayan, Inca, and Aztec civilizations in South America, the Roman road system, and even the organization of the Greek Olympic festival all bear testament to the fact that great management efforts have taken place throughout the recorded history of humankind. These projects involved thousands of individuals in projects that were sustained over extended periods of time—decades, if not centuries. What was different in each of these eras was how we viewed individuals and organized them to promote a given enterprise. The agricultural era was dominated by an authoritarian approach. The concept of the divine right of kings gave rise to a top-down style, which subjugated individuals to the arbitrary whims of their rulers or those in power. Management in medieval times according to Machiavelli (trans. 1952), was by physical force and through dividing and conquering.

The industrial model of organization led to greater efficiency and worker productivity. Yet this model was still built upon principles of hierarchical top-down control. At the turn of the 20th century, the only industrial model available was that used by the Prussian army (Drucker, 1996). This model encouraged individuals to comply with an authority system where supreme authority rested somewhere above the ranks and responsibility consisted of obeying orders and performing those tasks inherent in one's job (Rice & Bishoprick, 1971). The model did improve upon the previous authoritarian model by creating standardized policies and procedures that provided for more order and stability within organizations. Ideas such as task differentiation and specialization, hierarchical control, insistence on loyalty to the chain of command,

span of control, recordkeeping, an emphasis on vertical interactions, and a one-to-one management style all gave rise to the opportunity to the management of bureaucratically structured and managed organizations. Capital or money was the driving force behind this management structure.

In the knowledge era, we are faced with a different set of societal conditions; therefore, the way in which we approach the management of organizations must also be rethought. Today's environment characterized by rapid discontinuous change, use of technology, and more highly educated and aware individuals has created the need for new approaches to management. Lester C. Thurow (Thurow, 1996:279), has noted that in the twenty first century "brainpower and imagination, invention and the organization of new technologies" will be the new strategic key ingredients, replacing natural resources and capital. 21st century organizations will be required to promote cooperative relationships, promote ecologically sustainable development, and capture and harness the human mind and spirit in ways that enable us to take advantage of human potential. Such organizations will engage in a continuous task reassessment, use ad hoc communication and control mechanisms, be expansive and open in the sharing of information, and employ a collaborative team management approach. As Edginton (1998:5) has written:

> "Key concepts that emerge for managing leisure service organizations in the 21st century include the ability to be visionary, to be agile, to build collaborative partnerships, to promote independent learning and growth, and to create structures that liberate individuals from

top-down, hierarchical, bureaucratic structures. Hierarchical structures prevent independent action, ad hoc networks, and, in effect, block creative solutions to problems and issues affecting leisure service organizations. Management structures of the next century will create opportunities leading to more vibrant, relevant, and meaningful leisure experiences."

As one can see, there have been dramatic shifts in the assumptions used to manage individuals in organizations in each of these eras. Obviously, there was the need for less formal organization during the agricultural era, although there was a distinct division of labor. As organizations became more complex and capable of higher levels of productivity first during the industrial era and now the knowledge-based era, new ways of thinking began to be employed to manage individuals. We will continue to see an evolution of management assumptions in the future. The 21st century will be an exciting time for leisure service managers, with many challenges and opportunities.

Management and Leisure Service Organizations

What are managers? What is management? What are characteristics of admired leaders? What do leisure service managers do? What is a leisure service organization? These are complex questions and do not necessarily yield quick and easy answers. In this section, we will provide the reader with a background to help define these and other concepts generic to management in leisure service organizations.

What Are Managers?

Leisure service managers are individuals who have the responsibility and authority for providing direction to a leisure service organization and who have the ability to move it toward its goals and objectives. They are directly responsible for much of the success or failure of an organization. Indeed, a manager's competence, as reflected in his or her skills, knowledge, and ability to move an organization forward, and in meeting the needs of those served, will be echoed in the growth and achievement of the organization (or operation). Successful managers are able to identify trends, recognize problems, resolve conflicts, use opportunities, audit poor performance, reward excellent efforts, and lead an organization to its goals. However, there is no universal definition of a manager. In fact, there is some disagreement as to whether or not we should think of the individuals in management roles in leisure service organizations as leaders or managers. Kouzes and Posner (1995:8-18) have suggested that managers are involved in the following five key activities:

1. To Challenge the Process. As Kouzes and Posner note, managers venture out; they are pioneers. Managers are never satisfied with the status quo. An important role of the leisure service manager is to inquire critically in to the conditions of humankind that have an impact on their quality of life, especially related to leisure. Leisure service managers should seek to improve the quality of life of all human beings through their critical examination of these conditions.

2. To Inspire a Shared Vision. An important, if not critical, role of leisure service managers is instilling a common vision. As Bennis and Nanus (1985:20-28) indicate, to choose a direction a manager must first have developed a mental image of a possible and desired state of the organization. This image, which may be called a vision, may be as broad as an individual's dream or as precise as a goal or mission statement. The vision provides a realistic, attractive, and credible future for the organization.

3. To Enable Others to Act. An important role of the manager is to empower others to act. Today people working in leisure service organizations must work in teams to be successful. An important function and role of the manager is to remove barriers so that individuals can do what they are paid to do. Often this involves humanizing rules, policies, and procedures so that they are reasonable, prudent, and applicable to various situations. Enabling others to act often involves assisting the work of others in such a way that the work is easier or the labor of the task is able to be completed without impediments. This process is often one in which the leisure service manager acts as a facilitator.

4. To Model the Way. The actions of leisure service managers are symbolic touchstones for the work of individuals within leisure service organizations. Individuals look for the hidden meanings in every act of the leisure service manager. A note scribbled on the side of a memo, or a comment of praise or scorn carries with it deep symbolic meaning to individuals. Each of these acts gives meaning to an individual. The job of the manager is to help create meaning in the lives of employees by modeling the way. Above all, the leisure service manager must be a person who operates with a sense of integrity. This means that a person must act honestly, sincerely, and with forthrightness. The leisure service manager should remember that he or she is a role model.

5. To Encourage the Heart. An important part of the work of leisure service managers is to encourage individuals to give of themselves from the heart. As Naisbitt and Aburdene (1985:20) indicate, "intellectual strategies alone will not motivate people. Only an organization with a real mission or sense of purpose that comes out of an intuitive or spiritual dimension will capture people's hearts to inspire the hard work required to realize the vision." In a sense, the work of the leisure service manager involves giving individuals hope—that feeling inside of you when you know something good is going to happen!

Management Defined

There are a number of definitions of management. The classical way of studying management is to view it as a process. This idea has advanced by early management pioneers such as Henri Fayol. Fayol defined the management process as including five primary functions: planning, organizing, command, coordination, and control. In a more contemporary sense, these functions of management have been cast as planning, organizing, staffing, directing, and controlling. This historical view may or may not be relevant today.

What is management in contemporary times? Management can be thought of as a process of working with individuals to achieve organizational goals. It is about activating the strengths of individuals as they work in the organization and making their weaknesses irrelevant. It involves many complex and demanding tasks. It may involve helping individuals understand and focus on the organization's vision and goals. It may involve removing the barriers that prevent people from achieving these goals. Management often involves viewing the total resources of the organization—human, physical, fiscal, and technological—in a holistic sense and blending them together in such a way as to move a leisure organization forward toward its vision and goals. In this sense, the leisure service manager works to accentuate the strengths of an organization and its resources and minimize its deficiencies. This may involve ensuring that the person with the right knowledge, skills, and competencies is focused on the right place at the right time. Managers must have knowledge of the task to be achieved and the ability to motivate people toward the attainment of the task. They must understand the objectives that are to be accomplished and be able to focus on the processes that can be used to achieve them. When an individual becomes a leisure services manager, his or her function is to help people or groups to fulfill their leisure aspirations. The manager does this by working with and through other people.

Drucker (1994) has provided great insight into contemporary management. He suggests that the fundamental task of the manager is to make people capable of joint performance by providing them with a common vision or goal, an appropriate structure to work within, and training as needed to perform the appropriate task and respond to changing conditions within the environment. Management is about working with human beings. Managers create a climate of pride. They help individuals believe in what they do, as indicated above, by accentuating their strengths and making their weaknesses irrelevant. Management involves creating high expectations and high standards and helping individuals to understand the value and importance of focus and discipline.

Management is about achieving great things by harnessing available resources in such a way as to improve the quality and value of leisure services available. Successful leisure service managers often leave a legacy that finds their organization healthier, more able to cope with change, and infused with a capacity for higher levels of achievement and productivity. Management is the spark, the vigor, and the magic ingredient that stirs the pot and makes it all happen.

It is not enough that the manager directs the organization; the organization must be operated in a productive manner. Productive management can be defined as the relative effectiveness and efficiency of a leisure service organization. Effectiveness is measured by the degree to which an organization achieves its goals and objectives. Efficiency refers to the amount of resources consumed in achieving the organization's goals and objectives. A productive organization is effective and efficient; conversely, an unproductive organization lacks these elements. Productivity can be measured by assessing the relationship of inputs to outputs and comparing these to the organization's standards for effectiveness and efficiency.

Productive management is of great concern to the leisure service manager, whose job is to operate the leisure service organization so that its resources benefit those it serves. By integrating the goals and objectives of the organization with the personal needs of those working within it, effectiveness may be achieved. An efficient organization is one that achieves its goals and objectives at the lowest possible cost in terms of expenditure of human resources, fiscal resources, or both. Efficiency is sometimes tempered by humanistic considerations, however. It is quite possible for an organization to achieve a great deal of effectiveness without being efficient, and vice versa.

Hultsman and Colley (1995:3-4), reporting on the factors that will shape productive government organizations in the 21st century, have identified several elements of "best professional practice" that contribute to quality. They suggest that a focus on quality is gaining greater attention in the public sector and that organizations wedded to quality will be successful. They have suggested six management practices are desirable in order to be a highly productive leisure service organization:

1. Customer Focus. Leisure service organizations that are committed to their customers will be successful. This means that they need a clear understanding of the needs and desires of the clients that they serve. It also implies a need to find ways to gain feedback from customers so that organizational performance may be improved.

2. Leadership. The keys in this area are managers who take personal responsibility for motivating and leading an organization's workforce. Having a strong base of internal support from employees is important if managers are to succeed. Likewise, it is important for managers to support their subordinates.

3. Innovation. Seeking innovation will enable leisure services organizations to meet their mission more effectively. It is important for organizations to be open to new ideas, concepts, and ways of improving professional practice. Especially important is the need to involve employees by soliciting their ideas for change.

4. Employee Involvement. A part of the process of improving quality is ensuring that employees feel that they are empowered to affect change. It is important to develop ways to involve employees as well as to provide them with meaningful opportunities to be involved in the processes of decision making and evaluation of programs and services.

5. Process Improvement. Successful organizations are ones that have developed a system to promote improvement. This often involves ensuring that customers' involvement and ideas are incorporated into the process of improving programs. The work of W. Edwards Deming serves as a model here. Deming felt that organizations should find ways to improve their work on a continuous basis; as a result, programs such as Total Quality Management (TQM) and Total Quality Leadership (TQL) have evolved (Walton & Deming, 1988).

For example, *Camp Adventure™ Youth Services* employs a management strategy known as Total Quality Program Planning (TQP), which was built upon TQM and TQL strategies. Simply, the strategy suggests that every program should be improved in some way every day; that staff should exceed the expectations of customers day in and day out. The idea is to make the next day better, more magical, and more enticing than the day before. Those at *Camp Adventure™ Youth Services* say that magic begets magic, and quality begets quality. In other words, if you improve your organization a little bit each day, it will become better and better.

6. *Change Management.* Change within successful organizations is driven by customer needs and desires. For change to be embraced, individuals need to understand the impact it will have on them personally. When there is a clear understanding between the need for change and the action that employees are to take, it is easier to bring about change initiatives within organizations. This is often accomplished by encouraging the participation of employees and others in strategic and other planning initiatives.

These strategies to incorporate "best professional practice" can have a significant impact on the work or on the organization. There is a need to create work environments that are productive, leading to quality and value for customers. As Hultsman and Colley suggest, there are two components for manager/leaders; one is behavioral and the other is analytical. They write: "The behavior aspect of leadership entails fostering a positive work environment, developing a participative management style, ensuring employee involvement

in shaping organizational goals and directions, and creating a shared vision through the use of teamwork. The analytical aspect of leadership entails process identification (i.e., what does the organization do and why?), setting and using measurable process objectives, and the appropriate application of evaluation tools and statistical techniques" (1995).

Characteristics of Managers

What values, personal traits, or characteristics are valued? Over the past several decades, Kouzes and Posner (1995) have studied managers throughout North America, Mexico, Western Europe, Asia, and Australia. Their perspective on management or leadership characteristics that helps provide an understanding of perspective on what individuals admire in leaders. Their findings are found in Table 1.3. As one can see, the four most important traits are honesty, being forward-looking, being inspiring, and being competent. All of these traits together communicate the image that the leisure service manager sends to individuals. A person of integrity, who is visionary, can move people to action, and who is capable at his or her work is the profile to aspire to.

Classifications of Leisure Service Managers

There are three broad classifications in it which persons who manage leisure services can be categorized: the supervisor, the bureaucrat, and the manager.

1. *The Supervisor.* The primary function of the supervisor is to motivate the subordinates responsible to him or her.

Table 1.3
Characteristics of Admired Leaders

Characteristics	1995 Respondents	1987 Respondents
Honest	88	83
Forward-Looking	75	62
Inspiring	68	58
Competent	63	67
Fair-minded	49	40
Supportive	41	32
Broad-minded	40	37
Intelligent	40	43
Straightforward	33	34
Dependable	32	32
Courageous	29	27
Cooperative	28	25
Imaginative	28	34
Caring	23	26
Determined	17	20
Mature	13	23
Ambitious	13	21
Loyal	11	11
Self-controlled	5	13
Independent	5	10

Source: Kouzes, J. M., & Posner, B. Z. (1995). *The leadership challenge.* San Francisco: Jossey-Bass

2. The Bureaucrat. The responsibility of the bureaucrat is to manage an organization, adhering to its policies, procedures, and rules.

3. The Manager. The manager is differentiated from the supervisor or bureaucrat in that this person is selected for his or her intellectual capacity, not technical knowledge. Because the manager deals with the future, he or she needs behavioral flexibility (Reddin, 1974:9).

All these individuals are involved in management and, therefore, are all viewed as leisure service managers. Their individual roles or purposes may vary, but the goals sought are similar.

Skills of the Leisure Service Manager

A leisure service manager must possess certain skills, knowledge, and ability to be successful. Robert L. Katz (1955:33-42) identifies three areas of skill that are necessary to the management process—technical, human, and conceptual:

1. *Technical Skills.* This involves the ability to use one's knowledge in the performance of specific work tasks. Skills in the management of aquatic facilities, such as the ability to check pH and chlorine residuals, are examples of skills that can be learned from experience or through a formal education process.

2. *Human Skills.* Here the leisure service manager applies his or her ability to motivate people by working with and through them to achieve organizational goals.

3. *Conceptual Skills.* This involves an understanding on the part of the manager of how each of the organization's components fit together in order to meet its goals and objectives. It further implies that an

individual has an understanding of how the organization is affected by, and relates to, broader environmental factors.

According to Katz, individual management styles vary with the type of management position one holds. This phenomenon is shown in Figure 1.1

As one advances from supervisor to bureaucrat to manager, the mixture of skills needed to be productive changes. A park foreman must have technical knowledge relating to construction, turf care, and vehicle and equipment repair. He or she is usually responsible for the accomplishment of specific tasks and must train and develop others to complete these tasks. On the other hand, the manager must understand how all the components of the organization fit together. He or she must have the ability to interrelate various organizational functions in order to meet the overall goals of the organization. Although the technical and conceptual skills needed at each level may vary, all positions require equal ability in dealing with human beings. The ability to deal with people is vital; it is the key to productive management because it is primarily through others that work is accomplished.

What Is a Leisure Service Organization?

Leisure service organizations are formed to meet the individual and collective leisure needs of society. They provide a framework that allows individuals to do things collectively that they would not be able to do alone, thus serving as entities that overcome the limitations of individual action. Leisure service delivery systems are organized specifically to meet the objectives of those they serve. Goals will vary accordingly to meet the needs, desires, and expectations of the organization's constituents.

Figure 1.1
Management Skills

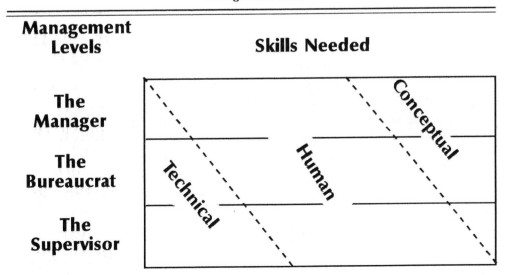

Source: Hersey, P., Blanchard, K. H., (1972) *Management of organizational behavior: Utilizing human resources, (2nd Edition),* 6.

Edginton, Hudson, and Ford (1999:6) have identified three basic types of leisure service organizations—public governmental organizations; nonprofit, nongovernmental organizations; and commercial/private enterprises. A brief explanation of each of these follows:

1. *Public Governmental Organizations.* This type of organization is concerned with community welfare, improving quality of life, service to the public, enriched community life, wide use of leisure, and protection and conservation of the environment. Typical funding strategies include tax revenues, fees and charges, donations, trusts, grants, contracts, partnerships, use of volunteers, and in-kind contributions. Typical settings include municipal park and recreation departments, county and state conservation and park systems, museums, art galleries, historical commissions, and nature or conservation agencies.

2. *Nonprofit, Nongovernment Organizations (NGO).* These organizations focus on social welfare, and benefits to members in terms of enriched living, community building, character building, and citizenship. Some typical funding strategies are membership fees and charges, donations, grants and contracts, community enhancements, use of volunteers, and in-kind contributions. Typical settings include the YMCA, the YWCA, Boys & Girls Clubs of America, Boy Scouts of America, Girl Scouts of the USA, Camp Fire Boys and Girls, the Salvation Army, Big Brothers Big Sisters of America, and Junior Achievement.

3. *Commercial/Private Enterprises.* These types of profit-oriented enterprises are market-driven, customer-oriented, and promote community development through enterprise. Funding strategies include fees and charges, and partnerships. Typical settings include amusement parks, hotels, convention centers, racetracks, professional sports arenas, outdoor-oriented businesses, casinos, resorts, theaters, bowling centers, play centers, retail outlets, and water parks.

Leisure Service as a System

A complex and diversified environment affects the management and organization of leisure services. Because they consist of a number of interacting systems (i.e., social, political, economic, and physical), environmental forces present a challenge to leisure service managers. A manager's work is greatly influenced by the interrelationships that exist among these various factors. Each system interacts with the others, influencing one another and the total environment. In discussing the interrelationships that exist within the environment, Murphy, Williams, Niepoth, and Brown (1973:1) wrote:

"The ecology of leisure service delivery systems is concerned with the interrelationships among people in their physical and social environment, and the ways these relationships influence, or are influenced by, particular social processes. It is therefore understood that the relationships of each component of the delivery system within any community are viewed as an ecological unit. It is holistic in the sense that any change in the population being served will affect the nature of programming and vice versa. Each component is an integral part of the overall delivery system, and each influences another segment of the unit. All elements mutually modify one another."

A dynamic leisure service organization is in constant interaction with the environment. The interaction that takes place between systems in the environment may be defined as an *interface*. When the leisure service organization contacts a participant in the delivery of services, such as when providing face-to-face leadership for an activity, an interface occurs. It also exists at a party or during a coffee break, when members of a leisure service organization discuss their activities.

An important function of the leisure service manager is to recognize the various systems that affect the delivery of leisure services. Further, it is extremely important that the leisure service manager identify and manage *critical interfaces* (i.e., where two or more systems interact with each other) that exist between and within systems of the total environment. This calls for a holistic approach to the management of leisure services.

Holistic Management

A holistic approach to the management of leisure service organizations involves identifying all the environmental factors that affect the organization and implementation of services. It has two basic components—the *external*, or *macro*, environment and the *internal*, or *micro*, environment—that relate to the delivery of leisure services. The macro environment includes those con-straints that surround, interact with, and influence a leisure delivery service organization. These constraints, including the economic, social, physical, and political systems, impose various sanctions and affect the delivery of leisure services. The micro environment includes the goals, processes, organizational structure (both formal and informal), and individual behaviors of managers and employees in the leisure service organization.

Figure 1.2 delineates the interacting components that have a bearing on the delivery of services. The role of the manager, using this approach to management, is to integrate these components by identifying and managing the critical interfaces to ensure the delivery of services in a productive manner. The manager is responsible for receiving such inputs as money, labor (professional, skilled, semiskilled, and unskilled), fixed capital resources, equipment, and land and transforming these into outputs in the form of leisure services. A discussion of each of the interacting components of the environment that influences the delivery of leisure services follows.

The Leisure Service Organization

Leisure organizations consist of a number of elements. In this section we will discuss the relationship of managers to employees and look at their individual behaviors. In addition, we will identify and discuss the importance of organizational goals, present information about the formal and informal organization structure, and also discuss work/transformation activities.

The Manager and the Employee

The individual behavior of leisure service managers and their employees is

Figure 1.2
The Leisure Service Organization Holistic Management Model

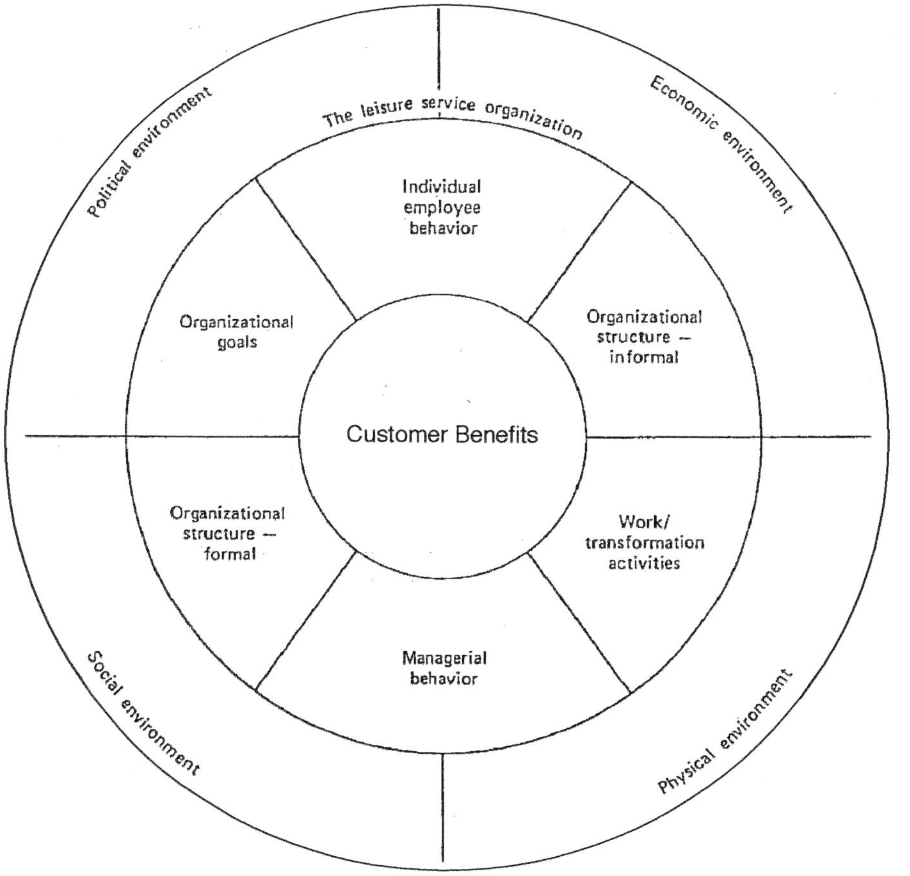

perhaps the most important element in the holistic management model. Human beings possess physiological and psychological variables that affect their behavior. One's physiological makeup includes inherited characteristics, such as the nervous system, organs, muscles, and glands. Psychological processes, including perception of others, self-image, ability to learn, and motivation, also affect behavior. Generally speaking, the manager potentially has greater impact on the psychological rather than physiological processes of his or her employees; therefore, this discussion will focus on the psychological processes that influence behavior.

Human beings interpret their environment in different ways; this is known as the process of perception. The way one perceives individuals and situations has a great impact on one's behavior toward others. For example, one leisure manager may perceive an individual employee as a deviant, capable of antisocial behavior; another manager may view the same individual as possessing worth. Individual perception influences sensitivity to the individual and, in turn, affects interpretation and action. This will affect the manager's decision-making role, in that all information he or she receives will be modified by the perceptual process.

A person's self-image will also have a bearing on his or her behavior and, in turn, the manner in which he or she deals with various environmental components. An individual who has a security-oriented self-image may behave differently than a person who conceives of himself or herself a independent and confident (e.g., a security-oriented individual may be a very authoritarian leader). Consequently, because all components of the system interact, the organization will ultimately be influenced by the individual leisure manager's self-concept.

Learning is another psychological factor that affects individual behavior. An individual's ability to learn has a direct bearing on his or her ability to understand concepts and absorb knowledge. Attitudes, skills, knowledge, and other forms of behavior are all learned within three domains: the cognitive, the affective, and psychomotor. To illustrate, knowledge of an organization's goals is gained through cognitive processes; loyalty between a manager and his or her subordinates is learned within the affective domain; and the learning of physical abilities used in the performance of tasks falls within the psychomotor domain. An individual's inability to understand and integrate such concepts or knowledge may seriously inhibit his or her ability to achieve organizational goals.

Motivation is the last element to be discussed that affects individual behavior. Motivation consists of three interacting factors—needs, drives, and goals. Needs may be defined as physiological or psychological deficiencies. Drives are directed toward initiating action to meet needs. Goals are the ends that drives and needs are directed toward. People are motivated by a host of needs, such as

security, status, power, and achievement. For example, a leisure service manager may exhibit a need for increased status by striving toward the attainment of higher levels within the organization.

Discussing the interaction that exists between an individual and the institution that employs the individual, Jacob R. Getzels and E. G. Guba (1957:425) suggest that two classes within a social system affect the processes of management—the institutional, or nomothetic dimension, and the individual, or ideographic dimension. They write:

> "There are, first, the institutions with certain roles and expectations that will fulfill the goals of the system. Second, inhabiting the system there are the individuals with certain personalities and needs dispositions, whose interactions compromise what we generally call "social behavior." Social behavior may be apprehended as a function of the following elements: institution, role and expectation (nomothetic dimension) . . . individual, personality and need dispositions (ideographic dimension)."

Figure 1.3 diagrams the interactive relationships that exist within a social system. Conflicts between individual needs and values on the one hand and organizational goals and role expectation on the other can create friction. Conversely, the role prescribed for an individual by the institution may be well suited to him or her. The point is that people bring different characteristics and personal needs to the organization, and these affect their ability to function within prescribed roles. When a conflict occurs within a management

Figure 1.3
Interacting Individual and Institutional Components

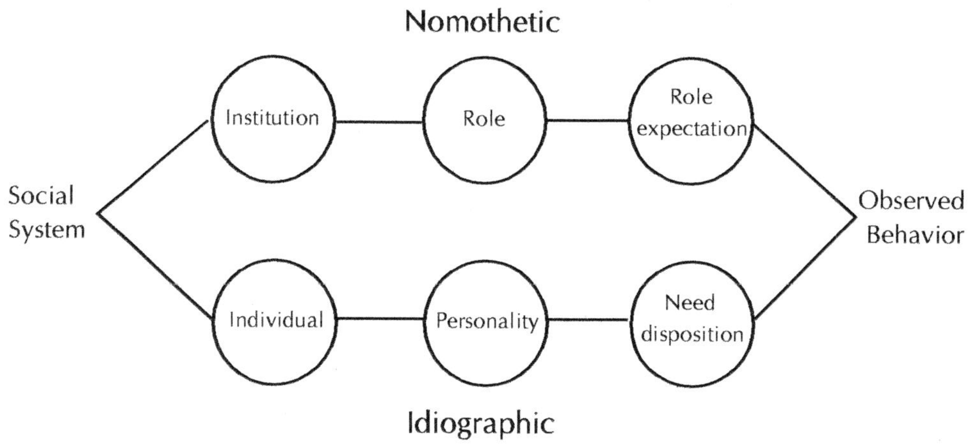

Nomothetic

[Diagram showing two rows of connected circles. Top row: Institution — Role — Role expectation. Bottom row: Individual — Personality — Need disposition. Left apex labeled "Social System", right apex labeled "Observed Behavior".]

Idiographic

Source: Getzels, J. B. and Guba, E. G. (1957) "Social Behavior and the Administrative Process," *School Review, 65*(4) (1957)

system because of an individual's behavior, one of two things can happen: The individual can change the behavior, or the organization can change its role expectations of the individual. The leisure manager's role is to find the common ground between institutional expectations and individual behavior.

Organizational Goals. The goals (ends, aims, and purposes) of an organization represent the desired outcomes toward which a leisure service system is directed. In the public sector, these goals are usually established and adopted by a legislative body. They are proven criteria for decision making and assist the leisure services manager in relating to the environment. The resolution of conflict in goals, between and within the external and internal environmental constraints, is a constant activity of the leisure service manager. The goals of a leisure service organization may be categorized into five types: output, adaptation, management, motivation, and positional goals (Edginton & Neal, 1983).

Output goals of the leisure service organization are reflected in the production or creation of services, which usually institute or facilitate behavior change in the participant. There are three types of output goals: direct service goals, participant expressive goals, and participant instrumental goals. *Direct service* goals are those goals that result in the provision of services directly to participants outside the leisure services organization. These include the creation and provision of any of the following: (1) leisure activities; (2) facilities, such as parks, recreation centers, and swimming pools; and (3) information services, including leisure counseling.

These services are used by the manager as tools to change or modify an individual's behavior in some way. They result in the instrumental and expressive types of behaviors. Instrumental behaviors can be thought of as being linked to a person's basic biological and psychological needs, such as skill development, security, and social affiliation.

The Leisure Service Manager and the Management System   19

Therefore, *participant instrumental* goals result in services that are directed toward the attainment of some skill or the reduction of basic needs, such as for food and security. Expressive types of behaviors relate to a person's needs for recognition, self-esteem, and self-realization. *Participant expressive* goals are, therefore, services that result in the acquisition of behavior directed ultimately toward self-actualization.

Adaptation goals reflect the interaction of the organization with environmental systems. Stated simply, an organization's ability to relate to and adapt to the various environmental subgroupings (which constantly change) will affect its ability to obtain resources that are necessary for its survival and stability. This may entail securing resources, such as finances, staff, capital fixtures, and equipment. Ensuring the confidence, and hence support, of those who contribute to the organization (e.g., taxpayers, consumers) is accomplished by making efficient use of resources and meeting the needs, interests, and values of the participants served.

Management goals deal with decision making in such matters as who should run the organization, how conflicts should be handled, and how resources should be distributed and accounted for. Management goals may involve both staff and participants in the governance of the organization, aligning the reward system (e.g., salaries, benefits, privileges) with the level of responsibility and maintaining harmony between individuals and functions within the organization.

Motivation goals endeavor to ensure the satisfaction of participants and staff and to inspire loyalty toward the organization as a whole. This is accomplished, in part, by developing pride in the organization and the ideals for which it stands. Protecting and facilitating staff and participants' rights, and ensuring that an individual has maximum opportunity to pursue his or her interests, also exemplify this type of goal.

Positional goals maintain the position of the organization as related and compared to other leisure service organizations. Such goals strive to maintain or increase the prestige of the leisure service organization. They are achieved by high-quality programs and services, responsiveness to changing trends, and preservation of characteristics unique to the organization. Leisure service organizations are subject to influences that are directed toward reducing or changing their position or status in the community. This challenge to an organization's position may come from other departments competing for tax dollars in the governmental sector or from those commercial organizations that strive for a greater percentage of the leisure market.

Organizational Structure—Formal and Informal.

The goals of an organization are achieved in large part through its structure. Two aspects of this subject are relevant to the productive management of leisure service organizations and to this discussion on formal and informal organizations.

The formal organization of a leisure delivery service system is established specifically to accomplish the system's goals. This type of organizational structure requires the collective effort of the entire membership of the organization. According to David Buchanan and Andrzej Huczynski (1997:316):

"Formal organization refers to the collection of work groups that have been consciously designed by senior management to maximize efficiency and achieve organizational goals. Decisions about job descriptions, organizational charts, types of authority, and so on, all relate to designing the formal organization."

Formal organizations are structured to increase productivity. But because of specialization, rules, and a hierarchy that at times stifles communication, formal structures may impede the attainment of an organization's goals. Rules and procedures can become ends in themselves, thus blocking individual initiative; specialization can lead to fragmentation within the organization. On the other hand, formal organizations are a means for orderly and controlled interactions among people. They provide clearly defined lines of authority and responsibility and may positively influence the achievement of an organization's goals and objectives. The nature and complexity of the goals that are to be achieved by a leisure service organization will dictate the degree to which a formal structure is necessary. To function, large systems must depend on having an extensive formal organization.

The goals of a leisure service organization may also be influenced by the informal organization present within the system.

> "Informal groups play a significant role in the dynamics of organizational behavior. The major difference between the formal and informal groups is that the formal group . . . has officially prescribed goals and relationships, whereas the informal one does not. Despite this distinction, it is a mistake to think of the formal and informal groups as two distinctly separate entities. The two types of groups coexist and are inseparable. Every formal organization has informal groups and every informal organization eventually evolves into some semblance of formal groups. (Luthans, 1998:282)"

Formal and informal systems exist side by side and should complement one another. An informal organization may contribute to the formal organization in the following ways:

1. It blends with the formal organization to make a workable system for getting work done.

2. It lightens the workload of the formal manager and fills in some of the gaps of his or her abilities.

3. It gives satisfaction and stability to work groups.

4. It is a very useful channel of communication in the organization.

5. Its presence encourages a manager to plan and act more carefully than he or she would otherwise. (Davis, 1981:257-259)

Because they may have conflicting sets of values, informal organizations can hinder the achievement of the goals of a formal organization. A group of individuals can organize around a concern, on an informal basis, and bring a great deal of pressure to bear on an organization. This can result in considerable expenditure of the organization's resources and may detract from its productivity.

The influence of organizational structure-formal and informal-on leisure service as a system as a whole is very important. Relationships that exist between and within an organization continually interact with each other. Individual behavior is modified by the formal and the informal organization, and vice versa. The leisure service manager should be aware of the potential and consequences of both formal and informal organizations and should be able to take advantage, when possible, of these types of organizations. Goal achievement can be enhanced or diminished by organizational design.

Work/Transformation Activities. Work/transformation activities are the actual functions performed by the manager. They refer to the actual effort put into procuring inputs and transforming these inputs into outputs (such as leisure-time activities) by the leisure service manager. Basic work functions of a leisure service manager include financial activity and the creation and distribution of leisure services. The management of fiscal resources (finance) is handled through the process known as "budgeting." There are three stages in the budgeting process: preparation, authorization, and execution. Two tasks, budget preparation and implementation, consume a great deal of a leisure manager's attention.

Creation and distribution of a service includes four activities: organizing, pricing, the distributing, and promoting a service. Essentially, this involves getting the right service to consumers when they want it, at the price they are willing to pay, and in the place that is most convenient for their participation. The work functions are accomplished through the processes of planning, organizing, staffing, directing, and controlling.

Planning is a process that involves identifying goals and developing the methods necessary to achieve them. It also entails decision-making responsibility in the allocation of an organization's resources. Once an organization has set its goals and has determined the direction in which it wants to go, it must ask itself what its priorities are with the resources available. In addition, it must assess the future and determine how the organization may meet its potential needs.

Organizing involves establishing specific roles and blending resources into a coherent organizational structure. The determination of roles allows for the delegation of management authority, responsibility, and accountability. Further, a well-defined organization provides for the coordination of activities among workers to accomplish the purposes of the organization and takes into account the resources available in determining relationships among individuals. Ultimately, organizing produces a structure that enables individuals to work collectively toward the achievement of leisure service goals. Tasks or roles that take into account the individual abilities and skills of the members of a leisure service organization contribute to its increased effectiveness and efficiency. Organizing is a dynamic process, however, and should constantly take place as individual competency within the leisure service organization changes and as the environment outside the organization evolves.

Staffing is a process whereby an organization's needs for labor are met. The process endeavors to meet both present and future personnel needs of the organization and, according to Ernest Dale (1978:370), includes several specific functions:

1. Recruitment, or getting applicants for the jobs as they open up.
2. Selection of the best qualified from those who seek the jobs.
3. Handling transfers and promotions.
4. Training of those who need further instruction to perform their work effectively or to qualify for promotion.

Directing is accomplished by encouraging, leading, motivating, and communicating with employees to achieve organizational goals. In general, the role of the leisure service manager is to work with subordinates, communicating to them the procedures necessary to carry out the plans of the organization. In other words, "telling people what to do and seeing that they do it" (1978:424). The manager works to help each subordinate use his or her skills and abilities to maximum potential, and to motivate employees toward the achievement of organizational goals.

In verifying the extent to which an organization conforms to its plans, a manager is involved in the processes of control. Control concerns the establishment of standards to guide performance. Standards serve as the criteria against which performance is measured. Following the establishment of performance standards, the control process proceeds to measure and evaluate performance. This can be accomplished through personal observation, financial accounting, or appraisal of the results achieved by an individual or organization.

The final factor involved in the control process is that of corrective action. Corrective action may require decisions to adjust and change or to integrate individuals into the organization. It also may entail the development of new standards or managerial methods that

increase employee motivation toward achievement of an organization's plan of action. Controlling depends on feedback from the various units that make up an organization. Without adequate management information systems to provide data on performance, the process of control is ineffective.

Factors Influencing the Work of Leisure Service Organizations

Numerous factors have an impact on the work of leisure service organizations and their managers. First and foremost are the needs, interests, values, and desires of customers. As previously indicated, having a customer-focused organization is important. Other factors that influence the work of leisure service managers are the social, political, physical, and economic environments. Implications of these factors will be discussed in this section.

The Customer. The needs, interests, values, and lifestyles of individuals served by a leisure service organization are central concerns of the leisure services manager. Age, gender, education, income, cultural traits, occupation, and biological and psychological factors affect leisure behavioral patterns.

Leisure activity interests vary with age. For example, younger persons are inclined to find strenuous physical activity, especially team sports, desirable. On the other hand, middle-aged adults are likely to prefer individual and dual sports, which are less demanding physically. Cultural traits and norms also affect individual behavior. Individual convictions or sentiments can serve as a basis for making decisions that affect leisure behavior. The drive for success within our competitive society and the view that activity is a worthwhile end in itself are two examples of value orientations that affect the leisure behavior of North Americans. Whether a function of biological or cultural factors, the gender of an individual will affect leisure interests. The development of roles through the process of socialization may well determine the types of activities in which males or females may engage. Although cultural values have changed recently regarding the involvement of women in strenuous physical activity, heretofore it was assumed that this type of activity was exclusively within the domain of men. Education, income, and occupation are all interrelated and are often linked to one's social status; activity preferences vary according to one's status. A discussion of the economic factor as it affects leisure patterns appears later in this chapter. In addition, it has traditionally been hypothesized that leisure behavior is modified by a number of biological and psychological factors.

The integration of these factors within social, economic, physical, and political systems provides the basis for increased awareness of leisure behavioral patterns. Efforts made by leisure service organizations aimed at providing adequate programs, activities, and facilities are made challenging by variances in leisure lifestyles among the individuals they serve. They must deal with differing needs, interests, and values, which are affected by a host of environmental factors. The insensitivity of some managers to these factors has greatly diminished the effectiveness of leisure services. In many cases, this problem has been compounded by individual prejudices (racial, political, religious, or otherwise) and by the delivery of services based on a limited understanding and knowledge of their con-

stituents gained only from perceptions. The need for interpretive efforts is paramount, whether oriented toward research tools and techniques or toward employing individuals who can relate directly to varying leisure lifestyles. Productive delivery of services depends greatly on development of a conscious effort to understand the needs of the consumer, especially as shaped by the systems within the environment.

The Social Environment. The social environment consists of the sum total of interactions that take place among individuals or groups of individuals and that results in the development of formal or informal organizational systems. This interaction produces many forms of human and societal behavior. A leisure service organization is affected by and can affect the activities that take place among individuals or groups as they interact.

Social behavior can be shaped greatly by leisure. Perhaps the most pronounced change in individual and group behavior affecting the social environment is that of changing attitudes toward work and leisure. Moving from a work-oriented to a leisure-oriented society has produced new social patterns among individuals and groups. For example, new forms of social behavior have resulted in a host of organizations dedicated to leisure pursuits. Television, professional sports, movies, and fast-food chains are all leisure-oriented agents that are contributing to the change in our social environment. Such institutions carry a distinct set of norms or roles that influence consumer values and hence behavior.

Formal organizations are another important component of our social environment that affects the delivery of leisure services. The leisure service manager is in constant interaction with governmental, social, political, and economic organizations, such as businesses and corporations. Surrounded by formal and informal organizations and groups, it is important to remember that the leisure service organization does not operate in a vacuum and that it is dependent on its relationships with other bodies. The relative success or failure of an organization may depend on its ability to manage its affairs properly with other organizations and groups.

Responsiveness to changes in the social environment is best achieved by recognizing that human behavior is not static, but dynamic. Activities, facilities, and services should be directed toward providing positive and enriching opportunities that satisfy individual and group needs for growth. Further, the value of an organization is reflected in the types of goods and services it offers. In creating and distributing selected goods and services, the leisure service organization affects the social environment and plays a role in shaping culture and society.

The Political Environment. Both the formal structure of government and the informal process that affects political decision making directly affect the leisure service manger. Formal governmental structures exist at the federal, state or provincial, and local levels. Their primary function is to establish laws and policies that enable, inhibit, or regulate the behavior of people in some way. In addition, governments, especially at the local level, have traditionally been providers of leisure services. An understanding of the laws formulated by legislative and judicial institutions is obviously vital to the leisure service manager.

Perhaps of equal importance is the leisure service manager's knowledge of the informal, or de facto, political process that directly affects or influences the initiation and implementation of policy. Theoretically, a representative form of government provides opportunities for the interests of all to be recognized. It rests on the belief that selfish interests are subservient to the common good. The democratic process, however, is often thwarted by a number of factors that do not contribute to the welfare of all. One of the most important political forces facing the leisure service manager today is the influence of special interest, or pressure, groups. Such groups have a profound impact on the functioning of the democratic process.

A special interest group exists when a group of people bands together around a mutual concern. Many groups in our society today affect the delivery of leisure services. Examples include swim clubs, hobby clubs, athletic teams, conservation and ecology organizations, and service and political organizations. These types of organizations allow individuals having common interests to share values and develop camaraderie and loyalty. Yet there are few value-free or altruistic groups. Because our society contains many special-interest groups having varying values and needs, the probability that these groups will interact and perhaps conflict with other groups and organizations is great. These conflicting organizational values give rise to pressure groups.

A pressure group is a special interest group that actively promotes its own interests. A political party can be defined as a pressure group. In many cases, pressure groups attempt to influence the distribution of organizational resources to reflect their personal interests rather than what is traditionally thought of as the common good. It is with this type of group that the leisure service manager must contend.

Public leisure service delivery systems are not value-free organizations. They are initiated to provide a variety of activities, facilities, and services that provide opportunities for use of persons' leisure. Because these exist to serve the leisure needs of the citizens within their legal jurisdictions, they do not cater solely to the specific interests or values of a particular group. This does not imply that this type of leisure service organization does not meet individual and group needs; rather, it implies that such organizations try to promote the concept of the greatest good for the greatest number.

Conflict may develop between a pressure group and a public leisure service delivery system when, in distributing resources to meet community needs, the specific requests of a pressure group are subservient to the welfare of the entire community. When this occurs, pressure groups exert their influence to affect the distribution of resources through the political process. A number of tactics can be used by pressure groups to influence organizations and the political process. They may try to influence the passage of legislation, sway public officials, or attempt to mold public opinion. By representing the values of the leisure service organization to the public at large, the manager attempts to counter the impact of pressure groups on the distribution of resources.

An example of the type of confrontation that can exist between a pressure group and a public leisure service organization involves the distribution of swimming-pool time. It is consistent with the aims of many public leisure service organizations to provide a variety of aquatic activities that meet the

varying interests and needs of a community. But in many communities, the formulation of a parents' swim club to support the activities of the competitive swim program provides a focal point for conflict between the values of the swim club and the public leisure service organization. The club may demand that the community's aquatic program be organized to serve *its* needs rather than the broad interests of all. Pressuring for increased access to the swimming pool, and demanding an increased amount of the leisure delivery system's time to organize their activities are types of pressure group conflict that must be dealt with. It may be that the representatives of the swim club are among the more powerful political leaders of the community, and they may use their positions of authority and influence to affect the distribution of resources.

Special interest groups need not *necessarily* be thought of as operating in conflict with the aims and values of the leisure service organization. In fact, there are numerous special interest groups whose values are complementary to those of a leisure service organization. In many cases, the leisure service organization and a given special interest group work together to their mutual benefit. Service clubs with a strong commitment to meeting community needs are often deeply involved with public leisure service organizations. Providing financial support as well as assistance in the form of voluntary work hours, service clubs are engaged in activities such as Halloween parades, Easter egg hunts, park clean-up activities, and support of capital improvements. They are an important resource to a public leisure service organization. To achieve its aims, a public service organization has the responsibility to use its community resources wisely and to provide opportunities for community service. It is thus able to effectively meet its own needs as well as those of the special interest group.

The Physical Environment. The planning of activities, facilities, and services depends greatly on a community's physical features. Climate, terrain, resources, spatial arrangements, and population density are components of the physical environment that affect the delivery of services. Regional variances in the physical environment provide conditions that foster differing lifestyles and hence promote the development of a broad range of leisure-time activities that suit the particular location in which an individual lives.

Climate affects leisure programming as much as any other component of the physical environment. In the San Francisco Bay Area, for example, the Mediterranean climate allows for a host of year-round outdoor recreation activities. Programs are operated out-of-doors during the school year as well as during the summer months. In contrast, communities located in the Toronto metropolitan area may operate programs in indoor facilities. As the seasons change in various locations, programming efforts take on new dimensions, reflecting the particular leisure needs that have been created as a result of differing climatic conditions. The topography or terrain of a given location may also affect leisure tastes. Persons living in mountain areas of the United States and Canada have available unique opportunities for particular types of leisure activities, such as hiking, mountain climbing, and orienteering. Individuals who reside close to large bodies of water are able to enjoy such activities as sailing and waterskiing. Modern technology has overcome some geographic limitations with the use of such innovations as wave machines for pools and

artificial snow and ice. Another alternative may involve the transportation of participants from one geographic area to another in order to involve them in seasonal or regional leisure activities.

Both man-made and natural resources affect individual participation in leisure activities. Natural wilderness areas, forests, lakes, and rivers all provide abundant opportunities for participation. The preservation of outdoor recreation resources has been a growing concern for the past several years. To insure that future generations have continued access to our natural areas, massive efforts have been undertaken to set aside some areas and to regulate the use of others. Man-made facilities, such as artificial lakes, picnic areas, swimming pools, parks, and recreation centers also provide opportunities for participation. Communities lacking in both natural and man-made resources are unable to provide adequate leisure services.

Spatial arrangements and population density are interrelated. Urban living characterizes a way of life for our society that presents opportunities for social interaction. Urban life provides a variety of individual choices that can lead to personal fulfillment. On the other hand, the conditions that are created as a result of crowding and overpopulation can initiate antisocial behavior. The leisure service manager plays an important role in improving the quality of the urban environment. The creation of certain environmental conditions promotes positive forms of interaction among people, and by preserving a community's natural beauty, life is enhanced.

The Economic Environment. The economic environment has a profound impact on the provision and consumption of leisure services. Between absolute poverty and complete affluence exists a variety of leisure lifestyles. Some individuals, enslaved by their economic circumstances, are denied opportunities for a fully enriched leisure lifestyle; others, born within the cult of affluence, are able to explore fully the potential of a leisure-oriented life.

Not only does individual income affect individual participation in various leisure activities, but it also determines the collective wealth of a community and the economic climate of a nation. Perhaps the greatest need for public leisure services is found in poor urban areas of North America. Although there has been a redistribution of financial resources through federal, state, and provincial agencies, the pressing economic conditions that exist in the inner-city areas of the United States and Canada adversely affect opportunities for leisure behavior. Conversely, more affluent suburbs are able to finance the development and operation of some of the nation's finest public leisure delivery systems.

The economic status of the nation also affects leisure lifestyles. One of the most dramatic upsurges in the consumption of and participation in leisure activities took place during the Great Depression. During this period, vast amounts of money were provided for the creation of recreation facilities and services. In more contemporary times, high levels of affluence—particularly in the 1960s—resulted in the creation of a multimillion-dollar leisure market.

Interpreting the economic environment involves: (1) understanding the effects that different levels of income have on participation in leisure activities, and (2) providing increased opportunities for participation in activities that are unattainable because of the economic circumstances of many would-be participants. In the latter role, the leisure service organization acts to fulfill its traditional function of providing collectively the services that are individually unattainable.

Management Challenges of the 21st Century

What challenges will leisure services managers face in the 21st century? There will be many uncertainties in the future. We live in a time of great change, and it is difficult to know in the future what may occur. Our basic values can be used as a foundation to guide our efforts. We are in the business of creating joy and happiness, promoting the wise use of leisure, protecting human dignity, conserving and protecting the environment, and encouraging ecologically sustainable activities.

Edginton (1997) and other noted authors such as Godbey (1997) and Mobley and Toalson (1992) have identified several management challenges, issues, and trends facing leisure service organizations in the 21st century. Table 1.4 provides an analysis of their recommendations in terms of the challenges that leisure service managers must face. Several consistent themes are identifiable from these recommendations. First, all authors speak to the importance of management strategies for working with individuals within leisure service organizations. The themes of attention to the need for new leadership techniques, managing knowledge-based workers, and promoting an entrepreneurial spirit are evident. It is also evident that these authors recognize the importance of responding to the changes that are occurring in society. One author suggests that we must not merely respond to change, but embrace it. Keeping organizations fluid, flexible, and agile was

Table 1.4
Management Challenges of the 21st Century

Mobley & Toalson (1992)	Edginton (1997)	Godbey (1997)
Park and recreation professionals must be able and willing to identify, analyze, promote, and respond to change in society	Developing market and customer-driven, high-yield leisure services	All leisure service organizations must become increasingly agile
New leadership techniques will be required of park and recreation professionals to facilitate consensus-building	Tracking the impact of quality of life improvements by measuring benefits and outcomes	All leisure service must increasingly cooperate with competitors
Parks and recreation must return to its heritage of serving all of the people	Outsourcing to promote flexibility and cost-effectiveness	Most leisure services will have to figure out what they are good at and outsource everything else
Renewed attention must be given to the poor and their impact on parks and recreation	Managing knowledge-based workers who are more sophisticated, intelligent, and involved	Reconceptualizing government-sponsored leisure services will require a change in management strategy toward benefits-based management
Parks and recreation must find ways to celebrate the variety of cultures within the community	Creating cultures of innovation that promote creativity, ingenuity, and embrace change	Leisure services must become enterprises
Parks and recreation programs must provide a choice other than the use of drugs and must develop self-esteem in our youth	Visioning and valuing, with managers acting more as coaches by inspiring, transforming, and focusing workers on shared values	The successful leisure service will treat people appropriately, not equally
Parks, recreation, and leisure services must facilitate, and identify directly with, the growing wellness movement	More fluid, flexible organizations that liberate the human spirit	The successful leisure service organization will customize services, information, and products
Park and recreation organizations must work with other agencies in building networks and coalitions to achieve success	Greater networking and collaboration, promotion of teaming, greater organizational communication, and linking of individuals to solve problems	The successful leisure service will rethink pricing, timing, and platforms
Parks and recreation must make a commitment to continuing education and professional development		
The future success of parks and recreation will depend on the quality of service provided to all of the people we serve		
It is essential to improve the image of the profession, both externally and internally, so that the relationship between parks and recreation programs and values and contemporary issues is clearly apparent		
Parks and recreation must be involved in partnerships mutually beneficial with tourism		

continued

Table 1.4 Continued
Management Challenges of the 21st Century

Mobley & Toalson (1992)	Edginton (1997)	Godbey (1997)
The park and recreation profession must take its rightful place as a leader in shaping environmental policy		
The park and recreation profession must develop and articulate clearly defined mission statements, goals, and objectives of the field		

Sources: Adapted from Mobley, T. A., & Toalson, R. F. (1992). *Parks and recreation in the 21st Century - (Chapter One).* Arlington, VA: National Recreation and Park Association, Edginton, C. R. (1997). Managing leisure services: A new ecology of leadership toward the year 2000. *Journal of Physical Education, Recreation, and Dance* 68(2), 29; and Godbey, G. (1997). *Leisure and leisure services in the 21st century.* State College, PA: Venture.

another challenge consistent among the authors. Another consistent theme was the importance of providing quality services that are customer-driven. Authors spoke to the notion of creating customer-driven, high-yield services, and customizing services. Networking, collaborations, partnerships, building coalitions, and encouraging consensus were all identified as being key themes for the future. Also, benefits management and outsourcing were identified by these authors as important challenges to meet in the 21st century.

Another perspective that may be offered regarding challenges is to view element, that may be identified as "certainties" in the environment. Obviously, there are many unknowns that leisure service managers will deal with in the future. However, there are also some known elements that managers can respond to in a timely and prompt fashion. Drucker (1999:44-63) has identified four "new certainties" that leisure service managers may address in the 21st century:

1. Collapsing Birthrate. Drucker notes a collapsing birthrate in the developing world. These changes will cause great turbulence in the workforce and in the marketplace. For example, productivity of workers, especially knowledge-based workers, will have to increase to make up for shortages in the workforce. Traditional employment patterns will also change, affecting, in turn, concurrent leisure patterns.

2. Disposable Income. According to Drucker (1999: 51), the four major growth sectors of the 21st century were government, health care, education, and leisure. He notes, "with leisure probably taking as much of the enormous expansion of economic productivity and output as the other three together," he projects that the leisure industry may be declining. The most rapidly growing industry is that of financial services.

3. Defining Performance. New definitions of performance will be required. These will be benefits-driven and, performance-oriented. Long-term commitment and values may have to be balanced with short-term values. In nonprofits, we will have to define performance more effectively in non-financial terms. This is especially important for knowledge-based workers, for whom financial incentives may not be as important as the amenities of the work environment.

4. Global Competitiveness. Although that is difficult to extract in terms of the management of government leisure services in the United States and Canada, increasingly global competitiveness in profit-oriented leisure industries is an important factor. Organizations are increasingly seeing themselves as international and transnational, with interests that transcend national boundaries.

Leisure service managers can respond to these certainties in the immediate future. We know that the nature of the workforce is changing. It is clearly far more diverse today than it ever has been. In fact, it has been reported that by the year 2050, all of the so-called minorities will together surpass, in numbers, the current Anglo majority (Yzaguirre, 1998). Further, the workforce will be older and will be motivated by factors other than financial incentives. Performance is a challenging element for leisure service managers to measure. It is relatively easy to define tangible "economic costs" and then define performance in terms of economic gains or losses to an organization. On the other hand, it is far more difficult to identify "social costs" and relate the success of the person's performance to the improvement of social ends in a more tangible way. Not impossible, just very challenging and sometimes difficult. The leisure industry has ridden the crest of the tidal wave of change that has occurred as we have

moved from the agricultural society to the industrial society and then to the knowledge-based era. However, increasingly we see inroads into the amount of leisure available to individuals in terms of time, and also the availability and access to quality leisure experiences. Individuals in developing countries today are often far more rushed, harried, and pressured in their lives than they were in previous decades. Last, it is evident that we will increasingly live in a global village. It is important to understand that we will be shaped by cultural, political, social, and economic events throughout the world. Today's leisure and popular culture is an amalgamation of the world's culture.

Summary

The arrival of the 21st century provides a great opportunity to review strategies used to manage leisure service organizations. The growth of leisure in North America has resulted in the creation of a vast number of organizations that deliver leisure services. In the past 150 years, a host of social innovations, from parks to community centers to amenities such as child-care programs, has emerged. Leisure service managers will continue to play an important role in the social transformation of society. Working with and through human resources, leisure service managers are charged with forming the effective and efficient, hence productive, management of these organizations.

The 21st century presents a new set of assumptions that will influence the work of leisure service managers. Greater emphasis on quality, doing more with less, technology and telecommunications, and rapid discontinuous change, coupled with a more sophisticated workforce, will create great challenges for leisure service managers. There will be a need for flexible, agile, and responsive organizational structures. Networking, collaboration, coalition building, teaming, and establishing partnerships with all be important activities of leisure service managers. Leisure service managers will be cheerleaders, coaches, teachers, facilitators, encouragers, and visionaries rather than policy enforcers, controllers or directors. Their work will be to encourage the best efforts of others rather than to coerce or force their employees.

Acting in a number of roles, it is important for the manager to be aware of the various environmental systems that can affect the delivery of leisure services. Environmental constraints include the participant and his or her social, political, physical, and economic factors; organizational elements include an individual's behavior, organizational goals, organizational structure, and work/transformation activities. An awareness of the patterns of interaction, or interfaces, that take place between and within these systems is crucial to the leisure service manager. The productive management of any leisure delivery service organization is dependent on the ability of the manager to work with these constraints and to move the organization toward its goals.

Discussion Questions

1. In what ways has the concept of "management" changed over the past eras? More specifically, how has management been transformed in the last 150 years?

2. Many early pioneers in the park and recreation field were also great man

agers. Explain and discuss this dimension of their professional activity.

3. How do current management practices differ from management practices of the past? How do management roles differ from management roles of the past?

4. How will a management model of the knowledge-based era differ from that of an industrial-based era?

5. Identify and describe five key activities of leisure service managers.

6. Define and discuss management and productive management.

7. What skills does a manager need to be successful?

8. Identify and discuss three types of leisure service organizations.

9. How is the leisure service organization a system? What are its component parts?

10. What challenges do leisure services managers face in the 21st century?

References

Bell, D. (1968). *Toward the year 2000: Work in progress.* Boston: Houghton Mifflin.

Bennis, W., & Nanus, B. (1985). *Leaders.* New York: Taylor & Ron.

Buchanan, D., & Huczynski, A. (1997). *Organizational behavior: An introductory text.* New York: Prentice-Hall.

Dale, E. (1978). *Management: Theory and practice.* New York: McGraw-Hill.

Davis, K. (1981). *Human behavior at work* (6th ed.). New York: McGraw-Hill.

Drucker, P. F. (1994, November). The age of social transformation. *The Atlantic Monthly.*

Drucker, P. F. (1996). The shape of things to come. *Leader to Leader.*

Drucker, P. F. (1999) *Management challenges for the 21ᵗ Century*. New York: Harper Business.

Edginton, C. F., & Neal, L. L. (1983). Park and recreation directors: Perceptions of organizational goals. *Journal of Park and Recreation Administration, 1*(1). 39–49.

Edginton, C. R. (1998, April). The art and science of managing leisure services: Reflecting, rethinking, and repositioning for the 21ˢᵗ century. J. B. Nash Scholar Lecture, AAHPERD Convention, Reno, Nevada.

Edginton, C. R., Hudson, S. D., & Ford, P. M. (1999). *Leadership for recreation and leisure programs and settings*. Champaign, IL: Sagamore Publishing .

Edginton, C. R. (1997). Managing leisure services: A new ecology of leadership toward the year 2000. *The Journal of Physical Education, Recreation and Dance. 68*(8), 29–31

Getzels, J. R., & Guba, E. G. (1957, Winter). Social behavior and the administrative process. *School Reviews,* 65, 425.

Godbey, G. (1997). *Leisure and leisure services in the 21ˢᵗ century*. State College, PA: Venture Publishing.

Hall, L. (1995). *Olmsted's America*. Boston: Bullfinch Press.

Hultsman, J., & Colley, J. A. (1995). Park and recreation management for the 21ˢᵗ century. *Journal of Park and Recreation Administration, 13*(2),

Johnson, M. A. (1989). *The many faces of Hull House*. Urbana: University of Illinois Press.

Katz, R. L. (1955, January/February). Skills of an effective administrator. *Harvard Business Review,* 33–42.

Kouzes, J. M., & Posner, B. Z. (1995). *The leadership challenge.* San Francisco: Jossey-Bass.

Kuhn, T. S. (1970). *The structure of scientific revolutions* (2nd ed.). Chicago: University of Chicago Press.

Kuhn, T. S. (1996). *The structure of scientific revolutions* (3rd ed.). Chicago: The University of Chicago Press.

Luthans, F. (1998). *Organizational behavior*. Boston: McGraw-Hill.

Machiavelli, N. (1952). *The prince*. New York: Mentor.

Meine, C. (1988). *Aldo Leopold*. Madison: The University of Wisconsin Press.

Mintzberg, H (1980). *The nature of managerial work*. New York: Harper & Row.

Mintzberg, H. (1973). *The nature of managerial work*. New York: Harper and Row

Mobley, T. A., & Toalson, R. F. (1992). *Parks and recreation in the 21st century- Chapter one*. Arlington, VA: National Recreation and Park Association.

Mobley, T. A., & Toalson, R. F. (Eds.) (1992). *Parks and recreation in the 21st century*. Arlington, VA: National symposium committee and NRPA.

Murphy, J. F., Williams, J. G., Niepoth, E. W., Brown, P. D. (1973). *Leisure service delivery system: A modern perspective*. Philadelphia, PA: Lea & Febiger.

Naisbitt, J. (1982). *Megatrends: Ten new directions transforming our lives*. New York: Warner Books.

Naisbitt, J., & Aburdene, P. (1985). *Reinventing the corporation*. New York: Warner Books.

Reddin, W. J. (1974, August). Management effectiveness in the 1980s. *Business Horizons, 17*(4), 9.

Rice, G. H., & Bishoprick, D. W. (1971). *Conceptual model of organization*. New York: Appleton-Century Crofts.

Thurow, L. C. (1996). *The future of capitalism*. New York: William Morrow.

Toffler, A. (1980). *The third wave*. New York: Bantam Books.

Walton, M., & Deming, W. E. (1988). *The Deming management method*. New York: Perigee.

Yzaguirre, R. (1998). The New America Identity. In F. Hesselbeien, M. Goldsmith, R. Beckhard, R. & R. Schubert (Eds.), *The community of the future.* San Francisco: Jossey-Bass.

Chapter

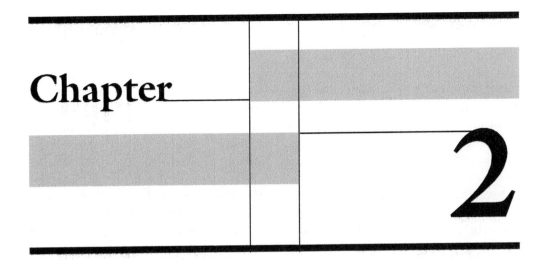

2

Management Theory and Practice

Early leisure service managers and planners meet with John Olmsted to formulate plans for Seattle (WA) Washington Park. Olmsted is pictured fourth from the left.

Introduction

New possibilities have been created in the areas of individual opportunity, material wealth, and leisure as a result of the social economic transformation that has occurred during the past 150 years. As we progressed from the agricultural era to the industrial era, a host of new social inventions emerged. Many of these social inventions influenced the way that we lived, worked and played. However, the assumptions that led to these industrial-based ideas and inventions are now giving way to new ideas and concepts. The information or knowledge era is currently reshaping our basic institutions, just as these evolved in the transition from the agricultural to the industrial era before it.

The evolution of management thinking roughly parallels the development of the leisure service profession. This occurred in roughly the same time frame, influenced by similar social economic conditions and thinking. We often think of management as being a concept derived directly from business. However, Drucker (1999) reminds us that the first practical applications of management theory did not take place in a business but in nonprofit and government agencies. He further points out that the term "manager" is an American invention dating back to the early years of the 20th century. We can learn much about the thinking of Americans and the work of our profession as we review the rich history of management and its relationship to the leisure service profession.

This chapter discusses the evolution of social ideas relevant to management and the historical development of the leisure service profession. In particular, the authors discuss the emergence of management in the contexts of the industrial revolution, the social reform movement, and the transfer of technology. We also include a thorough discussion of management history, as well as reviews of scientific management, human relations management, management science, human resources management, and contemporary management. Last, a review of management and leisure service organizations is presented.

The Evolution of Social Ideas and Leisure Service Management

The rise of modern management follows the development of complex organizations that emerged through-

out the industrial revolution. Drucker (1996) suggests that the prevailing model of management was one that emphasized command and control. The industrial model of organization was mechanistic in nature, emphasizing a need for authority and coordination. In Chapter One we learned that in the early and mid-1800s, the best model of organization available was that used by the Prussian Army (Drucker, 1996). This model emphasized downward delegated authority; hierarchically arranged superior–subordinate relationships; division of labor, and the creation of rules, regulations, and policies to guide behavior and to legitimize the work of the organization.

In this section, we will discuss the evolution of management and will present the evolution of management thinking within the context of the industrial revolution. Following this section, will be a short discussion of social reform and the resulting social innovations that lead to responses from early leaders of the profession. Much of their management thinking and ideology is revealed in the nature of their social reforms. Many early leaders were guided by a belief in scientific determination that emphasized the trainability of individuals and promoted the use of human capabilities to their fullest. Last, a discussion of social reforms and the transfer of social technology will demonstrate how our early leaders were influenced, as well as how ideas practiced in other settings, and in other countries influenced our programs of social reform.

The Context of the Industrial Revolution

The emergence of industrial society brought with it a wave of change in human affairs (Hall, 1998). The origins of the industrial revolution began with the emergence of capitalistic society. Capitalism as a type of economic system came into being in the 17th century in Europe. In general, capitalism refers to the economic theory advanced by Adam Smith in 1774. His historically important work, *An Inquiry into the Nature and Causes of the Wealth of Nations,* provided a foundation for the rise of an industrial society.

The Industrial Revolution created a wholesale change in the way business was conducted and, in effect, how life was organized. It brought about an increase in production that resulted in a vast array of material goods being available to the general population. In some respects, the Industrial Revolution gave individuals hope that they could improve their lives dramatically. The capitalistic system provided individuals with an opportunity to be inventive by using their talents and energies to improve their lot in life. Previously, individuals were tied to the land; in feudal society, they had few prospects beyond their station of birth.

Hall (1998:283) has suggested six characteristics that can be used to define industrial society:

1. A change in the nature of economy such that a very small primary sector can feed a population involved in the secondary and tertiary sectors

2. The dominance of machine production within factories

3. The urbanization of society

4. The growth of mass literacy

5. The application of scientific knowledge to production

6. An increase in the bureaucratic regulation of all aspects of social life

Industrial society resulted in a wholesale change in the way people lived their lives. Basically, industrialized societies were transformed from rural agrarian societies to urban industrial ones. Work and play in urban societies were vastly different than in rural ones. Rather than being tied to the seasons, individuals in work environments tended to be driven by machines, schedules or managers. The relationship between those in the management class, or the owners of businesses, and workers changed dramatically. In feudal societies, the relationship between landowners and the peasants was often paternalistic yet supportive. However, the rise of factories and corporations caused workers to become impersonal cogs in the machine of production.

As industrial might grew, organizations became much larger and more complex. There came a need for individuals with unique skills to manage such large and demanding organizations. The rise of management enabled owners to separate themselves from the day-to-day operations of businesses and place them into the hands of other individuals whom they held accountable for success or failure. In a sense, a body of knowledge was developed to assist managers in the implementation of their activities. As Drucker (1994:3-80) has written: "rarely in human history has any institution emerged as fast as management or had as great an impact as quickly. In less than 150 years, management has transformed the social and economic fabric of the world's developed countries."

The Need for Social Reform

Industrial society also created a great need for social reform. As urbanization, immigration, class distinctions, child labor, and boom and bust cycles in the economy affected people's lives, a need arose to address these concerns. The problems of poverty, unhealthy living environments, lack of open space, illness and disease, as well as the social chaos that emerged from sharply defined class distinctions, were well documented in American literature. Jacob Riis, writing in the *Battle with the Slum* (1902:3), reminds us that "great changes which the 19th century saw, the new industry, political freedom, brought on an acute attack which put that very freedom in jeopardy." Social advocate Jane Addams points out in her book, *The Spirit of Youth and the City Streets,* (1912:5) "industrialism has gathered together multitudes of eager young creatures from all corners of the earth as a labor supply for the countless factories and shops. . . . Never before in civilization have such numbers of young girls been suddenly released from the protection of the home and permitted to walk unattended upon city streets . . . never before have such numbers of young boys . . . [been] . . . in the midst of vice, deliberately described as pleasure. Into this void came the numerous social reformers, including individuals such as William Cullen Bryant, Luther and Charlotte Gulick, Joseph Lee, Ellen Starr-Gates, Henry Curtis, Clark W. Hetherington, and G. Stanley Hall, as well as the aforementioned individuals, Jacob Riis and Jane Addams.

These individuals and others advanced forward a host of social innovations to address the problems that had emerged from the industrialization of society. A wave of social reform brought with it many different strategies directed at solving problems, including settlement housing, parks, cleaner streets, better housing, regulation of working conditions, suppression of prostitution, prohibition of alcohol, new transportation systems, playgrounds, public baths (swimming pools), even ridding the streets of peddlers and the newsies (i.e., any boy or girl selling gum, shining shoes, etc.). Such reforms often resulted in the provision of essential social services aimed at "easing the troubles of every city dweller" (Baldwin, 1999:38). Public service managers including park and recreation administrators were "guided by human sympathy and scientific method . . . to meet the special needs of everyone."

Technology Transfer

The industrial revolution, with its origins in European communities, brought its full might and influence to bear on human affairs in America in full force by the late 1800s. As a result, there was a significant transfer of technology and other ideas between European communities and America. Americans often imitated the production and management methods of industrial Europe, in particular those found in the United Kingdom and in Germany. The transfer of technology was not limited to managing businesses and industry, but also extended to the social arena. Industrialization had created a whole new set of challenges that required new social innovations. Great social reform had occurred in Germany and England as a result of the municipalization of many basic services such as water, light, and sewage treatment as well as the provision of public open spaces. In a sense, municipal services were developed by linking with businesses and industries to develop these resources. In turn, these types of services were often run at the actual cost of the service to the citizens.

Daniel T. Rogers writing in *Atlantic Crossings: Social Politics in a Progressive Age* (1998) attributes the significant technology transfer between European countries and America to the return of young American graduate students educated in the best of Europe's universities, especially in Germany and England. The process of technology transfer was also aided by the ideas brought to America by its burgeoning immigrant population in the late 1800s and early 1900s. Further, the process of technology transfer was aided by Americans who toured European communities. In this latter case, Americans traveling freely to European communities observed, recorded, and ultimately replicated the social innovations of modern European industrial society.

Several examples support the contention that this extensive transfer of technology, which occurred not only in management theory and practice but more specifically in social inventions, lay the foundations for the park and recreation movement. The first is that of Frederick Law Olmsted's visits to European countries and their subsequent impact on his landscape design concepts. The second is the contributions of Dr. Maria Zakrzewska, a Prussian immigrant to the United States. And last are the management and organizational ideas of Max Weber and Henri Fayol and their subsequent influence on American business, enterprise, and government operations.

Fredrick Law Olmsted, widely recognized as the "Father of Landscape Architecture," was well traveled. As a young man, not only did he travel within the United States, but he also traveled to China, England, France, Belgium, Holland, and Germany. In England, he was particularly taken with the countryside and, in particular, with Birkenhead Park. Birkenhead Park was a public park developed in 1844 by Joseph Paxton. This park area, which covered 120 acres, was "bisected by a gently curving city street and circled by a carriage way. There were no formal vistas, no straight lines at all. The picturesque ponds, random clumps of tr rolling meadows, overgrown hilloc and meandering footpaths reminded Olmsted of the English countryside" (Rybczynski, 1999:93). Undoubtedly, this experience had a profound impact on Olmsted; it is evident that he brought these and other ideas to bear in his design plan for Central Park in New York, which was presented with his co-collaborator Calbert Vaux in 1857.

Dr. Maria Zakrzewska contributed her ideas to the establishment of unique social programs in many ways. In conjunction with Dr. Elizabeth Blackwell, she opened the first infirmary for women and children in the United States in 1853. Formerly "the chief midwife of Prussia's largest hospital, . . . Dr. Zakrzewska] . . . had immigrated, to New York City convinced that only in a republic can it be proved that science has no sex" (Burrows & Wallace, 1999:800). Dr. Zakrzewska is credited with "the general development of the provision for play . . . with the establishment of sand gardens in the yard of the Children's Mission in Boston in 1885 through the sponsorship of the Massachusetts Emergency and Hygiene Association. (Doell & Fitzgerald, 1954:70). Undoubtedly, Dr. Zakrzewska had been exposed to the thinking and social reforms of early education advanced by German educational theorists Freidrich Froebel and Johannes Pestulozzi.

Frobel's task was the systematizing of play under the leadership of adults, without robbing play of its freedom, or the child of his or her perfect spontaneity and independence of action (Hughes, 1897:125). The use of sand gardens fulfilled this educational end by providing play environments that gave children the opportunity for spontaneous behaviors.

More directly related to management theory and practice is the contribution of Max Weber. Weber, a German economist and social historian, formulated many of the founding principles of the bureaucratic form of organization. He viewed bureaucracies as being the most rational method of organization. According to Weber (1947:330-340), bureaucracies have five characteristics:

1. *Division of Work.* This involved breaking tasks into their smallest components so individuals with the minimum level of ability could perform them.

2. *Centralized Authority.* Weber believed that positions should be arranged in a hierarchy so that a higher position was maintained over each individual in the bureaucracy, that is, up to the ultimate source of authority-owner of a policymaking board.

3. *Rules.* Weber suggested that each organization should have a set of abstract rules to guide its internal and external actions. He felt that to operate rationally, an organization must be bound by a set of rules that promote adherence to a standard.

4. *Rational Personnel Policies.* Uniform policies allow each individual to be treated in an equitable manner. Weber believed, for example, that promotions should be based on one's ability rather than on one's social status. This notion supported his view that the bureaucratic form of organization was a rational one.

5. *Records.* Weber believed that bureaucratic organizations should maintain records as a method of increasing their accountability.

Weber believed that a bureaucracy was the ideal organizational structure. It provided a means whereby organizations could gauge their performance against a standard. If an organization was malfunctioning, its component parts could be compared with this standard and corrective action could be taken. Interestingly, Weber was also a professor at several prestigious universities, including Freiburg, Heidelberg, and Munich. As Rogers (1998) points out, many young American graduate students were exposed to different theories of economic thinking and undoubtedly were exposed to Weber's works.

The process of technology transfer in the management area was also supported by the work of the French industrialist Henri Fayol (1949). Fayol defined the management process as including five primary functions: planning, organization, command, coordination, and control. These management functions have come to serve as the foundation of the administrative process described in management literature. Believing that the process of management could be applied universally, Fayol developed 14 principles that he felt could be used by managers to solve problems in a number of situations:

1. *Division of Work.* Division of work refers to the principle of specialization of labor in order to concentrate activities for more efficiency.

2. *Authority and Responsibility.* Authority is the right to give orders and the power to exact obedience.

3. *Discipline.* Discipline is absolutely essential for the smooth running of business; without discipline no enterprise could prosper.

4. *Unity of Command.* An employee should receive orders from one superior only.

5. *Unity of Direction.* There should be one head and one plan for a group of activities, all having the same objectives.

6. *Subordination of Individual Interests to General Interests.* The interests of one employee or a group should not prevail over that of the organization.

7. *Remuneration.* Personnel compensation should be fair and, as far as possible, afford satisfaction both to personnel and the firm.

8. *Centralization.* Centralization is essential to the organization and is a natural consequence of organizing.

9. *Scalar Chain.* The scalar chain refers to the chain of superiors ranging from the ultimate authority to the lowest rank.

10. *Order.* The organization should provide an orderly place for every individual, in other words, a place for everyone and everyone in his or her place.

11. *Equity.* Equity and a sense of justice should pervade the organization.

12. *Stability of Tenure of Personnel.* Time is needed for employees to adapt to their work and to perform it effectively.

13. *Initiative.* At all levels of the organizational ladder, zeal and energy are augmented by initiative.

14. *Esprit de Crps.* This principle emphasizes the need for teamwork and the maintenance of interpersonal relationships. (Kast & Rosenzweig, 1974:58-59)

Fayol's perception of management functions and principles provides a means for analyzing the management process. His conceptual framework allows management methodology to be widely applied in industry and government. Emphasizing that management principles are not static, he stressed that managers should use their experience and insight in decision making.

Management History

There is a great deal of literature available regarding the practice and theory of management. Management techniques and thought can provide the leisure service manager with a foundation of theory that can be used to formulate a personal management philosophy. Although management principles can be traced to ancient times, this chapter focuses on modern management theory starting at the beginning of the 20th century.

Scientific Management

The rise of industry gave impetus to the "scientific management" movement. Stimulated by the need to create an increase in goods, the industrial revolution of the late 19th and early 20th centuries called for improved methods of production. The notion that management could be viewed as an exact science based on mathematical calculations was known as scientific management. It is based largely in the work of Frederick W. Taylor and his associates in the early 1900s. As initiated by Taylor, the scientific management movement was directed toward improving techniques of work and, ultimately, increasing worker efficiency. Although stressing the need for cooperation between management and subordinates, scientific management operationally dehumanized the worker and made work itself specialized in nature.

Taylor was concerned with developing incentive plans for employees that would reward them for extra effort above and beyond a normal day's output. The assumption of this theory was that in a work situation, individuals are motivated by the desire for financial rewards. Scientific management theory further incorporated the premise that once a work task had been analyzed objectively, specific procedures could be determined to complete the task. Once the most effective and efficient way to complete a task was determined, a worker was trained in the procedures. Workers were expected to contribute a fair day's work and were rewarded financially for output above the minimum standards of expectation.

Taylor's (1967:36-37) principles of scientific management included the following:

"First, the development of the science, i.e., the gathering in on the part of those on the management's side of all knowledge which in the past has been kept in the heads of the workmen; second, the scientific selection and progressive development of the workmen; third, the bringing of the science and the scientifically selected and trained men together; and fourth, the constant and intimate co-operation which always occurs between the men on the management's side and the worker."

It was assumed that once a worker understood the principle of increased financial incentives, the work output would increase. Enhancing an individual's opportunity for increased economic gains was assumed to be a prime motivating factor.

Scientific management's contribution to management theory is felt today throughout industry and government. By establishing a concern for effectiveness and efficiency, the scientific management movement drew attention to the need for management and organizational theory. Toward that end, the scientific management movement contributed a number of important theoretical concepts. Kast and Rosenzweig (1974:57) wrote:

"The scientific management movement provided many of the ideas for the conceptual framework later adopted by administrative management theorists, including clear delineation of authority and responsibility, separation of planning from operations, the functional organization, the use of standards in control, the development of incentive systems for workers, the principle of management by exception, and task specialization."

Further, the concept of cooperation between management and workers was another important by-product of the scientific management movement. (One fixture of contemporary management theory, employer–employee cooperation, will be discussed in chapters that follow.)

However, scientific management can be criticized from a number of different perspectives. Most notably, scientific management dehumanized the role of the worker and did not allow for such motivating factors as recognition, a sense of achievement, and the need for self-esteem:

"By the end of the scientific management period, the worker had been reduced to the role of an impersonal cog in the machine of production. The job became more and more narrowly specialized until the worker had little appreciation for his or her contribution to the total product. Naturally, the worker had very little, if any, involvement and pride in his job. Although very significant technological advances were made in . . . [this period], the serious weakness of the scientific approach to management was that it dehumanized the organizational member. The worker was assumed to be with-

out emotion and capable of being scientifically manipulated, just like machines." (Hicks, 1972:373-374).

Human Relations Management

Another approach to management, known as "human relations," emerged in the 1930s. Pioneered by Elton Mayo and his associates, the human relations theory suggested that workers can be motivated by nonfinancial aspects of the work environment. It further implied that the work situation can be viewed in behavioral terms and that the role of the manager is to create satisfactory interpersonal relationships.

The behavioral science approach to the study of management embraces a number of disciplines, such as psychology, sociology, and anthropology. The field of behavioral science is directed toward establishing

". . . evidence collected in an impersonal and objective way. . . . The ultimate end is to understand, explain, and predict human behavior in the same sense in which scientists understand, explain, and predict the behavior of physical forces or biological factors or, closer to home, the behavior of goods and services in the economic market." (Berelson, 1963:3)

Several important studies have contributed greatly to the development of a body of knowledge for the behavioral sciences as they relate to organizational management.

The Hawthorne Studies
Headed by Mayo, the Hawthorne research studies are generally consid-

ered to represent the beginning of the human relations approach to management. The Hawthorne research effort consisted of a series of experiments designed to study the relationship between employee conditions and productivity. The first study was organized to determine the effects of illumination on worker production. A sample of workers was selected and divided into two groups, one for control and the other for experimental changes. The experimental group was subject to increases and decreases in the amount of illumination. On the other hand, the control group had illumination held constant. Contrary to the hypothesis tested, both groups showed increases in productivity.

Following the illumination studies, another project known as the "relay room experiments" was undertaken. This experiment was initiated to determine the effects of a number of working conditions on production. Selected variables, such as the number of hours worked per day and the number of days worked per week, were manipulated. After reaching a conclusion similar to that of the illumination studies, it was suggested that the independent variables tested were not the only influences on worker productivity.

Two additional studies, a second relay room experiment and a bank wiring room experiment, were undertaken. The second relay room study was undertaken to determine the impact of wage incentives on production. Supervision, general working conditions, and the setting were held constant for both the experimental and control groups. The experimental group, which received wage incentives, showed a 12 percent increase in production at the conclusion of the study.

The bank wiring room studies resulted in findings opposite those obtained in the second relay room study. Studying the production of workers assembling bank wires, the researchers determined that output was restricted for a number of reasons, including fear of unemployment, fear of raising the job standard, and protection of slower coworkers.

Obviously, in both experimental situations, some factor was not being held constant or controlled. Of course, this factor was the human factor.

The Hawthorne studies marked the first time that an intensive systematic analysis had uncovered, by accident, the *human variable* in management and organizational behavior. Mayo and others concluded from the experience that two factors affected work and productivity. The first was the importance of group dynamics in the work situation. Behavior exhibited in work groups was by and large a by-product of individual and small-group interaction among workers. Second, it was suggested that the quantity and quality of job supervision affected employee job satisfaction and production.

The Hawthorne studies undermined the theory of scientific management, that is, that higher productivity could be achieved by financial reward alone. These further suggested that an understanding of the behavioral sciences could increase organization and management effectiveness and efficiency. The Hawthorne studies have been criticized because they did not directly relate employee satisfaction with employee performance. It has also been suggested that early behaviorists, such as Mayo, widely applied their theories to management without due consideration to actual worker productivity.

Management Science (Operations Research)

Management science is the second major area that affects management and organizational theory and practice. It is an outgrowth and extension of scientific management. Based largely on the application of mathematical equations and use of the computer, the study of management science is an important element influencing organizational and management decision making today.

A number of new techniques, such as Program Evaluation Review Technique– Critical Path Method (PERT–CPM), Total Performance Management, and Planning-Programming-Budgeting System (PPBS), are examples of management science techniques. These concepts are applied widely in the delivery of leisure services by both commercial organizations and governmental institutions. As an outgrowth of Taylor's scientific management, they involve application of "the scientific method as a framework for problem solving with emphasis on objective than subjective judgement" (Kast & Rosenzweig, 1974:87).

Management science and operations research is geared toward providing quantitative information that can be used in management decision making. Quantitative methods can complement or replace subjective methods, such as operating on hunches, operating by rule of thumb, and brainstorming. They can help the leisure service manager bypass decision making based on guesswork. Directed toward solving operational problems, these management techniques have been greatly enhanced by the increased capabilities of electronic data processing.

There are three general areas in which quantitative techniques and tools

for management have been developed. The first of these, general systems modeling, includes organizational design, simulation model building, accounting systems and models, and management information systems. The second grouping, scheduling models, includes conventional models such as milestone charts. Mathematical-statistical modeling, such as marginal analysis and network analysis, is the last general area in which quantitative techniques exist. Although it is difficult to specifically identify a body of knowledge in the field of management science, management science has nine key characteristics:

1. Emphasis on the scientific method

2. A systematic approach to problem solving

3. Mathematical model building

4. Quantification and use of mathematical and statistical procedures

5. Concern with economic-technical rather than psychosocial aspects

6. The use of electronic computers as tools

7. Emphasis on a total systems approach

8. Optimal decisions sought with closed-systems assumptions

9. An orientation to normative rather than descriptive models (Kast & Rosenzweig, 1974:89)

Management science was first applied successfully in England during World War II. It was introduced to help the British Royal Air Force intercept invading aircraft. With the aid of radar systems, researchers were able to calculate intercept routes mathematically. Following World War II, operations research techniques were applied widely to problems of business and industry in England. During the early 1950s, operations research was first applied in the United States. The following six steps are widely accepted as operations research techniques that can be used to solve a problem:

1. Formulate the problem.

2. Construct a mathematical model to represent the system under study.

3. Derive a solution from the model.

4. Test the model and the solution derived from it.

5. Establish controls over the situation.

6. Put the solution to work (implementation). (Churchman, Ackoff, & Arnoff, 1957:89)

A key concept in management science and operations research is that of modeling. A model is a "simplified representation of the relevant aspects of an actual system or process" (Donnelly, Gibson, & Ivancevich, 1971). It allows the decision maker the opportunity to simulate reality and therefore analyze potential effects with a great deal of predictability.

Network Modeling

The management functions of planning, scheduling, and controlling can be enhanced through the graphic means used in network models. These are tools designed specifically to help the leisure service manager determine the relationships that exist between the various tasks associated with any given project or program. Network models allow the leisure service manager to deal with the complexity and uncertainties involved in the organization of projects or programs. These techniques provide the leisure service manager with ideas to facilitate decision making. Network models do not make decisions for managers, but they can serve as a resource on which to base decisions.

There are three essential components involved in the use of network models. The first phase usually involves identifying or planning a project's or program's activities and events and arranging them in a logical sequence. An *event* may be defined as "a specific accomplishment that occurs at a recognizable point in time" (Levin & Kirkpatrick, 1971:393). *An activity* is "the work required to complete a specific event".

The second phase involved in network modeling is actually scheduling the estimated duration of each activity. By proceeding logically through a network and determining the time each activity will take, one is able to estimate the cumulative project or program time. As a program or project progresses, the third major component, controlling, enters the scene. By monitoring the completion of events, changes, or modifications in the entire project, an analysis can be undertaken to determine the future impact on the entire network. By updating the model periodically, a leisure service manager is able to effectively and efficiently control a project or program. Figure 2.1 illustrates a network.

Simulation

Although simulation is a broad term, it essentially involves the manipulation or reproduction of an organization's

Figure 2.1
A Network Diagram

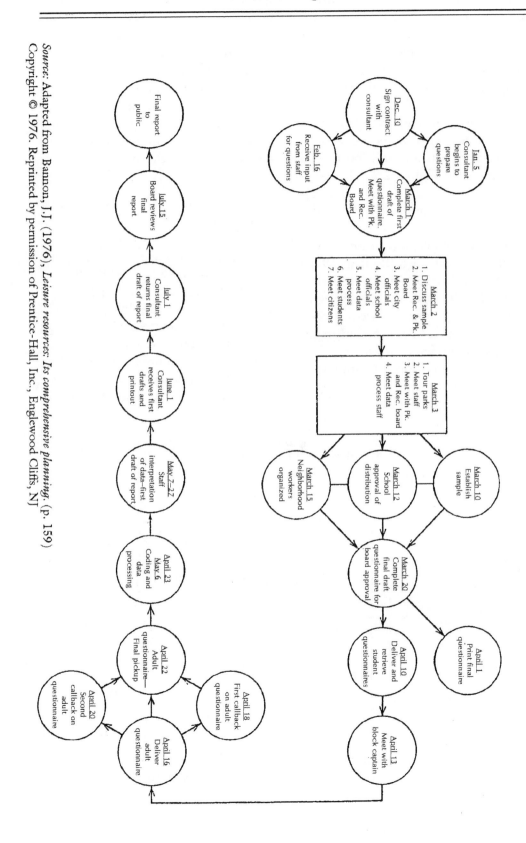

Source: Adapted from Bannon, J.J. (1976), *Leisure resources: Its comprehensive planning*, (p. 159) Copyright © 1976. Reprinted by permission of Prentice-Hall, Inc., Englewood Cliffs, NJ

potential operations as it moves through time. Simply, one may use simulation to model and represent a number of situations for the purpose of aiding decision making. Two methods of simulation—decision-making trees and sampling—are discussed as historical elements in this area of management.

A decision-making tree can help the manager deal with the potential alternatives involved in a decision-making situation (see Figure 2.2). It "is no more than a pictorial diagram that captures the uncertainty of the situation and enumerates the possible outcomes of making the decision in one way or another" (Peterson & Pohlen, 1973). By describing or simulating the various alternatives that face the leisure service manager, the potential consequences of a given decision can be illustrated graphically and identified in advance.

Another method of simulation comes through the use of sampling. It would, of course, be difficult to have a total population represented in every decision that affected the allocation of an organization's resources. As an alternative, one can use methods of sampling that accurately represent the entire population. Sampling is done with the use of random numbers. A random sample is a method of systematically taking a portion of a given population to ensure that each number has an equal chance of being selected.

Systems Analysis

Systems analysis is a technique that allows the leisure service manager to identify the variables that may be involved in the operation of an organization. Kraus and Curtis (2000:40) suggest that there are three types of systems: (1) natural; (2) physical, and (3) open. Systems analysis "is a method that reduces a total system into increasingly smaller components until the smallest unit making up the entire system is defined." (Hjelte & Shivers, 1972:290)

Figure 2.2
Model of Free-Time Activity Choice

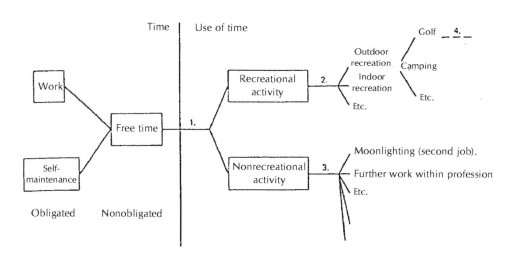

Source: Dr. Doug Crapo, Balmer, Crapo, and Associates, Waterloo, Ontario, Canada.

Systems analysis broadly applied, according to Kraus and Curtis (1973:26-27) seeks to do the following:

1. Establish detailed work objectives that specifically determine what, when, where, and how work is to be accomplished

2. Develop effective schedules for maintenance and repairing, and group functions together for efficient performance

3. Develop standardized methods for job performance in which work routines are programmed, with time standards for completion

4. Provide instruments and techniques for effectively measuring and determining the cost of job performance, to assist in evaluating employee work output and assigning tasks or planning budgets

There are five components necessary for constructing a system: inputs, process, output, feedback, and control. Output refers to the desired goals or objectives of the system. Inputs are the resources necessary to achieve the desired goals or outputs. Process refers to the procedure or procedures that consume resources and allow for the achievement of desired outcomes. Mechanisms for feedback are directed toward evaluation and modification of both type and amount of resources consumed to produce desired goals or outputs. The function of control is to regulate or change components of the system that can affect the desired outcome. Systems theory suggests that all these components are interrelated and dependent on one another. Figure 2.3 diagrams the systems approach to the management of recreation.

As Kast and Rosenzweig, (1973:109) note, systems can be viewed in one of two ways: "(1) closed, or (2) open and in interaction with their environment." Closed systems view management and organizational behavior as primarily centered around the internal organization and operation of the agency. Open systems, on the other hand, are characterized by constant in-

Figure 2.3
A Systems Approach to the Management of Leisure Services

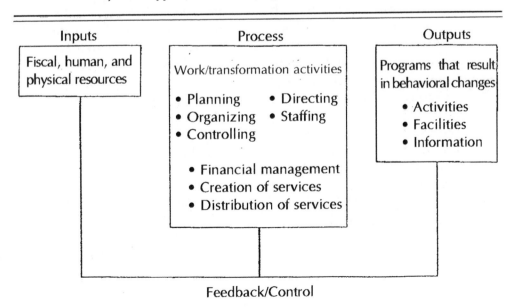

teraction among the various systems, such as the political, social, and economic environments. Closed systems tend to become static when lacking continual input, feedback, and stimulus from the environment. Open systems maintain a dynamic posture in regard to their environment. They react quickly to changes in the environment and modify the mission and function of the organization to the changing environmental inputs. The management model presented in Chapter One suggests that leisure delivery organizations should be open systems that respond to the various inputs and constraints, which result from continual interaction with the environment.

Human Resources Management

The idea of Human Resources Management (HRM) emerged as an extension of organizational science but combines previous work in the area of human resources with contemporary findings in the behavioral sciences. As Schuler suggests, human resources management "grew out of the organizational science trend and combines learning from the previous movements with current research in the behavioral sciences." HRM has become an important management strategy within modern organizations. According to Schuler (1992:) a strong HRM focus is necessary because of (1) rapid change, (2) high levels of uncertainty about basic business conditions, (3) rising costs, (4) rapid technological change, (5) changing demographics, (6) more limited supplies of highly trained labor, 7) rapidly changing government legislation and regulations, and 8) increased globalization of industries.

We can think of human resource management as decision making that has an impact on people working within an organization or, in short, its human resources. Fisher, Schoenfeldt, and Shaw (1999) have written that organizations need a number of elements to be successful, including physical resources, financial resources, marketing capability, and human resources. Human resources include "the experience, skills, knowledge, judgment, and creativity belonging to the organization along with the means of organizing, structuring, and rewarding these capabilities." Often human resources management involves five major areas:

1. *Planning for Organizations, Jobs, and People.* This includes strategic management of human resources, human resource planning, and job analysis.

2. *Acquiring Human Resources.* This involves equal opportunity procedures, recruiting and job search, measurement and decision-making issues in selection, and assessing job candidates.

3. *Building Individual and Organizational Performance.* This refers to human resource development and human resource approaches to improving competitiveness.

4. *Rewarding Employees.* This includes performance appraisals, compensation system development, and incentive compensation and benefits.

5. *Maintaining Human Resources.* This involves safety and health, labor relations and collective bargaining, and reductions in the workforce.

Miles (1975) has discussed the difference between classical or traditional models of management, the human relations model, and the HRM approach. In the HRM approach, people are viewed differently than in either the traditional or human relations model. The basic assumption of the HRM approach is that people will contribute to meaningful ends if they are involved in establishing the goals. And in fact, as Miles states, "most people can exercise far more creativity, responsible self-direction, and self-control than their present jobs command." The work of a manager, in this approach, involves creating an environment that helps individuals exercise self-direction and control in such a way as to release their unused work capacity. HRM claims that productivity may increase when people have greater influence and control over their work environment.

Contemporary Management

In the past two decades, management thinking has undergone great change. We have seen nothing short of a revolution in the way in which organizations are managed. Great emphasis is placed on innovation, change management, and pursuing excellence in quality in the delivery of leisure services. The growth in employment of knowledge- and service-based workers requires greater "teaming" amongst employees. Increasingly, the knowledge and expertise of individuals is valued over their formal positions, or authority within an organization.

Perhaps the individuals most influential in promoting this change in thinking are Thomas J. Peters and Robert H. Waterman, Jr. These authors' book *In Search of Excellence* (1982) gave us a new paradigm for managing into the 21st century. Their work provided the stimulus for a greater focus on releasing the work capacity of employees, improving quality, restructuring organizations in ways that were less bureaucratic, connecting with customers, promoting entrepreneurial behavior, and encouraging productivity by promoting action. As Drucker (1994) notes, contemporary management in the last decade of the 20th century made us both qualitatively and quantitatively different than we were in the first years of this century, and perhaps at any other time in our history.

Focus on Quality and Excellence

A focus on quality and excellence comes from the work of W. Edwards Deming, who advanced concepts related to quality in his work in Japan following World War II. The Deming method involves improving quality, productivity, and competitive positioning by focusing on improving processes of design, and production, as well as being in touch with customers to understand their needs. It involves having a longer-term perspective and establishing benchmarks, then measuring statistically an organization's progress against those benchmarks.

Perhaps the key management ideas emerging from a focus on quality and excellence have been the concepts known as Total Quality Management (TQM) and Total Quality Leadership (TQL) (see Chapter One). These management concepts require managers to take an active role in promoting quality within their organizations. Continuous, ongoing improvement is sought through this process. TQM and TQL seek to involve actively all stakeholders in the process. Workers are encouraged to team together to find ways to improve the quality of either the process involved in producing the service or the service itself.

Benchmarking, Measuring, and Evaluating

Increasingly, leisure service organizations are being held accountable for the expenditure of their resources. In order to measure success, organizations are challenged to create a framework to gauge their outcomes, usually against the inputs or resources they have expended. Luthans (1998:37) has written that "benchmarking is the process of comparing work in service methods against the best practices and outcomes for the purpose of identifying changes that will result in higher quality output." Kraus and Curtis (2000:44) have suggested that benchmarking is a "continuous process of measuring products, services, and practices against an organization's strongest competitors, or those recognized as industry leaders."

Camp (1995) has identified a five-step process that may be employed in benchmarking. The first step is planning, which involves identifying what is to be benchmarked, what are comparable organizations, and what data is to be collected. The second step involves analyzing the gap between current performance and future desired performance. The third step is decision making; it involves establishing goals and plans to close the gap between actual and desired performance. The next step involves implementing specific actions and monitoring progress. The last step focuses on fully integrating the process of benchmarking into an organization's operations.

An example of benchmarking as applied in the leisure service field is found in Figure 2.4. This strategy of benchmarking a variety of elements in the management of the Elk Grove (Illinois) Park District enables staff to determine how well the organization is performing in terms of its goals, roles and responsibilities, communication, cooperation and collaboration, leadership, conflict, efficiency, esprit, recognition systems, and quality.

Reorganizing and Reengineering Organizational Change

In the early 1990s, public, non-profit, and private organizations were challenged to reinvent themselves in light of the changing social economic conditions of the times. The knowledge era gave way to new and different expectations on the part of participants for services to be more customized and of higher quality. Basically, existing work methods, procedures, and strategies were being challenged. David Osborne and Ted Gaebler (1992) authored *Reinventing Government*, challenged government to become more entrepreneurial and less bureaucratically focused. Interestingly, concepts thoroughly discussed in the first edition of this book (published as *Productive Management of Leisure Service Organizations*), such as Sunnyvale, California's Total Performance Measurement system, were offered as examples of excellent management strategies.

What exactly is reengineering? Michael Hammner and James Champy (1993:32) have written in *Reengineering the Corporation: A Manifesto for Business Revolution*, that reengineering is "the fundamental rethinking and radical redesign of business processes to achieve dramatic improvements in the

Figure 2.4
Sample of Benchmarking

Snapshot

elk grove park district	1 – 5	6 – 10	11 – 15	16 – 20
Goals	Employees in disagreement on Company's mission or do not know what mission is. Employees question direction and leadership.	Employees challenge mission and direction; want to change things. "We do not live our mission."	Employees understand and work toward goals. High level of buy-in support.	Employees take joint pride in department and Company accomplishments. New goals emerge as old ones are reached.
Roles & Responsibilities	Individuals unclear on expectations and tasks. No group identity. Employees unclear on how they fit in the organization.	Individual roles become clearer, responsibilities emerge. Power and position battles take place.	Employees know and support each others' roles and work to support them. Sharing and learning take place often.	Department roles and responsibilities grow. Individuals grow to meet the new expectations.
Communication	Communications guarded and cautious. Many closed doors, suspicious discussions.	Participation levels vary widely. Some employees are open and trusting; others closed and cautious. Things to be done are often kept secret.	Communication is two-way, interactive and creative. Plans are acknowledged and handled.	Communication is constant and in all directions. Employees use all means available to assure desired results of dept. and Company are achieved. Face value communications.
Cooperation & Collaboration	No department cooperation, little trust, open hostility. Focus on self-preservation. Personal plans and positions important.	Need for teamwork acknowledged but seen as impractical and too hard. Small exclusive groups form and the "in" group gains power. Some trust in selected individuals.	Broad team begin to form - sub-groups dissolve and leadership is observed throughout the Company. Company wins seen as important.	Trust is high and unquestioned. Motives are taken at face value. Personal wants are deferred for Company needs. "We" orientation. "We can do it together" attitude.
Leadership	All employees look to official leader for decisions, direction, and conflict resolution. Dependent decision making.	Employees challenge leader. "Grapevine Leaders" emerge at the expense of formal leader. Some covert operations take place.	Leadership responsibilities shared and official leader is supported throughout the Company. Letting go and delegation skills used.	Leader delegates to employees. Leader defines role as supporting employees and removing roadblocks to accomplish joint objectives.
Conflict	People strive for individual recognition and exposure. Conflict is low as employees size up their competition.	Personal attacks occur. High level of competition and conflict. Individuals and departments strive for power and control. "Us vs. Them" attitudes seen.	Team decides on ground rules for resolving conflict productively and solves most problems. Non-team players are expelled.	Conflict is seen as energy and creativity. Disagreements are sources of great opportunity to work together to solve problems.
Efficiency	Very little team output. Individual contributions only source of productivity. Team seen as bother.	Work is accomplished by individuals or small exclusive groups. Team output is seen only on forced occasions.	Team is primary productivity tool. Strength productivity and expertise seen as strategic advantage.	Team productivity is seen as greater than the productivity of individuals working separately. Employees working as a team multiply the return on investment in productivity and skills.
Esprit	Team identify seen as "corny" or of low value. Individuals point to "That's the way it's always been done" as the reason not to cooperate or work together.	Employees occasionally see benefit in working together. Most group productivity is by small "in" groups.	Employees unify and develop identity as a team. Individuals feel good about group success and accomplishments.	Team seen as primary source of strength and accomplishment. Reputation throughout the Company grows and individuals are intensely proud of their team.
Recognition Systems	Rewards and recognition for individual accomplishments only.	Rewards designed for short-term successes with little regard for whether the accomplishments were the result of team or individual efforts.	Team rewards/members for efforts that enable the team to reach its objectives. High level of peer recognition.	High confidence in team process. Being a team player is seen as necessary for promotion and increased responsibility. People grow and develop by working together.
Quality	"I just show up and do what I'm told." "They don't pay me to think."	Some big improvement ideas implemented after much effort and politics.	Many small successes in quality of goods and services. Lead from the top of the organization.	Continual improvement every day. Fully integrated throughout the entire Company. Everyone involved.

Source: Elk Grove (Illinois) Park District

critical contemporary measures of performance, such as cost, quality, service, and speed." A great deal of emphasis in the reengineering of organizations is placed on the creation of new processes, products, and services. Organizations are virtually being reinvented in such a way that procedures are being revitalized, ineffective bureaucracies smashed, and networking encouraged.

Information Technology

With the spread of information technology, we are being affected in many different ways. The technology revolution has virtually no end in sight, and the rate of technological change continues to move in a rapid and significant fashion. The half-life of computer hardware is now projected at approximately 18 months. The impact of Internet services and the World Wide Web is transforming commerce and business dramatically. Cellular phones and other forms of communication are dramatically influencing our ability to connect with one another.

Hill and McLean (1999) have suggested that we are going through both evolutionary and revolutionary changes that involve technology. The unpredictability, if not chaotic nature, of these changes is making it difficult to assess with great accuracy the future impact on leisure. Nonetheless, Hill and McLean suggest that marketing will play a key role as leisure and technology are integrated in the future and that it is important to have a holistic perspective on the blend of technology and leisure. Blazey (1999:30) suggests that it is important to develop a set of core values to guide one's use of technology. He notes "the ability to access, use, manipulate, and transform Web-based data will, without question, contribute to the information explosion. Yet to be devised, however, is the ethical framework guaranteeing attribution, recognition, and compensation for authorship; the appropriate "fair use" guidelines; and, a more fundamental issue, the means to verify content accuracy."

The Learning Organization

Peter M. Senge, in writing *The Fifth Discipline* (1990); popularized the importance of organizations built around a culture of learning. As Senge notes "learning gets to the heart of what it means to be human. Through learning we re-create ourselves" (14). The learning organization, according to Senge, is one that "is continually expanding its capacity to create its future. The learning organizations do not learn to survive or even adapt, but rather their focus is on creating the future." Senge notes that five important technologies are required of learning organizations:

1. *Systems Thinking.* This implies an interconnectedness between elements within an organization. It is a conceptual framework used to make the full patterns clear and help us see how to change them effectively.

2. *Personal Mastery.* This is the discipline of continually clarifying and deepening our personal vision, of focusing our energies, of developing patience, and of seeing reality objectively.

3. *Mental Models.* Mental models are deeply ingrained assumptions, generalizations, or even pictures or images that influence how we understand the world and how we take action.

4. *Building a Shared Vision.* The practice of learning shared vision involves the skills of unearthing shared "pictures of the future" that foster genuine commitment and enrollment rather than compliance. In mastering this discipline, leaders learn that it is counterproductive to try to dictate a vision, no matter how heartfelt.

5. *Team Learning.* When the intelligence of the team exceeds the intelligence of the individuals in the team, and where teams develop extraordinary development for coordinated action, team learning has taken place.

Learning organizations are more capable of engineering change than organizations focused elsewhere. Creating an organizational culture focused on learning, hence innovation, draws the creative energies of individuals into its effort.

Strategic Management

The rate of change and the turbulence of the 1980s and 1990s gave rise to the need for a different strategy for managing organizations. This was particularly true in planning the work of leisure service organizations. Out of this environment of rapid and unyielding change emerged a concept known as strategic management or strategic planning. Strategic planning, unlike previous short-term focused management and planning efforts, was aimed at positioning an organization in such a way as to identify its core values, resources, and services so that it would be able to respond quickly in the marketplace to emerging trends. In other words, strategic management involved developing a favorable strategy for an organization that would position it in such a way that it achieved success.

Key to the process of strategic management was the development of a strategic plan. Most organizations followed what was known as the "SWAT" model of strategic planning. This involved several steps, including the identification of an organization's core values coupled with an ongoing scan of the environment to recognize changes advantageous to the organization. Planning usually involved identifying the vision or mission of an organization, the factors and trends that would affect its operations, its strengths and attributes, its internal and external threats, its goals and action plans, and last, the resources required to implement its programs.

Management in Leisure Service Organizations

Historically, the development of management ideas in the leisure service field roughly parallels those of modern management. Ideas expressed by the founders of our field Fredrick Law Olmsted, Jane Addams, Ellen Starr-Gates, Henry Curtis, Joseph Lee, Clark W. Heatherington, George Hjelte, J. B. Nash, George Butler, Harold D. Meyer, Charles K. Brightbill, and many others, help us to construct a unique body of knowledge related to leisure services management.

Our body of knowledge is found in professional practice, that is, in the application of management skills and knowledge that are germane to the delivery of leisure services. The skills and knowledge are also influenced by existing management theories and our values as professionals. Draper (1983) has argued that it is important to determine the appropriateness, generalizability, and implications of employing business management practices in leisure service provision. In this portion of the book, we will examine from a historical perspective the management literature as it relates directly to professional practice in the leisure service field. In addition, we will identify points at which management theory has been integrated into the leisure service literature and hence has had an impact on professional practice.

This section is divided into four parts. The first part traces management, literature, and thinking in the leisure service field from 1815 to 1920. The second presents information covering the Depression and war years of 1930 to 1950. The next part, entitled the Zenith of the Movement, covers a period from 1960 through the 1970s. The last covers 1980 to the present.

Early Perspectives on the Management of Leisure Services (1850–1920)

Many projects aimed at improving the welfare of individuals emerged during the late 1800s and early 1900s in the United States. As noted, such projects were often offered in response to the problems associated with urbanization, social economic stratification, ethnic and racial division, factory conditions, immigration, and the basic redefinition of daily life brought about by industrial society. The hubbub of urban life spawned such social innovations and programs as settlement houses, parks and open spaces, playgrounds, outdoor gymnasiums, field houses, and community and recreation centers in addition to cleaner streets, better housing, new transportation systems, and clean water and sanitation systems. Such successful projects were not only a reflection of great visionary thinking but also the application of other important management skills and abilities.

One of the ways that we can better understand early management thinking of the leisure service profession is to look at the practices of some of our founders. Frederick Law Olmsted has been described as being ambitious and goal oriented (Hall, 1995:66). Insight into his approach to management is offered by Hall, who writes that he was "considerate and fair in his dealings with workers, . . . nevertheless an autocrat, a boss who made decisions and disdained second-guessing or grumbling from subordinates." Writing to his son, John Olmsted, in 1862 and reflecting on his style of work, he wrote: "whenever you see a head, hit it." Rybczynski (1999:177) writes that Olmsted knew how to delegate authority to talented subordinates, and that one of his most valuable qualities was his capacity to engender intense loyalty in the people with whom he worked.

The work of Jane Addams and Ellen Starr-Gates, cofounders of Hull House in Chicago also provides interesting perspectives into managerial leadership practices of the founders of our profession. Addams has been described as calm and businesslike in her personality (Bryan & Davis, 1990). Starr-Gates' style, in contrast tended to be more emotional, more deeply religious, more committed to causes. Bryan and Davis (1990:5) note that without the passion of Gates it is unlikely that Addams "would have been able to translate her ideas into action." It seems that their flexibility and willingness to change were the key elements in their management styles that contributed to their success as well as enabling them to position themselves for leadership.

Henry S. Curtis writing in *The Practical Conduct of Play* (1915) and in *The Play Movement and Its Significance* (1917), provides valuable observations of the work of early leisure service professionals. Curtis noted that in "communities of Germany and Denmark, a special individual is employed who is known as a *Spiele Inspector*, or Play Supervisor, whose business it is to supervise the play of the community." It is evident that we draw our early ideas from the model provided by play supervisors in these two countries. Curtis (1917:218) pointed out that in 1906, less than 20 cities in the United States maintained playground programs, but by 1913, 342 cities had such programs.

What exactly did supervisors of playgrounds do as managers? Curtis (1915) wrote: "the person in charge will have to organize and plan a system as well as to administer" its programs (1915:16). He went on to note that "it is absolutely essential that . . . [the person] . . . should be a capable organizer and administrator" (1915:17). Curtis, referring to Joseph Lee, suggested that the great work that needed to be done was to "secrete the system." In order for this to be done, according to Curtis (1915-16), leisure service professionals of that era needed to create interest and enthusiasm for their work, be promoters, speak in public, secure cooperation, prevent friction, and maintain a state of discipline among play leaders.

The Normal Course in Play, prepared by the Playground and Recreation Association of America under direction of Joseph Lee, provided practical material that was used to train play-ground and recreation workers. First prepared in 1909, *The Normal Course in Play* was developed by a committee of individuals chaired by Clark W. Hetherington, with Henry S. Curtis serving as secretary. Chapters focusing on "Leadership" and "Organization and Organization and Administration" provide an overview of the role of administrators and details some fundamental principles of organizing community recreation. As noted, ". . . it is through organizations that facilities, leadership and agencies are interrelated and permanence given the play structure." (Lee, 1925). In discussing administrative responsibilities, such activities as maintaining records, securing land, and obtaining supplies are mentioned. Further budget planning is advanced as administrative responsibility. *The Normal Course in Play* details the duties of the recreation executives as follows:

"the selection, training and direction of employed play leaders; the purchasing and installing of apparatus and the laying out of playgrounds; the planning of buildings for recreation purposes and the securing of the use of school buildings and special buildings for use as community or neighborhood centers; the organization of neighborhood groups and cooperation with all community organizations and the encouragement and development of general recreation in the community and throughout community institutions of all kinds. The superintendent of recreation has the task of interpreting to the public through addresses, conferences, and play demonstrations the recreation work and needs of the community. On him or her falls the task of unitizing all the spare time available, thoroughly training volunteers to conduct recreation and vitalize the programs of local groups through the introduction of recreation, music, and drama, and to help in all phases of the movement. Finally, the recreation executive should be able to build up a group of volunteers back of the municipal work who will feel a responsibility for the whole movement."

It is evident in reviewing these responsibilities that the work of leisure service professionals during the early years of the movement was demanding and complex. It required a high level of ability in order to succeed. Interestingly, this literature does not incorporate any of that from the emerging body of knowledge in management. However, it does reflect an effort to distill roles, functions, and responsibilities of managers. In effect, early writers synthesized what they had observed into elements of "best professional practice" and acknowledged them in the literature of the day.

The Depression and the War Years (1930–1950)

The years 1930 through 1950 brought significant changes in the management of leisure services. In particular, during the Great Depression, the movement was enhanced by infusing into it federal funds for programs, such as the Work Progress Administration (WPA) and the Civilian Conservation

Corps (CCC). These programs enabled the expansion of programs and services at the local, state, and federal levels. Also, it marked a period of time wherein management knowledge was slowly incorporating the work of Mayo and his colleagues, as well as developments in operations research or management science. These elements, when combined with scientific management, provided a foundation for modern management thought and brought with them a host of new innovations that had the potential to influence the administration of leisure service agencies.

This period was marked by structural reform and reorganization in the park and recreation field. Numerous park departments were combined with playground or recreation commissions. For example, the City of Los Angeles, California, merged its Parks Department with its Playgrounds and Recreation Department in 1947. The management thinking of George Hjelte, general manager of this newly consolidated department, provides insight into the management ideas of the times: Hudson (1974:163) notes that "it was the character of George Hjelte to point out the human element in organizations. One of his administrative strong points was that he realized that organizations were run by human beings." Further, Hjelte pointed to the importance of coordinating and redefining an organization's function as a way of promoting management excellence. He wrote that:

"Effective administration is not only concerned with the operation of an existing institution, according to established precedents, but also in the definition and re-definition of its function, the improvement of its operations, the expansion of its services, and the adaptation of its work to changing needs" (Hudson, 1974:98).

In 1940, Hjelte authored the book *The Administration of Public Recreation,* which was concerned with the effective organization and administration of public recreation systems. It highlighted practices and problems common in the administration of public leisure services. Management, according to Hjelte (1940:133), "is concerned with the execution of the policies established by the commission and is clearly a function of the employed manager or superintendent of the department." Hjelte used terms such as "organization," "management," and "administration," and suggested that the services required to administer recreation included "planning, management, construction, maintenance, horticultural services, organization, promotion, and supervision" (1940:49).

During the same time period, books authored by George D. Butler, J. B. Nash, Harold D. Meyer, and Charles K. Brightbill also influenced management thinking in the public leisure service field. Nash, writing in *The Organization and Administration of Playgrounds and Recreation* (1938), provided a clear overview of the legislative mandates empowering public park and recreation organizations. Further, he discussed at great length how units were to be organized. In identifying the work of executives, he suggested four basic rules for managers:

1. Plan work intelligently.

2. Delegate authority wisely.

3. Follow up to make certain that results are being achieved.

4. In an emergency, be prepared to handle details personally. (186)

He suggests that the duties of managers in park and recreation systems are to inspire, to encourage, and to lead, not to spy on, to pick at, or to discourage (1938:199).

Butler (1936) suggested that the role of managers involved organizing the staff, planning the program, conducting staff meetings, and supervising. The manager was to help with publicity, ensure there was a well balanced program, and in general ensure that workers were focused on their work. Interestingly Butler suggested that "if the chief executive is a man, as is usually the case, a woman is frequently chosen" as the assistant. Obviously there was some gender bias in place that influenced this type of management thinking.

Meyer and Brightbill (1948) introduced into the management literature a clearer definition of the concept of administration and, in particular, recreation administration. Building on the historical management works of Fayol and others, they noted that "recreation administration is the act of planning, organizing, managing, and directing organized recreation" (25). Further, they suggested that "it is the task of administration to turn these elements into effective, organized recreation opportunities." The individual who assumes this high executive responsibility is called the "administrator." Administrators were to be involved in planning, personnel, facility and program development, and finance and business procedures, according to these authors. Some of the characteristics of able administrators identified by Meyer and Brightbill included:

1. A high regard for professional development.

2. Sound judgement of human nature.

3. Accuracy in sizing up situations, distinguishing readily between important and unimportant matters that results in well-considered opinions.

4. The ability to make difficult decisions on which others can depend.

5. Willingness to assume appropriate new and added responsibilities.

6. The ability to adapt to changing conditions and needs. (:29)

These authors also commented on factors that led to failure among administrators. They suggested that the following elements could contribute to the failure of administrators:

1. Impatient with anyone who did not quickly and readily comprehend what had been proposed.

2. Indiscreet, or at best not too concerned about personal behavior, when the administrator was "off the job."

3. Inclined to consider even constructive suggestions as personal criticism.

4. Too busy to orient or condition those whose approval he or she hoped to gain.

5. Determined to follow the rulebook rigidly, making no exceptions.

6. Interested mainly in pleasing everybody all the time.

7. A victim of mistaking personal publicity for effective departmental public relations.

8. Under the impression that his or her opinion had to be voiced on all matters, whether it was appropriate or not.

9. Not careful about keeping within budgetary allocations, even though the causes which he or she sought to serve were worthwhile.

10. Kept a record of his colleague's unfavorable actions in the event he or she ever came in major conflict with them.

Fitzgerald (1948:316) provided great insight into the work of recreation professionals in the 1940s and 1950s. He, like George Hjelte, suggested that professionals of the future "must be flexible enough to meet the changing needs of communities and to provide for the increasing numbers of relationships which recreation is encountering in community, state, national and world life." Fitzgerald suggested that the challenges of the future include the need for "higher salaries, greater security, more adequate recreation areas and facilities, longer professional careers, and larger staffs."

The Zenith of the Movement (1960s–1970s)

In many respects, the high point of the park and recreation movement occurred during the 1960s and 1970s. Spurred by the findings of the Outdoor Recreation Resources Review Commission (ORRRC) report released in the early 1960s and a similar study, the Canadian Outdoor Recreation Demands Study (CORDS) in the 1970s, great attention was drawn to the growth of leisure programs and services. In the United States, the acquisition and development of parks and other open spaces was enhanced dramatically by the passing of the Land and Water Conservation Fund Act in 1964. In addition there were numerous other significant legislative acts, including the Wilderness Act (1964), the Wild and Scenic Rivers Act (1968), the National Trail System Act (1968), and others especially related to water, air, and environmental quality that had a great impact on the expansion of services and also on management practices.

Despite the environmental gains of the 1960s and 1970s, it was also a period of taxpayer revolt and great inflation. An attempt at the general downsizing of government led by Proposition 13 in California in 1978 found park and recreation systems "doing more with less" and seeking strategies to establish a greater fee and charge base to support operations. Also, there was a turn away from the philosophical principles of social welfare and the greatest good for the greatest number in service delivery toward ones focused on using marketing strategies to guide the delivery of services. These changes brought forth the need for new management strategies and required a new set of skills—management skills that required visionary thinking, entrepreneurial managerial leadership, marketing, and in general greater emphasis on new and different ways of managing the fiscal activities of park and recreation systems.

In 1964, Lynn S. Rodney authored one of the most influential management books in the park and recreation field. *Administration of Public Recreation* was designed to provide an introduction to the general field of recreation administration. Its importance lay in that it incorporated a substantial amount of what could be defined as the "discipline of management" of the times. Rodney frequently cited noted management authors and related management concepts and their application to recreation. For example, quoting William Newman (1950) he suggested that administration involves guidance, leadership, and control. Citing John N. Pfiffner and Robert V. Prest (1960), he indicated that administration is an activity or process that is concerned with carrying out prescribed ends. Relating this to the field, he then went on to state that "recreation and parks administration must be concerned with this problem in mind: How can goals be reached with minimum effort and maximum efficiency?" (Rodney, 1964:26) Thus Rodney's writings became the first serious effort in the literature aimed at integrating management theory with recreation administration.

Discussing the administrative process, Rodney also draws on the work of Henry Fayol, Luther Gulick, and Ordway Tead. He suggests that management functions can be distilled into seven basic processes:

1. *Planning.* What are the objectives of the department? What program and activities should be provided to meet the objectives? What policies should be formulated? What should be the scope of operation?

2. *Organizing.* How should the plans be carried out? How will the work be allocated or divided? What organizational units should be established to carry out basic functions? What relationships should exist between units of operation?

3. *Staffing and Resourcing.* Who is to perform the many and varied tasks? What human and material resources are available? How are they to be allocated?

4. *Directing.* Who is to oversee how the work is being carried out? How are orders to be issued to get the organization operating and carrying out its functions? Who will direct general operations? How will this direction be given?

5. *Coordinating.* How will the various units of work be fused together into a team effort? What means should be used to ensure that divisions of work are functioning in harmony and are synchronized in effort?

6. *Controlling.* How are the assigned tasks being carried out? Are they conforming to agreed-upon plans? Are they meeting standards?

7. *Evaluating.* Were the objectives accomplished? Could the services be improved?

Rodney (1964:34) introduced many management concepts related to the organization of park and recreation systems. For example, he was the first author to introduce into the literature the idea of structuring organizations through: (1) the establishment of an integrated organization structure, (2) the identification of a unity of command, (3) the development of an adequate span of control, (4) the establishment of compatible relationships in the delegation of authority and responsibility, and (5) the use of staff units for research and specialization. Rodney also discussed such concepts as managerial

planning, decision making, and communications. He also introduced into the literature for the first time leadership theories, including discussions of the Trait Theory, Situational Theory, and Group Dynamics Theory. Overall, the impact of his writings was dramatic, as it significantly improved and advanced the body of knowledge related to park and recreation management by merging theories of the era with current practices.

Another important management work in the early 1960s was *Elements of Park and Recreation Administration* by Charles E. Doell. Doell was the former Superintendent of Parks for the City of Minneapolis, Minnesota. He brought a wealth of practical applied experience to discussing the essential elements involved in the administration of park and recreation systems. He did not incorporate contemporary management thinking in his writings, but rather relied on his great professional experience. Doell (1963:106) writes that "the operation of a park and recreation service at any and all levels of government is dependent on a systematic banning together of the many talents of people who possess those talents in such a way as to act as a unit. In a somewhat folksy manner, Doell wrote (1963:121-122) that the chief executive of park and recreation systems should pursue the following managerial guidelines:

1. Contrary to the situation in past generations, the present day public administrator cannot afford to be an autocrat.

2. Helpfulness, courtesy, and kindness must be constantly practiced.

3. Because a park and recreation service permeates all through soci-

ety, the manager of such a service organization, either personally or through other personnel with whom he is in daily contact, must be associated with a great many organizations.

4. There must be genuineness in his desire to be helpful.

5. Confidence is an essential element in leadership, but overconfidence and snobbishness are definite liabilities.

6. Most people are good citizens and most people are friendly and helpful, but they are all human and on occasion most anyone can participate in a sharp deal.

7. In all actions and consideration, the eye of the park administrator must be kept on the final goal.

To Doell's credit, he successfully integrated the body of professional knowledge related to park administration as practiced during this period of time. His work proved to be an invaluable source of information, which a student or professional could use to comprehend quickly the fundamentals of park administration.

The 1970s saw an explosion of management literature related to recreation and parks. In 1974, a quarterly publication entitled *Management Strategy* was developed specifically for park and recreation executives by Joseph J. Bannon through his organization, Management Learning Laboratories. Many useful ideas were advanced, including articles entitled "Philosophy of Recreation and Park Management," "Management and Organization of Parks and Recreation," "Personnel Administration in Parks and

Recreation," and "Financial Management in Parks and Recreation." In an article prepared for the *President's Commission on American Outdoors: A Literature Review,* Edginton and Williams (1986) analyzed the management literature related to the park and recreation field. Between 1960 and 1980, trends suggest that financing followed by planning, personnel administration, management general, evaluation, computers, and contracting were the leading topics discussed by authors in the literature.

Numerous books were also written in the 1970s, bringing opportunities for greater choice into the selection of teaching materials for classroom use. Many of these books were written by educators teaming their talents with practicing professionals. Hjelte and Shivers published *Public Administration of Recreation Services* in 1976. This book focused strongly on public administration, bringing into clear focus the factors that influenced it as it related to leisure services. Other significant contributions included discussions concerning computer technology, systems management, planning, and evaluation and research. Another book with a public administration focus was offered by Reynolds and Hormachea, *Public Recreation Administration* (1976). A more comprehensive, holistic perspective for the management of leisure services was presented in Murphy, Williams, Niepoth, and Brown's 1973 book, *Leisure Service Delivery System: A Modern Perspective.* This ecological perspective integrated, rather than separated, all of the components involved in leisure service delivery.

Also in 1973, Richard Kraus and Joseph Curtis authored *Creative Administration in Recreation and Parks.* This well-developed book, which would serve as the primary textbook for over two decades, is currently in its sixth edition. Kraus and Curtis had the unique ability to capture current concepts used in professional practice and coupled them with contemporary management theory to create a distinctive and unique perspective. Also the first edition of *Productive Management of Leisure Service Organizations: A Behavioral Approach* was authored by Edginton and Williams in 1978. This book was uniquely focused to assist managers and students in understanding ways of increasing the capacity of workers. Its major contributions were in its thorough discussions of motivation, the integration of individual needs and organizational goals, organizational design theory, and communication. It was the first textbook to include a discussion of marketing and its application to leisure services. The last contribution of great note was *Problem Solving in Recreation and Parks,* published by Joseph J. Bannon in 1972. This book provided a model for problem solving and, in addition, presented a hundred case studies that reflected problems encountered by park and recreation administrators. The book was an immediate success, as it provided practical strategies for solving organizational problems.

A Period of Reorganization and Growth (1980s–1990s)

The 1980s and 1990s were a period of great prosperity in America. Although concern for government debt was evident at the beginning of this period, and often required organizational restructuring, reengineering, and reorganization, by the end of the century the robust nature of the economy had addressed these economic concerns.

Greater emphasis was placed on providing high-quality, customer-focused leisure services. Outsourcing, expansion of the use of technology, benchmarking, innovation, networking, and a rethinking of managerial leadership strategies to enable excellence all became part of the focus of managers. Benefits management was prominent among managers in the park and recreation field. Much of the impetus came from the work of Driver et al. (1991) and, in Canada, from the work of the Ontario Parks and Recreation Federation and Alberta Recreation and Parks. The National Recreation and Parks Association (NRPA) established a benefits-based program known as Benefits-Based Management (BBM) to assist public park and recreation agencies.

In 1980, the American Academy for Park and Recreation Administration (AAPRA) was established. This organization was dedicated to the following goals: "to promote understanding of parks and recreation goals and methods, to increase knowledge through encouraging its gathering, organization, and dissemination, and to unify and strengthen our purposes, all toward improving the quality of life in America" (Hartsoe, 1992:1). This organization contributed to expanding the body of knowledge through several ways. Perhaps most important was the founding of the *Journal of Park and Recreation Administration.* Founding editors Joseph J. Bannon and Theodore R. Deppe brought "focus and credibility to the emerging unique body of knowledge in the management of parks and recreation" (Edginton, 1997:30). The journal bridged the gap between research in scholarly endeavors and professional practice. In the first decade, journal topics frequently included ones focused on personnel administration, fiscal management, computer applications, marketing, motivation, fees and charges, and employee productivity.

Another important contribution of the American Academy for Park and Recreation Administration has been the synthesis of the management philosophies of its members. For example, Doug Gaynor, former president of the Board of Trustees of the National Recreation and Park Association and director of Parks and Recreation, city of Modesto, California, provides a perspective on management philosophy related to park and recreation administration. Gaynor suggests that clearly and fundamentally, the mission of the park and recreation movement is to "implement our past generations' visions of parks, recreation, open space, and community service and to create a new and continued vision filled with challenges for future generations to implement and continue the legacy" (Pezoldt, 1991:25). Gaynor states that the basic mission of the park and recreation field includes the following:

1. To recognize that our employees are our most important asset

2. To have the highest caliber of employees

3. To have the best managed organization

4. To provide quality services to the community

5. To provide leadership (Pezoldt, 1991:29)

In addition, the American Academy for Park and Recreation Administration established a task force in 1989 to develop an accreditation procedure for agencies. This task force, under the direction of Professor Louis F. Twardzik, Michigan State University, developed standards and procedures for accrediting agencies. A National Commission on Accreditation for Park and Recreation Agencies (CAPRA) was established. This commission, operating in conjunction with the National Recreation and Park Association (NRPA), administers the CAPRA program. CAPRA consists of a board of 12 individuals appointed by the NRPA Board of Trustees, the AAPRA Board of Directors, the American Association for Leisure and Recreation (AALR), the International City/County Management Association (ICMA), the Council of Executive Directors (CED), and the National Association of County Park and Recreation Officials (NACO).

Their 10 categories of standards include more than 150 individual items. Of the total number of standards, 35 are considered fundamental to quality operations, and agencies seeking accreditation must be in 100 percent compliance with these basic standards. For the remaining standards, an 85 percent compliance rate is required. The ten basic categories are as follows:

1.0 Agency Authority, Role, and Responsibility

2.0 Planning

3.0 Organization and Administration

4.0 Human Resources

5.0 Finance (Fiscal Policy and Management)

6.0 Program and Services Management

7.0 Facility and Land Use Management

8.0 Safety and Security

9.0 Risk Management

10.0 Evaluation and Research

The standards have all been field-tested and are to be viewed as elements in the effective and efficient operation of park and recreation systems. These standards are reflected in a document published in 1999 by the NRPA entitled *Management of Park and Recreation Agencies*. The book was designed to integrate management practices found in CAPRA's standards for national accreditation.

Several significant developments in our bodies of knowledge occurred during this period of time. Perhaps the most important was the publication of *Financing, Managing, and Marketing Recreation and Park Resources* by Dennis R. Howard and John L. Crompton in 1980. No one textbook has so altered the practice of the profession as has this book. In particular, Howard and Crompton's focus on financing and marketing basically redirected the work of the park and recreation profession toward these ends in the early 1980s and beyond. Their book served as an authoritative source that effectively integrated examples of professional practice with emerging management and marketing theory. It was a document right for the times, with content appropriate to assist in redirecting park and recreation operations to reflect the needs of that era. Another book aimed at redirecting the profession was one by Frank Benest, Jack Foley, and George Wilton entitled *Organizing Leisure and Human Services* (1984). This book,

which focused on reorganization strategies, outlined "a plan for the future design and management of recreation and human services agencies" (Benest, Foley, & Wilton, 1984:). In addition, the book provided new alternatives for the future by recognizing that the goal of leisure services is to develop human potential. This approach did not gain as strong a foothold in leisure service systems in comparison with the emphasis now being placed on marketing strategies.

Also, the late 1970s 1980s and 1990s saw a rise in books related to subfields of management aimed at the delivery of leisure services. For example, titles such as *Park and Recreation Maintenance Management* (Sternloff & Warren, 1977), *Evaluation of Recreation and Park Programs* (Theobald, 1979), *Management Strategies in Financing Parks and Recreation* (Deppe, 1983), *Evaluation for Leisure Service Managers* (Lundegren & Farrell, 1985), *Managing Human Resources in Recreation, Parks, and Leisure Services* (see reference section Culkin & Kirsch, 1986), *Personnel Management in Recreation and Leisure Services* (Grossman, 1989), *Marketing for Parks, Recreation, and Leisure* (O'Sullivan, 1991) and *Financing and Acquiring Park and Recreation Resources* (Crompton, 1999) provided in-depth analyses on various topics and served to strengthen and expand the body of knowledge. Other titles of note included the International City Management Association's *Managing Municipal Leisure Services* by Lutzin (1980), *Public Parks and Recreation Administration* by Linn R. Rockwood (1980), *Introduction to Recreational Service Administration* by Jay S. Shivers (1987), *Leisure Systems* by James F. Murphy, E. William Niepoth, Lynn M. Jamieson, and John G. Williams (1991), and *911*

Management: A Comprehensive Guide for Leisure Service Managers by Joseph J. Bannon (1999). This last text was unique in that it provided individual chapters focused on specific topics dealing with three general categories—general management, human resource management, and executive development.

Summary

This chapter has provided an overview of management theory and practice. Both general management theories and management practices specific to leisure services have been reviewed. The rise of management follows the development of complex organizations during the industrial era. The initial management model employed methods of command and control. This model, known as the industrial model of management, involves hierarchical structuring, authoritarian decision making, and the creation of rules, regulations, and policies to legitimize the work of the organization.

Industrial society not only created a need for new management strategies, but also created a need for social reforms. A host of social innovations occured in both management and the leisure service professions in nearly parallel fashion. Many ideas were borrowed from European countries, especially England and Germany. There was a great technology transfer of ideas advanced by Americans who had visited European communities, and also a result of immigration to the United States. Settlement houses, parks, public baths, playgrounds, and other solid developments all had their origins elsewhere and were brought to the United States. The same is the case for many early management principles.

Management theory and practice may be viewed from a number of perspectives. Five approaches—scientific management, human relations management, management science, human resources, and contemporary management—provide a theoretical base for the leisure service manager. Each approach strongly influences the management of a leisure service organization. Scientific management provides a conceptual and historical perspective on the management process. Human relations management modifies scientific management thinking by introducing an increased concern for the human variable. Management science provides the leisure service manager with a number of specific tools and techniques to aid decision making. Human Resources Management focuses on staff development, recruitment, selection, and other elements related to enhancing the human capital within an organization. A brief overview of recent management theories was provided.

Last, a discussion of the evolution of management in relation to leisure service delivery was included. Management theory and practice related to leisure service organizations were explored in four time frames: 1850 to 1920, 1930 to 1950, the 1960s to 1970s, and the 1980s to 1990s. A review of the literature suggests an increasing level of crossover and sophistication of management concepts into the leisure service area. Further, it is evident that leisure service management thinking and practice has evolved in concert with changing societal conditions over the past 150 years.

Discussion Questions

1. What are the characteristics that can be used to define an industrial society?

2. In what ways did the rise of management theory and practice parallel the rise of social innovations related to leisure?

3. How did the concept of technology transfer influence the generation of social reform and the provision of?

4. Identify and discuss Max Weber's ideas of bureaucracy. How are they useful in organizations today? How are they dysfunctional?

5. Discuss the evolution of management thinking.

6. Describe early management thinking in the leisure service field. How would you characterize Frederick L. Olmsted's management style?

7. What were the essential elements of leisure service management from the 1900s to the 1920s?

8. How would you characterize leisure service management of the 1960s and 1970s?

9. What new concepts emerged in the 1980s and 1990s that had an impact on the management of leisure services? What issues did leisure service managers face that required a rethinking of their work?

10. Why is a historical review of management theories and practices useful in understanding the work of the profession?

References

Addams, J. (1912). *The spirit of youth and the city streets.* New York: Macmillan.

Baldwin, P. C. (1999). *Domesticating the street.* Columbus: Ohio State University.

Bannon, J. J. (1972). *Problem solving in recreation and parks.* Englewood Cliffs, NJ: Prentice-Hall.

Bannon, J. J. (1999). *911 management: A comprehensive guide for leisure service managers.* Champaign, IL: Sagamore Publishing.

Benest, F., Foley, J., & Welton, G. (1984). *Organizing leisure and human services.* Dubuque, IA: Kendall/Hunt.

Berelson, B. (1963). *The behavioral sciences today.* New York: Basic Books.

Blazey, M. A. (1999). Ethics and technology. *Journal of Physical Education, Recreation, and Dance,* 70(8), 29-31.

Bryan, M., & Davis, A. F. (1990). *100 years at Hull House.* Bloomington: Indiana University Press.

Burrows, E. G., & Wallace, M. (1999). *Gotham: A history of New York City to 1898.* New York: Oxford University Press.

Butler, G. D. (1936). *Playgrounds: Their administration and operation.* New York: Ronald Press.

Camp, R. (1995). *Benchmarking: The search for industry best practices that lead to superior performance.* Milwaukee, WI: Quality Press.

Churchman, C. W., Ackoff, R. L., & Arnoff, E. L. (1957). *Introduction to operations research.* New York: Wiley & Sons.

Crompton, J. L. (1999). *Financing and acquiring park and recreation resources.* Champaign, IL: Human Kinetics.

Culkin, D. F., & Kirsch, S. L. (1986). *Managing human resources in recreation, parks, and leisure services.* New York: Macmillan.

Curtis, H. S., (1915). *The practical conduct of play.* New York: Macmillan.

Curtis, H. S. (1917). *The play movement and its significance.* New York: Macmillan.

Deppe, T. R. (1983). *Management strategies in financing parks and recreation.* New York: Wiley & Sons.

Doell, C. E., & Fitzgerald, G. B. (1954). *A brief history of parks and recreation in the United States.* Chicago: The Athletic Institute.

Doell, C. E. (1963). *Elements of park and recreation administration.* Minneapolis, MN: Burgess.

Donnelly, J. H. Jr., Gibson, J. L., & Ivancevich, J. M. *Fundamentals of management: Functions, behavior, and models.* Dallas, TX: Business Publications.

Driver, B. L., Brown, P. J., & Peterson, G. L. (Eds.) (1991). *Benefits of leisure*. State College, PA: Venture.

Draper, D. J. (1983). The adoption and implementation of business and industrial management strategies and techniques. *Journal of Park and Recreation Administration*, 1(1),51.

Drucker, P. F. (1996). The shape of things to come. *Leader to Leader*, 1,16.

Drucker, P. F. (1994, November). The age of social transformation. *Atlantic Monthly*, 53-80.

Drucker, P. F. (1999). *Management challenges for the 21st century*. New York: Harper Business.

Edginton, C. R. (1997). Managing leisure services: A new ecology of leadership toward the year 2000. *Journal of Physical Education, Recreation, and Dance*, 68(8), 30–31.

Edginton, C. R., & Williams, J. G. (1978). *Productive management of leisure service organizations: A behavioral approach*. New York: Wiley & Sons.

Edginton, C. R., & Williams, J. G. (1986). Literature Synthesis: Changing management practices in urban recreation and parks. In *President's Commission on Americans Outdoors (pp. 53–57)*. Washington, DC: U.S. Department of Interior.

Farrell, P., & Lundegren, H. M. (1978). *The process of recreation programming: Theory and technique*. New York: Wiley & Sons.

Fayol, H. (1949). Administration Industrielle et Générale. In *General and industrial management*. London: Sir Isaac Petman & Sons.

Fisher, C. D., Schoenfeldt, L. F., & Shaw, J. B. (1999). *Human resource management* (4th ed.) Boston: Houghton Mifflin.

Fitzgerald, G. R. (1948). *Community organization for recreation*. New York: Barnes.

Grossman, A. H. (1989). *Personnel management in recreation and leisure services*. Reston, VA: American Alliance for Health, Physical Education, Recreation, and Dance.

Gulick, L., & Urwick, L. (Eds.). (1937). *Papers on the science of administration*. New York: Institute of Public Administration.

Hall, L. (1995). *Olmsted's America: An "unpractical" man and his vision of civilization*. Boston: Bulfinch Press.

Hall, J. A. (1998). Industrial society. In W. Outhwaite, & T. Bottomore, (Eds.), *The Blackwell dictionary of 20th century thought (pp.283-285)*. Oxford: Blackwell.

Hamner, M., & Champy, J. (1993). *Reengineering the corporation: A manifesto for business revolution*. New York: HarperCollins.

Hartsoe, C. E. (1992). *History of American Academy for Park and Recreation Administration*. Champaign, IL: Sagamore Publishing.

Hicks, H. G. (1972). *The management of organizations: A systems and human resources approach*. New York: McGraw-Hill.

Hill, J., & McLean, D. D. (1999). Introduction: Defining our perspective of the future. *Journal of Physical Education, Recreation, and Dance*, 70(8),15-17.

Hjelte, G. (1940). *The administration of public recreation*. New York: Macmillan.

Hjelte, G., & Shivers, J. S. (1972). *Public administration of recreational services*. Philadelphia: Lea & Febiger.

Howard D. R., & Crompton, J. L. (1980). *Financing, managing, and marketing recreation & park resources*. Dubuque, IA: W. C. Brown.

Hudson, S. (1974). *George Hjelte, Recreation administrator*. Unpublished doctoral dissertation, University of Utah.

Hughes, J. L. (1897). *Froebel's educational laws for all teachers*. New York: Appleton.

Kast, F. E., & Rosenzweig, J. E. (1974). *Organization and management: A systems approach*. New York: McGraw-Hill.

Kraus, R. G., & Curtis, J. E. (1973). *Creative administration in recreation and parks*. St. Louis, MO: Mosby.

Kraus, R. G., & Curtis, J. E. (2000). *Creative administration in recreation and parks*. Boston: McGraw-Hill.

Lee, J. (1909/1925). *The normal course in play*. New York: Barnes.

Levin, R. I., & Kirkpatrick, C. A. (1971). *Quantitative approaches to management*. New York: McGraw-Hill.

Luthans, F. (1998). *Organizational behaviors*. Boston: Irwin/McGraw-Hill.

Lutzin, S. G. (1980). *Managing municipal leisure services*. Washington, D C: International City Management Association.

Meyer, H. D., & Brightbill C. K. (1948). *Recreation administration: A guide to its practices*. Englewood Cliffs, NJ: Prentice-Hall.

Miles, R. E. (1975). *Theories of management*. New York: McGraw-Hill.

Murphy, J. F., Williams, J. G., Niepoth, E. W., & Brown P. D. (1973). *Leisure service delivery system: A modern perspective*. Philadelphia: Lea & Febiger.

Murphy, J. F., Niepoth, E. W., Jamieson, L. M., & Williams, J. G. (1991). *Leisure systems: Critical concepts and applications*. Champaign, IL: Sagamore Publishing .

Nash, J. B. (1938). *The organization and administration of playgrounds and recreation*. New York: Barnes.

Newman, W. H. (1950). *Administrative action*. Englwood Cliffs, NJ: Prentice-Hall.

Osborne, D. E., & Gaebler, T. (1992). *Reinventing government: How the entrepreneurial spirit is transforming the public sector*. Reading, MA: Addison-Wesley.

O'Sullivan, E. L. (1991). *Marketing for parks, recreation, and leisure*. State College, PA: Venture.

Peterson, J. A., & Pohlen, M. F. (1973). Agency management. In S. G. Lutzin & E. H. Storey (Eds.), *Managing municipal leisure services*(pp. 55–). Washington, D C: International City Management Association.

Pezoldt, C. W. (1991). *Management philosophies by members of the American Academy for Park and Recreation Administration*. Champaign, IL: Sagamore Publishing .

Pfiffner, J. M., & Presthus, R. V. (1960). *Public administration*. New York: The Ronald Press.

Peters, T. J., & Waterman, R. H., Jr., (1982). *In search of excellence*. New York: Harper & Row.

Reynolds, J. A., & Hormachea, M. N. (1976). *Public recreation administration*. Englewood Cliffs, NJ: Prentice-Hall.

Riis, J. A. (1902). *The battle with the slum*. New York: Macmillan.

Rockwood, L. R. (1980). *Public parks and recreation administration: Behavior and dynamics*. Salt Lake City, UT: Brighton.

Rodgers, D. T. (1998). *Atlantic crossings: Social politics in a progressive age*. Cambridge: The Belknap Press of Harvard University Press.

Rybczynski, W. (1999). *A clearing in the distance: Frederick Law Olmsted and America in the nineteenth century*. New York: Scribner.

Schuler, R. S. (1992). Repositioning the human resource function: Transformation or demise? In P. J. Frost, V. F. Mitchell, & W. R. Nord (Eds.), *HRM reality: Putting competence in context*(pp.8–12). Cincinnati: Southwestern.

Senge, P. M. (1990). *The fifth discipline*. New York: Doubleday.

Shivers, J. S. (1987). *Introduction to recreational service administration*. Philadelphia: Lea & Febiger.

Sternloff, R. E., & Warren, R. (1977). *Park and recreation maintenance management*. Boston: Holbrook Press.

Taylor, F. W. (1967). *The principles of scientific management*. New York: Norton. 36–37.

Tead, O. (1951). *The art of administration*. New York: McGraw-Hill.

The American Academy for Park and Recreation Administration. (1993). *21st Century Management*. Champaign, IL: Sagamore Publishing.

Theobald, W. F. (1979). *Evaluation of recreation and park programs*. New York: Wiley.

van der Smissen, B., Moiseichik, M., Hartenburg, V. J., & Twardzik, L. F. (1999). *Management of park and recreation agencies*. Ashburn.

Schuler, R. S. (1992). Repositioning the human resource function: Transformation or demise? In P. J. Frost, V. F. Mitchell, & W. R. Nord (Eds.), *HRM reality: Putting competence in context* (pp. 8–12). Cincinnati, OH: Southwestern.

Chapter

3

Managerial Leadership

Photo courtesy of the Stern Photography, Cedar Falls Iowa.

Enthusiastic managerial/leadership is a hallmark of contemporary leisure services managers.

Introduction

What is the essence of managerial leadership in leisure service organizations? Unequivocally, it could be said that managerial leadership is the pivotal force moving leisure service organizations forward. We have all witnessed highly performing, superbly led leisure service organizations. What differenti- ates these organizations from ones that are mediocre? The key is managerial leadership. Gifted leisure service managers are those individuals who have the energy, enthusiasm, and perseverance to move individuals to action in the pursuit of organizational goals.

What is managerial leadership? Warren Bennis and Bert Nanus (1985:21) clarify the work of managers as leaders: Managerial leadership "is what gives an organization its vision and the ability to translate the vision into reality." In a sense, managerial leadership is vision and action combined. Leisure service managers who have the ability to assist individuals by providing a positive direction to their efforts and encouraging them to act are successful ones. Managerial leadership is often thought of as the process of influence, in other words. Influencing others to action in order that they may achieve organizational goals. Also, in a more contemporary sense, managerial leadership is about transforming the lives of people. Real transformation is about creating dialogue between and among people, getting joint commitment, and promoting change within individuals and organizations.

In this chapter, we will explore key components and elements related to managerial leadership. Included will be discussions of the importance of managing or leading, empowerment, quality, learning organizations, and ethics. Further, managerial leadership roles will be discussed as well as numerous leadership theories, studies, and models.

Managing or Leading?

Bennis and Nanus, writing in their now famous book *Leaders* (1985:21), redirected management thinking regarding managers and their work as leaders. At a time when business and other environments were changing rapidly, they framed a new perspective that has given great meaning to the work of managers. The centrality of their ideas was captured in the phrase; "managers do things right, leaders do the right thing" (1985:21). In other words, Bennis and Nanus were saying that as a manager you could do everything correctly according to procedure and still be missing the boat. We have all worked at organizations where managers are policy driven, insisting on strict adherence to rules, procedures, and methods. The assumption is that if you do everything right, you will produce a quality product or service. The fallacy in this thinking is that you may be doing everything according to pre-scripted policies and procedures, but you may not be achieving quality or the ends that are desired. As Bennis and Nanus say: "the difference may be summarized as activities of vision and judgement—effectiveness—versus activities of mastering routines—efficiency" (1985:21).

In effect, Bennis and Nanus are implying that a need exists for a whole new theory of leadership. They suggest that leadership must be understood in the context of today's environment, and that it must be summarized in three major contexts: commitment, complexity, and credibility. Bennis and Nanus suggest that a *commitment* gap exists; that managers have failed to empower people and to enhance human resources effectively within their organizations. Increasingly, the world that we live and work in is a *complex* one. As Bennis and Nanus have written, we live in "an era marked by rapid and spastic change" (1985:8). The problems of organizations are increasingly complex. They have too many ironies, polarities, dichotomies, dualities, ambivalences, paradoxes, confusions, contradictions, contrarieties, and messes to understand and deal with. As far as *credibility* is concerned we have seen an erosion of confidence in government. The taxpayers' revolt, as discussed in Chapter two, started in the 1970s with Proposition 13 in California as a loss of faith in government. Lack of credibility among our national leaders in more recent times has added to this problem. These elements require a new idea of leadership and suggest that managers must operate differently in order to be successful.

Four areas of competency emerge for manager/leaders from the new Bennis and Nanus model: (1) attention through vision, (2) meaning through communication, (3) trust through positioning, and (4) the deployment of self. Vision can be thought of as the power of forward thinking that often involves creating symbols and metaphors to help communicate a desirable and attractive future. For a vision to be successful it must animate, expirate, and bring alive the work of people within an organization. As Bennis and Nanus have indicated, "by focusing attention on a vision, the leader operates on the emotional and spiritual resources of the organization, on its values, commitment and aspirations (1985:92).

Great leaders often inspire their followers to high levels of achievement by showing how their work contributes to worthwhile ends. It is an emotional appeal to some of the most fundamental of human needs—the need to be important, to make a difference, to feel useful, to be a part of a successful and worthwhile enterprise. Without effective communication, little can be accomplished in leisure service organizations. As Bennis and Nanus state: "success requires the capacity to relate a compelling image of a desired state of affairs—the kind of image that induces enthusiasm and commitment in others." They cite Walt Disney's strategy

which succinctly communicates his powerful vision in the statement, "If you can dream it, you can do it."

The third competency area identified by Bennis and Nanus is trust. As they indicate: "trust is a lubrication that makes it possible for organizations to work" (1985:153). We can think of trust as one person's belief or confidence and that of another, such as in the trust an employee has for the leisure service manager. It is built on the relationships of honesty, integrity, and reliability between people. When you are confident and can rely on another individual, you are said to have trust. When individuals have trust in the manager, it is possible to have consistency within the organization. Without trust, there can be no consistency or unity of action.

The fourth competency element is that of the deployment of self. The key issue here is the creative deployment of oneself as a manager. How one manages oneself—how one uses one's time, energies, and talents—has a great influence on the success of an organization. It is important for managers to know their strengths and weaknesses, and then to deploy those strengths in such a way as to influence productively the work of the leisure service organization. Effective managers are those who are able to grow and who learn to overcome their weaknesses. It is also important for an organization to have a sense of itself—a sense, its organizational strengths and weaknesses. Likewise, organizations need to become "learning organizations" (Senge, 1990) As Pinchot (1996:38) summarizes these four elements for us, "leadership focuses on communicating and inspiring values, on listening to and caring for followers, and on leading by personal example."

Empowerment and Managerial Leadership

Pinchot notes that as organizations become larger and more complex, there is less direct personal contact between managers and employees. It is as though the work of the leisure service manager is one of creating an environment wherein people are given freedom to identify work methods and pursue organizational goals. A key element in the work of successful leisure service managers is the ability to empower individuals. A framework for understanding the concept of empowerment can be borrowed from the Chinese philosopher Lao Tsu (25):

> The very highest leader is barely
> known by men.
> Then comes the leader they know
> and love.
> Then the leader they fear.
> Then the leader they despise.
> The leader who does not trust
> enough will not be trusted.
> When actions are performed without unnecessary speech
> The people say, "We did it ourselves."
>
> *Lao Tsu*

The wisdom above helps us understand the impact of indirect management on employees. As one can see, when employees are empowered they have a greater sense of ownership. Further, empowerment creates opportunities for others to lead and, in fact, to embrace and support the goals of the organization.

Pinchot (1996:26-30) suggests that the following three strategies can be employed for empowering leadership within organizations:

1. Delegating Within a Traditional Hierarchy. Delegating within any traditional organizational structure is a means of creating opportunities for empowering employees. It is important to match authority and responsibility when delegating. Although delegation may relieve others of work, it does not necessarily cultivate the development of leadership. However, it is a step in the right direction toward empowering individuals.

2. Creating Community. The development of community means having individuals embrace the work of an organization as an important part of their efforts. In other words, it is creating the idea that people are involved in a worthwhile endeavor. Creating community often involves transforming individuals so that they embrace loftier or higher goals. Building community helps people be committed to a common vision so that they are, in fact, self-managing and empowered employees.

3. Liberating a Spirit of Enterprise. In organizations today, expertise is based on knowledge as much as on position. When we liberate individuals to use their knowledge to guide the work of an organization, we are empowering them to bring their talents, skills, and competencies to bear in solving organizational problems. Further, by liberating individuals, we create space in organizations to enable them to pursue those ends that they feel are necessary for organizational success.

Pinchot reminds us that organizations of the future will be made up of entrepreneurs and intrapreneurs. Individual employees will need to be empowered to make decisions not only regarding their own work agendas, but also by suggesting and contributing to ways that help achieve the organization's goals. The challenge for leisure service managers will be to create environments or cultures within organizations that empower people, that in effect liberate the human spirit and potential for work capacity, new ideas, and innovation.

Commitment to Quality

As indicated in Chapter One, successful leisure service organizations are ones that are committed to quality. Quality is a perception of excellence that is usually measured against standards. By exceeding basic standards, we get higher and higher levels of quality. As mentioned in Chapter Two, W. Edwards Deming is the champion of quality principles in organizations. The Deming method of management basically focuses on establishing benchmarks to measure quality and then consistently finding ways to improve the work of an organization by building of quality control procedures. The Deming method also involves empowering employees by teaming them; this encourages them to cooperate by adding their creativity to the processes used in developing products and services.

Edginton and Edginton (1994) have adapted Deming's methods to the planning of leisure service programs. Their model, called Total Quality Program Planning, was designed to promote quality in youth programs, but it can be applied in all leisure service settings. Like Deming's strategies, their model is directed toward exceeding expectations by constantly improving both the impact and processes used in program planning. They suggest that technically sound programs are not enough; these must exceed expectations. They state that "high quality programs are not only technically correct, but have something more, something extra" (22). The extra quality suggested by these authors is found when programs strive to touch the emotional and spiritual side of individuals. According to Edginton and Edginton, this process requires the commitment of the leisure service manager to ensure its success.

What are the hallmarks of quality? Edginton and Edginton (1994:13-17) suggest that a commitment to quality can be found in the following 13 guidelines:

1. *Innovation.* Success in leisure programming stems from a commitment to innovation. No program should be the same from one year to the next. Programs should constantly evolve to meet the changing needs of children and youth. Innovative organizations are constantly looking for new and different services, equipment, areas, and facilities that improve the quality of services available to youth.

2. *Future Orientation.* Leisure service managers who address not only quality issues of today, but those of tomorrow will be successful. It is important that you include in your work not only the *immediate* needs of your organization for quality, but some focus on what can be done in the future to promote quality. Leisure service organizations that invest in the future are those that invest some of their resources in ensuring that their programs and services are successful and vibrant in months and years to come.

3. Getting Things Right the First Time. Perhaps the most efficient way to promote quality within your organization is to do things right the first time. Sloppiness and a "seat of the pants," last-minute approach to planning often lead to having to redo activities or services. This is not only costly, but results in poor performance. Some activities and programs and the opportunity they presented for customers, cannot be corrected if they are not planned effectively.

4. Continuous Improvement. The best way to achieve quality is to improve the processes associated with creating leisure services. The job of any youth leader should be to find ways to continuously improve upon programs and services, constantly searching out new ways of doing things better, more cost efficiently, and in a way that is more meaningful to customers. Improvement is a never-ending, dynamic process; it should not be thought of as a one-time event. Establish a goal of making one small change in every program every week to improve the quality.

5. Continuous Education. The continuous development of the leisure service manager in terms of knowledge and skill is essential to achieving quality. Good people make good programs, but the needs of youth are dynamic and changing, requiring continuous education and development. Leisure service managers should seek ways to improve their knowledge base.

6. Attention to Detail. Success in leisure programs is painted in small

steps as well as in broad strokes. The little things that you do to make a program of high quality make the difference between superior services and mediocre ones.

7. Pride. Believing in what you are doing is contagious. Pride is having a high opinion of yourself and your work. It comes from doing a job competently as well as having ownership in the effort.

8. Anticipatory Planning. Don't merely respond to the needs of customers as they are expressed from moment to moment. Learn how to anticipate needs in advance and meet them before they are requested. Anticipatory planning requires the leader to think in advance (days, weeks, months), and to visualize services as they will likely unfold and anticipate actions that may be needed.

9. Performance Measurements. Find ways to record your progress toward achieving quality by creating performance measurements. Graphs and charts provide opportunities for discussion, focus on opportunities for change, and may lead to the development of new programs or better methods and procedures. Participant numbers, outcomes related to performance measures, program costs, participant use hours, and participant survey results are all sources of data that can be charted to measure performance. Measuring achievement over a period of time enables the leisure service manager to see the gains in quality and performance, and possibility to justify future program developments.

10. *Elimination of Mistakes.* Mistakes are costly to an organization both in terms of funds and image. Mistakes made in program planning are costly to participants in terms of opportunities for development. *If play and leisure is powerful enough to help customers, it is powerful enough to hurt them.* When mistakes in program planning affect the quality of services, they also affect customers. Eliminating mistakes helps improve quality, morale, cost effectiveness, and other critical factors.

11. *Elimination of Negativeness.* Positive attitudes are important in the delivery of leisure services. Leisure service professionals should strive to be enthusiastic, energetic, and zestful. If you enjoy what you are doing, that quality will rub off on others; the reverse is also true. Positiveness is a "can do" attitude that promotes a willingness to find ways to serve customers effectively with quality programs.

12. *Assume Personal Responsibility for Quality.* The old way to get quality was to supervise and inspect services and manage change either from the top down or from without. The new way of promoting quality is to build it from within. The best way to promote quality from within is to ensure that *each individual* assumes personal responsibility and accountability for making sure that services are provided in an excellent, high-quality manner.

13. *Teaming: Doing What It Takes to Get the Job Done.* Leisure service managers as well as other staff must be willing to do what it takes to get the job done, and to get it done

right. The Total Quality approach is dependent on teamwork, cooperation, and supportive behavior. It is not "your job" or "my job," but rather "our job." All staff should be focused and have their eyes and efforts directed toward the *primary goal*—that is, providing the very highest quality of services for customers—and they should be willing to do what it takes to make that happen.

Edginton and Edginton have developed a unique three-step model for implementing programs in their TQP design. The first step involves *"creating the vision."* This involves knowing what one is trying to accomplish and visualizing the program or event in advance. The second step, *"creating the environment,"* involves structuring the physical, social, and abstract setting. For example this could involve, in simple way, decorating a room, adding music, or constructing rules or procedures for games that would promote interaction. The last step is *"creating the connection."* This step involves creating a quality "bubble of contact" with individuals. It is the genuine personal contact between the leader and the customer to which this element refers.

Learning Organizations and Managerial Leadership

Successful organizations in the future will be ones focused on innovations and that have the ability to cope and deal with change. Such organizations by nature will require a focus on continuous learning. Organizations that are not equipped to help employees develop, grow, and maximize their potential will be seriously handicapped in the future. As indicated, in a knowledge-based society, the human resources of an organization will be its most important asset. The development of human capital requires an investment and a commitment on the part of any leisure service organization. Further, organizations that do not know how to learn will be operating at a disadvantage.

Peter Senge's work entitled *The Fifth Discipline: The Art and Science of the Learning Organization* served to draw attention to the importance of learning within an organization. As Senge (1990:4) has written: "the organizations that will truly excel in the future will be the organizations that discover how to tap people's commitment and capacity to learn at all levels in an organization." He states that: "learning disabilities are tragic in children, but they are fatal in organizations. Because of them, few corporations live even half as long as a person—most die before they reach the age of forty". Senge suggests that government and nonprofit organizations may have less flexibility than businesses in this area. Confirming the importance of learning in leisure service organizations, Hultsman and Colley (1995:1-10) suggest that improvement-driven organizations will be required in the future for success.

What types of roles will be required of leisure service managers in leisure service organizations? How will these be different from those in the past? More specifically, what does it take to lead an organization that is focused on learning as its principal organizing strategy? First and most important is to recognize that the work of the leisure service manager will be different. It will require a greater degree of openness, an encouragement of critical thinking, information processing, and collective decision making. Certain roles become

clear. Senge (1990:341-357) identifies three roles that managers will play in improvement-driven organizations:

1. The Manager/Leader as a Designer. Senge suggests that the design of a learning organization is an important managerial function. If you were to design an organization that emphasized learning, how would you do it? Think of the best learning situations that you have ever been in: What were the hallmarks of these organizations? How would you design a leisure service organization to reflect these elements of "best professional practice" in terms of creating a learning environment?

2. The Manager/Leader as a Steward. A steward of an organization is one who establishes the vision. As Senge notes, it is helping individuals in the process of "becoming." As individuals we are all in the process of becoming. Life is about learning; life is about becoming who we are as individuals. The same could be said about an organization. All organizations are in the process of becoming, and it is the role of the manager to shepherd, steward, or mentor the organization through this process of becoming.

3. The Manager/Leader as a Teacher. Our role as managers is one of assisting individuals in the formation of their characters, as well as in the values, they will have and the approaches they will take in their work and in their lives. Teaching often involves helping individuals acquire lifelong skills of learning, thinking, and problem solving. Further, the manager teaches by virtue of who he or she is. We have all been influenced by those whose genuineness, integrity, loyalty, sincerity, and caring had an impact on our lives without them needing to tell us of these virtues. We can learn simply by being in another's presence.

As is the case with organizations committed to quality, leisure service organizations committed to learning will outperform those focused elsewhere. It is the leisure service manager's responsibility to ensure that learning environments are in place so that the organization and the individuals within it continue to grow, develop, and learn in order to meet the challenges of the future. The learning organization will rewrite the way that we view the work of managers in today's institutions. By focusing on learning, it is possible for organizations to stay abreast of change and be not only evolutionary in their processes but also—because learning often involves new discoveries—revolutionary in creating solutions to the complex challenges found in today's society.

Ethics and Managerial Leadership

Ethical behavior is not only required but also demanded of leisure service managers. Daily, leisure managers are drawn into ethical concerns. They are required to make decisions based on their values and the values of the organization. Ethics deals with standards of what is considered right or wrong in our society. Leisure service managers are responsible for creating an organizational climate that reflects ethical values. It is essential for leisure service managers and organizations to operate ethically because they're providing people that work within the organization and are served by it with a sense of dignity.

In the leisure service field, we pursue many values. From a historical perspective, our values include the wise use of leisure, the preservation and conservation of our environment, and the promotion and protection of human dignity. Further, we have a strong commitment professionally to promoting a higher quality of life for individuals and to improving the livability of our communities. We are committed to the value of building community life. Other values that are important in the leisure service field are the promotion of freedom, justice, and social democracy. We are also committed to creating safe environments for individuals while providing them with opportunities to grow by offering them opportunities to engage in risk-taking behaviors that promote development. And, we are committed to helping individuals better their self-concept, their sense of self-worth, and their sense of belonging. These values in general will guide the work of leisure service managers.

Bullaro and Edginton (1986) have identified three areas of ethics that should be addressed by leisure service managers:

1. Human—Social Responsibility. These refer to the ethical standards that are established for dealing with people. If we say that we will operate with integrity and fairness toward all people, this is a reflection of our values that will have an impact on our work as leisure service managers. For example, the U.S. Marine Corps Morale, Welfare, and Recreation Department in Okinawa, Japan, states that they will "operate with fairness and complete integrity . . . [and] . . . offer courteous, attentive, and efficient service in a pleasant atmosphere, with a professional and positive attitude". These are values regarding how the organization will treat individuals.

2. Community Responsibility. Community responsibility refers to the interaction between the leisure service organization and the community that it serves. All organizations operate in communities, a community can be a local municipality or it can be a world community. Organizations have the responsibility to contribute to these communities. As Bullaro and Edginton (1986:32) note, "leisure service organizations should provide leadership to contribute to the communities' growth, development, and enrichment." They note that this often involves maintaining community stability and well being. The Central Oregon Park and Recreation District objective concerning community is as follows: "to develop community stability by providing safe, positive environments that are conducive to socialization and fostering community pride."

3. Environmental Responsibility. The world that we live in is dramatically affected by how we manage our environment. Leisure service organizations by definition are committed to values that promote a strong land ethic. As indicated, the preservation and conservation of the environment is a foundational value of our profession. The Willamalane (Oregon) Park and Recreation District underscores this in stating that they "will be a leader in the progres-

sive development and care of attractive and hospitable places where people may enrich their lives. Willamalane will always treasure our heritage and natural resources and will preserve and protect priceless open spaces for the children of the future."

Figure 3.1 presents leadership standards from the Elk Grove (Illinois) Park District. These standards provide guidelines for the behavior of individuals in leadership roles.

As one can see, ethics play an important role in the work of the leisure service manager. Not only will his or her value system have an impact on the work environment, but also the stated values of the organization will have an impact on his or her efforts. In a world that is increasingly complex, uncertain, and ambiguous, it is important for leisure service managers to be grounded in a strong value structure. Such values provide the underpinning for ethical behavior and serve as a beacon that can guide the leisure service manager in day-to-day actions.

Managerial Leadership Roles

What do leisure service managers do? At first this would seem to be an easy question. In Chapter One we talked about the importance of managers challenging individuals, sharing a vision, enabling others to act, modeling the way, and giving others encouragement (Konzes & Posner, 1995). Further, the authors have suggested that technical, human, and conceptual skills are required of managers. However, these are broad, sweeping interpretations of the managerial leadership roles in which leisure service managers are involved.

Figure 3.1
Leadership Standards of the Elk Grove, Illinois, Park District

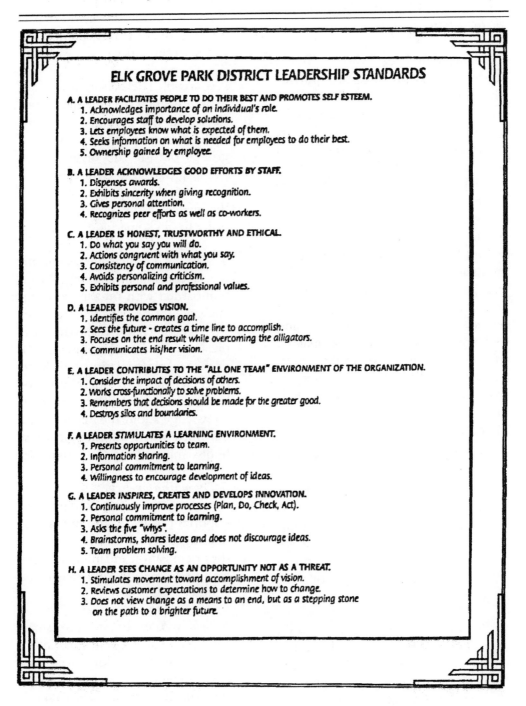

ELK GROVE PARK DISTRICT LEADERSHIP STANDARDS

A. A LEADER FACILITATES PEOPLE TO DO THEIR BEST AND PROMOTES SELF ESTEEM.
1. Acknowledges importance of an individual's role.
2. Encourages staff to develop solutions.
3. Lets employees know what is expected of them.
4. Seeks information on what is needed for employees to do their best.
5. Ownership gained by employee.

B. A LEADER ACKNOWLEDGES GOOD EFFORTS BY STAFF.
1. Dispenses awards.
2. Exhibits sincerity when giving recognition.
3. Gives personal attention.
4. Recognizes peer efforts as well as co-workers.

C. A LEADER IS HONEST, TRUSTWORTHY AND ETHICAL.
1. Do what you say you will do.
2. Actions congruent with what you say.
3. Consistency of communication.
4. Avoids personalizing criticism.
5. Exhibits personal and professional values.

D. A LEADER PROVIDES VISION.
1. Identifies the common goal.
2. Sees the future - creates a time line to accomplish.
3. Focuses on the end result while overcoming the alligators.
4. Communicates his/her vision.

E. A LEADER CONTRIBUTES TO THE "ALL ONE TEAM" ENVIRONMENT OF THE ORGANIZATION.
1. Consider the impact of decisions of others.
2. Works cross-functionally to solve problems.
3. Remembers that decisions should be made for the greater good.
4. Destroys silos and boundaries.

F. A LEADER STIMULATES A LEARNING ENVIRONMENT.
1. Presents opportunities to team.
2. Information sharing.
3. Personal commitment to learning.
4. Willingness to encourage development of ideas.

G. A LEADER INSPIRES, CREATES AND DEVELOPS INNOVATION.
1. Continuously improve processes (Plan, Do, Check, Act).
2. Personal commitment to learning.
3. Asks the five "whys".
4. Brainstorms, shares ideas and does not discourage ideas.
5. Team problem solving.

H. A LEADER SEES CHANGE AS AN OPPORTUNITY NOT AS A THREAT.
1. Stimulates movement toward accomplishment of vision.
2. Reviews customer expectations to determine how to change.
3. Does not view change as a means to an end, but as a stepping stone on the path to a brighter future.

In this section, we will explore three methods of appraising the work of leisure service managers. The first will be to review a conceptual framework developed by Henry Mintzberg (1980) which is applicable to all managers. Next, we will look at a research study conducted among municipal recreation managers. Last, we will examine several job descriptions to better frame the roles that leisure service managers play.

A Conceptual Appraisal of Managerial Roles

Henry Mintzberg (1980:58-90) has developed a set of roles that portray what, specifically, managers do. He suggests that managerial activities may be categorized into three areas. Within the first area are interpersonal roles, which encompass a set of interpersonal relationships between the manager, his or her subordinates, and his or her superiors. Specific roles assumed by the manager in this area are figurehead, liaison, and leader. The second area includes informational roles, within which the manager receives and sends information. Within these roles, the manager acts as a monitor, disseminator, and spokesman. Last, the decision-making role finds the manager performing as an entrepreneur, disturbance handler, resource allocator, and negotiator. Following is a discussion of each of Mintzberg's 10 roles:

1. *Figurehead*. The most basic and simplest of all managerial roles is that of figurehead. Because of his or her formal authority, the manager is a symbol, obliged to perform a number of duties. Some of these are trite, others are of an inspirational nature; all involve interpersonal activity.

2. *Leader*. The organization looks to its formal head for guidance and motivation. In the leader role, the manager defines the atmosphere in which the organization will work.... Leadership involves interpersonal relationships between the leader and the led. In the informal group, the leader is usually followed because of his or her physical or charismatic power. In formal organizations, where the manager is most often appointed from above, he or she must frequently rely on powers vested in the office.

3. *Liaison*. The liaison role deals with the significant web of relationships that the manager maintains with numerous individuals and groups outside the organization. These [relationships] are referred to as "exchange" relationships— the manager gives something in order to get something in return.

4. *Monitor*. The manager as a monitor is continually seeking, being bombarded with information that enables him or her to understand what is taking place within the organization and its environment. He or she seeks information in order to detect changes, to identify problems and opportunities, to build up knowledge about the milieu, to be informed when information must be disseminated and decisions made.

5. *Disseminator*. Access to information allows the manager to play the important role of disseminating, sending external information into the organization and internal information from one subordinate to another.

6. *Spokesperson*. In the spokesman role, the manager transmits information out to the organization's environment. As formal authority, the manager is called upon to speak on behalf of the organization; as nerve center, he or she has the information to do so effectively. The manager may lobby for the organization; he or she may serve as its public relations head, or may be

viewed as an expert in the trade in which the organization operates.

7. Entrepreneur. In the entrepreneur role, the manager acts as initiator and designer of much of the controlled change in the organization... . This role encompasses all activities where the manager makes changes of his or her own free will—exploiting opportunities, solving nonpressing problems.

8. Disturbance Handler. The disturbance handler role deals with involuntary situations and change that is partially beyond the manager's control.... The manager acts because he or she must, because the pressures brought to bear on the organization are too great to ignore.

9. Resource Allocator. Resource allocation is the heart of the organization's strategy-making system. For it is in the making of choices involving significant organizational resources that strategies are determined. As formal authority, the manager must oversee the system by which organizational resources are allocated.

10. Negotiator. The manager is responsible for representing the organization in major nonroutine negotiations with other organizations and/or individuals. (1980).

Mintzberg also delineates six reasons that justify the need for managers in the organizational structure:

1. The prime purpose of the manager is to ensure that the organization serves its basic purpose—the efficient production of specific goods and services.

2. The manager must design and maintain the stability of the organization's operations.

3. The manager must take charge of the organization's strategy-making system, and therein adapt the organization in a controlled way to its changing environment.

4. The manager must ensure that the organization serves the ends of those persons who cont[...]

5. The manager must serve as the key informational link between the organization and its environment.

6. As formal authority, the manager is responsible for the operating of the organization's status system. (95–96).

Do these more global definitions of the work of managers apply to the leisure service field? It is evident in reviewing the literature that little is known about what exactly leisure managers do.

Managerial Work Activities of Leisure Service Managers

What are the specific managerial work activities and competencies of the leisure service manager? Seminal research work in this area was undertaken by Smale and Frisby (1992). Studying the work of municipal recreation managers, these authors identified four managerial competencies specific to the field of recreation: planning, organizing, influencing, and controlling. They defined planning as the process of visualizing the future, setting goals, determining objectives, and developing action plans. Organizing, according to these authors "involves" devising ways of implementing plans" (81-108). Influencing has to do with the processes that move people to action, such as communicating, motivating, and working with groups. These are process-oriented activities. Last, controlling involves making sure that standards are met. Table 3.1 presents an analysis of each of these elements and the types of activities with which leisure managers would be involved.

In the study, respondents indicated that they spent most of their time in the planning area. Smale and Frisby noted that this fact is consistent with the busi-

Table 3.1
Management Functions and Associated Competency Areas in Municipal Recreation

Management function

   Managerial competency

Planning
   Planning and preparing budgets
   Attending planning meetings
   Planning programs and services
   Setting organizational objectives
   Planning special events
   Setting policy
   Marketing activities
   Keeping informed of technological advances
   Research methods

Organizing
   Setting plans into action
   Organizing and allocating paid staff
   Coordinating services
   Hiring and training paid staff
   Working with community groups
   Scheduling activities and programs
   Managing facilities
   Working with volunteers

Influencing
   Communicating with the public
   Motivating colleagues and paid staff
   Influencing others
   Supervising paid staff activities
   Negotiating and lobbying

Controlling
   Problem solving
   Monitoring of budgets
   Writing reports and manuals
   Reviewing operations
   Conducting performance appraisals
   Conducting program evaluations
   Safety and risk management
   Gathering information for service reviews

Source: Small, B. J. A. & Frisby, U. (1992) Managerial work activity and perceived competencies of municipal recreation managers. *Journal of Park and Recreation Administration 10*(4).

ness field; managers report spending a large percentage of their time (27.8 percent) in this area. They also report spending 24.5 percent in the organizing function, 21.03 percent in the influencing function, and 17.36 percent in the controlling function (see Figure 3.2).

These authors also looked at specific elements within each of the management functions. Level of involvement and perceived proficiency in each of the test items were rated by the respondents in the study. In the planning area, managers reported their proficiency as higher in planning programs and services, special events and research methods than their level of involvement. On only one item did they appear to be more involved than proficient—

planning and preparation of budgets. In the organizing function, individuals felt proficient in all areas except setting plans into action. For the management function, there were three areas in which respondents rated their proficiency lower than their involvement—communicating with the public, motivating staff, and influencing others. Last, in the controlling function, conducting program evaluations was the only area in which their proficiency was rated higher than their actual involvement.

Smale and Frisby also looked at the differences between upper, middle, and lower management. In the planning area, upper-level managers saw themselves as the most proficient in planning and preparing budgets, setting organizational objects, and setting policies. In

Figure 3.2
Percentage of Time by Leisure Service Managers in Various Functions

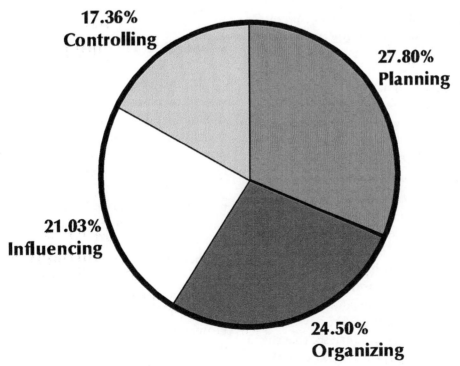

Source: Adapted from Small, B. J. A. & Frisby, U. (1992) Managerial work activity and perceived competencies of municipal recreation managers. *Journal of Park and Recreation Administration* 10(4).

the organizing functions, middle- and lower-level management saw themselves as being the most proficient in scheduling activities and programs. Smale and Frisby noted that the people skills of managers, as reflected in the influencing management structure, were not as strong as one would think. Conventional wisdom suggests that leisure service managers have strong people skills; however, this might be an area targeted for improvement. Upper-level managers reported greater competencies in the controlling function of measurement, especially in the areas of monitoring budgets, reviewing operations, problem solving, and gathering information for service reviews.

What Do Leisure Service Managers Actually Do?

Another way of gaining an understanding of managerial roles is to view actual job descriptions of leisure service managers. Rather than looking at conceptual models, a sampling of the content of job descriptions can help provide an understanding of the roles in which leisure service managers may be involved. Job descriptions from two different agencies were sampled.

Director of Parks and Recreation, Corporation of the City of New Westminster, British Columbia

As can be seen in Figures 3.3, the Director of Parks and Recreation for the Corporation of the City of New Westminster, British Columbia, works under the direction of the City Administrator, City Council and Parks and Recreation Committee. From viewing the job description, one can see that the position involves planning, coordinat-

ing, and directing activities. Further examples of work include organizing program services, preparing budgets, preparing policy recommendations, serving as a consultant or advisor to policymakers and advisory groups, and planning and designing facilities and areas. There is a level of specificity related to job requirements.

Superintendent, Willamalane Park and Recreation District, Oregon

As indicated in the general statement of duties, the Superintendent of the Willamalane Park and Recreation District is the chief executive officer of the organization. This person is responsible for the management and operation of the organization. The management functions include administration of parks, personnel, programs, services, areas and facilities, maintenance, planning and research, finance and budget, serial and bond issues, and public and community relations (see Figure 3.4).

Leadership Theories

In this section, we will review a variety of basic managerial leadership theories, studies, and models. Conceptual frameworks, such as the ones we present, help define, measure, predict, and even develop an approach to leadership (Hitt, 1988). Leisure service managers must have a theoretical foundation to base their actions on. The theories, studies, and models discussed will help establish that foundation. Remember, the essence of managerial leadership is moving individuals to action in order to achieve organizational goals. How one interacts with others and frames his or her own behavior as a manager/leader is the topic of this portion of the chapter.

Figure 3.3
Job Description of the Director of Parks and Recreation for the Corporation of the City of New Westminster, British Columbia

Corporation of the City of New Westminster

Director of Parks and Recreation

1. Nature and Scope of Work

This is administrative work in planning, coordinating and directing City parks and public recreation and museum and historic center programmes, operations, services and facilities in accordance with applicable policies, objectives, community needs and requirements. The Director of Parks and Recreation directs the activities of the Parks and Recreation Department: develops objectives, methods and procedures and plans and acts as advisor to the Parks and Recreation Committee and City Council on parks and public recreation matters. Work performance is reviewed and evaluated by the City Administrator, Council and Parks and Recreation Committee in terms of the effectiveness of departmental operations and programmes.

2. Illustrative Examples of Work

Plans, organizes, coordinates and directs parks and public recreation museum and Irving House operations, services and programmes; develops and implements plans and policies to accommodate the City's needs and requirements for parks and recreation services.

Plans, assigns, and supervises directly and through administrative staff the work of a large group of employees engaged in parks and recreational, operational and maintenance tasks.

Prepares departmental budgets, exercises control over expenditures, develops and implements new and/or improved work methods and procedures and reviews and evaluates all facilities, operations, services and programmes.

Prepares and presents policy recommendations, administrative reports, records and correspondence and provides a variety of information and assistance to the public, groups and organizations relative to policies, services and facilities.

Acts as advisor to the City Council, City Administrator and to the Parks and Recreation Committee on parks and recreation matters; attends management, staff and public meetings in an administrative or consultative capacity as required.

Hires, disciplines, lays off and terminates staff, and acts for the City in processing employee grievances, arbitration hearings and related labour relations matters.

Oversees the design and planning of parks and recreational facilities and areas and supervises developments on major facilities and projects.

Performs related work as required.

3. Required Knowledges, Abilities and Skills

Extensive knowledge of the procedures, methods, principles and practices involved in the administration of a moderate-sized public park and recreation system, and of the resources, interests and requirements of the City related thereto.

Thorough knowledge of the objectives of public park and recreation programmes and of trends and developments related thereto.

Thorough knowledge of rules, regulations, policies and bylaws governing departmental operations.

Working knowledge of the technical aspects of parks construction, maintenance and horticultural operations.

Ability to plan, administer and direct parks operations and a wide range of diversified recreation programmes and operations, and provides a high degree of effective leadership.

Ability to plan, coordinate and supervise directly and through delegation, the work of a large staff engaged in diversified parks and recreation duties.

Continued

Figure 3.3 Continued
Job Description of the Director of Parks and Recreation for the Corporation of the City of New Westminster, British Columbia

Ability to prepare estimates, budgets, correspondence and administrative reports covering departmental operations.

Ability to promote interest in parks and recreation services, prepare publicity material and speak effectively in public matters related to parks and recreation.

Ability to develop and maintain effective relationships with a variety of groups, contact associations and the a public.

Ability to develop, interpret and implement policies and regulations required for the administration of the Department.

4. Desirable Training and Experience

University graduation in Parks and Recreation Management or related discipline plus extensive related parks and recreation experience in a senior administrative capacity, or an equivalent combination of training and experience.

5. Required Licenses, Certificates and Registrations

Valid Driver's License for the Province of BC.

Basic Leadership Theories

A number of basic theories evolved during the previous century that help us understand managerial leadership. As Bennis and Nanus (1985:5) have suggested, "leadership skills were once thought to be a matter of birth. Leaders were born, not made, summoned to their calling through some unfathomable promise." As social conditions have changed—and, as some have suggested, the ability to lead has become more widely spread throughout the population—other theories have evolved to explain the leadership process. In this section we will discuss six theories that have been used to explain the process of managerial leadership.

1. Great Man Theory. This theory of managerial leadership is based on the idea that there are individuals who assume the role of leader because of certain historical events that provide them with an opportu-nity for leadership. In the recreation and leisure field, those individuals whom we credit with having great influence in the course of the history of our profession include Jane Addams, Frederick Law Olmsted, Luther Gulick, Joseph Lee, Stephen Mather and John Muir (Edginton, Hudson, & Ford, 1999).

2. The Trait Theory. This theory suggests that an individual can possess specific traits that would contribute to an effective managerial leadership style. The assumption is that if you can identify the traits, you can identify individuals with managerial leadership skills. In Chapter One, using Katz's model, we suggested that a manager needs a blend of conceptual, human, and technical skills to be successful. Other traits have been identified by Yukl (1981): (1) creativity, (2) or-

Figure 3.4
Job Description of the Superintendent of the Willamalane Park and Recreation District, Willamalane, Oregon

SUPERINTENDENT
Exempt

General Statement of Duties

The SUPERINTENDENT is the chief executive officer of the District and is responsible for its management and operation. Responsibilities include, but are not limited to: administration of parks, personnel, programs, services, areas and facilities, maintenance, planning and research, finance and budget, serial and bond issues, and public and community relations.

Supervision Received

Reports directly to the Board of Directors.

Supervision Exercised

Responsible for the indirect supervision of all District employees. Directly supervises the Recreation Services Division Director, Park Services Division Director, Human Resources/Finance Manager, Marketing Manager, and Executive Secretary.

Examples of Principal Duties

ADMINISTRATION: Organizes and directs the programs and services of the District; develops and administers a broad program of recreation activities for all age groups and interests; and maintains systematic, complete, and accurate records of District activities and services, personnel, property, and finances.

FINANCE: Prepares, submits, justifies, and controls the budget. Supervises the District's financial operation, including the maintenance of complete financial records for all District transactions.

PLANNING/RESEARCH: Directs the acquisition, planning, construction, improvement, and maintenance of all District areas, services, and facilities. Ascertains present and future needs. Prepares long-term plans to meet those needs, including budgetary requirements. Conducts, develops, and coordinates systems of internal and external research evaluation for the establishment of overall agency goals.

Administration Center • 200 South Mill Street • Springfield, OR 97477-7303
Ph. (541) 736-4044 • TDD (541) 736-4014 • FAX (541) 736-4025

Continued

Figure 3.4 Continued
Job Description of the Superintendent of the Willamalane Park and Recreation District, Willamalane, Oregon

SUPERINTENDENT
Page 2

PUBLIC RELATIONS/
COMMUNITY INVOLVEMENT: Provides an effective system of continuous interpretation, promotion, and publicizing of the services of the District. Establishes and maintains cooperative planning and working relationships with other local agencies—governmental, voluntary, and private—and with state, regional, and national agencies. Counsels with Districtwide groups and individuals to determine program needs, area, and facility requirements and improvements.

PERSONNEL: Recruits, selects, and employs all personnel. Develops, maintains, and coordinates systems of personnel policy, including job descriptions, evaluations, hiring and dismissal procedures, salaries, benefits, grievances, affirmative action, training, and workshops.

BOARD COMMUNICATION: Responsible for informing the Board of Directors on matters and issues pertaining to the District and their effect on the community.

Experience and Training

Master's degree in Park and Recreation Administration, or related field, and five years of progressively responsible park and recreation administrative experience, including public relations, park maintenance, landscaping, financial and budgetary management, and comprehensive planning/research.

Recruiting Requirements, Knowledge, Skill, and Ability

1.   Ability to establish and maintain an effective working relationship with an elected Board of Directors while implementing and carrying out the policies which they establish.

2.   Proven ability to give direction and guidance to District staff by defining standards and principles of operation.

3.   Administrative skill in the organization, interpretation, and coordination of sound financial accountability programs.

4.   Working knowledge of contemporary personnel practices and programs of professional enrichment.

5.   Working knowledge of administrative research and evaluation procedures which facilitate the establishment of common agency goals.

Continued

Figure 3.4 Continued
Job Description of the Superintendent of the Willamalane Park and Recreation District, Willamalane, Oregon

SUPERINTENDENT
Page 3

6. Must be able to coordinate comprehensive planning, acquisition, and development programs.

7. Ability to develop and coordinate a broad range of public relations, community involvement, and public education programs.

8. Ability to communicate, including public speaking and the writing of reports, manual, directions, and related materials.

03/01/97

---

ganization, (3) persuasiveness, (4) diplomacy and tactfulness, (5) knowledge of the task and (6) the ability to speak well. Further, it is evident that managers need cultural awareness and understanding as well as sensitivity of diverse populations. Other skills are emerging as being important in the 21st century: flexibility, self-managed learning, and creativity.

3. Group or Exchange Theory. The group theory of managerial leadership has its origins in the discipline of social psychology. Basically, this theory suggests that there is an interaction between leaders and followers within group environments. The leader is given this position, along with its status and rewards, in exchange for the benefits that he or she produces for the group. Basically, this theory views leadership as an exchange process.

4. Behavior Theory. This theory is an extension of the group or exchange theory. This theory suggests that

leadership must be viewed in the context of group behavior. Leaders exist when they are working within a group toward some common goal. Managerial leadership involves influencing others in the context of group behavior.

5. Situational or Contingency Theory. This model holds that situational factors influence the use of a given managerial leadership strategy. In this approach, there may be factors that guide a leader to use one style or another. For example, the task maturity of employees may enable a more open, laissez faire managerial leadership style. On the other hand, when individuals lack knowledge of a task they may have to be supervised in a more directive fashion.

6. Excellence/Transformational Theory. This concept of managerial leadership emerged in the 1970s. It basically suggests that leisure service managers are involved in a transformational process. In this model, leaders move individuals using symbols, and expressions of good will, and encourage individuals to operate at higher levels because the work they are engaged in is worthwhile and important. Advanced primarily by Peters and Waterman (1982) as well as Burns (1978), this concept has had a great influence on managerial leadership.

These basic theories have yielded numerous leadership models and basic studies. In fact, Bennis and Nanus (1985:4) report that after decades of academic analysis, there are more than 350 definitions of managerial leadership. Yet with all of the studies that have been conducted "no clear and unequivocal understanding exists as to what distinguishes leaders from nonleaders, and perhaps more important, what distinguishes effective leaders from ineffective leaders and effective organizations from ineffective organizations."

Leadership Models and Basic Studies

As indicated, numerous studies have been conducted from which many models have been developed to describe managerial leadership styles. In this section of the book we will review benchmark studies such as the Lewin, Lippitt and White studies of the late 1930s and the Ohio State studies of the 1940s. More contemporary theories such as William Hitt's Model of Leadership and Hershey and Blanchard's Tri-Dimensional Leader Effectiveness Model are also presented for discussion.

The Lewin, Lippitt, and White Studies

The landmark Lewin, Lippitt, and White studies (1939) marked the beginning not only of the study of leadership, but contributed to the development of the discipline of social psychology. These individuals were interested in determining the impact of various leadership styles on the behavior of individuals. In particular, they organized their studies to observe leadership styles in theatrical mask making and clubs organized around a variety of activities such as model airplane construction and mask making. They investigated the impact of three styles of leadership—democratic, authoritarian, and laissez-faire.

In the initial study, they compared the impact of the democratic leadership style with the autocratic leadership style. They found that the participants in the study were more hostile in the presence of the autocratic leadership style than the democratic leadership style. There was also more aggression displayed between the boys participating in the study. In their next effort, they included the laissez-faire leader and discovered the same pattern of aggressiveness. In addition, they found that the boys liked the democratic and laissez-faire leaders more than the authoritarian leaders.

It is interesting to note that the Lewin, Lippitt, and White studies have greatly influenced the work of leisure services personnel over the years. Numerous professional manuals and guidebooks tout the value and importance of using the democratic style of leadership. Edginton, Hanson, Edginton, & Hudson (1998:67) have written, "many texts on recreation leadership styles, and based upon the findings of this very limited sample, suggest that a democratic leadership style is most desirable and effective in all situations. However, the ideal leadership style will vary according to the needs of a given situation, as will become evident when shown against other leadership styles."

The Ohio State Studies

The Ohio State studies were developed by the Bureau of Business Research in the 1940s. A multidisciplinary group of researchers from disciplines such as psychology, sociology, and economics were drawn together to study leadership behavior. They developed the Leader Behavior Description Questionnaire (LBDQ) to study and analyze leadership behavior in a variety of settings. The project involved studying armed forces personnel, civil servants, educators, students, and blue-collar workers.

To study leadership, they identified two key components that contribute to a person's leadership style. These were called *initiating structure* and *consideration*. Initiating structure can be thought of as one's task orientation. In other words, it deals with how goals are established, work organized, and patterns of communication are established to support the work of a group. Initiating structures also deal with the work methods employed. The element of consideration has to do with the relationships developed between individuals in an organization. Building trust, promoting cooperation between people, and otherwise creating a comfortable work environment have much to do with the element of consideration. This is sometimes also referred to as the human relations element of a person's leadership style.

The importance of the Ohio State studies is that they helped identify these two essential components of leadership. Subsequent managerial leadership models have been built around these basic concepts. Other authors have suggested that a person's managerial relationship style can be a blend of these two elements, or that an individual's managerial leadership style can be high

in one element, such as the initiating structure, and low in the other. The Ohio State studies did not identify which mix of style would be appropriate or most effective in a given situation; rather they laid the groundwork for helping us better understand the components of one's leadership style (see Figure 3.5).

The New Managerial Grid

Developed by Robert R. Blake and Jane S. Mouton (1978), the Managerial Grid Theory suggests that successful managers are those who are concerned

Figure 3.5
The Leadership Style Model Portraying the Ohio State Studies Dimensions

	(Low) Task Orientation (High)
High human relations orientation and low task orientation	High task orientation and high human relations orientation
Low human relations orientation and low task orientation	High task orientation and low human relations orientation

(Low) Human relations orientation (High)

with both people (human relations) and production (completion of work task). Figure 3.6 shows the Management Grid that they developed. Along the vertical axis, concern for people is rated on a scale of 1 to 9. The horizontal axis measures concern for production, also on a scale from 1-9.

Blake and Mouton identify five management positions within the Managerial Grid. Position 1,1 represents a low concern for both people and produc-

Figure 3.6
Blake and Mouton's Management Grid

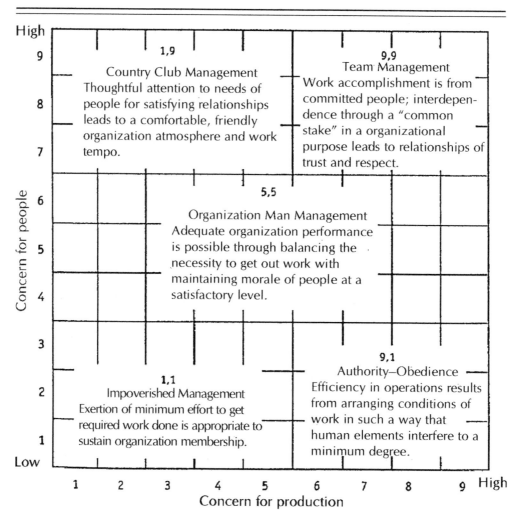

Source: Blake, R. R., & Mouton, J. S. (1978). *The new management grid* (p. 11). Houston: Gulf Publishing. Copyright © 1978. The Managerial Grid Figure reproduced by permission.

tion. High concern for both people and production is represented by position 9,9. A low/high score for the completion of tasks and the maintenance of satisfactory human relations would be reflected in position 1,9 or 9,1. The position of 5,5 indicates a managerial style that essentially tries to find a compromise between the concerns of people and the completion of a task.

The University of Michigan Studies

In the late 1940s, the Survey Research Center at the University of Michigan began to study leadership. Basically, this group was involved in helping to determine both worker productivity and satisfaction. They looked at factors such as morale, supervision, work conditions, methods, and productivity. They found that managers whose employees were more productive were more employee centered, showing genuine concern for people. On the other hand, they found that less productive groups were ones in which there was close supervision and great concern for productivity. Interestingly, they found that work satisfaction and productivity are not necessarily tied to one another.

The University of Michigan Studies extended the variables identified in the Ohio State Studies. Rather than using a grid-type format to show the relationship between managerial leadership variables (concern for people, concern for task) they suggested that these two variables should be viewed as existing on a continuum. Two models emerged in the literature from the University of Michigan work. They are the Rensis Likert System of Management and the Tannebaum and Schmidt Continuum of Leadership Behavior.

1. The Rensis Likert System of Management. This model of managerial leadership proposes four systems of styles, when viewed as existing on a continuum. System 1, Exploitive Autocratic, suggests that the manager is authoritarian, lacking confidence and trust in employees. The environment is very closed and controlling. System 2, Benevolent Autocratic, finds the manager viewing employees in a condescending manner. The manager using this style will sometimes involve employees in decision making and problem solving. System 3, Participative, is a more open, collaborative style. Managers usually solicit the involvement or participation of employees, and there is a freer and more open work environment. Last, System 4, Democratic, involves the full par-

ticipation of employees and is seen as one in which the manager has complete confidence and trust in his or her subordinates.

2. The Tannebaum and Schmidt Continuum of Leadership Behavior. The Tannebaum and Schmidt Continuum of Leadership Behavior presents a model that discusses use of authority by the manager and combines it with freedom that subordinates might have. As seen in Figure 3.7, at one end of the continuum, authoritarian, task-oriented managers use a great deal of authority, and at the other end of the continuum, managers are more democratic and relationship oriented. The point of this model is that managers at one end of the continuum make all the decisions and tell people what to do, and at the other end they empower employees with freedom to make decisions and to find their own work methods.

Transformational/Transactional Leadership.

Transformational/Transactional Leadership was proposed by Burns (1978) and constitutes an important advancement in management thinking that will have a great impact on the 21st century leisure service manager. Burns proposed two types of leadership styles: transactional and transformational. Transactional Leadership proposes that there is an exchange between the manager and his or her employees. The manager exchanges financial rewards or other units of value with individuals in exchange for their efforts. In a sense, the manager promises individuals that if they perform they will be rewarded and

Figure 3.7
Tannebaum and Schmidt's Continuum of Leadership Behavior

(Authoritarian) ← ————————————————— → (Democratic)
Task Oriented ———————————————————— Relationships-Oriented

Source of Authority

Use of Authority
by the Leader

Area of Freedom
for Subordinates

Leader
makes
decision
and
announces
it

Leader
"sells"
decision

Leader
presents
ideas and
invites
question

Leader
presents
tentative
decision,
subject to
change

Leader
presents
problem,
gets
suggestions,
and makes
decision

Leader
defines
limits,
asks
group to
make
decision

Leader
permits
subordinates
to function
within limits
defined by
superior

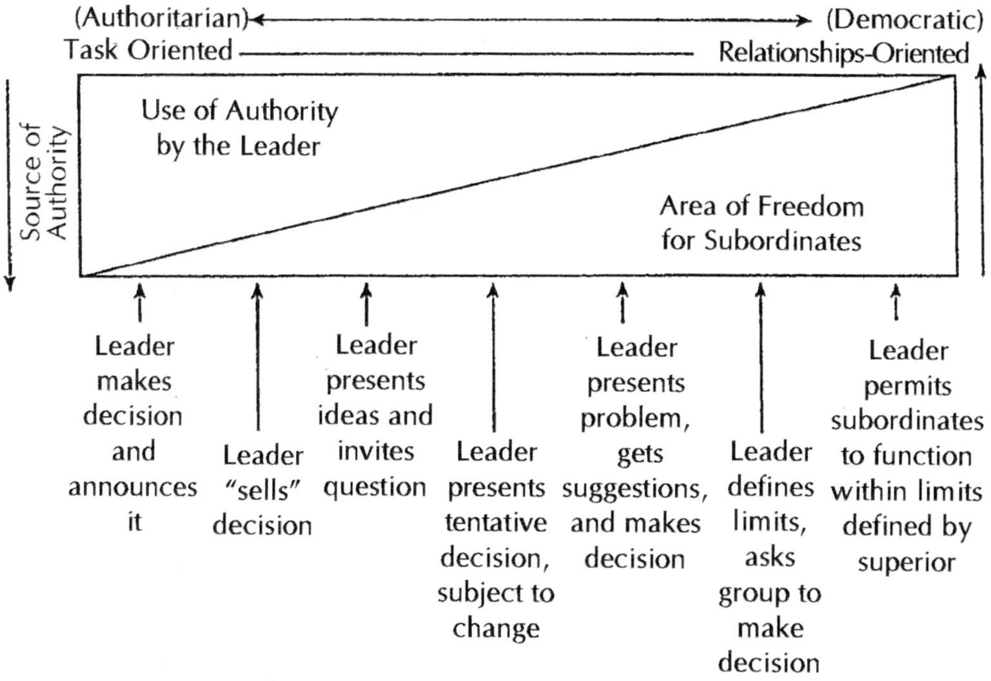

Source: Tannebaum and Schmidt's Continuum of Leadership Behavior

recognized. The fallacy in the Transactional Leadership model is that it may not inspire employees to higher levels of performance because it sets up a never-ending process of weighing the perceived value of rewards gained against one's work performance. Usually it creates the scenario that for individuals to perform at a higher level, they must gain greater external rewards for their performance.

Transformational Leadership is directed toward assisting individuals feel a sense of commitment to a worthwhile enterprise. The goal of leisure service managers using this method is vastly different than in the transactional strategy. The leisure service manager as a transformational leader encourages people to higher levels of performance and productivity. His or her job is one of drawing people into the enterprise because they are engaged in extraordinary opportunities to make a difference. This is communicated to people through the use of symbols and encouragement.

The manager's role as a transformational leader is one of coaching, advising, problem solving, promoting pride, and in general assisting employees rather than controlling types of behavior. Bass (1985) has suggested the following ways that transformational leaders can motivate employees: (1) by raising their levels of consciousness, (2) by getting them to transcend their self-interests, and (3) by raising their need level on Abraham Maslow's hierarchy of needs. Leisure service managers using this approach will often cheer their employees on to higher levels of productivity. The goal is to get employees to internalize the goals of the organization and to be motivated by these internal values. According to Luthans (1998:396), "transactional leadership is a prescription for mediocrity and . . . transformational leadership leads to superior performance in organizations facing demands for renewal and change."

Fiedler's Contingency Model of Leadership Effectiveness

This model of managerial leadership suggests that no single style fits every situation. Fiedler (1967) defined two basic styles. The first is the human relations, or lenient, style, in which the manager tends to be permissive. The second style is the task-directed or hard-nosed management style in which the manager tends to be more controlling and directive. Fiedler notes that there are three dimensions that influence which managerial leadership style is selected in a given situation:

1. Leader–Member Relations. This refers to the extent to which the manager feels that he or she is accepted by the group. According to Fiedler, this is the most important factor in determining the managerial leadership style to be employed.

2. Task Structure. Task structure is related to clarity of role expectations. In other words, when there is great precision and clarity in what needs to be done to implement one's tasks, jobs, or responsibilities, the task structure is high. In situations where this is not the case, great ambiguity is created. This is the second most important dimension in determining one's managerial leadership style.

3. Position Power. Position power refers to one's formal authority. Usually this is drawn from the positioning of an individual with in an organization, but it can come from other sources as well, including the ability to use rewards and punishments, one's knowledge and expertise, and one's attractiveness to the group.

Fiedler and his associates were able to determine in their research studies that the task-directed or hard-nosed style was effective in situations that were either favorable or unfavorable to the manager. In other words, when the relationship between the manager and employees is positive and when the relationship between the manager and employees is negative, the most appropriate style to employ is the task-directed one. On the other hand, in situations where there is an intermediate favorableness toward the manager, then the relationship-oriented style should be employed (see Figure 3.8).

Path–Goal Theory of Leadership

The Path–Goal Theory of Leadership is a situationally driven model. Basically, it suggests that managerial leadership is a function of motivation, satisfaction, and performance. In the same situation, the manager/leader may use different styles to influence employees. In other words, one employee may require a more directive, controlling type of managerial leadership style, whereas others may need to be challenged to produce at a higher level. The theory suggests four models that can be employed:

1. Directive Leadership. Directive leadership is authoritarian in na-

Figure 3.8
Fiedler's Contingency Model of Leadership

Task-oriented style	Relationship-oriented, considerate style	Task-oriented style
High assumed similarity or least preferred co-worker scores	Low assumed similarity or least preferred co-worker scores	Low assumed or least preferred co-worker scores

◄———————————	———————————	———————————►
Favorable leadership situation	Situation intermediate in favorableness for leader	Unfavorable leadership situation

Source: Fiedler, F. E. (1967). *A theory of leadership effectiveness* (p. 14). New York: McGraw-Hill.

ture. In this model, employees are told what to do in a direct and succinct fashion. There is no attempt to involve individuals in decision-making or problem-solving processes.

2. *Supportive Leadership.* In this model of leadership, the leader-manager expresses care and concern for the welfare of his or her employees. The manager is often open to suggestions and finds ways to involve individuals in decision-making processes by receiving their comments. Hallmarks of this style are being positive and supportive.

3. *Participative Leadership.* In this model of leadership, the leader-manager encourages individuals to actively contribute their ideas to the organization. Although the manager may maintain ultimate author-

ity in making decisions, attention is given to creating a more open, participative environment.

4. *Achievement-Oriented Leadership.* Creating high expectations, identifying clear performance goals, and creating challenging standards are all elements of the achievement-oriented style. Leisure service managers using this approach are seen as encouraging and able to instill confidence in employees.

Research conducted on Path–Goal Leadership has found that different styles do have an impact on employee motivation, satisfaction, and productivity. Luthans (1998: 392–393), summarizing the Path–Goal Theory of Leadership research findings, reports the following: (1) studies of seven organizations have found that *leader directiveness* is positively related to the satisfaction and expectancies of subordinates engaged in clear tasks; (2) studies involving 10 different samples of employees found that *supportive leadership* will have its most positive effect on satisfaction for subordinates who work on stressful, frustrating, or dissatisfying tasks; (3) in a major study in an industrial manufacturing organization, it was found that in nonrepetitive, ego-involving tasks, employees were more satisfied under *participative leaders* than under non-participative leaders; and (4) in three separate organizations, it was found that for subordinates performing ambiguous, non-repetitive tasks, the higher the *achievement orientation of the leader,* the more confident subordinates were that their efforts would pay off in effective performance.

Reddin's 3-D Theory of Management Effectiveness

The 3-D Theory of Management Effectiveness, developed by William Reddin (1970), maintains that a manager's style must remain flexible to be effective. Reddin's theory of management rests on his belief that empirical evidence demonstrates that there is no single appropriate management style. The 3-D Theory of Management Effectiveness incorporates the dimensions of concern for completion of a task (TO = task orientation) and the establishment of satisfactory human relations (RO = relationships orientation). These two basic dimensions are similar to the consideration factor and initiating structure identified in the Ohio State University leadership studies. They also relate to the Blake and Mouton Managerial Grid in its concern for people and production. To these two dimensions, Reddin added a third dimension that he identified as *managerial effectiveness,*

meaning "the extent to which a manager achieves the output requirements of his or her position" (1970s). The effectiveness of a manager is found in the ability to change one's behavior according to the needs and dictates of the situation.

The 3-D Theory of Management Effectiveness includes four basic types of management: integrated, dedicated, related, and separated (Reddin, 1970:39). Reddin notes that managerial effectiveness is determined by appropriate application of one of the four basic styles. Conversely, he notes that inappropriate application of the styles results in ineffectiveness. Reddin expands the four basic styles to eight styles in order to distinguish appropriate, effective management styles from inappropriate, ineffective management styles. He calls these the executive (high-task, high-relationship, effective), the compromiser (high-task, high-relationships, effective), the benevolent autocrat (high-task, low relationship, ineffective), the autocrat (high-task, low-relationship, ineffective), the developer (low-task, high-relationship, effective), the missionary (low-task, high-relationship, ineffective), the bureaucrat (low-task, low-relationship, effective), and the deserter (low-task, low-relationship, ineffective). (See Figure 3.9.)

The 3-D Theory recognizes that leisure services/managers must be sensitive to the situational demands of administering a leisure service organization. Working with professional as well as quasi-professional personnel and the public at large presents a variety of management challenges. Individuals who are involved in the actual creation of activities must be motivated in a different manner than park maintenance personnel, who are essentially involved in carrying out routine tasks.

Figure 3.9
The 3-D Style Model

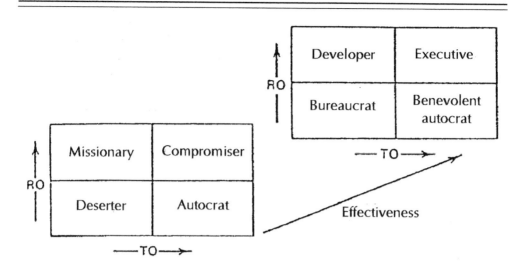

Source: Reddin, W. S. (1970). *Managerial Effectiveness.* New York: McGraw-Hill. Copyright © 1970 by William Reddin. Used with permission of McGraw-Hill Book Co.

Tri-Dimensional Leader Effectiveness Model

Hershey and Blanchard's (1977) Tri-Dimensional Leadership Effectiveness Model is found in Figure 3.10. The model effectively combines the dual elements of task-orientation and relationship orientation of the Ohio State Studies with a third element, effectiveness, as defined by an individual's task-relevant maturity. Task-relevant maturity is defined as "the capacity to set high, but attainable goals, willingness and ability to take responsibility, and education and/or experience" relevant to the task (1977:104). Thus, task-relevant maturity becomes an individual employee's knowledge, commitment, and experience to get the job done. Some individuals will have a higher-task relevant maturity on certain job functions when compared with other ones or with other individuals. An individual might have high task-relevant maturity in one area and lower in another.

Hershey and Blanchard identify four basic styles of leadership effectiveness, as indicated in Figure 3.11. The goal for the leisure service manager is to match his or her style with the needs of the individual. The four styles are as follows:

1. Telling Style. This approach to managerial leadership combines a high-task and low-relationship orientation. It is an effective style in situations where employees have a low level of task-relevant maturity.

2. Selling Style. This style of managerial leadership combines a high-task and high-relationship orientation. It is an effective style in situations where individuals have a low level of task-relevant maturity

3. Participating Style. This method of managerial leadership has a low-task and high-relationship orientation. It is an effective style in situations where subordinates have a high level of task-relevant maturity.

4. Delegating Style. This approach to managerial leadership combines a low-task and low-relationship orientation. It is an effective style in situations where leaders have a high level of task-relevant maturity.

This model of managerial leadership is useful in that it combines earlier studies with the notion of effectiveness, however, it has been criticized as being oversimplified. For example, there may

be elements in the work environment other than one's task-relevant maturity that influence the application of one's managerial leadership style.

Hitt's Model of Leadership

Hitt's Model of Leadership combines visioning with action. As Hitt (1988) notes, the two key dimensions of vision and ability to implement the vision can be displayed in graphic form, as shown in Figure 3.12. Discussing Hitt's Model of Leadership, Edginton, Hudson, and Ford (1999: 7) have written that this model emphasizes prag-

Figure 3.10
Tri-dimensional Leader Effectiveness Model

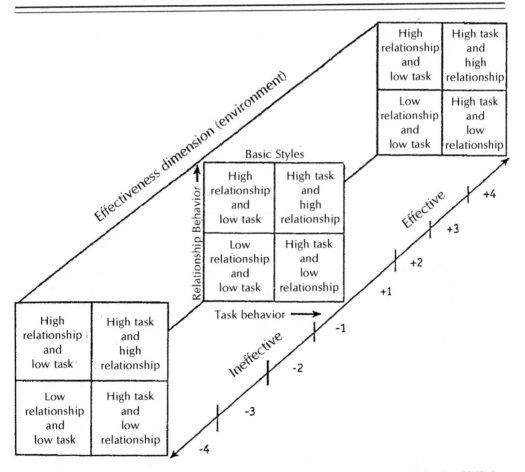

Source: Hersey, P. & Blanchard, K. H. (1977). *Management of organizational behavior: Utilizing human resources* (3rd ed., p. 106). © 1977. Reprinted by permission of Prentice-Hall, Inc., Englewood Cliffs, NJ.

Figure 3.11
Situational Leadership

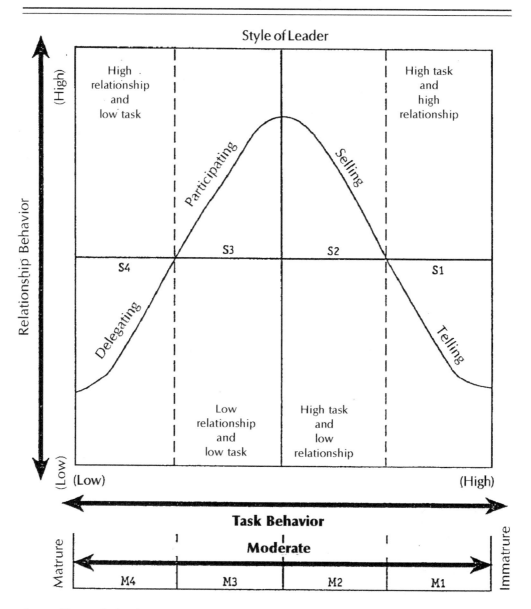

Source: Hersey, P. & Blanchard, K. H. (1977). *Management of organizational behavior: Utilizing human resources* (3rd ed., p. 170). © 1977. Reprinted by permission of Prentice-Hall, Inc., Englewood Cliffs, NJ.

matic idealism. In other words, "it is a leadership style that seeks higher ends, yet at the same time recognizes real-life conditions that influence the behavior of others. Leadership becomes a pro-cess of establishing a realistic, attractive vision for the future and then creating a plan of action to achieve desired ends." The four managerial leadership styles that emerged from Hitt's studies are as follows:

Figure 3.12
The Nature of Leadership

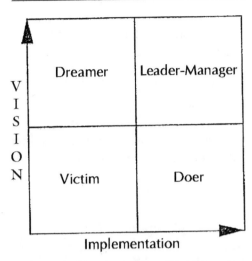

Source: Hitt, W. D. (1998). *The leader-manager: Guide lines for action.* Columbus: Battelle Press.

1. Victim. The person low on both vision and implementation, who complains that the organization is unfair

2. Dreamer. The person high on vision, but low on implementation

3. Doer. The person high on implementation, but low on vision

4. Leader Manager. The person high on both vision and implementation

Hitt's Model presents an interesting perspective on leadership in light of earlier studies showing the importance of visioning and transforming individuals in the work environment. In one dimension, the leisure service manager who is low on vision and implementation is seen as a victim. He or she is unable to create an attractive future for the organization and cannot move people to action. The dreamer is an individual who is very visionary, but who lacks the ability to move things forward. Usually this is a person with a lot of ideas, but lacks the knowledge of how to implement them. The doer is a person who can get things done, but does not necessarily have a strong vision. The optimal style is the leader - manager; one who combines great visionary skills with the ability to make things happen.

Collaborative Leadership Paradigm

The idea of collaborative leadership has been promoted among organizational behavior theorists. Best articulated in James A. Belesco and Ralph Stayer's book *Flight of the Buffalo*, collaborative leadership involves working with others in such a way as to promote a shared approach to decision making and problem solving. Using the metaphor of a flock of geese flying in a "V" formation, these authors suggest that the structure of the group and its leadership change depending on the group's needs. They point out that when flying, a flock of geese changes leadership frequently, with different geese taking the lead:

> "I could see geese flying in their "V" formation; the leadership changed frequently, with different geese taking the lead. I saw every goose being responsible for getting itself to wherever the gaggle was going, changing roles whenever necessary, alternating as leader, follower, or scout. And when the task changed, the geese would be responsible for changing the structure of the group to accommodate, similar to the geese that fly in a "V" but land in waves. I could see each goose being the leader." (1993:18).

From this metaphor for collaborative leadership, Belasco and Strayer deduced four important principles around which their idea of managerial leadership is built: (1) leaders transfer ownership for work to those who execute the work; (2) leaders create the environment for ownership where each person wants to be responsible; (3) leaders coach the development of personal capabilities; and (4) leaders learn fast themselves and encourage others to learn quickly.

Partnership Model of Leadership

This is a gender-based model of leadership that compares the masculinity-dominator model of leadership with the femininity-partnership model (Eishler, 1995). The traditional masculinity-dominating model emphasizes an authoritarian model of leadership. Basically, it is a model in which individuals are controlled through a more coercive form of leadership. The partnership model emphasizes freedom of choice and promotes mutual respect between individuals. Whereas the former model emphasizes punitive type control and behavior, the latter emphasizes giving support and providing empathy, care, and nourishment to others. In a sense, the partnership model provides the opportunity for individuals to connect with one another in a way in which unconditional support is the norm.

McKinney and Collins (1991) have researched the impact of gender and other variables on performance appraisals in leisure service settings. They have found few significant differences when viewing performance by gender. However, they do report that female leisure service managers tend to provide higher ratings when evaluating employees compared to male managers. This could be a result of different perspectives on management due to the partnership-nurturing model of managerial leadership. Henderson and Bialeschki (1990) and Henderson (1992) have discussed the challenges and opportunities faced by the feminization of leisure services. Henderson notes that "to suggest that differences in leadership between males and females can be attributed to gender differences is to oversimplify a complex situation." Further, she writes, "in examining leadership as an issue, individual differences among women, women's perceptions of themselves as leaders, and other's perceptions of women's leadership are factors that must be taken into account... . The typical feminine approach focuses on the process that results in outcomes, relationships among people and cooperation" (Henderson & Bialeschki, (45-59). However, Bialeschki and Henderson (1984) report that women in leisure services are no more masculine than feminine, or vice versa, in their personalities.

The Servant Leadership Model

The concept of servant leadership was proposed by Robert Greenleaf in the 1970s. Servant leadership involves creating caring environments by promoting teamwork, a sense of community, and finding ways to involve individuals in decision making and problem solving. In a sense, the servant leader is one who sees his or her managerial role as a manager as one of supporting, nurturing, and giving to others. The leisure service manager's responsibility as a servant leader involves serving his or her employees. It supports the idea that the work of managers is to remove the barriers that prevent them from succeeding in their responsibilities. Servant leaders, according to Spears (1995), reflect characteristics of listening, empathy, healing, awareness, persuasion, conceptualization, foresight, stewardship, and commitment to the growth of people and the community.

DeGraaf and Jordan (1999) have suggested that servant leadership can provide a sound philosophical underpinning for leisure service professionals' efforts. They write that servant leadership as a philosophical approach "emphasizes increased service to others by encouraging shared decision making and a sense of community. Such an approach emphasizes the three factors that have shaped all forms of leisure services at their best: the desire to help people, an entrepreneurial spirit, and the ability to respond to societal change." (15). The idea of servant leadership comes from a Christian theological perspective. At the last supper, Jesus Christ washed the feet of his Apostles as a way of demonstrating his humility and supporting them. An extension of this view is that the leisure service profession should adopt a "public servant" image by placing the needs of others before its own. This ideology can permeate the entire philosophy of a leisure service organization as well as its management structure.

Summary

Managerial leadership is key to the success of leisure service organizations. Leadership is about influencing others by creating a credible, attractive, and realistic vision for the future and then moving people toward action to achieve desired ends. Vision is the power of forward thinking and is fundamental to the work of a leisure service manager.

However, visioning by itself is not enough; managers must act and must influence others to do the same. As Bennis and Nanus (1985) have written, "managers do things right, leaders do the right thing." In this book, we have chosen to emphasize the latter, recognizing the importance of integrating the need for the leisure service organization not only to be effective but also efficient.

Key contemporary concepts for leisure service managers involve empowering others, promoting quality, establishing learning opportunities, and operating in an ethical fashion. Empowerment has to do with ensuring that individuals are given freedom and have a sense of ownership for their efforts. It involves delegating, creating community, and liberating individuals within leisure service organizations. Quality is of utmost concern to leisure service professionals. It involves pursuing excellence. The rate of change and the expansion of knowledge have required organizations to become learning centered. As human capital becomes an organization's most important resource, the development of this element becomes increasingly essential to its future success. Last, operating in an ethical fashion is essential for leisure service managers. Three ethical areas need to be addressed: (1) human-social responsibility, (2) community responsibility, and (3) environmental responsibility.

Several approaches to appraising managerial roles were offered. One conceptual model showed that a manager can serve as either a figurehead, leader, liaison, monitor, disseminator, spokesperson, entrepreneur, disturbance handler, resource allocator, or negotiator. The management functions reported in the leisure service literature include planning, organizing, influencing, and controlling. A review of actual job descriptions from leisure service managers suggests that they are involved in preparing budgets, overseeing staff, visioning and planning, and developing and maintaining areas and facilities.

Many leadership theories, studies, and models were given. Basic theories include the Great Man Theory, Trait Theory, Group or Exchange Theory, Behavior Theory, Situational or Contingency Theory, and Excellence/ Transformational Theory. A number of managerial leadership models were discussed. Many of these identified one's managerial leadership style as comprised of two components, relationship orientation and task orientation. More contemporary models suggest that one's managerial leadership style should be flexed in order to be effective, and that different conditions or situations may require different approaches. Many leisure service managers today see themselves as being in a transformational role, encouraging individuals to pursue higher ends. Other management models suggest that leisure service managers see themselves in the role of being servants to those with whom they work. This model suggests that the leisure service profession should take on more of a public service orientation.

Discussion Questions

1. What is managerial leadership?

2. What does the statement mean, "managers do things right, leaders do the right thing"?

3. What is vision, and why is it important in management leadership?

4. Define empowerment, and identify three strategies that may be employed to implement this concept.

5. What is quality? What methods are available to leisure service managers to promote quality in their work environments?

6. Why is creating a learning organization important?

7. How do ethics influence the work of the leisure service manager?

8. Identify and discuss the roles in which leisure service managers engage. Locate a job description in your community and identify management roles and functions.

9. Identify and discuss basic leadership theories.

10. How do leadership studies and models help provide a foundation for the work of the leisure service manager? What managerial leadership model reflects "best professional practice" in the leisure service profession?

References

Bass, B. (1985, Winter). Leadership: Good, better, best. *Organizational Dynamics*.

Belasco, J. A., & Stayer, R. C. (1993). *Flight of the buffalo*. New York: Warner.

Bennis, W., & Nanus, B. (1985). *Leaders*. New York: Harper & Row.

Bialeschki, M. D., & Henderson, K. A. (1984). The personal and professional spheres: Complement or conflict for women leisure services professionals. *Journal of Park and Recreation Administration, 2*(4), 45-54.

Blake. R. R., & Mouton, J. S. (1978). *The new managerial grid*. Houston: Gulf Publishing.

Bullaro, J. J., & Edginton, C. R. (1986). *Commercial leisure services: Managing for profit, service, and personal satisfaction.* New York: Macmillan.

Burns, J. M. (1978). *Leadership.* New York: Harper & Row.

DeGraaf, D. G., Jordan, D. J., & DeGraaf, K. H. (1999). *Programming for parks, recreation, and leisure services: A servant leadership approach.* State College, PA: Venture Publishing.

Edginton, S. R., & Edginton, C. R. (1994). *Youth programs: Promoting quality services.* Champaign, IL: Sagamore Publishing .

Edginton, C. R., Hudson, S. D., & Ford, P. M. (1999). *Leadership in recreation and leisure service organizations.* Champaign, IL: Sagamore Publishing .

Fiedler, F. (1967). *A theory of leadership effectiveness.* New York: McGraw-Hill.

Greenleaf, R. (1977). *Servant leadership: A journey into the nature of legitimate power and greatness.* New York: Paulist Press.

Hemphill, J. K., & Coons, A. E. (1957). Development of the Leader Behavior Description Questionnaire. In R. M. Stogdill & A. E. Coons (Eds.), *Leader behavior: Its description and measurement.* Columbus: Ohio State University, Bureau of Business Research.

Henderson, K. A. (1992). Being female in the park and recreation profession in the 1990s: Issues and challenges. *Journal of Park and Recreation Administration, 10*(2), 15-29.

Hershey, P., & Blanchard, K. (1977). *Management of organizational behavior—Utilizing human resources* (3rd ed.). Englewood Cliffs, NJ: Prentice-Hall.

Hitt, W. D. (1988). *The leader manager: Guidelines for action.* Columbus, OH: Battelle Press.

Hitt, W. D. (1990). *Ethics and leadership.* Columbus, OH: Battelle Press.

House, R. J., & Mitchell, T. R. (1974, Autumn). Path–goal theory of leadership. *Journal of Contemporary Business.*

Katz, D., Maccoby, N., & Morse, N. C. (1950). *Productivity, supervision, and morale in an office situation.* Ann Arbor, MI: University of Michigan, Survey Research Center.

Kouzes, J., & Posner, B. (1995). *The leadership challenge: How to keep getting extraordinary things done in organizations.* San Francisco: Jossey-Bass.

Lewin, K., Lippitt, R., & White, R. K. (1939). Patterns of aggressive behavior and experimentally created social climates. *Journal of Social Psychology.*

Likert, R. (1967). *The human organization.* New York: McGraw-Hill.

Luthans, R. (1977/1998). *Organizational behavior* (8th ed.). Boston: McGraw-Hill.

Mabey, C. (1994). Youth leadership: Commitment for what? In S. L. York & D. J. Jordan (Eds.), *Bold ideas: Creative approaches to the challenge of youth programming.* University of Northern Iowa, Institute for Youth Leaders.

McKinney, W. R., & Collins, J. R. (1991, Fall). The influence of race, sex, and age on performance appraisal bias in public parks and recreation. *Journal of Park and Recreation Administration, 10*(2), 45-54.

Mintzberg, H (1980). *The nature of managerial work.* New York: Harper & Row.

Peters, T. J., & Waterman, R. H. (1982). *In search of excellence.* New York: Harper & Row.

Pinchot, G. (1996). Creating organizations with many leaders. In F. Hesselbein, M. Goldsmith, & R. Beckhard, (Eds.), *The leader of the future.* San Francisco: Josey-Bass.

Reddin, W. S. (1970). *Managerial effectiveness.* New York: McGraw-Hill.

Rost, J. C. (1993). *Leadership for the twenty-first century.* Westport, CT: Praeger.

Senge, P. M. (1990). *The fifth discipline.* New York: Doubleday.

Smale, B. J. A., & Frisby, W. (1992). Managerial work activities and perceived competencies of municipal recreation managers. *Journal of Park and Recreation Administration, 10*(4), 81–108.

Spears, L. (1995). Servant leadership and the Greenleaf legacy. In L. Spear (Ed.), *Reflections on leadership: How Robert K. Greenleaf's theory of servant leadership influenced today's top management thinkers.* (pp. 1–16). New York: Wiley & Sons.

Stogdill, R. (1974). *Handbook of leadership: A survey of theory and research.* New York: Macmillan.

Tannenbaum, R., & Warren H. (1973, May–June). How to choose a leadership pattern. *Harvard Business Review, 106.*

Walton, M. (1986). *The Deming management method.* New York: Perigee.

Yukl, G.A. (1981). *Leadership in organizations.* Englewood Cliffs, NJ: Prentice-Hall.

Chapter 4

Managers, Goals, and Policy Development

Promoting a policy of inclusion, the City of Phoenix's River Rampage seeks to involve teens with disabilities as well as teens at-risk.

Introduction

Leisure service managers need an understanding of both the process of establishing a vision and the role that policymaking plays in leisure service management. They should be able to conceptualize the many facets involved in this process and integrate these as they pertain to the organization. Managers must understand the nature of visioning, the process of goal setting, the process of policymaking, the different types of policy structures, factors affecting the policy process, and their role in the policy process. A policy, like a budget, is a plan. It is a way for an organization to delineate a course of action that guides the behavior of both employees and consumers.

Vision and goal setting are covered in the first section of this chapter. This is followed by a discussion of values, policy, the process of policy formulation, and environmental factors of which managers must be aware. A later chapter will present a discussion of the legal basis for leisure service organizations. Any group of individuals has a set of rights and privileges, as well as power and the authority that allow it to operate within society. This is also the case with leisure service organizations. In many cases, these rights are derived from formal legal codes. Legal considerations fall within the subsystem of the political environment. Knowledge of legal parameters will enable leisure service managers to concentrate their efforts on areas that will serve their clients most productively.

Visioning and Goal Setting

As previously indicated, vision is the power of forward thinking. A vision can be thought of as a philosophical direction for an organization. It comes from the spiritual or intuitive as well as the cognitive dimension. A vision statement must be written boldly, giving direction to the efforts of individuals at all levels of the organization. As an essential element of a leisure service organization, a vision statement is organized around a widely shared set of values that, in effect, reflect the culture of the organization within the contextual framework of community values. Vision statements enable organizations to document their ideas, intentions, and values so that

they can be taught and reinforced. Vision is central to an organizations strategic plan, master plan, and comprehensive plan. Figure 4.1 depicts the relationships between values, vision, and goals relative to planning for leisure services. It is important to note that managers must be aware of the environmental conditions of their clients and the community in order to assess the values needed to formulate the vision of the organization. Second, it is important that leisure managers have a system in place to monitor societal trends in order to develop responsive organizational goals. The next section discusses

Figure 4.1
Relationships in Values, Vision, and Goals of a Leisure Service Organization

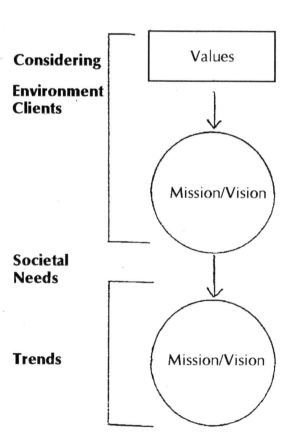

the vision and the importance of values within the context of leisure service management.

Developing a Vision for a Leisure Service Organization

How does one go about developing a vision for a leisure service organization? Written in broad terms, vision statements often focus on the values or benefits that leisure service organizations attempt to provide. Often such statements serve to inspire, uplift, encourage, and motivate, and to produce a level of commitment among employees and customers. As Naisbitt and Aburdene (1985:20) have written, "the first ingredient in . . . [an organization] . . . is a powerful vision, . . . a sense of where . . . [the organization] . . . is going and how to get there." They also note that "intellectual strategies alone will not motivate people. Only . . . [an organization] . . . with a real mission or sense of purpose that comes out of an intuitive or spiritual dimension will capture people's hearts. And you must have people's hearts to inspire the hard work required to realize a vision."

Basically, the process of developing a vision statement involves identifying the core values of both the organization and those it serves. Edginton (1987: 7) has written that a leisure service organization's core values may "focus on concern for quality, consistency, dependability, integrity, safety, and value." Usually vision statements answer the fundamental question, "What business are we in?" Leisure service organizations wishing to develop a vision statement will first identify values of importance relating to the following:

1. Broader Societal Values. Broader societal values include, for example, a Judeo-Christian ethic, a Protestant work ethic, democracy, freedom, liberty, social justice, and increasingly, recognition of living in a pluralistic, diverse culture.

2. Community Values. Every community develops a unique set of specific values that guide the work of leisure service managers. In some communities, quality of life, livability, open space, preservation and conservation, opportunities to promote the well-being of individuals, and other values are sought. Identification of these types of values often enables the development of community specific standards.

3. Customer Values. The vision statement of leisure service organizations should reflect the values of the customers whom they serve. Such values vary according to the population grouping served by a giving leisure service organization. Community park and recreation departments will reflect the values in a given geographic location, for example a city, a district, or a county. A private leisure service organization might serve a more narrowly focused clientele with a more discrete set of values.

4. Employee Values. Employee values are very important in the development of an employee statement. After all, employees are the ones who must believe first in the vision of an organization in order to bring it into being. An organization's vision must first be interpreted by employees to customers (see figure 4.2).

Figure 4.2
Sample of Organizational Values

Organizational Values

Fun
Just have fun. Enjoy work. This will reflect on our ability to deal with customers and co-workers in a positive way.

Innovation
Employees continuously work to improve processes and service. Be creative, stick your neck out and make a difference.

Teamwork
Within the organization we shall strive toward working together in the establishment and completion of common goals. External to the organization, we shall seek cooperation with organizations who also deliver services to the Elk Grove Community.

Opportunity
We will work in partnership with employees to foster growth and development. The investment of time in training and development will be of paramount importance to the organization. Our programs, facilities and services will be provided on the basis of accommodating unique needs of customers, which will create a variety of opportunities for customers to participate.

Respect
We are committed to including external customer opinions in our decision-making process. We value the information customers provide. In addition, internally within our organization, we shall value the opinions of each other. Every employee in the organization is important to the overall mission of the District.

Integrity
We strive for honest and open communication within our organization as well as with our customers. We shall work on maintaining the trust and respect of each other and our customers.

Trust
We vow to do what we say we are going to do. We strive for service reliability for our customers. In addition, we shall empower staff and create an environment in which employees' good judgment will be relied upon.

Source: Elk Grove Park District, Elk Grove, Illinois

Once these values have been identified, an organization's vision statement can be developed. Although there is no one best way of writing a vision statement, most are short and written in a concise ,direct manner. They must be written in such a way as to ensure an emotional involvement yet at the same time they should challenge others to loftier cognitive pursuits. An excellent example of a vision statement can be found from the city of Phoenix, Arizona (see Figure 4.3).

The Manager and Identification of Community Values

Should we use market-driven management models, environmental management models, or socially driven

Figure 4.3

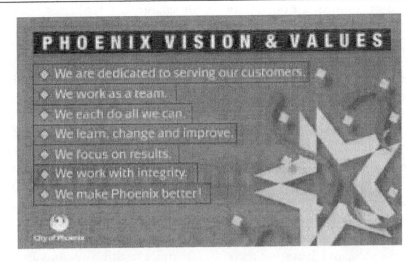

City of Phoenix Vision and Values

We Are Dedicated to Serving Our Customers
We succeed by focusing our attention on the customer. The city exists to serve the customer and our community. Their needs give us our direction and purpose. They need to feel and sense our commitment to them.

We Work as a Team
Teamwork is the basis of our success. We use cooperation as our first tool in working with other employees, departments, the private sector. We involve people because we value their commitment and ownership. We view successful performance as a group activity. There is nothing we cannot accomplish together. One unit of the city cannot be successful at the expense of another. Our teamwork and cooperative spirit reaches out to the customer - we include the customer in our team.

We Each Do All We Can
We are the city's most important resource. We are committed. We each have the opportunity and responsibility to develop and use our skills to the highest level. We value diversity. To be successful, we all contribute our ideas and creativity to improving the city. We are proud of the statement our work makes about us.

We Learn, Change and Improve
We are open to new methods and we listen and learn from others. We correct our mistakes and learn from them. We continually strive to be faster, smarter and better than we were the year before.

We Focus on Results
Each of us knows the level of our customer satisfaction, our response time in delivering service and the cost of those services. We use information about the results we provide so we can improve. There are times when bureaucracy is a barrier to achieving the desired result. Where rules do not add value, we want to change them to better focus on results and customer satisfaction.

We Work with Integrity
Whenever we make a decision, provide a service or deal with customers, we act with honesty and integrity. People learn from interacting with us that they can continue to trust us. We treat all people equally and equitably.

We Make Phoenix Better
We work to make Phoenix better. Improving transportation, the environment, public safety, educational opportunities and other parts of our community is the reason we come to work each day. It's the reason we want to change and improve. Making Phoenix a better place to live and work is our bottom line. We care about our community.

Source: City of Phoenix, Vision and Values Statement

management models? Cato (1992) has noted that just as we have integrated business practices into our operations, the pendulum is swinging toward social, humanistic, and altruistic concerns. We can offer programs that benefit youth, which concurrently act as catalysts in addressing related social problems concerning the family, racism, homelessness, and other issues. Dustin (1991) has recommended that the park and recreation profession ought to make more of a connection with peace, leisure, and recreation. However, Orams (1992) notes that we as a profession should address a conservation ethic and promote the value of leisure and recreation. Yet Orams further recommends that we should adopt marketing as well as effectiveness and efficiency principles to serve our clients. Finally, McAvoy (1990) has proposed a set of environmental ethics and recommends that the park and recreation professional's philosophy of service must be grounded in ecological principles, not in merchant values.

A considerable amount of discussion has also taken place with regard to the future. For recreation, park, and leisure services to prosper, proponents will have to identify a single concept within which to examine and interpret the consequences of their services (Godbey, 1991). The profession also needs to be recognized as a primary health care provider. Sessoms (1992) suggests that if the profession is to remain vital, we must provide the service that the public needs and expects, our leaders must advocate and interpret the value of what we do, and we must work cooperatively with our kindred professions.

Toalson and Mobley (1993) have proposed that park and recreation organizations should be required to commit resources to address social concerns. The suggested role would take the form of enabler or facilitator, due to the inability of most departments to undertake all the social issues and concerns that are prevalent within our communities. Additionally, is it recognized that the cultural diversity within our communities will require new leadership techniques to provide park and recreation services. Thaman (1993) supports the notion that support of and alignment with health care should be part of the mission of the park and recreation profession. Godbey, Graefe, and James (1993) found that because Americans are more health conscious and long for more of a sense of community, support for local parks and recreation will continue in that these services are considered part of the park and recreation profession's responsibility. The authors note that society is aging, yet we as a profession continue to provide most of the focus on youth. This may cause some change in the level of community support if services are not realigned.

Granted, the issues, goals, and needs for the profession to be community responsive are all important to the management of services. Park and recreation agencies must be stewards of community resources. Park and recreation issues should be at the forefront of community development and policy. We must also be prepared to provide the services our community desires (within certain guidelines and norms). This task requires us to understand marketing and needs assessment processes. Addressing social issues, homelessness, youth needs, and delinquency issues are also very important and central to the mission of parks and recreation. Professionals must also be prepared to provide community leadership, meet basic needs, understand community values, and become more policy astute.

It seems an impossible task to address all these concerns with increasing demands and limited resources. What is needed is a model designed to provide professionals a way to view the value orientations of the communities they serve. This value-driven model is opposed to the notion that we, as a profession, should embrace one direction, cause, or philosophy. In fact, Pfister and Ewert (1993) recommend that value orientations based on culture must be considered in managing lands to reflect both individual and larger cultural concerns. The authors go on to suggest that without an increased awareness of the differences, leisure professionals are not likely to formulate effective service strategies for diverse populations.

A Fan of Leisure Service Values

Consumer selection of leisure activities is influenced by values. If consumers are environmentally concerned, they are not likely to ride motorcycles on backpack trails. These people would rather walk on trails, conserve fossil fuels, and experience the quiet solitude of the forest. Conversely, others are oriented to high technology equipment. They may desire fast transport, excitement, and high risk. They may find these through the use of motorcycles, because it is perfectly acceptable within their social and cultural value structure.

If values are reflected through individual action, then it is reasonable to assume that values are reflected through societal action. Consequently, individual and societal values are transferred through professions, which in turn offer services based on an interpretation of these values. The leisure profession responds to the values of society and of individuals through the development of legislation, vision statements, policy, political action, education programs, and professional societies and associations.

Figure 4.4 presents the fan of values model by which the park and recreation profession can focus on benefits, needs, and issues to address in carrying out its mission of providing services to the community and caring for the land now and for future generations (Knowles-Lankford & Lankford, 1995). The fan of values illustrates an array of fundamental beliefs that influence community development; social services, such as recreation and leisure programs; and social reforms. Individuals and society are located at the center of the fan, at the point where all the values meet. These values shape us, both individually and as a society. The fan of values model indicates that individuals and society as a whole hold various beliefs and that they place relative importance on these beliefs and values.

These beliefs and values are then translated to individual and community goals, which are then translated into objectives. Often these objectives are more personal in nature and provide indications of a manager's own recreational emphases or choices of activities. However, many times these objectives are placed into action through public policy and by electing officials who support the value or values. These values help to define the public interest. The fan of values helps to ensure that community recreation and leisure service goals and objectives coincide with the community's values.

Figure 4.4
Individual and Societal Values and the Leisure Profession

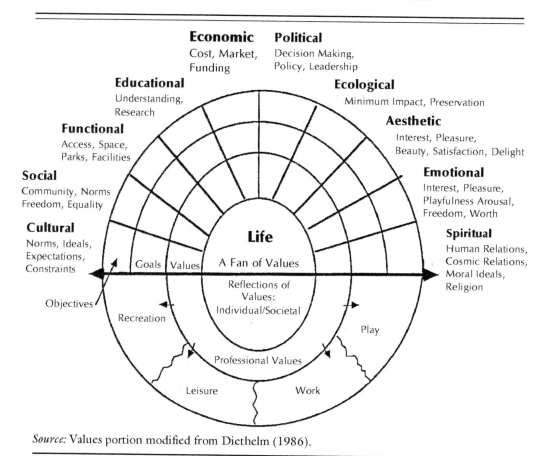

Source: Values portion modified from Diethelm (1986).

The public interest, which we serve as professionals, is a composite of a society's values—economic, social, political, educational, functional, ecological, spiritual, and aesthetic. Each had its time in the limelight. During the 1960s, social and political values were in focus. During the 1970s, ecological values became a national concern. During the 1980s, economic values dominated the value spectrum. During the 1990s, it appears that both social and environmental issues were predominate. The 21st century is surely going to present complex and interconnected value systems, which the leisure service manager must be able to interpret, develop actions and programs for, and operationalize internally (through goals, objectives, a vision, and policy).

In defining the public interest as a set of values, it follows that the more values a solution addresses, the more brilliant the solution. That was the beauty of the Works Progress Administration (WPA): Not only did it provide jobs for a huge unemployed workforce, the program addressed social and aesthetic as well as political values. Not all solutions can be so brilliant. Determining which values are to be given more weight at a certain time is a problem we continually face. The leisure manager's role in negotiating the milieu in which these values exist is precarious. Are we agents of the existing culture or of its evolution (Friedmann, 1987)? The public interest that has no voice is that of a future society's values. Who then assumes that voice? How is this voice reflected in action? It is the responsibility of the leisure service manager to help identify and address these value systems.

The answer lies in part in the process itself. If the process involves the public directly in creating the solution, then it must be a reflection of the public interest. The relationship between the planner and the planned for must be mutually responsive. It is through this process that the recreation planner and manager and the public are able to know more about the values that must be served. When asking who assumes the voice of a future society's values, we must ask how and if the voice of today's society is being reflected in its evolution. The process is educational in both directions. Action informs plans and experience informs theory. However, the opportunity to act and the effectiveness of that action relies on the accessibility to and responsiveness to the organization of power. Learning must be conducted on an intimate level. Planning, policymaking, visioning, and goal setting have to be brought down to the neighborhood level. It is through the social learning model implemented at a neighborhood level that a vision that serves multiple values can be created. This vision must place societal values above the individuals' values. By recognizing and working with community values, leisure service professionals help people to understand the nature of work and play, the value of work and leisure, and the worth of leisure and the environment. It is through this educational process that people become accustomed to the notion that leisure resources, parks, and recreation are integral to the quality of community life.

Leisure service management is an intentional activity, an intervention process. The intervention process takes place when and if the professional has determined the local values of the individual and the society. Leisure intervention is a process of offering opportunities for individual and societal change. We as professionals adjust, transform, interpret, understand, counsel, and consult in order to make life better for people. Within the profession, we seek to change the things we perceive society to be dissatisfied with. In other words, we act to provide the opportunity for the individual or society to change, and in doing so we help manifest the preferred future that people envision.

It is important for those in the park and recreation profession to view their services as a whole, guided by a common philosophy and driven by an environmental ethic (Lankford, 1993). An environmental ethic cannot rely solely on aesthetics for park development nor on public demand for recreational pursuits. We must understand our communities—the values residents hold—and apply our professional skills in resolving community problems. Today's community problems are immense, complex, and diverse. Being successful in planning, developing, and maintaining our natural resources while addressing the many leisure needs and social conditions will be our greatest challenge of the future.

The Role of the Leisure Service Manager in Promoting the Vision

Leisure service managers play an important role in the visioning process. They are responsible for identifying and maintaining the core values of an organization. Such values should be a part of the vision of any leisure service organization and should drive its culture. Again, Naisbett and Aburdene

(1985:20) have suggested that "usually the source of a vision is a leader, a person who possesses a unique combination of skills, the mental power to create a vision, and the practical ability to bring it about." Edginton (1987) has suggested ten functions that leisure service managers should pursue in order to promote an organization's vision and core values:

1. Ensure that there is a written vision statement. One cannot assume that the values in the mind of the manager are shared. They must be communicated in a tangible form. To ensure consistency, they must be in written form.

2. Ensure that policies, procedures and methods are reviewed periodically in relation to the vision statement. The core values of an organization should not change, but should be broad enough and developed with such wisdom that they endure social, cultural and political changes. However, application of the values to societal conditions requires evolving policies, procedures and methods.

3. Ensure that the vision statement is interpreted to and by the customers served by the organization. Customers should feel the impact of the organization's vision. This may require interpreting it to those the organization serves.

4. Ensure that mid-level managers interpret the vision statement to the staff. The values of an organization must permeate the entire unit. Middle managers often are responsible for ensuring that those involved in direct service delivery embrace the vision.

5. Ensure that the manager has the opportunity to interpret the vision statement to the staff. The interpretation of the vision throughout all levels of an organization must be actively supported by the chief executive officer. When the president and CEO of Hewlett Packard, Carly Fiorina, pitches the goal of this organization to "invent," she is not only speaking to her constituency, but to her employees. She is actively promoting the values of the organization in a symbolic manner.

6. Ensure that concrete goals and objectives are established that can be tied to the vision. Goals and objectives serve to translate the ideal into concrete, pragmatic processes and procedures. They enable the organization to move step-by-step toward achieving the vision in an observable, measurable manner.

7. Evaluate the achievement of goals and objectives. The measurement of goals and objectives is central to ensuring that the vision or values of an organization are pursued by the organization as a whole.

8. Ensure that an accountability system is established that ties the work of the staff and their rewards to the accomplishment of the vision. An organization that rewards performance and that is consistent with its vision, by and large, outperforms others who do not forge this relationship. Success in achieving the vision of an organization occurs by aligning the work of employees with desired ends.

9. The vision statement should influence decision making and guide the leisure service organization toward a common end. All decisions within the organization should be based on its core values. People committed to a common vision should work toward ends consistent with this vision.

10. The vision is an intuitive statement to be believed in. The vision statement is a spiritual statement. It must be believed in by the individuals who are engaged in the work of the organization. It should not be viewed as a superfluous statement, but rather one that provides meaning and structure to the work endeavors of individuals within the organization.

Figure 4.5 is a vision statement for *Camp Adventure™ Youth Services.* This unique organization outsources children and youth services worldwide. It produces a level of commitment from its staff that is reflective of a highly motivated group. The vision statement for Disneyland is presented in Figure 4.6. It is motivating and compelling; one can see in the statement the impetus that drove the development of this organization. Figure 4.7 is a vision statement for the Oregon Park and Recreation Society. It presents a high degree of commitment to the welfare of others and to the values of this organization. Finally, Figure 4.8 is a vision from the Honolulu Department of Parks and Recreation Department (1994). This vision is unique in that it embraces change, imagination, and hope for the future of the services and the organization. This vision was developed partly to help the Department become more self-sufficient and less reliant on tax dollars.

Goals and Objectives

Goals and objectives are fundamental to planning for leisure service delivery. Goals and objectives form the ba of the community and internal strateg planning process. Also, these sta nts of organizational intent comm te to the community the relevance of its programs, services, and operations (budget, public relations, acquisitions, dedications, etc.). Goals are broadly defined aims or intentions that move an organization to a desired state, whereas objectives are specific, narrow, and measurable. Goals can be thought of as articulated values. The most common organizational failings are in the areas of go roles, and communication. Lack of cl ity with regard to goals can lead to disorganization, inefficiency, and ineffectiveness. Figure 4.9 illustrates the strategic alignment of the primary mission, the strategic goal, and the overall objective of the Honolulu Department of Parks and Recreation. One can see that the approach is simple, straightforward, strategic, and forward thinking.

Murphy, Niepoth, Jamieson, & Williams (1991:271) suggest that a goal for a public recreation department might be "to provide all citizens of the community with an opportunity to engage in a wholesome recreation program during their leisure for the betterment of the individual and the total community." Obviously, this goal cannot really be evaluated without some specific objectives that assist in its implementation and eventual evaluation of success. These objectives guide the manager in making decisions for service delivery. Setting of organizational goals is most effective when carried out in the context of a strategic plan (discussed later in the book), which anticipates future

Figure 4.5

Camp Adventure™*Youth Services*

Vision Statement

Camp Adventure™ *Youth Services* is committed to enriching and enhancing the well being of children and youth. Our theme - Catch The Magic - suggests zeal, energy and enthusiasm. We will reach out with warmth, sincerity and genuine interest to those whom we serve.

We are committed to pursuing excellence in all of our endeavors. It is our desire to provide activities, programs and services that observe the highest standards of quality, creativity and safety. It is our intent to create a camp environment that emphasizes the joy of sharing, the thrill of discovery and the fun of companionship. We are dedicated to expanding the horizons of those we serve by enhancing and enriching their social, physical and emotional well-being.

We are dedicated as professionals, to operating with integrity, pride and sensitivity. We are committed to one another and to each others' success. Our team effort will be built on our loyalty to one another and to the dedication and commitment to the ideals of our theme - Catch The Magic!

---

needs and prepares to take actions. Some other examples of broad community leisure service goals are listed below:

1. To develop a sense of community to enhance the quality of life

2. To maximize individual and community potential by encouraging citizens to work together

3. To provide individuals with a range of social opportunities and a strong sense of community interation

4. To encourage and motivate self-supporting community groups to help themselves (Murphy, Niepoth, Jamieson, & Williams, 1991:271)

Figure 4.6

The Disneyland Story

The idea of Disneyland is a simple one. It will be a place for people to find happiness and knowledge.

It will be a place for parents and children to share pleasant times in one another's company; a place for teacher and pupils to discover greater ways of understanding and education. Here the older generation can recapture the nostalgia of days gone by, and the younger generation can savor the challenge of the future. Here will be the wonders of Nature and Man for all to see and understand.

Disneyland will be based upon and dedicated to the ideals, the dreams, and hard facts that have created America. And it will be uniquely equipped to dramatize these dreams and facts and send them forth as a source of courage and inspiration to all the world.

Disneyland will be something of a fair, an exhibition, a playground, a community center, a museum of living facts, and a showplace of beauty and magic.

It will be filled with accomplishments, the joys, and the hopes of the world we live in. And it will remind us and show us how to make these wonders part of our own lives.

McLean, Bannon, and Gray (1999) note that goals should be based on essential facts such as limitations under which the agency may operate, realistic views of options available for implementation, and a review of legal, financial, political and physical factors of the agency's options. The authors also note that actions such as strategy options (objectives) should be based on a thorough departmental and public review process. Furthermore, an analysis and consideration of the following factors would be necessary to develop meaningful and effective goals:

1. Fiscal, personnel, and maintenance impacts and implications

2. Health and safety implications

3. Partnership opportunities

Figure 4.7
Oregon Park and Recreation Society

It is our belief, as members of the Oregon Park and Recreation Society, that we have the unique opportunity to create within our diverse communities, environments in which citizens in Oregon can experience human dignity and true quality of life through readily accessible leisure experiences. IT IS THEREFORE OUR VISION:

- That we share knowledge and expertise freely through an educational ethic that transcends all boundaries;

- That we cultivate a fundamental respect for Oregon's exceptional cultural and environmental heritage.

- That we are advocates for a service ethic which demands equity of leisure opportunities for all.

- That we instill in Oregonians the passion for affecting change in their own lives.

- That we consciously link our sense of purpose to the resolution of significant social/cultural issues.

By dedicating ourselves to this vision we are committed to leisure participation because of the joy, self-esteem and sense of belonging it brings; life's enhancement by enthusiastic participation; and the people's recreation through a playful and meaningful approach to life at its fullest.

---

4. Planning implications related to the overall community long-range plan, land use restrictions, easements, and so on

5. Potential social impacts and benefits of offering programs for various socioeconomic groups of the population

6. Impacts on community livability (171, modified)

For goals to be used as a measure of organizational performance, the following conditions must be present:

1. Goals are derived from legitimate and formal public policy.

2. Goals are clearly defined and identified.

3. Goals must be few enough to be manageable.

4. Goals must represent consensus or general agreement.

5. Progress toward these goals must be measurable. (Jreisat, 1992:6)

Figure 4.8
Vision Statement

Vision: To Form Anew In The Imagination

Reinventing DPR begins with a vision.

For a brief moment, we ask you to just imagine...

Imagine a space-time continuum—
Imagine what our island looks like from above,

      hundreds and thousands of miles in space.

Imagine what our island looked like in times past,

      hundreds and thousands of years ago.

What do you see?

      Deep blue waters, sandy beaches, clear mountain streams, pristine
forests, harmony...

We envision our parks as islands in time connecting the past with the present—

      our natural and cultural heritage

      intertwined with what we wish the future to be,

      our legacy;

We envision our parks as islands in time connecting people with people—

      an extraordinary diversity of peoples and values

      intertwined with our sense of place,

      neighborhoods and family,

      our community; and

We ask you to imagine our whole island as a park, connecting us through gateways, greenways, streamways, beachways...

Imagine parks as an integral part of our community, connecting our legacy with destiny, a place with space to recreate, and time to enjoy.

Just Imagine...

Source: Honolulu Parks and Recreation Department

Managers must foster worker awareness of the relationships between community and organizational values and goals, objectives, and policies. In order for goals to be attainable and be used to guide organizational performance, the following are offered as guidelines for fostering awareness:

1. Provide training in goal and objective setting.

Figure 4.9

Strategic Focus

Primary Mission

We add quality to life.

Our primary mission is to enhance the quality of life for all people in our community through provisions for parks and recreation programs and services.

Strategic Goal

Our strategic goal is to ensure efficiency, effectiveness and responsiveness in local provisions for parks and recreation programs and services.

. . . that what we do is not only done the best that it can be done, but that what we provide is of significant importance and value and meets the community's needs.

Overall Objective

Our overall objective is to facilitate provisions for parks and recreation programs and services that are

- accessible,
- enjoyable,
- meaningful,
- safe,
- well-designed, and
- well-maintained.

Source: Honolulu Parks and Recreation Department

---

2. Model the process and procedures used to derive the goals.

3. Create situations in which all employees can be involved in goal setting.

4. Advocate organizational values during goal setting.

5. Assess the clarity of goals in all work-related encounters.

Priority and Measurement of Objectives

Leisure managers face the task of evaluating and ranking the importance of objectives in order to move toward goals. Managers in both the nonprofit and public sectors are concerned with the ranking of seemingly interdepen-

dent objectives (Pekar, 1982). For example, a leisure service manager must determine the relative importance of providing technical assistance services, self-help programs, or leader directed services in a given community. Obviously, determining objectives and priorities is a judgment based on the best available information. This prioritization of objectives must involve customers, the community, staff, and decision makers. Yet the manager must eventually make many of the decisions. Studies of objectives that managers have set for their organization confirm the difficulty of balancing the concerns of interest groups (Donnelly, Gibson, & Ivancevich, 1990). The answer lies in the process and in the values of the decision makers, managers, staff, and community.

Effective managerial performance requires establishing objectives in every area that contributes to overall organizational performance. Drucker (1980, 1985) has stated that objectives should be established in at least eight areas of organizational performance: (1) market standing, (2) innovations, (3) productivity, (4) physical and financial resources, (5) profitability, (6) manager performance and responsibility, (7) worker performance and attitude, and (8) social responsibility. Objectives for innovation, employee attitudes, and social responsibility present some difficulty in measurement. For example, an objective to become more socially responsible would be difficult to measure. Yet to say "to become more socially responsible by providing 25 percent more direct scholarships for the needy in summer camp this year" is measurable.

Clear goals and objectives can be converted into specific targets and actions. Note how management could align goals, objectives and indicators (see Table 4.1). These objectives can become more meaningful for specific departments. Objective 1 can become a target for the marketing department, whereas objective 2 can be a target for maintenance, and so on. Furthermore, not only specific targets but indicators of organizational performance are built into this system.

Management by Objectives

Directed at the management functions of planning and controlling, MBO is a process that can enable the leisure service manager to focus on achieving organizational goals while providing for satisfactory human relationships and experiences. As Edginton (1976:10) has written regarding leisure service organizations, MBO

". . . is a systematic approach to management whereby mission

Table 4.1
Development of Goals, Objectives and Indicators

Goal	Objective	Indicator
1. Maintain a majority of the market share of the summer day camp participants	a. Retain 80% of last years participants b. Obtain 20% of first-time customers	Percent of registrants Percent of registrants
2. Provide working conditions that Exceed safety levels	a. Automate trash pickup b. Reduce injuries by 15% by year 1	Automation 60% of facilities by1 January Ratio of labor days lost to total labor days
3. Develop front line managers for middle management positions	a. Develop a merit review system by 1 Jan. b. Select 10 managers to attend training	Report submitted on 1 November Number selected by 1 January
4. Maintain and improve employee satisfaction	a. Improve satisfaction levels by 15% by year end	Ratio of total employees to quitters Attitude survey of all employees

statements and job functions—that is, identification of objectives desired, results to be achieved, and courses of action—are mutually agreed upon at the administrative and operational levels. Mutually subscribed objectives and job functions provide for an exchange of information, development of understanding, building of acceptance and belief, and a commitment to action between administrative and operational levels."

Contributing to organizational unity, MBO allows for the identification and development of mutual concerns and interests of an organization's members. Responsive dialogue between manager and staff can lead to mutually determined courses of action. A cooperative and satisfying work environment usually can be achieved when a manager makes an effort to include the employee in a discussion of the work objectives to be achieved, rather than merely dictating exactly what the employee is to do. Figure 4.10 is a form that has been used by the Calgary (Alberta) Parks/Recreation Department in the implementation of its MBO program.

Policymaking

Policies provide leisure service organizations with guidelines that delineate such factors as the types of services to be offered, acceptable forms of employee behavior, the relationship between employees and consumers, and standards for consumer behavior (e.g., acceptable forms of consumer behavior in public park facilities). People make policies; they are not organizational monoliths. In this section, we will discuss policy structures, the policy process, policy units, what policymaking boards do, customers, and the policymaking process, the role of the leisure service manager, and factors affecting policy development.

What is Policy?

Policy is usually thought of as the formal guidelines an organization has established, but there may also be a set of informal policies within an organization. The definition used in this book maintains that a policy is a course of action that guides human behavior. For our purposes, this suggests that a policy, as a course of action, will govern the behavior of individuals within an organization. Formal policies, usually expressed as written documents, delineate the purposes, aims, goals, objectives, principles, procedures, and rules that provide direction to individuals within an organization. Informal policies consist of norms, mores, and customs present within an organization that affect individual and collective behavior. Informal policies may have a great impact on the organization because they have the potential to displace formal policies. Essentially, policies—formal and informal—may be thought of as the plan or plans that organizations follow.

There are three ways in which policy affects behavior in organizations:

1. *Enabling Behavior.* Policies serve to enable organizations and individuals to pursue goals or ends that would not be possible without them. For example, policies enable orga-

Figure 4.10
MBO Form

INFORMATION ON THE USE OF THIS OBJECTIVE FORM

These four functions are suggested for you to group your objectives.
It is not necessary to put in a sheet for all four function.
You may put in two sheets for one function
OPERATION___FINANCE___RELATIONSHIPS___PERSONNEL___
INDICATE WITH AN "X" THE FUNCTION RELATED
TO THIS SHEET
TO COVER THE PERIOD FORM_____ to_____
Suggest six month period: JANUARY to JUNE or JULY
to DECEMBER

POSITION: ___ of the employee
Date Submitted:
Date Delivered to immediate Supervisor

SHORT TERM GOALS:

	COMPLETION DATE:	INDICATORS:	EVALUATION DATE:	IF NOT COMPLETED ADJUSTED DATE:
(1) State your short term objectives	REPORT by	Measurable indicators of	Either	
for this function of your job	DATE	achieving the goal set		
			a July	
(2) Begin with – To achieve	or			
– To ensure	COMPLETED	Answer the question	or	
– To prepare, etc.	by DATE	"How do we know the goal		
	or	has been met?"	January Date	
(3) Ten to Fifteen words	Progress Report	Time percentage		
try to avoid "and" – "in addition"	Dates	cost etc.		
or double goals in one statement				

BRIEF DESCRIPTION OF ROUTINE DUTIES INVOLVED:

responsible for – what are your duties and responsibilities – related to this particular function.

Stress the less obvious.

LONG TERM OBJECTIVE: (Philosophical)

This objective should only require to be revised every two or three years.

It is the long range aim that you wish to achieve in this functional area for your particular section of the Parks & Recreation Service.

Signature of EMPLOYEE   Signature of   Date of APPROVAL
SIGNATURE   IMMEDIATE SUPERVISOR
                                     APPROVED   Date

nizations to hire staff, levy taxes, build facilities, develop areas, and manage various operations.

2. *Regulating Behavior.* Many policies are regulatory in nature; that is, they regulate routine behaviors. For example, stoplights regulate routine traffic behavior. In leisure service organizations, control points in buildings regulate the flow of participants in and out in a systematic fashion.

3. *Inhibiting Behavior.* Policies also inhibit behaviors. For example, access to a park may be limited to a certain time frame so as to ensure that there is proper supervision when people are in the park. Many rules and regulations that are established by leisure service organizations often inhibit behaviors that help maintain the safety of individuals.

An example of a policy that would enable behavior to occur is the adoption of a rule, that sets forth the hours and days of operation of a community swimming pool. Adoption of this policy *enables* the park and recreation director to open the facility at a certain time and use the resources of the organization to operate and promote the activity. It also *inhibits* certain types of behavior in that it restricts the hours the pool can be used. When formulating a policy, the manager must be cognizant of the complementary nature of inhibiting and enabling behaviors; the adoption of a policy that enables certain kinds of behaviors can, in fact, inhibit other activities.

Policies also serve the function of *regulating* certain types of behaviors. By routinizing certain patterns of activity, an organization is able to concentrate more of its resources on major issues. It reduces the need for repetitive decision making in areas that can be delegated to subordinates. If a manager were confronted with the task of having to make decisions on each matter of concern to the organization, his or her time and energy would be misused. A park manager can routinize maintenance procedures so that the maintenance staff knows what jobs have to be done and during what time period, rather than having to decide on a daily basis. On the other hand, routine can be equated with rigidity. Organizations must be extremely careful in this regard because ruts can be created. People can easily become creatures of habit, inflexible, and unable to respond to changing expectations. The manager must periodically review the tasks that have been routinized in the organization to ensure that they are, in fact, consistent with organizational goals and objectives.

Policies are useful to organizations for several other reasons. They help clarify relationships and patterns of communication by establishing networks of communication and levels of authority and responsibility. They can help an organization evaluate its goals and objectives by presenting a clear picture of the methods and procedures used to achieve them. Policies also provide for consistency. The resources of an organization, especially its human ones, can uniformly be directed toward achieving the goals of the organization. If all employees know the direction in which the organization is moving, they can contribute their work effort toward this end.

Once an organization has developed a documented set of policies and has set forth its philosophy, goals and objectives, and rules and procedures, its actions become somewhat predictable. Predictability can lead to the reduction of criticism both from within and without the organization because individuals understand what to expect from it (namely, consistency).

There are five important characteristics of successful policies:

1. Flexibility. A policy can be seen as existing on a continuum between rigidity and flexibility. Ones that are flexibly written can change as environmental conditions change. This is not to imply that policies do not have some degree of stability, only that they can be adapted. A manager's judgement (based on staff and community input) in determining the amount of flexibility needed in a given policy is the primary method used to determine this factor.

2. Comprehensiveness. The comprehensiveness of a policy is the extent to which it covers the actions that are necessary to implement a program. The degree of comprehensiveness will be directly related to the course of action pursued. The scope of the policy depends on the scope of action being controlled by the policy itself.

3. Coordinative. A policy must be interrelated and coordinated with other types of policies within the organization. Procedures, rules, and plans of operation do not stand alone, but are tied to policies that set forth the mission and objectives of an organization.

4. Ethical. Policies must be written to ensure that ethical practices are maintained (and formulated) based on fairness and equality. A policy

should be discharged impartially and comprehensively. The ethical concepts that are incorporated into a policy usually are written to conform to the norms, values, and mores that exist within society.

5. Clarity. A policy should be written in a manner that can be readily understood by the individuals or group that is intended to affect. A well-written policy will simplify the manager's task in communicating intent to staff and the community. This will save time and energy and lead to better relationships among the manager, staff, and community, in that all parties will know what to expect.

The ultimate effectiveness of any policy can be determined by the extent to which it fulfills its intended purpose. Policies that do not produce the type of behavior that is expected should be reevaluated. Thus, the process of policymaking can be viewed as an ongoing effort in which policies are regularly evaluated and revised as needed.

Policy Structures

The policies of an organization can be viewed as existing in a hierarchy, with general statements that deal with broad concerns at the top. As policies increase in specificity, they are placed lower on the hierarchy until the most detailed are reached at the base. Lower-order policies are derived from the policies that appear directly above them in the hierarchy. For example, a general policy advocating safety may be the catalyst for a series of specific safety rules related to smoking on the premises, necessity of safety goggles, and so on.

Hodgetts and Wortman (1980) have outlined a series of policy statements that range from the general to the specific. They identify these as major policies, secondary policies, functional policies, minor policies, procedures and standard operating plans, and rules. They suggest that a manager's effectiveness can be strengthened by developing policies based on knowledge of the policy hierarchy, as shown below:

Major Policies. This type of policy is a broad statement that reflects the aims of the organization. It delineates the type of services to be provided and their general purpose (e.g., "The purpose of a leisure service organization is to enhance the quality of life by providing leisure services").

Secondary Policies. These are derived from the broader major policies. They delineate the target market (e.g., "The leisure service organization will serve all ages and races by providing activities, facilities, and information").

Functional Policies. The management operations of an organization are spelled out in its functional policies. These may include the major services to be provided (e.g., activities, facilities, information, consultation), marketing (pricing and promotional factors), finance (how funds are to be appropriated and accounted for), and personnel (job specifications, hours of work, etc.). These types of policies are derived from secondary policies. Table 4.2 is an example of a minor policy used by The Maryland-National Capitol Park Planning Commission to create and abolish positions.

Minor Policies. The next level, minor policies, further details operational aspects of the organization. These may specify different activity areas (e.g., arts, sports, etc.), facility standards, or maintenance expectations.

Procedures and Standard Operating Plans. This type of policy is drawn from functional and minor policies. Procedures and operating plans detail the step-by-step methods necessary to organize, implement, and evaluate the various functions of an organization (e.g., the standard operating plan and procedures adopted in the management of a swimming pool may detail its hours of operation, program, and staffing requirements.)

Rules. In turn, rules are obtained from procedures and standard plans. They govern the day-to-day conduct of individuals within an organization. Rules are rigid and not subject to interpretation (e.g., "No smoking"). Table 4.3 is an example of regulations governing the use of park and recreation facilities operated by The Maryland-National Capital Park and Planning Commission

The Policy Process

The process of policymaking is carried out in three phases: *formulation, implementation,* and *evaluation*. These involve determining where the organization is going, what procedures should be used to get it there, and what corrective measures must be taken to keep it heading toward its primary mission. These three functions are interrelated,

Table 4.2

Chapter 400
Creation and Abolishment of Positions

410   Basic Concepts

The creation and abolishment of positions are Department Head actions initiated as a result of changes in work programs, organization, budget, and/or technology.

420   Creation of Positions

All Merit System positions are established by a Department Head subject to budgetary and organizational guidelines approved by the Commission/Planning Board. Positions are created as full-time career or part-time career and may not exceed the authorized personnel complement as approved by the Planning Board and/or Commission.

421   The Department Head shall consult with the Personnel Manager when creating new positions.

430   Reasons for Abolishing Positions

A career position may be abolished for any one or more of the following reasons:

431   Work program changes;

432   Reduction in funding;

433   Technological changes;

434   Reorganization or restructuring

440   Authority to Abolish Positions

A Department Head may abolish an encumbered full-time career or part-time career position with the approval of the Commission in the case of Central Administrative Services departments or the respective Planning Board in case of operating departments. The Commission or Planning Board may abolish a position that reports directly to it. Reasons for the abolishment actions shall conform to any one or a combination of reasons identified in Section 430 of these Rules and Regulations.

441   A Department Head may abolish a vacant career position.

450   Abolishment of Encumbered Career Positions

A Department Head shall follow the procedures of Chapter 2200, Reduction-In-Force, when abolishing an encumbered career position.

Source: The Maryland-National Capitol Park Planning Commission

---

and the success of an organization depends on the manager's ability to coordinate them.

When *formulating* a policy, a number of factors must be taken into consideration. The policy must be related to the overall mission or purpose of the organization. It must also be drafted with an understanding of its relation-ship to environmental subgroupings, both within and external to the organization. The resources that are needed must be taken into consideration when formulating a policy. Many policies are written that can never be implemented because their authors have not appraised the availability of resources. Finally, these questions have to be considered: Has

Table 4.3

Regulation of Public Use

Section 1. Use by the General Public

Park property and park and recreation programs are open to use by all members of the public regardless of race, sex, national origin, color or creed.

Section 2. Hours of Operation

A. Except for Commission employees or persons accompanied by Commission employees, no person shall be on Commission or Park property from sunset to sunrise unless that facility is officially open for public use.
B. Any park property may be closed by the Director to the public entirely or for certain uses and such closing shall be posted in advance for public notice.

Section 3. Permits

A. Permits are required for:
(1) the reserved use of athletic fields, recreation buildings, camping and group picnic areas and certain other facilities as designated.
(2) Solicitation of contributions or moneys.
(3) Conducting a parade, procession, rally or assembly for the purpose of protesting, demonstrating or disseminating any form of written or oral information.
(4) Conducting of surveys, interviews or polls
(5) Other activities and uses indicated as requiring a permit in Chapters V and VI of these Regulations including: use of model powered airplanes and rockets; cutting, sawing or removal of trees; use of alcohol; posting notices; commercial uses; erecting structures; planting vegetation; use of metal detectors and digging;

B. Procedure for permits
(1) Permit applications may be obtained from the Park Permit Section of Montgomery or Prince George's County for use of facilities or activities in the appropriate County.
(2) The permit shall be issued within a reasonable length of time following receipt of the application and all information requested by the Director, or the applicant shall be furnished a written statement indicating the reasons why the permit is denied, the applicant may apply to a court of record, having jurisdiction over the parties, within ten days of denial of permit, to obtain judicial review of such restriction and denial.

C. Permits are issued subject to these conditions:
(1) Permits may be issued for a single time use, seasonally, or on an indefinite time basis for regional parks, athletic fields, recreation centers or community buildings
(2) Permits will be issued upon a determination by the Director or his designee that the facilities or activity areas applied for are available and appropriate for the purpose specified in the permit, and that the proposed use or activity is consistent with the size, location and available amenities of the relevant park property and with public health, safety and welfare.
(3) The application may be granted and the permit may be issued unless one or more of the following facts is found to exist:
a. That one or more of the statements in the application is not true.
b. When the applicant or any agent or representative of the applicant who will participate under the permit has previously violated any portion of the Regulations of the Commission, or has violated any of the terms and provisions of any prior permit.
(4) Permits are issued subject to:
a. All regulations presently in effect, as though inserted as part of the terms of the permit.
b. Liability for any damage, injury or loss sustained by persons or property as a result of permittee's negligence or that of any member of that group.
c. Revocation at any time for violation of any provision of the permit.
(5) The permit must be in the possession of the permittee and shown upon request
(6) If the permit is for a charitable fund-raising activity, the expected cost of fund-raising shall not be excessive in relation to the gross amount to be collected.
(7) The activities referred to shall be conducted strictly in conformance with the terms and conditions of the permit issued by the Director.
(8) In conducting permitted activities no person shall:
a. In any way obstruct, delay or interfere with the free movements of any other person, seek to coerce or physically disturb any other person, or hamper or impede the conduct of any authorized business or activity on any Commission property.
b. Conduct any activities in a misleading or fraudulent manner.

Continued

Table 4.3 Continued

(9) Whenever rallies, demonstrations, pageants, ceremonies and entertainments are to be held on park property, special regulations as to the parking of vehicles and positions and movements of spectators may be promulgated by the Director. All persons within the area of such special regulations must obey or comply with the lawful orders of the Park Police or other authorized persons engaged in maintaining order.

(10) A fee may be assessed to defray the cost of policing certain events. Additionally, for a special event, the permittees assume personal liability for the costs of excessive cleanup of the premises; loss, breakage or removal of park property; and for the conduct and good order of the group.

Source: The Maryland-National Capitol Park Planning Commission

the policy been realistically conceived? Can it really work? Will it produce the type of behavioral outcomes expected? Will people accept the policy? After careful analysis of all these factors, an organization will be in a position to formulate a sensible set of policies, which can prove to be of invaluable aid to a manager in a leisure service organization.

Policy *implementation* occurs when a policy is put into operation. This is done through the design of an organizational structure from which positions of authority and responsibility are created. Once the assignment of roles within the organization has taken place, policy implementation is carried out through a system of rewards and penalties. The implementation of a policy, like the formulation phase, must take into account the organization's resources. Many well-conceived policies have failed because they ignored this important factor. The extent to which a policy represents the needs of the organization's members will determine its chances of success.

Policy *evaluation* represents the efforts of an organization to determine to what extent its policies have achieved their desired end. Essentially, this is a process of control. Control usually involves the establishment of standards, the measurement of performance against standards, and the correction of deviation from standards (Koontz & O'Donnell, 1972). Organizational outputs are measured against a set of standards in policy evaluation. In this sense, standards are absolutes toward which an organization strives; hence they are usually quantifiable.

The measurement of performance involves comparing the outputs of the unit with the standards to determine whether the policies have been achieved. As policies become stagnant and unproductive, corrective action should be initiated and the policy should be changed or abolished. This last factor suggests that the policy process is one wherein the manager maintains flexibility.

In any organization, there is an element of risk in the formulation and implementation of policies. Effective managers will calculate closely the risks involved in adopting one policy versus another. This is done to optimize the allocation of an organization's resources. It is important to note, however, that all organizations will be confronted with a certain amount of failure. We learn and grow by making errors. The lack of failure may be an indication that an organization is not extending itself to meet people's needs and is overly conscious of its security. There is a saying that "if you're not failing, you're not trying anything new."

Koontz and O'Donnell (1972) have suggested a number of guidelines that can be followed in the policymaking process. Noting that all organizations have policies, they suggest that it is virtually impossible for any given body to be effective without the existence of written policies. They further suggest that the use of written policy manuals does not guarantee effective management, that this is accomplished through the understanding that the policy process is dynamic and ongoing. All policies represent a form of communication among individuals within the organization. Like any form of communication, policies are dependent on the intentions of the sender and the receptiveness of the receiver. There must be an openness and willingness to engage in two-way communication. One cannot assume that an organization will have effective policies without attention to a number of basic guidelines governing them. Koontz and O'Donnell outline seven ways in which the policymaking process can be enriched and the management of policies made more productive:

1. *The policy process should contribute to the goals and objectives of an organization.* There is a need to ensure understanding of the relationship that exists between major policies, secondary policies, functional policies, minor policies, procedures, and rules. As each policy is developed and written, it should be linked to higher-order policies to maintain consistency within the organization.

2. *The policy process should not be ambiguous.* One policy should not conflict with or contradict another policy.

3. *The policy process should be adaptable.* It is extremely important that policies be formulated and implemented so as to accommodate change. This is not to infer that a policymaking body should vacillate in its decision making, catering to pressure from individuals and groups; rather, it should be cognizant of changing trends in society and how they affect the implementation of policy.

4. *The policy process should enable one to distinguish among rules, major policies, and procedures.* Earlier in the chapter, a hierarchy was presented linking major policies to procedures and rules. Major policies are written within a broad context to provide general direction to an organization. On the other hand, procedures and rules are action programs that are established as specific guidelines for employee behavior.

5. *Policies and the policy process should be in writing.* Written policies reduce the confusion that can arise from verbal direction.

6. *The policy process should be taught.* It is a poor assumption to believe that people will take it upon themselves to be knowledgeable about an organization's policies, procedures, and rules.

7. *The policy process should be controlled.* One cannot assume that

people will adhere to policy decisions or that a policy will stand the test of time. Policies can become obsolete, and it is important to recognize that policies, if they are to be effective, need to be used and kept up-to-date. (217-219)

Policy Units

The authority to make policy in public leisure services is usually vested in a board or commission appointed by another legislative body or elected by the public at large. In private leisure delivery systems, policy is formulated either by the owners of the organization or by a board of directors elected or appointed to represent the owner's interests.

Public Policymaking Board, Council, or Commission

This type of policymaking unit is usually appointed by a legislative body or elected by the public at large to provided direction and control of the public park and recreation services. It receives its legal powers to collect and assess tax levies and to provide certain select services through state or provincials enabling acts, city charters, special legislation, or local ordinances. Some boards have complete authority and independence to make policy in their designated area. Other boards, known as "semi-independent boards," have partial powers and are usually tied closely to other legislative units within the governmental structure. For example, a semi-independent board may have authority to determine its program policies, but will not have the ability to levy taxes to provide these services.

Public Advisory Board or Commission

This type of board has no final power or authority, but it can exert considerable influence over policy decisions by other legislative bodies. Advisory boards are appointed to provide a policymaking unit with an in-depth perspective of the community's leisure-time needs. Basically, they serve a resource function. By providing information and making recommendations, advisory boards affect policymaking at various levels. This type of board allows for citizen participation within the governmental structure.

The Corporation and Board of Directors

A corporation is a method of organizing profit- or nonprofit-oriented enterprises. The corporation has a legal existence of its own. In a corporation, the elected or appointed board of directors is responsible for management. Board members are morally responsible to the corporation rather than the shareholders that elected them. The board is given the power to make the rules that will govern the conduct of business. In addition to determining the functions and duties of personnel, board members may also determine the allotment of shares and the payment of dividends to shareholders. Policy established by the board of directors is subject to the approval of the shareholders of the organization. A corporation is required by law to hold a shareholders' meeting annually and to provide each shareholder with an annual report of the company at least three weeks before this meeting.

What Policymaking Boards Do

Policymaking boards perform a number of important functions. Their responsibility varies according to the nature of the organization. Businesses having a prime function of making a profit require slightly different responsibilities of its board member than public nonprofit organization. According to Ward (1991), the responsibilities of board members in private enterprises include the following:

1. Actively supporting the Chief Executive Officer (CEO) and his or her polices, both within the organization and to outside parties, as long as his or her performance is judged to be satisfactory.

2. Replacing the CEO promptly if the board concludes that his or her performance is, and will continue to be, unsatisfactory

3. Participating actively in the decisions to elect and re-elect board members

4. Determining compensation of senior management, including bonuses, incentives, and compensation of the CEO; reviewing recommendations of the CEO; and ratifying compensation of other executives

5. Discussing proposed major changes in the organization's strategy and direction, major financing proposals, and other crucial issues, usually as proposed by the CEO

7. Requiring the CEO to explain the rationale behind operating budgets, major capital expenditures, acquisitions, investments, personnel matters, and similar important plans (accepting these proposals if they are consistent with the organization strategy and if explanations are reasonable; otherwise, requiring additional information)

8. Formulating major policies regarding ethical or public responsibility matters, conveying to the organization the fact that the board expects adherence to these policies, and assuring that violations of these policies are not tolerated

9. Analyzing reports on the organization's performance, raising questions to highlight areas of possible concern, and suggesting possible actions to improve performance, but with the understanding that the CEO, and not the board, is responsible for performance

10. Assuring that financial information furnished to the relevant parties fairly represents the financial performance and status of the organization and assuring that internal controls are satisfactory

These examples are very general. It should be realized that each of these responsibilities may entail more specific action in regard to personnel, finance, public relations, and so on.

Wolf (1990) has identified the responsibilities and duties of board members involved in nonprofit organizations. In reviewing the list of responsibilities below, one will note that they are somewhat similar to the responsibilities of board of directors working in private commercial organizations. Helping establish direction, evaluating management personnel, reviewing fiscal matters, and others are all consistent among different types of organizations. As Wolf writes, there are nine areas of responsibility:

1. Determining the organization's mission and setting policies for its operation, ensuring that the provisions of the organization's charter and the law are being followed

2. Setting the organization's overall programs from year to year and engaging in longer range planning to establish its general course for the future

3. Establishing fiscal policy and boundaries, with budgets and financial controls

4. Providing adequate resources for the activities of the organization through direct financial contributions and a commitment to fundraising

5. Selecting, evaluating, and, if necessary, terminating the appointment of the chief executive

6. Developing and maintaining a communication link to the community, promoting the work of the organization

7. Engaging in the day-to-day operation of the organization

8. Hiring staff other than the chief executive

9. Making detailed programmatic decisions without consulting staff.

As one can see, there is a wide range of activities in which board members are involved, including policymaking, fundraising, activity on board committees, recruiting new board members, engaging in community relations, evaluating the organization's budget, training new board members, and conducting personnel practices. Board members of nonprofit organizations are often challenged to increase participation of inactive members, recruit other members, broaden the range of skills in the makeup of the board, and make board membership more representative of the community. Also, board members are challenged to ensure financial stability, improve the relevancy of program offerings, build membership, and assist with evaluations. Board members also are often involved in board member activities, especially ones tied with fundraising.

Reynolds and Hormachea (1976), discussing public recreation boards, identified a number of basic functions that all public recreation boards undertake. They note that these functions may vary according to which legislation and local laws are being enabled. The functions they identify include the following:

1. To employ the recreation and park executive and to establish his or her duties and responsibilities

2. To establish the purposes, objectives, policies, procedures, and other guidelines for the management of the agency programs and services, refer them to the executive for execution, and give him or her support

3. To establish the standards of quality and the scope of the services to be rendered

4. To serve as a liaison between citizens and agency; to interpret

citizen needs and interests and provide programs, facilities, and services to serve their needs; to interpret the value of recreation to the public in order to gain their interest, understanding, and assistance

5. To establish a sound fiscal plan satisfactory to the community; to recommend sources of income and to approve the budget and fiscal matters

6. To keep the general public and public officials informed concerning the status of the recreation and parks programs

7. To receive and evaluate reports from the executive, and to act as a board of appeals on any action not resolved satisfactorily by the executive. Its actions are final, as it is the highest authority related officially to the department

8. To represent the department at ceremonials and official events, including budget matters

9. To make rules for the conduct of the commission's business and meetings (84-85).

Customers and the Policymaking Process

An important component in the process of policymaking in the public sector is to involve the public being served. Historically, the customer has played a small role and has even been ignored in the formulation and evaluation of policies. A number of problems arise with regard to customers' involvement in the policy process. The first

revolves around the determination of which individuals should be involved in the process. Does a public leisure service organization open its process only to those specifically affected by a given program, or is it necessary to consider the views of the entire political unit that the board represents? If the latter view represents the position of an organization (and this is usually politically safer), the problems created by the scope of this undertaking may prohibit effective policy development. On the other hand, if all individuals are not included in the policymaking process, they may feel that their interests are not effectively being represented.

Another concern that occurs as a result of customers' participation in the policy process is that their presence may make objective and rational planning and evaluation difficult. The average customer is without expertise in the leisure delivery field and may cloud rather than clarify the issues at hand. Individuals tend to be interested in their own gains rather than the whole; therefore, program planning becomes adaptive and incremental rather than being accomplished on a holistic basis. As a result, organizations are often unwilling to include customers because their subjectivity biases the process of policy development.

Another factor that may prevent customers from participating in policy processes is that of political expediency. Politicians have often ignored citizen input so that their particular programs or philosophies are not jeopardized or questioned. If a politician wants to push through a program, the quickest way may be to bypass customer involvement. If the program or policy is to be evaluated and a politician has endorsed it, he or she may wish to avoid the risk of involving dissatisfied individuals. Even though a citizen group may be supportive of a particular policy, its initial involvement may result in the creation of a cohesive unit that is capable of dissention in future policy evaluation.

What can be done to overcome these problems? Scioli and Cook (1975) have identified five factors that can help strengthen customers' involvement in the policymaking process. They suggest that first, policymaking must include not only the population who will benefit directly from a program, but also should be open to those individuals or groups who will not benefit. Second, there must be a method whereby the expected outcomes of the program can be measured. This part of the process should emphasize the reaction of the customers served by the program. Third, the future needs of individuals must be taken into consideration in evaluating a program or policy. Fourth, the process should include a step that allows for resolution between the second and third factors (how present needs are being met and what direction an organization plans to take in the future). Fifth, policymaking is a dynamic process; it cannot be conceptualized as taking place within a finite period, but should be viewed as a continuous social process.

Mechanisms that can be used to encourage participation in the formulation of policy in public leisure service organizations following.

Citizen Advisory Groups. Citizen advisory groups have traditionally been used by community parks and recreation departments to encourage participation. Their main function is to assist elected government bodies by serving as consultants. It is not unusual for a citizen advisory group to serve or represent the needs of a geographic area

within a community or to provide assistance in the operation of a facility or program area.

Task Forces. The task force is an extremely popular way to involve consumers in the formulation of policy. Task forces are usually created to investigate a specific issue or problem. They may produce recommendations that the elected officials of a government agency may find useful in decision making.

Focus Groups. Focus groups are often used by commercial leisure service organizations to gauge customers' reactions to services. As Edginton, Hanson, Edginton, and Hudson (1998:133) have written, focus groups consist of six to nine people with a moderator who asks questions and records answers.

Electronic Mail. Electronic mail, or e-mail, is pervasive in society today. The Internet provides an opportunity for individuals to be connected worldwide. Leisure service organizations can establish Web pages, home pages, Web sites and other ways of connecting electronically with their constituents.

Polls and Surveys. Polls are directed toward determining the attitudes of individuals on specific issues, whereas surveys are directed toward the measurement of a broader set of concerns. These mechanisms offer opportunities for participation, although there have been cases in which statistics have been manipulated to suit the ends of pollster. Nonetheless, if used properly polls and surveys can be a valuable tool to encourage participation in policy formulation.

Public Meetings and Hearings. Opportunities for individuals to voice their opinions at official meetings and hearings also encourages consumer involvement. Although public meetings can be a one-way form of communication, they can also be opened up in order to establish dialogue in which viewpoints are exchanged, issues made known, and consensus sought.

Community Forum. This open type of meeting format can be used to solicit a wide variety of responses from community members. It is similar to a public meeting or hearing and usually provides opportunities for an exchange of information between officials and individuals.

Written Submission. Petitions and briefs are also useful tools that can be used to promote consumer involvement. A petition carries the signatures of a large number of individuals and reflects their opinion on a specific issue. A brief is a concise statement relating to the concern of an individual or group on a specific issue.

Plebiscites. One of the most direct methods for obtaining consumer involvement is via the use of a plebiscite. A plebiscite places the decision of a given issue directly in the hands of the voter. A referendum to secure funds for the development of a community center is an example of a plebiscite.

The Media. The media, including newspapers, television, and radio, are perhaps underused for involving consumers in the policymaking process. The media can be an effective tool for disseminating information and receiving consumer feedback.

By involving consumers in the process of policy formulation and evaluation, it is hoped that program offerings and policies will be linked more closely to consumer needs. By increasing an organization's sensitivity toward consumer interests and concerns, effective-

ness and efficiency may be increased. But one must be cognizant of, and prepared to deal with, the problems that arise from consumer involvment. It is important to remember that the framework that is established for consumer input will dictate the appropriateness and accuracy of the information received. Policymaking can be enhanced if mechanisms that ensure validity and viability are used.

The Role of the Manager

There are a number of perspectives on the role that a leisure service manager should take in formulating policy. Some suggest managers have no role in policy formulation and serve only in the implementation of policy that has been created by others. In the case of an organization that has a policymaking board, the manager simply administers the policy decisions. Others advocate that the leisure service manager should have some involvement in the function of policymaking in that he or she, because of his or her training and background, is in a more knowledgeable position than the nonprofessional.

Many people have suggested that because numerous types of policies exist, formulation and implementation might be undertaken by people at different levels within the two policymaking units of an organization: the legislative body and the administrative body. Legislative bodies deal with policy divisions regarding values; value judgements are those that represent the aims, purposes, and general direction of an organization. Administrative bodies deal with what are known as "factual policies"; factual policies represent the practical means and technical knowledge that are needed to carry out policies that represent values. Within this approach to policymaking, the manager usually makes precise decisions regarding how things are to be run and where and when they are to be done. The legislative body presents policies in the form of guidelines and directions, which are intended as a general guide for the manager to follow.

Bannon (1973) maintains that a manager and a policymaking board should develop a cooperative relationship in order to effectively use the knowledge available from both parties. If a board member has sufficient knowledge in technical areas, Bannon recommends that this individual be allowed to contribute his or her expertise. If the manager can better interpret the interests of the target market, he or she should be allowed to contribute to the process of making value-oriented policy. Bannon (1973:31-32) writes:

> "A close and cooperative relationship should exist between a director and the recreation and park board. A joint policymaking relationship does not imply impingement by either party on the other's prime responsibility; rather, it implies a sharing of knowledge and experience and a logical overlap of functions for organizational enhancement."

The area of policy implementation is clearly the major management function of a leisure service manager. The basic work activities, financing, and the marketing of services, are primary areas in which the manager carries out the policies of the organization through planning, organizing, directing, staffing, and controlling. The manager plans and organizes the leisure deliv-ery system by determining its long-, middle-, and short-term objectives and by carefully designing its organizational structure to meet the mission of the system. The manager then staffs the organization by hiring and training the personnel needed to carry out various policy assignments. This then sets the stage for the manager to direct the organization, especially in human resources, toward the achievement of its goals. The final function, control, finds the manager measuring the achievement of policies and taking whatever actions are necessary to correct deviations from them.

The responsibility that managers assume in formulating and implementing policy should not be taken lightly. They must recognize that their actions will influence people and affect their leisure behavior. Leisure service managers, as a result of their position of influence in the community, have to be more cognizant of the impact of their actions. Managers should realize their social responsibilities to the individuals, community, and society within which they operate. Managers cannot afford to live in a vacuum, unresponsive to the broad implications of their actions for the total environment. The process of decision making must incorporate a strategy whereby the manager can take into consideration the above concerns.

The following examples serve to illustrate different types of policy structures. The first one is a major policy; the examples then work progressively from more minor ones to rules and regulations.

Palo Alto, California. A statement of the general aim of the Recreation Division of the Palo Alto Community Services Department is shown in Table 4.4. This statement may be considered

**Table 4.4
The Philosophy of the Palo Alto Recreation Division,
Palo Alto Community Services Department**

General Aim
The general aim of the Recreation Division is to provide leisure pursuits that are creative, meaningful, and satisfying; to help individuals discover themselves, maintain their human dignity, and attain their optimum physically, mentally, emotionally, and socially.

a major policy reflecting the general direction or purpose of the organization. It is a broad statement that gives direction to the organization.

Kitchener, Ontario. Table 4.5 represents a portion of the resource-oriented goals and objectives of the Kitchner Parks and Recreation Department. This statement reflects three types of policies: major, secondary, and functional. The goals of the organization can be considered its major policies. The objectives listed for each goal statement are examples of policies that are derived from the broader goal statements. The section on physical resource implications spells out a number of functional activities that may affect the operation of this organization. This document is an excellent example of the manner in which different types of policies are linked within a hierarchical policy structure.

Glenview, Illinois. The policy presented in Table 4.6 represents the Glenview Park District's policy concerning standards for community parks. It is a minor policy that is based on the Park District's functional policy concerning land and facilities. It defines the standards that have been established for this particular type of park.

Marshalltown, Iowa. Table 4.7 depicts, in part, operating procedures of the Marshalltown Park and Recreation Department. This type of policy details the procedures that employees are to follow. Included is a discussion of hours of work, attendance requirements, and rest periods. The items presented serve the function of inhibiting, regulating, and enabling certain kinds of behavior.

Arlington Heights, Illinois. Table 4.8 presents rules that can be found within an organization. This selection was taken from Ordinance 260, which defines misdemeanors in the Arlington Heights Park District. It specifically spells out a rigid set of guidelines that are subject to extremely limited interpretation. For example, Section 9 (not shown) is very explicit, stating that "No person shall throw a stone, brick, or other missile in or upon any park." This rule is designed to inhibit certain types of behavior.

The Constitution states that certain powers are reserved exclusively for state governments and that, in some cases, the federal and state governments may concurrently provide these services. It is under this provision of the Constitution that states have the power to focus their efforts on the leisure needs of their constituents. These relationships between the federal government and individual states have provided a framework whereby the aims of government and the steps in achieving these aims are facilitated.

Summary

In the first part of this chapter, we explored goals, objectives, values, and

Table 4.5
Resource-Oriented Goals and Objectives of the
Kitchener Parks and Recreation Department

Goal	Objectives	Physical Resouce Implication
Goal 1—To coordinate the roles of groups and individual providing the various forms of park and recreation experiences and resources in the city of Kitchener, so as to maximize the availability and utility of these opportunities for the benefit and overall enjoyment of the citizens of Kitchener.	1-1. To establish and maintain liaison with providers of park and recreation opportunities in Kitchener. 1-2. To form ongoing working relationships with community recreation associations and other community-oriented groups providing park and recreation experiences and resources with Kitchener, so as to insure a comprehensive park and recreation supply system for the residents and to limit unnecessary duplication of resources. 1-3. To create and continuously update an inventory of all park and recreation resources and opportunities within Kitchener as a base for determining levels of supply and areas of deficiency. 1-4. To provide technical and financial assistance, wherever required and deemed feasible, to insure continuous, high quality, beneficial park and recreation experiences and resources for all citizens of Kitchener. 1-5. To insure community awareness and to encourage communication from residents on matters related to park and recreation opportunities and resources.	1-1. Must develop coordination mechanisms with board of education, separate school board, YM/YWCA, private golf clubs, ethnic associations, churches, commercial operators, Grand River Conservation Authority, etc. Joint development/operation agreements with other suppliers to optimize return on municipal expenditure. 1-2. Must encourage the development of and support (financial and advisory) representative community recreation associations in each community. Encourage participation in physical resource planning, development, and operation. 1-3. Work with all "providers" to develop and maintain an inventory classification and reporting system. 1-4. Support other suppliers capable of providing opportunities more efficiently (cost) or effectively (community response). 1-5. Community involvement in all major planning and development decisions, particularly at the neighborhood or community level.

policies of which the leisure service manager should be aware. A policy is a plan that inhibits, enables, or regulates behavior in some way. Policies can be seen as existing in a hierarchical fashion, with major policies at the top and rules at the bottom. Major policies give broad direction to an organization, whereas rules spell out specific rigid regulations that are to be followed. The leisure service manager plays a dual role in the policy process by helping policymaking bodies formulate policies, while carrying the responsibility for their implementation and enforcement. This dual role requires a high order of ability, as the leisure service manager is placed in the somewhat tenuous position of both setting policy and enforcing it.

Table 4.6
Policy Concerning Community Parks, Glenview Park District

Definition: A large park area providing broad expanse of natural scenery and capable of accommodating large numbers of people; often includes special features of district wide interest.

Examples of Provided Features: Picnic areas, bridle paths, nature trails, zoos, band shells, fishing and sports areas.

Principles of Location and Design:
1. Each major section of the community should be within convenient distance of a community park, and it should be easily accessible from a major thoroughfare.
2. The community park should be large enough to take the urban dweller away from the noises and rush of urban environment.
3. The park should be developed for both active and passive use for all ages, but the development of active play areas should not destroy the primary purpose of the park.

Recommended Standard: One community park for at least each 40,000 population or one acre per 400 minimum. Size—100 acres or more where possible, within one to two miles of every home where possible.

Example: Harms Woods Forest Preserve.

Table 4.7
Working Hours, Conditions, and Workweek,
Marshalltown Park and Recreation Department

Section 1: Hours of Work
The hours during which the Park and Recreation Department shall be open for business and service shall be determined in the department's best interest by the director.

Section 2: Worksheet
The working time per week shall be 40 hours, with special provisions for additional hours uniformly to meet existing conditions or a living wage.

The above rules apply only to hourly people and all salaried people having the result and productivity clause to regulate and determine their hours for continued betterment and growth of the department.

Section 3: Attendance
All employees shall be at their station in accordance with these rules at the appointed time and with regularity. Failure to comply is adequate reason for dismissal.

Section 4: Rest Periods
If authorized by their superintendent, employees may take two 15-minute coffee breaks or rest periods each workday, under provisions and in accordance with the limitations as set by their department heads. Such breaks shall be considered a privilege and not a right, and shall never interfere with proper performance of the work responsibilities and work schedule of the department.

Discussion Questions

1. Discuss the process of identifying core values for a leisure service organization's vision statement.

2. What is the role of the manager in promoting an organization's vision?

3. What is the leisure service manager's role in goal setting?

4. What is a policy? How does it affect behavior in organizations?

5. Discuss the policy process.

6. Identify the role of different policy units.

Table 4.8
Arlington Heights Park District Ordinance No. 260
An Ordinance Defining Misdemeanors and Providing Penalties for Such Misdemeanors

Be it ordained by the Board of Commissioners of the Arlington Heights Park District, Cook County, Illinois:

Section 1. For the purpose of this ordinance, the following terms shall have the definitions given herein:

A. "District" is the Arlington Heights Park District, Cook County, Illinois.
B. "Board" is the Board of Commissioners of the Arlington Heights Park District.
C. "Director" is the Director of Parks and Recreation, the chief administrative officer of the District.
D. "Park" is any playfield, playground, swimming pool, ice skating rink, open area, building or parts thereof or other facility and the materials and equipment therein owned, leased or in use by the District.
E. "Person" is an individual, firm, partnership, group, association, corporation, governmental unit, company or organization of any kind, except the District, its employees and Board members while said employees and Board members are engaged in the performance of District duties.
F. "Vehicle" is any conveyance, whether motor powered or self-propelled, except baby carriages, and conveyances in use by the District.

Section 2. No person shall engage in any sport, game, amusement or exercise in any Park, except in such parts thereof as are designated for that purpose by the Director.

Section 3. No person shall enter a Park or part thereof posted as "Closed to the Public," nor shall any person use or abet the use of any such Park or part thereof in violation of posted notices.

Section 4. No person shall hinder, interfere with or cause or threaten to do bodily harm to any employee or the District while such employee is engaged in performing his duties in and on behalf of the District.

Section 5. No person shall expose or offer for sale any article or thing, nor shall any person station or place any stand, cart, or vehicle for the transportation, sale, or display of any such article or thing in any Park, except a regularly licensed concessionaire or other person acting under an official permit of the Board; nor shall any person within any Park or on its borders announce, advertise, or call the public attention in any way to any article, or service for sale or hire.

Section 6. No person shall paste, glue, tack or otherwise affix or post any sign, placard, advertisement, or inscription, whatever, nor erect or cause to be erected any sign whatever on any structure or thing in a Park, except as authorized by the Director.

---

7. What do policymaking boards do in public, nonprofit, and private leisure service organizations?

8. What is the role of policy-making in the process?

9. Identify and define eight ways that customers may be involved in the policy-making process.

10. Discuss community values. How do they influence organizational goals, objectives, and policies?

References

Bannon, J. J. (1973, July). Who really makes policy? *Parks and Recreation, 7*; 31–32.

Cato, B. (1992). Double jeopardy or another unique opportunity? *Parks and Recreation, 27*(12), 25.

Clements, M. (1992, June). How much do we care? *Parade Magazine,* 16–17.

Corcoran, T. (1990, March). Sustainable development: A dump site for ideas. *The Globe & Mail,* 44.

Donnelly, J. H., Gibson, J. L., & Ivancevich, J. M. (1990). *Fundamentals of management* (7th ed). Homewood, IL: BPI-Irwin.

Dustin, D. L. (1990). Looking inward to save the outdoors. *Parks and Recreation, 25*(9), 86–89.

Dustin, D. L. (1991). Peace, recreation and leisure. *Parks and Recreation, 26*(9), 102-104.

Drucker, P. (1980). *Managing in turbulent times.* New York: Harper & Row.

Drucker, P. (1985). *Innovation and entrepreneurship.* New York: Harper & Row.

Edginton, C. R. (1974, February). Management by crisis: There is an alternative. *Journal of Iowa Parks and Recreation,* 10.

Edginton, C. R. (1987). Creating an organizational structure. *Management Strategies,* 11(1).

Friedmann, J. (1987). *Planning in the public domain: From knowledge to action.* Princeton, NJ: Princeton University Press.

Gardner, J., & Roseland, M. (1989). Acting locally: Community strategies for equitable sustainable development. *Alternatives, 16*(3), 36–47.

Godbey, G. (1991). Redefining public parks and recreation. *Parks and Recreation, 26*(10), 56-59.

Godbey, G., Graefe, A., & James, S. (1993). Reality and perception—Where do we fit in? *Parks and Recreation, 28*(1), 76–83.

Hodgetts, R. M., & Wortman, M. S. (1980). *Administrative policy: Text and cases in the policy sciences* (2nd ed.). New York: Wiley & Sons.

Honolulu Department of Parks and Recreation (1994). Reinventing DPR—Strategic plan for action: Creating an agency that works better and costs less. Honolulu, HI: City and County of Honolulu.

Jreisat, J. E. (1992). *Managing public organizations: A developmental perspective on theory and practice.* New York: Paragon House.

Knowles-Lankford, J., & Lankford, S. (1995). Our professional responsibility for a preferred future. *World Leisure & Recreation Association Journal, 36*(4) pp. 40–44.

Koontz, H., & O'Donnell, C. (1972). *Principles of management* (5th ed.). New York: McGraw-Hill.

Lankford, J. K. (1993). The role of parks and recreation in sustainable community development. *World Leisure & Recreation Association Journal, 35*(2), 13–17.

McAvoy, L. (1990). An environmental ethic for parks and recreation. *Parks and Recreation, 25*(9), 68–73.

McLean, D., Bannon, J., & Gray, H. (1991). *Leisure resources: Its comprehensive planning.* Champaign, IL: Sagamore Publishing.

Moiseichik, M., & Bodey, K. Legal authority and jurisdiction. In van der Smissen, M. Moiseichik, V. J. Hartenburg, & L. F. Twardzik, (Eds.), *Management of park and recreation agencies.* Ashburn, VA: National Recreation and Park Association.

Murphy, J. R., Niepoth, E. W., Jamieson, L. M., & Williams, J. G. (1991). *Leisure systems: Critical concepts and applications.* Champaign, IL: Sagamore Publishing.

Naisbett, J., & Aburdene, P. (1985). *Reinventing the corporation.* New York: Warner Bros.

Newman, P. (1991, Fall). Sustainable settlements: Restoring the commons. *The Urban Ecologist,* 3–14.

Orams, M. B. (1992). Peace, leisure, and recreation: A response. *Parks and Recreation, 27*(2), 54–56.

O'Sullivan, E. (1991). Marketing experiences: It's the how not the what. *Parks and Recreation, 26*(12), 40–42.

Pekar, P. P. (1982, March–April). Setting goals in the non-profit environment. *Managerial Planning,* 43–46.

Pfister, R., & Ewert, A. (1993). Ethnicity and environmental concerns of forest visitors. [Abstracts from the 1993 Symposium on Leisure Research]. Arlington, VA: National Recreation and Parks Association.

Reynolds, J. A., & Hormachea, M. N. (1976). *Public recreation administration.* Englewood Cliffs, NJ: Prentice-Hall.

Rodney, L. S., & Toalson, R. F. (1981). *Administration of recreation, parks, and leisure services.* New York: Wiley & Sons.

Schultz, J. H., McAvoy, L. H., & Dustin, D. L. (1988, January). What are we in business for? *Parks and Recreation,* 52–54.

Scioli, F. P., & Cook, T. J. (1975). *Methodologies for analyzing public policies.* Lexington, MA: D.C. Heath.

Sessoms, H. D. (1992). Lesson from the past. *Parks and Recreation, 27*(2), 46–53.

Thaman, M. B. (1993). The health care issue—Part of the solution. *Parks and Recreation, 28*(5), 30.

Toalson, R. F., & Mobley, T. A. (1993). The 21st century, part 2. *Parks and Recreation, 28*(5), 56–60.

Van der Ryn, S., & Calthorpe, P. (1986). *Sustainable communities: A new design synthesis for cities, suburbs, and towns.* San Francisco: Sierra Club Books.

Ward, J. L. (1991). *Creating effective boards for private enterprises: Meeting the challenges of continuity and competition.* San Francisco: Jossey-Bass.

Wolf, T. (1990). *Managing a nonprofit organization.* New York: Fireside.

Zeiger, J. B. (1990). Environmental equilibrium. *Parks and Recreation, 25*(9), 36.

Chapter 5

Motivation: Inspiring Excellence

Motivation is about inspiring and encouraging others to reach their full potential.

Introduction

Have you ever wondered why some individuals are more dedicated, committed, hard working, and action oriented than others? Why do some individuals invest greater amounts of time, energy and effort in their work performance when compared with their colleagues? Much of the answer to this question has to do with whether or not an individual is motivated. Motivation is an extremely complex, challenging, and sometimes even difficult and demanding task to address as a leisure service manager. What moves individuals and an organization toward excellence?

Clearly, many variables can influence whether individuals are motivated within their work environments. Do employees have a clear understanding of the goals to be achieved? Are they enthusiastic, even "gung-ho," about their work environment? Are they prone toward action? Are their actions aligned, fused, and integrated with the goals of the organization? These and other questions have to do with the concept of motivation.

Motivation plays an exceedingly important role in moving an organization toward excellence. What is the difference between a mediocre organization and one that truly strives for excellence in all its endeavors? Leisure service organizations seeking excellence create environments where individuals are transformed, tapping into their potential in ways that unleash greater energy, effort, and in effect create greater commitment to the organization's effort. In this chapter, we will explore the concept of motivation. Specifically, motivation will be defined; ways of defining and understanding primary and secondary motives will be presented, and theories of motivation will be discussed. Further, a review of pertinent studies linking motivation to leisure service personnel and a model for promoting excellence will be included.

Motivation: Why Is It Important?

Why is motivation important in leisure service organizations? What factors challenge managers today to unlock greater potential within an organization's human resources? Without question, the most important resources in any organization today are its human ones. The success of an organization will rest on the efforts of individuals within organizations. The abilities of such individuals to respond to challenges, to put forth effort, to be action oriented, and to learn and grow are all factors related to motivation.

It has been estimated that motivation has a tremendous influence on the work of employees within organizations. Hershey, Blanchard, and Johnson (1996) have suggested that most individuals can perform their jobs by using as little as 20 to 30 percent of their ability. Studies have shown that about one out of every four say they are working to full capacity. Nearly half of the individuals in the workforce indicate that they do not put more into their positions than is minimally required. Further, many people do not believe they are working as hard as they did in the past. Interestingly, the majority of individuals indicate that their performance would improve under the right conditions. In other words, in the proper environment where they are motivated, their work performance would increase.

Today the leisure service field and society in general are challenged by a number of factors that relate to the need for creating motivating environments. First, and perhaps most important, is the need to create work environments that draw, attract, and retain individuals because they are part of a worthwhile endeavor—one that they feel is serving valuable ends not only to them personally, but to society as a whole. People want to be a part of a worthwhile endeavor. From an individual perspective, Peters and Waterman (1982:56) in their now classic book *In Search of Excellence,* have written:

> "We desperately need meaning in our lives and will sacrifice a great deal to institutions that will provide meaning for us. We

simultaneously need independence to feel as though we are in charge of our destinies, and to have the ability to stick out."

As these authors point out, individuals will sacrifice a great deal to an organization in order to have meaning in their lives. In other words, the context of working within an organization that provides worthwhile work opportunities gives rise to meaning in life. Interestingly, Peters and Waterman have also pointed out that individually, people need to feel as if they are valued and capable of excellent performance. As they note:

"All of us are self-centered, suckers for a bit of praise and generally like to think of ourselves as winners, but the fact of the matter is that our talents are distributed normally— none of us is really as good as he or she would like to think, but rubbing our noses daily in that reality doesn't do us a bit of good." (55)

Thus, as one can see, motivation not only involves creating worthwhile experiences for people, but providing opportunities for recognition, achievement, growth, and so on. Creating motivational environments may directly involve cheering on the best efforts of others or removing the barriers that prevent them from succeeding at their work. Drucker (1980: 24) has reminded us that our work as managers involves one thing and one thing only, and that is "to ensure that employees do what they get paid to do." In addition to being involved in worthwhile work, other important reasons for focusing on motivation are:

1. Improving Organizational Harmony. A motivated, dedicated staff will contribute in a positive way to organizational harmony. People who share a common vision and are working toward the fulfillment of that common ideal are usually happier than individuals working in organizations in which the mission is diffused and work efforts dispersed.

2. Increasing Productivity. As indicated, individuals within an organization can work adequately and use only 20 to 30 percent of their capability. Having high standards provides a basis for high productivity. Encourage people to do more and they will. It is a self-fulfilling prophecy.

3. Providing Opportunities for Employee Growth. Human beings are constantly in a state of growth. They are not static: They are in movement toward a goal. Their growth can be channeled so that it is aligned with the goals of the organization.

4. Improving Quality of Excellence. Quality is a perception of excellence. It is an attitude. It is free. People are motivated to perform at an excellent level, thereby increasing the quality of services.

5. Increasing Employee Retention. Individuals who are highly motivated, who are involved in the work and goals of the organization, are likely to stay in the organization.

6. Doing More with Less. Increasingly, leisure services organizations are being asked to do more with less. Technological innovations help here; however, operational budgets are not keeping pace.

7. *Worthwhile Work.* As mentioned, creating opportunities for individuals to engage in worthwhile work may be the most important element in creating a motivational work environment.

As one can see, there are many different reasons why motivation is important.

The Basic Motivation Process

Motivation comes from the word *motive*, the Latin word *movere*, "to move." Therefore, motivation is anything that moves people to perform. If employees are trying to perform, it is because they are motivated to one extent or another. Motivation is usually connected with some desire. Desire means, "to express a wish to." But desire, or wanting to do, does not qualify as the sole prerequisite to motivation. Motivation is that which actually moves a person toward a goal (doing a job), not that which just makes him or her want, or desire, to move. Motivation is not to be measured or considered in terms of desire, interest, attitude, or morale, but in terms of actual effort to perform. If the individual is not trying to perform, he or she is not motivated.

The concept of motivation is usually associated with having individuals meet their needs. When individuals' needs are not met, they are in a state of psychological or physiological imbalance. To move to a state of balance, persons will act on their needs. Luthans (1998:161) has written: "motivation is a process that starts with the physiological or psychological deficiency or need that activates a behavior or a drive that is aimed at a goal or incentive." Thus according to Luthans, to understand the process of motivation, it must be viewed in terms of the basic process of understanding how needs are translated into drives to meet goals that help restore balance in a person's life. Of course, such a balance is a theoretical goal that, in fact, may never be obtained. As one goal is achieved, another is identified. As Csikszentmihalyi (1991) teaches us, individual behavior is always framed between the skill and ability of an individual and the challenges the person is presented.

The basic motivation process can be viewed as a cyclical one, as represented in Figure 5.1. An individual has a need, which results in a drive directed toward some end or goal. Each of these elements interacts with one another to move or motivate people. Needs create action or drives toward a goal. Each of these elements can be defined as follows:

1. *Need.* A need can best be defined as a form of deficiency. A need exists when there is either a psychological or a physiological imbalance. Needs can be complicated or simple.

2. *Drive.* A drive is action oriented, usually resulting in some form of behavior. Where there is a need or deficiency, this usually results in a drive to alleviate the deficiency or meet the need.

3. *Goals.* Likewise, goals are ends at which drives are directed. Thus, obtaining a goal or meeting a particular need restores the psychological and physiological balance and ends the drive.

Understanding this simple yet valuable way of viewing motivation sets the process for helping individuals effectively meet the needs of employees. Every individual has needs—young or old, rich or poor, employed or unem-

Figure 5.1
The Basic Motivational Process

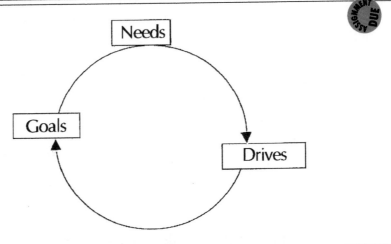

ployed, and regardless of race. Needs must be met in one fashion or another. Every waking hour of every individual's day is directed toward meeting personal needs. An individual has conscious and unconscious needs. Needs are met in different places and during different time periods. Some needs are met at work, some are met during leisure, and some are met in daily maintenance (eating, sleeping, bathing, etc.). It is important for the leisure service manger to understand what the individual needs of his or her employees are and how to go about meeting them. When individuals' needs are not met, it may result in frustration, anxiety, and other problems.

Integrating Needs and Organizational Goals

A challenge to leisure service managers is the alignment or the integration of individual needs with organizational goals. In an ideal world, these two elements would be fused with one another. Leisure service managers should

be aware that employees come to work to meet their own needs. Individuals do not come to work only as employees to help meet organizational goals. They are individuals first and come to work to meet needs that can best be met through employment. The dual function of a leisure service manager is to help employees meet their work-oriented needs and to help consumers meet their leisure needs. To plan services that meet the needs of people, managers must be able to recognize participants' needs and their level of development. Only if managers understand this concept can they truly offer meaningful leisure services.

Thus, a major responsibility of the leisure service manager is to attempt to coordinate or fuse the needs of the individual with the goals of the organization. The concept known as work alignment is a very important part of the motivation process. It requires the leisure service manager to do the following:

1. Know the needs of each individual employee.

2. Know the needs of the organization.

3. Know the abilities of each employee.

4. Know the limitations of each employee.

5. Understand the resources of the organization.

6. Understand how all these factors can be interrelated.

7. Understand that people release work capacity in order to meet needs.

Leisure service managers, as professionals in the field of leisure as well as managers of employees, do the following: (1) help individuals meet their needs through leisure services, and (2) help their employees meet their needs through work experiences. Managers who understand the needs of people and help employees meet their work-oriented needs will release the work capacity of employees that will provide leisure services for the constituents.

Understanding Motives

What moves individuals? There are two types of motives: primary and secondary. Primary motives are generally unlearned and physiologically based (Luthans, 1998). Therefore, when we think of primary motives, we should think of them as the more basic ones. They are focused on such basic physiological elements as hunger, thirst, sex, shelter, and so on. Secondary needs are ones that have an impact on an individual in terms of his or her own individual interests. They are very important elements in terms of work motivation, as they provide opportunities for

stimulation beyond an individual's basic needs. In this section, we will focus on the latter types of motives, as they are the ones that leisure service managers have the greater ability to influence.

Affiliation. Individuals have a great desire to be with other people as well as to be associated with a cause that provides meaning, structure, or value to their lives.

Power. Power in the context of motivating means that individuals seek to influence or control others. Power can be used positively or negatively. Positive use of power is essential in achieving organizational goals.

Achievement. Achievement is often thought of as seeking a challenge; being goal oriented; and establishing moderate, realistic, and attainable goals.

Financial Rewards. Financial rewards are monetary incentives. They are motivators in that they reflect a degree of achievement, or status and may result in security.

Status. Individuals are often motivated by the status of the title or a position that they assume. Further, there is great status in working for organizations that are perceived to be excellent and are held in high esteem by the public or the profession.

Recognition. Individuals are motivated because they receive recognition, praise, stroking, and acknowledgment of their efforts.

Worthwhile Work. Many individuals suggest that engaging in worthwhile work is an important motivator in their lives. Individuals want to feel that they are part of a valuable enterprise contributing to the well-being of society.

Growth and Learning. The opportunity to continue to grow and learn is becoming a powerful motivator. In a knowledge-based society, the opportunity to continue to learn may be a very strong motivator for individuals.

Opportunities to Innovate and Create. Curiosity is a primary motivator of individuals. Human curiosity as reflected in desire to innovate and create new concepts or ideas and, in the case of leisure services, new programs or activities can be a strong motivator.

Defining Motivation

How do we define motivation? How is human performance maximized in an organization? Motivation is often thought of in the context of creating some types of incentives that move people. It is our belief that motivation is far more complex than creating rewards or punishments, including incentives such as rewards, salary structures, or other benefits. Human beings are complex by nature, and what moves one individual to action may be vastly different than what moves another. In general, we can think of motivation as a process of influence in one's life—influence to move, to act, to respond to the moment-to-moment, daily, and longer-term elements that affect our behaviors.

Work motivation is often culturally defined, as Edginton and Griffith (1983: 166) have written:

"Humans have a large capacity for activity. This activity can be manifested in a number of different ways. When it is organized and results in the creation of products or services, for which individuals are paid, it is known as work. Definitions of work are culturally based; what constitutes working in one society may be different from what con-

stitutes work in another society. The way in which work is manifested may also vary from culture to culture. In North American society, religious precepts have historically been the primary cultural determinant of work. Currently, however, we view work more in terms of citizenship. For example, a good citizen is one who is employed and thereby is perceived as contributing in a positive sense to the general welfare of society.

. . . work is a primary factor shaping a person's life both now and in previous times... . Fundamental cultural values and norms have been primarily defined by the work in which people have engaged... . Throughout the history of humankind, work has had a more influential role in shaping individuals' behavior than other factors, such as food or sex. Recognizing the impact of other variables such as religion and education, Smith suggests that work is the central factor shaping human behavior."

Then what is the definition of motivation in a work situation? Motivation can be thought of as the provision for work opportunity whereby individual employees can meet their individual needs while meeting the goals of the organization. In other words, as Edginton and Griffith (1983:1965) have written, motivation is the process whereby an environment is created that enables individuals to be stimulated to take action that fulfills the goals of the organization. Essentially, an effective

Exhibit 5.1
The Analogy of the Acorn and the Oak Tree

An analogy to the motivation process would be the planting of an acorn to grow an oak tree. The individual wanting to grow the oak tree is similar to the individual wanting to motivate an employee. The oak tree can be likened to the employee whom the manager wants to motivate. The individual who plants the acorn does not actually cause it to grow. He or she cannot get inside the acorn and force it to grow if the acorn itself is not viable; no matter how much the person who planted it wants it to grow, it will not. The same situation exists in the case of an employer wanting to motivate an employee. If an employee does not have the skill or desire to accomplish a particular task, no matter how much that employer wants him or her to, he or she will not; if the acorn is not viable, no matter how much the planter wants it to grow, it will not. You do not get inside the employee, nor do you get inside the acorn and force it to grow. You create an environment in which the acorn grows. You plant it in good soil, water it, fertilize it, place it where it will gain a certain amount of sunlight, and as a result, the acorn grows itself. It has inside itself all the necessary properties to grow, provided the environment in which it was planted is conducive to growing. The same can be said of an employee. The employee must have the necessary skills, attitudes, knowledge, and intelligence to perform a given task. If the employee does not have the capacity for a given task, no matter how much incentive you offer, he or she cannot be motivated to do it. On the other hand, if an individual does have the right skills, aptitude, and so on, and if the employer creates the right environment, he or she can be motivated. The employer or manager can create an environment in which an individual is self-motivated.

leisure service manager creates an environment wherein people can be self-motivated. Exhibit 5.1 presents an analogy of the motivation process with the planting of an acorn and the growth of an oak tree.

Fallacies of Motivation

There are many fallacies about motivation. To help the reader achieve a clearer understanding of the dynamics of motivation, some of the fallacies will be discussed. For example, many individuals feel that if they could instill the proper attitude in the employee, that he or she would show an increase in performance. It is based on the assumption that attitudes produce behavior, when in actuality behavior develops attitudes. Therefore, an individual's attitudes are always appropriate in that they are part of his or her value system. Behavior produces values; people essentially believe in what they do because it justifies their behavior. People's experiences and environment determine behavior.

Another false assumption is that work is something done to the worker,

be it positive or negative in terms of a reward or punishment. Over the years, this has been described as the carrot-and-stick or "reward" theory. The basic problem with this theory is that an employee will work only as long as the carrot is dangling in front of him or her. The minute the reward is taken away, the employee may stop working. Another problem is that maybe the person is full of carrots (particular rewards) or does not like them and is not going to be motivated by them. On the other hand, the individual may run out of carrots. This type of problem is very apparent today. In our society, people's expectations have increased, making them difficult to meet. A striking union wanting more wages may price itself right out of the market, to the point that the product involved can no longer be made and sold in the public market. There is a limit to how far an organization can go in motivating people purely by some sort of monetary reward (see Figure 5.2).

The "stick," or "punishment," or "negative motivation" theory also has many shortcomings. It is based on the premise that an individual moves, works,

Figure 5.2
The Carrot Approach to Motivation

the man got the donkey to move, the donkey did not keep moving far enough to make it worthwhile; the idea backfired and the workload was lost.

Employees who fear their supervisors or dislike them may engage in spiteful, vengeful activities. They may deliberately sabotage or slow down work when the supervisors are not around. They may break tools, break rules, or

Figure 5.3
The Punitive Approach to Motivation
Leading to Employee Resentment

or is motivated as long as fear or threat is hanging over his or her head. However, when the threat is removed or the employer turns his or her back, the employee, because he or she is not self-motivated, will tend to slow down or stop movement altogether. In addition, use of the punishment theory creates frustration within the employee, which in turn breeds aggression. The aggression can be covert, but it nonetheless will affect production and the work environment. Building a fire under someone to get the person moving is good only for initial movement; ultimately, it backfires in the attempt to create motivation. Figure 5.3 shows a fire that was built under a donkey to get it to move the cart. The problem is that the donkey moves forward only enough to stop the pain and pulls the cart, or the workload, right over the fire. Although

break gold brick. Negative motivation leads to movement, but not for long and not necessarily in the right direction.

Factors Influencing Motivation

Numerous factors influence the creation of a motivating environment. One can think of many different elements in the environment that influence the process that leads individuals to be motivated. We have identified four distinct factors:

1. A Function of Needs. As indicated, we all have needs. We move to meet these needs. We are directed first toward the accomplishment of the need that is most outstanding. In an attempt to meet this need, we are moved to action; that is, we are self-motivated. The strongest impact or influence on motivation is the need that an individual has at a particular point in time. Suppose an employee has the following needs: (1) less harassment from the boss, (2) more independence, and (3) more salary. The desire to get away from the manager, who he/she cannot stand, is the most pressing need at the time. So the employee makes a lateral move, even though it involves neither more salary or more independence.

2.   A Function of Opportunity. No matter how strong an individual's need may be, if the opportunity to satisfy that need is not present, the motivation is decreased considerably, if not lost. The more available the goal or opportunity to meet the need, the stronger the motivation. If employees know there will be new jobs open in the next three months at a higher rank and salary, they are apt to be motivated toward working hard for one of them if they feel they stand a good chance of getting a promotion.

3.   A Function of Ability. This involves the individuals' capabilities in terms of the skills, training, and knowledge he or she has to perform a particular task. No matter how much an individual may have the desire to do something, if physically or intellectually the person does not have the ability to do it, his or her motivation is hindered significantly. No matter how much a person wants to become a great singer, if he or she does not have a good voice, he or she will never be a great singer. Training and practice may help, but not necessarily.

4.   A Function of Reinforcement. Suppose an individual who has a need strives to meet that need and gets reinforcement in the way of praise or a reward of some sort. This reinforcement will cause him or her to be similarly motivated again at another time.

Thus, the four factors behind motivation are need, opportunity, ability, and reinforcement. It might be stated differently: motivation is a function of potential; the potential of an individual to meet his or her needs, use his or her abilities fully, have opportunities to meet his or her needs, and receive reinforcement. These factors are interrelated, and we will discuss them in more detail later. The manager's job is to find ways to organize both the work and the abilities of employees to maximize their work capacity. This is done by humanizing work, making it more interesting and challenging, and by creating an environment in which employees want to work. The manager has two choices: *to make people work* or to try to *make people want to work.*

Creating a Motivating Environment

What are the characteristics of a motivating environment? Do people need to be challenged? Must the environment be a dynamic, fun place within which to work? Do people need to get along with one another, treating one another with respect and dignity? Is trust required? In general, a motivating environment has three characteristics:

1.   Shared View of Organizational Goals and Contributions. A harmonious worker–management view is what a good job consists of and to what it contributes. These goals are determined mutually by the employer, on the one hand, and the supervisor, on the other. For these goals to be met, there must be supportive management and reinforcement of individual needs.

2. Support of Management. Supportive rather than coercive management. Rather than simply pushing workers to perform, the supportive management assists them in finding ways to meet their goals and objectives by helping them remove obstacles.

3. Ensuring that Employees Feel Worthwhile. Reinforcement of employees' needs for feeling worthwhile. This involves giving employees recognition in a way that reinforces their efforts to work and move toward the accomplishment of the goals and objectives of the organization. The most influential recognition will come from an employer's immediate supervisor, who should regularly reinforce him or her on a job well done.

In a work environment where there is mutual agreement and trust, the worker–management view of good work contributes to the goals of the organization and of the individual. There is real and sincere concern with work that contributes to organizational as well as to individual goals. There is also concern for the approach to work and the work results. The key to a harmonious worker–management view of what is good work, and to what it contributes, is mutual determination. Therefore, *both* the supervisor and the employee should participate in developing goals for the employee's job and how to accomplish them. The supportive manager or supervisor removes unnecessary obstacles

and provides resources to help employees do what they want to do. Therefore, the supervisor will ask, "How can we help you do your job more productively?"

Motivation and Views of Human Nature

An important part in the process of motivation is how we view our fellow human beings. If individuals are perceived as lazy or disinterested in their work, as contrasted with viewing them in a more robust fashion, this will affect the leisure service manager's activities in moving people toward the organization's goals. On this topic, Edginton and Griffith (1983:172) have written the following:

"The way in which human behavior is viewed is very important in the motivating process. If the manager views individuals as being inherently lazy, incompetent, immature, and lacking in self-discipline, this perception will influence his or her treatment of employees. The manager with this perception and managerial leadership style would tend to be discipline- and control-oriented. Further, the manager might believe that the best way to motivate such individuals is through disciplinary measures. However, a manager who views individuals as being capable of being self-disciplined, industrious, and competent might attempt to motivate employees by facilitating his or her behavior."

Three models can be useful in helping the reader understand how one's view of human nature can influence the process of motivation. These are Douglas McGregor's (1970) Theory X and Theory Y, Chris Argyris' (1957) Immaturity–Maturity Theory, and from a leisure service manager's perspective, James MacGregor Burns' (1978) Transactional/Transformational Model.

Theory X and Theory Y

Douglas McGregor's (1960) Theory X and Theory Y postulated that there were two basic assumptions of human behavior. If either of these theories is adopted by a leisure service manager, it affects his or her management style. Theory X assumptions concerning the behavior of human beings are characterized by McGregor as follows:

1. The average human being has an inherent dislike of work and will avoid it if he can.

2. Because of this human characteristic of dislike of work, most people must be coerced, controlled, directed, and threatened with punishment to get them to put forth adequate effort toward the achievement of organizational objectives.

3. The average human being prefers to be directed, wishes to avoid responsibility, has relatively little ambition, and wants security above all. (33–34)

A leisure service manager using Theory X assumptions about the nature of human beings will have essentially an authoritarian, punitive, and controlling approach to management. The theory presumes that people are basically lazy and crave security. Job performance can be achieved only when the manager controls and directs the work environment. Further, Theory X suggests that once a worker is secure in the work environment and free from decision-making responsibility, he or she will be satisfied.

It is important to recognize that once the basic needs of security and safety are satisfied, a worker will not be motivated solely by offers of financial incentives. For a worker to produce more, a manager must appeal to that person's individual needs for recognition, status, self-esteem, and self-actualization. Certainly, every leisure service manager has had an employee who is motivated without threats, or implied threats, of punishment or by increased financial incentives. This concern is characterized in McGregor's Theory Y. Theory Y assumptions about the behavior of human beings are basically an outgrowth of the research of behavioral scientists. They include the following:

1. The expenditure of physical and mental effort in work is as natural as play or rest.

2. External control and the threat of punishment are not the only means for bringing about effort toward organizational objectives. People will exercise self-direction and self-control in the service of objectives to which they are committed.

3. Commitment to objectives is a function of the rewards associated with their achievement.

4. The average human being learns, under proper conditions, not only to accept but also to seek responsibility. (47–48)

Theory Y indicates that work is as natural as play, that employees want to perform well in their jobs, that they are creative, and that most employees are self-motivated. Thus, the manager using Theory X assumptions of behavior views the employee as existing in an immature state. The reverse is the case when the manager uses Theory Y assumptions.

Immaturity–Maturity Theory

Chris Argyris' (1957) immaturity–maturity theory indicates that individuals require a management style appropriate to their particular maturity level (see Figure 5.4). Argyris has determined that several changes take place in an individual's personality as he or she matures; these changes are based on the person's experience in the environment, and his or her mental and physical growth. The first of these changes finds the individual moving from a passive state as an infant to a state of increasing activity as an adult. The second change takes place as the person matures, as he or she moves from a dependent state to an independent state. A third change that occurs as the individual matures is that he or she moves from behaving in a few ways to being capable of

behaving in many ways. The fourth factor is that an immature person has erratic, shallow interests, whereas the mature person has deeper and stronger interests. Fifth, Argyris states that an immature person has a short time perspective, whereas the mature person has a long time perspective for both past and future activities. The next factor is that the immature person is willing to assume a subordinate position, whereas the mature person requires an equal or superordinate position. Finally, the immature individual lacks awareness of self, whereas the mature individual has awareness and control of self at all times.

Transactional/Transformational Model

This model presents two basic approaches to motivation. The transactional approach is one of employing the carrot-or-stick strategy. In other words, people are viewed as pawns to be manipulated, and this often results in inadequate performance. In the transactional model, the leisure service manager uses rewards or punishments as a

Figure 5.4
Immaturity–Maturity Continuum

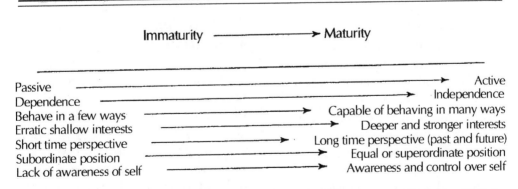

Source: Hersey, P., & Blanchard, K. H. (1972). *Management of organizational behavior: Utilizing human resources* (2nd ed., p. 51). Englewood Cliffs, NJ: Prentice-Hall. Model by Chris Argyris (1957). *Personality and the organization.* New York: Harper and Row. Reprinted here by permission of Prentice-Hall, Inc.

method of motivating people. In its simplest form, the manager exchanges something of value for an individual's labor. The problem in this model is that it creates the potential of an environment of threat, fear, or punishment if a person doesn't perform adequately. On the other hand, the transformation approach suggests that people should be enabled to pursue higher ends or goals. In other words, they should be empowered in such a way as to feel that they are part of a worthwhile program, activity, or organization. People should be transformed to higher levels through this process of commitment, dedication, and effort. The leisure service manager viewing individuals through the transformational prism sees individuals as capable human beings worthy of greater effort. As Edginton, Hudson, and Ford (1999: 45) have commented, this idea is:

> ". . . built on the concept that individuals can be empowered to do greater works. They can be encouraged by appealing to more altruistic ends, which promotes a greater sense of commitment that leads to greater productivity, more intense involvement, and higher levels of satisfaction. In a sense, transformational leaders appeal to the spiritual or emotional side of individuals by encouraging them to pursue ends that are worthwhile, present a greater sense of value to individuals, or contribute in some meaningful way to more global visionary ends. By empowering people to pursue a more visionary enhanced pathway, transformational leaders unlock the reservoir of potential within individuals."

Thus, one can see that the use of a transformational approach has the potential to elevate, and in fact motivate, people to higher levels of achievement and performance.

Theories of Work Motivation

During the 20th century, numerous theories of work motivation emerged in the management literature. Work motivation can be distinguished from other concepts of motivation previously presented in this chapter, which dealt primarily with basic psychological processes. At the turn of the century, Fredrick W. Taylor and others proposed incentive strategies to motivate workers. In turn, these gave rise to the development of a host of conceptual frameworks to define work motivation. In general, work motivation theories can be broken down into three (3) categories: (1) content theories, (2) process theories, and (3) contemporary theories. Table 5.1 presents a summary of the various models of work motivation that are prominent in the management literature today. The following is a brief description of the characteristics of these three types of theories of work motivation.

Content Theories of Work Motivation

Content theories of motivation are primarily concerned with identifying the needs or drives that move individuals to work. They ask the question: "What are the conditions or work elements that are required for individuals to be motivated?" The theories in this classification include Fredrick W. Taylor's Scientific Management Theory

Table 5.1
Work Motivation Theories

Content Theories of Motivation	Scientific Management, 1900s Human Relations, 1930s Maslow's Hierarchy of Needs, 1940s Herzberg's Motivation/Hygiene Theory, 1950s ERG Motivation Theory, 1970s	Focused on the factors or elements that individuals identify which are motivating
Process Theories of Motivation	Expectancy Theory, 1960s Performance/Satisfaction Model, 1960s Smith/Cranny Model, 1960s	Links performance and satisfaction. Often indicates that performance is a measure of ability and effort. Satisfaction is derived from comparison of inputs with outputs and expectations of rewards.
Contemporary Theories of Motivation	Exchange Theory, 1960s Equity Theory, 1960s Reinforcement Theories, 1950s, 1990s	Suggests that individuals can be externally motivated. Uses positive reinforcement to condition desired behaviors.

focused on wage incentives, Elton Mayo's Human Relations Theory, Abraham Maslow's Hierarchy of Needs, Fredrick Hertzberg's Motivation/Hygiene Theory, and Clayton Alderfer's ERG Theory.

Scientific Management as a Motivation Theory

As discussed in Chapter Two, Frederick W. Taylor's scientific management theory was developed in the early 1900s. Taylor's theory maintains that if you totally understand a job, break it down into parts, and improve on the skills and the methods of performing the job, and then pay an individual according to his or her ability to produce work, you can motivate (Taylor, 1967). Taylor spent many years analyzing small tasks that workers perform, breaking them down into component parts, and improving on each

part. Based on this job analysis and improved training, the individual could learn to perform a task at a rapid speed. The employee was paid for faster work on a piecemeal basis, resulting in an ability to make more money through increased productivity. This theory of motivation was popular for a number of years, and many industries picked up on the Taylor approach to improve work productivity.

One of the greatest shortcomings of this method was that it was contingent on the incentive approach to work. If you paid an individual enough, he or she would work at a rapid rate. It did not take into consideration any of the individual's personal needs; it took into account only the need for financial reward. Although this method, or theory, of motivation produced good results in a number of situations, in many other situations it did not. It was found that individuals who were paid on a piecemeal basis increased productivity only when they were paid for greater work rates; never did they increase work rates because of self-motivation. Only external or extrinsic reward encouraged them to work at a higher rate.

Human Relations as a Motivation Theory

The human relations approach to motivating individuals emerged in the 1930s. As shown in Chapter Two, the Hawthorne Studies recognized the importance of individual behavior in organizations and how the attention that individuals receive can influence their performance. This approach to motivation failed to recognize the importance of underlying psychological processes, however it was based on three simple adaptive assumptions:

1. Personnel are primarily economically motivated, and, secondarily, they desire security and good working conditions.

2. Provision of the above reward to personnel will have a positive effect on their morale.

3. There is a positive correlation between morale and productivity. (Luthans, 1998)

Based on these three assumptions, the motivational problems facing management were relatively clear-cut and easy to solve. Theoretically, all managers had to do was devise monetary incentive plans, ensure security, and provide good working conditions. Morale would be high and maximum productivity would result. Unfortunately, these human relations approaches to motivation did not work out in practice. Although no harm was done and some

good actually resulted in these early stages of human relations management, it soon became evident that such a simplistic approach fell far short of providing a meaningful solution to the complex motivational problems facing managers. It became clear that motivation is more complex than simply trying to meet employees' needs for certain economic, security, and working conditions.

Maslow's Hierarchy of Needs Theory

Abraham Maslow's Hierarchy of Needs depicts a structure with the more basic needs at the bottom of the model and the higher or more refined needs at the top. As can be seen in Figure 5.5, there are five distinct categories of needs:

1. *Physiological Needs.* These are survival needs—air, water, food, clothing, shelter, and sex. Examples of how the organization can satisfy these needs are through pay, benefits, and working conditions.

2. *Safety Needs.* This refers to protection against danger, freedom from fear, and security. Examples may include such things as benefit programs, including insurance and retirement plans; job security; safe and healthy working conditions; and competent, consistent, and fair leadership.

3. *Social Needs.* These needs include belonging, love, affiliation, and acceptance. Friendly associates and organized employee activities are examples here.

4. *Self-Esteem Needs.* This refers to the need for achievement, recognition, and status. Titles of responsibility, praise and recognition for

work done, promotions, competent management, pay as related to status, and a prestigious work environment are examples here.

5. *Self-Actualization Needs.* This refers to the realization of one's potential growth using creative talents. Examples include providing a challenging work environment and allowing creativity, as well as opportunities for growth and advancement.

Maslow indicated that people's motivational needs could be arranged in a hierarchy. He believed that it was essential that lower-level needs were met first. Then, once those lower-level needs were met, the individual would begin to strive for higher-level needs. To motivate an individual using this approach, an attempt is made to determine the level of need for which the individual is reaching. Once the proper level of need is determined, the manager or employer attempts to use that level of need to release the work capacity of the employee.

There is no question that Maslow's hierarchy theory has had a tremendous impact on various management approaches to motivation. By using Maslow's hierarchy in pyramid form, as show in Figure 5.5, the needs that are described can be associated with various motivational terms. Psychological, or basic, needs can be associated with salary. Security needs can be associated with seniority, union subsidy, severance pay, and so on. Social or belonging needs can be associated with title, status symbols, and promotion. Finally, the highest level, self-actualization, is associated with employee achievement wherein the employee gets satisfaction out of the work itself.

Herzberg's Motivation/Hygiene Theory

Fredrick Herzberg's Theory of Motivation was conceptualized in the 1950s. Building on Maslow's Theory of Motivation, Herzberg concluded that employees had two different categories of needs that could be met in the work environment, and that these were independent of one another and affected behavior in different ways. Those elements that caused job dissatisfaction were associated with environmental factors and came to be called "hygiene factors." When employees felt good about their jobs, this feeling generally had to do with the work itself; these Herzberg called the "motivators." Thus, his theory became the "Motivation/Hygiene Theory" (see Figure 5.6).

As you will see later, much of the research work in the leisure service field has used Herzberg's Motivation/Hygiene Theory. Hygiene factors include policies, the type of administration, the type of supervision, the working conditions, the interpersonal relationship among individuals (superiors, coworkers, and subordinates), and employees' salary, status, and security. These factors are not an integral part of the job, but they affect the conditions under which the job is performed. Herzberg related these to hygiene in the sense that they are preventative and environmental. He found that hygiene factors produced no motivation from workers, but prevented loss in work performance because of work slowdown. If they were not provided for, they did not necessarily move employees to outstanding performance; these factors just kept them working at a steady capacity.

The motivators, on the other hand, are factors that involve a sense of achieve-

Figure 5.5
Maslow's Hierarchy of Needs

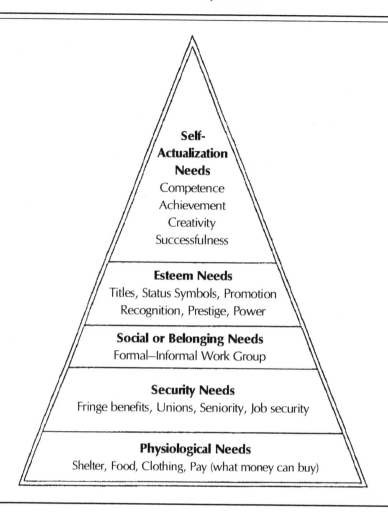

Self-Actualization Needs
Competence
Achievement
Creativity
Successfulness

Esteem Needs
Titles, Status Symbols, Promotion
Recognition, Prestige, Power

Social or Belonging Needs
Formal–Informal Work Group

Security Needs
Fringe benefits, Unions, Seniority, Job security

Physiological Needs
Shelter, Food, Clothing, Pay (what money can buy)

ment, professional growth, and recognition. They offer a challenge, and therefore were referred to by Herzberg as "motivators." He called these factors motivators also because they seemed capable of having a positive effect on job satisfaction, often resulting in increased work capacity and total output.

Herzberg's theory appears to have a close relationship with Maslow's Theory of the Hierarchy of Needs. The hygiene factors—company policy, administration, supervision, salary, interpersonal relationships, and working conditions—all seem to be affected by the first three levels of Maslow's needs: physiological, security, and social needs. The hygiene factors prevent dissatisfaction, but they do not lead to satisfaction; they tend to bring motivation up to a theoretical zero level. On the other hand, the motivators seem to be aligned with esteem and self-actualization needs. Herzberg's theory indicates that to motivate employees, the top two levels of Maslow's needs have to be dealt with. An individual must have a job that is challenging in content to be truly motivated.

The Herzberg theory brought new interest to the area of motivation. Prior

Figure 5.6
Motivation Hygiene Theory of Frederick Herzberg

I.	Hygiene factors Job dissatisfaction	Motivators Job satisfaction
II.	Provide for job dissatisfaction when not maintained	Motivate employees

III.	1. Supervision
	2. Company policy and administration
	3. Working conditions
	4. Interpersonal relationships with
	  (a) Peers
	  (b) Subordinates
	  (c) Superiors
	5. Status
	6. Job security
	7. Salary
	8. Personal life
		1. Achievement
		2. Recognition for achievement
		3. Work itself
		4. Responsibility
		5. Advancement
		6. Possibility of growth

to this time, in both the scientific management and the human relations approaches, attempts to improve motivation dealt with hygiene factors and the environment; Herzberg's theory indicated that if one truly wanted to motivate an employee, one had to deal with the higher-level needs. The management approach prior to this point indicated that if you had a morale problem or were not attaining high production, you should initiate higher wages or more fringe benefits or provide better working conditions. This solution did not work. Oftentimes managers found that they were already paying higher wages than their competition and had a better fringe benefit package, yet the organization still suffered from lack of motivation. For the first time, Herzberg's theory offered an explanation for this dilemma. By considering only the hygiene factors, managers were

not really motivating their personnel; they were just keeping them from being "job dissatisfied."

The Herzberg theory does not indicate that hygiene factors are not important; indeed, they are very important. But also important are the motivators contained in the job itself, making it interesting and challenging to the employee. Are employees turned on by their jobs? Are they getting the praise, recognition, and status they need? Are they provided with opportunities for advancement, achievement, and responsibility? These are the motivators that keep employees working harder and striving for bigger and better things.

ERG Motivation Theory

This model of motivation was advanced by Clayton Alderfer. Alderfer's model basically advances the work of Herzberg and builds on Maslow's Hierarchy of Needs. Like Maslow and Herzberg, he suggests a need typology that can be hierarchically ordered. He suggests that individuals have lower- and higher-order needs. His need structure is organized in three core areas: existence, relatedness, and growth. These three terms give rise to the term "ERG" and are the basis of his concept.

Existence needs are similar to Maslow's physiological needs. In other words, they are related to a person's basic human needs—ones that deal with survival, such as having shelter, food, sex, and so on. Relatedness needs focus on those elements that build relationships with others. Growth needs are ones that are focused on an individual's need for personal growth and development. The ERG Model sees these categories as falling on a continuum, rather than having sharp demarcations between them. Further, unlike Maslow's Hierarchy, the ERG model suggests that a person's higher needs might be met before their lower order needs are met, or are in parallel with them. For example, a person might seek opportunities for appreciation and recognition while striving for job security.

Process Theories of Work Motivation

Process theories of work motivation focus on the relationship of inputs to outputs. As Luthans (1998: 175–176) writes, process theories "are more concerned with the cognitive antecedents that go into motivation or effort and, more important, with the way they relate to one another." Theories in this area include the following: (1) Victor Vroom's Expectancy Theory of Motivation, (2) the Porter and Lawler Performance/Satisfaction Motivation Model, and (3) the Smith and Cranny Model.

Vroom's Expectancy Theory of Motivation

Vroom's (1964) theory is built on the concept that motivation is a direct result of three factors: valence, expectancy, and force. His assumption is that choices made by an individual among alternative courses of action are related to psychological events occurring simultaneously with the behavior. Figure 5.7 summarizes the Vroom theory of work and motivation. Vroom indicates that force and motivation are basically the same; they are shown to be the algebraic sum of the products of valence multiplied by expectancy.

Vroom defines *valence* as the strength of the individual's preference for a particular choice. Other words that might be substituted for valence include incentive, attitude, or desire. For valence to be positive, the individual must prefer obtaining the out-

Figure 5.7
Vroom's Expectancy Theory of Motivation

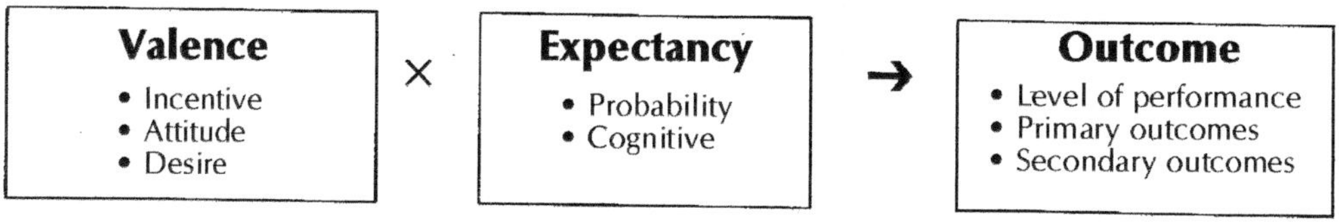

come to not obtaining it. *Expectancy,* the other variable in Vroom's theory, is the probability that an individual might achieve a particular outcome.

As mentioned, the strength of motivation to perform a certain act depends on the algebraic sum of the products of valence and expectancy. To use an example that might better explain the Vroom theory, let's assume that an employee has a desire for promotion. This desire can be strong, medium, or weak. Obviously, the stronger the employee's desire for promotion, the stronger his or her preference. The same goes for expectancy; the possibility that he or she will gain the promotion can vary from a good chance to a very poor chance.

Vroom, in *Work and Motivation* (1964), indicates five properties of work roles: They (1) provide financial remuneration, (2) require the expenditure of energy, (3) involve the production of goods and services, (4) permit or require social interaction, and (5) affect the social status of the worker. Vroom indicates that there is no judgement regarding the priority of these different work roles as they affect the employee's strength of preference for working, but they are contributing factors in why people work. Vroom also maintains that employees who are involved in the decision-making process and have opportunities to interact on the job have lower rates of absenteeism and turnover.

In general, Vroom (1964) made three assumptions about motivation as it relates to ability: (1) People prefer tasks and jobs that require the use of their abilities; (2) people prefer consistent information about their abilities (consistent standards and evaluation) to inconsistent information; and (3)

people prefer receiving information telling them that they possess valuable abilities to receiving information telling them that they do not possess valuable abilities.

Porter and Lawler Performance/ Satisfaction Motivation Model

The Porter and Lawler Performance/Satisfaction Motivation Model basically extends the Vroom Model. They suggest that motivation is very complex and that there may not necessarily be a relationship between job satisfaction and performance, as suggested in the content theory of Herzberg. They suggest that motivation, satisfaction, and performance are variables that need to be addressed as a part of the process. Their model indicates that the value of a reward and the perceived probability of a reward will in turn influence an individual's effort. This, in turn, will be affected by an individual's ability and his or her role perceptions, which then influence performance. Performance, in turn, is tied to rewards, whether they are intrinsic or extrinsic and whether or not a person perceives the reward structure as being equitable. If there is a sense of equitable return between a person's performance and rewards, then they are satisfied.

As one can see, the Porter and Lawler Model involves multiple variables, stressing that many relationships exist between motivation and job effectiveness. Their theory counters some of the traditional, simplistic assumptions made about the positive relationships between satisfaction and performance. They deal with effort, performance, reward, and satisfaction, all of which are interrelated and have an effect on motivation (Porter & Lawler, 1968).

Smith and Cranny's Theory

A motivation model formulated by Smith and Cranny (1968) presents a more simplistic, three-way relationship among effort, satisfaction, and reward. Their model is triangular: each variable is in a corner of the triangle, and each has a causal effect on the other (see Figure 5.8).

A new benefit package (reward) may lead to an increase in satisfaction. In turn, a satisfied, cooperative worker may become eligible for promotion. Performance is affected only by effort, not by reward or satisfaction, as shown in the

Figure 5.8
Smith & Cranny, Motivation Model

Source: Smith, P., & Cranny, C. J. (1968). Psychology of Men at Work. *Annual Review of Psychology, 19,* 469.

model. Performance is in the center of the model and can influence rewards and satisfaction, but can itself be influenced only by the effort of intention. The Smith and Cranny model is a simplistic model; it stresses that a manager's job is to administer rewards. Yet this alone does not have a direct impact on performance and falls short as a way for managers to motivate employees.

Contemporary Theories of Work Motivation

Contemporary theories of motivation focus on perceptual issues related to social equity, locus of control, and factors such as how we interact with others, organizational symbolism, and so on. Prominent among these theories is Festinger and Homans' Exchange Theory of Motivation, J. Stacy Adam's Equity Theory of Motivation, Harold Kelly's Attribution Theory of Motivation, and Reinforcement Theory.

The Exchange Theory of Motivation

This theory of motivation comes from the work of Homans (1961). Basically, this theory suggests that people view each relationship in their work environment as having both benefits and costs. Benefits or rewards can be thought of as the positive elements gained from interactions. In a work environment, these might include being engaged in worthwhile and meaningful work, making friends, earning a salary, and other elements. The costs to an individual would be expressed in terms of time, fatigue, pressure, stress, or in other elements that distract from the individual's well-being.

In Exchange Theory, basically, people measure the benefits against the costs and determine the likely outcomes. If the benefits outweigh the costs, they are likely to maintain the relationship. If not, they are likely to move in another direction. It is difficult to measure the outcomes of any situation, including one's work environment, because there are multiple benefits and multiple costs that don't necessarily yield a linear relationship for measurement. People do, however, compare their experience with previous situations to establish a minimum baseline or standard. For example, in a work situation, a person might ask the question of whether or not the stress of the environment is equal to, less than, or more than in previous work situations. This provides a basis for comparison. They may also assess their current situation in the light of other available alternatives.

This theory helps us understand how people balance different situations that influence their work and life circumstances. It does not explain how people achieve satisfaction in the environment or how performance is linked to satisfaction. It merely helps us understand that tradeoffs are being made when viewing the anticipated costs juxtaposed with anticipated benefits.

Equity Theory of Motivation

The Equity Theory of Motivation is built on the work of J. Stacy Adams. This theory suggests that individual performance and satisfaction in the work environment is affected by the degree of equity or inequity individuals perceive in the rewards that they receive. Basically, the Equity Theory of Work Motivation is built on the notion of social comparison. The idea of social comparison is that individuals' feelings or perceptions of whether or not they are being dealt with fairly occur as they view themselves in relationship to other people. It is based on three basic assumptions:

1. People evaluate their social relationships similar to the way they evaluate their economic transactions.

2. Social relations are an exchange process in which people make an investment and expect certain outcomes in return.

3. People compare their own situation or exchange balance with others to determine their own relative balance.

How does the Equity Theory apply to work motivation? When individuals perceive an inequity in the amount of work that is performed in relation to the awards they receive, it creates a level of dissatisfaction. This dissatisfaction is usually proportionate to the individuals' perception of their conceived inequity. Individuals will attempt to reduce the dissatisfaction by altering their effort or their performance. Cognitively, people also can change the measures that they use to measure their rewards when contrasted with their efforts and performance. Further, it is possible that individuals may irrationally perceive that their effort and performance is greater than the reward structure will allow.

The Equity Theory of Motivation helps us understand how a person's perception can influence the process and, in turn, his or her effort, performance, and job satisfaction. It is difficult to align all of these elements effectively within the work environment for all employees. This is the major challenge for leisure services managers in crafting environments in which individuals are self-motivated. Much of the success of an organization depends on whether or not individuals feel valued, either intrinsically or extrinsically, for their efforts. Also, whether or not people feel valued depends on their perceptions of how they are treated. Often people will leave an organization when they perceive they are undervalued.

Attribution Theory of Motivation

The Attribution Theory of Motivation is built on the work of social psychologist Harold Kelley. What are attributions? We can think of attributions as a process by which we link behavior to its causes—to the intentions, dispositions, and events that explain why people act as they do. Attribution theory helps us understand how, when we interact with others, we interpret their behavior. In other words, attributions help people understand the behavior of others as well as their own. There are two different types of attributions: dispositional and situational. Dispositional attributions refer to internal factors such as an individual's personality, motivation, or ability. On the other hand, situational attributes focus on external factors such as peer influence.

Attributions have a strong influence on how individuals perceive others in the environment. Further, the external symbolic attributions of an organization (its culture) will have a great influence on the work of individuals. People use symbols within the environment to form their opinion of its climate. In addition, individually perceived attributes have a great influence over a person's performance and satisfaction. Luthans (1998:183) uses the concept of locus of control to explain the impact of internal versus external attributions. He suggests, "employees who perceive internal control feel that they personally can influence their outcomes through their own ability, skills, or effort. . . . Employees who perceive external control feel that their outcomes are beyond their own control; they feel that external forces control their outcomes."

The success or failure of a leisure service manager is not determined by their achievements alone, but also by their attributions. Attributions or perceptions can be attributed to many different factors—ability, effort, task comprehension, and even luck. For managers, the quality of their work is perceived as being due to their ability, effort, and task clarity, then they probably feel they would be viewed in a more positive light. On the other hand, if their successes or failures are attributed to luck or even timing, then they might be viewed less positively. Attributions are important because they have an influence on our reaction to others, and they serve as a basis for our perceptions of others' success or failure in their environment. The same can be said of a leisure service manager's attributions of his or her employees.

Reinforcement Theory

It would be difficult to say that Reinforcement Theory of motivation is a completely contemporary model. The ideas are directly traced to the work of the psychologists Pavlov and Thorndike and later to the work of Skinner in the 1950s. Reinforcement Theory is basically built on the idea that people are motivated by external factors. An individual responds to stimuli that lead to a change in his or her behavior. The response to a given stimulus is called a "response." When a person learns ways to respond to a given stimulus, this is called "conditioning." In other words, through the process of learning, certain behaviors can be reinforced through the process of rewards and punishments.

It is interesting to note how individuals will respond to a leisure services manager when they are offered support for their efforts. Reinforcing individuals often involves giving them support in a positive way. It involves recognizing their basic worth, dignity, and value in an organization. Edginton and Griffith (1983:171) have written:

> "Recognition of the inherent value or worth of the individual is central to effective motivation. Each person within a recreation and leisure service organization likes to feel that he/ she is an important part of that

agency's efforts. By reinforcing either the work of individuals or their personal disposition, feelings of self-worth can be enhanced. It is important to recognize that not all jobs have been designed to permit the individual to derive satisfaction from the work itself. Consider the case of a secretary who may do an excellent job, but does not find the work itself challenging. Such a person may be motivated more by reinforcement than by the work itself. By letting that person know that he or she is competent, well-liked, and appreciated, the manager can increase the probability that the individual will continue to function effectively."

Again, Reinforcement Theory focuses on the factors that will increase desired behaviors. The goal is to reinforce the behavior that is desired and encourage it on a repeated basis. This is done by rewarding desired behaviors, and often by ignoring those that are irrelevant to the goals of the organization.

Motivation Studies and Leisure Services

Over the past several decades, numerous studies have been conducted concerning work motivation among leisure service personnel throughout the world. The chief proponent of this work has been Larry Neal (1984) and his associates at the University of Oregon. Neal and others have studied and reported on municipal park and recreation workers, therapeutic recreation specialists, Armed Forces personnel, seasonal camp staff, volunteers, and oth-

ers. Studies have been conducted in Australia, Canada, Hong Kong, Greece, and in the United States. Nearly all of these studies (as described in Table 5.2) have been theoretically based on Hertzberg's Motivational/Hygiene Theory. In general, these studies have focused on what factors motivate individuals, and on the differences in perceptions between workers and managers about what motivates employees.

Neal and his compatriots have found systematically that leisure service personnel are motivated by factors that can be defined as "motivators," in other words, the elements in the work environment that provide for job satisfaction. Such factors as the opportunity to be engaged in "worthwhile work," "opportunities for job growth," "achievement," "recognition," and "having responsibility" are rated highly by respondents in nearly all studies. There are minor exceptions across cultures. For example, Edginton, Neal, and Edginton (1989) reported that leisure service professionals in Hong Kong placed a higher emphasis on salaries or income than on other factors. These findings were consistent with other professional workers in Hong Kong, especially those in the business environment (see Table 5.3).

Many of the motivational studies also looked at the differences in perceptions between leisure service workers and their supervisors. One of the assumptions in many of these types of studies is that there is a difference in what a manager thinks motivates an employee and what the individual employee might feel is important to him or her. The idea is that if this gap can be closed then higher productivity will ensue. Contrary to this assumption, there is little evidence in the studies completed of a difference in perceptions

Table 5.2
An Analysis of Motivation Studies in Leisure Services in the 1980s and 1990s

Author(s)	Theoretical Model	Setting	Research Focus	Findings
Neal, Williams, & Beech (1982)	Herzberg Motivation/ Hygiene Theory	Municipal Parks & Recreation	Compared perceptions of managers and employees on what motivates employees.	There is consistency in perceptions between managers and employees. Motivators rank highest.
Rothschadl (1983)	Herzberg Motivation/ Hygiene Theory	Volunteers	Compared perception of managers and volunteers on what motivates volunteers.	Little difference between motivators & hygiene. There is consistency in perceptions between managers and volunteers.
Voight (1983)	Herzberg Motivation/ Hygiene Theory	Therapeutic Recreation	Compared perceptions of managers and employees on what motivates employees in both clinical and community therapeutic recreation settings.	There is a consistency in perceptions between managers and employees. Difference between hygiene & motivators slight, emphasis on motivators.
Neal (1984)	Herzberg Motivation/ Hygiene Theory	Municipal Parks & Recreation	Compared perceptions of managers and employees on what motivates employees.	Consistency in perceptions between employees and managers.
Cannon (1985)	Herzberg Motivation/ Hygiene Theory	Boy Scouts of America	Compared perceptions of managers and employees on what motivates employees in a non-profit setting.	There is consistency in perceptions between managers and employees. There are differences between and among professional's & volunteers
Summers (1986)	Core job dimensions, job involvement and work motivation.	Municipal Parks & Recreation Business Management	Job satisfaction.	Public park and Recreation managers report greater job satisfaction than their business counterparts
Hoff, Ellis, Crossley (1988)	Herzberg Motivation/ Hygiene Theory	Seasonal Staff	Work motivation of potential summer staff.	Demonstrated that the motivation/hygiene theory is valid when used with seasonal employees
Nogradi & Anthony (1988)	Vroom's Typology	Municipal Parks & Recreation	Core job dimensions, job involvement, and work motivation Job satisfaction of seasonal park and recreation staff	Job design is closely related to work motivation

Continued

Table 5.2 Continued
An Analysis of Motivation Studies in Leisure Services in the 1980s and 1990s

Edginton, Neal & Edginton (1989)	Herzberg Motivation/ Hygiene Theory	Municipal Parks & Recreation	Cross-cultural, Australia, Canada, Hong Kong & United States.	Cultural differences were found amongst respondents
Edginton, Madrigal, Lankford & Wheeler (1990)	Herzberg Motivation/ Hygiene Theory	Municipal Parks & Recreation	Tied to organizational goal study.	Emphasis placed on activities that contribute to organizational motivation
DeGraaf & Edginton (1992)	Herzberg Motivation/ Hygiene Theory	Camps Part-time seasonal staff; viewed different types of camps (public/private)	Motivation of seasonal staff to accept a camp job, work throughout the summer, and return in future years.	Found that similar factors motivate individuals throughout the entire summer.
Lankford, Neal & Buxton (1992)	Herzberg Motivation/ Hygiene Theory	Public, private/commercial, nonprofit and armed forces leisure services organizations	A study between five (5) diverse groups.	Placed a higher emphasis on hygiene factors such as working conditions.
Henderson & Bialeschki (1993)	"Flow"	Camping	Creating "flow" seasonal staff.	Potency, affect, creativity & motivation promote flow.
Nogradi, Yardley & Kanters (1993)	Vroom's Typology Focus on work related attention, job effectiveness and job effectiveness outcomes	Municipal parks and recreation; correctional and health care settings	Core job dimensions, job involvement and work motivation.	Poor job design promotes low motivation Enriched jobs are a way of enhancing motivation
Williams & Neal (1993)	Importance Performance- Technique	Municipal parks and recreation	Proactive survey creation & methodology; MAPS = Motivation, Assessment & Performances Scale.	Little difference between managers and employees with respect to the importance of work motivators in the work environment MAPS is a tool to identify & interpret employee user data; user friendly
Costa (1996)	Herzburg two-factor	National Sports throughout Greece	Within/between superior/subordinates. Compared with USA.	Greek superior/subordinates showed a marked difference; significant difference between USA/Greek respondents
Williams, Lankford, & DeGraaf (1999)	Multiple Work Motivation Techniques	Public, private & non-profit organizations	Exploratory study using NGT Herzberg expert panel; & Pathfinder Analysis.	Multiple theoretical models help us understand work motivation Expands the decision-making of employees' motivation

Table 5.3
**Differences and Similarities Among Professional Park and Recreation Workers in
Australia, Canada, Hong Kong, and the United States as Related to Herzberg's Two-Factor
Motivational Hygiene Theory**

Motivation statement	Australia	Canada	Hong Kong	U.S.	K-W H*
Appointed leader of group	16	20	20	20	143
Quality work	5	1	10	3	69
Increased freedom on the job	15	14	7	13	371.4
Important/worthwhile work	1	2	1	1	NS
Interesting work	4	4	4	4	NS
Personal/work-related goals	6	5	11	6	118.8
Get along with supervisor	8	9	17	7	277.8
Chance for promotion	18	18	5	16	606
Job growth	2	3	2	2	NS
Good working conditions	13	10	9	10	430
Good wages	17	15	3	14	419.4
Get along with co-workers	13	10	9	10	430
Appreciation by supervisor	12	12	15	11	421.6
Help agency attain goals	7	6	19	12	342
Raises and other rewards	20	19	18	19	950
Being part of a team	9	8	16	8	296.7
Job security	10	13	6	9	219.6
Feedback on performance	14	16	14	17	611.1
Shared decision-making	3	7	8	5	76.2
Good benefits package	19	17	12	18	658.8

*Results shown are significant at the .01 level.

Source: Edginton, Neal & Edginton, 1989

between workers and managers. In fact, in studies completed by Voight (1983), Rothschadl (1983), Neal (1984), and Cannon (1985), these authors suggest that there is great synchronization in perceptions between workers and managers in terms of factors that motivate individuals.

It is interesting to note that leisure service managers report different levels of satisfaction with their positions than their counterparts in other professions. For example, Summer (1986) reports that park and recreation managers have greater satisfaction with their jobs than their counterparts in other professions. Further, there is a relationship between high levels of job satisfaction and motivation. Several studies, including ones conducted by Nogradi and Anthony (1988) and Nogradi, Yardley, and

Kanters (1993), report that higher levels of job satisfaction lead to job motivation.

Studies completed among seasonal employees in leisure service settings, especially camp environments, by DeGraaf and Edginton (1992) and Henderson and Bialeschki (1993) have addressed the topic of motivation. DeGraaf and Edginton using Hertzberg's Motivation Hygiene Theory discovered that seasonal employees are motivated by similar factors as full-time employees. They seek "worthwhile work opportunities," "chance for growth," "achievement," and "recognition." Interestingly, these authors have also discovered that, in general, the factors that motivate people at the beginning of their seasonal experience are the same that motivate them at the conclusion of their experience.

Henderson and Bialeschki (1993) applied the theoretical construct of "flow" in relationship to motivation. They found that potency, affect, creativity, and motivation were highly related to enabling individuals to experience flow.

Making the Motivation Process Productive

The motivation process can be made productive by three factors: (1) creating a job and an environment that will be most conducive to employee motivation; (2) creating jobs that are directed toward meeting individuals' needs; and (3) creating an environment that permits employees to perform their jobs while working toward the goals of the organization. In a work situation, individual needs and organizational goals are dependent on each other; if either one is compromised, it will affect efficiency and productivity. The idea is "to make work productive and the worker achieving" (Drucker, 1974:169). Accomplishing this task is not a simple matter. It requires the managerial skills of good leadership and communication.

Employees' needs must always remain central in the thoughts of the leisure service manager. (It must be remembered that as the employee strives to meet his or her needs in a work situation, it may result in released work capacity.) The work capacity of a group of employees channeled in the right direction by the leisure service manager accomplishes the goals of the organization. If employees' needs are not being met, there is a good possibility they will not be motivated, and thus their work capacity will be used in a nonproductive manner. As stressed earlier, the leisure service manager has to find a way to meet employees' needs while also meeting organizational goals. The most successful leisure service manager accomplishes organizational goals by meeting individual employee needs first. Trying to fit employees into jobs that do not meet their individual needs can result in a waste of time, energy, and other resources.

Let us assume that a leisure service manager is assigned a particular task and consequently directs a park supervisor to construct a small building. The leisure service manager's goal is to complete the building. He or she could, with the skills and the time, complete the building himself or herself. The job can be done better and accomplished more quickly by a group of employees, however. The leisure service manager should first analyze the tasks necessary to construct the building. It takes digging and forming for a foundation, pouring cement, bringing water and electricity to the building, laying cement blocks, installing doors and windows, placing the roof, and installing shelves and cabinets, as well as other tasks.

The park supervisor, in assigning the various employees to the various tasks, does not assign them arbitrarily. He or she assigns the tasks to the employees based on their skills. The carpenter constructs the forms, the mason lays the blocks, and so on. To do otherwise would be a waste, and the job might be done poorly and unproductively. Likewise, it would be unproductive to assign an engineer with 20 years' experience to dig the foundation, even though he or she could do the job. If the engineer is not motivated, he or she might do it slowly and poorly and would be overpaid for the job. Although this is an oversimplified example, it makes the point that the abilities of the employee should be matched with the abilities needed for the task at hand to maximize effectiveness, efficiency, and employee satisfaction.

To release work capacity in the employee, the leisure service manager has to design a job that will be conducive to employee motivation. The first step in job design is to find out what the employee wants from his or her job. Designing a job may involve the following: (1) the employee can be asked to list a number of things he or she wants from the job in terms of priority; (2) the leisure service manager and the employee can outline what the goals and objectives of the organization are, and (3) the leisure service manager and the employee can outline or reaffirm the specific tasks of the job for which the individual was hired. The employee should be asked what he or she desires from the job, what goals are to be sought, what ambitions he or she is pursuing, and what he or she hopes to accomplish in the job. By determining and understanding the answers to these questions, the leisure service manager can begin to design a job that will motivate the employee.

After the employee has been on the job for a period of time and the leisure service manager has formed a working relationship with the employee, the manager will begin to recognize certain factors that motivate the employee. It might be a pat on the back, a word of encouragement, or some other form of recognition. Some employees are motivated by added responsibility. In this case, the leisure service manager should attempt to design more responsibility and more independence into the job. Whatever the need may be, the leisure service manager should begin to design into the job the things that meet the employees' needs in order to, in turn, meet organizational goals. In other words, the leisure service manager must manage both work and the employee at the same time, integrating the goals of the organization in the overall work design.

In today's society, "working" is no longer just a matter of earning a salary to provide security. No longer can managers motivate employees by salary, security, and fringe benefits alone. Leisure service organizations must provide work that is meaningful, satisfying, and worthwhile by making the work productive and giving workers the opportunity to achieve. Employees may not necessarily expect work to be enjoyable, but they do expect work to be worthwhile and to accomplish something they feel is of value. On the other hand, to have employees feel a sense of personal achievement while the goals and objectives of the organization go unaccomplished is futile and unprofitable. If this situation exists, ultimately there will be no job for these employees. The leisure service manager must recognize that individuals' needs change, so he or she must constantly change the job to make it motivating and must also provide an environment that is motivating to employees.

Peter F. Drucker, in his book *Management: Tasks, Responsibilities, Practices,* indicates that four separate activities are necessary to make work productive. First, work requires analysis. The leisure service manager should know the specific operations needed for work, their sequence, and their requirements. Second, it is necessary to synthesize the individual operations into a process of production. Third, the process of control must be built in order to maintain and encourage quality, quantity, and standards of excellence. Fourth, the appropriate tools have to be provided. To make work productive, one must start with the end product or service desired. Skills, information, and knowledge are tools of the leisure service manager. When they are applied, these tools must always be related to the desired end product or service.

To enable employees to achieve and find satisfaction in their work, the leisure service manager must provide them with opportunities to take on responsibility in their jobs. This requires meaningful work, reinforcement of positive growth, and continuous learning because it is nonproductive to ask an employee to take responsibility for a job that is boring, meaningless, and unfulfilling. To facilitate employee responsibility, employees should be part of the planning process. They should have input into the work design and the work process. The more the leisure service manager encourages employees to take responsibility for their own jobs, the more responsibility they will take for meeting the goals of quality and quantity.

The role of the leisure service manager is not one of making employees work. It is a fact that employees today are more knowledgeable and have better information and more training than their predecessors. The threat of losing the job is no longer an effective way to make employees work. Also, job security and income stability are no longer factors that motivate employees to work because society has guaranteed these things. Thus, the role of the leisure service manager must be to facilitate the positive development of employees, with organizational well-being as a by-product, so to speak. This is especially critical in a knowledge-based society where employees respond to their opportunities for learning and growth with job satisfaction.

Motivation and Excellence

Have you ever worked in a situation where you couldn't wait to get to work the following day? Have you ever been involved with a group of people who were so exciting to be with that you were drawn to them because of their creativity, dynamism, and enthusiasm? Have you been in an organization that demanded your best performance daily and set high standards? On the other hand, have you dreaded being at work? Have you been in situations where the level of energy and effort put forth by your colleagues was minimal? What's the difference between these two situations? One is an organization that encourages excellence, whereas the other one is mired in mediocrity.

Leisure service organizations that are focused on and wed to excellence will outperform ones focused elsewhere. Excellence implies being superior in some quality, skill, or achievement. Excellence means performing at an extraordinary level. Organizations that focus on excellence seek to raise the level of performance of all individual employees. Leisure service organizations of exceptional merit are ones that have great pride in their effort and do everything they can to ensure that it is done in the best way possible.

To build excellence within a leisure service organization, a manager must cultivate a climate committed to innovation, openness, and a willingness to examine one's internal and external operations on a continuous basis. It requires cultivating a positive and open attitude toward change. To pursue excellence requires the leisure service manager to ask the question, "What attitudes or behaviors are you trying to cultivate within the organization?" An organizational culture that is committed to excellence will challenge individuals in a positive way to grow, develop, and set high performance standards. It is interesting to note that when people are challenged in this way, they often feel good about themselves and their accomplishments. This is not only true for organizations, but also for individuals. When individuals feel good about themselves, they are more productive than when they are depressed. Likewise, when a leisure service organization feels good about itself, it will be more productive.

Many variables are required to build environments committed to excellence. As Edginton and Griffith (1983) have suggested, positive support in work environments can be characterized by many different variables. Environments that do not have a strong commitment to employee development, good interpersonal relationships, and a consideration for each individual as a uniquely contributing member of the organization are ones that often fail the test. These types of environments do not support excellence. Positive, supportive work environments are ones in which common commitments to the needs of the individuals and the goals of the organization are forged.

Exhibit 5.2 outlines some of the elements required of excellence in a positive work environment, as identified by Blanchard and Bowles (1998), Peters and Austin (1985), and Edginton and Griffith (1983). These include the ability to develop trust, promote freedom, respect the style of others, create a commitment to similar goals, promote high output goals, have open communication, share information, engage in group or participatory decision making, create opportunities for posi-

tive interpersonal relationships, engage in team building, develop goals and delineate tasks, provide opportunities for growth, create an appropriate and safe physical work environment, offer recognition, develop positive attitudes, give active support, engage in constant innovation, actively cheer on the support of others, engage in worthwhile work, and promote enthusiasm. These elements create a work environment in which people can be self-motivated and can commit themselves to higher output goals. Excellence occurs when people are self-motivated and they are committed to higher levels of performance.

One of the most effectively managed leisure service organizations is the Girl Scouts of the USA. Rear Admiral (USN Ret.) Marty Evans, National Executive Director of this organization, has developed a leadership model that creates an environment committed to excellence in that organization. Her seven-step process is found in Figure 5.9. This seven-step process has "striving for excellence" as its lead action step to more effective leadership and also includes the following: "to earn trust," "communicate vision," "mentor others," "reflect optimism and enthusiasm," "practice ethical decision making every day," and last, to "keep hope alive." Hope is that feeling inside of you when you know something good is going to happen! Excellence and hope! This is an outstanding set of guidelines, by which to enable people to be self-motivated while encouraging a high level of performance.

Summary

Motivation occurs when individuals are enthusiastic and excited about

Exhibit 5.2
Elements Promoting Excellence in the Work Environment

Trust. Trust is developed when decisions are perceived as being in the interests of all individuals. It is present when individuals have confidence in one another.

Freedom. People need an opportunity to exercise discretion in carrying out the specific details of their jobs. Nothing is more frustrating than having someone looking over your shoulder, dictating your agenda.

Respect for the Styles of Others. People do different things in different ways. It is important to accept the styles of other people. It is possible to disagree without being disagreeable or attacking.

Commitment to Similar Goals. When individuals move in separate directions without a unified purpose or common goal, it is difficult to create a positive work environment.

Commitment to High Output Goals. When expectations are high, performance is also high. Challenge individuals to perform their best.

Open Communications. Avoid hidden agendas, talking behind individuals' backs, double talk, and other negative forms of communication. Be open and honest with one another.

Sharing Information. People have a desire to be informed. Feelings of insecurity, of being left out, and of being unimportant are often associated with negative work environments that do not share information.

Group Decision Making. People want to be involved in decisions that affect their lives. Group decision making may take more time, but it builds stronger commitment.

Interpersonal Relationships. People like to have an opportunity to interact with one another and want to enjoy their relationships with colleagues.

Team Building. Promoting staff unity helps build a positive work environment. Team unity results in a greater commitment on the part of employees to achieving the goals of the organization.

Goal & Task Delineation. Basically, people need to understand clearly what is to be done and have available the means to achieve it. It is the role of the manager to help employees understand their jobs.

Opportunities for Growth. Perhaps the number one reason that people choose to work in one environment over another is its opportunities for growth and development. People want to be stimulated; they want to be intellectually challenged.

Healthy Work Environment. The physical work environment can have an impact on employees. A clean, safe work environment is essential in creating a positive work setting.

Recognition. People need to be recognized for their contributions to the organization. Individuals' self-esteem is enhanced when they feel that they are contributing. Recognition can be an acknowledgement of individual's contributions.

Positive Attitude. Positive mental attitudes are essential in a work environment. Life is too short to be subjected to constant whining, complaining, and other unpleasantness. Approach and live your life with elan.

Active Support. Giving active support means that you are willing to understand the viewpoints, concerns, and needs of others. It implies giving of oneself to others in order to help them grow.

Constant Innovation. In a world of change, organizations that are not committed to innovations will not survive. As Peters and Austin (1985) write, "innovation in business and nonbusiness is highly unpredictable, and the context and configuration must be predicated on uncertainty and ambiguity."

Actively Cheering on Others. Blanchard and Bowles (1998) have written that cheering each other on is an important element in the success of an organization. Congratulations are affirmations that who people are and what they do matter, and that they are making a valuable contribution toward achieving the shared mission.

Engaging in Worthwhile Work. Research studies in the leisure studies field reveal that there is nothing more important to individuals than engaging in worthwhile work. To be involved in organizations that are committed to higher ends or goals and to feel a part of an altruistic endeavor is very motivating.

Enthusiasm. Enthusiastic individuals are ones who can arouse the interest of others. To be enthusiastic is to be inspired. Enthusiasm is contagious and spreads throughout organizations.

Source: Blanchard, K., & Bowles, S. (1998). *Gung ho!* New York: William Morrow: Edginton, C. R., & Griffith, C. A. (1983). *The recreation and leisure service delivery system.* Philadelphia: Saunders; and Peters, T., & Austin, N. (1985). *A passion for excellence: The leadership difference.* New York: Random House.

Seven Action Steps to More Effective Leadership

1   Strive for excellence.

2   Earn trust.

3   Communicate vision.

4   Mentor others.

5   Reflect optimism and enthusiasm.

6   Practice ethical decision making every day.

7   Keep hope alive.

Marty Evans

National Executive Director
Girl Scouts of the U.S.A.

place when the leisure service manager understands the motivation process, recognizes the needs of his or her employees, and is aware of what behavior will result when the employees go about meeting these needs. To be effective, the leisure service manager should know what incentives to include in the job in order to release work capacity from within employees. The leisure service manager who is aware that the only way to accomplish the goals and objectives of the organization is through employees will be productive.

The leisure service manager knows that motivation is a function of the employee's needs, the opportunities available to the employee, the employee's ability, and reinforcement of the positive growth of the employee. In this chapter, we have emphasized that motivation is important because it contributes to organizational harmony, increased productivity, opportunities for growth, improving excellence, increasing employee retention, doing more with less, and providing worthwhile work. The leisure service manager can provide a number of opportunities for employees that will influence the process of motivation. They can set goals that individuals strive toward, provide training and educational programs, and reinforce desired behaviors.

We can think of the process of work motivation as one whereby individuals meet their individual needs while meeting the goals of the organization. Many factors influence motivation. It is a function of needs, opportunities, ability, and reinforcement. To create a motivating environment, one must work to create a shared view of organizational goals, provide a supportive management structure, and make sure that employees feel valued. The effective leisure service manager understands that

the tasks by which they are challenged. Work that contributes to employees' satisfaction, growth, and development while contributing to the accomplishment of organizational goals and objectives is the leisure service manager's aim. Motivation of employees takes as employees strive to meet their needs, it results in behavior that is work capacity. Working with the employees, the effective leisure service manager designs jobs that will meet the employees' needs while accomplishing at the same time the organization's goals.

There are three basic categories of work motivation theories: content, process, and contemporary. Content theories of motivation deal with the elements that move individuals to work. Process theories of motivation compare inputs to outputs and help us understand more effectively the relationship between job satisfaction and performance. Contemporary theories of motivation focus on issues related to one's cognitive perceptual processes, especially as related to issues of equity. Included in the latter category is Reinforcement Theory, which suggests that people may be motivated by external factors and that their behavior may be shaped by conditioning.

In the leisure service field, much of the research has used the Herzberg Motivation/Hygiene Theories. Studies conducted in multiple settings have found that most leisure service professionals identify work elements related to what Herzberg defines as motivators, or higher-order needs. For example, many studies suggest that leisure service professionals value being engaged in worthwhile work opportunities and having opportunities for job growth. Interestingly, there are some differences when compared across cultures in different countries.

Discussion Questions

1. Why is motivation important?

2. Identify and define the basic motivation process.

3. Identify and discuss primary and secondary motives.

4. Define work motivation.

5. Discuss fallacies and motivation.

6. How does a manager's view of human nature affect the creation of motivation in work environments?

7. Identify and discuss theories of work motivation.

8. Trace the evolution of research related to work motivation in the leisure service field. Discuss implications that influence professional practice.

9. How is motivation tied to excellence?

10. How do you create a motivating "gung ho" work environment?

References

Argyris, C. (1957). *Personality and the organization*. New York: Harper & Row.

Blanchard, K., & Bowles, S. (1998). *Gung ho!* New York: William Morrow.

Burns, J. M. (1978). *Leadership*. New York: Harper & Row.

Cannon, E. C. (1985). *A study of perceived motivational factors and the degree of perceived influence of professional administrators within the western region of the Boy Scouts of America*. Unpublished doctoral dissertation, University of Oregon, Eugene.

Costa, G. (1994). A cross-cultural analysis of work motivation by Greek and U. S. recreation employees. *European Journal for Sport Management* (1). 1

Csikszentmihalyi, M. (1991). *Flow: The psychology of optimal experience*. New York: HarperCollins.

DeGraaf, D. G., & Edginton, C. R. (1992). Work motivation and camp counselors. *Journal of Park and Recreation Administration*, 10(4), 37–57.

Drucker, P. F. (1974). *Management: Task, responsibilities, practices.* New York: Harper & Row.

Drucker, P. F. (1980). *Managing in turbulent times.* New York: Harper & Row.

Edginton, C. R., & Griffith, C. A. (1983). *The recreation and leisure service delivery system.* Philadelphia: Saunders.

Edginton, C. R., Hudson, S. D., & Ford, P. M. (1999). *Leadership in recreation and leisure services organizations* (2nd Ed.). Champaign, IL: Sagamore Publishing.

Edginton, C. R., Madrigal, B., Lankford, S., & Wheeler, D. (1990). Organizational goals: Differences between park and recreation managers and board or commission members. *Journal of Park and Recreation Administration, 8*(2), 70–84

Edginton, C. R., Neal, L. L., & Edginton, S. (1989). Motivating park and recreation professionals: A cross-cultural analysis. *Journal of Park and Recreation Administration, 7*(3), 33–43.

Henderson, K. A., & Bialeschki, M.D. (1993). Optimal work experiences as "flow": Implications for seasonal staff. *Journal of Park and Recreation Administration,* 11 (1), 37–48.

Hersey, P., Blanchard, K. H., & Johnson, D. (1996, April). *Management of organizational behavior: Utilizing human resources.* Prentice-Hall.

Hoff, A., Ellis, G., & Crossly, J. (1988). Employment motives of summer job seekers in recreation settings: A test of Herzberg's Motivation/Hygiene Theory. *Journal of Park and Recreation Administration.* 6(1), 66–73.

Homans, G. C. (1961). *Social behavior.* New York: Hardcourt, Brace, Jovanovich.

Lankford, S. V., Neal, L. L. & Buxton, B. B. (1992). An examination and comparison of work motivators in public, private/commercial, non-profit, and Armed Forces leisure service organizations. *Journal of Park and Recreation Administration, 10*(4), 57–70.

Luthans, F. (1998). *Organizational behavior.* Boston: Irwin McGraw-Hill.

McGregor, D. (1970). *The Human Side of Enterprise.* New York: McGraw-Hill.

Neal, L. L. (1984). Motivational discrepancy between staff levels in municipal leisure services. *Journal of Park and Recreation Administration, 2*(4), 25–29.

Neal, L., Williams, J., & Beech, S. (1982). How managers perceive subordinates. *Journal of Health, Physical Education, Recreation, and Dance, 53*(4), 56–58.

Nogradi, G. S., & Anthony, P. (1988). Perceived job characteristics, job involvement, and work motivation: An examination of the relationships for seasonal municipal recreation employees. *Journal of Park and Recreation Administration, 6*(3), 113.

Nogradi, G. S., Yardley, J. K., & Kanters, M. A. (1993). The relationship between work related attention, motivating potential of jobs, and job effectiveness outcomes. *Journal of Park and Recreation Administration,* 11(3), 37–50.

Peters, T., & Austin, N. (1985). *A passion for excellence: The leadership difference.* New York: Random House.

Peters, T., & Waterman, R. H. (1982). *In search of excellence: Lessons from America's best-run companies.* New York: Harper & Row.

Peters, T., & Waterman, R. H. (1988, October). *In search of excellence: Lessons from America's best-run companies.* Warner Books.

Porter, L., & Lawler, E. (1968). *Managerial attitudes and performances.* Homewood, IL: Richard D. Irwin.

Rothschadl, A. M. (1983). *A comparison of volunteers' and their supervisors' perceptions of volunteer motivation in the city of Salem, Oregon, Regional Parks and Recreation Agency.* Unpublished master's thesis, University of Oregon, Eugene.

Smith, K. V. (1965). *Behavior, organization and work: A new approach to industrial science.* Madison, WI: College Printing and Typing.

Summers, D. (1986). Recreation and park administration versus business management: A comparative job analysis. *Journal of Park and Recreation Administration, 4*(4), 8–22.

Taylor, T. F. (1967). *The principles of scientific management.* New York: Norton.

Voight, A. E. (1983). A national study of perceived motivational factors and the degree of perceived influence of supervisors and subordinates. Unpublished doctoral dissertation, University of Oregon, Eugene.

Vroom, V. H. (1964). *Work and motivation.* New York: Wiley & Sons.

Williams, A. E. (1992). *Motivational assessment in organizations: An application of importance-performance analysis.* Unpublished doctoral dissertation, University of Oregon, Eugene.

Williams, A. E., & Neal, L. L. (1993). Motivational assessment in organizations: An application of importance-performance analysis. *Journal of Park and Recreation Administration,* 11(2), 60–71.

Chapter

6

Structuring the Leisure Service System

Structuring leisure service organizations often involves arranging human and other resources to effectively achieve organizational goals.

Photo courtesy of the Orange County (Montgomery, NY) Dept. of Parks, Recreation and Conservation.

Introduction

Effective leisure service organizations structure their activities in such a way as to encourage productivity. The structure of an organization often reflects and supports its culture. Certain organizational structures are open, whereas others are closed. Certain types of organizations enhance innovation, creativity, and the flow of information, others promote close control and direction. In this chapter, we will explore the structuring of leisure service organizations and discuss the interrelationships that exist among a number of environmental factors. More specifically, discussion will center on the char acteristics of formal organizations, the types of organizations providing leisure services, and the factors involved in structuring leisure service organizations. In addition, four organizational structures—bureaucracy, systems theory, decentralization, federation, network, and virtual—are presented, and examples of their application to leisure service delivery systems are discussed.

Organizational Culture

Schein (1985) has suggested that the idea of culture can be applied to any social unit. We can think of a leisure organization as a social unit, deliberately constructed to provide benefits in the form of leisure experiences, areas, and facilities to those it serves. When we think of an organization's culture, we think of its basic assumptions, in other words, the way it views itself and relates to its environment. The concept of culture permeates all of our being. At the broadest level, we think of civilization in the context of developed versus undeveloped countries, eastern societies versus western societies, open democratic societies versus closed totalitarian societies, and so on. According to *Blackwell's Dictionary of 20th Century Social Thought,* "the most striking single fact about the history of humankind is the extraordinary diversity of social forms produced by beings of either the same or very nearly the same genetic type" (Outhwaite & Bottomore, 1994). This diversity is possible because culture provides us with an opportunity to transmit and learn differences.

The culture of a leisure service organization may be the most powerful factor influencing its success or failure (Edginton, 1987:129). It helps define expected behaviors and relationships between and among employees and those served by the leisure service organization. Some leisure service organizations have very strong and easily identifiable cultures. Others are more fragmented and difficult to understand. Deal and Kennedy (1982:4) note that "every organization has a culture. Sometimes it is fragmented and difficult to read from the outside . . . whether weak or strong, culture has a powerful influence throughout an organization. It affects practically everything—from who gets promoted and what decisions are made, to how employees dress and what sports they play. Because of this impact, we think that culture also has an major effect on the success of an organization."

Exactly what is an organization's culture? Schein (1985:9) has indicated, an organization's culture can be thought of as "a pattern of basic assumptions—invented, discovered, or developed by a given group as it learns to cope with its problems of external adaptation and internal integration—that has worked well enough to be considered valid and, therefore, to be taught to new members as the correct way to perceive, think, and feel in relation to those problems." Six common ways that meaning is transmitted within leisure service organizations and other social units are the following:

1. Observed behavioral regularities when people interact, such as the language used and the rituals around deference and demeanor

2. The norms that evolve in working groups, such as the particular norm of "a fair day's work for a fair day's pay" that evolved in the bank wiring room in the Hawthorne studies

3. *The dominant values espoused* by an organization, such as "product quality" or "price leadership"

4. *The philosophy* that guides an organization's policy toward employees and customers

5. *The rules* of the game for getting along in the organization; "the ropes" that a newcomer must learn in order to become an accepted member

6. *The feeling or climate* that is conveyed in an organization by the physical layout and the way in which members of the organization interact with customers or other outsiders

As Edginton (1987) has noted, a leisure service organization's culture can be planned, or it can occur by happenstance. The culture of a leisure service organization can be embedded in or reflected in its organizational structure or design. The organizational design promotes ways of interacting and communicating with one another within the organization. The organizational structure can be top-down and hierarchical, or it can be more open, fluid, and organic. Structure influences culture; culture influences structure. They should reflect one another. Because the culture of any leisure service organization can be managed, it can be planned, taught, and transmitted to its employees. The structure of an organization often reflects its core values, its basic assumptions about how it operates.

The Formal Organization

The way that a leisure service organization is formally structured can have great impact on its effectiveness and efficiency. The formal organization can best be thought of as encompassing *the roles that are assigned to individuals* working within the system. This means that each individual within an organization is given a functional responsibility to carry out. Thus, members within the organization can be held accountable for their actions. Further, the manager can identify patterns of communication among individuals and an organizational member's status can be identified. The role of the manager in a formal organization is to staff it, train members of the organization in their various responsibilities, and evaluate members' performance to ensure that the goals and objectives of the organization are being achieved.

Obviously, each individual brings to the organization different skills, interests, and personality traits that will affect his or her perception of organizational goals. Dissatisfaction within organizations commonly occurs when there is a discrepancy between the employees' and the manager's concept of their respective roles. In many cases, the rigidity found in organizational structures is the cause of this dissatisfaction. Can anyone recall when a job description was tailor-made to an individual? The function of the manager is to integrate the goals of the organization and the design chosen to achieve these goals with the individual needs of the members of the organization. When these factors are well integrated and compatible, success is assured.

As indicated, leisure service delivery systems, as organizations, are deliberately constructed social units designed to attain a set of goals and objectives. They are made up of individuals and have a unique set of characteristics. These elements are universal, they can be identified in any organization. Identification of these factors allows us to differentiate between an organization and a social grouping, such as a family or church group. Four key elements can be identified that are characteristic of organizations:

1. Goal Seeking. Leisure service organizations are goal seeking. Typically, they are involved in the creation of leisure services to satisfy the needs and desires of a given set of consumers. They are constructed to bridge the gap between people's needs and the organizational resources to achieve those needs.

2. Assignment of Tasks. Leisure service organizations are involved in the assignment of tasks. To accomplish the goals set forth by an organization, there must be a division of labor whereby the responsibility for completing the various work units of the organization is assigned. This commonly allows for the creation of specialized subunits within the organization to carry out the organization's work efficiently and effectively.

3. Power Centers. Within leisure service systems are positions of authority, responsibility, influence, and status. These positions ensure that decision making is possible, and that the allocation of the organization's resources is undertaken by individuals or units within the organization that are held accountable.

4. Interlinked with the Environment. Leisure service organizations are interlinked with other environmental contingencies. Leisure service organizations interface with a host of environmental subgroup and these subgroup affect the decision-making process within the organization. The methods used to determine goals and objectives and the way resources are acquired and distributed are examples of factors that can be strongly influenced or determined by external environmental factors.

Structuring Leisure Service Organizations

The form of any leisure service organization must be related to the goals and objectives it strives to achieve. To carry out tasks and assume responsibility within the leisure service delivery system, people must be organized. The establishment of a formal organizational structure allows the leisure service to integrate and coordinate its resources and direct its activities toward the attainment of goals and objectives. The structuring of an organization may well determine the degree to which it is productive. Certainly, human energy, fiscal resources, and technical resources might be used in an ineffective and inefficient manner because of an inadequate formal organization. For example, consider the plight of a park maintenance worker who is locked into a slot on an organizational chart that involves routinized work and that lacks opportunities for recognition and achievement. Further, leisure needs of many people go unmet because some organizations are organized too rigidly to respond to changing behavioral patterns. Several other factors should be taken into consideration when determining contingencies. These include goals and objectives, basic work activities, environmental factors, and structural variables.

Goals and Objectives

Goals and objectives are the ends toward which a leisure service organization directs its efforts. Goals are broad statements that provide general direction to an organization. Objectives are specific statements that set forth a reasonable set of expectations that can be achieved. They usually include some dimension of time; as such, they are quantifiable and can be evaluated or assessed. The process of setting goals and objectives is involved in the establishment of a goal hierarchy. Usually the goals of a system are derived from its basic vision, mission, or purpose. Then its objectives, both long-range and short-range, are determined. Any objective within an organization is tied to and dependent on a higher set of goals. Frequently, the relationship between goals and objectives is misunderstood. In many cases, the day-to-day operational aspects of the leisure delivery systems are not related to the broad, general goals of the system. This results in confusion because questions of decision making, responsibility, and accountability do not follow any systematic or consistent framework.

What is the relationship between the goals and objectives of a leisure delivery system and its organizational structure? The structure is dependent on the goals and objectives; however, the goals and objectives are defined, to a degree, by the structure. Therefore, it is extremely important that the structure of an organization reflect or take into account its goals and objectives. If a leisure delivery system emphasizes grassroots participation in the decision-making process, then perhaps a flexible organizational structure that allows for external input is appropriate. On the other hand, there are instances in which input needs to be focused through one channel within the structure; this may call for a more rigid organizational structure that controls input, allowing it to take place only within certain limitations, to avoid chaos.

Basic Work Activities

As mentioned in Chapter One, all leisure service organizations are involved in a number of basic work activities. These fundamental work activities are: (1) the management of financial resources, (2) the creation of a leisure service, and (3) the distribution of the services. They provide a basis on which leisure delivery service can be formally organized. This approach to structuring leisure services is called the "functional approach" to organization.

Consider the provision of leisure services by a private organization. The organization performs a service by creating activities and facilities. Structured activities such as instruction in macramé or building a swimming pool, illustrate the provision of services. For the consumer, these activities represent something of value that has been brought into existence by this type of organization. For the leisure delivery system, the activity of creating services is its reason for existence. Work that results in the creation of services is the primary function of the organization.

Once the service has been created, the next important function is to distribute it to those who wish to consume it. The service must be packaged and promoted appropriately if it is to reach those it is intended to serve. Macramé instruction may be organized in a formal classroom setting, at a specific time, with a specific set of dates, and may have structured lessons, all of which allow for the attainment of a specific set of skills. On the other hand, it may be organized as a club to provide opportunities for advanced skill development. Or a macramé program may be organized in an arts center on a drop-in basis, being structured informally to allow the participant to set his or her own goals. These activities may be offered at different times during the day and at different days of the week or times of the year. Further, the activities may be promoted through a variety of methods, including newspaper articles, brochures, and flyers. The general idea is that the service will be distributed to the consumer in an appropriate form, at the right time, and at the right place. Finally, the organization must manage the finances needed to create and distribute the service. It charges fees and invests funds as a way of acquiring the capital to provide services. In addition, the financial resources accumulated must be accounted for properly to ensure that they are dispersed in an appropriate manner.

These three activities (also known as line functions) provide a foundation on which formal organizational structures are developed. They must be performed in some manner if an organization, any organization, is to exist.

Staff functions, on the other hand, are those that support the three basic work activities. As an organization increases in complexity, support functions such as personnel and research usually increase. The expertise that is necessary to manage these support areas ensures the prominence of the three basic work functions. Hiring a specialist to manage the personnel functions of an organization, for example, allows other individuals within the structure to concentrate on performing their basic work activities.

Environmental Factors

One of the most important factors to consider when designing an organization is change in the environment. Change has become a dominant factor influencing institutions, as it forces society to reexamine or reevaluate its attitudes and beliefs. Expanding technology has resulted in a flow of new goods and services and has brought about the creation of new knowledge that affects organizations. For example, Dent (1998) notes that today 25 percent of youth earn college degrees compared with 2 percent in the early 1900s. Also, the work ethic is changing. Religious beliefs that in the past have affected society's attitudes toward work, leisure, and play are rapidly evolving. Perhaps the most cherished of our traditional institutions is that of the Protestant work ethic. By aligning hard work with righteousness, the Protestant work ethic indirectly glorified material gains. A new ethic, emphasizing "personal responsibility and situational ethics," has emerged (Ryterband & Bass, 1973:69). This is forcing organizations to look at their authority structure and allow individuals to assume more responsibility.

Other institutions that are undergoing change include the family and educational institutions. The movement from an extended family structure to a nuclear family structure has produced a reaction to predetermined roles such as authoritarianism, and has led to a host of new attitudes. This trend in behavior has extended into the work environment. In addition, whereas the family was the center of life in past decades, organizations may have to assume this responsibility in the future.

Structural Variables

A number of organizational structures can be used in the delivery of leisure services if the appropriate factors for their use are in evidence. The effectiveness and efficiency of an organization will, in large part, depend on the manager's ability to use structure that is appropriate for the needs of his or her constituents. In the past, the responsibility for organizational failure, has been directed mainly toward the people in the organization rather than the organizational design. Park and recreation departments have traditionally relied on one method of organizing services, rather than selecting more appropriate forms. In a society characterized by change, a high rate of mobility, highly educated people, and sophisticated technology, meeting leisure needs requires a flexible and innovative organizational design. The dynamics of leisure are such that organizational responsiveness is tied to the survival of the organization. Organizations that can evolve to meet changing leisure trends and needs will flourish; those that cannot will experience diminished productivity.

Mechanistic versus Organic Organizations

Organizational designs can be viewed on a continuum. Certain types of organizational structures operate more effectively and efficiently when the environment is stable. Others are better suited to environments in which change is a factor. Those that are capable of dealing with change are known as "organic organizations" (Litterer, 1973:335–336). "Mechanistic organizations," on the other hand, are more appropriately used in stable situations.

Organic structures are best able to deal with rapid and unpredictable changes in the environment within which they operate. When an organization produces a variety of goods or services for a large cross section of individuals, its need for flexibility is great. It demands a structure that is adaptable to "changing conditions where the problems to be faced are not predictable and are usually new, removing the possibility of establishing, in advance, programs for their solutions" (Litterer, 1973: 336). Organic structures do not have fixed roles that are defined in hierarchical form. Litterer describes ten characteristics of an organic organization:

1. Special knowledge and experience possessed by organization members is looked at in light of what they can contribute to the common or overall task. That is, expertise is not evaluated in terms of how well a person can meet the requirements of a job, but what he or she can contribute to the goal to be accomplished.

2. Closely connected with this is the idea that each individual's task is looked at from the point of view of what it contributes to attaining the overall goal in terms of the current situation or problem. The question is, "Is it relevant?" not, "Is it glamorous?" Assignments or methods are not rigidly fixed.

3. The set of rights, obligations, and methods become more limited as defined fields of responsibility diminish or disappear. People tend more often to ask: "What needs to be done?" rather than: "What am I responsible for?" Individual tasks are less sharply defined and are continually being redefined. People feel a responsibility or commitment to the overall work at hand and not just to their specific jobs or areas of technical expertise.

4. Typically, problems are not pushed off upward, downward, or sideways as someone else's problem. The continual redefinition of tasks occurs through interaction with others, most of whom are not supervisors.

5. Control, authority, and communication move through a wide network rather than a single hierarchical structure. Sanctions may be applied by many people other than hierarchical superiors, and these are derived from a community of interest rather than a contractual relationship with a central authority.

6. Omniscience is no longer imputed to the head of the organization. Knowledge of what is appropriate can exist anywhere in the organization, depending more on individual information and skill rather than hierarchical position. The locus of this expertise becomes the ad hoc center of authority and communication. Authority may be decentralized or polycentralized.

7. Interaction tends to be much more lateral than vertical. Commu-

nication between people of different ranks involves much more consultation than command.

8. Content of communication consists of information and advice rather than instructions and decisions. This is in keeping with the concept of local units maintaining control by using local feedback rather than by instructions or plans.

9. People are committed to the organization's task and "technological ethos" of material or service progress and expansion rather than to loyalty and obedience. They would not say: "My organization, right or wrong," but rather: "My organization, I want it to be right."

10. Prestige is attached to the expertise and affiliations that individuals have in the general or social milieu external to the organization (337–339).

Mechanistic organizations operate more successfully in an environment that has stabilized. When an organization produces the same good or service for a defined set of individuals with similar interests and needs, it is said to be operating within a stable environment. The consistency in problems facing the organization allows it to prepare standard responses to those situations. The work of the organization becomes fixed, routine, and systematic in nature. The 10 characteristics of a mechanistic organization are as follows:

1. The overall goal or problem the organization is working on is broken into tasks differentiated by the functions they fill, and specialization is carried as far as possible.

2. Each functional role, or each task, has precisely defined rights, obligations, and technical methods; that is, there is a high order of standardization.

3. People in positions of carrying out these tasks are concerned with doing their job as defined. Furthermore, they take pride in developing their technical expertise in doing the task, as contrasted with having a concern for the overall goal of the endeavor.

4. When problems between positions occur, they are settled by referring them to superiors, who reconcile differences in a way that is relevant to their own special part of the overall task.

5. Control, authority, and communication usually follow hierarchical patterns.

6. There is a general assumption throughout the organization that higher-ups are in a better position or are better equipped to make decisions. Hence, they can handle the more difficult decisions, and their decisions should take precedence over decisions made at lower levels because they are more likely to be correct. This reinforces the hierarchical structure and makes things centralized.

7. Interaction tends to follow hierarchical lines, primarily between superior and subordinates.

8. Operations and working behavior tend to be governed by instructions and decisions issued by superiors, which in turn may come from an overall plan.

9. There is a strong insistence on loyalty to superiors and to the organization as a condition of membership.

10. Prestige is attached to expertise in the rules and procedures of the organization or on one's hierarchical position in the organization, as contrasted with having general knowledge about a field or what one can contribute to the overall objective. Prestige is attached to local or internal rather than general or cosmopolitan knowledge, experience, and skill. (337-339)

Because organizations are viewed as being on a continuum, moving from rigid and mechanistic to flexible and organic types, a number of factors must be taken into consideration when developing the organizational structure. Of importance is the degree to which these factors are applied in the development of form of organization. For example, certain types of organizational structures require a higher degree of specialization than others.

Pugh, Hickson, Huntings, & Turner (1968) identified six dimensions involved in structuring formal organizations. These dimensions—specialization, standardization, formalization, centralization, configuration, and flexibility—are discussed below:

1. *Specialization.* This involves the division of labor in such a way that the tasks performed in an organization are distributed or concentrated within a number of positions. The

extent to which an organization has specialized may be recognized by the number of positions within the organization relative to its size.

2. *Standardization.* This entails a system of rules and regulations that allows an organization to maintain consistency within its structure. Adherence to a set of abstract rules ensures that an organization will maintain stability, on the one hand, but on the other, it may render an organization inflexible and unable to meet change.

3. *Formalization.* When an organization's philosophy, principles, policies, and procedures are documented carefully, it is said to be a highly formalized organization. Organizations that have not precisely delineated their methods in written form are said to be less formalized.

4. *Centralization.* This dimension can be determined by locating the positions in an organization that have the authority to make decisions. Highly centralized organizations find decision-making concentrated in a few individuals. Decentralized organizations find decision making authority dispersed throughout the organization. Obviously, this authority can be placed on a continuum, with certain types of organizations having decision making more highly concentrated than others, and vice versa.

5. *Configuration.* This term refers to the placement of positions within the organization. Certain organizational structures look like pyramids; others are linear in appearance.

6. *Flexibility.* Flexibility involves the ability to accommodate to change. Certain types of organizations adapt readily to changes in the environment, whereas others adapt poorly, if at all. Flexibility can also be placed on a continuum. Organizations that are rigid are mechanistic; those that adapt to change readily are organic.

Figure 6.1 illustrates how each of the factors of goals and objectives, basic work activities, environmental change, and structural variables affects the delivery of leisure services. First, the goals and objectives of the organization are affected by environmental factors. Changing attitudes toward work force an organization to be more concerned about its management goals. The organization is forced to become more receptive to employees' needs for creativity, expression, self-esteem, and recognition. As leisure behavioral patterns change, the output goals and objectives will in turn affect not only what is produced in terms of goods and services, but also how they are produced. Variables within the organizational structure will be modified, producing a new structural form that meets it goals. This cycle may be continuous in an environment where change is the dominant factor. Structures that are rigid and not adaptable to changing traditions are generally not effective. However, in an environment where stable conditions are present and change is not a dominant factor, rigid mechanistic structures may be appropriate.

What form of structure should a leisure service organization take—organic or mechanistic? At first it would seem that the answer to this question is obvious. Certainly, we live in a period

Figure 6.1
Factors Influencing the Structuring of a Leisure Service Organization's design

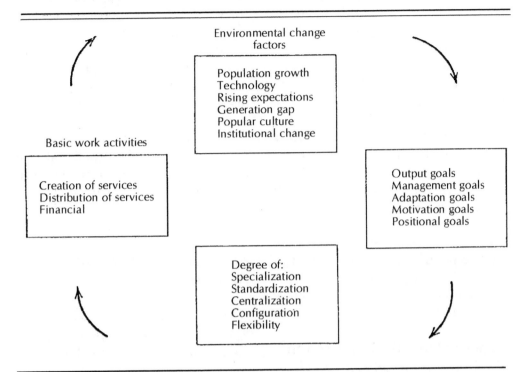

Environmental change
factors

Population growth
Technology
Rising expectations
Generation gap
Popular culture
Institutional change

Basic work activities

Creation of services
Distribution of services
Financial

Output goals
Management goals
Adaptation goals
Motivation goals
Positional goals

Degree of:
Specialization
Standardization
Centralization
Configuration
Flexibility

when change is a dominant factor affecting society. Leisure behavioral patterns change rapidly and are thought to be addressed by a dynamic delivery system that is also standard and routinized in nature. Parks have become an accepted governmental service. Individuals expect parks to be included among those services provided at the local, state or provincial, and federal levels. The procedures used to maintain these facilities have been delineated clearly, and fixed routines have been established, so it would seem that the type of organizational structure to be used would depend on the specific service being offered to the public.

The maintenance of park areas may be better organized into a mechanistic structure, where a set of fixed standards can be applied. For example, the quartz lamps used to light a baseball diamond have a predictable number of burning hours. A maintenance schedule can be established to systematically replace these bulbs based on number of hours of usage. In this case, the maintenance function is predictable and can be organized using a rigid structure. Many park and recreation departments have established work schedules that outline their daily, weekly, monthly, and yearly work operations. Therefore, a mechanistic structure that provides for systematic control may be useful in this particular situation.

On the other hand, behavior that results from any one person's involvement in leisure activity is highly individualized. The establishment of predictable norms of behavior, from which standards can be developed, is limited. The relationships that develop between a recreation leader and the persons participating in the activity are highly personalized ones. The ability of the leader to adapt general theories and concepts to the needs of each person being served requires a high degree of flexibility.

Because of the highly personalized nature of the recreation and leisure experience and the rapid change taking place in society, especially as it relates to the consumption of leisure services, there is a need to organize services that are highly adaptable. The need for a flexible structure may indicate that the programs should be developed in an organic organizational manner. Of course, there are exceptions to this suggestion. In programs where participant safety is of prime importance, as in aquatic programs, a more rigid set of rules and procedures must be applied. A mechanistic organizational structure would probably be better in this case.

Types of Organization Used in the Delivery of Leisure Services

Four organizational forms that are used in the delivery of leisure services will be described in the latter part of this chapter; the bureaucratic model of organization, the systems approach to organization, decentralization, and the federation method of organization. As shown in Figure 6.2, they can be distributed along a continuum with the bureaucratic form of organization, which is the most rigid structure, at one end, and the virtual approach which is the most flexible, at the other. Several other organizational methods can be used in the delivery of leisure services, including the free form model of organization, the collegial model of organization, the egalitarian approach to organization, and still others. Although discussion of all the models of organization has not been undertaken, this should in no way diminish their importance or their potential applicability in the delivery of leisure services. The forms of organization chosen for discussion represent the four most distinguishable forms currently practiced.

Bureaucratic Model of Organization

The bureaucratic model of organization has perhaps been the most widely implemented and analyzed form of organization. It is based on the assumption that authority rests at the top of the organization and flows downward throughout the organization. In this way, superior and subordinate relationships are developed among individuals within the organization. As such, each individual is subject to:

> ". . . an authority system where supreme authority rests somewhere above an employee, and the employee's responsibility consists basically of obeying orders and performing those tasks

Figure 6.2
Organizational Forms Used in Delivery of Leisure Services

Mechanistic: Rigidly Structured Organizations	Bureaucratic	Decentralization	Network	Organic: Flexibly Structured Organizations
	Systems	Federation	Virtual	

which are inherent in his particular job." (Rice & Bishoprick, 1971:20).

This division of labor allows for the establishment of an organizational hierarchy. The establishment of superior–subordinate relationships makes adherence to the lines of authority in an organization possible. This arrangement allows each of the organization's work activities to be subdivided into a specific set of tasks. From this arrangement, roles entailing responsibility and authority can be determined.

Max Weber's principles, along with those of Henry Fayol, have provided the foundational principles of classical organizational theory (as discussed in Chapter Two). Many of the characteristics of Weber's bureaucratic model of organization are inherent in the following management principles: (1) unity of command, (2) span of control, (3) authority and responsibility, and (4) scalar and functional processes. These principles, on which the bureaucratic model of organization is based, are discussed below:

1. *Unity of Command.* Unity of command implies that each individual in the organization is responsible to one single supervisor. In this way, authority is distributed throughout the hierarchy of the organization from the highest to the lowest position. This is known as "the chain of command." It has been suggested by many that individuals work more effectively when they are responsible to only one person. Without adherence to this arrangement in a bureaucratic organization, confusion results.

2. *Span of Control.* This may be defined as the number of individu-

als who are directed by a manager. It is generally believed that the number of subordinates an individual should oversee should be limited. Although there is not a fixed number of people that can be identified as a "manageable" group, it is generally assumed that supervising more than six individuals will diminish a manager's effectiveness and efficiency. A number of factors may influence the ability of a manger to supervise any given number of people. Lynn S. Rodney and Robert F. Toalson (1981:41-42) write that these factors include the following:

a. *Diversity of Services.* When division of work is complex or diversified, there is more need for supervision than if the work is repetitive and requires few decisions or personal conferences.

b. *Executive Skill.* The energy, adaptability, and skill of some executives vary from those of others; hence, the span of supervision of these people will vary.

c. *Skill of Employees.* Untrained and unskilled employees require more time and effort to manage than those who are more highly competent.

d. *Non-supervisory Relationships.* A person's duties other than those related to a supervisory function seriously cut down on the time spent in supervision.

e. *Stability of Operation.* A highly dynamic work situation in which turnover of employees is high calls for more coordination and control; hence, it limits the time available for supervision.

f.   *In-Service Training.* Some units require considerable on-the-job training; hence, less time can be spent on supervising others.

g.   *Type of activities.* Supervision of other executives or other administrative activities entail different responsibilities than of supervision of operating employees. Each process requires a different amount of time; hence, there is a variance in the span of control.

3. Authority and Responsibility. Once a person is obligated or has the responsibility to perform a task, he or she must be given commensurate authority to complete it. It is frustrating to be required to perform a certain function without the proper support. Managers need authority to make decisions, direct subordinates, and expect accountability from their subordinates, because in a bureaucratic organization, authority is passed down the hierarchy from one level to the next. For example, an aquatic supervisor receives authority from his or her superior, who may be the superintendent of recreation. If authority cannot be delegated, hierarchical structures cannot develop. Delegation of authority is a continuous activity of organizations. But in one respect, responsibility cannot be delegated: When a manager delegates authority within an organization, he or she does not relinquish responsibility for the successful completion of those tasks assigned to the individuals under his or her direction.

4. Scalar and Functional Processes. Scalar and functional processes deal with the horizontal and vertical growth of the organizational form. What is suggested by this principle is that the functions of the organization can be placed in a coordinated hierarchical structure. This provides for the establishment of lines of authority from the top of the organization to the bottom. Managers occupy the top level of the organization, supervisors the middle level, and those individuals providing direct services the lower levels (see Figure 6.3). The lines of authority in this arrangement run from the manager at the top through the supervisory level to those at the direct-service level on the bottom. Communication travels from either end of the hierarchy through these channels of authority.

Figure 6.3 shows how various functions within a bureaucratic structure are arranged in a hierarchy. Depicted in pyramid form, the authority to develop policy rests at the top of the structure and the primary service of the organization is located at the bottom. At the policy level within this structure, legislative guidelines are created that affect the organization's activities. Individuals working as managers are responsible for directing and implementing the guidelines as developed at the policy level because they straddle the policymaking and administrative levels. At the next level, the administrative level, is involved in the organization, promotion, and development of services. Here, administrators provide direction to an organization by enforcing policy. The third level in the bureaucracy is known as the supervisory level. Although supervisor may directly orga-

Figure 6.3
Levels of Bureaucracy

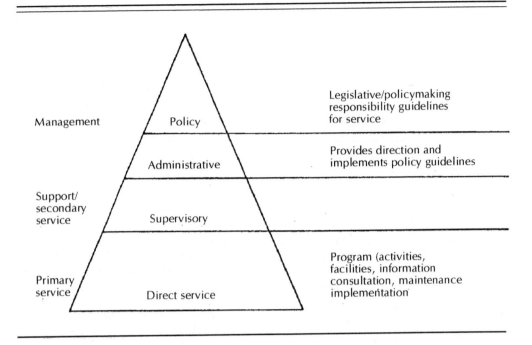

nize and implement services, their role usually does not entail providing face-to-face leadership. Primarily, they act in a supporting role, providing information, direction, supplies, motivation, inspiration, and control to individuals involved in the creation or distribution of the good or service. The last level in the bureaucratic structure comprises those people who actually create or distribute the product or service. These individuals may be operators of machines or recreation leaders engaging in face-to-face leadership.

Types of Ownership in Private Leisure Service Organizations

In profit-oriented organizations, the type of ownership will have great bearing on the way the organization is structured as a bureaucracy. There are three types of business ownership in the United States and Canada: the sole proprietorship, the partnership, and the corporation.

Sole Proprietorship

When the management and ownership of an organization are the same, it is known as a sole proprietorship. In this form of ownership, one individual is responsible for the organization's debt and management practices. It allows one individual to claim all the profits of the business, as well as to use the tax benefits available. This method allows a great deal of freedom of action for the individual who owns the company, because he or she is able to make all decisions that affect the creation and distribution of services. Seventy percent of all businesses in North America are organized in this way. Obviously, it is technically the easiest method to use when formulating a profit-oriented enterprise. Sole proprietorship is fundamental to ensuring competition in the free market.

Eighty percent of the businesses organized as sole proprietorships fail. Therefore, it is important to explore some of the disadvantages of this method of ownership. The primary disadvantage is the unlimited liability of the owner. Unlimited liability refers to the responsibility of the owner for all business debts incurred, even if such financial obligations require his or her *personal* assets (e.g., home, car, savings). Another limitation of the sole proprietorship concerns the restrictions inherent in a business run from only one person's perspective; the talents (managing, marketing, etc.) necessary to successfully operate a business may not all be possessed by one person. It is true that the owner may be able to hire such help, but without the chance for advancement—potential partnership, partial ownership of the business, and so on—as an incentive, qualified talent may be difficult to attract and hold. Another significant drawback to this type of ownership is its lack of continuity in the event of the owner's death.

Partnership

A partnership exists when two or more people decide to join together to form a business. It is the least popular form of ownership. Although a specific written agreement between the partners is not legally required, most partnerships have a written document that spells out the liabilities and responsibilities of each partner. This prevents misunderstandings and helps individuals avoid problems in the operation of their business.

There are four types of partners found in this type of business ownership:

1. At least one partner must assume unlimited liability for the activities of business. He or she is known as the "general partner."

2. "Limited partners" are individuals who have assumed a limited role in the business; they do not have the same financial responsibilities as the general partner. As a result, their authority is usually limited.

3. When a partner keeps his/her identity unknown to the public, he or she is known as a "secret partner." A secret partner can participate in management, but usually has limited financial responsibility.

4. The partner who invests only money is known as the "dormant partner." A dormant partner is not involved in the management of the organization and is liable only for the amount of his or her investment.

A partnership has several advantages, among which are ease of formation, increased availability of financing, diversification of management skills, certain tax advantages, and a high level of personal interest as partners in the business. In addition, a partnership has a clearly defined legal status. The main disadvantages of a partnership are the mandatory unlimited liability of at least one of the partners, possible discord between partners, and difficulties that arise in conjunction with dissolving a partnership or the withdrawal of one partner. If, for some reason, one partner wishes to withdraw from the business, he or she must gain the approval of the other partners. This can make it difficult to withdraw one's investments and can be time-consuming. When a partnership is dissolved, the entire business must be liquidated, which may represent a loss of the entire investment. A great disadvantage may occur when a partner dies, because the partnership may have to be liquidated as part of his or her estate.

Corporation

Corporations constitute approximately 20 percent of all businesses and account for 80 percent of the annual sales of all businesses. The corporation may be defined as a legal entity existing only on paper and in the eyes of the law. A corporation has all the rights and privileges of an individual; it is an artificial being. A corporation can buy, sell, own, manage, and dispose of property. It can sue or be sued. A corporation, as the legal owner of the business, is made up of shareholders who are liable only up to the amount of their investments.

The structure of a corporation is hierarchical in nature. At the top of any corporation are its shareholders. These shareholders are represented by a board of directors; the board is responsible for representing the rights and interests of the shareholders. It oversees the day-to-day operation of the organization, formulates its short- and long-term goals and objectives, and hires the corporation's management team.

The major advantage to organizing a business as a corporation is the factor of limited liability, that is, liability only up to the unit of one's investment; there is no personal liability required by law. Another advantage is the increased ability of a corporation to obtain capital; it may sell shares of stock and borrow money using corporation assets as collateral. Corporations also provide an efficient method for transferring ownership. One's shares may simply be sold in order to liquidate one's investment in a given corporation redidly. Because a corporation is not dependent on one or more individuals, it has almost unlimited continuity. In other words, if one owner (shareholder) dies, the corporation continues to operate. Corporations may employ a professionally trained management team, which usually results in more effective and efficient management practices.

There are a number of disadvantages to organizing a business as a corporation. For one, not only is the corporation itself responsible for paying taxes, but individual shareholders are also taxed on their investments. Essentially, this results in double taxation. Another disadvantage may be the costs associated with incorporating. At the level of the very small corporation, these costs may not appear great; but costs increase proportionately with the size of the organization that wishes to incorporate. There is a standard percentage per share issued that the company must pay in addition to other fees. Corporations must also adhere to a number of governmental regulations, which are policed quite heavily (e.g., equal employment, truth in advertising). Last, corporations are essentially public entities. They must publish their financial statements and company activities, which reduce the amount of privacy within the corporation. With the proper court order showing just cause, any shareholder has the right to inspect the corporation's financial accounts.

The Public Administration Model of Bureaucracy

In North America, the goals, objectives, and policies of public leisure service delivery systems are determined by the constituents served. The right to influence public institutions is inherent in the democratic way of life. Services important to society's welfare have, in many cases, come under the direct control of the public. The public administration model of bureaucratic organization has evolved to accommodate this fact.

The public administration model of organization provides direct opportunities for participation in the establishment of goals and objectives and in the formulation of policy. To control its activities, a group of individuals is elected or appointed to a board or commission to guide the bureaucracy. Their responsibility is in the formulation of policy, and the bureaucracy's function is to carry out or implement policy. Although there is not always a division today between the formulation and implementation of policy, this system affords a rational approach to involving consumers within the rigid framework of the bureaucratic structure. It provides an opportunity for individuals to influence those institutions that affect their lives. Any public leisure service system that uses the bureaucratic form of structure operates, at least in principle, with a public administration model of organization.

There are three types of boards or commissions that are found in public leisure service delivery systems: separate and independent boards, semi-independent boards, and advisory boards (Artz, 1973). Separate and independent boards are autonomous units that have the authority to develop and enforce policy. Those who serve on this type of board may be elected by the constituents they serve, or they may be appointed by a governmental functionary. They are able to operate independently of other governmental bodies and are usually given jurisdiction to exercise certain rights, including the levying of taxes.

A semi-independent board does not have the full powers that separate and independent boards have. Although this type of board may be charged with the establishment and implementation of policy, ultimate authority may rest with another decision-making body. To control the activities of this group, final financial authority is usually held by another legislative body.

Advisory boards serve as a means for individuals to participate in a bureaucratic structure. They make recommendations to other legislative bodies; however, these suggestions have no formal authority.

Development of a Bureaucratic Structure

Public nonprofit and private profit-oriented leisure service organizations do not necessarily follow similar patterns in the establishment of a bureaucratic structure. Figure 6.4 illustrates the arrangement of the work activities of a private leisure organization governed by a board of directors. In a smaller organization, the board may be able to directly supervise those individuals who are hired on a part-time basis to handle each of the basic work activities. As the organization grows in scope, size, and complexity, the board may employ a manager on a full-time basis to implement the directions of the board. Figure 6.5 shows this new organizational arrangement. The manager supervises those functions that are formally handled by the board. No longer is the board involved in the organization and implementation of services. This responsibility has been delegated to the manager, and the bureaucratic structure has begun to grow vertically. Assuming that the organization continues its growth, the manager may have to hire individuals on a full-time basis to supervise each of the work areas. Thus, the organization has again expanded in a vertical fashion.

Figure 6.4
The Basic Work Activities of a Profit-Oriented Leisure Service Organization

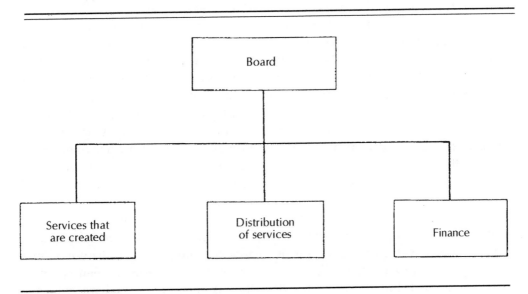

Figure 6.5
An Expanded Profit-Oriented Leisure Service Organization Bureaucratic Organization

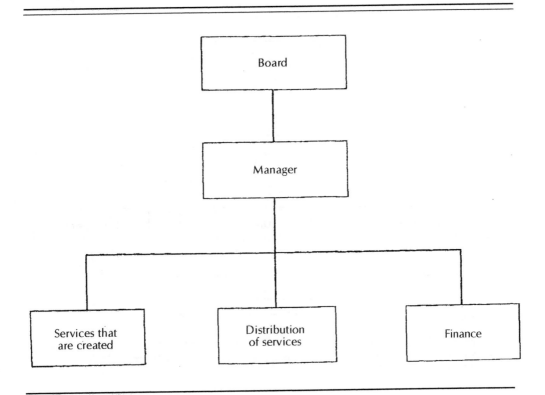

As the workload continues to increase, the organization continues to grow taller and taller. The work activities regarding the creation of services might be subdivided into two sections. One section might have an individual in charge of youth services only, and the other might have someone in charge of adult services only. Not only can a structure be subdivided along functional lines, but activities can also be geographically distributed. The work activities relating to the distribution of services (see Figure 6.6) might be subdivided into two districts, which represent the geographic areas the organization serves. The organization is still growing, even though the tasks have been subdivided, but the growth has been horizontal as well as vertical.

The organization may grow further by adding other functions to assist the three areas. These new services, which are created to provide support, are known as "staff functions." The three basic activities are known as "line functions" and must be performed for the organization to survive. As previously mentioned, the two staff functions are personnel and research. As an organization grows, a full-time personnel manager may be needed to hire and train staff, manage employee benefits, and monitor employee problems.

As public parks, recreation, and leisure services have stabilized, becoming an accepted and permanent fixture of local government, patterns of organization reflecting their functions have emerged. Rodney and Toalson (1981) write that

Figure 6.6
An Enlarged Profit-Oriented Leisure Service Bureaucratic Organization

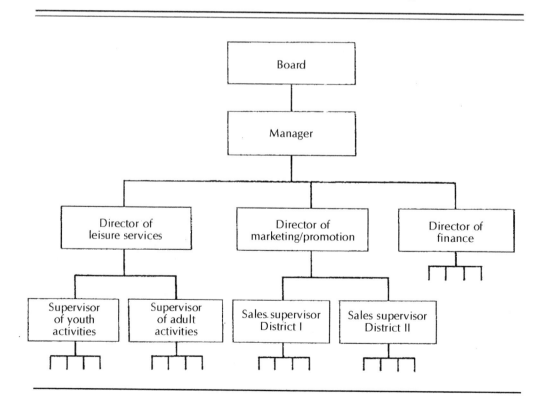

there are 11 divisions commonly found in parks and recreation departments: special facilities, aquatics, playgrounds and centers, construction and maintenance, special programs and facilities, administration, engineering, horticulture, police, forestry, and botanical gardens and arboretum. Figures 6.7 through 6.13 are organizational charts that show differences in the way the various tasks found in public park and recreation departments are organized. These charts represent departments in Joliet, Illinois; Willamalane, Oregon; Cedar Falls, Iowa; Coronado, California; Burnaby, British Columbia; Black Hawk County, Iowa; and Phoenix, Arizona.

Joliet (Illinois) Park District. Established in 1922, the Joliet Park District is administered by a separately elected board of commissioners. This independently elected board serves as the governing body of the district in charge of establishing services, hiring and evaluating staff, and developing strategies for revenue acquisition. The district is organized into four major units: natural resources, revenue facilities, recreation and parks, and golf operations. The Joliet Park District serves a population of 95,000 (see Figure 6.7).

Willamalane (Oregon) Park and Recreation District. Another example of an organizational structure governed by a separate, independently elected board of directors is the Willamalane Park and Recreation District. Founded in 1944, this leisure service organization has two basic divisions: recreation services and park services. The district serves a population of 58,000 and includes several unique areas, such as the historical Dorris Ranch and the Splash Swim Center. Support services such as public affairs, human resource management and financial management are op-

erated in a sub-unit within the Office of the Superintendent. (See Figure 6.8)

Cedar Falls (Iowa) Department of Human & Leisure Services. The Cedar Falls Department of Human and Leisure Services operates as one of five departments within the government of the City of Cedar Falls. The organizational chart for the Department of Human and Leisure Services is found in Figure 6.9. As one can see, there are three primary divisions: recreation, parks, and cultural services. The department comes under the direction of the mayor and city council form of government and is supported by an advisory park and recreation board. Cedar Falls is a midwestern community of 35,000.

Coronado (California) Recreation Department. Coronado, California, is an oceanside community in southern California with a population of 26,000. Established in 1886, this unit is a part of the city government supported by an advisory recreation commission appointed by the mayor and the city council. This Recreation Department has three divisions: aquatics, activities, and beach management. It is supported by an administrative staff. The Recreation Department works closely with the Public Services Department, which is responsible for maintaining areas such as parks (see Figure 6.10).

Burnaby (British Columbia) Parks, Recreation, and Cultural Services Department. This Canadian community of nearly 180,000 operates a complex and diverse leisure service system. Figure 6.11 presents the organizational chart for the district. It includes six divisions: parks, cultural services, recreation services, food services, golf operations, and support services. Operating as a part of city government, this unit is

Figure 6.7
Joliet (Illinois) Park District Organizational Chart

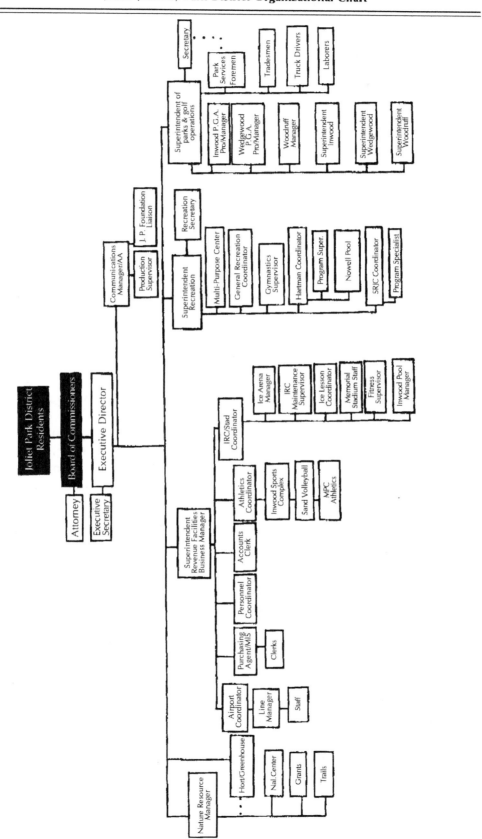

Figure 6.8
Willamalane (Oregon) Park and Recreation District Organizational Chart

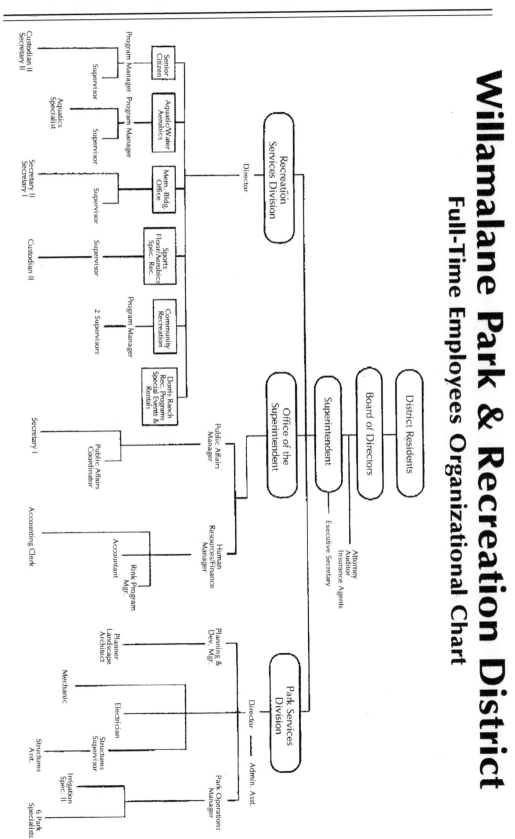

Figure 6.9
City of Cedar Falls (Iowa) Organizational Charts for (a) Department of Human and Leisure Services, (b) City Government Divisions and Departments, and (c) City Services

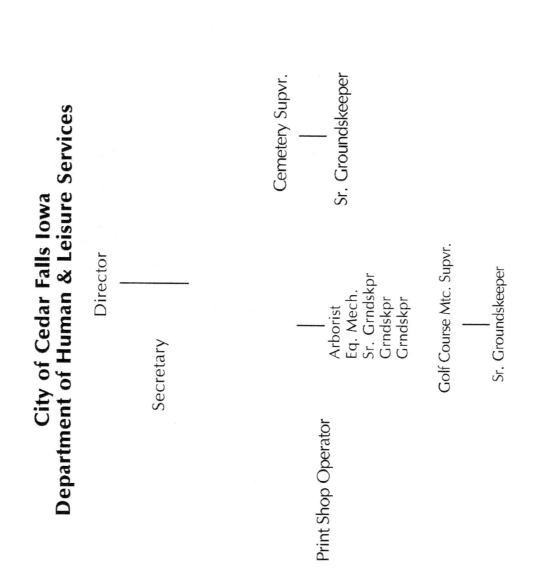

Figure 6.10
Coronado (California) Recreation Program Organizational Chart

Recreation

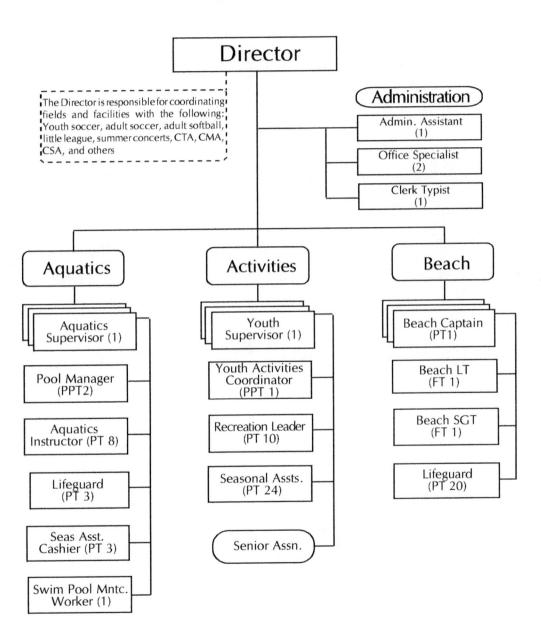

Director

The Director is responsible for coordinating fields and facilities with the following: Youth soccer, adult soccer, adult softball, little league, summer concerts, CTA, CMA, CSA, and others

Administration

Admin. Assistant (1)

Office Specialist (2)

Clerk Typist (1)

Aquatics

Aquatics Supervisor (1)

Pool Manager (PPT2)

Aquatics Instructor (PT 8)

Lifeguard (PT 3)

Seas Asst. Cashier (PT 3)

Swim Pool Mntc. Worker (1)

Activities

Youth Supervisor (1)

Youth Activities Coordinator (PPT 1)

Recreation Leader (PT 10)

Seasonal Assts. (PT 24)

Senior Assn.

Beach

Beach Captain (PT1)

Beach LT (FT 1)

Beach SGT (FT 1)

Lifeguard (PT 20)

Figure 6.11
Burnaby (British Columbia) Parks, Recreation, and Cultural Services Department

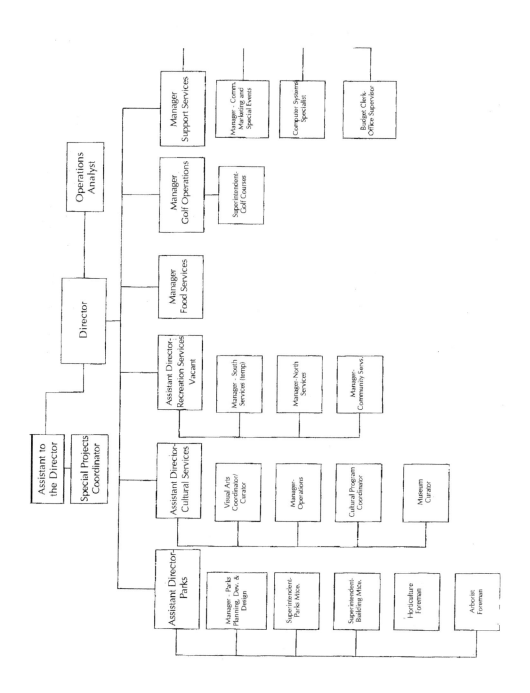

Figure 6.12
Black Hawk County (Iowa) Conservation Board Organizational Chart

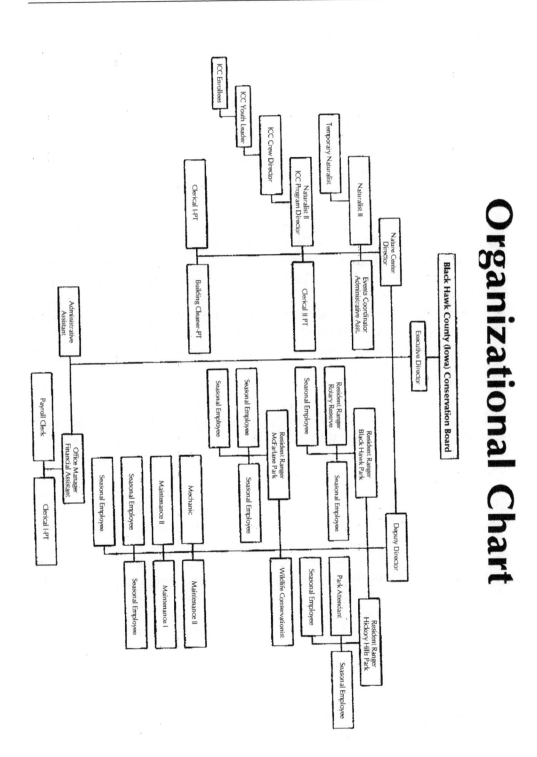

supported by a seven member park, recreation, and cultural services advisory commission. The Park, Recreation, and Cultural Services Department traces its establishment back to 1932.

Black Hawk County (Iowa) Conservation Board. Figure 6.12 presents the organizational chart for the Black Hawk County Conservation Board. Governed by the board of supervisors of Black Hawk County, this board appoints a five-member board of directors to direct the affairs of the unit. Founded in 1957, this park and recreation system manages over 7,000 acres of park lands for a county population 125,000. The organization is broken into two basic units: one dealing with nature center operations, and the other with park maintenance functions.

Nonprofit organizations also have characteristics similar to government agencies in terms of organization. However, because their funding patterns are different, they often are attentive to membership development or resource development. The organizational chart presented in Figure 6.13 demonstrates this design feature.

Boys & Girls Club of Waterloo (Iowa). The Boys & Girls Club of Waterloo is a private, nonprofit agency, affiliated with Boys & Girls Clubs of America and the Cedar Valley United Way. Founded in 1966, the mission of the Boys & Girls Club of Waterloo is to inspire and enable all young people, especially those from disadvantaged circumstances, to realize their full potential as productive, responsible, and caring citizens. With a membership of over 1,000, the Boys & Girls Club is focused on youth development. Figure 6.13 showns the organizational chart of the unit and reflects its two primary divisions: program development and re-

source development. Waterloo is a community of approximately 64,000.

Systems Approach

A systems analysis allows the manager to look at the interrelationships that exist among the various components of the environment. As indicated in the systems model, leisure services can be viewed on a macroscale or a microscale. By viewing the interrelationships that exist within the total environment on a macroscale, the manager is able to make more productive decisions. This allows the manager to acknowledge the relationships that exist among various subsystems within the environment, then to integrate their effects into the leisure service organization. With this information, the leisure service manager is better able to recognize, interpret, and act on those factors that can affect the organization. The manager may position the organization's resources to adapt to constraints, based on his or her ability to view the leisure service organization as part of a larger environment.

The leisure service organization itself is also a system. It is a microenvironment operating within a larger system. As such, the activities of the organization can be thought of as being composed of many subsystems. These subsystems, operating internally, are interconnected within a hierarchy. Each subsystem produces a set of expectations that ultimately result in behavioral outcomes. For example, staff behavior may result in the creation of leisure services or in the establishment of a supportive work environment, or it may breed a nonsupportive work environment. An infinite number of behavioral outcomes can be produced because there are many

Figure 6.13
Waterloo (Iowa) Boys & Girls Club Organizational Chart

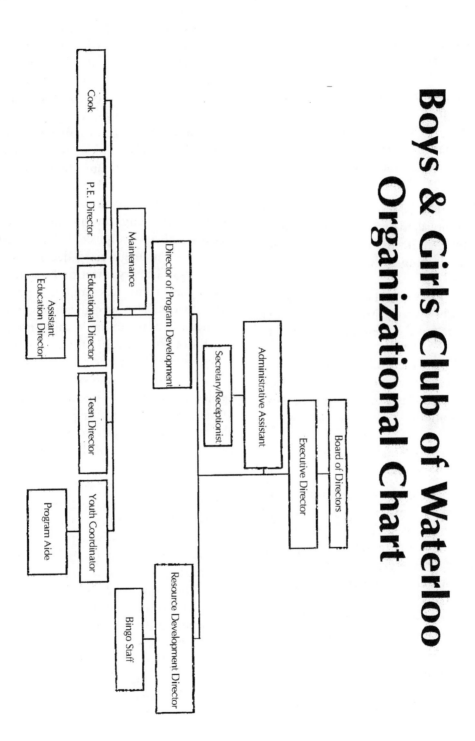

potential subsystems within an organization. The critical factor in using systems theory is to recognize that subsystems can be deliberately constructed to produce a specific set of outcomes, such as the completion of selected tasks or the creation of a supportive work climate.

Applying systems theory to the management of park maintenance, Gerald Bethal (1971:12) outlined the procedure that is illustrated in Figure 6.14. The flowchart indicates the following steps:

1. The tasks that need to be accomplished (inventorying the maintenance needs of each facility and developing a task list)

2. How each task is to be accomplished with consideration for materials and equipment to be used

3. The methods of integration of tasks to be accomplished with organizational standards and available resources

4. A work schedule based upon the above factors

The Marshalltown (Iowa) Parks and Recreation Department has made use of the systems method in their park maintenance operation. This approach involves the integration of a general set of maintenance standards with specific work procedures, which in turn yield a routine, for each of their facilities.

Edginton and Eldridge (1975) have described how systems theory can be applied in creating a more humanistic environment via the provision of a program of developmental training in park and recreation systems. They suggest that a developmental training program not only can contribute to the output objectives of an organization, but can also provide opportunities to satisfy human needs, both intrinsic and extrinsic (see Figure 6.15)

An extension and refinement of systems theory practiced today is known as "modular organization." In this approach to organizing services, the manager organizes each of the tasks of a specific process or project into functional units. Modular organizations are comprised of a number of units whose activities are coordinated by an established management hierarchy. Functional units may vary in size and composition, depending on the project or process to be accomplished. The initial role of the manager is to decentralize the work of the organization by assigning the authority to complete a given unit of work. This specialization allows an increase in flexibility because it creates the opportunity for alternative structures within each project team.

There are five types of modular, or project, structures. The first is "individual project organization," in which the individual project manager completes the assignment by himself or herself without the assistance of other staff members or support teams. The second type of project organization is called a "staff project organization." The individual is involved in leading the project and is given enough support and backup services to complete the task. The third type exists when the manager has the joint responsibility of overseeing line and staff functions and selected projects, or modular units. This is known as "intermix." The fourth type is known as "aggregate project organization." In this arrangement, the project manager is responsible for all the functions necessary to complete a given assignment. The fifth, the "matrix organization," occurs when the project

Figure 6.14
Process of Developing a Maintenance System

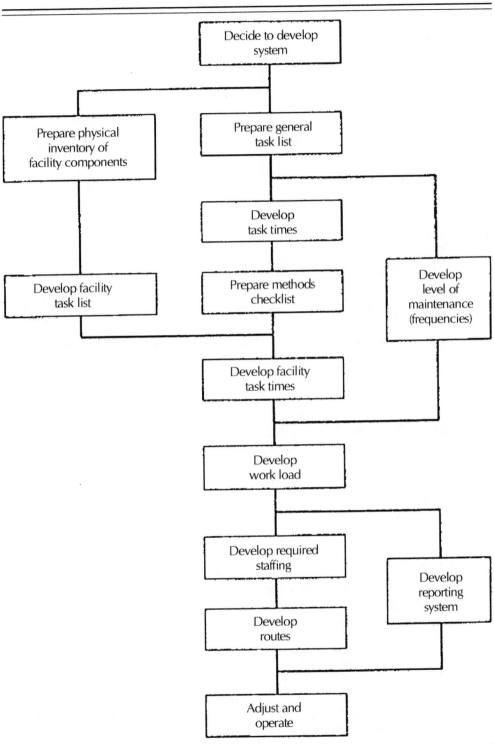

Source: Bethel, G. (1971, April). A systems approach to management of park maintenance. *Park Maintenance,* p. 12. Used with the permission of *Park Maintenance Magazine,* Box 1936, Appleton, WI.

Figure 6.15
Matrix Organizational Structure

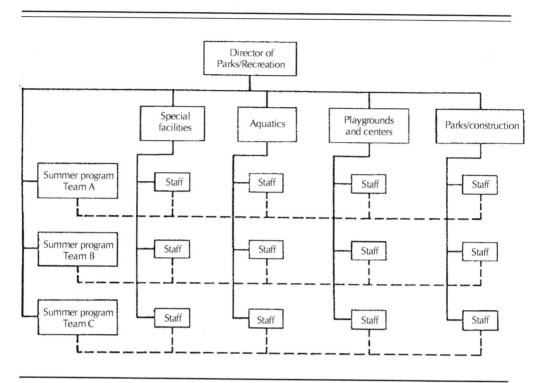

organization exists side-by-side with the more traditional bureaucratic structure (see Figure 6.15). Individuals operating within this type of organization may have dual responsibilities. One is the normal or regularly assigned responsibility, and the other responsibility would be the work of the project team.

The Borough of North York (Ontario) Parks and Recreation Department has adopted project management as a method of using its resources and expanding services. This method of organization created flexibility and freedom within its structure, which allowed it to develop new ideas and approaches in meeting the leisure needs of the constituents it served. By establishing project teams, staff members were not fitted to prescribed jobs; rather, they were assigned to groups of appropriate individuals. This allowed the supervisors directing administrators and park per-

sonnel to work directly with recreation programmers. Groups were formed to meet shifting leisure patterns brought about by a changing environment. As these groups fulfilled their goals and objectives, they were dissolved. As new challenges came into being, new groups were formed.

Decentralization

The drive to make the delivery of leisure services more effective and more efficient has turned the attention of many managers toward the concept of decentralization. As organizations have become more complex, there has been increased concern for finding ways to place individuals in decision-making positions closer to the people receiving services. As a bureaucratic structure grows vertically, there is a tendency toward inefficiency. The structure becomes an end in itself rather than a means to an end. Rules and procedures are established and enforced rigidly, with no apparent relationship to one another, even as layering within the bureaucratic structure increases.

Jack W. Perez (1970) has suggested that parks and recreation departments need to develop organizational structures that have the ability to respond quickly to local cultural needs. He writes that large communities are made up of many cultural groups requiring specialized services. To deal with each of these groups in a meaningful way, parks and recreation departments must focus resources effectively on each group's concerns. He notes that decentralization has proved to be a successful leisure delivery strategy in the following ways:

1. It provides gauge of local feelings and attitudes through instant communication and feedback

2. It promotes special programs of community interest

3. It provides a rapport between recreation administrators and the people who receive recreation services

4. Local business is expedited with dispatch

5. Each of the directors of the centers in the area is afforded the opportunity to meet with the supervisor regularly, with the knowledge that his or her boss, so moved, can act on any concerns. (20)

Why would a leisure delivery system want to decentralize its operations? Leisure is dynamic, and there is a need for organizations to be flexible and have the ability to respond to change quickly. Organizations that have concentrated authority at levels closest to the constituency they serve may be more effective. Further, by providing opportunities for individual initiative and responsibility among lower-level staff, job satisfaction is increased. As previously mentioned, people today tend to be more highly educated, thereby having the capability to make their own decisions. Young people are less willing to accept authoritarian direction. They desire work environments that are democratic and that allow individuals to have responsibility commensurate with their potential. A highly motivated group of individuals, having authority and operating at levels close to the constituents they are serving, should increase the effectiveness and efficiency of a leisure delivery system.

What Is Decentralization?

The concept of centralization/decentralization is tied to the methods used to delegate authority within an organization. In a centralized organization, authority is concentrated among a few individuals. Decentralized organizations are ones in which authority has been dispersed in the structure in some way. In determining whether an organization is centralized or decentralized, it is very important to be aware of how much and in what ways authority has been dispersed. As indicated in Chapter One, organizations are affected by and respond to a variety of environmental constraints. These factors may vary from community to community. Thus, the degree to which organizations decentralize will vary, In addition, the methods used to decentralize will vary, according to the circumstances involved. For example, a public leisure delivery system may be organized to respond to the needs of people in different geographic areas or from different cultural groups.

Fred Luthans (1998) writes that there are three types of centralization/decentralization. The first involves the geographic arrangement of a system's operation. The term "centralized," in this case, refers to the placement of all an organization's operations in one location. In contrast, decentralized geographic location disperses the organization's operations throughout the locale of the constituency it serves.

The second type of centralization/decentralization deals with functional units within an organization. Referring again to maintenance in community park and recreation departments, certain departments centralize the maintenance function by locating it administratively under a superintendent of parks. All the maintenance functions within the organization are then directly under his or her authority. Decentralization would occur if the authority and responsibility for handling maintenance functions were to be assumed by each program area within the department. For example, the custodian at a recreation center would be placed under the supervision of the center director in charge of that facility.

The third type of centralization/decentralization deals with the "retention or delegation of decision-making prerogatives or command" (Luthans, 1998:522). This involves determining the amount of decision-making power that is placed at the various levels within an organization. Within certain leisure delivery systems, a great deal of authority, hence decision-making power, is placed at various levels within the organization. In others, power is concentrated only in the management posi-

tions. This particular concept may not be apparent, according to Luthans, merely by seeing the structure of an organization.

This last factor, the delegation of authority, is perhaps the fundamental concept of decentralization. In many situations, managers are unwilling to delegate authority because they lack self-confidence or fear their employees. Many individuals are accustomed to making their own decisions and do not want to give up this power. This conflict makes decentralization difficult. Thus, even if an organization has dispersed geographically or functionally, if authority to make decisions does not accompany this dispersion, decentralization may not really have occurred. The rate at which decisions are made may, in fact, have increased, rather than the efficiency increasing. According to David Buchanan and Andrzej Huczynski (1997:326), the following are advantages of decentralization:

1. lower-level decisions can be made more easily

2. lower-level management problems can be dealt with on the spot

3. lower-level managers have an opportunity to develop their decision-making skills

4. the motivation of lower-level managers is greater when they are entrusted to make decisions rather than always following orders issued at a higher level

5. an organization's workload is spread to allow top-level managers more time for strategic planning.

The plan of decentralization adopted by the Calgary, Alberta, Parks

Figure 6.16
Decentralization Plan of Calgary (Alberta) Parks and Recreation Department

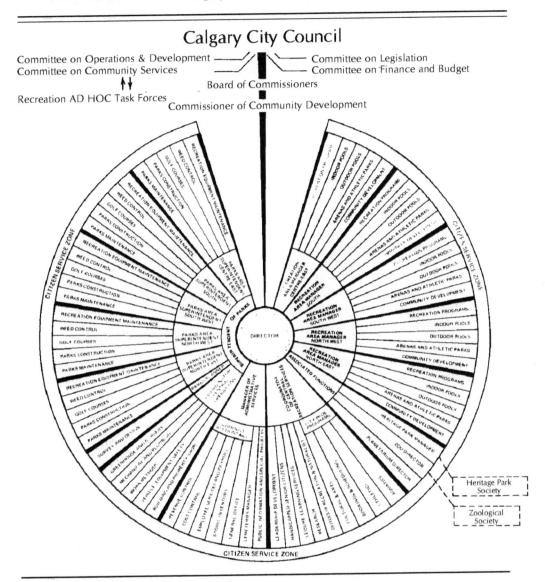

and Recreation Department (see Figure 6.16) is an example of how this concept can be implemented from a philosophical, methodological, and structural perspective.

Federation Model of Organization

The federation model of organization allows several specialized groups to associate freely with one another in a flexible organizational framework. It is a method whereby specialized groups having independent modes of operation and interest can combine with each other to pursue a set of common goals. In this way, each group within the federation may contribute the talent, abilities, and skills of its members to a larger extent. Organized within a loose democratic structure, specialized groups are autonomous units that have very little authority over other specialized groups within the federation. Each group is thought to be an equal partner with the other groups. The key features of the federation concept of organization include the following:

- Specialized groups work cooperatively toward a set of common goals.

- Specialized groups are autonomous, independent, and self-sufficient.

- Because of the voluntary nature of involvement, the authority structure of the federation lacks the coercion found in the mechanistic method of organization.

Specialized groups in the federation must work in concert with each other to pursue the goals established. The cooperative nature of involvement in a federation is therefore a key factor. The success of each specialized group will contribute to the achievement of the federation's overall goals, so the welfare of each group is important to every other group. If one specialized group fails in some way to successfully fulfill its purpose, its downfall will affect the other groups. Thus, it is beneficial for groups within a federation to take an interest in the activities of the other groups. It is not uncommon to find one group advocating the concerns of another group while pursuing its own interests. This cooperative approach to the delivery of leisure services is perhaps most appropriate in a society characterized by great demand and dwindling resources. In many cases, organizations have operated competitively in the delivery of leisure services. Naturally, in other cases, this has diminished the organization's effectiveness because it has resulted in the diluting of resources and has led to confusion on the part of consumers.

Another key feature of this concept of organization is that specialized groups remain autonomous and free to conduct their own activities. Groups are free to choose any form of organization that best suits their needs. They are free to pursue their own goals and objectives while working toward the overall mission of the federation. In this way, they are allowed to retain their freedom in making decisions that will affect their group's specific activities. This independence allows groups within the federation to respond in a manner that is consistent with their own goals and objectives. In addition, each group is responsible for running its own organization, and the federation is freed from the responsibility of internal administrative problems.

The federation method of organization results in a loose democratic structure. Because of this, authority is not coercive in nature. Groups participate voluntarily. They are involved because they want to be, not because they are forced into the organization. This results in an affiliation of groups that are highly motivated. Individuals and groups are more likely to be productive when their participation in activities is of their own volition.

What is the role of the manager in the federation? Primarily, this person serves as a facilitator, catalyst, and enabler to the group. The manager has no authority to direct any group to do a specific task within the federation. Thus, his or her role is to act in a coordinating capacity by providing services that help those within the federation. Information and specialized technical resources are the types of services managers are likely to provide. For example, the manager of a federation might identify, collect, and distribute information regarding opportunities for federal funding to each of the groups. This person might act as an agent on behalf of the federation, representing its interests to the community. In addition, the manager is in a position to help formulate the general policy of a federation. However, the manager's ability to enforce policy is limited to his or her ability to inspire the members of the group to work as a cohesive unit in implementing federation activities.

Figure 6.17 delineates a federation of leisure services that involves a number of community institutions that are engaged in the delivery of leisure services. All have an interest, whether it be for altruistic reasons or otherwise, in creating and distributing services. The federation method of organization allows these institutions to meet or discuss common problems, issues, and concerns. Further, it can act as a clearinghouse for programs in order to prevent the duplication of activities. It can collectively pool resources to provide services in areas where independent groups are not capable of doing so. The broad goals and objectives of each group can also be promoted through the federation.

Figure 6.18 shows how a specific program area—sports—can be organized into a federation. The activities of this federation would be similar to those in Figure 6.17, but would focus on a different level of concern.

Figure 6.19 illustrates how a community park and recreation department might organize some of its line functions into a federation (see page 222 for a definition of line functions). The key feature is that each facility can determine its own internal organizational structure. Thus, this approach avoids imposing a rigid structure where inappropriate, and uses a flexible structure in facilities that demand flexibility. In the management of a golf course, the tasks are routine, and the structuring of permanent roles is relatively simple; therefore a bureaucratic structure is inappropriate. On the other hand, personnel operating in a community center are subject to a relatively unstable environment. In this situation, it may be appropriate to establish short-term ad hoc groups to deal with the problem of change. In this case, the beauty of this approach is that it allows those performing specific functions to develop appropriate organizational structures; at the same time, it provides a way to coordinate their activities. The Federation Plan of Community Organization for Leisure adopted by the City of Fremont, California, illustrates how the federation plan can be put into effect in a community park and recreation system (see Figure 6.20 and the Appendix).

Network Organization

One of the newest organizational models to be proposed is the "network organization." This type of organizational structure has evolved directly from the beliefs of the knowledge era. The focus of network design is to create organizational structures that are closest to the customer. They are not top-down and hierarchical; rather, they focus on creating teams or networks that are made up of front line professionals with entrepreneurial leadership abilities. Luthans (1998:539) writes "newly emerging network designs go beyond horizontal structures and totally abandon the classical, hierarchical, functional structure of organization."

What exactly is a network design? Miles and Snow (1995:5-18) have writ-

Figure 6.17
A Federation of Leisure Services

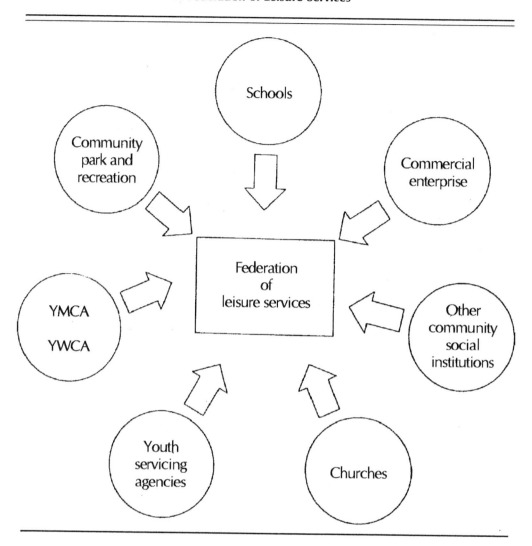

ten this about a network design: "delayered, highly flexible, and controlled by market mechanisms rather than administrative procedures, firms with this new structure arrayed themselves on an industry value chain according to their core competencies, obtaining complementary resources through strategic alliances and outsourcing." Godbey (1997), Edginton (1997), Edginton and Jiang (1999) have all confirmed the importance of the need for flexibility in de-

signing park and recreation organizational structures for the future. For example, discussing the process of outsourcing, Edginton and Jiang have suggested that there will be a need to reshape leisure service organizations in the future in such a way as to promote quality and cost effectiveness while increasing flexibility through outsourcing. A network design and outsourcing go hand in hand. As Dent (1998:137) has indicated, "the new network organization consists of leaders, guiding entre-

Figure 6.18
A Youth Sports Federation

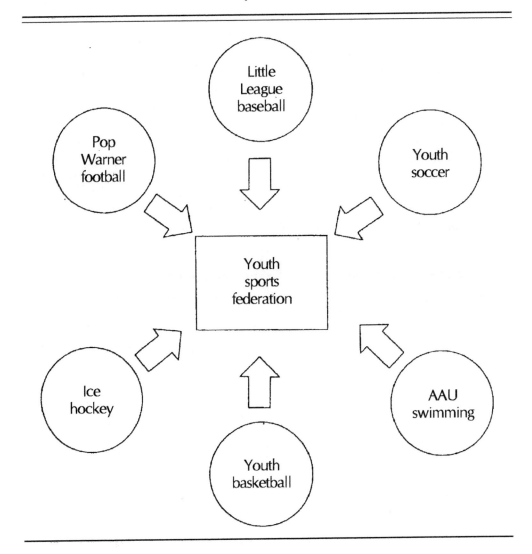

preneurs, and self-managed teams in a chaotic, real-time process that is organized around the ever-changing needs of individual customers." Terms used to define the new network design include: open, dynamic, changing, self-managed, empowered, team-oriented goals, a focus on broader competencies, and competence. As Tapscott and Caston (1973:106-115) have suggested, network designs are "based on cooperative, multidisciplinary teams and businesses networked together across the enterprise. Rather than a rigid structure, it is a modular organizational architecture in which business teams operate as a network of what we call client and server functions."

Dent (1998:137-138) has suggested that there are four key components to successfully operating network organizations:

1. Leadership at the Center. Dent notes that leadership is where the action is—not removed, as is the case in a hierarchical organization where decision-making rests at the top. This supports Bennis and Nanus' (1985) idea that managers do things right and leaders do the right thing. The idea is that an organizational structure should empower those closest to the customer to take action, to be self-regulating, and to be entrepreneurial. In this type of organizational design, "leaders establish the focus of the organization, an effective culture and network structure to support that focus, and rules for decision-making within the network" (Dent, 1998: 138). This places the action with the front line of the organization. As is the case in the University of Northern Iowa's *Camp Adventure™ Youth Services* program, its organizational culture is built around the theme, *"Our front line is our bottom line."*

2. Front-Line Customer-Oriented Teams. This concept suggests that the organization operates from the customer back, rather than the reverse. Network organizations call

Figure 6.19
A Community Park and Recreation Department Organized as a Federation

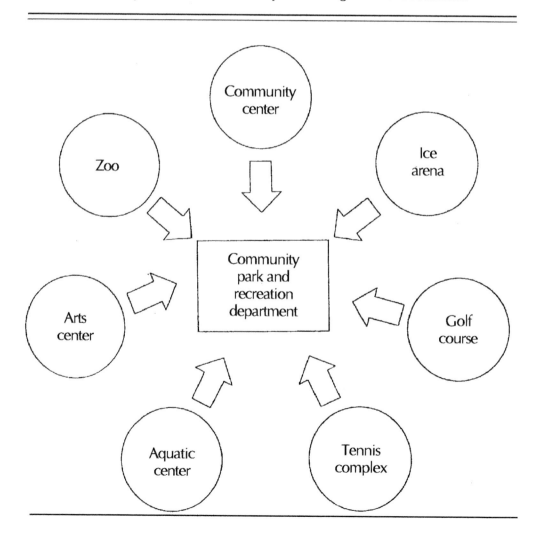

Figure 6.20
Federation Plan for Community Organization of Recreation and Leisure Services
in Fremont (California)

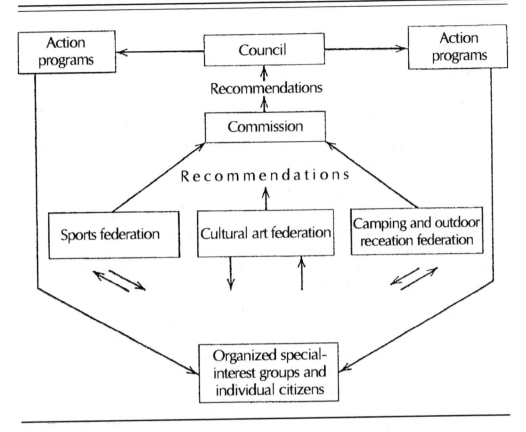

for the establishment of smaller teams or networks focused on a particular segment of the market-place. Such teams become experts at working with these unique niches in the marketplace. Front-line teams, as Dent (1998:138) has written "become expert at knowing and serving such customers, and make most of the key decisions, right there on the front-line. The idea is to create frontline teams who can respond in a rapid, customer-focused manner to provide customized services and programs that are focused on individual needs." This strategy would seem to support the work of leisure service organizations in that many

leisure activities have short product life cycles and are fad oriented.

3. Elimination of Bureaucracy. Critical to the concept of the network organization is the flattening out, or even the elimination, of bureaucracy. Layers of bureaucracy prevent rapid response, timeliness, and even innovation in responding to customer-driven needs. Essentially, networked organizations are very flat organizations with little or no bureaucracy. Each front-line network team is backed by support staff or support teams who provide resources that enable them to move rapidly to meet customer needs.

The idea is to have all routine support functions, as well as the processing of information for decision making, being provided to front-line network teams for instantaneous decision making. Dent (1998:139) writes, "Routine, repetitive, left-brain tasks are automated and assumed by sophisticated computers, which free individuals at all levels of the organization to engage in more right-brained customer-oriented work." The flattening of the bureaucracy gives the ability to provide quick action, which creates greater flexibility and may improve an organization's competitive position. As Dent has written, "in a network organization it is not simply streamlined, it is eliminated altogether" (139).

4. Focus on Customer Satisfaction by Increasing Personal Accountability. A key factor in the establishment of network organizational designs is to ensure that personal accountability is achieved throughout the organization. In order for this to occur, each individual needs to become an entrepreneur with ideas about how to improve customer satisfaction. In this sense, the organization becomes a free marketplace of ideas for all front-line staff. As ideas are implemented with the clear goal of establishing customer satisfaction, there is likewise greater personal accountability for each individual within teams. Information regarding performance is critical. Benchmarking becomes an important factor in measuring performance. The establishment of a base or standard of minimum performance against which to measure achievement is a prerequisite of the

network type system. Again, as Dent (1998:139) has noted: "A network organization understands that its most valuable commodity is knowledge and information, and it therefore provides the communications infrastructure needed to wire together the front and back lines for real-time decision making. The information system simultaneously feeds key performance data to management to ensure that there is ongoing accountability for both qualitative and quantitative bottom-line results, from customer satisfaction to productivity."

The Virtual Organization

Another organizational design, or concept, to emerge in recent years is that of the "virtual organization." This term draws its inference from the technological or information era. Computers operate in virtual space. The idea is that organizations appear to be more than they are. Through the use of such management strategies as partnering, outsourcing, and other strategic management alliances, an organization can create a temporary network of resources that provide it with a presence greater than its actual internal resources. As Luthans (1998:541) has suggested: "the word virtual as used . . . comes not from the popular virtual reality but from virtual memory, which has been used to describe a way of making a computer's memory capacity appear to be greater than it really is." Thus, a virtual organization can align resources by developing through outsourcing or strategic partnerships, and therefore deliver programs and services to meet the ever-rapid changes in the environment.

A good example of a virtual organization that occurs through outsourcing is the work of the Wisconsin Department of Tourism. Like many other tourism, parks, and recreation agencies, the Wisconsin Department of Tourism has benefited for many years from the expertise of external sources in such areas as advertising, public relations, and market research. Likewise, Lands' End, a catalog company, has conducted its own inbound telemarketing for eight years. It has also outsourced its fulfillment to River Front, a sheltered workshop for people without certain abilities. In this case, the benefits are not just limited to cost-effectiveness. By helping those in need, they gain a sense of being a better corporate citizen. Also, lacking facilities and staff time, the Greater Madison Convention and Visitors Bureau's fulfillment job was outsourced to Madison Packaging and Assembling.

In creating a virtual organization, the park and recreation organization must identify its core competencies. This usually involves investigating what the park and recreation organization is legally responsible for implementing. In some situations it may be illegal to create a virtual organization because the responsibilities are specifically restricted to the agency. The next step would be to define all programs and services that could be designated as direct services. Direct services are those that engage the customer in some way to facilitate a leisure experience. This could be the identification of specific programs, activities, areas, or facilities. Following this, the organization would need to identify its indirect or support service functions. All of the above could be arranged into partnerships or outsourced as a part of the virtual organization.

The five key attributes of a virtual organization are as follows:

1. *Technology.* Informational networks will help far-flung companies and entrepreneurs link up and work together from start to finish. The partnerships will be based on electronic contracts to keep the lawyers away and speed the linkups.

2. *Opportunism.* Partnerships will be less permanent, less formal, and more opportunistic. Companies will band together to meet all specific market opportunities and, more often than not, fall apart once the need evaporates.

3. *No Borders.* This new organizational model redefines the traditional boundaries of the company. More cooperation among competitors, suppliers, and customers makes it harder to determine where one company ends and another begins.

4. *Trust.* These relationships make companies far more reliant on each other and require far more trust than ever before. They share a sense of "co-destiny," meaning that the fate of each partner is dependent on the other.

5. *Excellence.* Because each partner brings its "core competence" to the effort, it may be possible to create a "best of everything" organization. Every function and process could be world-class – something that no single company could achieve. (Luthans, 1998: "The Virtual Corporation," 1993).

There are few examples of virtual organizations that we can provide as examples in the park and recreation field. However, for decades leisure service organizations have engaged in the process of contracting for services. In this sense, leisure service organizations have been forerunners in the creation of virtual organizations by attracting resources and staff on contract to supplement their basic core staff.

The Leisure Service System as a Learning Organization

What will the leisure service organization of the future look like? This is a difficult and challenging question to answer. Certainly, leisure service organizations of the future will have to be highly flexible, innovative, agile, and responsive to change. The leisure service organization of the future will have to be a highly adaptable organism. Key in this process will be the ability of organizations to learn how to change. To be successful, organizations will need to become what Peter M. Senge refers to in *The Fifth Discipline* as "learning organizations." (See also Chapter Three for an introduction to these principles.) Learning organizations are ones that have the ability to transform themselves, to make themselves anew in the environment of discontinuous, ongoing, rapid, and dynamic change.

What do learning organizations look like? What do they emphasize? Table 6.1 compares the characteristics of the traditional versus the learning organization. As one can see from this table, critical components of the organization are shared between management and employees. There is less distinction between those who manage the organization and those who deliver the services. Clearly, the emphasis is on shared deci-

sion making, collaborative thinking, and joint conflict resolution, with a basic focus on building a common commitment to the endeavor. Learning organizations are ones that can make mistakes and overcome these to move forward. They are organizations that are sensitive to information and can respond to changes in the environment. Learning organizations understand the importance of developing a long-term strategy and enhancing their reflective powers to improve decision making. They build on past knowledge and experience to forge new strategies to cope with changes in the future.

Luthans, Rubach, and Marsnik (1995:27-32) define three key characteristics as important ones for designing leisure service organizational structures in the future:

1. Creative Tension. As Senge (1990) suggests, there is a need for creative tension within organizations, a perceived gap between the organization's vision and its accomplishments. Recognition of this difference leads to the process of inquiry, the process of questioning. It also encourages a challenging of the status quo and promotes the opportunity for reflection.

2. Culture Facilitating Learning. This suggests that the culture of the organization supports the idea of continuous, ongoing learning. As Luthans (1998:45) suggests, "the culture of the organization . . . [must] . . . place a high value on the process of learning and go beyond mere lip service by setting mechanisms in place for suggestions, teams, empowerment, and most subtly, but importantly, empathy."

Table 6.1
Characteristics of Learning Organizations

Criteria	Classical Organizations	Learning Organizations
Vision, goals, and objectives	Top-down Hierarchically oriented	Shared Emerges with support from all
Problem-solving and idea-generating strategies	Narrow Controlled by top management	Open Encourages partnerships with all employees
Leadership	Creates reward structure Formulates transactional relationships	Transformational Encouraging personal responsibility Commitment to higher ideals
Relationship with customers	Views customers as commodities	Views customers as partners in the process of idea generation
View of change	Views change as incremental, reactive	Views change as continuous, proactive, anticipatory behaviors
Organizational culture	Encourages specialization, individual competence, focused thinking	Encourages collaborative activity, teaming, broader, more cosmopolitan thinking
Orientation to learning	Views learning for its utilitarian value to accomplish specific ends and tasks	Views learning as a way of encouraging innovation, change, an ongoing part of the organization's way of operating

3. Systems Thinking. Learning organizations have a vision that is shared throughout the organization. In other words, there is understanding and commitment in the organization from the top to the bottom. Further, there is a commitment to openness in the organization for a shared dialogue. Also, individuals within learning organizations have a commitment to the entire work of the organization, not just to their component or specialized tasks. They see themselves as a part of a broader whole.

A key feature in the establishment of learning organizations is how information is processed. Argyris (1990) distinguishes between two distinct types of organizations in terms of how they approach learning. He differentiates between first-order or single-loop learning and second-order or double-loop learning. A single-loop organization learns without significant change to the organization's basic mode of operation. In other words, it may change, but only the routine operations and strategies. However, a double-loop organization reevaluates its basic assumptions and changes its culture as it learns. This type of learning creates greater opportunities for adapting to change because it provides an opportunity to continually review it vision, goals, and objectives in light of rapid, ongoing changes in the environment. Senge (1990) discusses the idea that learning should be generative. In other words, it should lead to innovation, change, and going beyond merely reacting to change to actually anticipating change.

Employees in learning organizations find themselves engaged in ongoing, continuous activities aimed at improving operations, policies, and procedures. Their role is to examine each component of the organization to determine strategies to enhance and improve each component part. Learning organizations encourage experimentation, constructive criticism, and continuous open dialogue between individuals. Employees in learning organizations see themselves as a part of a continuous learning process. Sometimes they are the teachers, sometimes the learners. Key in this process is the creation of sincere, genuine relationships between individuals so that learning can take place. When we think of positive learning environments, we see them as being stimulating, exciting, dynamic, and upbeat but also places where we are allowed to explore our ideas and concepts without fear of failure. Such environments often reflect a great deal of empathy, support, caring, and compassion between the learner and the teacher. They also often en-

courage the best efforts of individuals, that is, they create challenges for individuals, problems to solve, mountains to move, and so on.

"Learning organizations are also characterized by human-oriented cultural values such as these: (1) everyone can be a source of useful ideas, so personnel should be given access to any information that can be of value to them; (2) the people closest to the problem usually have the best ideas regarding how to solve it, so empowerment should be promoted throughout the structure; (3) learning flows up and down the hierarchy, so managers as well as employees can benefit from it; (4) new ideas are important and should be encouraged and rewarded; and (5) mistakes should be viewed as learning opportunities. The last point of learning from failures is an especially important cultural value for people in the learning organization" (Kramlinger, 1992).

Summary

In this chapter, we have presented a discussion of organizational designs. It is important for a manager to recognize that its goals and objectives, basic work activities, and other environmental factors will affect the structuring of any leisure service organization. These elements will affect the amount of specialization, standardization, centralization, formalization, flexibility, and type of configuration chosen within a given structure. It is important for the reader to remember that organizational structure may be viewed as existing on a continuum that runs from mechanic (rigid) organization on one end to organic (flexible) organization on the other. In addition to the goals and objectives of an organization, it appears that the critical factor in the choice of design is the relative stability of the environment. When the environment is thought to be stable, mechanistic designs are appropriate; conversely, when it is unstable, organic structures should be used. Each manager must evaluate those factors that influence his or her particular situation and apply the principles to determine the most appropriate structure.

It is critically important that the human element in organizations be acknowledged. Managers who take into consideration the unique interests and needs of their organization's membership, while focusing on the organization's goals, will be successful.

Discussion Questions

1. How does the culture of an organization influence its operations? What exactly is an organization's culture?

2. What are five key characteristics of formal organizations?

3. What key factors must be taken into consideration when structuring leisure service organizations?

4. Identify and define the characteristics of mechanistic versus organic organizations. How might these concepts be applied to the structure of leisure service organizations?

5. What are the characteristics of the bureaucratic model of organization?

6. Identify and define three types of ownership in commercial or private leisure service organizations.

7. Locate a local leisure service organization and obtain a copy of its organizational chart. Analyze the chart to determine how its component parts relate to the theories presented in this chapter.

8. What are the advantages to decentralizing the organizational structure of a leisure service system?

9. What elements characterize network organizations? What is the difference between a network organization and a virtual organization?

10. What implications do learning organizations have for the management of leisure services?

References

Argyris, C. (1990). *Overcoming organizational defenses*. Needham Heights, MA: Allyn & Bacon.

Artz, R. M. (1973). Boards, councils, and citizen involvement, In S. C. Lutzin & E. H. Storey, (Eds.), *Managing municipal leisure services* (pp. 60-67). Washington, DC: International City Management Association.

Bennis, W., & Namus, B. (1985). *Leaders: The strategies for taking charge*. New York: Harper Row.

Bethal, G. I. (1971, April). A systems approach to management of park maintenance. *Park Maintenance*, 24(4), 12.

Buchanan, D., & Huczynski, A. (1997). *Organizational behavior: An introductory text*. London: Prentice Hall.

Deal, T. E., & Kennedy, A. A. (1982). *Corporate cultures*. Reading, MA: Addison-Wesley.

Dent, H. S. (1998). *The roaring 2000s*. New York: Simon & Schuster.

Edginton, C. R. (1987). Defining an organizational culture. *Management Strategy*, 11(1), 1-8.

Edginton, C. R. (1997). Managing leisure services: A new ecology of leadership toward the year 2000. *Journal of Physical Education, Recreation and Dance, 68*(8), 30-31.

Edginton, C. R., & Eldridge, R. C. (1975). Developmental training: Methods and procedures for your department—Part 2. *Park Maintenance, 28*(9), 8-10.

Edginton, C. R., & Jiang, J. (1999, September). Outsourcing for parks and recreation agencies." *Ifpra Bulletin, 7*(14) 46-49.

Godbey, G. (1997). *Leisure and leisure services in the 21st century.* State College, PA: Venture.

Kramlinger, T. (July, 1992). Training's role in a learning organization. *Training.*

Litterer, J. A. (1973). *The analysis of organizations.* New York: Wiley & Sons.

Luthans, F. (1998). *Organizational behavior.* Boston: Irwin McGraw-Hill.

Luthans, F., Rubach, M. J., & Marsnik, P. (1995, January). Going beyond total quality: The characteristics, techniques, and measures of learning organizations." *The International Journal of Organizational Analysis,* 22-44.

Miles, R. E., & Snow, C. C. (1995, Spring). The new network firm: A spherical structure built on a human investment philosophy *Organizational Dynamics,* P. 5–18.

Outhwaite, W., & Bottomore T. (1994). *The Blackwell dictionary of 20th century social thought.* Oxford: Blackwell.

Perez, J. W. (1970, December). The decentralization of recreation. *California Parks and Recreation,* 20-22.

Pugh, D. S., Hickson D. J., Huntings, C. R., & Turner, C. (1968). Dimensions of organizational structures. *Administrative Science Quarterly, 13*(1), 65-105.

Rice, G. H., & Bishoprick, D. W. (1971). *Conceptual models of organization.* New York: Appleton-Century-Crofts.

Rodney, L. S., & Toalson, R. F. (1981). *Administration of recreation, parks, and leisure services* (2nd ed.). New York: Wiley & Sons.

Ryterband, E. C., & Bass, B. M., (1973). Work and nonwork: Perspectives in the context of change. In M.D. Dunnette (Ed.), *Work and nonwork in the year 2001* (pp. 69-89). Monterey, CA: Brooks/Cole.

Schein, E. H. (1985). *Organizational culture and leadership.* San Francisco: Jossey-Bass.

Senge, P. M. (1990). *The fifth discipline: The art and practice of the learning organization.* New York: Doubleday Currency.

Tapscott, D., & Caston, A. (1993, February). The modular corporation. *Fortune,* 106-115.

The virtual corporation. (February, 1993). *Business Week,* 98-102.

Weber, M. (1947). *The theory of social and economic organizations.* New York: Free Press Oxford University Press.

Chapter

7

Planning, Decision Making, and Organizational Effectiveness

Fulfillment in the planning process often comes with the dedication of a new park and recreation resource.

Introduction

What is planning? How can planning inform decision makings? How can planning, in its various forms and processes, enhance the effectiveness of leisure service organizations? Highly functional and effective organizations plan for the future. These organizations rely on comprehensive community plans, recreation park and leisure ser-

vices master plans, and strategic plans to promote organizational effectiveness. Leisure service managers must become informed about planning in order to manage their facilities, resources, and services effectively. As Drucker (1987:146) noted: "It is precisely because the real problem is fear of the unknown, fear of being abandoned in a world the worker does not know or understand, that such organized planning is so badly needed." Of particular importance is the notion that leisure managers must link community values, needs, and priorities with organizational goals, policies, and plans. The planning function provides the leisure service manager with a means to make these important linkages in a systematic and effective manner.

This chapter addresses decision making, the manager and planning, local values, and problem solving through planning, and strategic change to promote organizational effectiveness. Characteristics of effective leisure service planning are presented. No matter whether the leisure services manager is engaged in internal strategic planning or development of a community-wide recreation element as part of the community comprehensive plan, there are key and fundamental practices necessary in carrying out effective plans.

Second, information is provided that highlights strategic planning, due to the fact that leisure managers often find themselves conducting this type of planning.

Relationship Between Planning and Decision making

As most practitioners and academics would agree, these two topics usually require a book or series to describe. These two topics are interrelated in various and meaningful ways in the delivery of leisure services. Importantly, in planning for leisure, one usually directs attention to issues such as community involvement; process; standards; classification of lands, resources, and facilities; and long-range issues and criteria pertinent to the leisure service

system. In leisure management, one attempts to develop policies and procedures for the efficient and effective delivery of leisure services, areas, and facilities. Within both of these areas, technical aspects are prominent.

A distinct and deliberate process of decision making exists. Figure 7.1 depicts this process and highlights the tasks that require managers and staff to make decisions (Donnelly, Gibson, & Ivancevich, 1990). It should be noted that Bannon (1976), Lankford (1981), and Bannon and Busser (1992) have described basic problem-solving models and planning processes that incorporate these same generic steps. Problem identification requires an analysis of the situation. Donnelly et al. (1990:540-541) note that the following factors complicate this process:

1. Perceptual problems we hold that may prevent the manager from facing realities

2. Defining the problem in terms of solutions, or jumping to conclusions without adequate review

3. Identifying symptoms of the problem, not the real problem

Problems are usually of three types: opportunities, crises, or routine. Managers must deal with crises and routine problems (Tjosvold, 1984). Opportunities must be found or discovered. This only occurs when managers focus less on crises and more on the larger perspective of the organization and vision. Planning offers the manager an opportunity to view the larger picture and consider opportunities.

Next, the manager must consider alternatives to solving the problem or seeking out the opportunity. Managers must evaluate the alternatives based on

Figure 7.1
The Process of Decision Making

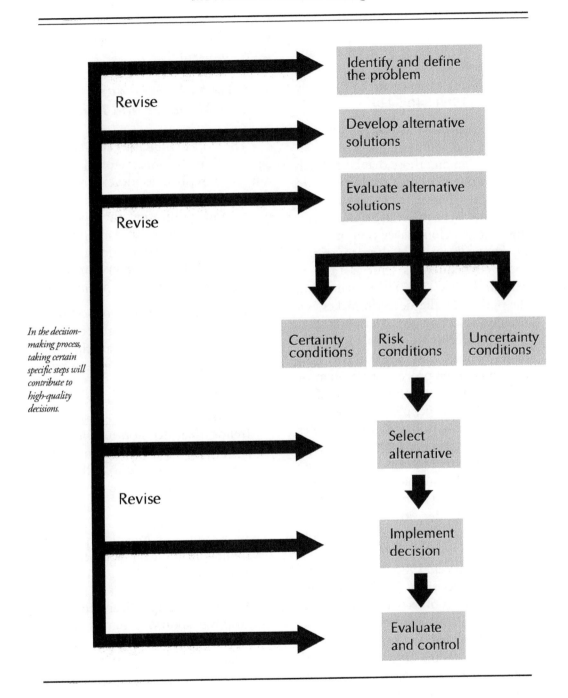

In the decision-making process, taking certain specific steps will contribute to high-quality decisions.

preliminary goals and objectives that are defined within step one. This is a research process and must consider these possible conditions:

1. The decision maker has certainty about the outcome of each alternative;

2. The decision maker has no knowledge of the probability of the outcome of each alternative; and

3. The decision maker has some probabilistic estimate of the outcomes of each alternative. (Donnelly et al., 1990:540-541)

The manager must then work with the staff and community to choose alternatives among those that best match organizational goals, resources, and constraints. Optimal solutions are often impossible in managerial decision making. The decision maker cannot possibly know all available alternatives and their consequences (Shrivastava & Mitroff, 1984). Thus, rather than being the optimizer, the decision maker is a satisfier, selecting the alternative that meets an acceptable (satisfactory) standard (Donnelly et al., 1990). Finally, an implementation process or action must occur to achieve the objectives specified earlier. Because people are involved in the implementation and consequences of action, a manager's job here is really choosing good solutions and also transforming such solutions into behavior in the organization (Donnelly et al., 1990). The test of the decision and implementation is the behavior of the people affected by the decision (Taggart, Robey, & Krocek, 1985). Finally, evaluation of the decisions, implementation, and impact on objectives is necessary. This is explained elsewhere in the book.

We feel that the act of planning offers a basis for making decisions in the delivery of leisure services at any scale. It is important to note that many authors (Dimaggio & Useem, 1980; Driver & Knopf, 1981; Mitra & Lankford, 1998; Rossi, 1978) believe that information and research generated to influence the decision-making processes is often irrelevant. Whatever your belief, we will

attempt to provide illustrations that help you to understand the primary question: To what extent is planning more or less an approach to management decision making?

The Work of the Leisure Service Manager and Planner

The work of the leisure service manager, within the context of planning, can be described as developing and initiating a goal-setting process, preparing and monitoring the operating and capital budgets, and monitoring and evaluating citizen participation involvement. Slater (1984) notes the manager's role in fostering planning as:

1. Setting aside time to meet with staff to brainstorm future scenarios; encouraging staff to participate in professional activities and associations;

2. Identifying emerging issues and trends that decision-making and policy-making bodies should be aware of, and speaking with other organizations that have faced similar issues;

3. Reading as much as possible about impending developments and issues in society; and

4. Encouraging citizens and civic groups to sponsor programs and to think about what they want for the future.

Figure 7.2 provides a perspective on the actors in the planning process and their planning roles (Slater, 1984). It is important to note the various levels of management, staff, and elected officials and their corresponding planning responsibilities.

Figure 7.2
Actors and Their Planning Roles in the Planning Pyramid

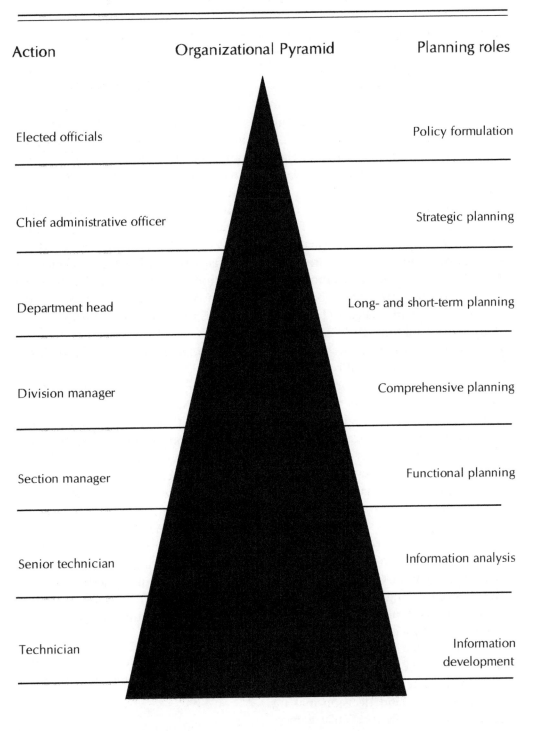

Action	Organizational Pyramid	Planning roles
Elected officials		Policy formulation
Chief administrative officer		Strategic planning
Department head		Long- and short-term planning
Division manager		Comprehensive planning
Section manager		Functional planning
Senior technician		Information analysis
Technician		Information development

Source: Slater 84

Management

To approach the discussion of "To what extent is planning more or less an approach to management decision making?" requires that a perspective through which management decision making is viewed be clarified. Management decision making may be seen as a point in time when the ball starts rolling, this being a more traditional perspective. It may also be viewed as a sequence in time that determines the course of the ball's path.

In either case, management decision making is a creative process. However, how could a purely rational process "booby trap the planet with some 60,000 nuclear weapons—far more than enough to jeopardize the global civilization" in the name of peace (Lankford & Knowles-Lankford, 1989–90). How could a purely rational process support major efforts in industrial recruitment as the primary strategy for economic development when it has been established that small business is the largest contributor to the local economy? Granted, these decisions do have some rational basis. At different times in history, nuclear threats have been real if the particular leader's stated visions were to be interpreted as true intentions. Also, certain level of economic stability may be attained from the establishment of a few large industries. Nevertheless, the decision-making process is informed by rational and nonrational thought and is assuredly a creative process. The extent to which it is rationally driven or driven by creative thought is never constant and is related to the type and range of the planning and decision-making processes adopted by a particular agency.

Planning

Concurrently, the perspective through which planning is viewed and how the nature of planning is characterized must be clarified. Planning is traditionally thought of as the development of several possible futures or alternatives and the alternative courses toward a selected, preferred future. However, in this more conventional view, planning does not adequately address the process of transferring thought into reality. The planned reality and the reality that results from the plan, are quite different. As with decision making, the process of planning can be viewed as a sequence in time in which the direction of action informed through planning is continually adjusted based on the new realities that the action reveals.

Dominant Planning Theories

Planning theory has been dominated by two major and two subsidiary streams of thought: planning to guide society through regulation in the social reform movement, and planning to transform society through revolt in the social mobilization movement. Within the social reform movement, policy analysis and social learning were outcomes. Social reform concentrated power and information to monitor private interests without destroying individual freedom. The theory is flawed, according to Friedmann (1987), in the following ways:

1. The belief that rationality alone can drive planning towards social change;

2. The one-way flow of information—from the top down; and

3. The belief in the conception of a master plan.

Essentially, it was believed that society could be guided by rational thought and that fact had to be tempered by value. Unfortunately, we cannot escape making value statements, for facts must be selected and interpreted (Mill, 1974). In planning and subsequent management decision making for social change, we use values in order to configure facts and interpret them. This notion of social reform relies on the "expert" to relay "appropriate" information to the public, from plan to implementation. As Quade (1975) has noted, analysis of information must be used alongside experience, judgment, and intuition.

Social reform, as noted earlier, is tied to a grand master plan. Master plans suggest that plans and management decisions occur at one point in time, and are difficult to change. Perloff (1980) argues that in addition to the usual economic, social, political, physical, and environmental components, time must be incorporated into the planning and management decision-making framework. However, this comprehensive stance does not move the plan and decision any closer to implementation, because it is not intended to be informed by action (Friedmann, 1987).

Social mobilization is the only stream in planning theory that has questioned the dominant order—namely, the economic, political, and social order. Instead of beginning with goals and objectives, we start with citizen involvement and social criticism (Friedmann, 1987). Therefore, leisure service planners and managers begin to operate outside the framework of the established order to facilitate direct involvement in various phases of the process.

What should the nature of leisure planning be in practice? As with management decision making, it is neither a purely rational nor nonrational process. Although planning has traditionally strived to be a purely rational process, it could never achieve this goal, because no matter what the plan is or was, it reflects the values of those who conceived the plan. Therefore, values are subjective, as is the interpretation of those values. It is important to note that changes have occurred primarily in how we work with and value community input, and in process. An old saying goes: "the process is more important than the product." Today, we can compare the traditional and new view of planning as follows:

- *Traditional View*
  Static, linear process
  Emphasis on product
  Token citizen involvement
  Professionals apply personal values

- *New View*
  Dynamic, incremental process
  Emphasis on process
  Citizen participation is essential
  Professionals translate values into alternatives (Knowles-Lankford, 1999)

Planning as Management Decision making

With these simplistic views of decision making and planning, we are able to address the question: "To what extent is planning more or less than an approach to management decision making?" Given the traditional model of decision making as a point in time, the more planning is able to supply a range of alternative futures that influence the decision, the more effective it is as a process to inform decision making. This assumes that the more options there are, the more responsive the process will be to reaching a creative solution. This is not to say that what is perceived as the best idea, at a given point in time, should not be revealed. Rather, all the aces should be on the table with the expectation that the ace of spades is yet to be played. In other words, good ideas should be revealed early so that good qualities may be extracted and used in the formation of better ideas.

If, however, the planning approach applied to this traditional view of the decision-making process is based on the premise that action informs thought, then the relationship changes. In this combination, there is no congruency, because a continually adjusting planning approach requires that the decision-making process occur over time. This planning approach applied to the decision-making process over time is effective to the extent that the decisions made are molded by the course formed by planning and action.

There is also a certain level of compatibility between decision making, which occurs over time, and the more traditional planning approach. In this combination, planning informs merely the first level of decision making. It is ineffectual to the extent that responses to the first showing of alternative solutions will reveal another layer of the problem—the public interest.

The public interest is a composite of a society's values—economic, social, political, educational, functional, ecological, spiritual, and aesthetic values (Knowles-Lankford, 1993). Each, in its time, has had its turn in the limelight. During the 1960s, social and political values were in focus and at issue. During the 1970s, ecological values be-

came a national concern. During the 1980s, economic values dominated the value spectrum. During the 1990s, it appears that both social and environmental issues are predominant. The important point is that the degree to which we, as a profession and a society, serve or place a priority on a particular value or configuration of values is always in flux. It is a test of balance—a balance that can only be temporary. Once an expression of a given value reaches a critical peak through policy or some other physical manifestation, that value is served, temporarily, and the interest shifts to another value.

In defining the public interest as a set of values, it follows that the more values a solution addresses, the more brilliant the solution (Knowles-Lankford, 1993). That was the beauty of the Works Progress Administration (WPA) during the Great Depression of the 1930s in the United States. Not only did it provide jobs for a huge unemployed workforce, the program addressed social, aesthetic, as well as political values. Not all solutions can be so brilliant. Determining which values are to be given more weight at a certain point in time is a problem we continually face.

The leisure service planner and manager's role within this milieu of values is precarious. Are we agents of the existing culture or its evolution (Friedmann, 1987)? The public interest, which has no voice, is that of a future society's values. Who then assumes that voice? How do you marry these potentially disparate perspectives?

The answer lies in the process itself. If the process directly involves the public in creating the solution, then it must be a reflection of the public interest or, as stated above, societal values. This appears to be a developing trend of the future. The call for public participation in the planning process is frequent. The tone of that call has been shifting to *meaningful* public participation in the planning process. Although the methods continue to evolve, the relationship between the planner and the planned for must be mutually responsive. It is through this process that the leisure planner and manager and the public are able to know more about the values that must be served in providing leisure services (Knowles-Lankford & Lankford, 1995). This approach allows planners and managers to know more about the world of the problem and perhaps identify the interrelationships among the worlds of many problems in aim for the brilliant solution.

It is instructive to look at how the ideals of individual freedom and equality are expressed in the world around us. What makes them so visible is our narrow interpretation of these ideals. We have the suburbs and with it, unequal access to the land. We have an ever-increasing investment in the road system to provide for individual freedom of mobility. Jackson (1994) has shown the extreme lack of variety in our human-made environment. These examples illustrate for us how the lack of a community vision can destroy the potential for individual freedom. The suburb is an illusion, providing us with neither the countryside nor the urban experience. The road has become so popular that the freedom it professes is stifled by congested roadways. The problem that the world around us reveals is the lack of a diversified interpretation of freedom and equality. This interpretation can bring about diversity through the dispersal of power, in a regional, community, or neighborhood sense, through meaningful citizen involvement

programs and through social mobilization and learning opportunities in the leisure planning and management arenas (Knowles-Lankford, 1993).

When asking who assumes the voice of a future society's value, we must ask how and if the voice of today's society has evolved from a planned perspective. The process is educational in both directions—from the planner, and manager to the public. Action informs plans and experience informs theory. Importantly, however, the opportunity to act and the effectiveness of that action rely on the accessibility to and responsiveness to the organization of power. Learning must be conducted on an intimate level. Planning and management functions have to be brought to the neighborhood level. It is through the social mobilization and learning model conducted at the neighborhood level that a vision, which serves multiple values, can be created. This vision must place societal values above individual values for the enhancement of leisure services.

Essentials of Effective Leisure Services Planning

High-quality and responsive recreation and park plans, derived from an effective recreation resource planning process, are critical for the creation of a community leisure service system that significantly affects the quality of peoples' lives. Recreation park and leisure services planning can be defined simply as a process of developing and using information for leisure service delivery. This information may have to do with historical leisure trends or problems (and how the community should solve them), with existing conditions of the resources, or with issues that appear to have a bearing on the future of recreation, parks, and leisure services at the local community level. Recreation, parks, and leisure services planning is a method of evaluating problems and opportunities and suggesting action about them. Too often, leisure service organizations rely on planning processes that are not flexible or realistic to address local leisure needs, desires, and values (Lankford, 1989). Inflexibility in recreation and park planning means the government will not be able to respond adequately to changes in the community's desire for services. Opportunities for service adjustment will be lost due to the government's inability to respond quickly. There is no single formula for the planning process. However, a planning effort can be positively influenced by many factors including: community and technical support; detailed work plans; systematic data collection and analysis; development of alternatives based on preliminary goals; and a future perspective (vision).

Brooks (2000), a well-respected and accomplished recreation planner in Northern California, offers what we believe to be a time-tested and comprehensive, yet flexible, planning process. Figure 7.3 shows the critical path used

Figure 7.3
Critical Path For Developing the Cedar Grove–Bidwell Park Enhancement Master Plan, City of Chico, California

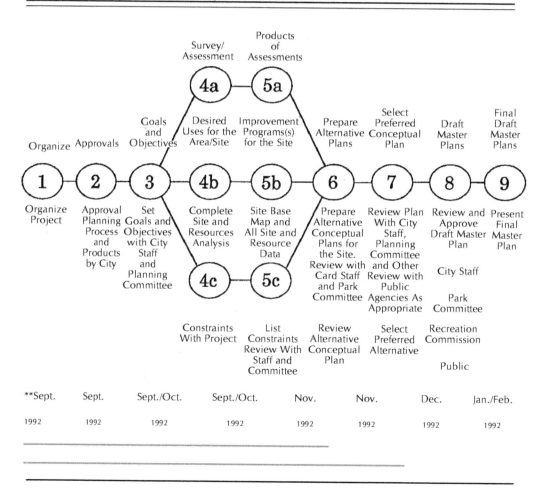

for developing the Cedar Grove–Bidwell Park Enhancement Master Plan for the City of Chico, California. Brooks has used this process for many planning projects, both small and large scale. Brooks notes that the process can be adapted for site development plans, master plans, and comprehensive plans. In fact, Brooks used a similar process in programming work in both Davis and Pasadena, California. There are basically nine steps (this varies based on the project and client): detailing organizational and approval tasks (step 1 & 2); setting goals and objectives (step 2); conducting site resource, constraint, and needs assessments (steps 4a-c), using products of assessments (steps 5a-c); preparing alternative plans based on assessments (step 6); selecting preferred conceptual plans (step 7); drafting the master plan (step 8); and finally, presenting the plan (step 9). It is instructive to note some of the important and unique features of this process. First, there is involvement by both the community and a steering committee. This involvement takes place at crucial decision-making junctures. Second, the products of assessment steps allow the community and planner to work in an integrated fashion. Finally, there are numerous opportunities to discuss the recommended actions.

Well-developed and implemented recreation, parks, and leisure services plans enhance the government's ability to foresee and respond to changes in service needs and desires, potential acquisitions, and potential opportunities for service improvement. What follows is a review of eight essential features and ideas that should be reflected in local recreation, parks, and leisure services plans, general plan recreation elements, and master plans. Lankford, Neal, and

Knowles-Lankford (1995) and Lankford (1981, 1989) suggest that the following eight elements are essential to any leisure service planning effort.

Essential Element 1: Recreation, Park, and Leisure Services Plans Should Be Based on Local Values

Different communities have different values and needs. Different neighborhoods or districts within cities have different values and needs. For example, the amount of open space in one community may be totally unacceptable to that community, whereas it may cause no problems in another community. The leisure service matters that are issues in your community might not be issues in communities with different values. Public hearings, group work sessions, surveys, and personal interviews are good ways the park and recreation agency can identify local values toward leisure services. This information will enhance the local recreation planning process.

Value statements (from the point of view of the users) should be developed with regard to ecological conditions, social issues and conditions, outdoor or environmental education values, economic needs and conditions, aesthetic issues, and finally political constraints and realities (Knowles-Lankford & Lankford, 1995). Knowles-Lankford (1993) has indicated that the recreation profession should be the overseer of community decisions that affect the quality of life of the resident. What is needed to improve the quality of life in our communities is to facilitate future visions or a preferred future of community life. A value-driven process helps recreation professionals identify needs and values in order to create this vision of sustainable, livable, and healthy communities.

Essential Element 2: Recreation, Park, and Leisure Services Plans Should Reflect Local Approaches to Problem Solving

Two communities may share values and concerns for similar leisure delivery problems, yet they may respond to those problems in totally different ways. Interagency cooperation or intergovernmental service agreements may be a good solution for one's community's leisure service delivery, but other communities might prefer the establishment of one comprehensive agency for leisure service delivery. It is important to know the values of the community in order to develop responsive solutions to problem solving and policy development. Recreation and parks policies and problem-solving solutions will most likely fail without due consideration of local values and needs (Lankford, 1994).

Too often, national park and recreation standards are used to telling local communities and cities what types and levels of leisure services and facilities they should be providing to address potential deficiencies. National standards are useful reference tools and guides; however, programs and solutions should reflect local expectations, needs, differences, values, and standards.

For example, Figure 7.4 presents a set of 11 community specific park standards and service areas for the city of Phoenix, Arizona Parks, Recreation and Library Department. These outline neighborhood, community and district facility and service needs.

Essential Element 3: Participation from Local People in the Recreation, Parks, and Leisure Services Planning Process is Essential

A recreation, park, and leisure services plan could be based on local values and reflect local standards, yet could be developed without participation of the local people. Even if the recreation planners, managers, staff, and decision-makers know all there is to know about the problem or situation, citizens should be involved in developing recreation plans and strategies. When citizens are involved in developing a recreation, parks, and leisure services plan or strategy, they are much more likely to be committed to implementing the plan and supporting the leisure service agency's efforts (Harper, 1993; Lankford, 1994). People can be involved through committees, public hearings, informal reviews of plans, and neighborhood councils. Harper (1993) presents a comprehensive example of working with citizens in the development of a park (see Figure 7.5).

Citizen involvement can be defined as the opportunity for all citizens of the community to have access to all stages of the planning process—from gathering raw data to final plan adoption—and to have the opportunity of having their views made known to decision makers prior to the actual decisions being made (Lankford & Cramb, 1992). Local recreation planners and managers should make available to citizens all necessary working papers, plan elements, and technical reports. Meetings should be publicized through the following means: (1) releases to news media; (2)

display ads in the newspaper, and (3) radio and television announcements. Informational meetings are also helpful in establishing public support and awareness. This type of meeting can be informal: "drop-in" or open house type. The format and purpose emphasizes person-to-person contacts rather than lecture type presentations (Lankford, 1990c). A number of observations have been made with regard to planning and working to enhance community access to the planning process:

1. Use surveys to identify issues and concerns of residents;

2. Use the Nominal Group Technique (NGT) to refine process. This is not a brainstorming process—*there is a difference;*

3. Help citizens and the decision-making body be visionary with regard to the desired results;

4. Use public balloting for designs and plans;

Figure 7.4

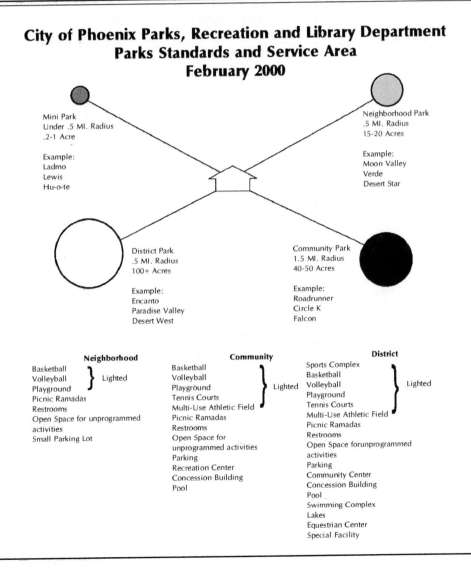

City of Phoenix Parks, Recreation and Library Department
Parks Standards and Service Area
February 2000

Mini Park
Under .5 MI. Radius
.2-1 Acre

Example:
Ladmo
Lewis
Hu-o-te

Neighborhood Park
.5 MI. Radius
15-20 Acres

Example:
Moon Valley
Verde
Desert Star

District Park
.5 MI. Radius
100+ Acres

Example:
Encanto
Paradise Valley
Desert West

Community Park
1.5 MI. Radius
40-50 Acres

Example:
Roadrunner
Circle K
Falcon

Neighborhood
Basketball
Volleyball   } Lighted
Playground
Picnic Ramadas
Restrooms
Open Space for unprogrammed activities
Small Parking Lot

Community
Basketball
Volleyball
Playground   } Lighted
Tennis Courts
Multi-Use Athletic Field
Picnic Ramadas
Restrooms
Open Space for unprogrammed activities
Parking
Recreation Center
Concession Building
Pool

District
Sports Complex
Basketball
Volleyball   } Lighted
Playground
Tennis Courts
Multi-Use Athletic Field
Picnic Ramadas
Restrooms
Open Space forunprogrammed activities
Parking
Community Center
Concession Building
Pool
Swimming Complex
Lakes
Equestrian Center
Special Facility

Figure 7.5
The Forks Renewal Corporation Public Consultation Process Phase II—Development Plan

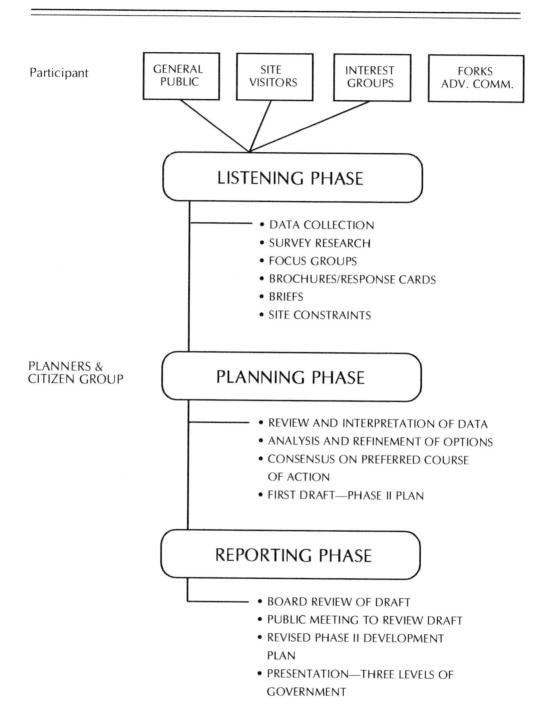

Participant

GENERAL PUBLIC

SITE VISITORS

INTEREST GROUPS

FORKS ADV. COMM.

LISTENING PHASE

- DATA COLLECTION
- SURVEY RESEARCH
- FOCUS GROUPS
- BROCHURES/RESPONSE CARDS
- BRIEFS
- SITE CONSTRAINTS

PLANNERS & CITIZEN GROUP

PLANNING PHASE

- REVIEW AND INTERPRETATION OF DATA
- ANALYSIS AND REFINEMENT OF OPTIONS
- CONSENSUS ON PREFERRED COURSE OF ACTION
- FIRST DRAFT—PHASE II PLAN

REPORTING PHASE

- BOARD REVIEW OF DRAFT
- PUBLIC MEETING TO REVIEW DRAFT
- REVISED PHASE II DEVELOPMENT PLAN
- PRESENTATION—THREE LEVELS OF GOVERNMENT

Source: Harper, J. (1993). The Forks: A unique inner-city development focus on public participation. *Journal of the World Leisure & Recreation 35*(2), 5-9.

5. Listen to resident–*remember* if they feel they are listened to, they tend to support change;

6. Provide as many means as possible for public access to the planning and decision-making process;

7. Be prepared to provide training sessions for citizens;

8. Ensure an atmosphere that encourages citizens to speak freely

9. Be precise about what you mean by citizen participation, how it works, and what voice citizens have; and

10. Total congruency of opinion may not be possible, but a fair, effective and accessible planning process that includes participation and representation of the public is possible. (Lankford, 1990c)

A great deal of effort on the part of tourism planning and development organizations is needed in order to solicit input on development proposals that identify and respond to the public interest in the context of contemporary values and issues. Tourism plan development and adoption should reflect shared responsibility of citizens, elected officials, and professional staff. Oftentimes, planners and developers assume, conveniently so, that the public interest is defined by the decision-making body and various commissions. An effective citizen participation program may be defined as one that enhances the legitimacy of the planning process and acceptability of the decisions and recommendations, and that improves decision making.

Essential Element 4: Recreation, Park, and Leisure Usage Data Are Required.

The feelings of citizens and leisure service professionals (staff as well as management) are very important in the recreation planning process. However, their opinions have to be compared with available recreation and park data. Both the perceptions of citizens and empirical data should be used to describe the current local situation and to project a vision of the future. Use of only one type of data can be misleading. Local citizens, decision makers, and leisure service providers may believe in a myth which "hard" data about recreation and park usage may dispel. However, in many instances, deeply held convictions may not be affected by contrary evidence, no matter how accurate the data. In these instances, convictions and their consequences must be dealt with as realities in the planning process, in spite of other evidence to the contrary.

The private personal interview is an excellent way to collect data and develop issue statements. In addition, the interview provides the recreation planner with an opportunity to establish relationships with community members and decision makers. Obviously, one cannot interview an entire community; therefore, a mix of data-collection techniques is required and will prove most beneficial to the recreation planner. Community surveys (either mail or telephone, or a combination) are effective in collecting important quantitative and qualitative recreation and park information. Qualitative research methods such as observation studies and case studies are also important and are complementary to survey data collection methods.

Basic to the development of any recreation, park, and leisure services plan is the quantity and quality of information on which decisions can be based. This information will serve as a source for identifying problems or opportunities that the recreation, park, and leisure services plan will need to deal with, and will also provide suggestions for dealing with these problems or opportunities (Knowles-Lankford & Lankford, 1995).

Essential Element 5: Recreation, Park, and Leisure Services Plan Alternatives and Recommendations Should Be Clearly Defined

An important function of a recreation and park plan is to help government, planners, and managers make rational, informed choices regarding leisure service delivery for the citizens of your community. Leisure service professionals, government officials, and citizens have to be given significantly different, alternative ways of dealing with problems, opportunities, or the achievement of goals. Meaningful alternatives may involve a range in cost, timing, doing nothing, doing a little, or doing a lot. Sometimes it is beneficial to present conservative to radical alternatives in response to situations in order to show the decision makers and community the range of options and the extent or seriousness of the situation. In any event, there is seldom only one way of addressing a situation; rather, there are many ways that are appropriate, timely, and effective.

Essential Element 6: Keep Recreation, Park, and Leisure Services Plans and Issues Clear and to the Point

Recreation, park, and leisure services issues are complex. The range of local values, funding problems and priorities, open space acquisition possibilities, agency personnel problems, and service delivery issues creates the need for clear and concise problem identification and description. Recreation, park, and leisure services issues have to be understood in a clear and simple way by members of the government, decision makers, members of the community, and others outside the profession. Technical reports with an abundance of data, tables, graphs, charts, economic models, and such are helpful for planners and managers, but they are of little practical value for the layperson. Decision makers have little time to read lengthy documents and usually prefer executive summaries, which highlight key findings and recommendations (Lankford & Cramb, 1992). If decision makers are interested, or if questions about recommendations arise, the technical supplement and the plan are readily available for reference and clarification.

Common mistakes in plans and technical reports include poor organization and format, mixing of factual information with conjecture or recommendations, excessive jargon, excessive or incomplete information, and redundancy. An effective park and recreation plan and technical report should be well-organized with a clear and simple format. The agency should: (1) keep factual information separate from analysis and opinion; (2) use an easy-to-read format to organize the presentation of information; (3) use the same basic format for all future park and recreation plans and documents, with some minor adaptations when necessary; and finally, (4) keep the narrative to a minimum when presenting factual information.

Essential Element 7: The Recreation, Park, and Leisure Services Plan Must Reflect Leadership and Commitment

It is critical that the plans identify positions and divisions within the park and recreation agency that will be responsible for implementing and monitoring portions of the plan. Schedules for phased implementation, criteria for evaluating the plan's success, and identification of responsible positions and divisions within the agency should be detailed in the plan.

The park and recreation departments are identified as the lead agency in the community that will be responsible for the plan. In other words, it must be shown within the plan that the department is committed to the plan's successful implementation. Without committed and concerned leadership for the plan and process, change will be painful and sometimes politically costly for the agency. Leisure service professionals must exhibit a commitment to the vision and mission as expressed in the plan (Lankford, 1990a, 1990b; Neal & Lankford, 1995). Commitment to promoting employee and citizen involvement in decision making concerning future leisure service delivery should be established in the plan. Government agencies that are successful in recreation planning are those that use staff and citizen knowledge and input to determine potential problems and op-

portunities and to develop realistic and workable solutions to these situations.

Essential Element 8: The Recreation, Park, and Leisure Services Plan Must Be Practical and Realistic

If the recommendations and strategies contained in the plan are not realistic, they are of little or no use to the community. If, for instance, the plan calls for the development of a multi-use community facility to be built, and the residents desire a gymnasium or park, then this recommendation is not realistic or compatible with local values. In reality, the costs of proposed services and facilities have to be reasonable in relation to community income levels and willingness to pay. In addition, professional personnel have to be available for the new services proposed. Technical recommendations such as the total computerization of the agency must be appropriate given the current skills within the agency. Dissatisfaction and decreased work motivation will occur if employees are pressed into using new technology without adequate training and time to become accustomed to the "new way" of doing business (Edginton, Neal, & Edginton, 1989; Lankford, Neal, & Buxton, 1992; Neal 1984). Citizens and leisure agency staff should be receptive to the proposals and plan recommendations. The proposals have to be politically feasible in the context of the local political environment. In other words, the recommendations have to be "realistic."

Recreation planners know how to produce plans and studies about local leisure service delivery. The problem, however, is how to produce a plan that can or will be accepted and carried out by the community. Although no single planning approach can guarantee implementation, the local planners, with the assistance of the interested citizens of the community, can develop a process that will ensure that the results, at a minimum, will be taken seriously by the decision makers and the community. Well-developed recreation and park planning processes and plans improve community public relations (Lankford, 1994).

How can leisure service organizations enhance the chances that their plans will be implemented? First, the agency must involve citizens, decision makers, business leaders, and leisure professionals (staff and managers) at the beginning and throughout the planning process. Second, the agency must develop recreation plans that are focused on the serious concerns of citizens and community leaders, and on issues and opportunities confronting the leisure delivery system. Third, the agency should use the recreation planner's technical knowledge and skills to help citizens, other leisure professionals (staff and managers), and decision makers better understand the issues and opportunities, and the alternative methods for dealing with the issues identified. Finally, the assumptions, values, attitudes, language and specific concerns of the people who will use the services and the people who will implement the plan must be built into the plan from the beginning of the process. The recreation, park, and leisure services planner must be a leader. A proposed framework for the leader or planner follows:

1. The leader or planner must develop a process to identify internal and external strengths and weaknesses of the leisure service system;

2. The leader/planner must develop a process for identifying future trends, opportunities, and issues for service provision;

3. The leader or planner must develop a process for decision making that uses staff;

4. The leader or planner must develop a process for innovation; and

5. The leader or planner must develop a process for organizing tasks, setting priorities, and establishing goals and objectives. (Lankford, 1990a; 1990b; Neal & Lankford, 1995)

Quality recreation, park, and leisure services plans can help government agencies serve the needs of their community, now and in the future, by assessing current and possible future leisure needs, and comparing those needs to current and possible future deficiencies in the system. Essentially, planning is decision making which helps to solve problems (Lankford & Knowles-Lankford, 1989–1990). Many times it is the process that helps solve park and recreation problems, not the plan itself. In order to save critical park open space systems, it is imperative that recreation, park, and leisure services officials embark on a well-structured and process-oriented park planning effort to serve the needs of future generations. As we envision the future of parks and recreation and the relationship to community development, leisure service managers need to look further to the next generation (Knowles-Lankford, 1993). As leisure service managers, we need to project ahead to see the implications of our decisions over time and with a longer perspective than we do today.

The Maryland-National Capital Park and Planning Commission has developed an excellent strategy for enhancing their trail system. The planning process involves the establishment of a general vision for the program. This is related in their statement "Parks for Tomorrow, The Next 70 Years" (See Figure 7.6). The organization of the plan is found in Figure 7.7. Further, the general goals, objectives and strategies related to the plan are found in Table 7.1. Table 7.2 provides a summary of proposed trail projects to take place between 1999 and 2009.

Strategic Planning

This section describes the process for strategic planning. This process is of particular importance to managers in addressing the internal and external environmental influences that affect the way in which the organization functions and prospers. This material is based on the U.S. Army Presidio Morale Support Activities (MSA) Strategic Plan (Lankford & Knowles, 1988). Figure 7.8 depicts this process.

There are seven basic distinct steps in the strategic management planning process. It should be noted that there are many variations of this process in the literature and in management planning practice. For more specifics on this topic, one should refer to McLean, Bannon, and Gray (1999). However, the following seven steps provide the basis for strategic planning within leisure organizations:

Step 1. *Organize, Scan or Scope Out the Environment.* Establish objectives, definitions, and expectations of the planning effort. Establish time frame for the project, focus of the planning effort, and area to be covered by the plan (geographic or departmental). Identify future important trends and determine external environmental factors that will affect these trends. Getting organized to plan will include some or all of the following:

- Get support from decision makers, managers, and staff;
- Define expectations (your intentions and desires);
- Select a planning team (MSA staff and community members); and
- Define how long the process will take.

Step 2. *Select Critical Issues or Opportunities.* Using the information in Step 1, choose the most critical or important issues to resolve or address. The list of issues should be prioritized based on MSA resources, staff strengths and weaknesses, realistic time frames, and the political (internal and external) environment.

Step 3. *Establish a Mission Statement and a Set of Broad Goals.* This step establishes the direction for strategy development to keep the MSA on track during the planning program. The mission statement should be "a marriage of external demands and internal limitations, a combination of dreams and reality." Mission formulation should answer:

- What does the organization do?
- For whom?
- How?
- Goals should clarify the agency mission and what the MSA hopes to aspire to.

Step 4. *External and Internal Assessment.* Identify forces outside and inside the MSA affecting change and achievement of mission or goals. The MSA should conduct a situational analysis consisting of:

Figure 7.6
Parks for Tomorrow: The Next 70 Years

The Next 70 Years

- Provide a system of interconnected, volunteer patrolled and maintained trails and greenways
- Acquire additional parkland suitable for active recreation facilities.
- Balance recreation development with protecting environmental features.
- Provide parks to meet upcounty recreation needs and revitalize downcounty urban areas.
- Cluster local park facilities for maximum efficiency in maintenance.
- Provide urban and neighborhood open spaces by the private sector.
- Build and maintain parks through public/private partnerships.
- Interpret natural, historic and cultural resources.
- Provide park information to the public through the Internet, computer stations in malls, parks, etc.

The First 70 Years

- Primary emphasis on land acquisition for conservation purposes in the 30s, 40s, 50s, and continuing through the 90s.
- Emphasis on provision of active recreation facilities for downcounty developing areas in the 60s, 70s and 80s.
- New regulations and increased concern about the environment in the 90s.
- Publicly constructed neighborhood parks to serve walk-to recreation needs of local residents.
- Local parks located within neighborhoods/Many parks built within downcounty floodplains.
- Trails that lack regional connections.
- Parks maintained by public park staff.
- Information provided through printed brochures.

Figure 7.7
The Planning Process

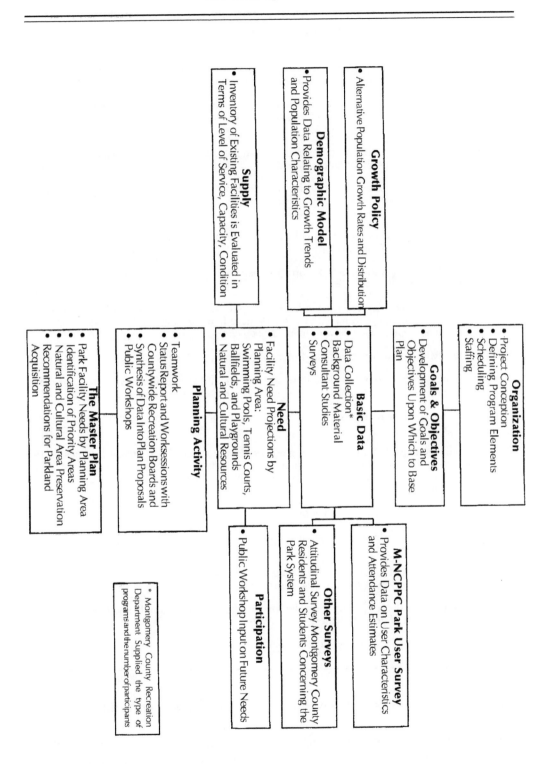

Growth Policy
• Alternative Population Growth Rates and Distribution

Demographic Model
• Provides Data Relating to Growth Trends and Population Characteristics

Supply
• Inventory of Existing Facilities is Evaluated in Terms of Level of Service, Capacity, Condition

Organization
• Project Conception
• Defining Program Elements
• Scheduling
• Staffing

Goals & Objectives
• Development of Goals and Objectives Upon Which to Base Plan

Basic Data
• Data Collection*
• Background Material
• Consultant Studies
• Surveys

Need
• Facility Need Projections by Planning Area: Swimming Pools, Tennis Courts, Ballfields, and Playgrounds
• Natural and Cultural Resources

Planning Activity
• Teamwork
• Status Report and Worksessions with Countywide Recreation Boards and
• Synthesis of Data Into Plan Proposals
• Public Workshops

The Master Plan
• Park Facility Needs by Planning Area
• Identification of Priority Areas
• Natural and Cultural Area Preservation
• Recommendations for Parkland Acquisition

M-NCPPC Park User Survey
• Provides Data on User Characteristics and Attendance Estimates

Other Surveys
• Attitudinal Survey Montgomery County Residents and Students Concerning the Park System

Participation
• Public Workshop Input on Future Needs

* Montgomery County Recreation Department Supplied the type of programs and the number of participants

Table 7.1
General Plan Refinement Goals, Objectives & Strategies Related to Park Trails

Provide a coordinated and comprehensive system of parks, recreation, and open space (Land Use Objective 8).

- Give priority to open space, park, and recreation investment in areas with the greatest existing or proposed residential density and in areas with important environmental features.

- Use open space, parks, and recreation facilities to shape and enhance the development and identity of individual neighborhoods, cluster developments, existing communities, and transitions between communities.

- Integrate open space, parks, and recreational facilities into urbanized areas to promote public activity and community identity.

- Plan for and encourage the provision of greenway to connect urban and rural open spaces, to provide access to parkland, to connect major stream valley park areas, and for recreational purposes such as walking and biking.

Provide pedestrian and bicyclists safe, direct, and convenient means of travel for transportation and recreation (Transportation Objective 6).

Connect parks and conservation areas to form an open space and conservation-oriented greenway system (Transportation Objective 2B).

- Conserve County waterways, wetlands, and sensitive parts of stream valleys to minimize flooding, pollution, sedimentation, and damage to the ecology and to preserve natural beauty and open space (Environment Objective 4).

- Identify and protect wetlands and other sensitive parts of watersheds.

- Prohibit development too close to streams, in the 100-year ultimate floodplain, and in flooding danger reach areas of dams, unless no feasible alternative is available.

- Maintain the natural character of drainage areas in the immediate vicinity of streams, rivers, and lakes.

- Minimize impacts from construction and operation of public and private facilities located in stream valleys, buffers, and floodplains; first priority should be given to preserving natural areas (avoidance), second priority to mitigation, and third priority to replacement with functional equivalents.

- Mandate "no net loss" of wetlands.

Preserve and enhance a diversity of plant and animal species in self-sustaining concentrations (Environment Objective 6).

- Plan a system of parks, conservation areas, subdivision open space, and easements to support a diversity of species in self-sustaining concentrations.

- Ensure protection of environmentally sensitive habitats and unbuildable land through the master plan and development review process.

- Minimize forest fragmentation to protect habitat continuity.

- External constraints and opportunities;
- Who or what is impacting your organization and how;
- What forces you must be aware of and prepared for;
- Internal strengths and weaknesses; and
- Get input for the entire organization (i.e., conduct an employee survey).

Table 7.2
Summary of Proposed Trail Project Completions 1999-2009

Plan Corridor	Hard Surface Trail Completions	Miles	Natual Surface Trail Completions	
Patuxent Corridor	NA		Jurisdiction of WSSC and State	
Seneca Greenway Corridor	NA		Seneca Trail	7.40
Northwest Branch Corridor	None		Kemp Mill Road to Ednor Road	4.80
C & O Canal Corridor	None		Muddy Branch Watts Branch	5.50 5.30
Rock Creek Corridor	• Rock Creek Trail Extensions • Gude Connector • Lake Needwood-Lake Frank Connector	1.25 1.10 0.20	Ag History Farm Park/Airpark Drive Underpass/Pope Farm Rachel Carson Park Lake Needwood to Ag History Farm	2.00 3.20 2.00
Capital Crescent Corridor	• Capital Crescent Trail • (interim) • Metropolitan Branch (interim)	2.20 1.20		
Eastern County Corridor	• Matthew Henson • Wheaton Regional to Randolph Road • Paint Branch Extension	4.80 0.70 0.40	Fairland Recreational Park	1 to 2
Upcounty Corridor	Magruder Branch Extension	0.90		
Total Miles		12.70		31.20

Step 5. *Develop Objectives, Policies and Strategies.* Using the information from the above step, develop action-oriented statements with respect to each strength and weakness identified and how action will be achieved. Objectives should be specific, measurable, and lead to the attainment of goals. Policies should express values of the recreation services and programs, and define why they exist. Strategies should include assumptions and targets for achievement.

Step 6. *Develop and Adopt an Implementation Plan.* This step identifies timetables, responsibilities, budgets, resources and so on for carrying out the actions identified above. Action plans should identify who does what, when, and how within specified time increments. Action plans might address communication, facilities, programs, finances, and resources.

Step 7. *Monitor the Plan and Scan the Environment.* This step is merely a monitoring of plan accomplishments. It is critical that the strategies adopted are working or carried out. When the environment changes, the MSA should be prepared to adjust strategies and update the plan. This monitoring system sets

Figure 7.8
Strategic Planning Process

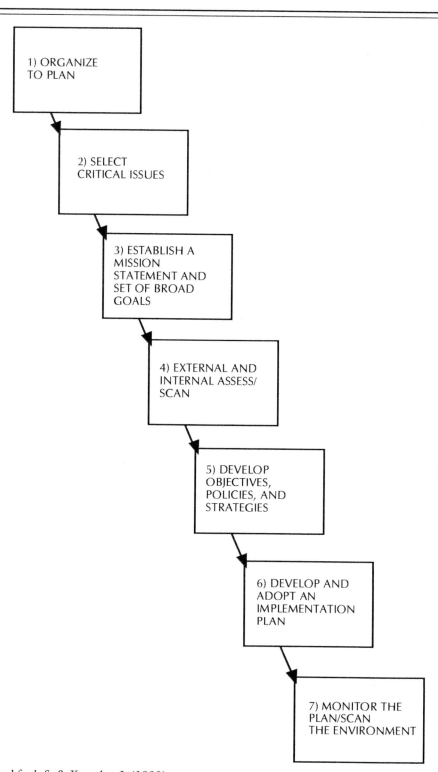

Source: Lankford, S. & Knowles, J. (1988).

up controls for review of action plans and objectives, strategies, and so on using the expertise of all staff. Basically, this step is the evaluation phase of the planning program.

Essentially, strategic management planning is:

1. A process for identifying internal and external strengths and weaknesses of an organization;

2. A process for identifying future trends, opportunities, and problems, internally and externally;

3. A process for identifying a means to innovate and create opportunities in management and service provision;

4. A process for decision making using those staff who are closest to problems, opportunities, customers, and facilities; and

5. A process for organizing tasks, and setting priorities, goals, and objectives.

Local Recreation Plans in Relationship to the Community Comprehensive Plan

The following section describes the relationships to local planning and development, and the recreation system. It is imperative that leisure service managers and their staff become more involved in local development efforts. We are the overseers of quality of life issues and livability (Edginton & McDonald, 2000).

Purpose of the Recreation Element of the Comprehensive Plan

Recreation, park, and leisure services issues, within a community comprehensive plan, are usually addressed in what is called the "recreation element" of the comprehensive plan. For the purposes of this section, "element" is interchangeable with "plan." It is important to note that comprehensive plans are also known as master plans (although sometimes this refers to a design plan for an area), development plans, the general plan, or simply the city plan. Of particular interest to leisure managers is that no matter what it is called, the content and process and subsequent decision-making procedures have a significant impact on the leisure service system in the community.

The purpose for the development of the recreation element is to help provide for both present and projected recreation needs. It is designed as a guide for future planning decisions and actions. This plan contains findings based on community surveys, policies that address citizen needs and concerns, and an implementation program to put these policies into effect. These policies are aimed at fulfilling the overall objective of the element or plan.

In order to help address present and projected needs, the element provides information to support the environmental, social, and economic significance of recreation, parks, and tourism at the community level. Inflation, diminished financial resources, and changing public attitudes heighten competition for the tax dollar. Decision makers and the general public should be aware of the benefits of establishing recreational outlets for everyone. Yet the recreation manager often takes it for granted that decision makers and the public realize the importance of community recreation services. Therefore, a recreation element to the general plan must be explicit in stating how parks and recreation are tied to economic development, community livability, and positive social change.

The remainder of the element addresses issues such as improving recreational facilities and resources in the area. Recreational standards, which are designed to determine deficiencies rather than the adequacy of the recreational outlets available, are also identified.

Values of Recreation, Parks, and Leisure Services Appealing to Decision Makers

To provide recreation, park, and leisure services outlets for citizens of the community, a system of parks and facilities should be established. These areas characterize the community, improve aesthetic quality, and soften the urban landscape. Open space, often established as recreational areas, provides relief by mitigating reflection, noise, and pollution. Vegetation absorbs pollutants and replenishes the oxygen supply.

In addition to the environmental advantages of establishing parks and recreation facilities, these areas provide the means for personal outlets and self-expression. It is often noted that if positive recreational pursuits are available, the problems of drinking, vandalism, and crime can be diminished. Social, physical, and cultural activities strengthen the "community" feeling.

Most people seek out open space and parks for emotional and physical renewal, the discharge of nervous energy, and as a relief from daily responsibilities. Leisure experiences improve physical, mental, and emotional health. They enhance motor, language, and recreational skills, promoting a healthy social community. Although open space and park lands have come under attack as locations for the increase of crime and vandalism, there is no evidence that the frequency and magnitude of crime and vandalism is concentrated in these areas. Importantly, the poorly designed open spaces, those which do not accommodate a diversity of uses and social interaction, are those that are more likely to become a void for increased crime and vandalism. Therefore, design, location, supervision, and the amount of open space available will determine how the area is used. Leisure service managers must be attuned not only to the planning, but also to the actual design of areas and facilities.

The provision of adequate and appropriate recreational programs, services, and facilities based on community needs and desires far outweighs the costs to the city, considering the costs of vandalism, crime, and so on. Public open space does not produce taxable income or become taxable real property. Increasing adjacent property values and lowering vandalism, alcoholism, crime, juvenile delinquency, and other disruptive social behaviors offsets this loss of tax base. Public open space requires few to no public services as compared to the public service costs required by more extensive developments.

Some level of discussion with decision makers on the environmental, social or community, personal, and economic benefits of recreation is necessary. Driver's benefits research (Driver,

Brown, & Peterson, 1991) is of use in this task. The Program for Recreation Research and Service (PRR&S) at the University of Hawaii has developed an extensive report for use at the city and county level (Lankford, 2000). This report documents both primary and secondary data on the environmental, social or community, personal, and economic benefits of recreation. The intent of the effort is to help local leisure service managers influence policy and budget allocations in favor of local leisure services.

Relationship to Other Recreation Plans

The city general plan (or comprehensive plan) is a statement of development policies in the form of a text, maps, and diagrams explaining objectives, standards, growth issues, environmental concerns, and alternative development proposals. The general plan consists of a number of related elements. The recreation element, in particular, is more directly related to the land use, circulation, housing and open space elements.

The Land Use Element. Trails and parks are part of the physical development pattern of the uses of land. Trails and parks are also a primary category of the quantity of land owned by government. Additionally, the quantity of park land is directly related to the standards of population density in this element.

The Circulation or Transportation Element. The effectiveness of recreational programs and the use of parks and trails are highly dependent on the degree of accessibility to their users. A comprehensive bicycle network plan will allow the city to study parallel trails for equestrians and hikers.

The Housing Element. The appropriate location of parks relative to housing helps create neighborhood and community focal points. In addition, housing locations relative to a network of open space enhances community livability.

The Open Space Element. Park sites and trails are part of the open space system. The outdoor recreation component of the open space system includes areas of outstanding scenic, historical, natural, and cultural value. The element addresses areas particularly suitable for park and recreation purposes, such as rivers and streams, wildlife habitats, and areas that serve as links between major recreation and open space reservations, including utility easements, abandoned railroad easements, and scenic highway corridors.

The elements of the general plan are all to some degree related and interdependent. Together they provide the policy framework to direct development needed to serve people and their activities within a given political jurisdiction and its area of influence. There are relationships evident between conservation of natural resources and open space. A fundamental purpose of the general plan is to promote harmony and balance between and among conflicting forces of growth and change, conservation and development.

Broad Recreation and Park Objectives and Policies Related to Planning

Objective. To provide adequate recreation facilities and programs, and open space for both present and future residents of the city and community.

Policies

1. To ensure that recreation facilities are compatible with adjacent land uses, the maintenance of environmental quality, and protection of property rights.

2. To formulate a park and recreation master plan for the optimum use of existing facilities and programs.

3. To attempt to ensure that those people who use recreation facilities contribute to the cost of providing and operating facilities.

4. To provide recreation programs that cater to local needs, desires, age groups, and all citizens in general.

Roles and Responsibilities for Providing Leisure Services in the Community

The responsibility for providing parks and recreation is intergovernmental, involving school districts and city, county, state, and federal governments. Responsibility and opportunity also lie within the private and commercial sectors, and with the landowner, developer, citizen, and entrepreneur.

The authority and responsibility to conduct public park and recreation programs is not reserved by the federal government and is, therefore, delegated to the states by the Tenth Amendment to the U.S. Constitution. In turn, the State of California for example, by law, has allowed local government (cities and counties), as well as special districts and schools, to conduct public recreation in addition to the role played by the state.

The federal government draws its authority to be in the recreation business, as it does in education, from the General Health and Welfare Clause in the U.S. Constitution. Although the lines of responsibility are sometimes undefined, it is apparent that all levels of government and education recognize the importance of recreation facilities and positive recreation activities as a significant condition for the well-being of our society.

School Districts. The seven cardinal principles of education, one which states that the school is responsible to "educate for the worthy use of leisure," illustrates the deep concern and responsibility of the schools to prepare, train, and provide programs and facilities for people to use their leisure time constructively. One of the roles of schools is to provide facilities and equipment for the use of recreation. In some areas, schools are given the authority and direction and an allowed finances to assist in providing recreation.

There are many ways in which school districts and cities can or should cooperate to make the most efficient and effective public recreation possible. Below are the ways in which these entities should cooperate, in the best interests of the taxpayer:

1. Establishing community recreational goals and objectives;
2. Assessing recreation program and facility needs;
3. Assessing resources available to help meet recreational needs;
4. Facilities–
   a. Master planning (determining overall facilities needed)
   b. Location of facilities
   c. Setting priorities for development

d. Design of facilities for joint use

e. Construction and improvement

f. Financing overall facilities

g. Financing facility improvements

h. Use of facilities;

5. Maintenance–
a. Grounds
b. Special facilities (pools, etc.)
c. Training of grounds personnel
d. Purchasing of maintenance supplies and equipment;

6. Program–
a.Design of activities and priorities
b.Articulation between school and recreation programs
c.Teaching of leisure skills
d.Financing recreation programs
e.Publicizing recreation programs
f.Leadership–
(1) Recruitment of personnel for recreation
(2) Selection of person nel for recreation work in the schools
(3) Training of personnel in recreation activities and schools concerns
(4) Evaluation of recreation leadership against set objectives
g. Supervision of recreation programs
h. Evaluation of programs; and

7. Paying utility, insurance, and overhead costs

The following presents some of the roles of local government with respect to recreation planning concerns.

City Government. A city general plan addresses the individual responsibility for providing parks, recreation, and leisure services facilities, and activities within its city limits. Additionally, in accordance with local public need and demand, cities may establish recreational programs to include sports. These include both instructional and expressive activities.

Special Districts. In unincorporated areas, a special district can be formed that allows a collection of taxes in order to provide recreation services. The special recreation district would have both the authority and responsibility to provide for unmet recreational facilities and program needs in the unincorporated areas of the county. A comprehensive recreation plan for the special district would be developed that identifies needs, deficiencies, policies, and strategies for service delivery. The special district is governed by an elected board of directors.

County or Regional Government. A county has both the authority and responsibility to provide for unmet recreational facilities and program needs in the unincorporated areas of the county, and to address itself to the protection and provision of recreation resources that will benefit the county as a whole. Under California state law, for example, each county may adopt a recreation element as part of its general plan to serve as a guide for providing recreational areas, facilities, and programs. It is important to note that some states (Oregon, for example) require counties and cities to adopt a recreation and park plan or element to the general plan. The county may subsequently develop ordinances and policies to help achieve the goals and objectives set forth in its general plan recreation element. Additionally, the county may provide, through dependent or independent recreation and park districts or through joint-powers agreements, services to residents of county areas outside of cities that are not provided with such services.

State Government. The state's primary area of responsibility is in the acquisition, development, maintenance, and conservation of park and recreation, and historical areas and facilities, which have both resource and participant values. These are normally of statewide significance or overlap county boundary lines. In addition to providing facilities, the state stocks county rivers and creeks with fish and enhances game refuge habitats for wildlife reproduction.

Federal Government. The federal government has responsibility for the preservation and development of park, recreation, and historical resources of areas that have nationwide recreation, cultural, or historical values, regardless of their location. Communities that are located adjacent to these resources benefit from the possible tourist attractions and expenditures. Yet it is crucial that local recreation resources are well-planned, allocated, and managed for the public (taxpayer) good (Lankford, Williams, & Knowles-Lankford 1997).

Planning Definitions for the Leisure Service Manager

Some definitions useful in the planning process are offered in the short paragraphs below.

Comprehensive Plan. A plan that indicates the principal acts by which all of the most important ends are to be attained; or the official statement of a governmental body that sets forth its policies concerning resource allocation for operation and development.

Critical Path Method. A flowchart illustrating all of the successive steps in a plan or a program, from beginning to end.

EIS/EIR. Environmental Impact Statement (EIS the required by the National Environmental Protection Act NEPA); Environmental Impact Report (EIR, required by California Environmental Quality Act, CEQA). Both define existing conditions, impacts of proposed plans or developments, and alternatives to proposed actions, and describe mitigation measures needed to eliminate or minimize adverse impacts.

Goals. A desired state, condition, end, or purpose toward which progress is directed.

Impact. The influence of one project or condition on another. Potential degradation of the environment.

Issue. A conflict between the objectives of different individuals or groups on a given topic.

Land Use. The occupation or reservation of land or water area for any human activity or any defined purpose. It also includes the use of air space above the land or water.

Master plan. A comprehensive, overall, detailed policy statement or program guide that considers all influencing factors in taking action to accomplish objectives and move toward the goal. (See Comprehensive Plan.)

Objectives. Measurable ends or means that can be reached or accomplished in moving toward goal achievement.

Plan. A program or course of action that can be put into effect and that is expected to accomplish desired objectives and lead to the attainment of the ends sought. A means to reach or move toward an end or goal.

Planning. The process of developing, monitoring, appraising, maintaining, and updating, as necessary, a plan of action.

Planning Process. The sequence of steps that is necessary to develop a plan. In practice, these are not discrete steps, and the sequence may vary. Feedback between the steps is continuous, and each step is interconnected with all the other steps. Citizen participation and input are key parts of every step in the planning process.

Policy. A statement or framework for guiding action and decisions for organizations or legislative bodies.

Programs. Time-phased organization and allocation of resources to accomplish objectives and move towards a goal.

Public involvement or Citizen Participation The opportunity for the maximum feasible participation by citizens in decision making regarding resource allocation or land use planning. This includes public hearings, advisory committees, and procedures that may be necessary to provide desired public input in a particular instance or situation.

Recreation Resources. Land and water areas and associated flora, fauna, climate, and environmental conditions, as well as facilities, people, organizations, and financial support that provide opportunities for recreation.

Recreation Resource Planning. A process that relates to planning for the leisure and recreation needs of people as related to land use, resources, and facilities. The use of information to facilitate decision making that results in the allocation of resources to accommodate the current and future leisure needs of a population and planning area growth.

Summary

This chapter discussed the relationships between decision making and planning. It is of particular importance to note that managers make decisions that affect the organization in both short- and long-term perspectives. They need information to make those decisions. Managers also need to use planning processes and subsequent plans to provide the necessary structure in order to make relevant, timely, and educated decisions. This chapter emphasized that planning really is decision making, and that decision making really is a form of planning. It was noted that many times the process of planning is more important than the actual plan produced. It is the interaction of staff, management, citizens, and decision makers, that makes planning useful in managing leisure organizations.

The chapter highlighted a critical path method that can be used in comprehensive, master, or site planning situations. In addition, eight essential elements of effective community recreation planning were identified. These elements should be prevalent within any planning procedure or process. It was stressed that citizen involvement is necessary and of the utmost importance in planning for leisure service organizations. Strategic planning was introduced using an example from a leisure service organization. The necessary steps for strategic planning were noted, and suggestions were made regarding how this type of planning is useful in leisure service management.

Linkages were made between recreation planning and land use, transportation, open space, and housing at the community level. It is important that the leisure service manager become involved in local development issues and projects. It is equally important that leisure service managers educate the decision makers on the value of recreation in the context of community planning. Finally, roles and responsibilities of various levels of government were identified with respect to planning.

Discussion Questions

1. What is planning?

2. What is decision making?

3. What makes organizations effective?

4. How can planning enhance the effectiveness of decision making?

5. What do managers do in their work that relates to a planning function?

6. List and discuss the essential elements of any planning project or effort.

7. Describe the steps in the critical path model presented in this book.

8. Describe the steps in the strategic planning model.

9. Describe the problem-solving process and how is relates to planning.

10. How are land use, housing, transportation, and open space planning related to leisure service delivery?

References

Bannon, J. (1976). *Leisure resources: Its comprehensive planning.* Englewood Cliffs, NJ: Prentice-Hall.

Bannon, J., & Busser, J. A. (1992). *Problem solving in recreation and parks.* Champaign, IL: Sagamore Publishing .

Brooks, F. A. (2000). Critical path method for facility and area planning [Telephone interview]. Chico–Bidwell Park Planning Project, and Lake Tahoe and the Lassen National Forest Projects.

Dimaggio, P., & Useem, M. (1980). Small-scale policy research in the Arts. In *Policy analysis.* Sage.

Donnelly, J. H., Gibson, J. L., & Ivancevich, J. M. (1990). *Fundamentals of management* (7th ed.). Homewood, IL: BPI/Irwin.

Driver, B., & Knopf, R. C. (1981). Some thoughts on the quality of outdoor recreation research and other contraints on its application. In *Social research in national parks and wilderness areas.* Atlanta, GA: U.S. Department of Interior, National Park Service, Southeast Regional Office.

Driver, B., Brown, P. J., & Peterson, G. L. (1991). *Benefits of leisure.* State College, PA: Venture.

Drucker, P. (1987). *Managing in turbulent times.* New York: Harper & Row.

Edginton, C. R., Neal, L. L., & Edginton, S. R. (1989). Motivating park and recreation professionals: A cross cultural analysis. *Journal of Park and Recreation Administration, 7*(3), 33-43.

Edginton, C. R., & McDonald, D. (2000). Community coordination and cooperation. In C.R. Edginton (Ed.), *Enhancing the livability in Iowa communities: The role of recreation, natural resource development, and tourism* (pp. 86–99). Cedar Falls, IA: University of Northern Iowa.

Friedmann, J. (1987). *Planning in the public domain: From knowledge to action.* Princeton, NJ: Princeton University Press.

Harper, J. (1993). The FORKS: A unique inner-city development focus on public participation. *Journal of the World Leisure & Recreation Association, 35*(2), 5–9.

Jackson, J. B. (1994). *A sense of place, A sense of time.* New Haven, CT: Yale University Press.

Knowles-Lankford, J., & Lankford, S. (1995a). Our professional responsibility for a preferred future. *World Leisure and Recreation Association Journal, 36*(4) 40–44.

Knowles-Lankford, J., & Lankford, S. (1995b). Sustainable Practices: Implications for tourism and recreation development. In S. F. McCool, & A. E. Watson, (Eds.), *Linking tourism, the environment, and sustainability (pp. 18-*

22). [Proceedings of a special session of the annual meeting of the National Recreation and Parks Association; October. 12–14, 1994. Minneapolis, Minnesota. Gen. Tech. Rep. INT-GTR-323]. Ogden, UT: U.S. Department of Agriculture, Forest Service, Intermountain Research Station.

Knowles-Lankford, J. (1993). The role of parks and recreation in sustainable community development. *Journal of the World Leisure and Recreation Association, 35*(2), 13–17.

Knowles-Lankford, J. (1999). *Planning lecture.* University of Hawaii, School of TIM.

Lankford, S. (1981). A study of planning processes used by selected resource management agencies. Unpublished master's thesis. Department of Parks and Recreation, California State University, Chico, California.

Lankford, S. (1989, May). Customize your park program. *Parks and Recreation, 24*(5), 52–53.

Lankford, S. (1990a). Leadership: A requirement for strategic management. *Management Strategy, 14*(1), 1.

Lankford, S. (1990b). Promoting innovation in public organizations: The benefits of strategic thinking and planning. *Leisure Watch, 5*(2), 5–6.

Lankford, S. (1990c). Public hearings and the park and recreation commissioner. *Management Strategy, 14*(2) 1.

Lankford, S. (1994). Attitudes and perceptions toward tourism and rural regional development. *Journal of Travel Research, 32*(3), 35–43.

Lankford, S., & Knowles, J. (1982). *General plan.* Corning, CA.

Lankford, S., & Knowles-Lankford, J. (1989–1990, Winter). To what extent is planning more or less decision-making? *Leisure Watch, 4*(4), 2–3.

Lankford, S., & Cramb, D. (1992, July). Municipal park and recreation advisory committee effectiveness. *Recreation Canada, 50*(3), p. 12-17.

Lankford, S. V. (1992, May 9–11). *Community participation in planning for tourism and the arts—Observations and discussion.* Presentation at The Economics of Tourism and the Arts: 2000, University of Oregon Continuation Center and the Department of Recreation and Tourism Management, Eugene, Oregon.

Lankford, S., Neal, L., & Buxton, B. P. (1992). An examination and comparison of work motivators in public, private/commercial, nonprofit, and Armed Forces leisure service organizations. *Journal of Park and Recreation Administration, 10*(4), 57–70.

Lankford, S. V., Neal, L., & Knowles-Lankford J. (1995). Essential elements of recreation and park planning. *Journal of Leisure and Recreation Studies (Korea), 12*(1), 13–20.

Lankford, S. V., Williams, A., & Knowles, J. (1997). Perceptions of outdoor recreation opportunities and support for tourism development. *Journal of Travel Research, 35*(3), 65–69.

Lankford, S. V. (2000). Benefits of parks, recreation and leisure services in Hawaii. Honolulu, HI: University of Hawaii, Program for Recreation Research and Service.

McLean, D., Bannon, J., & Gray, H. (1999). *Leisure resources: Its Comprehensive Planning.* (2nd ed.). Champaign, IL: Sagamore Publishing .

Mill, J. S. (1974). *On liberty.* Harmondsworth, England: Penguin Books.

Mitra, A., & Lankford, S. V. (1998). *Research methods in recreation, parks, and leisure services.* Champaign, IL: Sagamore Publishing .

Neal, L. L. (1984). Motivational discrepancy between staff levels in municipal leisure services. *Journal of Park and Recreation Administration, 2*(4), 25–29.

Neal, L. L., & Lankford, S. (1995). To lead followers: A key requirement for strategic management of leisure programs and facilities. *Hong Kong Recreation Review, 7,* 12–15.

Perloff, H. (1980). *Planning the post-industrial city.* Washington, DC: Planners Press (APA).

Quade, E. (1995) *Analysis for public decisions.* New York: American Elsevier.

Rossi, P. H., Wright, J. D., & Wright, P. H. (1978). The theory and practice of applied social research. *Evaluation Quarterly 2, 171–191.*

Shrivastava, P., & Mitroff, I. I. (1984, January). Enhancing organizational research utilization: The role of decision makers assumptions. *Academy of Management Review, 18–26.*

Slater, D. C. (1984). *Management of local planning.* Washington, DC: ICMA.

Taggart, W., Robey, D., & Krocek, G. (1985, April). Managerial decision styles and general dominance: An empirical study. *Journal of Management Studies, 175–192.*

Tjosvold, D. (1984, March). Effects of crisis orientation on managers' approaches to controversy in decision-making. *Academy of Management Journal, 130–138.*

Chapter

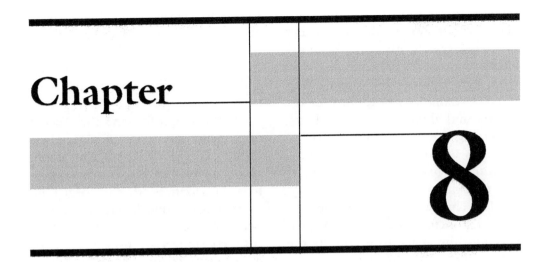

8

Marketing Leisure Services

Photo courtesy of the Battle Creek (MI) Parks and Recreation Department.

Marketing is about knowing the customer's needs so well that your services pre-sell themselves.

Introduction

Just as it is important to understand the principles of management, motivation, communication, leadership, and financing, it is also essential to understand the concept of *marketing* as it applies to the delivery of leisure services. Marketing is a method of directing the activities that take place in an organization toward the satisfaction of consumer needs and demands. To survive and succeed, leisure service organizations must do the following: (1) attract sufficient resources; (2) convert those resources into programs, facilities, or services; and (3) distribute those programs or services to various consuming publics. This system relies on the concept of *voluntary exchange*. That is, in exchange for services or programs delivered, the leisure service organization receives resources in the form of tax dollars and direct user fees. Thus, marketing may be defined as a set of activities aimed at facilitating and expediting exchanges with target markets (Crompton, 1983).

This chapter will examine the various components of the marketing process and how marketing impacts the delivery of leisure services

The Nature of Exchanges

Exchange requires two conditions. First, there must be two or more parties for the transaction to take place. Second, each party in the exchange must have something that might be valued by the other party. In a profit-oriented organization, one party provides a service in order to obtain revenue from another. In this case, marketing is based on the assumption that satisfying cus-

tomers will ensure profitability. Thus, marketing activities are based on trying to find out what an organization's specific customers or target markets want and then providing services that meet those wants.

In the nonprofit arena, the concept of exchange is more complex. Members of the target audience for a nonprofit agency are being asked to incur costs or to make sacrifices (that is, to give up something valuable) in return for promised benefits. In general, the kinds of costs consumers are usually asked by nonprofit marketers to "pay" are one of four types (see Figure 8.1):

1. *Economic Costs.* Consumers are simply asked to give up money or goods to a nonprofit or to buy a product or service (e.g., Girl Scout cookies, Boy Scout popcorn);

2. *The sacrifice of Old Ideas, Values, or Views of the World.* Consumers give up traditional attitudes about social causes (e.g., environmental awareness versus consumerism, as proposed by the Sierra Club);

Figure 8.1
Cost/Benefit Matrix for the Profit/Nonprofit Sectors

| | **Benefits** | | | |
Costs	A Product	A Service	Social	Psychological
Give up economic assets	Buy a poster	Pay for surgery or an education	Donate to alma mater	Donate to charity
Give up old ideas, values, opinions	Receive free Goodwill	Support neighborhood vigilantes	Support Republicans	Oppose abortion
Give up old behaviors, undertake or learn new behaviors	Practice birth control and receive a radio	Undertake drug detoxification treatment	Go to geriatric group once a week	Wear seat belts
Give up time or energy	Participate in a study and receive a coffeemaker	Attend a free concert	Volunteer for Junior League	Give blood

3. *The sacrifice of Old Patterns of Behaviors.* Consumers give up physical or psychological habits that may be damaging (e.g., stop smoking campaigns led by the American Cancer Society); and

4. *The sacrifice of Time and Energy.* Consumers provide needed volunteers for the agency (e.g., who volunteer for a variety of community organizations).

In exchange for these kinds of sacrifices, consumers in nonprofit enterprises can receive three types of benefits:

1. Economic benefits in the form of both goods and services;

2. Social benefits in terms of forming community and individual relationships; and

3. Psychological benefits or a sense of well-being.

The National Recreation and Park Association's commitment to Benefits of Leisure is an example of trying to promote these types of exchanges (see Figure 8.2).

Types of Markets

As mentioned above, markets are specific groups of people. They consist of individuals who have certain needs and are willing to exchange something of value to satisfy those needs. Markets may be differentiated from one another by identifying subclusters of individuals who consume a specific type of service. Thus, persons consuming leisure services may be referred to as existing within the subcluster known as the "leisure market."

As Crompton (1983:8) points out, historically, the importance of target marketing has not been widely recognized in the field of leisure services. Instead, programs and services have been directed at "everybody" or "the average user" rather than at target groups of "some specific bodies." This has resulted in the following patterns:

1. Standardized services are offered at uniform prices;

2. Services reach only a small number of an organization's potential target markets; and

3. Potential resources are lost from missed opportunities for meaningful exchange.

In general, not-for-profit organizations have a more difficult time in defining the target market, because they have more than one public to serve. A public may be defined as "a distinct group of people or organization that has an actual or a potential interest in, or impact on, the agency." Most nonprofit organizations seek support from a number of such distinct groups. Among these potential publics are the following:

1. *A Reciprocal Public.* This represents a public that is interested in the agency, with the agency interested in the public;

2. *A Sought Public.* This refers to a group from which the agency is interested in gaining support, but one that is not necessarily interested in the agency; and

3. *An Unwelcome Public.* This is a collection of individuals who are interested in the agency, but in whom the agency is not interested.

In addition, certain publics have an impact on the input of resources into

Figure 8.2
Benefits of Leisure Promotion

T-shirts are "walking billboards" and a great way to change public perception, increase awareness, and communicate to internal and external audiences that what you do is so much more than fun and games! Great for staff, volunteers, and summer campers. Join more than 800 park and recreation agencies and put "The Benefits Are Endless . . . " to wor for you. Everything available to fit your needs—add your logo too!

Call The ADvisors Marketing Group today at (760) 721-3737 for complete ordering and pricing information!

Mention this ad and receive a FREE Benefits Sports Bag with your first purchase!

the agency, for example, support, supplier, and employee publics; certain groups that are involved in the output of services, namely, various consumer publics; and certain groups that sanction the actions of an agency, such as the general, competitor, special, or government publics. Although not all these publics will be directly related to marketing activities, they have to be considered within any marketing strategy because of their potential positive or negative effects on the viability of an agency.

Market Segmentation

What exactly is the "leisure market"? Do all individuals in this area seek the same goods and services? Obviously, the leisure market is a heterogeneous mix comprised of even smaller groups of individuals having similar wants and needs. Thus, leisure service managers need to segment the larger group into these smaller groups in order to better facilitate the exchange process.

Marketing segmentation, as defined by Pride and Ferrell (1980: 147) is the process of dividing a total clientele into market groups consisting of people who have relatively similar service needs, for the purpose of designing a marketing mix (or mixes) that more precisely matches the needs of individuals in a selected segment (or segments). How are these segments determined?

Kotler (1980) states that three criteria must be met if meaningful market segments are to be developed. The first criterion used is that of size. Specifically, each segment should be sufficiently large—or in the case of nonprofit organizations where the resource base is small, sufficiently important—to be worth considering for the develop-

ment of distinct programs or services. In these cases, size must be practical in terms of economics to tailor it to a separate marketing mix.

The second criterion used is that of measurability. That is, the leisure service manager should be able to quantify a market size. Generally speaking, demographic variables such as age, gender, income, race, and ethnicity should be easily obtainable and may provide fairly concrete measures.

The third criterion used is that of accessibility. A key ingredient in creating an exchange process is the ability to communicate with potential consumers. Isolated senior citizens, people who do not speak English or youth who have dropped out of school are often difficult to reach even though they may be important markets for public and nonprofit recreation services. Thus, imaginative and unusual marketing approaches may be needed.

Haley (1968) has identified two benefit approaches (macro and micro) that can be used in market segmentation (see Table 8.1). In the macro approach, the agency identifies the benefits sought by the total potential clientele, and then defines the groups of people who seek each set of benefits by using sociodemographic, geographic or behavioral descriptors. This fulfills the criteria of measurablility and accessibility. In the micro approach, the agency first looks at market segments according to geographic, sociodemographic, or behavioral descriptors, and then identifies the benefits that each of these market segments seek. This approach is more widely used in agencies where little sophisticated research and few analyses are conducted.

There is no set formula for determining which descriptors are likely to

Table 8.1
Two Approaches to Market Segmentation

Macro Approach

Identify the benefits sought
by the total potential clientele

Define the group of people
who seek each set of benefits
using some combination of
geographic, sociodemographic,
and/or behavioral descriptors.

Macro Approach

Define the groups of people
using geographic, sociodemographics,
and/or behavioral descriptors

Identify the benefits sought by
each of these defined groups

be most useful for segmenting a particular market. Professional experience and judgment by the leisure service manager is probably the most important tool in the decision-making process. However, the following discussion of sociodemographic, behavioral, and geographic descriptors will provide insight into how market segmentation might occur.

Sociodemographic Descriptors

The most common descriptors used are those that divide a group by observable personal characteristics. For instance, Crompton (1983:17) cites the Fat Men's Basketball League established by the City of St. Petersburg, Florida, as a way of using these descriptors to reach a target population. All participants in the league had to weigh over 220 pounds and be shorter than 6'1" in order to play. The city identified a target market that wanted to play basketball but whose members could not compete in the regular leagues. The game was adapted to their needs (zone defenses and no fast breaks) and resulted in the agency's

being able to reach a group of citizens who would otherwise have been excluded.

It should be recognized that although demographics can provide a starting point for market segmentation, not all demographic variables affect the individual in similar ways. Rather, it is usually a combination of items that provides a clearer picture of various markets. For instance, looking at the variables of age, gender, and martial status, one might select groups that are seeking very different leisure benefits (see Table 8.2). It is important that the leisure manager understand not only sociodemographic variables, but the interaction between these variables and leisure behavior.

Behavioral Descriptors

The source of leisure behavior is both intrinsic and extrinsic (Edginton, Hanson, Edginton, Hudson 1998). Leisure behavior is influenced by the leisure competencies that an individual possesses and is encouraged by the availability of leisure activities and facilities.

Table 8.2
Common Demographic Segmentation Variables

Characteristic	Typical Breakdown
Age	Under 6, 6-11, 12-19, 20-34, 35-49, 50-64, 65+
Gender	Male, Female
Family Life Cycle	Young, single; young, married, no children; young, married, youngest child under 6; young, married, youngest child 6 or older; older, married, with children older; older, married, no children under 18; older, single; other
Income	Under $2,500; $2,500-$7,500; $7,500-$15,000; $15,000-$20,000; $20,000-$30,000; $30,000-$45,000; $45,000-$55,000; $55,000-$65,000; $65,000-$75,000; over $75,000.
Occupation	Professional and technical managers; officials, and proprietors; clerical, sales; craftsmen, foremen; operatives; farmers; retired; students; housewives; unemployed.
Education	Grade school or less; some high school; high school graduate; some college; college graduate; postgraduate work; graduate degree.
Religion	Catholic, Protestant, Jewish, Muslim, Other.
Race	Caucasian, Oriental, Hispanic, African-American, American Indian, other.
Nationality	North American, European, African, Asian, South American, Australian.

Four behavioral descriptors commonly used to segment markets are usage rate, level of ability, level of specialization, and lifestyle.

Usage Rate. Usage rate segments potential clientele by the extent to which a particular service offering is used. For instance, common descriptors used are nonusers, potential users, first time users, regular users, and so on. These categories enable an agency both to focus the efforts on delivering the benefits sought by a particular group, and to attempt to broaden its base of support by encouraging other types of users to become regular users. Although there is a temptation to try to focus on potential users, those who use a facility on a regular basis generally represent a more solid core than the larger potential market. In terms of efficiency of effort and cost, regular users should not be overlooked.

Level of Ability. Level of ability has frequently been used as a market descriptor. Especially in athletic leagues, an attempt is made to provide different levels to accommodate the abilities of all participants. Thus, it is not uncommon to see A, B, and C leagues set up to maximize the satisfaction, learning, or progression of participants. By encouraging participants to join activities with others of like ability, the level of satisfaction is likely to be improved and the ability to sustain regular users is increased.

Level of Specialization. Inherent in any recreation activity are benefits that range from general to specific. The more general the benefits sought, the easier it is for an agency to substitute activities or environments. For example, if one is a novice in the area of hiking, an agency needs to expend very few resources for equipment or organization. For this individual, the agency would serve as an information source, providing guidance about the types of trails available for day hikes, suggestions on footwear, and basic safety instruction. On the other end would be the experienced backpacker who desires to blaze his or her own trail in the wilderness. For this individual, the agency must be much more directive and structured in the information that is delivered and the way that the program is packaged. Most participants in local programs seek general, not specific, benefits. When specialized benefits are available, individuals are generally willing to pay a higher price, invest more time and effort, and are responsive to different kinds of promotional messages. But careful analysis should be made to ensure that the specialized market is large enough to warrant the cost, time, and effort needed to cultivate it.

Lifestyle. This is based on human profiles of potential clientele. As mentioned in the sociodemographic section, a leisure service manager gains only limited information from demographic variables. In other words, even though these variables describe who potential markets are, they do not help describe the whys of their participation. The most widely used approach to lifestyle measurement and segmentation is based on activity needs, interests, and preferences on questionnaires. Thus, potential clientele are asked to describe lifestyle needs, interests, and preferences on a 5-point scale with a range from "strongly agree" to "strongly disagree". Depending on the items on a questionnaire, the manager is then able to construct specific profiles of potential users based on the answers.

Geographic descriptors. These are segments of potential markets by geographic boundaries such as neighborhood, city, county, and region. The basic assumption underlying this type of segmentation is that there are limits to how far different client groups are prepared to travel for particular types of services. Thus, distance and travel time to a specific facility or event helps to identify potential users of the services. It should be noted, however, that not all activities or facilities have the same drawing power. A "tot lot" in a neighborhood where there are very few children will not have the same usage as one in a neighborhood that caters to young families, even though both areas are within easy walking distance of community members. Thus, simply looking at geographic distance and space standards does not give the leisure manager a clear picture of potential markets.

Selection of Target Markets

After target markets are identified, the next decision step for the leisure service manager is to determine how the agency's resources will be allocated among the various segments. In the private sector, an agency usually gives priority to developing those market segments that are most likely to be responsive to particular offerings, and thus that will provide the largest profit. However, public park and recreation agencies, as well as those in the nonprofit sector, face a more complicated dilemma. Because these agencies seek to serve multiple potential markets, they need to decide who receives what messages, whether groups that are least responsive should be ignored, and which markets should be given service priority. These are policy questions that must guide the methods used in the selection of target markets.

The three basic strategies used to select target markets are called undifferentiated, differentiated, and concentrated (see Figure 8.3). *Undifferentiated marketing* means that the same marketing mix is developed and offered to all potential client groups. This strategy is employed once a leisure manager has reviewed all the differences between potential target markets and has concluded that the common needs of all these markets are greater than the individual wants and preferences. Unfortunately, many times this strategy is employed by default; that is, an agency does not take the time or effort to analyze potential markets. Although there may be a few occasions when a single marketing mix can effectively serve everyone, this "one size fits all" approach rarely satisfies the majority of potential markets.

Differentiated marketing allows an agency to develop a variety of marketing mixes, each tailored to a particular target market. Although this method enables an agency to adapt its services to the wants of a particular client group, it is expensive both in terms of time and money. Ideally, this strategy allows an agency to match specific benefits to specific needs of potential clients.

A concentrated strategy is a compromise between undifferentiated and differentiated marketing. It allows the agency to focus on only one client group for a specific event or activity. For instance, not all members of the target market may be interested in a rock concert. Chances are that, in this case, a promotional and pricing strategy directed at a specific target segment will be more cost-effective and successful in the long run than trying to reach everyone. However, such a strategy cannot be exclusionary. The courts have held that once a public service is offered, that service must be made available to all residents who are eligible. Thus, an agency must not use a concentrated strategy that directs the resources only to one specific segment all of the time.

Marketing Positioning

As previously discussed, recreation, park, and leisure agencies cannot be all things to all people. Rather, their primary goal is to serve those citizens who are underserved by other organizations. In theory, all community leisure and recreation agencies should complement rather than compete with one another. In actuality, competition can be fierce unless agencies realize that they should find a market niche through which they can truly serve the needs of the community. In order to do this, a leisure service manager needs to look at what other agencies are doing and whom they are serving in order to determine the distinctive contribution that the agency can make in enhancing the community's quality of life. This is done through a process called *position marketing*. Position marketing entails:

1. Determining the expectations and desires for various program services and facility features;

2. Assessing target markets' current perception (positive and negative) of the program services and or facilities about those features;

3. Identifying other similar or substitute programs and facilities and

Figure 8.3
Three Alternative Market Selection Strategies

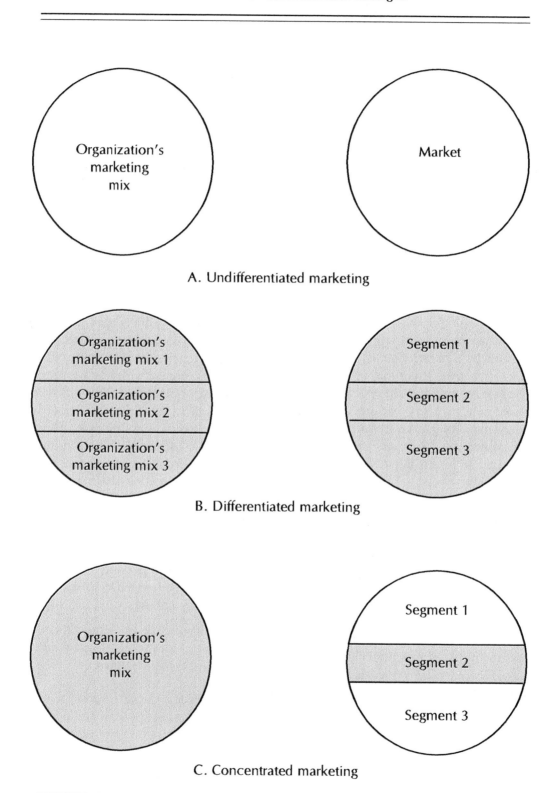

A. Undifferentiated marketing

B. Differentiated marketing

C. Concentrated marketing

their strengths and weaknesses for those same features;

4. Developing a position matrix that delineates underserved market segments; and

5. Determining the ways to enhance or change different elements of the marketing mix to improve services or facilities.

Figure 8.4 provides an example of the market positioning for an after-school child care service sponsored by a local park and recreation agency. This example depicts a relatively large number of organizations competing in Segment 1, which is characterized by above average family incomes and 8:00 to 5:00 work schedules. Abundant opportunities appear to be available to this segment of the market. Fewer opportunities are available to those with below average family incomes and whose schedules are either earlier or later than the typical work day. Hence, a possible positioning mix might be to provide services in a neighborhood school extending past 5:00 p.m.

A matrix approach to position marketing allows a leisure service manager to look at several different variables at one time in order to determine who the underserved groups may be. The more information available to the manager, the clearer the profile that can be developed. As new programs and services are added by other community agencies, the position matrix will need to be reevaluated.

Marketing Mix

The next step in the marketing process is to determine the correct marketing mix for achieving the goals and objectives targeted to selected markets. Traditionally, the marketing mix consist of the four P's: product, price, place, and promotion. Through the manipulation of these four elements, the leisure service manager can design a mix that fits the needs and preferences of the various market segments. It should be noted that the failure of a particular recreation service might not necessarily mean that the targeted group was not interested in the activity. Rather, it may be the result of poor service (product), high cost (price), availability (place), or poor communication (promotion). Many times, a readjustment of one of these elements can lead to increased success.

Product

The most basic marketing decision that organizations make is which products (i.e., goods and services) to offer to the target market. A product is defined as anything that can be offered to a market to satisfy a need. It includes physical objects, services, persons, places, organizations, and ideas. Other names for a product include the offer, the value package, or the benefit bundle (Kotler, 1982). The fundamental product of park and recreation agencies is their program services and facilities. It is through the various program activities that leisure service managers deliver the benefit of leisure to the clients. These programs need to be reviewed periodically in order to ensure that they are relevant to the mission of the organization. In addition, it may be necessary to modify or eliminate old programs and institute new ones regularly. However, it should be recognized that each new program involves risk, which can be

Figure 8.4
Market Positioning—A method for determining priorities among potential client groups to be served

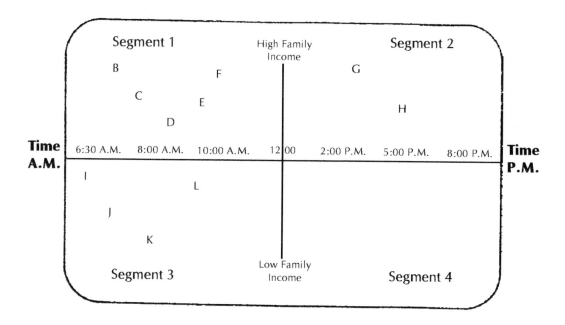

reduced by better marketing research, product development, and communication.

Product Life Cycle

It is not possible for a product's characteristics and marketing approach to remain optimal for all time (Kolter, 1982: 296). Just as human beings have a life cycle, so do products and services have a time of high acceptance and expectations and then a time of decline. The life cycle through which recreation programs are likely to pass consists of five stages (Shown on Figure 8.5). The first stage is the *introduction*. In this stage, considerable effort is needed to generate support and acceptance for the new program. Many times, leisure service managers try to jump-start this stage by offering special promotions

(e.g., two admissions for the price of one) to attract clients into the building to try the service. It is imperative that good customer relations be employed during this initial stage, as a bad experience will kill a new program faster than anything else.

Growth stage occurs if the new program satisfies the market. The early participants will continue their attendance and others will follow their lead. In this stage, program participants promote the activity more efficiently and effectively through word of mouth than most promotion efforts. As a result, the marketing effort changes to one of trying to sustain market growth as long as possible. This is accomplished in four ways:

1. The agency undertakes to improve the program quality and add new features;

Figure 8.5
Product Life Cycle

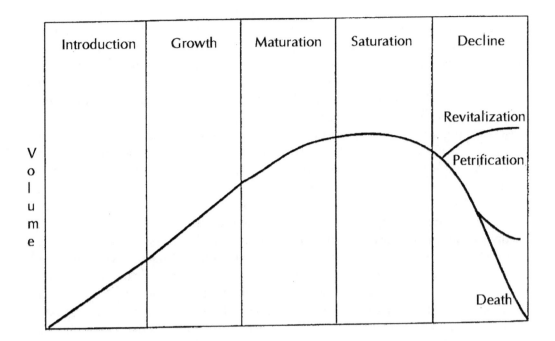

2. The agency vigorously searches out new market segments to enter;

3. The agency keeps its eyes open for new distribution channels to gain additional program exposure; and

4. The agency shifts its promotional efforts from building program awareness to trying to bring about program conviction and purpose.

The length of the first two stages varies. However, when the rate at which participation increases begins to slow down, the program cycle enters into the third stage, *maturity*. During the maturity stage, the number of participants continues to increase, but typically the rate of increase declines. This stage normally lasts much longer than the previous stages, and it poses some of

the most formidable challenges to marketing. According to Kotler (1982), most products are in the maturity stage of the life cycle; and therefore, most marketing management deals with the mature product.

It is at this point in the life cycle that imitators begin to appear, especially in the commercial sector. Because the rate of increase is in decline, an oversupply appears, which causes fierce competition. Simultaneously, various strategies are employed by all, including price-cutting and other tactics, until some of the weaker competitors start to drop out. At this point, the marketing strategy for the public agency shifts from attempting to attract participants into the program to one of getting them to prefer the program.

At the *saturation* stage, no new participants are entering the program. Now the agency is relying on repeat participants. It is at this stage that the agency needs to make the decision whether to modify the program or allow it to decline. The leisure service manager needs to examine whether the agency can continue to compete with the commercial sector in providing quality service or whether other elements can be instituted to revitalize the program. Unless strong retention reasons exist, carrying a weak program can be very costly to an organization. The cost of maintaining a weak program involves not just the amount of uncovered costs; the weak program tends to consume a disproportionate amount of management time and resources. It may also cast a shadow on the agency's image. Thus, the biggest cost of all may lie in the future, where an agency is seen as living in the past rather than planning for the future.

In the *decline* stage, other programs or activities become more attractive to participants, and the number of people involved in the activity significantly decreases. Decline may occur for many reasons. For instance, the program format may have become stale and routine, leading to psychological disengagement. In turn, participants turn to other activities in search of new experiences and stimulation. When the program has been singled out to be dropped, the leisure service manager faces further decisions. One alternative to completely eliminating the activity may be to offer it less frequently. Or a decision might be made to drop the program quickly and move on to the next one. Finally, a decision might be made to allow the program to disappear, simply through nonexistent enrollment.

Despite the evidence indicating that a program should be eliminated, there appears little evidence that many park and recreation agencies formalize this procedure. There are two predominant reasons why this occurs. (1) personal or political considerations, and (2) a lack of information. Established programs or services become sacrosanct. They are retained because of inertia, management sentiment, or the influence of vested interests. Figure 8.6 provides evidence of what can occur when an agency tries to change the status quo of services, in this case playgrounds. In 2000, the Department of Education in the State of Hawaii attempted to bring school playgrounds up to the safety standards stated in the Consumer Product Safety Commission Guidelines. As can be seen in the letter, this caused a political controversy concerning the elimination of play spaces, even though these play spaces were deemed unsafe for children. Many times, leisure service managers will face fallout in the political arena for trying to change programs or services.

This example makes it clear that an educational process involving constituents in the reasons for the change must accompany program or service elimination. Otherwise, an agency may face the ill will of the public that they need for support. Simply providing no alternatives can cause a serious public relations problem. In the case cited previously, some of the furor over the situation could have been minimized if a plan had been put in place that would replace unsafe equipment with new, safer playgrounds.

Price

The second P in the marketing mix is that of price. Prior to the late 1960s, many leisure service agencies paid little

Figure 8.6

March 31, 2000

From: Member H
House of Representatives
State of Hawaii
Honolulu, Hawaii

To: Department of Education

Re: Removal of Playground Equipment from Elementary Schools

Dear Sir:

On March 22, 2000 I received an email from another very angry set of parents regarding the removal of the playground equipment from U.S.A. Elementary School.

I and others with children or grandchildren at U.S.A. are stunned. "No way," we said, "there's always been playground equipment at U.S.A." But, to our shock, it is GONE. Most was removed last summer, some is being removed during these few weeks. I had to ask what has been/is happening.

A June 18, 1999, memo from your office to "All Elementary School Administrators" states that "attached sheets provide you with pictures of equipment which must be removed or carefully checked." It also states that "some equipment must be immediately restricted." The sample letter provided by your office for principals to notify parents (attached to your memo) states that "we (principals) have been directed by certified personnel of the State to remove some equipment and restrict use of other equipment" (emphasis added). It is not surprising that principals at 179 elementary schools statewide proceeded to order the removal of all or most of their playground equipment.

BUT THERE IS NO FEDERAL MANDATE for removal of playground equipment.

The "standards" regarding playground equipment are actually GUIDELINES or RECOM-MENDATIONS! The Consumer Product Safety Commission Handbook for Public Playground Safety says, "the guidelines are not a mandatory standard."

Parents across the state are frustrated and enraged. Most of the State's playground equipment has been DEMOLISHED. Parents are staring at the need to fundraise some $100,000 to replace their school' equipment. NO ONE knows when that will be, if ever.

There is no way that we should allow guidelines or recommendations (by CPSC or anyone else) to become MANDATES for DEMOLISHING nearly 17.9 million dollars of our kids playground equipment.

Please halt all further removal immediately, pending appropriate review and decision.

With best regards,

Senator H

(Editor Note: During the 2000 legislative session, the legislature passed funding of 3.1 million dollars to help schools replace playground equipment that the Department of Education deemed unsafe for children. Within the next three years, playgrounds at school sites in Hawaii will be some of the safest in the nation.

attention to setting prices for services. They basically offered programs free of cost or at a nominal fee. However, in the 1970's, when budgets across the country were drastically cut, being able to set a competitive price for services became an important element for the survival of many public agencies. Despite this fact, pricing is still one of the more difficult and politically sensitive areas for most leisure service managers.

It should be recognized that although price is used here to describe the actual charges set by the agency, these are not the only costs to participants. Adam Smith noted long ago, "The real price of everything, what everything really costs to the individual who wants to acquire it, is the toil and trouble of acquiring it" (as cited by Kolter, 1980: 305). Thus, in addition to the price, participants might have to face three other costs: effort costs, psychic costs, and waiting costs. Consider the case of a program participant in a physical fitness class who needs a physical exam prior to joining the class. A potential participant's resistance to joining the class might involve the following: (1) the actual cost of the program plus a $100 outlay for the physical exam; (2) the time, cost, and trouble of traveling a long distance to get a physical exam; (3) the fear of hearing bad news concerning one's physical health; and (4) the wait in the doctor's office for the physical exam to begin. Thus, the cost of joining the physical fitness class is much higher than the price of the class.

Pricing should be done in three stages. First, an agency needs to determine the pricing objective; that is, what are the reasons for charging a fee? Second, an agency needs to determine a pricing strategy. Third, it should determine when and whether a price change is needed and how to implement it.

Pricing Objectives

When setting a price, the first thing that a leisure service manager needs to ask is, "What are my objectives in pricing the program?" Many times, objectives may be in conflict and a choice must be made. Consider the following statement made by an after-school care provider:

"I want to keep my fees as low as possible to enable as many children of working parents an alternative to being latchkey children, but I must also keep the price high enough to ensure that the program will not lose money in the long run."

In this case, the provider has a conflict between an objective of maximizing audience size and an objective of maximizing cost recovery. It is apparent from this illustration that a leisure service agency must explicitly define pricing objectives for programs and services and also prioritize those objectives. Unfortunately, very few public and nonprofit leisure service agencies have established clear price objectives.

Pricing is critical in terms of marketing a program or service. Putting too high a price tag on a program can deter participation. At the same time, too low a price tag may signal that the program is not worthwhile. We will discuss the psychology of pricing later in this section, but first an examination of typical pricing objectives is in order.

Howard and Crompton (1980:420) list the following six possible pricing objectives for leisure service organizations:

1. *Efficient Use of All Financial Resources.* Charging a fee can provide an alternative source of revenue for an agency. In many cases where resources are tight, charging a fee may be the only way to get new programs financed. It should be noted that pricing can ease financial pressures in two ways. Not only can prices serve to increase revenue, but also more indirectly, they can reduce the level of costs. This may occur because the costs of operating a particular program presumably will be reduced as the number of participants declines in response to higher user prices.

2. *Fairness or Equitableness.* This objective is based on the assumption that those who play should pay. In other words, by charging a fee, those citizens who do not wish to participate or use the service are not forced to pay for those who do. Although nonusers still subsidize services through taxes, they still pay less than users. In addition, user pricing is the only way of making people who live and pay taxes outside the community contribute toward the cost of the recreation services they use.

3. *Maximizing Participation.* This objective is concerned with adopting a pricing policy that will encourage relatively large numbers of potential clientele to participate. One way to increase participation is to deliberately underprice an activity that has the potential to draw a large number of people to a facility. In doing so, the agency can expose a large number of current nonusers to the activities in the facility and thus gain new users of the agency's

services. Thus, there may be occasions when a very low price encourages large numbers to participate and leads to more revenues being collected than would a higher price, which would lead to having few participants in the program.

4. *Rationing.* User pricing may be used to ration services in two ways. First, it may exclude those potential users who are not willing to pay as high a price as other potential users. Thus, it serves as a way to discover the real need for a particular program based on the number who are willing to exchange money for perceived benefits. Second, user pricing may be used to reduce crowding at particular times in particular areas. For instance, charging more for the use of racquetball courts between the hours of 11:00 a.m. and 1:00 p.m. and 4:00 p.m. and 7:00 p.m. may be a way of rationing out a finite number of courts during peak demand times. The objective of this pricing strategy would be to bring about better use of the resources or facilities by influencing users to choose certain times, areas, or activities.

5. *Positive User Attitudes.* Many people are suspicious of the "free lunch." In other words, they feel that if something is free, it is not worth as much as something that is paid for. It is also suggested that people take better care of items if they have to pay for them. Additionally, it is felt that by imposing a fee, people are more likely to show up for services because they paid for them.

6. *Commercial Sector Encouragement.* Pricing that offers incentives for private investment can release crowding pressures by increasing the supply. However, this can only occur when the prices are competitive. For instance, if both a public leisure service agency and a private commercial agency are offering fitness classes, but the public agency is charging $20.00 less for the activity, the commercial agency is likely to have fewer customers.

Pricing Strategy

After an agency has defined its pricing objectives, it can consider the appropriate pricing strategy. There are two approaches for determining price: ignoring costs or basing the price on costs. In the first approach, ignoring costs, two methods are generally employed: demand-oriented pricing, and competitive-oriented pricing.

Demand-Oriented Pricing. This looks at the condition of demand rather than at the level of cost to set the price. Using this method, an agency estimates how much value potential participants see in a service or program, then offers a price accordingly. For instance, a concert that brings in a renowned performer would have ticket prices set at a higher level than a concert featuring a local artist. The premise of this method is that the price should reflect the perceived value in the consumer's head. Inherent in this method is also the concept that an agency should invest in building up the perceived value of the offer if it wants to charge a higher price. In other words, the more prestigious an item becomes, the higher the price can

be charged. This is anaglous to the price differential between a good car and a luxury model.

This type of pricing can also involve differential pricing. Differential pricing requires the ability to divide the clientele into distinct groups. The four major groups usually found in leisure services are those divided by participant, product, place, and time.

Many leisure service agencies feel that a child's ability to participate in activities should not be based on his or her ability to pay. Thus, it is not uncommon to find a different fee charged for adults than for children. In the past, this price differential has also been accepted for senior citizens. However, as the large baby boom generation ages, perceptions of who is entitled to price breaks is becoming a greater subject for debate. Not only are people over 50 the largest growing segment in society, they also are much more wealthy than their predecessors. As American values change, the issues surrounding price differentials for various participant groups are likely to become more complex.

Differential pricing by product occurs when more is charged for the use of a facility or service in one area than in another. For instance, the cost to rent a centrally located ball field may be higher than one to which the participants have to travel a longer distance. This price differential may also help in rationing, because the usage of the ball field in closer proximity to the participants would in all likelihood be used the most heavily. In this case, the people who want to pay for convenience in service must pay more for that quality of service.

The most common use of differential pricing by place occurs at spectator events. Fifty-yard line tickets in a football stadium are often 10 times the cost of bleacher seats in the end zone. Likewise, first orchestra seats in a theater are much more expensive than those in the balcony.

Differential pricing by time was discussed previously under the rationing objective. A variation of this pricing method may be the "free day" during the week, which is used to remove or reduce financial barriers among the more disadvantaged clients.

For price differentials to work, certain conditions must exist. First, the market must be segmentable, and the segments must show different intensities of demand. Second, there should be no chance that the members of the segment paying the lower price could in turn, and resell the product to the segment paying the higher price. Third, there should be little chance that competitors will undersell the firm in the segment being charged the higher price. Finally, the cost of segmenting and policing the market should not exceed the extra revenue derived from price differential (Kolter, 1982: 332).

Competition-Oriented Pricing. This occurs when an agency sets its prices chiefly on the basis of what its competitors are charging. There are three options for the agency employing this method. They may choose to charge the same as the competition, a higher price, or a lower price. The bottom line in this method is that the agency is not relying on its own costs or demand to set a price; rather, it is looking to the actions of its competitors. Thus, when the competition changes prices up or down, the agency follows suit, regardless of its own costs or demand.

The most popular type of competition-oriented pricing occurs when an agency institutes the *going rate* for a particular program or service. It is felt that this price generally represents the collective wisdom of the marketplace concerning the price that would yield a fair return. For a leisure service manager who pays little attention to actual costs of activities, this is a simple way to set a price. In addition, it avoids controversy, because the going rate is predicated on what people expect to pay for a service.

Pricing Strategies Based on Recovering Costs. This strategy is based on covering fixed costs, variable costs, or a combination of fixed and variable costs. *Fixed costs,* sometimes called overhead costs, are those costs that do not vary with the number of participants. Examples of fixed costs are equipment, facilities, and utilities. *Variable costs* are costs that change according to the number of people who participate. An example of this would be art supply costs, which increase as the number of participants increases. *Total costs* are the sum of fixed and variable costs.

Average Cost Pricing. This is a method by which an agency tries to cover all fixed and variable costs associated with a service. In this method (see Figure 8.7), the agency needs to determine all internal costs incurred by an agency in providing the service. This would involve allocating not only the direct variable costs associated with a service, but also attributing an equitable proportion of the agency's fixed costs to the service. These fixed costs would include both a share of the capital costs associated with financing the facility or equipment, and a share of the administrative and executive overhead of the agency. For instance, using this method, it could be argued that salaries, fringe benefits, and office costs of such personnel should be distributed across the full range of agency services

Figure 8.7
Average Cost Pricing

Average Cost price is determined by using the following formula

Average Cost Price=Average Fixed Cost + Average Variable Cost

Where

Average fixed costs= $\frac{\text{Total Fixed Costs}}{\text{Number of Participants}}$

Average variable costs= $\frac{\text{Total Variable Costs}}{\text{Number of Participants}}$

Example: If fixed costs   = $2000
            variable costs   = $1000
            Total Participants = 100

$$ACP=\frac{2000 + 1000}{100 + 100}$$

ACP=$30.00

so that an equitable proportion is added to the cost of each program. Because of the difficulty of trying to identify the extent of all fixed costs, this method is generally not used in large agencies. Second, if all programs were priced according to this method, the price charged would be higher than most participants would be willing to pay. However, it should be noted that this is the primary method used by commercial enterprises in determining price.

Variable Cost Pricing. This is used to try to recover only variable costs instead of both variable and fixed costs. In this method, the established price is equal to the average variable cost of providing the service (see Figure 8.8).

This is the most popular method used, for several reasons. First, by charging only for variable costs, the overall price for a program or service is lower. Second, it upholds the principle that those who use the service pay for the service, because variable costs recover costs consumed during the course of a program.

Partial Overhead Pricing. This is used to recover all variable costs and some proportion of fixed costs. The remaining share of the fixed costs represents the tax subsidy given to the particular program (see Figure 8.9). As Howard and Crompton (1980) noted, conceptually, the proportion of fixed costs that should be subsidized is de-

Figure 8.8
Variable Cost Pricing

Variable Cost Pricing is determined by using the following formula

$$VCP = \frac{\text{Total Variable Costs}}{\text{Number of Participants}}$$

If Total Variable cost = $750
Projected Participants = 50

Then: Total Costs Pricing = $15.00

Figure 8.9
Partial Overhead Pricing

Partial Overhead Pricing (POP) is established by using the following formula

POP = Average Fixed Cost + Average Variable Cost - Average Subsidy

(where: Average Subsidy represents the amount to which each user is subsidized out of tax funds)

If: Average Fixed cost is $10; Average Variable cost is $5 and Average Subsidy is $4

POP = $10 + $5 - $4   Price of Service: $11.00

pendent on the extent to which the nonuser public benefits. As the benefits that accrue to nonusers increase, the proportion of fixed costs met by the subsidy should increase.

Several important points need to be made about trying to institute a pricing strategy based on costs. First, a leisure service manager must have the ability to classify and allocate the costs associated with each program and service. Second, accurate records must be kept concerning participation in activities, because all these formulas are based on the projected number of participants in the program. This may be easily available for existing programs but might be problematic for new programs.

Changing the Price

Pricing becomes more of a challenge to the leisure service manager when a decision is made that a price change is needed. This change might be a price reduction in order to stimulate demand, to take advantage of lower costs, or to gain on weaker competition, or it may be a price increase in order to take advantage of strong demand or to pass on higher costs to participants. Whether the price is to be moved up or down, the action will affect participants, competitors, distribu-

tors, and suppliers. Yet their responses are among the most difficult to predict.

Price Elasticity of Demand. Price elasticity of demand refers to the relative sensitivity or responsiveness to changes in the number of participants relative to changes in price. If demand is *elastic,* a change in price causes an opposite change in total revenue: an increase in price will decrease total revenue, and a decrease in price will increase total revenue. An *inelastic* demand results in a parallel change in total revenue: An increase in price will increase total revenue, and a decrease in price will decrease total revenue (Pride & Ferrell, 1977). This implies that revenue can either fall or rise depending on the elasticity or demand for the particular service. In other words, if the purpose of the price increase is to increase total revenue, then prices can only be raised in those programs or services for which demand is relatively inelastic.

The price elasticity of demand depends on the magnitude of the proposed price change in the public's mind. For instance, a change from $6.00 to $7.00 for a movie theater ticket may not elicit great fallout. On the other hand, a change in gasoline prices from $1.50 a gallon to $1.75 a gallon causes great outrage. The elasticity of demand for a service is largely dependent on the existence of substitute services and their prices. For instance, a fitness facility may have difficulty raising prices if there are several fitness centers in the same area. This is an example of elasticity of demand. On the other hand, if the nearest fitness center is 45 miles away in another town, there will be an inelastic demand, as few substitutes are likely to be available.

In practice, price elasticity is extremely difficult to measure. One problem is that long-run price elasticity is apt to be different from short-run elasticity. Participants may have to stay with the agency immediately after a price increase, because choosing a new program takes time—but eventually they will change. In this case, demand is more elastic in the long run than in the short run. Conversely, participants may drop an agency in anger after prices increase but return to the agency later. The significance of this distinction between short-run and long-run elasticity is that the leisure service manager might not know how wise a price change has been for a period of time.

Psychology of Pricing. Psychology of pricing refers to the fact that the decision by the clientele to choose or not to choose a service is based many times on emotion, not rational thought. One example might be a person who quits a program in anger after a price has been raised, only to return a week later. Six psychological aspects of pricing (cited by Howard & Crompton: 442) are as follows:

1. *Expected Price Threshold.* Participants have an expected range of prices that they are willing to pay for a particular program or service. If a price is set above a threshold price in that range, then they will find it too expensive. On the other hand, if a price is set below the expected level, potential participants will be suspicious of the quality of the service. An important factor in establishing the expected price threshold might be the initial price an agency charges for the service. Thus, the leisure manager must be careful about the initial price established, because it may become the relevant midpoint of an expected price threshold.

2. *Tolerance Zone.* Similar to expected price threshold, tolerance zone refers to the concept that if the price increases within a certain range or zone are sufficiently small, they will not significantly influence participation. Price increases within the tolerance zone are those that are perceived by the participants to be too small to be of concern. Thus, this type of price increase or decrease results in no change whatever in demand. The importance of this concept for the leisure service manager is that a series of small, incremental increases in price over a period of time, which fall within the tolerance zone, are less likely to meet with participant resistance than a single major increase.

3. *Price–Quality Relationship.* People equate money with quality. Thus for many, the higher the price, the better quality is present. In some situations, a higher price might add prestige and make a contribution to improving the image of a specific service or of the agency. Many times, it may be possible to stimulate greater participation in programs by increasing price rather than by reducing it.

4. *Change in Perceived Value.* Many times, an increase in price is tolerated if the participants perceive that the service that they are purchasing has increased in value commensurate with the price increase. Sometimes the perceived value may be the result only of better communication between the agency and participants. For instance, using specific names of participants when mailing a newsletter instead of just blanketing the city in a mass mailing may give the impression that the participant is part of an elite group. In actuality, the mailing costs might be the same, but the change in perception is priceless.

5. *Customary Pricing.* People become accustomed to paying a certain price for a certain service. For instance, most people are used to paying an admission fee to a skating rink. If a the skating rink has charged the same price for 10 years, trying to raise the price due to rising costs might prove difficult. In effect, prices are determined by custom. It is up to the agency to produce programs or services that can be offered economically at those prices.

6. *Odd Pricing.* It is a common practice to price something at an odd price rather than an even price. Thus, a person may be willing to pay $4.99 for an item but not $5.00. In some cases, however, a person might take exception with getting a penny back from a $5.00 bill. There is no research to substantiate the idea that odd pricing attracts more participants than even pricing.

Place

The third P in the marketing mix is that of place or distribution. Every agency has to think through how it will make its services *available* and *accessible* to its target markets. Marketers call this the *place* or *distribution decision.* In leisure services, this is defined as a leisure delivery system and includes all those facilities (e.g., parks, recreation centers, swimming pools, etc.) and services that serve as points of contact with the client. There are four major decision problems that arise in designing and operating an efficient distribution system.

Level and Quality of Customer Service

The first decision that the leisure service manager must make is the level and quality of service to offer the target market. An agency must balance the need for participants' convenience against the cost of distribution. For instance, offering a personal trainer for fitness might be convenient for the participant, but cost-prohibitive for the agency. The alternative is to offer smaller programs in a variety of sites around the city to cut down on the cost to clients. Thus, it is important to begin distribution planning with a conceptualization of the level and quality of service that the agency will offer.

The Number and Location of Branches

The agency needs to decide on the number of sites in which it will operate its programs. By operating only one major facility (e.g., a recreation center) duplication of programs, staff, and building costs is avoided. Participants gain, in that the cost of services is lower, but they pay the price in convenience. A system of strategically placed recreation centers throughout the city would attract more users. Many large cities have multiple recreation centers. In addition, some have mobile recreation units that are placed in underserved parts of the city to promote recreation activities, especially in the summertime.

The relative importance of locating recreation and park facilities so that they are easily accessible depends on the type of facility under consideration. People often expect to drive long distances to national and state parks. On the other hand, in an urban environment, the most important consideration for leisure agencies is the accessibility of a site. For instance, a recreation center in Denton, Texas, once had a difficult time attracting children to its site. The major problem was that the center was located at the fringe of a neighborhood area, and children had to cross three major roads to get there. The parks and recreation department eventually removed the game room and redesigned the area for adult fitness. Participation picked up, because adults could drive their cars to the site. Ten years later, the recreation site is now surrounded by homes as the population of the city has grown from 38,000 to over 80,000. The site has again been redesigned to accommodate children, who can walk to the center without worrying about crossing busy streets.

Many communities are returning to the idea of community recreation programs at school sites, because elementary schools are designed to be within walking distance of the children in a given neighborhood. These shared facilities not only make good economic sense, but also help to rebuild the sense of community in many urban areas.

The Design of Facilities

The "look" of facilities can affect participants' attitudes and behavior. Areas that are run-down and unattractive invite vandalism and other antisocial behavior. When the grass in the park isn't mowed, the playground equipment is rusting, and the broken windows aren't replaced, the public will choose to go elsewhere. *Atmospherics* describes the conscious designing of space to create or reinforce specific effects on the consumer, such as feelings of well-being, safety, intimacy, or awe. A leisure service organization that is designing a new facility should consider four major design decisions:

1. *What should the building look like on the outside?* If it is a neighborhood center, perhaps it should blend in with the surrounding area. In contrast, a major sports venue or museum might be more awe-inspiring or ornate. The design should be influenced by the message that the agency wants to convey about leisure services in general.

2. *What should be the functional and flow characteristics of the building?* The planners must decide what type of leisure environment they wish to create. Small rooms imply intimate and personal services, whereas large gymnasiums allow crowds, noise, and spectators.

They have to decide whether to separate the more passive activities, such as arts and crafts, from the more active programs, such as sports and games. Corridors must permit good traffic flow, and the entire building must allow ease of supervision.

3. *What should the facility feel like on the inside?* Every building conveys a feeling, whether intended or unplanned. Leisure service planners need to consider whether the facility should feel awesome and somber, or bright and modern, or warm and intimate. Each feeling will have a different effect on the participants and their overall satisfaction with the facility.

4. *What materials would best support the desired feeling of the building?* The feeling of a building is conveyed by visual cues (color, brightness, size, shapes), aural cues (volume, pitch), olfactory cues (scent, freshness), and tactile cues (softness, smoothness, temperature). Leisure service planners must choose colors, fabrics, and furnishings that create or reinforce the desired feeling.

Each facility will have a look that may add to or detract from participant satisfaction and employee performance. The latter should not be overlooked. Because employees work in the facility all day long, the facility should be designed to support them in performing their work with ease and cheerfulness. Paying attention to small details, and helping employees be more effective in their jobs, improves the overall atmosphere of the facility. Every facility conveys something to the users about the attitudes the service providers felt toward them.

The Use of Third Parties

In deciding how to distribute its services, many leisure service agencies enter into either joint agreements or contracts with a third party. The third party might be a local school district, a YWCA, or even a private facility such as an ice-skating arena. These agreements usually mean relinquishing some control over how and to whom the services are distributed. There are several reasons why a leisure service agency would choose to involve a third party in the distribution of services.

First, many agencies lack the financial resources to carry out a full program of direct marketing. Thus, it is better to turn over the marketing of youth soccer to the community soccer association, whose main objective is to promote youth soccer.

Second, even if the agency has the funds to build its own channel of distribution to the final markets, it might not be able to do it as economically as through the use of an existing distribution system. For instance, why try to reach school children by building a new distribution channel when working with the school districts would allow this to occur?

Third, funds saved by avoiding the duplication of distribution channels can be put to better use. Instead of duplicating the work of schools, it is wiser to develop new programs that enhance the lives of school-age children.

The decision to enter into third-party agreements involves some important considerations by the leisure service manager. The first problem is choosing the best group to work with. Many times, commercial ventures will contact leisure service agencies to help sponsor events. The underlying motives of the commercial venture are to link their company's name to a positive, wholesome image. The leisure service manager needs to consider carefully whether a link with the company will help or hurt the agency's image. For example, having a cigarette manufacturer as a sponsor and distributor of a leisure service community brochure may not be the most acceptable move in a community.

Second, the leisure service agency must carefully establish the terms and responsibilities of third-party involvement. This is called the trade–relations mix; it consists of the price policies, conditions, territorial rights, and specific services to be performed by each party.

The next requirement is that the agency provides periodic evaluation and communication concerning the roles and responsibilities of each member of the agreement. Without such checks, the distribution message may get distorted, resulting in a reduction of participants in both parties' programs.

Promotion

The fourth important P in the marketing mix is that of promotion. Promotion can be thought of as communication. The most essential purpose of this communication is to inform—to let people know what programs and services are being offered by the leisure delivery system. Communication must be directed to target markets to keep them informed and to promote market exchanges. However, the agency's communication responsibilities go beyond communicating with target markets. The leisure service organization must communicate effectively with other publics in its external environment, such as the press, governmental agencies, and the financial community. It must also communicate effectively with its internal publics, particularly its board members, middle management, and professional and clerical employees. In short, the leisure service agency must know how to market itself to various groups in order to gain their support and goodwill.

In a sense, all four of the P tools in the marketing mix—product, price, place, and promotion—are communication tools. Thus, messages are carried to the market by how programs and activities are formatted, their price, and the places where they are available. However, some functions are primarily promotional in nature. It is to these elements that we next turn our attention.

A wide variety of promotional tools are available to the leisure service manager. Specific types of leisure service agencies may use distinct promotional tools. Thus, nonprofit agencies that rely heavily on donations may use benefit dinners and dances, auctions, bazaars, concerts, telethons, walk-run races, and direct mail campaigns to raise money. In contrast, summer camps make heavy use of camp brochures, get-acquainted parties, T-shirts with the camp name, camp movies, and direct mail.

Because of the varied ways that promotional activities take place, it would be impossible to thoroughly review all of them here. Rather, this section will provide a brief overview of important points to remember in planning promotional efforts.

One can classify promotional tools into four groups:

1. *Advertising.* This refers to any paid form of nonpersonal presentation and promotion of ideas, goods, or services by an identified sponsor.

2. *Publicity.* This refers to nonpersonal stimulation of demand for a product, service, or unit by planting commercially significant news about it in a published medium or obtaining favorable presentation of it on radio, television, or stage that is not paid for by the sponsor.

3. *Sales promotion.* These promotions are short-term incentives to encourage purchase or sales of a product or service.

4. *Personal Selling.* This refers to oral presentation in a conversation with one or more prospective purchasers for the purpose of making sales or building goodwill.

To use these tools effectively, they should be seen as falling into a communication framework (see Figure 8.10). Communication is an exchange between two entities (such as two individuals, or an individual and an organization) that carries meaning (Edginton et al., 1998). The exchange process is the vital link that enables an individual to express his or her needs to the organization and allows the organization to identify its program services. The exchange that exists between the leisure service organization and the customer must be a two-way process. Effective communication means that the organization communicates *with* the prospective customer rather than *to* the prospective customer. That is to say, the communication process is not complete until the prospective customer acts on the message that he or she has received. The customer digests and evaluates the information being sent and either accepts or rejects it, based on his or her own values, norms, interests, and needs. Figure 8.11 are examples of advertising/publicity aimed at customers. The first one advertises golf courses advertised by the city of Phoenix, Arizona. The next figure presents a newsletter of activities from the Hearst Center for the Arts, Cedar Falls, Iowa. The last brochure advertises a celebration run/walk sponsored by the YWCA, Waterloo, Iowa.

The processing of information for promotional purposes can be conceptualized as comprising four elements: the communicator, the message, the

Figure 8.10
A Model for Processing Information

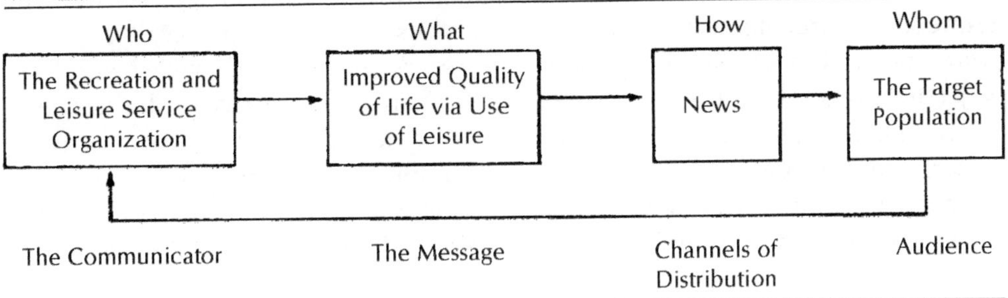

Figure 8.11

channel of information distribution, and the audience. The *communicator* is the leisure service organization—its professional staff and other associated members (such as persons in policymaking positions). In addition, program customers (current and prospective) can also serve as communicators. In general terms, the message communicated by a leisure service organization is one of improving quality of life through the wise use of leisure. Specifically, the *message* communicated will depend on the particular activity and the values to be derived from involvement. For example, the message used to promote a jogging class will center on physical fitness benefits, physical and mental challenges, relaxation, and so on.

Channels used to distribute information include the ones mentioned above: advertising, sales promotion, personal selling, and publicity. These topics will be examined shortly. Finally, this model shows that the communicator directs his or her message through various channels to a selected *audience,* or target population. In other words, the communicator asks the question, Toward whom is the information being directed—an age grouping, persons in a geographic area, a lifestyle clustering or interest group, or males and females.

Through the communication process, information is targeted toward individuals in an attempt to stimulate involvement in a particular service. As prospective customers become aware of the information being communicated to them, they may relate to it in terms of their own needs and view it as a way of fulfilling those needs. The promotional process often not only informs individuals, but also persuades them. Frequently, the persuasion aspects are viewed negatively, with the assumption that promotional efforts are only for the benefit of the provider of the service. In some instances—few, we hope—this may be the case. It is probably more apparent in the promotion of some commercial recreation enterprises, where profit may have a higher priority than the welfare of the customers. However, most leisure service organizations have a humanistic philosophy; as a result, they are interested primarily in the provision of services that are beneficial both to the customers and to the organization. In this sense, the promotional efforts are not directed toward the exploitation of individuals, but toward the provision of services that are in the best interests of the consumer.

The four channels of distribution have some common characteristics, especially in terms of the media employed, so they should be used simultaneously; however, they each serve distinctly different ends. To successfully promote a program, the leisure service manager should carefully design a strategy that incorporates each of these channels effectively. Promotional efforts should be well-planned; productive professionals will avoid an ad hoc approach.

Advertising

Advertising consists of nonpersonal forms of communication conducted through paid media under clear sponsorship. It involves such varied media as magazines and newspapers, radio and television, outdoor effects (such as posters, signs, skywriting), novelties (matchboxes, calendars), cards (car, bus), catalogs, directories and references, programs and menus and circulars and direct mail. It can be carried out for such diverse purposes as long-term buildup of a particular program, information dissemination about a service or event, or announcement about a special occurrence.

O'Sullivan (1991:123–24) suggests several factors for creating good advertising. She writes: "The message itself is a very important component of the advertisement." It should create attention and promote interest on the part of the customers targeted for a program. Further, the advertisement "should also foster a desire to take part in the program or service" (124). Last, an advertisement should lead to action on the part of the customer. This is known as the AIDA approach: attention, interest, desire, and action.

Advertising is an important aspect of a leisure organization's promotional efforts in that it enables the organization to reach large numbers of people rapidly with its message. This channel of promotion has been used primarily by commercial enterprises as a mechanism to persuade individuals to join in various pursuits; and these principles and methods can also be applied successfully in the public and nonprofit sectors. Advertising can be beneficial in a number of ways. It increases the customer's awareness of programs and services available. The customer is also able to make comparisons among the services offered based on quality, cost, and location.

There are basically two types of advertising: direct action and indirect action. *Direct action* advertising encourages the individual to act immediately on the information presented. For example, direct action advertising might inform the prospective customer of the need to sign up immediately for swimming lessons at the local pool or for day camp at the YWCA. *Indirect action* advertising tries to create long-term interest in a service. In other words, an indirect advertisement merely cites the availability of certain services or programs available from an organization. Special advertising for Park and Recreation Month in July or National Playground Safety Week in April are examples of indirect action advertising.

Publicity

"Publicity [may be] the most enduring promotional channel, the least expensive, and perhaps the easiest to use," write Rubright and MacDonald (1981:169). It consists of *media coverage of the events, activities, and services of a leisure service organization.* Rubright and McDonald note that "Publicity embraces news releases and features, speakers' messages, and press conferences. Agencies find countless outlets for news releases in daily and weekly newspapers, in regional tabloids, in an ever-growing number of radio stations, and in some television markets" (169). The organization that uses publicity effectively conveys information to various media sources in such a way that the organization is presented to the public in a favorable light. Newspaper coverage of a public meeting in which policy issues are discussed, a feature story highlighting the efforts of an individual within the organization, or a picture of the winning junior softball team are all examples of positive and productive publicity. On the other hand, an exposé on ineffective management practices, or an editorial condemning an organization and its efforts, could wound an organization severely.

How does one develop a favorable publicity posture? Many tools can be employed—news releases, photographs, press conferences—to provide the various media sources with positive information. Basically, the professional must sell the media on the newsworthiness of the various events and activities of his or her organization. To accomplish this, the professional should actively cultivate sources or contacts within various media. Obviously publicity is not paid for, so the organization is placed in a competitive position for newspaper space, for radio time, and for TV time. An organization should compete by exemplifying excellence and by extending itself courteously to the media.

Does the organization or professional create news? The answer to this question is definitely yes. However, creating news does not imply the staging of news. News is created by providing programs, by informing the media of the programs, and by conveying to the media the human interest features of these programs.

Publicity can also be generated by a leisure service organization in the form of brochures, flyers, reports, and newsletters that are distributed at various times and for various purposes to customers and potential program users. Although there are costs involved in producing these publicity items, they are generally less expensive than if the information were delivered through advertising.

Sales Promotion

Sales promotion comprises a wide variety of tactical promotional tools of a short-term, incentive nature designed to stimulate an earlier or stronger target market response. These tools can be subclassified into tools for *consumer promotion* (e.g., samples, coupons, money refund offers, prices off, gifts, contests, trading stamps, demonstrations), *dealer promotion* (e.g., free goods, merchandise allowances, cooperative advertising), and *sales force promotion* (e.g., bonuses, contests, sales rallies). Although a variety of sales promotion tools exist, they commonly have two distinctive qualities:

1. *Insistence Presence.* Many sales promotion tools have an attention-getting, sometimes urgent quality that can break through habits of consumers' inertia, causing a favorable response toward a particular service. They tell the consumer of a chance that they won't have again to get something special. This appeals to a broad spectrum of consumers, although particularly to the economy-minded, with the disadvan-

tage that this type of consumer tends to be less loyal to any particular brand in the long run.

2. *Product Demotion.* Some of these tools suggest that the seller is anxious for the sale. If they are used too frequently or carelessly, they may lead consumers to wonder whether the program is desirable or reasonably priced.

Sale promotion tools are used for a multitude of purposes. However, they make three distinct contributions to the promotional effort. First, they help in the communication process, because they are usually designed to gain attention and provide information that will lead to trying a service, program, or facility. Second, they are based on some concession, inducement, or contribution that is designed to represent value to the receiver, thus facilitating the exchange process. Third, they include a distinct invitation to engage in the transaction within a short period of time.

Sales promotion activities, if successfully arranged, enable an organization to generate a great deal of interest and enthusiasm for its service. These types of activities represent short-term promotional efforts and should be used sparingly rather than on a continuous basis, or they will lose their edge.

Personal Selling

One of the most effective channels for promoting programs is through personal selling. Usually, personal selling involves making direct, face-to-face contact with an individual or group. One should not underestimate the potential of the direct personal contact. It is perhaps the most pervasive, effective form of promoting a program's service.

In leisure service organizations, personal selling is not directly identified as such. It most commonly occurs within the context of public speaking to various community groups. It also occurs when prospective customers make direct contact with organizational staff members for information or clarification.

What makes a successful "salesperson" for the organization? Basically, an effective salesperson must be personable and able to relate to people. He or she must be aware of customer needs and how to communicate effectively the ways in which the services or the organization can meet those needs. This implies that a good salesperson understands not only people but also how the organization's service line can be employed to meet individual needs. The successful salesperson tailors his or her presentation to the audience, environment, and other relevant factors. Personal selling is often one of the more pleasurable and self-rewarding channels of promotional communication. It permits the organization's personnel to experience the impact that the agency is making on its customers" (Rubright & MacDonald, 1981:170).

The Role of Public Relations in Marketing

Public relations should be viewed as an important organizational tool that affects the total marketing process. Public relations touches every part of an organization's operations; it deals with items such as the caliber of services, the manner in which the public is dealt with on the phone, the manner in which leaders interact with customers, and so on. Because public relations is involved in so many organizational areas, it should not be left to chance.

Sometimes the lines between public relations and marketing become blurred, but they are not the same. Public relations is another type of communication tool used to advance the marketing objectives of the organization. Kolter and Andreasen (1996:543) define the differences between public relations and marketing as the following:

1. Public relations is primarily a communication tool, whereas marketing also includes needs assessment, product development, pricing, and place (distribution);

2. Public relations seeks to influence attitudes, whereas marketing tries to elicit specific behaviors, such as purchasing, joining, voting, and so on; and

3. Public relations does not define the goals of the organization, whereas marketing is intimately involved in defining the business, mission, customers, and services.

As a management process, public relations efforts are directed toward engendering goodwill toward the organization and establishing an understanding of its operations. Public relations efforts seek to develop a positive rapport with the public served by establishing management policies and practices conducive to the public interest and well-being. Such policies might, for example, deal with the following topics by specifically delineating guidelines for staff and behavior:

1. Interactions with the public;

2. Standards for dress and grooming;

3. Standards for building and grounds maintenance;

4. Rules regarding press release clearance; and

5. Clearance for special projects.

The good name of an organization is its greatest asset. An organization should try to cultivate good community relations in order to attract customers. A negative public image will, obviously, seriously affect the ability of an organization to serve a community effectively. Thus, an organization should have an active program to communicate with and relate to each public. Figure 8.12 outlines the public relations process.

Who Are the Publics?

The first step in the public relations process is to identify relevant publics. Given the limited resources of most leisure service agencies, they usually have to concentrate their attention on certain publics more than businesses do. As such, most organizations distinguish between their primary, secondary, and tertiary publics. An organization's primary publics are those to whom it relates on an active and continuous basis. The primary publics of a leisure service agency comprise its clients, employees, board of directors, and community. If the goodwill of any of these groups disappears, the leisure service agency is in deep trouble.

Figure 8.12
Steps in the Public Relations Process

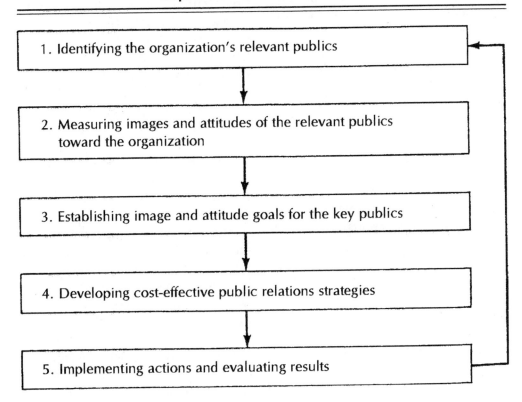

1. Identifying the organization's relevant publics

2. Measuring images and attitudes of the relevant publics toward the organization

3. Establishing image and attitude goals for the key publics

4. Developing cost-effective public relations strategies

5. Implementing actions and evaluating results

This is especially true for nonprofit agencies that rely heavily on donations and gifts from the public at large.

Also important to the leisure service organization are the secondary publics that indirectly affect the ongoing activities of the organization. These groups include government officials, competitors, and suppliers. These groups can affect the organization through legislation, competitive practices, and providing items necessary to carry on the organization's daily operations.

Finally, a leisure service agency will have to deal with various tertiary publics from time to time. These are publics who seek to advance the interests of their members at the expense or benefit of the agency. For instance, an environmental group might seek to have the leisure service organization refrain from using pesticides in parks. The agency will have to decide what the public relations fallout will be if they appease or oppose the request.

One thing that a leisure service manager must understand is that these publics are related not only to the agency but also to each other in important ways. For instance, a particular public (the environmental group) might have a great deal of influence toward the organization on the attitudes and behavior of other publics (the community, clients, and employees). Based on this influence, it is important to set up relations with its valued publics that produce satisfaction. The leisure service organization's task is to consider what benefits to offer each of its valued publics in exchange for their valued resources and support. Thus, once an organization begins to think about cultivating the support of a public, it starts thinking of that public as a market where an exchange might take place.

What Are the Public's Perceptions?

Once the publics have been identified, the leisure service agency needs to find out how each public thinks and feels about the agency. Although a good leisure service manager will have some idea of each public's attitudes through regular contact with the public's members, these impressions may be inaccurate and incomplete. To really uncover the attitudes of a public, the leisure service organization needs to undertake some type of formal marketing research. This may take the form of focus groups, public opinion surveys, or open forums.

How to Determine the View of the Organization?

Through periodically researching its key publics, the organization will have data on how these publics view the organization. These findings can then be assembled in the form of a scorecard, such as the one shown in Figure 8.13. The scorecard, in turn, becomes the basis for developing a public relations plan for the coming period. For instance, the participation in a youth soccer league is dependent first on parents' attitudes toward competitive sports, second, on the perception of the child; and third, on the influence from the community at large as well as from competing agencies.

Looking at the scorecard, we can see that it is important to have a communication program that will improve parents' knowledge and attitudes toward organized sports for youth. Looking at the next item on the scorecard, we see that communication with youth is fine, but the agency still needs to communicate with this group to keep the enthusiasm high. As with the com-

Figure 8.13
Scorecard on Youth Soccer Publics

Public	Knowledge	Attitude	Public's Importance
Parents	Medium	Negative	High
Youth	High	Positive	High
Community	Low	Neutral	High

munity, better communication also needs to occur to enable parents' positive feelings to be reinforced by other adults.

What Form Should the Public Relations Effort Take?

A leisure service organization usually has many options in trying to improve the attitudes of a particular public. Its first task is to understand why the attitudes have come about so that the causal factors can be addressed by an appropriate strategy. For instance, parents might have negative attitudes toward youth sports because they have read about the overcompetitive nature of some youth sports programs. Thus, a strategy needs to be employed that dispels these beliefs and presents the benefits of their children's participation in a program. This might include offering neighborhood soccer clinics that provide children with a chance to learn basic skills in a nonthreatening and noncompetitive way; restructuring the games so no score is recorded; ensuring that all children have a chance to participate in each game, or establishing a parent advisory board to help deal with issues that emerge concerning the program. The agency will need to estimate the amount of expected attitude improvement with each project in order to arrive at the best mix of cost-effective actions.

How Do We Know That the Public Relations Effort Is Working?

Evaluating the results of public relations activities is not easy, because it occurs in conjunction with other marketing activities. Thus, the public relations contribution is hard to evaluate separately. For instance, how does one measure the amount of exposure or awareness of a publicity effort? One way is by calculating the number of exposures created in the media. Most publicists supply the client with a "clippings book" showing all the media outlets that carried news about the organization and a summary statements, such as the one shown in Figure 8.14 for the National Program for Playground Safety.

The purpose of citing the equivalent advertising cost is to make a case for the cost-effectiveness of publicity, because the total publicity effort must have cost less than a given amount of money. Furthermore, publicity usually creates more reading and believing than ads. Still, this measure is somewhat limited, as there is no indication of how many people actually read, saw, or heard the message or what they thought afterward. Furthermore, the multiple venues used mean there was overlapping readership.

A better measure calls for finding out what change in public awareness, comprehension, or attitude has occurred as a result

Figure 8.14
National Program for Playground Safety PR Value Report January-May 2000

Television

National		Audience (EST)	Media Value
April 24, 2000	Later Today	3,000.000	$80,000
April 25, 2000	CNN Early Edition	3,000,000	$75,000
April 25, 2000	CNN Headline News	2,500,000	$50,000
April 25, 2000	CNN Morning News	4,000,000	$100,000

Satellite Television Tour

See attached VMS report for itemized coverage		28,488,134	$1,125,000
April 18 - April 30	Including NY, LA Chicago, Phili, SF... Plus more than 50 other regional markets		

Newspapers	**Circulation**	**Media Value**
	14,581,885	$475,450

Media Impressions & Values

Total Impressions	**43,070,019**	
Total Media Value		**$1,600,450**

of the publicity campaign. This requires survey research, which measures certain elements prior to the publicity campaign and after. As a result, certain public relations activities may be found to be too costly in relation to their impact and might be dropped. Also, several efforts might need to be modified. Furthermore, new problems will arise with certain publics that require redirection of the public relations resources. Thus, the public relations process is a continually recycling one.

Summary

Marketing is a method of directing the activities that take place in an orga-nization toward the satisfaction of consumer needs and demands. It is based on the concept of voluntary exchange. In order for an exchange to take place, two conditions must exist. First, there must be two or more parties for the transaction to take place. Second, each party in the exchange must have something that might be valued by the other party. In a profit-oriented organization, one party provides a service to obtain revenue from another. Thus, marketing activities are based on trying to find out what specific customers or target markets want, then providing services that meet those wants.

A market is defined in terms of specific groups of people. These groups consist of individuals who have certain needs and are willing to exchange something of value to satisfy those needs. Markets can be differentiated from one another by identifying subclusters of individuals, each of whom consumes a specific type of service. These subclusters form the basis for market segmentation. Sociodemographic, behavioral, and geographic descriptors are all generally used to segment markets.

Once markets are identified, three basic strategies (undifferentiated, differentiated, and concentrated) are used to select the methods for communicating with target markets. Position marketing means determining what the leisure service agency's distinctive contribution is for enhancing the community's quality of life. The marketing mix refers to the four P's of the marketing effort: product, price, place, and promotion. It is through the manipulation of these four elements that the leisure service manager can design a mix that fits the needs and preferences of the various markets segments.

Public relations interrelates with marketing but is a distinctive operation. Public relations involves communication. It is an attempt to engender goodwill with the target markets and the community at large.

Discussion Questions

1. Define marketing.

2. Marketing relies on the concept of a voluntary exchange. What does this mean?

3. Identify typical types of markets sought by leisure service organizations.

4. What does market segmentation refer to?

5. What does position marketing involve?

6. Identify and define the market mix.

7. Identify various types of pricing used by leisure service organizations.

8. What is the role of public relations in marketing?

9. Identify four types of promotional tools used by leisure service organizations.

10. Is there a difference between nonprofit, government, and leisure service organizations?

References

Crompton, J. (1983). Selecting target markets - A key to effective marketing. *Journal of Park and Recreation Administration,* Vol. 1 No. 1: 7–25.

Edginton, E., Hanson, C., Edginton, S. & Hudson, S. (1998). *Leisure programming: A service centered and benefits approach.* (3rd ed.) Boston, MA.: WCB McGraw-Hill.

Haley, R. I. (1968). Benefit segmentation: A decision-oriented research tool. *Journal of Marketing 32* (July): 30-35.

Howard, D., & Crompton, J. 1980. *Financing, managing and marketing recreation & park resources.* Dubuque, IA: Wm. C. Brown Co.

Kolter, P. (1980). *Marketing management.* (4th ed.). Englewood Cliffs, NJ: Prentice-Hall.

Kolter, P. (1982). *Marketing for nonprofit organizations.* (2nd ed.). Englewood Cliffs, NJ: Prentice-Hall.

Kolter, P., & Andreasen, A. (1996). *Strategic marketing for nonprofit organizations.* (5th ed.). Englewood Cliffs, NJ: Prentice-Hall.

O'Sullivan, E. I. (1991). *Marketing for parks, recreation and leisure services.* State College, PA: Venture.

Pride, W. M., & Ferrell, O. C. (1980). *Marketing: Basic concepts and decisions.* Boston: Houghton Mifflin.

Rubright, R., & MacDonald, D. (1981). *Marketing health and human services.* Rockville, MD: Aspen Systems Corporation.

Chapter 9

Financial Practices For Leisure Service Organizations

Effective fiscal practices are essential to successful leisure service management.

Photo credit PhotoDisc Mature Lifestyles Vol. 33.

Introduction

Financial management is concerned with managing the economic resources of a leisure service organization for the purpose of influencing future outcomes of its operations. In order to carry out this responsibility, the manager engages in a number of diverse activities, including (1) *planning*—determining short-range and long-term strategies for the fiscal solvency of the agency; (2) *importation*—gathering in the human, material and economic resources by the agency; (3) *allocation*—distributing resources imported into the agency; (4) *control*—establishing standardized policies and procedures relating to all trans actions and events involving monetary items to insure that generally accepted accounting principles and procedures are followed by the agency; (5) *recording and reporting*—listing all transactions of a financial nature in journals and ledgers and to generate periodic financial statements and reports; and (6) *evaluating*—periodically reviewing financial activities in order to assess their efficiency and effectiveness in meeting agency and funder requirements for fiscal accountability.

Even though many leisure managers have individuals who are hired to oversee the day-to-day financial operations of the organization, managers are still responsible for the financial well-being of the agency. As such, it is important that leisure service managers understand some of the fundamental principles concerning the acquisition, control, and allocation of funds needed to run the organization. This chapter will examine the principles and practices involved in the financial management of leisure service organizations.

For Profit versus Nonprofit Organizations

Both profit and nonprofit organizations are concerned with the matter in which their resources (assets) are used. Both types of organizations seek to maximize their operating efficiency. The profit-oriented organization does this to increase its profit margin; the nonprofit organization does this to minimize its costs and maximize its impact regarding the delivery of goods and services. Other similarities between the two are as follows:

1. Both acquire external resources in order to maximize income.

2. Both provide similar goods and services.

3. Both distribute goods and services.

4. Both incur financial obligations.

5. Both must stay financially viable.

6. Both have a limited pool of resources and resource providers.

7. Both may charge fees for services.

However, major financial and philosophical differences drive the financial practices of both types of organizations. Thus, in some cases, the for-profit finance theory does not fit the nonprofit organization and cannot be transferred with good effect.

For Profit Practices

A for-profit firm generates its income through the economic activity it conducts internally, namely, from producing and selling goods and services and from investments. In terms of mission and objectives, the for-profit agency seeks to maximize its revenues and minimize its costs in order to provide the greatest financial return to its investors, usually called shareholders. Although regulated by state and federal laws, for-profit organizations have a great degree of latitude in how they conduct financial transactions. They are accountable only to their shareholders, not to society at large.

Nonprofit Practices

In contrast, a nonprofit agency may have an internal flow of funds in addition to a legally required external source. In fact, a nonprofit agency cannot legally have only internal funding. To maintain its legal and tax status as a nonprofit, it must demonstrate an external source of support. Thus, fundraising and development serve an extremely important function for the nonprofit organization. But external sources often place restrictions on the use of their money. As a result, a nonprofit manager is faced with more scrutiny and accountability issues than his or her for-profit counterpart. It should also be noted that all financial return to the nonprofit organization must stay within the organization. In other words, no one individual can benefit by the financial practices of the organization.

Along with these financial differences are real philosophical distinctions between the two types of agencies that influences financial practices. In terms of mission, nonprofit agencies are seen as private voluntary organizations whose primary aim is to provide a social welfare service rather than to make a profit. As a result, a nonprofit organization operates to achieve a "multiple goal set" rather than a single goal. Thus, the primary goal of the manager in a nonprofit agency is for the operation or the delivery of societal benefits to the organization's clientele; the secondary goal is to maintain liquidity and solvency and to formulate budget constraints in making asset selection decisions. The professional goal, then, should be perceived as the dominant operating goal of the organization, with the financial goal and finance function taking on a supporting role. When a

nonprofit agency reverses the order of these goals, it can quickly lose its direction and sense of purpose.

Sources of Revenues

As noted above, both for-profit and nonprofit agencies need to acquire funds (revenues) in order to become financially solvent. For-profit agencies are free to garner resources in a free enterprise system, whereas nonprofit agencies rely on direct and indirect subsidies from public monies, as well as on the development of internal and external sources.

Taxes

Although declining in recent years, most revenues that are used to support governmental leisure service organizations come from taxes. There are a number of different types of taxes, including property taxes, income taxes, sales taxes, and other special taxes. But the majority of income for operating expenses at the local level of the government comes from property taxes. Property tax are of two types: *the real property tax* and *personal property tax*. Personal property can be divided into two categories for taxation: tangible and intangible. Tangible personal property, which can be taxed, might include automobiles, jewelry, equipment, and merchandise; in other words, physical assets. Intangible personal property includes accounts, stocks, bonds, and other similar assets, which are not taxed.

Much of the income for local government leisure service organizations comes from the real property tax. This is a tax assessed against such "real property" as homes, land, industry, and commercial enterprises that are within the jurisdiction of the organization. It not only includes land, but also anything that can be permanently attached to it (e.g., buildings and other improvements). Real property tax is assessed by determining the value of the property; this is known as the "assessed valuation" and is evaluated on a regular basis by a local tax assessor. The assessor appraises the property to determine its value based on factors that indicate its worth. In most cases, property is not assessed at its full value, but at a percentage of its actual, or real, value. State or provincial legislative authority usually sets the figure or percentage used by the assessor to determine the value of the property. Whether the local legislative authority uses the full percentage allowable under law is usually subject to its discretion.

Once the assessed value of the property is determined, this figure is multiplied times the tax rate. State or provincial legislative authorities also usually establish tax rates, and their application is subject to local government discretion. Local government authorities are not able to set a tax rate higher than the allowable maximum as indicated by law unless approved by the voters of a community.

Tax rates are expressed in terms of mills. One dollar would equal 1000 mills. Figure 9.1 presents figures for the conversion of various monetary units into mills. To give an example of this concept, a house in Cedar Falls, Iowa, with an actual property value of $50,000, would be assessed at 80 percent of the actual value, giving it an assessed valuation of $40,000. The tax rate in Cedar Falls is $1.13 per $100. Therefore, the taxpayer would owe the city $452 in real property taxes.

Property taxes are usually levied within a community to provide revenue for a general fund from which the local subdivision of government operates its services. The general fund is used to finance all general governmental services. Leisure services in a local community usually finance their operations through this fund. In certain states, special legislation exists that allows for a tax levy to support specific services, including park and recreation services. State statutes usually allow the local subdivision of government some discretionary power in the assessment of such taxes.

Another type of tax that may be used for leisure services is the special tax. This type of tax is levied specifically for park and recreation services. Other taxes used to finance local park and recreation services include sales taxes, amusement taxes, and special product or service taxes. These types of taxes are usually collected by a state or provincial government and reimbursed to the local subdivisions of government.

It should be noted that nonprofit agencies such as YWCAs, YMCAs, Boys & Girls Clubs, and others rely indirectly on taxes. These organizations are tax-exempt, according to the Internal Revenue Service (IRS) Section 503 of the tax code. Although they do not receive tax monies directly from local government authorities, they do not have to pay property taxes for their land and buildings to those same authorities. So unlike in for-profit leisure organizations, they are able to remove an expenditure item from their budgets.

Fees and Charges

As tax revenues have declined, fees and charges have become increasingly

Figure 9.1
Tax Rate Summary

1.00 = one dollar
0.10 = one dime
0.01 = one cent
0.001 = one mill
0.00150 = one and one half mills
0.01 = one cent (10 mills)
0.05% (of 1%) = 0.0005 mills
0.1% (of 1% = 1/10 of one percent or 0.005 (5 mills)
1.0% = 0.01 or one cent per dollar (10 mills)

important to help offset the costs of operations. For example, an organization might have a fee to enter a swimming pool or to participate in a special class or other type of activity. However, as Manning, Callinan, Echelberger, Koenemann, and McEwen (1984: 20) note:

"A user fee for public park and recreation services is an issue fraught with controversy. The traditional view among park and recreation professionals has been in favor of free or low-cost pricing of such services. Access to leisure, it is argued, provides important benefits to other individuals and society at large, and these benefits should not be denied to any segment of society based on income or other limitations."

Needless to say, there are varying philosophies concerning the basis on which fees are to be charged (see Figure 9.2). In many communities, these fees are imposed only for a specialized or more advanced activity or program; the premise is that the introductory or beginning level should be underwritten by the general operating funds of the community, and that fees and charges should be set only for specialized activities or more advanced instruction, equip-

ment, or facilities. The user is asked to pay for the costs related to more sophisticated programs rather than the taxpayer, who may not use the specialized facility or program. Generally, such programs as golf courses, special tennis programs, and high-skill classes in recreation are offset by such charges (see Figure 9.2 for fee policy).

A study by Brademas and Readnour (1989) found that despite the controversy around fees and charges, community recreation agencies seem to be uniting in their philosophies concerning the use of fees and changes. In their study of recreation agencies in the NRPA Great Lakes Region, they found that 95 percent of the agencies felt justified in charging fees, and 77 percent felt that these fees were consistent with the agency's basic philosophy.

Fees and charges may be classified as follows:

1. *Entrance Fees.* These are fees charged to enter a large park, botanical garden, zoological garden, or other developed recreational area. The areas are usually well-defined but are not necessarily enclosed. The entrance is the patron's first contact with the park. It may contain additional facilities or activities for which fees are charged.

Figure 9.2
City of Reno (NV) Policy Regarding Fees

City of Reno
Parks, Recreation & Community Services
Fees and Charges Policy

Department Mission Statement: To plan, develop, coordinate and deliver effective parks, urban forestry, recreation, aquatic and golf programs and facilities, cultural and special events for the use and enjoyment by Reno's diverse citizenry and visitors.

Philosophy of Need: Parks and Recreation services are essential for an urban government to provide its residents and visitors. The City's General Fund contribution for support of department programs and services has been capped. In order to continue providing and expanding services, fees and charges are necessary.

Basis for fees and charges: Those who benefit from the goods or services provided should pay in proportion to the benefits they receive. The fundamental basis for fees and charges decision making is a determination of who benefits from the service. It is recognized that pricing decisions may be influenced by practical considerations such as collections costs, market effects, legal constraints, or ability to pay.

Determining Community Benefits: If all, or substantially all, of the benefits accrue to the community as a whole (a "Public Good"), the community as a whole should pay for the service through taxes. "Public good" is a value determined by Reno citizens and established by City Council policy and budgetary appropriations. If all, or substantially all, of the benefits are to an individual or group that is to consume the good or service, not for the benefit of the general public, fees & charges should be paid whether by the individual or group or other means such as donations, scholarships etc. Where the benefits accrue to both the community and specific users, the costs should be shared on a basis of proportional benefit.

Scholarship Program: All Reno residents who desire access to programs and services will have the opportunity to participate. Therefore, a scholarship program should be in effect for those Reno residents who do not have the ability to pay either all or part of the established fee or charge. The scholarship policy will establish a program which provides staff the guidelines and procedures to provide reduced fees for those residents who do not have the means to pay in full. The guidelines will be based upon established standards, such as the Federal rules for school free lunch program. The guidelines will respect the privacy of the individual/family and will be applied consistently. There will be certain programs and activities where it is impractical to implement a scholarship program; for example, drop in programs like daily open swim. Attachment A is the Reno Scholarship Policy and forms.

Cost to Collect Fee: The revenue collected from fees and charges must always be greater than the costs of collection of the revenue.

Social Implication: It may be desirable to use the fees & charges system to encourage particular behaviors which enhance the recreational experience for all users; e.g., alter demand patterns, encourage reasonable uses of staff time, or alter behaviors which disturb other participants.

Fee Establishment: City Council will establish all fees and charges during the adoption of the annual budget. Flexibility is needed to accommodate changing factors which impact the approved budget and fees. The department must respond to market trends in a timely manner. If during the fiscal year the costs or demand for a particular program or service needs to be adjusted, or if a new program is offered, staff will modify or establish the fee after consultation with the Recreation and Parks Commission.

Park Usage: Parks are generally free and open to the public for general park use. Fees for specialized facilities in parks, and additional services beyond the normal park use itself, will be assessed. The use of public recreation areas and facilities by private groups should be considered secondary to general public use or usage by nonprofit recreation or service organizations. Only under unusual circumstances should a private use hamper ongoing Department programs, general park use or recreation facility rental. The community has a right to profit on the use of its facilities when public resources are utilized by profit motivated individuals, organizations, or businesses.

Special Interest Groups: Individuals and special interest groups will not receive special or preferential treatment in the waiving or reduction of fees that is inconsistent with established policy.

Costs: When establishing fees and charges, all costs will be considered.

Continued

Figure 9.2 Continued
City of Reno (NV) Policy Regarding Fees

Definitions:

Direct
Costs which if the program or service were not offered, would not be expended.

Overhead
Cost which support the provision of the program or service such as office support for registration, supervisory and/or administrative staff to plan, supervise and evaluate programs/services, marketing and advertising costs associated with the program/service, as well as special or program related park maintenance.

Indirect
Costs which support the overall department operations including support from other City departments which cannot be attributed to any particular program or service the department offers.

Financing Park Facilities: Costs for the provision (acquisition, development and routine maintenance) of traditional park facilities will not be factored in when determining fees. However, (individuals or organizations) desirous of specialized and/or new facilities beyond existing city resources may be required to pay the costs for the acquisition, development, operation, maintenance and program costs associated with the new facility.

Golf: Golf courses will generate enough revenues to cover all direct, indirect and overhead costs as well as any debt service for the development and future capital needs.

Program and Service Cost Allocation:
Youth Programs and Services
Youth programs and services will generate enough revenues to cover all direct and overhead costs. For most programs, youth is defined as 18 years old or younger.

Adult Programs and Services:
Adult programs and services will generate enough revenues to cover all direct and overhead costs plus a percentage of indirect costs. For most programs, adult are defined as 19 years or older.

Senior Programs and Services:
Senior programs and services will generate enough revenues to cover all direct and overhead costs plus a percentage of indirect costs. For most programs specifically offered for seniors, senior may be defined as age 55 and older.

Meeting Community or Neighborhood Needs:
Occasionally, the Director of Parks, Recreation and Community Services may reduce or waive fees and charges for activities/events which benefit the overall community and/or meet specific neighborhood needs. Fees will not be waived or reduced for events/activities which serve a limited or specific interest group. An organizer must be a not-for-profit agency with 501(c)3 status, community or neighborhood organization (i.e., NAB's) recognized or affiliated with the City.

Meeting Targeted Needs:
Programs specifically provided for those who are unable to pay will generate enough revenue, through fees, scholarships and other methods, to cover the direct costs.

Meeting Department or City Needs:
Some programs and services which serve as a marketing tool for the department, or the City as a whole, may be offered free or with reduced fees to the public. When collaborating or co-sponsoring a program or service, the costs attributed to all parties will be factored in when determining fees and charges. An equitable distribution of revenues will be maintained.

Gifts and Donations:
Corporate and individual sponsorships, gifts and scholarships can be accepted to reduce or offset the costs of a program, service or facility.

Satisfaction Guaranteed:
With the exception of child care programs, sports leagues, and aquatics, any participant not completely satisfied with a program will receive a full refund. As our customer we are committed to providing you the highest quality of services. If you are not satisfied with the program or service, a refund will be provided. For a complete copy of our refund policy call 334-2262.

Early Bird Discount:
To encourage customers to register prior to or by the established deadline for class cancellation, the department may establish an early bird discount. The fee for the program will be established and

Figure 9.2 Continued
City of Reno (NV) Policy Regarding Fees

published as the "early bird" rate and any registration received after the deadline will be charged a higher fee based upon the overall cost of the program. For example: for a recreation class a $5 fee could be charged and for a softball league team a $30 fee could be charged.

Equal Opportunity & Non Discrimination:
The fees and charges policy and implementation will comply with the city's equal opportunity and nondiscrimination policy.

Resident versus Non-Resident Fees and Charges:
There will be no distinction between resident and non-resident in the access or use of the department parks and recreation facilities. For the establishment of fees and charges, there are circumstances which warrant a non-resident fee or reduction in fees for residents.

When demand for recreational services exceeds the resources available, a non-resident fee can be established; for example, picnic and facility rental. When a program or facility can be fully utilized by residents, or there is a need to limit use, a non-resident fee can be established. Special services for residents may be provided including preferential registration times or special discounts such as season swim passes.

Scholarships provided for individual or families should be limited to Reno residents when the City's General Fund is the source of scholarship funds.

When demand for leisure education programs exceeds resources available, with pre-registration required, there can be different fees for non-residents. In general, a 50% increase for non-residents should be charged to non-residents.

Programs or services which are in the introductory stage may not differentiate between resident and non-residents in order to build interest in a new activity.

Programs that serve the region as a whole, such as a jointly sponsored program with the County or Sparks or a region-wide golf marketing effort, should not have a non-resident fee.

Drop-in programs such as open swim, open skate, teen clubs, special events or general youth programs where it is impractical to require identification should not have non-resident fees.

When the costs to administer a different fee system is greater than the revenues produced there should not be non-resident fees.

When facility operation and maintenance is subsidized with General Fund tax dollars, a non-resident fee can be established.

2. *Admission Fees.* Charges made to enter a building, structure, or natural chamber are designated as admission fees. These locations usually offer an exhibit, show, ceremony, performance, demonstration, or special equipment. Entry and exit are normally controlled and attendance is regulated.

3. *Rental Fees.* Payment made for the privilege of exclusive use of tangible property of any kind is considered a rental fee. This fee gives the patron the right to enjoy all the advantages derived from the use of the property without consuming, destroying, or injuring it in any way.

4. *User Fees.* When a charge is made for the use of a facility, participation in an activity, or as a fare for controlled use, it is referred to as a user

fee. The patron usually enjoys the privilege simultaneously with others. It is not the patron's exclusive right, as in the case of the rental fee.

5. *Sales Revenues.* All revenues obtained from the operation of stores, concessions, or restaurants and from the sale of merchandise or other property are included in this category. Unconditional ownership of the item must pass from the seller to the buyer with each sale.

6. *License and Permit Fees.* License and permit are considered synonymous here. A license is a written acknowledgment of consent to do some lawful thing without command; it grants a liberty or privilege and professes to tolerate all legal actions. It usually involves permission to perform an action. It seldom grants authority to occupy space or use property.

7. *Special Service Fees.* The charges made for extraordinary articles, commodities, services, or accommodations to the public are considered special service fees. Such accommodations must be unusual in character and not normally considered a required governmental service.

An excellent example of a fee and charge policy is that provided by the city of Reno, Nevada's Department of Parks, Recreation and Community Services. This policy thoroughly outlines strategies for collecting fees and charges, including useful definitions. This policy structure can be a major component of any leisure service organization, as the generation of revenues has become increasing important in terms of overall operational strategies.

Grants

Another method of financing leisure service programs is through grants from federal, state, or provincial governments. As Crompton (1999:303) notes: "Grant programs are authorized because there are political pressures for elected representatives to address particular problems. They tend to be authorized for limited periods of time and are allowed to lapse when the political pressure on that issue has dissipated or when there is widespread belief that they have not been effective." Thus, one can trace which social upheavals have become major issues by the nature of grants made available at any given time. Presently, the types of grants that have had direct impact on leisure services tend to be those involved with youth, after-school programs, capital improvements, and park land acquisition.

The one grant program directly related to public parks and recreation that has been sustained over time is known as the Land and Water Conservation Fund (LWCF). This fund was created on January 1, 1965, for the express purpose of assisting all levels of government in the acquisition and development of outdoor recreational resources. Specifically, the fund provides for:

1. Funding for the National Park Service, U.S. Fish and Wildlife Service, U.S. Forest Service, and (to a lesser extent) the Bureaus of Land Management to acquire lands for their systems.

2. Grants-in-aid to states and, through them, to local jurisdictions, and development of outdoor recreation facilities.

The legislation required that at least 40 percent of the annual LWCF appropriation be expended on federal projects and that up to 60 percent of it be distributed to state governments. In turn, the state governments were required to provide matching funds to local jurisdictions for outdoor recreation facility development.

Although this program has been ongoing for over 30 years, there have been several problems with it, mostly related to the monies that Congress has authorized for the fund. Initially, three sources of revenue for the fund were designated: proceeds from the sales of surplus federal land, boat fuel taxes and fees from recreational use of federal lands. When revenues generated from these sources proved to be insufficient, Congress added the use of outer continental shelf mineral leasing and royalty receipts as well as monies from other sources to attempt to add $900 million to the fund. However, as Crompton (1999) points out, there has never been one year in which annual appropriations of Congress reached the authorized spending level of $900 million. The highest appropriations were made in 1978 and 1979, which amounted to $805 and $737 million, respectively. In recent years, the stateside funding has been minimal.

There are some financial lessons to be learned from the issues surrounding the LWCF. Although it has helped to provide needed recreation facilities around the country (2.4 million acres of park land and open spaces, and development of over 25,000 recreational sites), the funding base for the program has always been tenuous. Thus, state and local entities that have received monies have been provided with a bonus rather than a reliable source of funding. It also means that this type of political funding is at the mercy of the appropriations process in Congress.

Some precautions should be given in regard to the use of grant funds as a revenue stream for park and recreation agencies. Foremost is the fact that grant programs are established for a limited time period and will eventually be terminated. When grant funds are used for programs that cannot be terminated, the local agency has to be ready to continue them and pick up the funding when federal funds stop. Many times, it is difficult, if not impossible, to stop a program once it is started, particularly if it is a popular program. One of the intents of a grant program is to help communities that are overburdened by taxes, but to start a federally funded program that ultimately will increase the local tax burden does not indicate a good management decision.

Communities and agencies that use grant funds to supplement the ongoing operations of their agencies, such as employing individuals to fill regular job vacancies, are hurting, not helping, the organization. When the source of those grant monies disappears, the agency will ultimately have to lay off these individuals or provide local funding. This is generally not the intent of grant programs and reflects poor management.

In any program that is undertaken with local, state, or provincial funds, the manager responsible for the program must realize what the commitment is to the future in terms of personnel, dollars, and facilities in starting the program. For this reason, many communities have used federal and state funds that are of a one-time or short-term nature for capital projects. When these capital projects are complete, it is the end of the commitment, except for the operation and maintenance costs, which can generally be absorbed by the local agency.

Donations

It is not unusual for leisure service organizations to accept donations. Financial arrangements can be made within an organization to receive gifts and other donations. Usually the establishment of a special fund or account accomplishes this. Often an organization will establish a special fund for the purposes of soliciting monies to develop a facility or acquire park acreage. Sometimes an organization may even establish a foundation for this purpose. The operation of the foundation is set up outside the governmental agency and is administered by private citizens, who can attract large donations and gifts because they have nonprofit, tax-exempt status. Thus, donations to such foundations or special funds are ordinarily tax deductible.

Sellers, Gladwell, and Pope (1999: 618) point out five advantages of establishing park and recreation foundations for soliciting donations:

1. Foundations are not "government";

2. Foundations can offer tax benefits to the contributor;

3. Foundations are in a position to leverage gifts;

4. Foundations can act without political impediments; and

5. Foundations are good public relations tools.

Public leisure service organizations can also establish special accounts that permit individuals or groups to give donations toward the purchase of special items. This type of fund is often held in a special account and used only for the specific purpose for which the account was established. Many parks and recreation departments have established special funds to accept donations for tree replacement, playground equipment, and the like.

Many youth-serving agencies depend heavily on donations to finance operational activities. In most other organizations, however, donations are ordinarily used to finance capital expenditures. Organizations that must rely primarily on donations for their day-to-day operations spend a great deal of time in fund-raising activities. This can diminish the impact of a leisure service organization, because the effort spent in acquiring donations may very well drain the creative energy and time of the staff.

Investments

Progressive nonprofit organizations may invest unneeded revenues in order to increase their ultimate revenue. During any given period of time, an organization needs only a certain cash balance to maintain its operations. Excess cash revenues can be invested, and the interest paid on these investments can serve as an additional source of revenue for the organization. Organizations can determine what funds can be invested on a long- or short-term basis. Long-term investments are usually made for six months to two years. Short-term investments can be made from one day to one year, but they are typically made for a period of 30 to 60 days.

Bond Programs

Bond programs that require referenda by the general public, to determine whether it wants to be taxed for such facilities, fund the majority of the capital improvements that are made in most public leisure service organizations. The procedures for bond programs are usually established by the laws of the state or province as well as by local agencies, which govern the requirements for such bond programs in terms of the percentage of the electorate that has to endorse a program before it can be undertaken.

Banks that lend money to individuals for personal use have credit ratings on individuals that indicate how much a risk that individual is in terms of lending. Likewise, cities and governmental agencies have bond ratings that indicate how well they finance and manage their money and how good a risk they are. Standard & Poor's has a rating criteria that starts with an AAA rating, which is the best rating a city can have. An AA is next best, and ratings go all the way down to an NCR rating for poor risks. Table 9.1 shows the various ratings.

The higher the city or agency's rating, the more easily it can borrow money, usually at a lower interest rate. A one percent difference in interest rate on $1 million for 20 years would amount to a savings of $200,000. Most communities have a bond indebtedness limit that they cannot go above. Most cities use as a rule of thumb a bond indebtedness limit of no more than 5 percent of the fully assessed value of the city for bonds at any one time. Bonds are the major source of revenue for capital improvement programs and serve as a basis of borrowing money for 15 to 30 years.

Generally, there are two major types of bonds used in governmental bonding. The first of these is the *general obligation bond.* This type of bond is one that is guaranteed with full faith and credit by a municipality to insure payment. The municipality guarantees to pay out of its general operating budget a certain amount of money on an annual basis for the privilege of borrowing the money. Such a system permits the municipality to acquire several million dollars at a time to acquire land and construct capital facilities that it could not otherwise acquire or provide out of its operating budget.

The other form of bond is the *revenue bond.* These bonds are often used to finance such facilities as golf courses, swimming pools, and other facilities that would produce revenue; hence the term "revenue bond." The revenue produced by the facility is pledged to pay off the bond indebtedness. Golf courses are probably the most common example of facilities that use revenue bonds.

Bonds may also be classified according to the method in which they are retired. There are three methods of bond retirement, or types of bonds, used by municipal leisure service organizations: term, callable, and serial bonds. Richard Kraus and Joseph Curtis (2000:164) describe the differences between these types of bonds:

Term Bonds. In this type of bond, the government agency promises to pay off the entire principal at the end of a given period of time. Normally, it would use the "sinking fund" method, under which an annual sum is put aside each year, with the amount accumulating each year until the full principal has been set aside at the end of the term of the bonds.

Table 9.1
Standard & Poor's Municipal Bond Ratings

Rating Criteria

AAA, prime.	These are obligations of the highest quality. They have the strongest capacity for timely payment of debt service.
AA, high grade.	The investment characteristics of general obligation and revenue bonds in this group are only slightly less marked than those of the prime quality issues. Bonds rated "AA" have the second strongest capacity for payment of debt service.
A, good grade.	Principal and interest payments on bonds in this category are regarded as safe. This rating describes the third strongest capacity for payment of debt service.
BBB, medium grade.	This is the lowest investment grade security rating.
BB, speculative grade.	Bonds in this group have some investment characteristics, but they no longer predominate. For the most part this rating indicates a speculative, noninvestment grade obligation.
B, low grade.	Investment characteristics are virtually nonexistent, and default could be imminent.
D, defaults.	Payment of interest and/or principal is in arrears.
NCR.	No contract rating. No ratings are assigned to new offerings unless a contract is applied for.
Provisional ratings.	The letter "p" following a rating indicates the rating is provisional, where payment of debt service requirements will be largely or entirely dependent upon the timely completion of the project.

Source: Pamphlet by Standard and Poor's Corporation, 345 Hudson St., New York, NY, p. 5-7.

Callable Bonds. This is a special type of bond in which the government has the option of calling in the bond issue for payment at a specific period of time before the end of its term, or at any time it chooses. Because bond interest rates tend to fluctuate, it is thus possible for the issuer to call in a bond and reissue it at low interest rates, depending on market conditions.

Serial Bonds. Under this method of financing capital outlays, the government pays the bond purchaser a specific portion of the principal, plus interest, each year that the bond issue is in effect. Thus, a percentage of the bond is reduced each year through payments of approximately equal sums.

As already stated, bond programs are regulated by laws, and the leisure service manager only has to understand the laws that govern his or her agency to place a bond issue before the public.

The secret of managing successful bond programs is getting them approved by the public.

There is only one reason why bond issues fail: They get more no votes than yes votes. There are many reasons why an individual may vote no:

1. The bond program does not provide anything of interest to that individual;

2. The voter does not want his or her taxes increased;

3. The voter does not have confidence in the agency sponsoring the bond issue;

4. The voter does not understand the issue; and

5. The bond program is poorly timed.

Generally, people vote for bond issues for only one reason: *There is something in it for them.* In most cases, it is a waste of time to try to change the mind of a person who is against a bond program. Except in the case of misunderstanding, you will not change his or her opinion.

To pass a bond program, the following procedures should be followed:

1. *Make sure the timing is good.* Depending on the situation, timing is very important. If a large voter turnout will help pass the issue, it would best be presented at a general election. If the taxpayers are overburdened, it is not a good time to put the issue on the ballot. If the image of the leisure service organization is poor at the time, it would be bad timing to place the issue on the ballot (Edginton & Williams , 1979).

2. *Provide a factual and informative public information document.* This should be provided to all voters. In many states and communities, government agencies themselves cannot take a stand on bond issues. No public funds can be spent on trying to sell the issue because of a conflict of interest. The public agency *can* provide the facts about the program, what it will cost the taxpayers, what it will provide, and what its purposes are. Figure 9.3 is an example of such a fact sheet.

3. *Provide for a citizen committee to support the program.* This may sound contradictory to the previous point; however, it is understood that at some point in time there is a decision that the public should be give an opportunity to

vote on a particular bond issue. Usually the parks and recreation staff make such a proposal. This is presented to the city council or governing board that decides whether to put the proposal before the voters. If it decides to put it to the voters, the council (or board) is the one to appoint a committee to support the bond issue. The committee should raise funds to support the program, publicize it, and engage in any other activities that will promote the program.

4. *Provide a bond program that is of interest to enough citizens that it stands a chance of passing.* As indicated earlier, people are going to vote for an issue only if it offers them something. One of two swimming pools in isolated areas of a large community will not pull enough voters to pass a bond issue. It is a good idea to examine past issues and determine how many individuals voted, which areas passed issues, and which did not, as well as to try to gain any other information that will help the leisure service manager determine how he or she can best present the bond issue so it will stand the best chance of passing. Usually a proposal for a large number of facilities distributed strategically throughout a community stands the best chance of passing.

5. *Do not spend a lot of energy and time trying to convince no voters to vote yes.* Most no voters have their minds made up, and you are not going to change them. You may change the few who have been misinformed with a good factual information pamphlet.

Figure 9.3
Open Space Bond Issue: Questions and Answers

Q. **What is the amount and purpose of the proposed bond issue?**

A. $5,000.000—to acquire undeveloped land with the city limits of Sunnyvale for open space purposes.

Q. **How much of the $5 million will be used for land acquisition and how much will be used for improvements to the land?**

A. The bond measure limits the use of bond sale proceeds for improvement of property to 10% or $500,000.

Q. **How much land is available for acquisition?**

A. Parcels identified as priority open space sites total approximately 93 acres plus two school sites of approximately 20 acres.

Q. **Can there be a tax rate increase?**

A. Once the bonds are sold, the City may raise property taxes in an amount sufficient to meet the annual cost. It is estimated that the general tax rate will be increased from its present $1.31 per $100 assessed valuation to $1.39 per $100 assessed valuation or an 8¢ increase. It does not require the City Council to increase taxes if other revenues are adequate.

Q. **What would be the increase in property taxes for the average Sunnyvale homeowner?**

A. Assuming a $10,000 assessed valuation ($40,000 home) this would mean an additional $8.00 per year in property taxes.

Q. **In the event the bond issue fails, will the City still attempt to buy the parcels that are available?**

A. Each year the City Council allocates community resources to various programs. The budgeting of funds to acquire open space or any capital or operating items is subject to the decisions of the the City Council each fiscal year. If revenue sharing continues, it may be possible to purchase additional sites from those available at the time.

Q. **Will the City develop the property for parks and other uses in future years?**

A. This determination will be made by city councils at the time each annual budget is adopted.

Q. **What are the maintenance and operating costs?**

A. Maintenance and operating costs are dependent solely upon the level of development and the level of maintenance that is determined as proper by each city council for each fiscal year.

Q. **In view of the unfavorable market conditions, will it be possible to sell the bonds in the event the citizens approve the issue?**

A. The city of Sunnyvale has an "AA" credit rating which is very high and places the City in the preferred customer category with respect to municipal bond issues. The maximum rate that can be paid is 7%. It is unlikely, unless the money market continues to deteriorate, that there will be any problem in marketing the bonds.

Q. **Why does the City have to purchase surplus school sites? Has not the public already paid for them?**

A. The sites were purchased with state bond money or through local school financing. Unless the state loan has been paid off, the schools are required by law to sell surplus sites at an auction to the highest bidder. The money can only be used for school capital improvements or loan re-payment. Schools are paid for by residents of the school district—not residents of the city.

Q. **Must the City pay the highest price for school sites?**

A. No. The City pays only the fair market value as determined by independent appraisals.

Q. **How much land does the City presently have in neighborhood parks and other types of open space?**

A. 153 acres in neighborhood parks
250 acre Mountain park
145 acres, Sunnyvale Municipal Golf Course
30 acres, Sunken Gardens Golf Course
172 acres, Bayland Park (future development)
220 acres, Bayland Park (county ownership)

6. *Develop a sound park and recreation program.* The best publicity for selling a bond issue is a citizenry that is convinced that the parks and recreation program makes the best use of public funds.

Whatever the type of bond issue, be it revenue or general obligation bonds, if it is a "good deal" for the community, it will pass; if it is not, it won't. Figure 9.4 outlines a bond funding process employed by the city of Phoenix, Arizona's Parks, Recreation and Library Department. This step-by-step procedure provides for multiple routes of citizen input in the decision-making process.

Budgets

Leisure service organizations accomplish their work through the use of human, fiscal, and material resources. If the leisure service manager is to work effectively and efficiently, he or she must have information about these resources and whether their use results in the achievement of organizational goals. In other words, organizations need some mechanism to provide a manager with resource information so that he or she has a reliable basis for decisions. The system that allows a manager to plan and control the use of organizational resources is known as the process of "budgeting."

In terms of budgeting, we can again classify leisure service organizations into two basic categories; profit-oriented and nonprofit-oriented. The purpose of a profit-oriented organization is essentially to earn a profit; that is, a profit-oriented organization, to be effective, must ensure that its revenues are greater than its expenditures. On the other hand, a nonprofit organization (NPO) is not primarily concerned with earning a profit; rather, it is concerned with providing goods or services to meet a societal need. However, NPOs must also be concerned with ensuring that expenditures do not exceed the revenues that it produces or acquires for its operation. It should be noted that the process of budgeting is basically the same in profit and nonprofit organizations.

Information Needed by the Manager

The specific type of information needed within a given organization will vary depending on the particular needs of the agency. However, a number of common types of data are needed by most leisure service organizations. Generally speaking, information required by leisure service managers can be categorized into three classifications. The first is *operations information*. In order to conduct the day-to-day operations of a leisure service organization, a manager needs a considerable amount of information, including the daily status of the organization's resources. For example, he or she must be aware of whether the organization has the resources it needs to make certain purchases, pay bills, and cover other expenditures. He or she also needs to know precisely what bills the organization must pay and on what dates, and the income the organization is likely to have and when it will be received.

The second type of information required by the leisure service manager is *management information*. In the transformation of resources into programs, the manager needs information that allows him or her to plan, control, and coordinate the work of the organiza-

Figure 9.4
Public Documents Supporting a Bond Program for a Construction Project
Bond Flow Chart

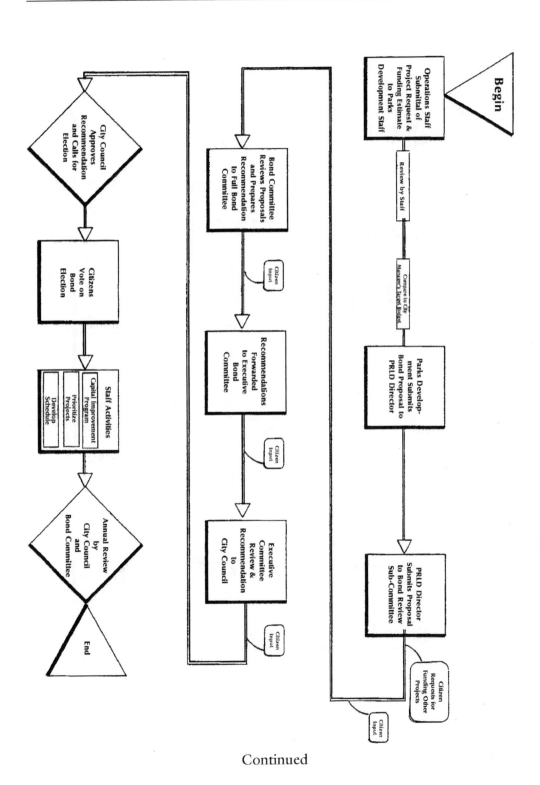

Continued

Figure 9.4 Continued
Public Documents Supporting a Bond Program for a Construction Project
Facility Needs Process

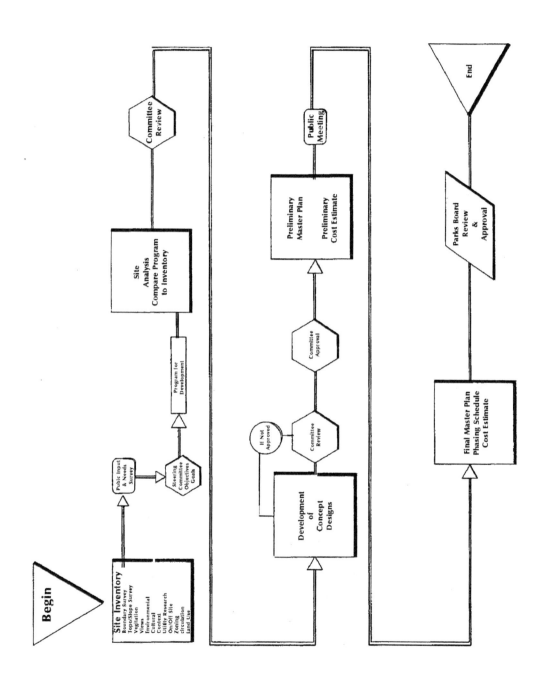

Continued

Figure 9.4 Continued
Public Documents Supporting a Bond Program for a Construction Project
Actualization

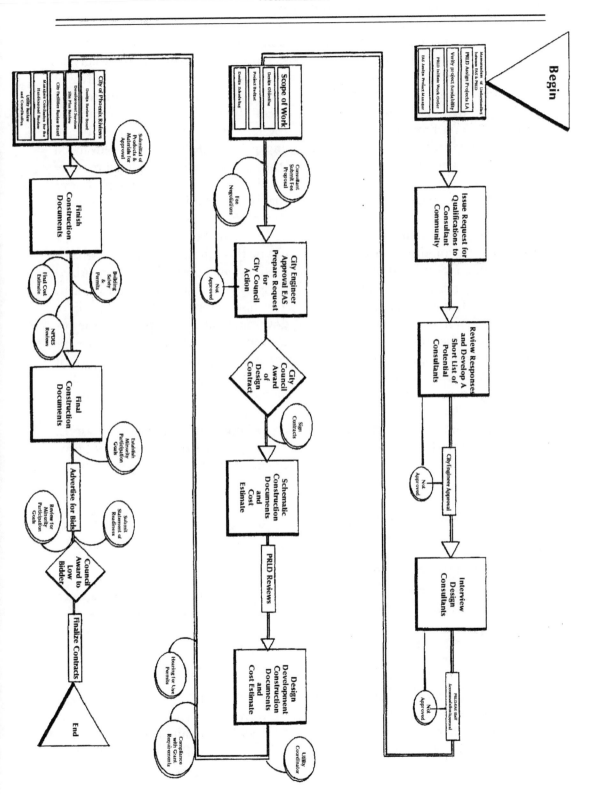

tion. For example, as a planning mechanism, the budget allows the manager to establish a program to meet the organization's objectives. In this manner, the manager is able to tie the goals of the organization to the resources available to achieve them. Planning and decision making go hand in hand. Thus, the budget that serves to guide the organization's operations provides managers with vital information affecting short- and long-term decision making.

The third type of information required in the management of leisure service organizations is *financial information*. Financial information about an organization is important, primarily so the manager may establish the credibility of the organization to outside appraisers. Most, if not all, organizations are involved in making financial transactions with other organizations. This may range from simply engaging in an agreement, to purchasing a given resource, to borrowing money on a long-term basis to finance the development of a facility. It is in the best interests of an organization to have a reputation for financial integrity. As was discussed in this chapter, municipal corporations are appraised and rated in terms of their credit risk. A lower credit rating may restrict an organization's ability to acquire resources, thereby seriously hampering the achievement of its goals.

What Is a Budget?

A budget may be thought of as a statement that allows an organization to plan and control its resources for a specific period of time. It may be stated in dollars, works hours, units of production, or any other descriptive or measurable unit. The budget provides in-formation about what resources the organization will acquire, how they will be acquired, how these resources will be spent, and what services will result. A budget is not a static document. Rather it represents the manager's ability to estimate or predict how the resources of the organization are to be acquired and spent. In making financial estimates, the leisure service manager is able to engage in the development of advanced strategies that allow him or her to more accurately predict and control actions that he or she might take in relation to the delivery of program services. In governmental organizations, a budget can be thought of as a legal tool that is used by an appropriately authorized body to finance a stated set of services. The final adoption of a budget by a governmental agency provides the organization with an estimate of the income it is to produce or acquire, how it will expend this income, and usually a method or plan of financial operation.

Budgeting is used by agencies for many important and practical reasons. The advantages of the budgeting process are numerous but, generally speaking, they can be listed as follows:

1. Budgeting allows the manager to organize the financial operation of the agency in a systematic fashion;

2. Budgeting requires a manager to think ahead to the work that must be accomplished within an organization and the costs that will be incurred in these efforts;

3. Budgeting provides a manager with a basis from which to develop a work schedule and organize the resources within the organization to meet its goals;

4.   Budgeting promotes standardization within financial operations. The desire for efficiency dictates the necessity for a unified approach to the acquisition and expenditure of resources. Standardizing financial operations allows an organization to increase its efficiency;

5.   The budget allows the manager to communicate with subordinates and coordinate their activities in monetary terms, which are commonly understood by both the management and subordinates;

6.   The budget serves as a reference that the manager and his or her subordinates can refer to in order to help clarify or support decisions;

7.   The budget provides legislative decision-making bodies with information necessary to the evaluation of organizations' programs and services;

8.   The budget in the public sector provides the taxpayer with an explanation for how resources are produced, acquired, and expended; and

9.   The budget, as a point of reference, serves as a legislative body's mechanism of control. In other words, the budget can serve as a guideline and measuring device that determines the level of effectiveness and efficiency in a given area of the organization. (Lynch, 1995)

The budgeting process oftentimes seems overwhelming, mysterious, and complex to the prospective leisure service manager. The budget and financial processes of any organization are extremely important and should be well-managed; but the budgeting process

does not have to be overwhelming, complicated, or complex, and it should be easily understood. It involves three basic steps:

1.   Developing a budget plan expressed in dollars that anticipates results of a future period;

2.   Coordinating these dollar estimates into a well-balanced program; and

3.   Comparing actual performance with the estimated balance programs

Almost any organization that the new leisure service manager might join in which he or she will have responsibility for budgeting and financial matters will have a section or division that has budgeting and financial matters as its primary function. This division will probably have existing procedures, policies, and a format that it follows in the preparation, execution, and control of the budget.

In many organizations, the budget process and procedures are spelled out in detail. During budget preparation, a budget manual is usually given to those who are responsible for developing the budget. It provides the manager with a format, timetable, and method by which the budget will be submitted. During the year, there will be controls and procedures to assure that the budget is adhered to, not overexpended, as well as methods to evaluate what has been accomplished.

The Budget Cycle

Budget planning can be developed for a fixed number of days, weeks, or months. Generally speaking, a budget plan is associated with a period of time or a cycle that covers an entire year's operation within an organization. This yearly cycle is known as a "fiscal year." A fiscal year can start at any time during the year and end with the settling of financial accounts. A fiscal year may run concurrently with the calendar year, starting January 1 and ending December 31, although it would still be called a fiscal year. In the United States, in many governmental organizations the fiscal year starts on July 1 and runs to June 30 of the following year. The Federal Budget runs on a fiscal year starting on October 1 and running to September 30.

In addition to budgets covering one year, many leisure service organizations project their budgets anywhere from three to eight years in the future, depending on the planning cycle adopted. Budgeting more than one year at a time enables an organization to get an indication of the types of commitments it is going to have in the future so it can anticipate the revenues it will need to meet these commitments. Also, looking into the future helps the manager determine other effects, such as inflation, a shift in program emphasis, the effects of new programs, and what adjustments have to be made as a result of additional revenue or decreasing revenue in the future. On the other hand, it is impractical to try to think too far into the future. As Peter F. Drucker (1973:123) has written:

"... planning is not forecasting. It is not masterminding the future. Any attempt to do so is foolish. The future is unpredictable. We can only discredit what we are doing by attempting it. No one can forecast what's going to happen ten years from now, which is proven by the many surprises that face the world every day. . .

On the other hand, by analyzing what we do today we certainly have a better idea of what effect it might have in the future. We know that it takes 99 years to grow a Douglas fir in the Northwest for pulpwood size; planting seedlings today is the only way we can provide for pulp supply for 99 years from now."

So it becomes obvious that we need to look into the future in order to determine what impact the things we are doing today will have on the ongoing viability of the organization. There is no better example of a management tool to use for this forecasting than the budgeting process. Not only is it necessary and valuable to look into the future, it is also helpful to examine what has happened in the past and see what trends have taken place. For this reason, most budgets show two or three years of past history in terms of accomplishments, expenditures in both work hours and other resources, and indications of trends and present needs. Figure 9.5 shows a budget with three year's history, an estimate for the present year, the requests for funds of a given year, and seven years of future projections.

Budget Design

There are many types of budget formats that can be used by leisure service organizations. However, they generally fall into four basic designs: line item, program, performance, and zero-base. Each format provides the manager with different types of information. For example, a line-item bud-

**Figure 9.5
What is a Budget?**

Program: 265.08 Parks maintenance
Function: Environmental services
Objective: Keep parks safe, attractive, and usable

Fiscal Year	Work Hours	Total Cost	Production Units (Work-Hour Output)	Costs per Unit	Unit Cost in Constant Dollars 2001-2002
Actual 2001-2002	80,811	807,564	108,634	7,43	7.43
Actual 2001-2002	80,576	819,747	108634	7.55	7.18
Actual 2001-2002	176,685	869,776	108,634	8.01	6.93
Estimated 2002-2003	81,654	979,455	116,445	8.41	6.60
Proposed 2002-2003	76,825	1,169,480	124,965	9.36	6.77
Projected 2003-2004	76,825	1,257,680	124,965	10.06	6.80
Projected 2004-2005	76,825	1,349,801	124,965	10.80	6.83
Projected 2005-2006	76,825	1,430,007	124,965	11.44	6.82
Projected 2006-2007	76,825	1,504,078	124,965	12.04	6.83
Projected 2007-2008	76,825	1,578,917	124,965	12.63	6.82
Projected 2008-2009	76,825	1,658,103	124,965	13.27	6.82
Projected 2009-2010	76,825	1,740,618	124,965	13.93	6.82

get provides a broad perspective of revenues and expenditures but little detail, whereas a program or performance budget provides information about the outputs or benefits that result from a specific aspect of the organization's efforts but does not provide a holistic financial view of the organization. Each of these formats has strengths and weaknesses.

What budget format should the leisure service manager choose? Simply, it depends on the information that is needed. Should a manager find that he or she needs information beyond the day-to-day operational type, it may be that a program budget is most appropriate. On the other hand, if a manager in a certain situation needs only operational information, it may be that he or she should use the line-item budget approach. In most organizations, some combination of these budget formats is used because the information needs vary.

Line-Item Budgets

The oldest budget format is the line-item or object classification design. This format came into existence during the early 1900s in an effort to hold municipal governments accountable for the expenditure of public funds. Although it may seem hard to believe today, prior to the introduction of line-item budgeting, municipal agencies were simply allocated an amount of money to spend during a fiscal year. This lump-sum approach provided no controls or safeguards to regulate whether the monies were being spent in an appropriate manner.

The creation of a line-item budget allowed legislative bodies and the public to scrutinize more closely the financial transactions of agencies by listing all revenues (monies coming into an agency) and expenditures (monies leaving an agency) by categories or accounts. This budget design is traditionally referred to as line-item budgeting, because each element of the budget has a specific line that describes the type of classification and the amount of money associated with that particular element. Typical classifications include such services as the following:

1. *Personnel Services.* This classification includes the direct labor of individuals who are employed within the organization on either a regular or a temporary basis and are paid on either an hourly wage basis or a fixed salary.

2. *Contractual Services.* This classification includes those services that are performed under an expressed or implied contract. The contractual arrangements of a leisure service organization range from postage, telephone, print-ing, and repairs to the cost of heat, light, and power. A contractual arrangement between a leisure service agency and another organization not only involves the use of that organization's equipment, but also the personnel necessary to implement a said service.

3. *Supplies.* Supplies are commodities that are entirely consumed or that show rapid depreciation in a short period of time. Examples would be fuel, office supplies, cleaning supplies, or turf-care products.

4. *Materials.* Materials are commodities that have a more permanent and lasting quality than supplies. These may include such things as materials used in construction and repair parts for equipment.

5. *Current Charges.* This type of expenditure includes the cost of clothing allowances, insurance, rental of typewriters, dues, and any other charges that are contracted at the option of the organization.

6. *Current Obligations.* These consist of fixed charges that have resulted from previous financial transactions entered into by the organization. For example, the payment of the organization's share of social security (United States) or social insurance (Canada) and its contribution to the organization's retirement or pension program are found in this classification. Also included may be the cost of interest on the organization's debt, which may have resulted from borrowing money for capital improvements.

7. *Properties.* This classification includes the cost of improvements

that are made to an organization's physical resources. It also includes the direct purchase cost of any new equipment or other physical resources, in other words, anything that is appreciable and has a calculated period of usefulness. This might include such things as playground equipment, machinery, office equipment, the cost of real estate, and any improvements made to existing properties.

8. *Debt Payment.* Debt payments may be distinguished from current obligations in that debt payments refer to the organization's payments on the principal of a given debt rather than the interest.

A system that an organization might follow in laying out an objective classification budget is shown in Table 9.2.

There are political strengths and weaknesses to this type of budget format. On the positive side, line-item budgets allow an astute manager to hide potentially volatile programs or personnel decisions under broad categories such as supplies and personnel. Indeed, the cost of programs may be spread out among many categories, as the focus of line-item budgeting is on the allocation of funds, not on the service benefit outcomes. Thus, the line-item budget makes it difficult to see a direct relationship between expenditures and program results. As Wildavsky (1986: 136) writes:

"It is much easier [for budget reviewers] to agree on an addition or reduction of a few thousand or a million than to agree whether a program is good or not. It is much easier to agree on a small addition or decrease [in a specific item] than to compare the worth of one program to that of all others."

This also points out one of the downsides of line-item budgets. Because politicians and decision makers can make sanitized cuts without seeing the pain or impact that such reductions have on people, they do not have to face the consequences that their actions have in human terms. Thus, in times of financial exigency, it is easier to wield the cutting ax without regard to the impact such cuts will make in programs and services.

The other problem that occurs with this format is that expenditures usually rise incrementally without regard to the value of specific programs and services. Thus, it can allow the leisure service manager to request an increase of expenditures during good economic times without having to justify the worth of these programs. As Holdnak, Mahoney, and Garges (1999: 681) write:

"Line-item budgets also encourage certain strategies on the part of those who prepare and review budgets that may not result in efficient allocation of resources, such as:

1. Never ask for less money than currently allocated;

2. Spend all the monies that are allocated;

3. Never encourage legislative or central office scrutiny by suggesting major changes in programs;

4. Ask for more than is needed in order to provide budget reviewers with something they can suggest to be cut;

5. Eliminate requests for new personnel or capital expenditures that will be a continuing expense; and

Table 9.2
Example of Objective Classification System

1000 Personnel Services

1100	Wages and salaries, regular
1200	Wages and salaries, temporary
1300	Other compensations

2000 Contractual Services

2100	Communication and transportation
2200	Power, water, and sewage
2300	Printing and advertising
2400	Repairs, janitorial services, and other services

3000 Supplies

3100	Fuel and lubricants
3200	Office supplies
3300	Cleaning supplies
3400	Food

4000 Materials

4100	Building materials
4200	Repair parts

5000 Current Charges

5100	Insurance
5200	Equipment
5300	Clothing allowances
5400	Subscriptions on dues
5500	Taxes
5600	Refunds

6000 Current Obligations

6100	Pensions and retirement
6300	Interest

7000 Properties

7100	Building structures and improvements
7200	Equipment
7300	Land

8000 Debt Payment

8100	Serial bonds

6. Allocate reductions and increases equally across departments."

Program Budget

In order to emphasize outcomes rather than costs, more and more agencies have been moving toward a program budget format and away from line-item budget presentation. The idea behind the program budget is to put more emphasis on dealing with programs that are desirable, and on associating costs with each of these programs in terms of the resources necessary to carry them out. In other words, it helps to determine which programs the policymaking or governing boards want to offer and permits the manager to determine how to finance these programs and assure accountability.

In a program budget, analysis is focused primarily on output, and the budget is structured in such a manner that the outputs are related directly to the goals and objectives desired. A program can be defined as a specific group of activities that is organized to meet a distinguishable goal. Thus, a program budget could reflect either a major program area (Athletics, Aquatics, Special Events) or a specific program within these major areas (softball, swim lessons, an Easter egg hunt). These budget groupings are analyzed and evaluated independently in terms of the costs.

In developing a program budget, the following steps are undertaken:

1. Identification of each program that the agency provides; and

2. Determination of the cost associated with the provision of each program.

It should be noted that many program budgets use line-item classifications but place the direct costs under the program heading. Thus, one is able to see the direct salary cost for an aerobic instructor rather than having it hidden in a general line-item budget under personnel. Depending on the budget philosophy of the agency, indirect costs such as lighting, electricity, room use, and so on will also be portioned out on a percentage basis.

Program budgets provide decision makers with greater information as to the cost-effectiveness of programs, facilities, and services by matching program objectives to full costs. These also help them determine the cost–benefit ratios of various programs and make comparisons. An example of a program budget that combines line-item budgeting is found in Figure 9.6. This recreation program budget worksheet from the city of Reno, Nevada's Department of Parks, Recreation and Community Services provides a guideline for budgeting for their at-risk youth programs. Line item categories include salaries, supplies and personnel.

Performance Budgeting

The performance budget format is a mechanism whereby an organization breaks down its work activities into detailed subunits for the purpose of determining the specific costs of each of these units. In other words, the manager using a performance approach to budgeting would further subdivide or arrange the functional and objective classifications of budgeting to get a detailed cost of a given program. It is not unusual for organizations to have a cross-reference system that shows objective classifications on the vertical axis and functional classifications on the horizontal axis. Performance budgeting is often used in organizations where the user pays the cost of a given activity. For the organization to have an idea of the total cost and appropriate cost for a given program, all the expenditures for that activity must be calculated. Once this has been accomplished, the organization can suggest a fee or charge to cover the expenses that are incurred. Some of the key features of performance budgeting are the following:

1. Performance budgeting does not preclude budgeting according to a classification of functions, subfunctions, and objectives of expenditures;

2. The data supplied by the process of performance budgeting are more valuable to top administrators and to the appropriating body than to administrators of single programs who are close enough to the enterprise to make judgments without performance budget data;

3. Formal procedures used in performance budgeting are more valu-

Figure 9.6
Recreation Program Budget Worksheet

| Program: Parks, Recreation & Community Services | Name: |
| Division: At Risk 1365 | Project Code: |

Revenue
Description

	Number	Fee	Frequency		Total
Program Fees (5482-2000)				$	0.00
Facility Fees (5480-1000)				$	0.00
Concession Sales (5480-1020)				$	0.00
Grants				$	0.00
Other:				$	0.00
Other:				$	0.00

Revenue Total: $ 0.00

Expense
7104-0000 Temp Salaries:
800

# of Sites	# of Staff	Pay Rate	Hrs. or Games	Weeks		Total
					$	0.00
					$	0.00
					$	0.00
					$	0.00
					$	0.00
					$	0.00
					$	0.00

900

					$	0.00
					$	0.00
					$	0.00
					$	0.00
					$	0.00
					$	0.00

Number

7104-0000 Total: $ 0.00

7106-0000 Overtime:

Hours	Regular Rate	Factor		
		1.5	$	0.00
		1.5	$	0.00

7106-0000 Total: $ 0.00

7202-0000 Retirement: (Total salaries × .1875)   **7202-0000 Total:** $ 0.00

7210-0000 Medicare: (Total salaries × .0145)   **7210-0000 Total:** $ 0.00

7211-0000 FICA: (Total salaries × .062)   **7211-0000 Total:** $ 0.00

7300-0000 Supplies:
Description

# of Sites	# of Items	Cost	Frequency		
				$	0.00
				$	0.00
				$	0.00
				$	0.00
				$	0.00
				$	0.00
				$	0.00
				$	0.00

7300-0000 Total: $ 0.00

7400-1000 O/S - Personnel:
Description

# of Items	Cost	Frequency		
			$	0.00
			$	0.00
			$	0.00
			$	0.00
			$	0.00
			$	0.00
			$	0.00
			$	0.00

7400-1000 Total: $ 0.00

Continued

Figure 9.6 Continued
Recreation Program Budget Worksheet

7400-2000 O/S - Other:

Description # of Items   Cost   Frequency

Staff expense teen

$ 0.00
$ 0.00
$ 0.00
$ 0.00
$ 0.00
$ 0.00

7400-2000 Total: $ 0.00

7410-0000 Communication:

Description # of Items   Cost   Frequency

$ 0.00
$ 0.00
$ 0.00

7410-0000 Total: $ 0.00

7412-0000 Public Utilities:

Description # of Items   Cost   Frequency

$ 0.00
$ 0.00

7412-0000 Total: $ 0.00

7420-0000 Rentals:

of Items   Cost   Frequency

$ 0.00
$ 0.00

7420-0000 Total: $ 0.00

7420-1000 Motor Vehicle:

Description # of Items   Cost   Frequency

$ 0.00
$ 0.00

7420-1000 Total: $ 0.00

7484-0000 Training & Travel:

Description # of Items   Cost   Frequency

$ 0.00
$ 0.00

7484-0000 Total: $ 0.00

7499-0000 Miscellaneous:

Description

$ 0.00
$ 0.00
$ 0.00

7499-0000 Total: $ 0.00

7460-0000 Capital Mach. & Equip.:

$ 0.00
$ 0.00

7460-0000 Total: $ 0.00

Expense Total: $ 0.00

Percentage of Division Overhead
Allocated to THIS Program (use %)

Overhead
% of 0001** $ 1%
Full Time Staff & Benefits in Program
Division Manager
Non Program Supplies
Non Program Contractural
Insurance
In Direct

$ 0.00

Overhead Total $ 0.00

Final Program Net Cost

Grand Total $ 0.00
Net +/(-) $ 0.00

able to those who are removed from the operating process than those involved in the operations;

4. The existence of a formal system of performance budgeting tends to encourage thinking of expenditures in relation to unit costs; and

5. The need for a performance budget system diminishes as cities or agencies decrease in size.

Zero-Base Budgeting

Zero-base budgeting is a process, rather than a budget format, that emerged in the early 1970s. It was developed in private business in 1969 by Texas Instruments, Inc., and first adopted for governmental use in 1973 in the state of Georgia by then-governor Jimmy Carter. Its wide application in a relatively short period of time, in both public and private organizations, made it an important budgeting technique that had an impact on the approach to management of leisure service agencies. It can also be thought of as a program budget.

The usual process of determining annual budget increases within an organization is accomplished by adding the projected cost of new programs and inflation to the organization's base budget for the previous year. In this way, the organization does not have to rejustify its previous year's appropriations. For example, if an organization has a budget of $2 million, and the projected inflation is 6 percent and the projected cost for new programs was 10 percent, its budget would be increased automatically by 16 percent, or $320,000. Such increases had been made traditionally without due consideration of the effectiveness of past programs relative to their cost.

The zero-base approach to budgeting does not allow an organization simply to request an automatic increase because of inflation or as a result of the development of new programs. Rather, using this approach the organization is required to *justify* its total request for funds from a zero base. An organization must look at each program or service and its relationship to its cost as if it were considering placing the item on the budget for the first time. In this way, the organization is forced to look at and evaluate its program and service offerings to ensure that they are effective in meeting organizational goals and are being operated efficiently.

The zero-base budgeting method also asks the organization to determine whether a past program is of sufficient impact to retain it, or whether it should be replaced by a higher-priority program. The technique forces an organization to constantly reassess its activities. Not only does this allow an organization a method of budgeting that maximizes the effectiveness of its expenditures, but—on a year-in, year-out basis—it encourages the organization to remain fresh, vigorous, and competitive in its approach to providing services. Many organizations rely on tradition in developing their programs and, as a result, become stale in their approach to meeting the needs of those they serve.

The zero-base technique should be thought of as more than a budgeting process. It is a total thought process that involves the development of organizational goals and objectives, evaluation of programs and services, and ultimately, managerial decision making. The process suggests that there is a linkage between many of the management activities within an organization and that, in the end, these will be reflected in the budgeting process, and vice versa. In many organizations, the budgeting process is thought of as a separate and distinct activity that takes place some distance from the operational activities of the organization. The zero-base approach, however, ties operational activities directly to the budgeting process.

The zero-base approach to budgeting can serve as an aid to legislative bodies, as well as to management and operational units within an organization. Each of these units will have unique and special types of informational needs. According to Peter Pyhrr (1977), to initiate the zero-base approach to budgeting, each of these decision-making units must focus on two primary concerns:

1. Are the current activities efficient and effective?

2. Should current activities be eliminated or reduced to fund new, higher priority programs or to reduce the current budget?

These two concerns are the essence of the zero-base approach to budgeting. An organization must ask itself, "Are our programs, activities, and services meeting the stated goals of the organization?" "Are the resources that are used to produce these programs being consumed in an appropriate manner?" In addition, the organization must ask itself whether the expenditures it is making are as important as other potential uses for the financial resources of the organization.

The zero-base budgeting process requires four basic steps: (1) identification of decision-making units within an organization, (2) development of an analysis of the decision-making packages within designated decision-making units, (3) analysis and evaluation of all alternatives within all decision-making packages, and (4) preparation of a detailed operational budget.

Identify Decision-Making Units. Decision-making units are any groups within an organization that have the authority and responsibility for planning and controlling financial resources and programs. Decision-making units may be led by division heads (e.g., the superintendent of parks, superintendent of recreation) or the coordinator of a set of functions, facilities, or activities. The zero-base approach to budgeting is built around these decision-making units; its purpose is to provide information to the manager or governing board so the person or persons can use the data that is generated in making decisions.

Analyze Decision Making in a Decision-Making Package. The "decision package" is the building block of the zero-base concept. It is a document that identifies and describes each decision unit in such a manner that management can evaluate it and rank it against other decision units competing for funding, then decide whether to approve it or disapprove it. To comparatively evaluate one decision-making unit with another, a common denominator must be established. Without a criterion that can be used in the measurement and evaluation of the various units in an organization, comparative decision-making is difficult. The purpose of a decision-making package is to provide management with information that is comparable for each decision-making unit so that management can evaluate one request for funds versus another. In this way, a manager or a legislative body is presented with a number of clear alternatives that can be evaluated in terms of achieving the organization's goals. Decision-making packages can develop the following types of information:

1. Purpose and objective of the decision-making unit.

2. Description of the proposed actions or activities. In other words, what is the unit going to do and how is it going to do it?

3. Cost and benefits of various levels of funding. Simply, what is the relationship between input levels and output levels?

4. Work load and performance measures.

5. Alternative means of accomplishing the objectives.

Evaluate and Rank All Alternatives Within Decision-Making Packages. Assuming that all organizations operate on limited resources, they must evaluate proposals from decision-making units and determine what activities should be approved and how much these activities will cost. Essentially, managerial decision making involves weighing the alternatives. In determining which course of action an organization will follow, its funding requirements are developed. Comparing the decision-making packages and alternatives within these packages allows the manager to identify the benefits that can be accrued from the selection of one alternative over another. In this way, the organization is better able to predict the potential consequences of a given alternative within a package. Further, comparing decision-making packages and alternatives allows an organization to weigh differences in terms of cost. It may be that one decision-mak-

ing unit within an organization can accomplish the same outputs at a lower cost than another unit. Thus, it would be possible to reduce the overall cost of providing services.

In prioritizing alternatives, the manager or legislative body of the organization ranks these according to their relative benefit to the organization. This ranking process is the backbone of the zero-base budgeting process, because it allows the manager to engage in systematic decision making. Decision making in many organizations occurs by default. Without information that can be compared and ranked by its potential contribution to the goals of the organization, a manager is not in a position to make effective decisions. He or she is simply reacting to the organizational environment, as opposed to actively directing the organization by choosing among alternatives in a careful, systematic manner.

Prepare a Detailed Operational Budget for the Selected Alternatives Within Decision-Making Packages. Once the organization has selected alternatives within the decision-making packages, the next step within the zero-base approach to budgeting is to establish a detailed operational budget for the items that have been selected. This budget may reflect traditional approaches to budgeting, including use of the standard classification type of budget.

The zero-base approach to budgeting should not be viewed as a short-term project that can be implemented without adequate staff development and training. Rather, it is a long-term management process by which an organization can identify alternatives aimed toward achieving stated goals. As such, it ensures that an organization will identify in advance the costs and benefits of potential services, and that existing programs and activities will remain effective. By ranking nonessential or low-priority activities, an organization is in a position to justify their elimination. As a result, an organization may redistribute its resources in such a way that it concentrates on high-impact programs, thus increasing its overall effectiveness.

The process also encourages an increase in an organization's efficiency. This occurs primarily because of the systematic approach detailing the potential actions of the organization in relation to costs and benefits. Also, costs are reduced as a by-product of the healthy competition that is introduced among decision-making units. The savings that an organization realizes because of increased efficiency can be put back into the agency to increase its services, or these can be used to reduce the burden on the taxpayers.

Budget Procedures

The budget process basically consists of four activities: (1) budget preparation, (2) budget design, (3) budget presentation, and (4) budget implementation.

Budget Preparation

Budget preparation is the first phase of the process. Most agencies have a budget manual that gives a timetable of the budget process: when it is to be submitted, in what form, and various other procedures that are part of the budget process. The budget procedure is usually developed by the finance agency in accordance with a timetable that will meet the requirements of the governing authority. The budget manual gives general instructions, a timetable for submission, and examples of forms to be used, as well as other instructions to aid the manager in submitting the budget.

The budget process is ongoing throughout the year. One of the best ways to assure that the budget is an ongoing process is for the leisure service manager and other top-level personnel to establish a budget folder in which ideas and suggestions can be accumulated throughout the year. When needs become apparent, the manager can write a memo covering the subject area and include it in the budget folder for consideration at budget time. To try to remember all the ideas and submit them at one time during the year is impractical, if not impossible. Establishing some procedure whereby ideas are accumulated on a year-round basis gives much greater assurance that everything will be included when the budget is submitted. In addition, other ideas, changes, corrections, deletions, and additions can be included in the budget folder; these will help the manager at the time of preparing the budget to modify and make necessary changes. The budget folder is more or less an ongoing tickler file that helps the manager to do a better job.

Another procedure that is helpful in budget preparation is the initiation of public hearings to get citizen input prior to submission of the budget. Such meetings should be public and held in various parts of the community to obtain ideas as well as support from residents. At such public hearings, the manager can review past programs and activities and present ideas he or she may have for the future, then open the meeting to the public for general discussion. Such public meetings impart to the community the feeling that the agency is concerned with its needs and interests. To have public support at the time the budget goes before the governing board is important. Recreation, parks, and leisure services programs are for the public, not the professional staff, and when supported by the public, are given more credibility.

Budget Design

Budget design or technique will vary from one agency to another depending on the type of budget process that is adopted. In most instances, the budget consists of a number of parts. The first of these is usually a *budget message,* a description of a budget in terms of the highlights, changes, or new programs that are being suggested. It gives the reader, whether a city council member or member of the general public, an overview and basis for understanding what is included in the budget in capsule form.

After the budget message, there is usually a one-page *budget summary.* The summary sheet reports the major categories within the budget. For example, in an objective classification budget, under expenditures, this sheet would summarize estimates for personnel services, supplies, materials, and so on; under revenues, it would indicate tax figures, fees and charges, grants, and the like.

In addition to the budget message and summary, there is sometimes a *budget narrative* that accompanies each subprogram or activity, such as sports, special services, aquatics, and playgrounds. The narrative, similar to a budget message, describes the highlights of each activity. Its purpose is to center on each activity in a more descriptive fashion than just in terms of dollars and cents.

Following the budget narrative, or sometimes in concert with the budget narrative, is the *budget detail.* Again depending on the type of budgeting process used, the budget detail will include a specific accounting of all the proposed expenditures and program elements within the budget design. It is this portion of the budget that takes the most time to develop; it serves as the primary guide for organizational finances and program operation. The budget detail may be so specific that it may indicate the number of pencils and basketballs needed, and their cost. It also lists such costs as personnel in terms of the specific number of people to be employed, how many hours they are to work per day, and how much they will be paid per hour. In a line-item budget, such proposed expenditures would be detailed by classification or function. In a program budget, they are detailed according to units designated within an organization.

Various graphs also can be used as part of the design of the budget to visually help the reader understand trends or what the budget is trying to accomplish. Using graphs or charts to show productivity trends or unit cost increases or decreases can be more helpful than presenting only dollar figures. Graphs can help justify budget changes of one form or another (see Figure 9.7).

Budget Presentation

The next aspect of the budget process is the *budget presentation,* which is usually made to the governing board that has to approve it, and which details budget appropriations. Prior to its presentation to the governing board, the budget is usually presented to the city manager or other administrative officers who have administrative control over the funds. In either case, the budget presentation is generally the same. Although budget presentation is extremely important, more important is the reputation that the agency develops on a year-round basis. Few agencies receive large appropriations based on the kind of presentations they make. More importantly, they receive appropriations based on the quality of services they offer throughout the year.

In terms of selling a budget, the type of services offered on a year-round basis, the competence with which programs are operated, and the thoroughness and follow-up provided to assure the public of worthwhile, well-run services goes a great deal farther than a flashy presentation once a year. The purpose of a budget presentation is to summarize, in narrative form, what the budget includes, particularly any new programs or changes made. Prior to the presentation, the governing body has usually studied the budget; the budget presentation is meant to summarize and highlight specific programs and answer questions.

Various methods are used in making the presentation. They may include slide presentations, verbal presentations, and tours of facilities. During the formal presentation, it is wise to try to avoid talking about dollars and cents and to concentrate more on program accomplishments and goals and objectives of the department. To spend a great deal of time talking about how many baseball bats are needed for the sports program is a waste of time. Again, if the governing board has confidence in the administrator and in the agency, the budget is generally accepted much more readily than if there is a lack of confidence. As indicated earlier, bud-

geting is a year-round process. Although the budget presentation is important, it is only a small part of the total budget process.

Budget Implementation

The last aspect of the budgeting process is implementation, once the budget is approved by the governing board. Usually, after the budget presentation, the governing board formally adopts the budget through a budget resolution. A budget resolution is a legal document that provides the funds with which the agency operates for a given year. Once the budget is approved, it is necessary to provide the necessary controls and procedures to see that it is administered properly and that carelessness, waste, and misappropriation are not permitted. These controls will be reviewed in the next section.

Budget Transfers. Once the governing board approves the budget, the manager is expected to stay within the limitation set relative to the amount of money within the given program. To add or transfer funds, a request has to be made of the governing board. Within a given program account, however, transfers can usually be made between activities, such as moving money from one line item to another. To move money from the sports account to the neighborhood recreation programs account requires action by the governing board in the form of a resolution. This assures that the money is spent according to the plans set by the governing board and does not leave this type of activity to the discretion of the administrator.

Methods of Expending Funds. The last aspect of the budget and financing ac-

Figure 9.7
Productivity/Cost Trends for Neighborhood Programs

Quality Goals
- Improve productivity measurement for neighborhood recreation programs
- Replace 5% of total program with new programs based on population changes
- Train 100% of staff
- Train 100% of part-time staff

Fiscal Year Production Plan
- Provide 1,957,591 participant hours at 12 park sites year-round and 9 summer school sites
- Provide 78,738 participant hours for 6 junior high programs
- Provide 259,440 participant hours for 12 summer teen programs
- Provide 91,303 participant hours for 4 teen centers
- Provide 42,092 hours of assistance through Sunnyvale Voluntary Action Corps

Special Notes
* Includes 3,961 CETA employee hours

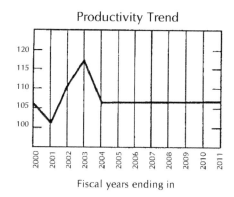

Productivity Trend

Fiscal years ending in

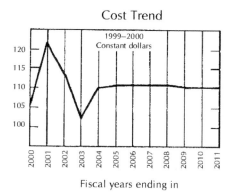

Cost Trend

Fiscal years ending in

tivities of an agency are the various methods of expending funds once approved by the governing board. There are various methods for initiating action to pay for the services, supplies, equipment, and salaries provided for in the budget.

The payment of salaries is usually handled by submitting some sort of document that indicates the number of hours an employee has worked in a day, week, or month, which the employee's supervisor signs. Without such a control, individuals could be paid for more time than they have worked. Some agencies use daily time cards; other agencies use payroll forms submitted to the finance department or payroll division once a month or every two weeks.

A purchasing division, established by the city charter that governs how monies are to be expended, handles most materials and supplies purchased. Controls are usually placed on making purchases. For example, the amount of petty cash that can be expended may have a set limit of $25.00 or less; anything above that would have to be submitted to the purchasing department on a standard purchase requisition. The requisition usually states the item wanted, and the quantity and description of the item. Depending on the procedure of the given agency, the item may require advertising for a formal bid on a competitive basis, or under a certain amount, may be acquired on an informal basis by calling three vendors to get the lowest bid. But again, in most agencies there are policies and procedures established by the governing board that indicate how purchases will be made and the controls set to make these purchases. Most public agencies require bidding procedures for purchases over $1000 or $2000, or they advertise on a formal basis with people submitting sealed bids to secure the best price. These methods eliminate dishonesty and corruption on the part of any employee.

Whatever the procedure, steps should be taken to ensure that controls are provided to eliminate dishonesty and insure that the agency gets the greatest value for the least cost. In most agencies, procedures are set by the governing board. In some cases, the state sets procedures that must be adhered to ensure honesty and to ensure that the public agency gets the most service possible for the least amount of money.

Budget Audit. At the end of the budget year, an outside firm does an audit to assure that honesty and integrity have been adhered to in the handling of public funds. An outside private firm of good reputation usually does the audit to give credibility to the auditing process.

Expenditures

Although the organization of an agency's budget will vary depending on the type of process adopted (e.g., line or program budgeting), the basic structure of a budget consists of two components. The first of these is the *revenues* that are produced or acquired by the leisure service organization. As mentioned in the beginning of the chapter, revenue or income sources for an agency include the following: taxes, fees and charges, grants, interest earned on in-

vestments, and donations. The other component is *expenditures.* There are two basic types of expenditures made by leisure service organizations: *operating expenditures and capital expenditures.*

Operating Expenditures

Operating expenditures are made for personnel, materials, supplies, and services, as well as other regularly occurring costs. Figure 9.8 shows some of the items that would typically be budgeted as operating expenses. Usually the largest single expenditure in the operating budget is for personnel services. Leisure services can be thought of as a *labor intensive* operation; therefore, a large percentage of an organization's operational expenditures goes to pay full-time, temporary, and seasonal personnel and the necessary overhead costs, such as retirement, leaves, social security, and insurance programs. The remaining percentage of the budget is for all other needs. Some budgets may not reflect these percentages, as other needs may run much higher. This usually happens when programs use a great deal of equipment or a number of supplies that are extremely costly, or when the rental of buildings or equipment is extremely high. Remembering percentages is not important; the main point is that the cost of personnel usually is the largest cost incurred year after year. With inflation, personnel costs can easily get out of control. The competent manager does all that he or she can to monitor personnel costs and plan for the future, making sure that adequate revenue is provided to cover personnel costs.

If revenue begins to drop, it will become necessary to cut operating costs.

Although some costs can be cut in the form of materials, supplies, and equipment, if there is a need to cut a great amount it will ultimately be necessary to cut human resources. This should always be the last, not the first, cut made, as "downsizing" a service organization's personnel will have a major impact on the overall quality and delivery of services. It is sometimes hard to recapture the energy, enthusiasm, and commitment of the remaining workers when they have been demoralized by layoffs and firings of respected colleagues.

Using the statistics in Figure 9.8, 61,290 work hours in the 2001 to 2002 fiscal year are equivalent to 29 full-time employees. Dividing $432,707 (the cost of salaries of the 29 employees) by 29 equals a $14,920 annual salary. In addition, the city has to pay for leaves, retirement, and other benefits in the amount of $74,642 plus $159,104, which totals $233,746, or an additional 35 percent ($5,222 per employee). This places the cost of an average full-time employee at $20,142 per year. The cost for supplies, materials, and equipment that an employee needs to work with is approximately $11,063 per year. The total cost to the city for an employee in salary and benefits and in materials, supplies, and equipment is $31,205 per year. Assuming that an employee works 25 years, this would cost the city $780,125.

By cutting one employee, you would be able to save approximately $20,142 in salary and benefits and $11,063 in material, supplies, and equipment. To cut supplies alone does not make sense because, first of all, they are not the most expensive items; also, if you don't have the supplies and equipment, the employee probably can't perform the work. It is also apparent that cutting human resources or other resources will affect production and effectiveness to some extent. But when revenues do not match expenses, something has to be done. It is the manager's job to determine which is the proper balance—to cut human capital or another resource. The other alternative is to increase revenue, which will be discussed later.

The second item that must be considered in operating costs is the factor of inflation. Comparing 2001–2002 with 2003–2004 in Figure 9.8, a two-year period of time, there is an increase of $299,704, or 34.5 percent. This is an increase of a little over 17 percent per year. The total work hours increased only 140 hours.

Certain other resources increased substantially: Fertilizer and chemicals (code 4234) increased 28 percent; gas and electricity (code 4331), 64 percent; and water (code 4333), 66 percent. Some of this increase was due to use, but most was a result of inflation.

An increase in inflation of 6 percent per year on an $868,776 budget equals $52,187 per year, with no increase in service. In other words, it would take approximately $52,000 more per year to deliver the same amount of service. In 10 years, this would be an increase of half a million dollars.

Figure 9.9 shows a program budget summary for the recreational services of the Department of Recreation and Parks for the City of Baltimore, Maryland, and is also an example of operational expenses. This budget provides information concerning the past actual budget, the present budget, and the future or requested budget. In addition, the total costs of the department's 21 programs are listed. Each of the programs would be further explained as shown in Figure 9.8 in order to provide additional detail and allow for control.

Figure 9.8
Line Item Detail

Program: 265.08 parks maintenance
Function: Environmental services

	2001-2002 Actual	2002-2003 to 4/3/03	2003-2004 Proposed
Work Hours			
4111 Regular salaries—work time	59,348	44,270	61,290
4112 Temporary personnel	16,829	12,775	15,160
4113 Overtime	508	310	375
Total Work Hours	76,685	57,355	76,825
Resources			
Human Resources			
4111 Regular salaries—work time	$328,671	$277,803	$432,707
4112 Temporary personnel	65,558	49,125	78,074
4113 Overtime	4,474	3,010	4,256
Subtotal	398,703	329,938	515,037
4116 Leave time	56,671	47,891	74,642
4117 Retirement/payroll insurance	92,917	94,478	159,104
Total Human Resources	548,291	472,307	748,783
Other Resources			
4201 Custodial supplies	5,343	4,990	6,000
4204 Special activity supplies	10,846	9,039	16,275
4215 Clothing	1,397	1,483	2,186
4231 Materials—buildings	3,843	3,758	4,200
4232 Materials—office equipment	196	394	543
4233 Materials—other equipment	1,661	2,105	2,062
4234 Materials—land improvements	52,969	33,927	68,117
4235 Materials—repair facil-vandals	7,359	3,178	10,000
4245 Small tools/implements	2,265	2,143	4,069
4270 Services—mtn buildings	3,737	1,578	5,968
4271 Services—mtn land improvements	30,279	18,317	39,724
4280 Services—mtn other equipment	5,045	3,445	4,557
4282 Services—repair vandalism	7,815	3,658	5,534
4306 Weed abatement contract	425	—	—
4331 Gas/electricity	28,036	30,737	46,000
4332 Telephone	5,761	4,937	5,043
4333 Water	33,832	30,138	54,250
4340 Travel/meeting expenses	77	6	96
4344 Equip rental—private	—	—	100
4372 Laundry	545	523	942
4501 Rent	4,800	5,760	5,760
4504 Taxes/licenses	6,149	6,190	7,000
4505 Fire insurance	5,790	5,668	6,500
4531 Equip rental—city pool	103,315	87,544	125,771
Total Other Resources	321,485	259,518	420,697
Total Resources	$869,776	$731,825	$1,169,480

Figure 9.9
Program Budget Summary

| Agency: Department of Recreation and Parks | Program: Recreational Services | | | 480 |

Program Budget Summary

(1)	(2)	(3)	(4)	(5)	(6)
		Actual 2001-2002	Budget 2002-2003	Requested 2003-2004	Recommendation
	Employment Summary Authorized salaried positions Man-years:		335.0	367.0	465.0
	Salaried positions Labor			348.9	
	Part-time, temp, & overtime Total man-years				
Code	**Summary By Object**				
01-15	Salaries and wages	2,399,800	2,901,435	3,992,820	
16-25	Other personnel costs	219,058	278,165	385,549	
26-50	Contractural services	277,095	238,441	444,110	
51-65	Materials and supplies	168,817	108,991	240,940	
66-75	Equipment—replacement	9,467	—	5,874	
76-85	Equipment—additional	9,520	47,027	95,404	
86-88	Grants and subsidies	2,400		2,000	
89-91	Debt service				
92-94	Land				
95-97	Buildings				
98-99	Improv. excl. bldgs.				
	Annual Total	3,086,157	3,574,059	5,166,697	
	Summary By Function				
01	Administration	92,787	78,791	93,208	
02	Central office & Storeroom serv.	165,387	159,576	215,431	
03	Municipal sports	126,864	154,859	160,298	
04	Street clubs for problem youth	35,392	267,002	373,649	
05	Recreation centers	1,990,394	2,080,430	2,739,521	
06	Recreation for handicapped	44,951	29,076	47,947	
07	Senior citizens activities	37,260	33,929	48,814	
08	Traveling play leaders	6,987	25,624	35,620	
09	Swimming instruction	21,125	53,523	221,580	
10	Music (group participation)	24,009	27,642	33,994	
11	Dramatics	6,397	8,293	13,064	
12	Dancing	28,405	18,742	21,650	
13	Arts and crafts	34,416	28,290	50,225	
14	Nature and gardening	15,968	17,278	18,615	
15	Physical fitness	23,299	34,581	44,315	
16	Playgrounds	432,516	511,423	564,680	
17	Modernization of existing facilities	—	45,000	14,800	
18	Operation Champ	—	—	—	
19	Accessory enterprises	—	—	264,286	
20	Community schools	—	—	264,286	
21	Municipal Athletic Association	—	—	15,000	
	Annual Total	3,086,157	3,574,059	5,166,697	
	Summary By Fund				
01	General	2,929,749	3,394,059	4,976,697	
02	Special	156,408	180,000	190,000	
03	Motor vehicle revenue Working capital				
	Annual Total	3,086,157	3,574,059	5,166,697	

The operating portion of the budget is used to finance the day-to-day operations of the organization on a pay-as-you-go basis.

Capital Expenditures

These expenditures are made to finance projects that are extremely costly, such as land acquisitions, park and building construction, and other projects that could conceivably use all the revenue during any one given year. The capital portion of the budget is sometimes used for such equipment as automobiles, trucks, and recreation equipment or a capital project. Anything under those amounts would be paid for out of the operating budget. Figures 9.10 and 9.11 show several examples of capital expenditures and how different agencies account for these types of costs.

Figure 9.10 shows the City of Baltimore's capital improvement program for land acquisition and facility development. A similar program is presented for each year for five years into the future. Before the program or project can be completed, it must be approved by the parks and recreation board, the city planning commission, and the city council, then approved by the public in a bond election by either a majority or a two-thirds vote, depending on state or provincial law.

Each year, the Department of Parks and Recreation submits an update of the capital projects program, which includes an additional year in the future. Projects are placed on the program in accordance with the city's 20-year look into the future, to determine needs based on changes in population, the need to replace old facilities, and other sociological and demographic information.

In addition to planning for capital projects, the manager of a leisure service agency also has to plan for the effect these capital projects will have on operating costs. If new facilities are built, they will require staffing and maintenance on an ongoing basis, and these costs have to be built into the operating budget. This is one of the reasons why it is necessary to budget for several years into the future. It is also necessary to anticipate revenues in the future so it can be determined if there will be adequate funds to pay off the debt of capital projects as well as pay the operating costs that the capital projects will incur.

Figure 9.11 illustrates an example of a specific project in great detail. The figure shows when the project will be built and the source of funding for its construction. The example also shows what the operating costs will be on an annual basis.

Different leisure service organizations may handle operating and capital expenditures slightly differently. The operational and capital expenditure methods are similar to an individual's personal finance practices. An individual usually has a salary and other forms of income, such as investments, rental property, savings accounts, and stocks and bonds. This income during a given year totals a specific amount. For the sake of explanation, let's assume that it is $30,000 a year. The $30,000 a year is the revenue that must be used to pay for the various items and expenses the person needs or wants. He or she needs a home, an automobile, and life insurance, and possibly such luxuries as a boat and a summer cottage. These items total more than the $30,000 income that this person will have for a given year. To purchase such items as a house, a boat, or an automobile, he or she

Figure 9.10
Capital Improvement Program

G indicates General Funds
L indicates Loan or Bond Funds

Bureau of Parks

L	Zoo—Continuation of master plan	$1,000,000
L	Park acquisition & development	500,000
L	Small playgrounds	100,000
G	Security park lighting	100,000
	Sub-total, Parks:	$1,700,000

Bureau of Recreation

L	Rec. center and playfield, Clifton Park	$ 400,000
L	Rec. center, Callaway School	300,000
L	Rec. center, Brehms Lane	300,000
L	Rec. center, Patterson Park	300,000
L	Rec. center, Medfield Heights	300,000
L	Rec. center addition—gym—Curtis Bay Center	200,000
L	Rec. center, Fairmount Ave. and Ann St.	300,000
	Subtotal, Recreation	$2,100,000

Grand total, Department of Recreation and Parks, Fiscal Year 1975:

$3,800,000

Breakdown of Funds

G $100,000
L   3,700,000
Total: $3,800,000

borrows money for several years: the house, 25 years; the automobile, 3 to 5 years. Similarly, with capital expenditures, it is impossible for any agency to buy all the land or parks or to construct all the facilities needed in any given year. Therefore, these items are financed over a period of time. In the case of an individual's house and automobile, a person borrows from a bank and pays back the debt over a certain time period. The debt consists of the principal, which pays back the money borrowed and the interest, which is for the privilege of borrowing money. Likewise, the leisure service organization borrows money from lending firms, banks, and other financial institutions and pays this money back on a timely basis—the principal as well as the interest.

The daily expenses of the individual for food, clothing, entertainment, and other such items can be compared to the operating expenditures and are paid for from the salary. The house, boat, automobile, and summer cottage are paid for with the borrowed money, and the principal and interest are paid back over a period of time out of the salary. The individual has to plan how much of the salary he or she can afford to spend on capital items, and how much of the salary he or she needs for daily operating expenses. Be it a personal budget or an agency budget, a determination has to be made as to what percentage of the budget will be expended for the operating versus the capital expenditures.

Figure 9.11
Tennis Court Budget Forecast
City of Sunnyvale, California

Project: 710 Serra Park Tennis Courts
Function(s):   Environmental Services

Resources/Element	Expended to 6-30-00	Proposed 2001-2002	Projected					
			2003-2004	2004-2005	2005-2006	2007-2008	2009-2010	2010-2011
Workhours	–	150	–	–	–	–	–	–
Resources (Dollars)								
.49 Parks	–	40,000	–	–	–	–	–	–
Total Resources	–	40,000	–	–	–	–	–	–

This project would provide for two tennis courts with lights at the Serra Park addition. City Council authorized project in 2001.

Operating costs this project will incur: $10,000 per year

Cost-Benefit Analysis

With the advent of program budgeting and zero-base budgeting, an understanding of cost-benefit analysis is extremely important to the leisure service manager. In traditional approaches to budgeting, the manager was concerned primarily with balancing expenditures with revenues. Little thought was give to the relationship between the expenditures made and the social impact or benefit of programs, services, or activities. The newer methods of budgeting tie finances directly to the impact or effectiveness of a given service. Therefore, an understanding of the methods that can be used to determine the qualitative relationship between the benefits and the costs of services must be developed. This qualitative relationship must be measurable in quantitative terms to be useful in decision making, however.

L. Hale Meserow and associates (1975:30) have noted that cost-benefit analysis can be useful to park and recreation organizations in a number of ways. It can accomplish the following:

1. Foster valid comparisons within and between operational facilities and departments;

2. Permit the assignment of priorities to specific programs and services;

3. Provide targets and guidelines for management decision making and resource allocation;

4. Assist in continual evaluation of agency objectives and procedures;

5. Provide valuable support data for justifying budget requests;

6. Identify high- and low-cost programs and services as related to maintenance, administrative, and direct leadership costs per participant-hour of service rendered; and

7. Provided essential data for policy formulation and revision.

There are essentially two ways to approach cost-benefit analysis. First, it can be viewed simply as an analysis of the economic efficiency within an organization. This approach can be useful should the purpose of the analysis be to compare alternatives primarily on the basis of cost. A manager could compare two similar program proposals that are aimed at achieving common goals, or appear to have the same impact, in order to choose the alternative that can be accomplished at the lower cost. In this way, the organization is able to increase its efficiency simply on the basis of choosing between alternatives, one of which can be implemented more frugally than the other. But most organizations do not have a single goal (i.e., economic efficiency); rather, most organizations are concerned with the accomplishment of a variety of goals. Therefore, the application of cost-benefit analysis should be considered from a nonefficiency standpoint.

Nonefficiency cost-benefit analysis should be used in addition to measurements of financial efficiency. In establishing nonefficiency cost-benefit programs, one is basically concerned with making value judgments about the impact the agency desires to achieve. A number of faulty assumptions are made when comparing the nonefficiency approach to the efficiency approach by using cost-benefit analysis. The most common faulty assumption is that the cost of individual programs can be equated to one another. Some programs may cost more, but may also have a higher social value. For example, a swimming program for persons with disabilities will cost vastly more than a swimming program for the general public. A public agency may, however, charge the same fee for both programs and underwrite the majority of the cost for the former program, having decided that its social value is worth the added investment.

In other words, an organization must look at the potential benefits of a program as it relates to the overall goals of the organization (servicing the community as a whole). Evaluating and choosing among alternative benefit packages or proposals becomes extremely important. The organization should not simply determine the cost of services based on their marginal cost; rather, it should consider the broader effect of its social programs. In fact, one might ask, *"What would the social cost be if the organization did not provid the service or program?"* This is one of the great differences between profit organizations and nonprofit organizations. In the case of the former, the task is to maximize the price of the service in relation to its actual cost in order to earn a profit. The nonprofit organization may have to underwrite the entire cost of the program.

Of the two types of cost-benefit analyses, efficiency analysis is more fully developed in the leisure service field in terms of methodology. One such system—efficiency cost-benefit analysis—has been developed for the Surrey, (British Columbia), Park and Recreation Department. Discussing the procedure, William Webster and Charles Reich (1977) write that cost/benefit data are based on the number of user hours of service rendered per dollar cost. Further, they suggest that specific application to the leisure service field depends on an understanding of the following key concepts:

1. *Participants* may be either active (i.e., taking part in a sponsored recreation activity, or otherwise making use of the department's facilities), or passive (i.e., spectators).

2. *Participant-Hours or User-Hours.* That includes both spectators and participants. It is a term that refers to the number of participants multiplied by the duration of their stay at the facility or program (e.g., 10 participants in a ceramics program for two hours a week over two weeks equals 200 participant-hours).

3. *Net Cost.* Net costs refers to the total expenditures, minus all revenue collected (p. 25).

As indicated in Figure 9.12, the participant hours are combined with spectator hours to determine the total user hours for the program indicated. The next step is to calculate the net cost of the program. This is accomplished by subtracting income produced by programs from their gross costs. The total user hours are then divided by the net cost to determine the net cost per hour of service rendered.

There are various forms of control that can be used to assure good management of the budget once it is approved.

Control

It is important to budgetary control to have a system whereby an organization records the collection of its revenues and expenditure of its funds. The procedure or system used to ensure that an organization has information regarding these transactions is known as *accounting.* Accounting may be defined as the classifying and recording of financial transactions that take place within an organization and between it and other agencies. The concepts of accounting and budgeting are often confused. For the purposes of this text, accounting can be thought of as a tool that enables the manager to collect, summarize, and report certain types of information, primarily for the purposes of controlling the budget.

There are a number of approaches to accounting, each providing different types or combinations of information to the manager. Two types of accounting methods commonly used are *cost accounting* and *accrual accounting.* Cost accounting has evolved as a result of the growth of program and performance budgets. In this approach to accounting, the report of expenditures is broken down into the functions, programs, or specific activities that the agency has designated in its budget. In this way the manager is able to view the expenditure in each of the units and thus maintain control over their activities. Cost accounting is also used as a mechanism to compare cost and benefits.

Accrual accounting is the standard method used in most leisure service organizations. Discussing the accounting procedures used in this method, Thomas Hines (1974:101) writes:

"Unpaid bills are obviously shown and charged against the proper account item, thus a current and accurate appraisal of the department's financial condition is evident. The department executive should receive each month a statement of the agency's financial status, and this statement should not require any additional computations on his part. Certainly, the statement should provide current information as it relates directly to the original budget, and it should be designed so that it will point to and suggest the procedures that should be taken to expedite the department's program development and services."

A system of monthly or regularly scheduled statements of expenditures can assist the control procedure. With the assistance of computers, expenditures can be kept track of accurately and paid promptly. Figure 9.13 is an example of the City of Sunnyvale's oper-

ating statement, which is produced by a computer every 28 days. It is basically a line-item budget in which costs and expenditures are shown for how much money has been spent or how much is left. It is important for the manager to review the expenditures on an ongoing basis so as not to overexpend or underexpend the budget.

Also shown on the operating statement are work hours planned and used, unit costs, and production units planned and actually accumulated. This report gives total expenditures in personnel services, other resources, and a grand total. By evaluating this report on a regular basis, the manager can see where he or she stands at all times so as not to overexpend or underexpend the budget. Most leisure service agencies use computer software packages that can give them daily, weekly, and monthly

Figure 9.12
Summary of Benefit and Cost Evidence Collected and Analyzed for North Surrey Indoor Pool

	Participant Hours +	Spectator Hours =	Total User Hours	Gross Cost −	Income =	Net Cost	Net Cost per Hour of Service Rendered
Public Swims	8,126	642	8,768	4,312	2,681	1,631	$0.19
Lessons	3,041	2,770	5,811	4,521	2,299	2,222	.38
School bookings	0	0	0	0	0	0	.00
Rentals	345	0	345	436	35	401	1.16
Club Programs	77	50	127	258	117	141	1.11
General nonassigned	0	0	0	2,401	578	1,823	—
Total Operations	11,589	3,462	15,051	$11,928	$5,710	$6,218	$0.41

For Cloverdale Town Center for January through March Quarter

Cultural programs	2,421	0	2,421	$2,623	$1,320	$1,303	$0.54
Sports and Fitness	2,579	0	2,579	2,766	1,421	1,345	.52
Outdoor programs	849	0	849	757	608	149	.18
Social programs	4,067	0	4,067	1,883	795	1,088	.27
Meetings	450	0	450	215	150	65	.14
Special events	0	0	0	0	0	0	.00
Miscellaneous nonassigned	0	0	0	1,852	0	1,852	—
Total Center Operations	10,366	0	10,366	$10,096	$4,294	$5,802	$0.56

Source: Webster, W. D. and Reich, C. M. (1977, Jan.). Benefit/Cost Analysis—Its uses in parks and recreation, *Recreation Canada*, No. 35, p. 25.

Figure 9.13
City of Sunnyvale Operating Statement

10 General Operating Fund   09 Dept. Recreation   305 Special Recreation Service

Account	Description		Appropriation	Encumbrance	Expenditure	Prior MO. Adj.	Variance	Hrs Planned & Used
4111	Regular Salaries-WT	CUR			3,218.97		3,218.97-	632.5
		YTD	135,187.00		104,144.10		31,042.90	5,384.4 / 3,760.0
4112	Temporary Personnel	CUR			8,711.88		8,711.88-	1,532.1
		YTD	22,710.00		26,661.34		3,951.34-	25,081.0 / 19,721.4
4113	Overtime	CUR			50.60		50.60-	
		YTD			554.77		554.77-	4.0
4116	Leave Time-Applied %	CUR						
		YTD	3,917.00		4,596.13		679.13-	
4117	Retre & Ins-Applied %	CUR			1,218.37		1,218.37-	
		YTD	10,823.00		11,050.46		227.46-	
	Total Amounts Personal Serv	CUR			13,703.99		13,703.99-	
		YTD						2,164.6
4203	Office Supplies	CUR			151.04			
		YTD	400.00				248.96	
4204	Special Activity supplies	CUR						
		YTD	18,864.00		12,572.04		6,291.96	
4210	Books & Publications	CUR			79.48		79.48-	
		YTD	240.00		514.91		274.91	
4215	Clothing	CUR						
		YTD	90.00				90.00	
4245	Small Tools & Implemts	CUR			299.16		299.16-	
		YTD	700.00		516.90		183.10	
4252	Photography & Blueprint	CUR			164.46		164.46-	
		YTD	800.00		701.27		98.73	
4280	Serv Maintain Other Eq	CUR			16.00		16.00-	
		YTD	500.00		42.10		457.90	
4305	Staff Development	CUR						
		YTD	580.00		238.00		342.00	

Continued

Figure 9.13 Continued
City of Sunnyvale Operating Statement

10 General Operating Fund
09 Dept. Recreation 305 Special Recreation Service

Account	Description		Appropriation	Encumbrance	Expenditure	Prior MO. Adj.	Variance	Hrs Planned & Used
4334	Hydrant Rental	CUR			162.00		162.00-	
		YTD						
4380	Travel & Meeting Exp.	CUR						
		YTD	144.00		94.00		50.00	
4342	Mileage	CUR			94.67		94.67-	
		YTD	200.00		531.03		331.03-	
4344	Equip. Rental-Private	CUR			136.00		136.00-	
		YTD	4,500.00		802.87		3,697.13	
4345	Postage	CUR			31.99		31.99-	
		YTD	1,302.00		179.60		1,122.40	
4346	Rec. Excursions	CUR			59.50		59.50	
		YTD						
4375	Dance Band Services	CUR			644.00		644.00-	
		YTD	5,600.00		2,785.98		2,814.02	
4383	Special Services	CUR			765.00		765.00	
		YTD	7,600.00		5,186.50		2,413.50	
4391	Rec. Instructional Serv.	CUR			510.00		510.00-	
		YTD	6,100.00		3,286.00		2,814.00	
4500	Prof. Tech. Serv. Fee	CUR			35.00		35.00-	
		YTD	70.00		76.00		6.00-	
4530	Print Shop Charges	CUR			871.59		871.59-	
		YTD	8,240.00		9,847.50		1,607.50	
4531	Equip. Rental-City	CUR			174.60		174.60-	
		YTD	1,343.00		3,883.14		2,540.14	
4538	Rental Serv.-Comm. Ctr.	CUR			6,895.71		6,895.71	
		YTD	74,274.00		69,486.17		4,787.83	
Total Amt. Other Oper. Cost		CUR			12,065.29		12,065.29-	
		YTD	131,547.00		110,997.55		20,549.45	
Total Amt. This Activity		CUR			25,769.28		25,769.28-	2,164.6
		YTD	304,184.00		257,500.18		46,683.82	25,109.8
Production Units Planned/Used		CUR		2,995			2,995-	
		YTD	28,100	28,726			626-	28,841.0
Cost Per Unit		CUR		8.60				
		YTD	10.83	8.96				

reports of all accounts. A general ledger of all funds or money transactions gives the manager good control over the budget. This report shows from what account a transaction was made, the date, amount, check number, to whom it was paid, a description of the item, and a voucher number. Figure 9.14 shows an example of the general ledger.

As indicated earlier, the largest expenditure in a budget is the cost of salaries. Full-time salaries usually have good controls. On the other hand, part-time salaries can easily get out of hand, and an agency can overexpend its budget if these are not carefully governed. Sunnyvale has developed a *work-hour part-time control report* accounting system to help with this concern (see Figure 9.15). An attempt is made to plan how the hours are going to be used throughout the year on the basis of a reporting period, which is usually monthly. In this example, every 28 days is the reporting period. This turns out to be 13 equal reporting periods per year. In each of the reporting periods, the number of work hours that are going to be used is shown and indicated as *hours by period*. The *hours to date* are indicated in the second column and are the accumulation of all the preceding work hours used to date. This process is followed for each program activity, 300.09, 302.09, and so on. Once the entire plan is prepared, it becomes a guide for the entire year and should be adhered to. If adjustments are to be made, the entire plan should be revised. Figure 9.15 is an example of the projection report completed every 28 days. Each program activity is reported indicating *hours planned for period* taken from the master plan (see Figure 9.15) *hours used for period* taken

from the operating statement (Figure 9.14), *hours planned to date*, and *hours used to date* are then calculated.

A *year to date variance* is then shown, which tells the manager if the plan is being followed. By doing this report every 28 days, the manager of each program—as well as the director of parks and recreation—can keep track of what is happening and take corrective action before any program gets out of control. If halfway through the year the manager finds that he or she has overexpended in a given area, it can be caught and slowed down before it is too late. On the other hand, if a surplus of hours builds up, additional programs can be planned. Whatever the case, a close watch needs to be kept on part-time hours.

Summary

The entire budget and financial process is intended to give the manager a financial plan to follow and a system to ensure that it is followed. The best assurance of having a good plan, procedures, and controls is a good manager. The budget is a financial plan, which consists of an operating and a capital budget. To support the plan, there have to be revenues. The budget process consists of budget preparation, budget design, budget presentation, and budget implementation and control. However, an agency's budget and financial system are only as good as the services it renders to the public, because the final determination of how much financial support an agency will receive is in the hands of the taxpayers.

Figure 9.14
General ledger activity report by account

City of Sunnyvale

General Ledger Activity Report By Account

Account Number	Date	Transaction Descr.	Debits	Credits	Check	Vendor Name	Item Description	Voucher
10-4346-304-09	05/14/00	Cash Disbursement	307.75		13820	Marine World	Rec. Trip	CD536
			323.75					
10-4531-304-09	05/13/00	0	2.40-	.00				ERO357
			2.40-					
10-4204-305-09	05/11/00	Cash Disbursement	10.99		13555	Terry Shimuzu	Reimburse Inst.	CD527
10-4204-305-09	05/12/00	Cash Disbursement	11.12		13605	J. C. Penney Co.	SG	CD529
10-4204-305-09	05/14/00	Cash Disbursement	31.81		13727	Alpha Beta Co.	SG	CD532
10-4204-305-09	05/14/00	Cash Disbursement	26.97		13726	Bayshore Ceramic	SG	CD532
10-4204-305-09	05/14/00	Cash Disbursement	7.36		13731	Craftsman	SUP	CD532
10-4204-305-09	05/14/00	Cash Disbursement	11.52		13780	Safeway Stores	REC SUP	CD534
			99.77	.00				
10-4210-305-09	05/11/00	Cash Disbursement	15.98		13551	Bala	PA	CD527
10-4210-305-09	05/12/00	Cash Disbursement	7.50		13673	Suburban Newspaper	Subscrip.	CD530
			23.48	.00				
10-4245-305-09	05/12/00	Cash Disbursement	299.16		13650	Cyndy Goldsborough	Serv.-Rec.	CD530
			299.16	.00				
10-4342-305-09	05/11/00	Cash Disbursement	9.84		13528	Linda Pedroncelli	Statement of Exp.	CD526
10-4342-305-09	05/11/00	Cash Disbursement	28.88		13588	Patricia L. Plant	Statement of Exp.	CD528
10-4342-305-09	05/11/00	Cash Disbursement	11.55		13589	Rae Dickson	Statement of Exp.	CD528
10-4342-305-09	05/14/00	Cash Disbursement	11.40		13717	Dee Volz	Mileage	CD532
10-4342-305-09	05/14/00	Cash Disbursement	8.85		13865	Sylvia Bustmante	Statement of Exp.	CD537
			70.52	.00				
10-4345-305-09	05/14/00	Cash Disbursement	19.50		13537	Postmaster	Postage Expense	CD526
			19.50	.00				
10-4375-305-09	05/11/00	Cash Disbursement	200.00		13536	Tom Taylor	PA	CD526
10-4375-305-09	05/11/00	Cash Disbursement	200.00		13536	Jack Johnstone	PA	CD526
10-4375-305-09	05/12/00	Cash Disbursement	200.00		13711	David Adams	PA	CD531
			600.00	.00				
10-4383-305-09	05/11/00	Cash Disbursement	300.00		13533	David Wayne	PA	CD526
10-4383-305-09	05/11/00	Cash Disbursement	300.00		13535	Joe Leon	PA	CD526
			600.00					
10-4391-305-09	05/11/00	Cash Disbursement	50.00		13534	Elizabeth Luce	PA	CD526
10-4391-305-09	05/11/00	Cash Disbursement	200.00		13577	Angela Dewree	PA	CD528
10-4391-305-09	05/11/00	Cash Disbursement	10.00		13662	Dwight Wrench	Award	CD530
10-4391-305-09	05/12/00	Cash Disbursement	10.00		13657	Oneida Hammond	Awards-Park & Rec.	CD530
10-4391-305-09	05/12/00	Cash Disbursement	50.00		13664	Greg Reuter	Award	CD530
10-4391-305-09	05/12/00	Cash Disbursement	10.00		13658	Guin Rasmussen	Award	CD530
10-4391-305-09	05/12/00	Cash Disbursement	10.00		13661	James Daly	Award	CD530
10-4391-305-09	05/12/00	Cash Disbursement	10.00		13659	Nancy Crowley	Award	CD530
10-4391-305-09	05/12/00	Cash Disbursement	10.00		13660	Albert Senzatimore	Award	CD530
10-4391-305-09	05/12/00	Cash Disbursement	10.00		13663	John Martinez	Award	CD530
			370.00	.00				
10-4530-305-09	05/12/00	Cash Disbursement	197.68		13594	Xerox Corp.	Mar. Rent	CD528
			197.68	.00				

Figure 9.15
City of Sunnyvale, work-hour part-time control report

Period Covered	306.09 Hours By Period	306.09 Hours To Date	310.09 Hours By Period	310.09 Hours To Date	312.09 Hours By Period	312.09 Hours To Date	317.09 Hours By Period	317.09 Hours To Date
7/1-7/24	1,349	1,349	2,777	2,777	5,000	5,000	515	515
7/25-8/21	1,580	2,929	1,370	4,147	5,600	10,600	515	1,030
8/22-9/18	100	3,020	572	4,719	1,800	12,400	473	1,503
9/19-10/16	388	3,417	1,570	6,289	1,100	13,500	458	1,961
10/17-11/13	388	3,805	1,939	8,228	500	14,000	497	2,458
11/14-12/11	162	3,967	1,421	9,649	100	14,100	497	2,955
12/12-1/8	262	4,229	1,269	10,918	300	14,400	352	3,307
1/9-2/5	334	4,563	2,670	13,588	500	14,900	515	3,822
2/6-3/5	316	4,879	2,733	16,321	500	15,400	544	4,366
3/6-4/2	334	5,213	2,017	18,338	550	15,950	540	4,906
4/3-4/30	216	5,429	2,329	10,667	600	16,550	529	5,435
5/1-5/28	414	5,843	3,823	24,490	1,200	17,750	492	5,927
5/29-6/30	993	6,836	2,897	27,387	3,650	21,400	469	6,396
Total	6,836		27,387		21,400		6,396	

Discussion Questions

1. Define financial management.

2. What are the similarities between profit and nonprofit organizations in the area of financial management?

3. What philosophical ends drive the financial management orientations of profit and nonprofit organizations?

4. Identify and discuss different sources of revenue available to leisure service organizations.

5. What is a budget?

6. Identify the differences between a line-item budget, a program budget, performance budgeting and zero-base budgeting?

7. Identify and discuss four basic activities found in the budget process.

8. What types of expenditures are typically proposed in a budget?

9. How can cost-benefit analysis be useful to leisure service managers?

10. Describe the role of accounting as a process of control in the budgetary process.

References

Brademus, D. J. & Readnour, J. (1989, Winter). Status of fees and charges in public leisure services organizations. *Journal of Parks and Recreation Administration, 7*(4), 42–55.

Crompton, J. (1999). *Financing and acquiring park and recreation resources.* Champaign, IL: Human Kinetics.

Drucker, P. (1973). *Management tasks, responsibilities, practices.* New York: Harper & Row.

Hines, T. (1974), *Revenue source management and recreation,* Arlington, VA: National Recreation and Park Association.

Holnak, A., Mahoney, E., & Garges, J. (1999). Budgeting in management of park and recreation agencies. In B. van der Smissen, M. Moiseichik, V. Hartenburg, & L. Twardzik (Eds.), *Management of parks and recreation agencies.* National Recreation and Park Association.

Kraus, R., & J. Curtis, (2000). *Creative administration in recreation and parks.* (6th Ed.). St. Louis, MO: Mosby.

Lynch, T. D. (1995), *Public budgeting in America* (4th Ed.). Englewood Cliffs, NJ: Prentice-Hall.

Manning, R., Callinan, E., Echelberger, E., Koenemann, E., & McEwen, D. (1984, January). "Differential fees: Raising revenues, distributing demand. *Journal of Parks and Recreation Administration, 2*(1), 20–37.

Meserow, H., Pompel, D. T., Jr., & Reich, C. M. (1975, February). "Benefit–cost evaluation. *Parks and Recreation, 10*(4), 30.

Phyrr, P. A. (1977, January/February). The zero-base approach to government budgeting. *Public administration review. 37.*

Sellers, J., Gladwell, N., & Pope, M. (1999). Financial management. In (Eds), *Management of park and recreation resources.*

Webster, W. D., & Reich, C. M. (1977, January). Benefit-Cost analysis—Its uses in parks and recreation. *Recreation Canada, 35,* 25.

Wildavsky, A. B. (1986). *Budgeting: A comparative theory of budgetary processes.* New Brunswick, NJ: Transaction.

Chapter

10

Human Resource Management

Photo courtesy of the City of Phoenix (AZ) Parks, Recreation and Library Department

Teamwork is required for the effective use of human resources in leisure service organizations.

Introduction

A productive leisure service organization is only as strong as the individuals in the organization. Since at least 50 percent of most operating budgets cover direct and indirect expenditures for personnel, it behooves the leisure service manager to be knowledgeable about human resource management practices.

Leisure service organizations need to employ persons with a variety of skills and knowledge in order to meet the leisure needs of their constituents.

In most leisure service organizations, there are generally three broad areas of function and responsibility. The first of these is the organization and delivery of program services. The second one involves supervision and leadership in program services and administration. The last responsibility pertains to business-related duties and activities. These three functions may be interrelated. In other words, you need human resources to operate program services, and there is a need for human resource management applied to programming to take into consideration physical resources.

Employees in the last occupation are recruited from the general pool of skilled workers available to all enterprises, but are not necessarily people with degrees in the leisure services field. However, it is valuable if these individuals (e.g., secretaries, accountants, human resource managers, etc.) have an affinity for the field and a commitment to the professional and organizational mission.

Human resource management can be thought of as a staff function within the organization, supporting the primary line functions of creating, distributing, and financing services within the leisure delivery system. Every organization is involved in human resource management, and the successful operation of various personnel functions may very well determine the productivity of an organization. McKinney and Yen (1989:23) have noted that the more agency–specific a leisure organization is, the more personnel functions it performs in house, in contrast to those leisure service agencies that are part of a larger governmental body such as a department within a city structure. This chapter will cover the topics of personnel planning and job analysis, recruitment and hiring procedures, performance appraisals and promotions, compensation, disciplinary actions and grievances, and in-service training and development.

Human Resource Management

Human resource management is concerned with the "people" resources within a leisure service organization. Whenever people are involved within an organization, the tasks that are carried out under the heading of "personnel services" play an important role in its productivity. When an organization has developed an awareness of the importance of human resource management services, the employees will, generally speaking, have high morale and job satisfaction. Such awareness allows for an organization to interact with its employees in a positive manner, recognizing that people are the most important resource within an organization.

Although large organizations may have separate personnel departments, the personnel functions that are undertaken within any organization, regardless of its size, are fairly uniform. These functions include:

1. Position analysis and classification;

2. Recruitment, selection, and orientation;

3. Assignments appraisals and promotion;

4. Compensation;

5. Disciplinary action and grievances; and

6. In-service training and development.

Position Analysis and Classification

There are three important components involved in planning for the personnel needs of a leisure service organization. The first is that of identifying and forecasting personnel needs. The second involves a job analysis of the specific work activities to be accomplished and the resulting job description upon which to base recruitment of personnel. The third component involves the development of a sound, detailed plan to meet future personnel needs due to expansion, specific future short- or long-term projects, the normal rate of turnover, and so on.

Forecasting an organization's personnel needs can be a difficult and extremely sensitive area. It is difficult to predict fully or accurately changes in the economy that will affect both business and government. Further, it is difficult for organizations to predict changing consumer expectations in an area such as leisure, which is dynamic and fluid. In spite of these problems, organizations should attempt to project their future work-force needs and determine the amount and type of employees they will require. In a business, this is accomplished by multiplying the expected growth by the ratio between the amount of work currently done and the number of individuals required to do it.

In the government sector, personnel planning needs are usually based on two factors. The first factor, which is somewhat stable, is the amount of tax revenues that will be generated over a fixed period of time. A city can determine with a certain degree of accuracy the increase in land values and, hence, the assessed valuation of property. With this figure, government organizations can predict their potential revenues for

the future, which allows personnel forecasting to be undertaken. Further, government organizations can predict personnel needs based on projected capital improvements in the leisure service area. This is especially true in the development of revenue-producing facilities that are self-supporting. A slight modification of this factor can be done in stable nonprofit agencies. If the agency has a stable source of income over a period of time (e.g., United Way funding, sustained membership, etc.), then it can also predict potential revenues for the future.

The second factor—political change—is somewhat more difficult to deal with effectively. The political programs of elected officials can have a significant impact on personnel planning. Certain politicians advocate the reduction of governmental services, whereas others suggest that they should be expanded. This uncertainty in political philosophy makes planning difficult but not entirely impossible. An organization usually will try to forecast its personnel needs over a five-year period. In nonprofit agencies, the politics of the board members come into play, because they are generally responsible for overseeing the funding of new positions. Thus, if a board member representing a specific constituency has a pet project that he or she wants undertaken, the nonprofit agency may find itself in a personnel crunch.

An important step in personnel analysis is to determine the specific work required. To adequately plan for future personnel needs, and ultimately, screen and select new employees, an organization must know what specific jobs are to be done, and the specific talents and abilities required to do them. The process of integrating these two concerns is known as "job analysis." This is usually undertaken by an organization in an attempt to identify the activities that an individual will engage in while performing a specific task. Once this has been done and has been linked to the competencies necessary to complete a given task, a job description is usually written. A job description states the title of the job, spells out the activities or duties that are to be performed in the job, and delineates the skills and abilities required to complete the job (see Figure 10.1). It is from the job description that future personnel recruitment is done. The specifications found in a job description serve as a basis on which a leisure service manager can fulfill the organization's future personnel requirements.

Once an organization has completed its projection of future personnel needs, its next task is to develop a plan to meet these future needs. This may involve an analysis of the organization's current workforce. The amount of expected turnover for a variety of reasons, including retirements, job transfers, and normal attrition, can be determined. Once this task has been completed, a plan that incorporates these findings with the forecasted human resource needs can be completed. This plan should spell out the positions that are necessary to meet the organization's future needs and the mechanisms necessary to secure employees to meet these future demands. This plan should also identify the step-by-step procedures that organizations will take to recruit new employees.

Classification Systems

In those agencies that fall under civil service requirements, another type of job classification occurs.

The civil service system was instituted in the 1880s to try to curb some of the political abuse and patronage that existed up until that time. In order to ensure fair and equitable treatment of all employees, most civil service systems established two categories of employees: classified and unclassified. Classified employees are generally thought of as the permanent skilled and professional staff of an agency. Unclassified personnel are usually political appointees or elected officials who head the department or division for a specified period of time. For instance, the Secretary of the Interior is a political appointee of the President of the United States. However, the undersecretary and other professional members of the department are classified individuals.

Classification systems were an attempt to equate dissimilar job titles across an agency or organization. Thus, in a city that follows a civil service classification plan, the city engineer might be classified at the same level as the park superintendent or the recreation supervisor. This type of classification system is used to decide wages, promotion, orientation, and in-service training.

The following definitions are generally used in civil service classifications:

1. *Position.* This is a job that demands specific performance. Its duties, responsibilities, and relationships are enumerated in a job description. This job can be full-time or part-time; it can be established or abolished. The job of a recreation supervisor is an example of position.

2. *Class.* This is a collection of positions with duties and responsibilities similar enough to warrant

Figure 10.1
Wooster (OH) Parks and Recreation Department, Job Description for
Director of Parks and Recreation

General Description: The Director of Parks and Recreation is the chief executive officer of the Parks and Recreation Department. He is responsible for the supervision, coordination, and leadership required to implement the efficient operation of the department under the policies and guidelines established by the Parks and Recreation Board.

Major Duties:

1. To inform the board on all matters germane to the functioning of the department as requested by the board.

2. To recommend courses of action, plans, and policies required to insure the smooth operation of the department and its purpose.

3. To direct the operations of the department and include the staff, programs, maintenance, financial, and facilities.

4. To recruit, select, and employ or to recommend employment of department personnel.

5. To administer the budget—directing, controlling, and accounting for the expenditure of department funds in accordance with budget appropriations. Supervising the keeping of complete financial records for the department.

6. The director will assume the perpetual goal of upgrading the staff through in-service training.

7. Improving the public awareness of the department's services through good public relations.

8. To enlighten the department's philosophy and objectives and stimulate the total growth through a planned program of acquisition, planning, design, and construction of recreation and parks facilities.

9. To study and analyze the effectiveness of the department's services, upgrading programs and facilities in keeping with conditions, needs, and trends that affect leisure services in the community.

10. To establish and develop a program for continuing use of volunteers and to act as a consultant on leisure resources with public and quasi-public agencies.

11. To prepare and issue regular and special reports for use by staff, board, community officials, and others, and for the information of the community.

12. To perform other duties as may be assigned by the board.

Desired Qualifications

College graduate in the field of Park and Recreation Administration. A minimum of three (3) years of progressive experience in the park and recreation field. A director must have the ability to organize and supervise a wide range of administrative functions and the ability to develop leadership within the staff and have attributes of personal leadership himself.

comparable education, experience, skill and practice. An example of class would be all city employees in supervisory positions (e.g., recreation supervisor, park supervisor, utility supervisor, water department supervisor, etc.)

3. *Vertical Classification or Series.* These encompass all positions that are related to a particular technology or professional group. The level of position can differ by the difficulty and responsibility of performance. There can also be a rank within classification. An example of this in a leisure service department might be as follows: recreation specialist, recreation coordinator, recreation supervisor, recreation superintendent, and recreation director.

4. *Horizontal Classifications or Grade.* This arranges classes of positions without regard for precise occupational resemblances but by attributes in terms of responsibility, supervision given and received, and complexity of work. Grade bisects series. The grade should rise as the work becomes more difficult and the responsibilities greater. For example, a secretary may be classified as a Secretary I, Secretary II, Secretary III, and so on in any city department. However, a Secretary I, Grade 3 may have more responsibility than a Secretary I, Grade 1.

It would be important then, in those leisure service organizations under a civil service system, not only to project future needs, but also to classify the positions of future employees.

Recruitment, Selection, and Orientation

To meet the personnel needs of an organization, a manager must spend considerable energy and time in the recruitment and hiring of new staff. The recruitment and hiring process involves locating qualified individuals to assume positions that have been authorized within the organization. Once sources of employees have been located, the next step is to screen employees by reviewing their applications or resumes. Interviewing prospective employees is the next procedure, and investigation of the backgrounds of potential employees is undertaken. Finally, the candidate selected for the position is hired. This process may vary, depending on the level and type of job the manager is recruiting for. Further, the intensity with which organizations pursue each of these steps will vary according to the needs of the organization and its resources.

Recruitment of Qualified Individuals

There are two main sources an organization can use to secure individuals for positions within the organization. It can look internally for individuals who can be promoted. Simultaneously, it can enlist the assistance of external sources to locate potential employees. Depending on the type of position available within an organization, a variety of resources may be tapped. In the case of professional positions, the National Recreation and Park Association's job referral program is an excellent source. Similarly, state and provincial professional organizations maintain job listings or publish journals in which job openings can be advertised. Another source of potential professional employees is through the colleges and universities having recreation or leisure service curricula.

For nonprofessional employees, an organization may advertise in a newspaper, receive referrals from state or provincial employment agencies, or review referrals from private employment agencies. Another method for locating qualified individuals is through personal referrals. Often individuals within the organization will know of potential candidates for a given job.

The recruitment of leisure service personnel may range from nationwide selection efforts to a local campaign to hire part-time instructors for activity classes. The recruitment of highly qualified staff plays an important role in the development of an organization's human resource base. Without competent staff, a key building block in the success of any leisure delivery system, an organization's efforts will be diminished. The process of selecting employees may be based on the establishment of elaborate criteria or on the individual preferences of managers. In either case, the selection of personnel is a necessary and important function and needs to follow fair employment practice laws.

Laws Pertaining to Employment

Since 1964, several federal laws have been passed to try to ensure fair employment practices in the recruitment and retention of qualified employees (see Table 10.1). All leisure service managers have a legal and ethical responsibility to be familiar with these laws and make sure that those in charge of the recruitment and hiring processes are aware of them.

Civil Rights Act of 1964 (Title VII).

This comprehensive act makes it unlawful for employers to discriminate against any qualified job applicants or employees because of their race, color, national origin, religion, or gender. It also prohibits employers from retaliating against an employee who files a charge of discrimination, participates in a discrimination investigation, or opposes an unlawful employment practice. The types of agencies covered by the law include federal, state, and local governments, public and private educational institutions, and private organizations employing 15 or more individuals who work 20 or more weeks per year. The Equal Employment Opportunity Commission (EEOC) was established by Title VII to interpret and enforce this law.

Employers are allowed to request exemptions in employment decisions under Title VII if they feel that they have a "bona fide" occupational qualification (BFOQ) that is essential to the normal operations of the organization. For instance, one could request a BFOQ to ensure the hiring of a male attendant for the men's locker room or a person of a specific religion to teach at a private religious institution. However, these BFOQs are few and far between. One would have a hard time for instance, insisting that a little league coach could only be male or female.

Table 10.1
Federal Employment Laws

Law	Year	Provision
Equal Pay Act as by the Equal Opportunity Act of 1972	1963	Requires employers to pay men and women similar wage rates for similar work in terms of their skill, effort, responsibility, and working conditions.
Title VII of the Civil Rights Act	1964	Unlawful for employers to discriminate based on an individuals race, color, national origin, religion, or sex.
Age Discrimination in Employment Act	1967	Prohibits discrimination in employment against individuals above the age of forty.
Rehabilitation Act, as amended in 1974	1973	Prohibits private employers with federal contracts or subcontracts valued over $2,500 from discriminating against qualified persons with disabilities.
Pregnancy Discrimination Act	1978	Prohibits employers from discriminating against women affected by pregnancy, childbirth, or related medical conditions, including abortion.
Americans with Disabilities Act	1990	Prohibits employers from discriminating against qualified persons with disabilities who can perform the "essential" job functions.
Civil Right Act	1991	Allows victims of intentional discrimination based on race, sex, religion, and disability to ask for compensatory damages, punitive damages, and to demand a trial.
Family and Medical Leave Act	1993	Requires employers to allow eligible employees to take a total of twelve weeks leave during any twelve-month period for one or more of the following: (1) birth, adoption, or foster-care placement of a child; (2) caring for a spouse, child, or parent with a serious health condition; (3) serious health condition of the employee.

Equal Pay Act of 1963 as Amended by the Equal Opportunity Act of 1972

This act was passed to address the concern that women were being paid lower wages than men for the same job positions and responsibilities. It is unlawful to pay dissimilar wages to men and women if they are performing similar jobs in terms of their skill, effort, responsibility, and working conditions. This act applies to federal, state, and local governments as well as to private employers with two or more employees. The EEOC also enforces this act. According to the guidelines, employers are allowed to make pay distinctions as long as they are based on such factors as seniority, meritorious performance, and quantity and quality of performance.

Age Discrimination in Employment Act (1967)

This act prohibits discrimination in employment against individuals who are above the age of 40. Specifically, it is unlawful for employers to: refuse to hire an individual based on age, reduce an older worker's wage rate, print or publish an employment notice or advertisement based on age, require older workers to pay more than younger workers for benefit programs, or eliminate or reduce the rate of an employee's benefit accrual because of age. If an employer can prove that an exception is necessary for the normal operation of the agency, he or she can request a BFOQ as outlined above. However, most leisure service organizations would have few, if any, jobs that would meet this stipulation. This act applies to federal, state, and local governments as well as private

employers with 20 or more employees. Enforcement of the Act is done through the EEOC.

Pregnancy Discrimination Act of 1978

This act was passed by Congress to protect women, both single and married, affected by pregnancy, childbirth, or related medical conditions (including abortion) against discriminatory employment practices. Under this act, employers may not refuse to hire, and may not fire, a woman just because she is pregnant or has had an abortion. They also may not change any of the benefits such as health insurance, vacation time or leaves of absence connected with the position occupied by a woman. In other words, under this act women affected by pregnancy, childbirth, or abortion have the same rights as workers who, because of a medical condition, are temporarily disabled and unable to perform their jobs.

Americans with Disabilities Act (1990)

The first legislation covering the rights of the disabled in employment was passed as early as 1973 (Rehabilitation Act) but was rather narrow in scope. The Rehabilitation Act applied only to employers receiving federal financial assistance over $2,500. The much more comprehensive ADA provides people with disabilities greater access to employment opportunities and protection against discriminatory employment practices. The fundamental provisions of ADA prohibit employers from discriminating against qualified persons with disabilities who can perform the essential functions of a job. The Act also prohibits organizations from using qualifications, standards, employment tests, or other selection criteria to screen out persons with disabilities unless the standards and criteria are job related. In addition, employers must make "reasonable accommodations" for job applicants and workers with disabilities. Examples of reasonable accommodation would include: (1) making areas at the workplace accessible (e.g., offices, restrooms, conference rooms, etc.), (2) buying or modifying office furniture and equipment, and (3) modifying work schedules.

Several positive results have occurred because of this Act. Not only has it allowed people with disabilities a chance to become productive workers in leisure service organizations, but it has also forced managers to write more definitive job descriptions that clearly identify the essential functions of all positions. In addition, it has brought about an awareness of how to plan and design an efficient work area to accommodate the needs of all workers.

Family and Medical Leave Act of 1993

Although not directly related to the hiring of employees, another law passed in the 1990s that directly affects employment practices is the Family and Medical Leave Act of 1993. This act was passed in recognition of the growing dilemmas that many Americans faced in terms of working and trying to care for family members. The act applies to both males and females, allowing qualified employees to take up to 12 weeks of unpaid leave during a 12-month period for family and health reasons. Family reasons include the birth of a child, the adoption of a child, or the acquisition of a foster child. Health reasons include serious medical conditions affecting either the employee or immediate family members such as bypass surgery, severe respiratory distress conditions, and serious nervous or mental disorders. The Department of Labor enforces the Family Leave Act. This act applies to all government employers, as well as private employers with 50 or more employees.

Selection Process

In the selection process, the employer tries to determine which potential qualified applicant will best fit within the organization's culture and work environment. Although the primary criteria are based on the extent of job-related qualifications of an applicant, a secondary consideration has to be the positive or negative interaction of the individual with members of the organization. As Beeler (1999: 505) noted: "All organizations have a culture which is formed by the values, beliefs, attitudes, and personality traits of the individual staff members." Effective organizations use in-depth interviews to assess how well job candidates organizationally fit within an existing culture. For example, an organization may place high value on teamwork. The organization may use the in-depth interview to determine if job candidates are capable of working as team members and contributing to the overall goals of the organization. Job candidates who appear to be extremely competitive and prefer to work alone may not be as attractive as those who have the ability to get along well with others, and work cooperatively toward accomplishing team goals.

Because the hiring of personnel has a lasting affect on the organization, it behooves the leisure service manager to have a plan in place to select the best possible applicant for the position. This means that both the screening and interview processes must follow legal guidelines while also allowing the best possible candidate to rise to the top.

Screening of Prospective Employees

Obviously, the criteria used to screen future employees will vary from position to position. The initial screening of potential employees should be based on the advertised minimum qualifications for the position. It is important that only people who meet the criteria are left in the pool. Thus, if the job announcement states that one requirement of the position is that candidates have a bachelor's degree, applicants with a high school diploma or an associate's degree should be taken out of the pool of potential prospects.

Once the initial screening has been made, a more detailed examination takes place to identify those applicants who exceed the minimum qualifications and have the best combination of education, training, and experience. This is an informed judgment call by leisure service professionals in the organization. Either the manager or a committee comprised of professional staff members has the best understanding of the job duties and responsibilities pertaining to a professional position. If this second screening process results in a large number of qualified individuals remaining in the applicant pool, a pre-interview process might take place in order to choose the lead candidates in the pool. This process might involve contacting potential applicants by phone, mailing out pre-interview questionnaires, or doing preliminary background checks. It is important that this be a fair and equitable process. Thus, if one applicant is contacted by phone, all applicants need to be contacted by phone.

The agency may want to run a preliminary background and reference check at this time or wait until the final list of candidates is selected. Either way, it is imperative that an agency do the following: (1) verify academic degrees and certifications; (2) check public records to ensure that applicants have no criminal records; and (3) check references to verify past work performances.

Interviewing Prospective Employees

Once the pool of applicants has been narrowed to a specific number set by the organization, an in-depth, face-to-face interview generally takes place. The interview process should be a structured conversation(s) among the job applicant, immediate supervisor, and other members of the professional staff who will be working closely with the new employee. The purposes of the interview are these: (1) to provide an exchange of job relevant information; (2) to assess job-relevant knowledge, skills, and abilities of potential candidates; (3) to provide the candidate with a realistic overview of job duties, responsibilities, and issues; and (4) to create a positive impression of the organization.

In order to achieve these purposes, an interview plan must be developed. This plan should detail the who, what, when, and where of the interview process, as shown below:

1. Who will be involved in the interview process? What roles will

these individuals play in the interview process? How will they be trained to be effective and fair interviewers?

2. What will be covered in the interview session, including the need to formulate job-relevant interview questions and forms?

3. When will the interview take place? Is the schedule designed to provide sufficient time for all people involved in the interview process to participate?

4. Where will the interview take place? Is a neutral site to be used? If done in a private office, will phone calls or people dropping by interrupt the interview?

It is extremely important that interviewers use uniform interview questions to avoid asking illegal or discriminatory questions (see Figure 10. 2). In addition, having a uniform set of questions avoids redundancy and can help ensure that needed information is both given and received during the interview process.

Personnel Assessment Center

The personnel assessment center concept is often employed in leisure service organizations in the selection of staff. Basically, an assessment center can be thought of as a "carefully coordinated comprehensive battery of selection techniques" (Jarrell, 1993:36). As Cook and Spencer (1992) have written: "a person's intelligence, education, training, experience, skills, aptitudes, and so on, are fairly obvious from the resume, application, and interview. But

it is the personal will do characteristic—drive, determination, stability, maturity—that determines whether or not the person will put those abilities to good use." In other words, the emphasis is on a person's ability to do or perform in a simulated work environment.

Personnel assessment centers often require individuals to carry out behaviors that are similar to the work environment. Activities include "simulations, in-basket exercises, and role-playing, undergoing psychological testing and engaging in group discussions, and self-evaluation" (Tracey, 1992:52). Individuals who are interviewing are observed by evaluators who assess and record their behaviors. *Camp Adventure™ Youth Services* has successfully adapted this concept in its selection process by operating a Leadership Assessment Center (LAC) to screen individuals. The LAC program helps the *Camp Adventure™ Youth Services* staff discover individuals who have leadership potential.

Orientation

Having spent a considerable amount of time in the recruitment and selection process, many leisure service agencies ignore the last important step—that of familiarizing the new employee with the practices, procedures, and culture inherent in the new job. As Busser (1999: 545–555) states: "orientation is critical to new employees' success and to protecting the investment the organization has made."

The purposes of an orientation program are as follows:

1. *To understand job expectations such as specific job duties and responsibilities, rules and regulations, and*

Figure 10.2
Interview Questions
What's Legal?

Many times it is not only what you ask but how you ask the question that makes it legal or illegal. It is always a good idea to have your questions on paper in advance to insure a legal interview.

Area	Lawful	Unlawful
1. Address, Length of residence	Applicant's address, place and length of current and previous residence. "How long in (city)?"	Specific questions about foreign address, whether applicant owns or rents home. Relationship of persons with whom applicant lives.
2. Age	If age is a legal requirement "If hired can you submit proof of age?" If applicant is a minor, proof of age in form of work permit or certificate of age.	Requirement that birth certificate or baptismal certificate be produced as proof of age.
3. Ancestry	Languages read, spoken or written.	Inquiries into ancestry, mother tongue, national origin of parents or spouse.
4. Arrests		Any inquiry relating to arrests.
5. Birthplace	"Can you produce birth certificate or other proof of citizenship after employment?"	Birthplace of applicant or relatives. Requirement that birth certificate, baptismal record or naturalization paper be submitted prior to employment. Questions which identify customs or denomination.
6. Citizenship	"Are you a citizen of the U.S.?" If not, do you have the legal right to remain permanently in the U.S.?	Of what country are you a citizen? Are you naturalized or native born? Requiring naturalization papers.
7. Convictions, Court Records	Inquiry into actual convictions which relate to ability to perform specific job.	To ask about or check arrest conviction or court records if not substantially related to specific job functions.
8. Credit rating	None	Any questions regarding credit.

Continued

Figure 10.2 Continued
Interview Questions
What's Legal?

Area	Lawful	Unlawful
9. Education	Academic, vocational or professional education; schools attended; language and office skills.	Questions about the nationality or religious affiliation of schools. How language skill was learned.
10. Emergency Contact	Name of person to contact in an emergency.	Name of relative to be contacted.
11. Experience	Applicant's work experience; other countries visited.	
12. Handicaps	"Do you have any physical, mental or sensory handicaps which might affect work performance or which should be considered in job placement?	"Do you have any handicaps?" or questions which might divulge handicaps which do not relate to the job.
13. Marital Status	Whether applicant can meet specific work schedules; any committments which might hinder attendance. Anticipated duration on job or anticipated absences if made to both males and females.	Inquiries about specific marital status, number of children; questions concerning pregnancy or birth control.
14. Military Record	Military experience and education related to a particular job.	Type of discharge
15. Miscellaneous	Notice that misstatements, ommissions, false information on application may result in discharge.	
16. Name	"Have you ever worked for this organization under another name?" Is additional information concern- nicknames or change of name necessary to check work record or education? If yes, explain.	Inquiries about names which would indicate national origin. Inquiries about names which have been changed by court order, marriage or otherwise.
17. Organizations	Organizations, membership in which might relate to a particular job.	List all organizations, clubs or societies you belong.
18. Photographs	May be required after hiring.	Required prior to hire.
19. Race	General distinguishing characteristics such as scars, etc.	Applicant's race; color of skin, eyes, or hair; height or weight where not job related.

Continued

Figure 10.2 Continued
Interview Questions
What's Legal?

Area	Lawful	Unlawful
20. References	Who referred you here?	Requiring religious references.
21. Relatives	Name of relatives employed here. Name and address of parents of a minor	Name or address of any relative of an adult applicant.
22. Religion	None	Inquiry into religious affiliation, holy observances, name of minister, etc.
23. Sex	Inquiry permissable only where bona fide occupational qualification (BFOQ) exists. BFOQ is interpreted very narrowly by the courts.	Sex of applicant. Inquiries which would indicate sex. Sex is not a BFOQ because a job requires physical labor.

policies and procedures. Simply handing a new employee a personnel manual and expecting him or her to understand the important items that will impact the new work environment is a poor way to introduce an employee to a new job.

2. *To introduce the new employee to the organizational culture.* Every new employee needs to know "how things are done around here." He or she needs to be socialized into the norms of behavior, values, and work etiquette that are expected in the organization. It is helpful if the new employee is assigned an experienced co-worker who can act as a mentor, answer questions, and respond to concerns that the new employee might have regarding work responsibilities.

3. *To start the formation of work relationships.* New employees need to be able to form positive work relationships with co-workers and

supervisors in a nonthreatening environment. This should be done gradually rather than in a day or half-day brief introduction.

To be effective, an orientation period should span several days or even weeks. It also needs to be done in segmented time periods. There is simply too much information for the new employee to absorb all at once. Orientation programs that are integrated into the normal workday schedule (i.e., two hours every day) are much more effective than all-day marathons.

Many times, it is assumed that internal candidates who have been promoted to a new job position do not need orientation. This assumption can end up causing serious problems. Even though someone familiar with the organization may not need the same indepth introduction to policies and procedures, he or she still needs time to adjust to new work relationships and new place within the organization. These "old hands" may experience as much work-related stress and anxiety as new employees from outside the agency. An effective organization recognizes this possibility and tailors an orientation program to their needs to help alleviate most of the anxiety and foster confidence in their ability to handle new job responsibilities and expectations. Specific information concerning orientation training is given later in this chapter.

Assignments, Appraisals and Promotions

The essence of the scientific management approach (see Chapter Two) was to select the right person for the right job. In reality, this is still the most important staffing consideration for today's leisure service organizations. The basis for having an efficient and effective organization is to have competent professionals developing and operating creative programs and services that carry out the organization's mission and goals. In order to do this, a leisure service manager must accomplish the following:

1. Assign the right people to the right job tasks;

2. Evaluate how employees are carrying out assigned tasks; and

3. Promote individuals into new positions with responsibilities and job duties as the organization evolves.

Assignment of Employees

This is a process that involves integrating the individual abilities that people bring to a work setting with the organization's needs. It is naive to think that an organization can tailor a job to fit each person's particular skills, knowl-

edge, abilities, and interests. On the other hand, it is also naive for an organization to assume that it can locate individuals with the specific skills, values, and attitudes necessary for particular jobs. Therefore, there is a tremendous need within organizations to find the best way to use each employee's skills. This may involve changing a job by expanding or making it more flexible to meet a particular individual's interests. It may also mean moving an individual from one position to another one. Generally, an organization should attempt to use its human resources effectively by integrating individual abilities and needs with organizational requirements.

Performance Appraisals

An important role in the management of personnel is the periodic evaluation of staff. Every leisure service organization expends vast sums of its fiscal resources on personnel. To ensure that an organization is run effectively, the performance of its personnel must be audited and either corrected or rewarded, depending on the situation. An effective performance appraisal system can provide the leisure service manager with information that can be used to guide decision making regarding promotions, training, and long-range planning.

Performance appraisal has served for many years primarily as a mechanism whereby an organization decides who merits salary increases or promotions. This device has been used as a rational method of linking the expectations of an organization with the performance of individual employees. It was thought that by establishing selected criteria, an organization could systematically identify and reward outstanding performance. In addition, it was thought that this approach would reduce the amount of favoritism and bias that occurred in organizations without a systematic approach.

One of the recent shifts in the use of performance appraisal techniques is the movement toward using them to aid in developmental training programs. Many organizations are concerned about the development of their employees. To aid in the task of constructing effective employee-oriented developmental training programs, performance appraisal techniques are being used to help employees better understand their own strengths and weaknesses. Rather than simply viewing these mechanisms as tools to evaluate a person's work performance for merit considerations, they are being used to help point out areas in which they can improve.

This added perspective is changing the nature of employee appraisal. In the past, an employee's evaluation was viewed strictly in black-and-white terms; his or her work was either good or bad, and depending upon this appraisal, he or she either got an increase or did not. Today organizations are using appraisal systems in a much more positive sense. They are no longer viewed as potentially negative or undesirable by either managers or employees; rather, they are seen as opportunities for managers to work with their subordinates, and vice versa, to improve the effectiveness and efficiency of the organization.

Another trend in the use of a performance appraisal has been in the area of long-range planning. There are two ways that it contributes to the planning process. First, it allows an organization to identify potential problem areas and take corrective action. If, for example, an organization has a morale problem, or certain of its employees lack the skills

to perform certain jobs, resources within the organization can be shifted to counter these concerns. In this way, an organization can determine some of its long-term needs and proceed accordingly.

The second way a performance appraisal contributes to an organization's long-range planning efforts is by identifying individuals within the organization who have promise for the future. Organizational resources can be allocated to help groom likely management prospects. Not only does the organization invest in a long-term training activity, but it is also able to compare and contrast current organizational personnel resources with future needs. If an organization finds that it does not have sufficient internal resources to meet its long-term personnel needs, it can plan long-term recruitment strategies that will enable it to find the needed resources.

Performance Appraisal Techniques

Performance appraisal techniques can be seen as existing on a continuum that runs from those emphasizing an individual's personality traits (inputs rather than outputs) to those stressing results-oriented performance (outputs rather than inputs). The latter is concerned with measuring what an employee produces, and the former focuses on identifying what the employee brings to the job in terms of personality. The trend in performance appraisal is clearly shifting from approaches used to measure personality traits to results-oriented appraisal mechanisms. Five methods will be discussed—rating scales, forced distribution, forced choice, critical incidents, and Management by Objectives (MBO).

Rating Scales

This technique involves the use of a form having a list of selected criteria, usually a list of words that can be used to describe an employee's performance. These words are placed in checkerboard style with the criteria that have been developed for appraisal. The manager simply checks the appropriate word that he or she feels describes an employee's performance. For example, if the criterion is "leadership," the form may present options ranging from "unsatisfactory" to "exceptional." The manager would check the term that best describes an employee's leadership ability (see Figure 10.3).

There are two types of rating scales. The first is known as the "additive" approach to performance appraisal. In this method, an employee's overall performance score is determined by adding up all the scores given for the criteria established. For example, descriptive terms are given a numerical score: "Unsatisfactory" might have the value of 1, and "exceptional" might be given the value of 5. The manager records the number of each of the selected criteria (leadership, loyalty, etc.) and determines a total, or overall, score. Despite the simplicity of this approach, it presents a number of problems in effective performance appraisal. For one, it assumes that all the factors being evaluated are of equal importance. But in certain jobs, loyalty may be more important than leadership; in other jobs, creativity may be more important than loyalty.

The other type of rating scale avoids the problems found in the additive approach. Rather than lumping all the criteria together to achieve an overall score, this approach allows a manager to evaluate an employee's performance on those criteria that relate specifically to an employee's position. In other words, an individual's appraisal is more tailor-made to the specifics of his or her job. The manager can simply ignore the criteria that are not applicable or that he or she is unable to evaluate effectively. In both approaches to performance appraisal, the stress is placed on the intention or personality traits of individuals, rather than on concrete job accomplishments.

There are numerous problems associated with using the rating scale approach to performance appraisal. Among the more significant drawbacks, as identified by George Strauss and Leonard Sayles (1972:511), are the following:

1. *Clarity of standards.* Frequently, individuals using the rating scale approach vary in their perception of what constitutes unsatisfactory or exceptional performance. For one person, exceptional performance may be viewed as theoretically unattainable. Another person may use a comparative approach to determine exceptional performance. The result is that these terms mean different things to different people and present a problem in accurate evaluation of individuals.

2. *Insufficient Evidence.* Because this approach is essentially a one-way mechanism that finds the manager rating his or her subordinates, it is slanted toward the manager's viewpoint. That is to say, the manner in which the employee interacts with the manager will be the primary determinant of the employee's rating outcome, regardless of the way he or she may interact with co-workers, or indeed the manager with his or her own subordinates.

Figure 10.3
Example of a Rating Scale for Performance Appraisal

		Excellent	Good	Fair	Poor	Not Observed
Employee _____	Recreation ☐					
Home Address _____ Phone ____	Pool ☐					
Employment Period: from ____ 20__ to____ 20__	☐ Rated by:					
Position Held _____	Date . ____ (Title)					
Previous Position with Wooster Parks and Recreation Department	Salary $ ____					

		Excellent	Good	Fair	Poor	Not Observed
1. Personality and Attitude						
A. Cheerful and friendly with everyone	A.					
B. Alert for new ideas	B.					
C. Coorperative attitude toward fellow workers, supervisors, and patrons	C.					
D. Suitable personality for recreation	D.					
E. Interest in and loyalty to the district and discretion in discussing it and its policies	E.					
F. Loyalty to superiors	F.					
2. Administrative Ability						
A. Plans and carries out suggested programs to full extent of ability and facilities	A.					
B. Shows originality and initiative in program	B.					
C. Receptive to suggestions from superiors	C.					
D. Submits reports promptly	D.					
E. Works with an encourages volunteers	E.					
3. Leadership						
A. An example to others	A.					
B. Not content with the status quo; constantly trying to improve both the program and himself	B.					
C. Has an ability to provide leadership	C.					
D. Enthusiastic	D.					
E. Skills and past experience enrich program	E.					
F. Attendance raises or remains constant	F.					
4. Reliability						
A. Is punctual in meeting all time schedules	A.					
B. Accepts full share of responsibility	B.					
C. Carries out, in cooperative spirit, policies and requirements	C.					
5. Appearance						
A. Presents a good personal appearance	A.					
6. Facilities						
A. Keeps facilities and supplies in good condition	A.					

Remarks: _____

_____ Rehire: ____ Not Rehire: ____

3. *Different Perception.* It is extremely difficult for individuals to be impartial in the evaluation of others. One's own particular prejudices, biases, and values can distort evaluation or make impartial evaluation impossible.

4. *Excessive Leniency or Strictness.* The perception that a manager has of himself or herself the job will affect his or her approach to appraisal. Some individuals see themselves as being hard managers re-

sponsible for maintaining discipline within the organization. As a result, their evaluations may be overly harsh. On the other hand, there also managers who try to create a country club atmosphere and be "one of the guys." Their evaluations may be very lenient.

5. *Halo Effect.* This problem is created when a manager allows himself or herself to be influenced by the success of an employee in one particular dimension of appraisal. What happens is that the manager carries over the success of the individual's performance in one area to all other areas. The reverse of this can also occur.

6. *Influence of a Person's Job.* There is a tendency to rank individuals operating in higher-level jobs as being more effective. It is important to remember that each job within an organization has specific requirements, and appraisal should consider these factors rather than where one is located in the organizational hierarchy.

Forced Distribution

In this approach to performance appraisal, the manager ranks employees within a given class against one another and places them on a hierarchical scale. It is similar to the procedure of grading on a curve. For example, using the employee's overall performance appraisal score, 10 percent of the individuals may be forced into the top category, 30 percent in the next category, 40 percent into the "average" category, 10 percent in the next lowest category, and 10 percent at the bottom. This mechanism is commonly used to distribute the funds available to pay for merit increases, dividing the funds according to staff ranking on a curve.

This approach allows managers to overcome some of the problems associated with the rating scale method. It usually assures that all managers apply the standards found in appraisal systems equally. Further, it eliminates the possibility that employees in one job classification will be compared with those of another. In addition, it eliminates some of the biases that occur as a result of the different perceptions individual managers have of employees by actively making them compare the work of one individual to that of another in the same job class. Further, this system is a relatively straightforward way of evaluating employees and, although it may take considerable time to rank employees, it is a mechanism that is usually understood by those being evaluated.

Obviously, there are also drawbacks to this system. First, and perhaps most important, it may set one employee against another, reducing the cooperative efforts necessary for an organization to achieve its goals. This approach also assumes that not everyone within an organization is *capable* of achieving a maximum standard of performance. Because there is no absolute set of criteria by which to measure effectiveness, employee productivity may decline. Within any organization are peer pressures to keep the "rate busters" in line. As a result, this approach to performance appraisal may create considerable tension within an organization.

Forced Choice

The U. S. Army at the conclusion of World War II developed this approach to performance appraisal. It is a procedure that is directed toward eliminating prejudice and bias in the evaluation of individuals. Essentially, the manager is presented with a number of statements that describe the behavior of an employee. He or she is given a dichotomous choice for each statement and must check one of two items, "one of which is the most and the other least characteristic of the person being rated." Certain choices that are included in the list of statements have no relevance to the performance appraisal. If a manager responds to a statement that does not relate to the task required in a given job, this ranking is disregarded. Conversely, the manager does not know which statements have bearing on job performance and which are bogus and have no bearing. Thus, the bias of the manager is partially eliminated. The manager has no way of knowing in advance which statements will contribute to a positive or negative performance appraisal, that also contribute to objective evaluation.

This approach to performance appraisal seems to be one of the more effective mechanisms that can be used. It has not been incorporated in leisure delivery systems with any degree of significance for a number of reasons. For one, it is an extremely costly method of evaluation because it requires an organization to specifically delineate the task necessary for a given job. Herein lies one of its strengths and one of its weaknesses. It is very time-consuming for managers to detail the requirements of a given job and is therefore very expensive. On the other hand, each set of statements must be custom-developed for each position or set of positions within an organization; this ensures that the evaluation criteria used will be relevant to the job being performed.

Another reason this approach has not been used widely is that it is based on the assumption that managers do not have the capacity to evaluate individuals without injecting their own biases. This naturally makes them leery of using the method because it seems to indicate their inability to operate competently. Another problem is that the manager may not answer honestly, thinking he or she has figured out which statements will count and which won't. This problem revolves around the fact that it is extremely difficult to discuss the contents of the evaluation form with employees if the manager himself or herself doesn't know which items are meaningful and which are not.

Critical Incidents

As mentioned in Chapter One, an important function of the leisure service manager is the management of the critical interfaces that exist between the leisure service organization and various environmental subcomponents. The same could be said about any employee's job. There are a number of critical interfaces that each individual must direct his or her efforts toward to ensure that the organization operates productively. The identification and evaluation of these critical interfaces is known as the "performance appraisal technique of critical incidents." Each job has a select number of critical job requirements. Once these have been determined, the next step is to analyze to what extent an individual organizational member has fulfilled these requirements. For each individual, the manager maintains a record of how the employee handles the critical requirements found in his or her job. There is no attempt in this approach to qualify the results in any way. The record of successes and failures of an individual serves as a basis for interaction between the manager and his or her subordinates.

The strength of this approach to performance appraisal is that it allows the manager to use objective information. The manager can point out specific instances in which an employee dealt with a given situation in a positive or negative manner. It allows the manager to appraise individuals based on actual observed activities rather than personality traits. The weakness of this method is that managers can become overly concerned with recording what people are doing. In a sense, this mechanism can create tension between a manager and the employees because they may perceive his or her record-taking activities as a way of maintaining a file on each of them.

Management by Objectives (MBO)

MBO is a results-oriented performance appraisal system that has evolved from the need to provide clearer and more effective measures of evaluation. It is based on the notion that an employee should be appraised on what he or she does rather than on his or her personality or position in the organization. MBO is based on the concept that managers and their subordinates can determine the outcomes or goals of a given job in relation to the overall goals of an organization. It involves identifying precisely the objectives to be accomplished by a given staff member during a specific period of time. Objectives are usually developed in such a way that they can be measured. The individual employee is then evaluated on his or her ability to achieve mutually agreed on objectives. For example, if an aquatic

supervisor in a municipal park and recreation department wanted to improve the effectiveness of his or her operations, he or she might specifically design an objective that would allow her to increase the number of participants coming to the facility while at the same time stabilizing the cost of operating it. In this case the aquatic director and the manager might fix a specifically targeted increase of participants and stipulate that the cost of operation cannot increase over the previous year. Further, he or she might specifically delineate the step-by-step procedures necessary to achieve this objective. The aquatics supervisor would be appraised on his or her ability to achieve this objective.

The essence of MBO is that individual employees participate in the development of an appraisal program that is tailor-made to their specific job requirements and abilities. It is a mechanism that allows for two-way communication between individuals and managers. In this way, the appraisal system is meaningful to the individual employee and is also tied to the needs of the organization. In addition, it allows an individual to concentrate on what is required of him or her in the future rather than what he or she has done in the past. A person's prior performance—which cannot be changed—is minimized, and the expectations for future performance—which he or she can control—are maximized. The manager using this system changes his or her role from overseeing individuals to that of helping them, enabling them to achieve their individual objectives. Again, the emphasis of MBO is on performance rather than personality.

There are a number of problems in developing an MBO system. It is an extremely time-consuming and costly program to implement initially. It requires a wholesale change in thinking, moving from non-quantifiable appraisal into highly measurable performance indicators. Individual goal setting can also be a misleading activity. All organizations have certain needs and goals, and it is folly to think that individuals can be turned loose without an effective way of controlling their activities. Usually, the goal-setting process in MBO starts from the top down and, therefore, reduces individual initiative in setting objectives.

Managers must be extremely careful not to manipulate individual employees involved in the objective-setting process. It must be a mutually subscribed to activity, which takes a lot of time and requires a manager to shift his or her management style. Another problem is that not all factors in organizations can be measured statistically. Creativity is extremely hard to quantify, as is employee morale. Further, because of the heavy emphasis on statistics, organizations often become more concerned with quantity rather than quality.

In spite of its limitations, the MBO process, in the opinion of the authors, is an effective tool that can be used in the delivery of leisure services. It is a procedure that allows individuals to link their activities with the overall goals of an organization. It provides opportunities for people to have input into the activities of an organization and also be evaluated according to their efforts rather than their personality characteristics.

Conducting Evaluation Interviews

Regardless of the technique used in performance appraisal, the manager and subordinate should sit down and openly discuss the employee's evaluation. Appraisal is an opportunity for the employee to receive feedback and identify factors that can potentially improve performance. Evaluation interviews, if structured properly, can be extremely useful mechanisms to help individuals improve themselves. On the other hand, if improperly conducted, they can serve to create tension and broaden the gap that exists between managers and employees. Strauss and Sayles (1972:512) developed a standardized procedure, which can be used in an evaluation interview. The process is as follows:

1. The superior tells the subordinate the purpose of the interview, and that it is designed to help him or her do a better job.

2. The superior then presents the evaluation, giving the strong points first and then the weak points. (There is no reason why the superior has to show the entire evaluation to the subordinate, nor . . . does he or she have to be 100 percent frank about the subordinate's prospects.)

3. Next the superior asks for general comments on the evaluation. He or she anticipates that the subordinate may show some hostility to negative evaluations and allows him or her to blow off steam.

4. The superior then tries to encourage the subordinate to give his or her own picture of progress, the problems he or she is meeting, and how these can be solved.

5. The interview ends with a discussion of what the subordinate can do by himself or herself to overcome his or her weak points and what the superior can do to help.

The superior tries to accept any criticism or aggression on the part of the subordinate without argument or contradiction. He or she helps the subordinate save face and does not expose his or her unjustified alibis.

Promotions

The advancement of employees from one position to another is a way of rewarding excellence within an organization and recognizing potential for growth. Promotions contribute to the overall morale of individuals by providing examples of opportunities for upward mobility and growth. Generally speaking, all organizations should try to promote individuals within the organization rather than pursue potential candidates from the outside. Obviously, this cannot be adhered to in all cases, but it is a policy that has merit. Rewarding effective employees is a good way to increase organizational morale. Occasionally however, this can create resentment when two employees vie for the same position.

Two factors can be considered in the selection and promotion of an individual. The first is *merit*. Merit is offered when an individual has demonstrated an ability to perform and has proved that he or she has the knowledge, skills, and ability to perform and has proved that he or she is promoted on the basis of merit. The second factor is *seniority*. Seniority involves giving preference for promotion to an individual who has a long service record with the organization. When individuals of equal ability are reviewed for potential advancement, usually the one with longer record of service to an organization will be rewarded. But when

seniority is the prime criterion for promotion, it can work to an organization's disadvantage. It prevents aggressive, young, and talented employees from advancing in the organization beyond a certain level. Thus, the organization may risk losing some of its most talented individuals to other agencies. Using seniority as the sole criterion has the added disadvantage of narrowing the organization's selection process. The senior person may not be the best person for the job. Seniority is used primarily in the promotion of nonprofessional employees, especially in organizations where workers are represented by labor unions.

Compensation

Individuals are motivated on the job by both intrinsic and extrinsic factors. Remuneration in the form of financial incentives can play an important part in the overall productivity of employees. For this to be the case, equitable pay programs must be established and administered. This may involve the structuring of objective wage systems and merit programs. Other forms of remuneration may include employee fringe benefits, such as paid vacations, holidays, health insurance, and recreation services. Fringe benefits are usually thought of as supplementary to an individual's basic wage.

Wages and Salaries

Wages and salaries are used by leisure service organizations to attract high-quality employees in order to achieve stated goals and objectives. A well-thought out wage and salary plan can serve to meet the extrinsic needs of employees and, as such, contribute to employee motivation and job satisfaction. A wage and salary schedule that is updated periodically can allow an organization to remain competitive with other organizations that are vying for the same professional and nonprofessional individuals. The salary and wage schedule may also compensate employees for changes in the cost of living, longevity of service, and outstanding contributions.

Wages are usually paid to nonprofessional employees who are involved in manual, semiskilled work; payment is generally made on a weekly basis and is based on the number of hours an individual has worked during that period of time. A *salary* is usually paid to professional employees who are involved in tasks in which the work is not routine and the work hours are not fixed; salaries are dispersed on a biweekly or monthly basis. The interplay of supply and demand may determine the amount paid in either salaries or wages to a given set of employees. For example, there are fewer skilled carpenters than there are individuals who can perform general laborer tasks. As a result, a carpenter is paid a higher wage than a laborer. Further, salaries and wages can serve as an indication of the relative importance of a job within an organization. The wages and salaries of many organizations will depend on the agreement negotiated between them and the labor unions that represent employees.

To determine what one individual or group of individuals ought to be paid in relation to others in an organization requires an evaluation of the jobs within the organization. Job evaluation is a systematic method of determining the importance of work positions within an organization. Archer (1974) identifies four methods commonly used by organizations to determine how jobs should be compared with each other—job ranking, job classification, factor comparison, and the point system.

1. *Job Ranking.* Job ranking involves identifying each job within an organization and ranking it hierarchically. Simply, this approach allows a manager to rank jobs in order of their relative importance. Wages and salaries are then based on this ranking. In this approach, there is no effort to accommodate comparable positions on the same level within an organization's hierarchy, and thus it has limited potential as a method to be employed in anything but small organizations.

2. *Job Classification.* In this approach, the manager establishes a number of job categories based on the difficulty of a job or its value to the organization. Within each job classification, allowance is made for an individual with advanced skills to be paid more than a person who is just beginning the job. An employee's pay would be determined by the level within the classification in which he or she is placed, depending on his or her skill or length of service to the organization. The value of this approach is that it allows individuals to increase their wage earnings by demonstrating increased knowledge or skill.

3. *Factor Comparison.* This method of job evaluation involves identifying the various factors an individual must possess to successfully undertake a given job. Managers might identify the amount of experience and education, the physical and mental demands involved, and the

amount of responsibility an individual must assume in a certain job. Other factors may be the number of employees a person is responsible for supervising, the amount of money within his or her jurisdiction, and the number of facilities and pieces of equipment he or she must operate. All these factors serve as a basis for comparing the various jobs found in an organization. Once this comparison has been undertaken, a standard wage is established for key jobs that represent different wage levels within the organization. The amount of money paid to each individual will vary depending on his or her relationship to these key positions and the input and output requirements of each position.

4. *Point System.* This approach consists of the establishment of job classifications based on points, which are determined by identifying the relative importance of a job. For example, a job may be broken down by the input requirements (education, experience, etc.) and points assigned to each of these factors. The total number of points for a given job will determine the class in which it is to be placed. Each class is then assigned a certain wage. For example, Class I employees might be paid $10.00 per hour and Class II employees receive $12.50 per hour. This system clearly delineates the inputs required for a job and relates them equitably with other jobs within an organization. The relative worth of all jobs is then linked to the wage system. The system allows jobs from one classification or category to be compared with those of another. Thus, there

is an equitable determination of the importance of each job within an organization. This allows the manager to pay individuals equally for work that requires comparable abilities, skills, and knowledge.

Fringe Benefits

Fringe benefits are used by an organization to help improve employees' psychological and social well-being. They compensate employees above and beyond their normal wage or salary. Although fringe benefits cost the organization money, many individuals perceive them as an organizational ploy to distract the worker from the issue of wages or salary. This is certainly not the case; fringe benefits have long been sought by employee and labor groups and can be thought of as contributing to the overall welfare of employees.

Why do organizations have fringe benefits? First, and perhaps most important, fringe benefits contribute to both the mental and physical health of an organization's employees. By providing an insurance program, for example, an organization can relieve the individual employee of the tension that arises from the concern for personal and family health. As another example, employees who are rested as a result of paid vacations or holidays are more fit psychologically for the work environment. Another important reason for fringe benefits is that organizations can purchase such things as insurance in a very large quantity and thus get it at a much lower price than the employees would have to pay individually. Organizations are always in competition with one another for personnel. It is to their advantage to attract and hold employees. Fringe benefits represent a means of instilling in employees satisfaction with their situation and an inclination to remain with the organization over many years.

There are at least nine different types of fringe benefits:

1. *Paid Vacations.* It is common practice among many organizations to provide full-time employees with a minimum of two weeks paid vacation. The length of a vacation period may be increased in direct relationship to the amount of service an individual has given an organization.

2. *Paid Public Holidays.* There are a number of holidays throughout the year that occur as a result of national legislation. Independence Day in the United States and Dominion Day in Canada are examples of holidays that are legislated. In addition, states and provinces celebrate certain events in their history, and employees are granted time off with pay for these occasions. Certain religious days are also declared as holidays (e.g., Christmas, Good Friday).

3. *Employee Breaks.* Many organizations give their employees short periods of time off during the day, for examples, coffee breaks and lunch periods. There is no reduction in salary or wages.

4. *Sick Leave.* Another fringe benefit that many organizations provided is paid sick leave. Individuals are allotted a specific number of days per year that they can take off for medical reasons.

5. *Reduced and Flexible Worksheet.* Historically, one of the earliest fringe benefits was the reduction of the workweek from 60 to 48 hours. Today the 40-hour week is standard, and some organizations have reduced this still further. An innovation in the hours spent on the job has been the restructuring of the workday from the normal 8:00 a.m. to 5:00 p.m. routine. Many organizations are experimenting with longer workdays and shorter workweeks. Flexible work hours enable individuals to schedule their work patterns to correspond with their lifestyles.

6. *Overtime Payment.* Organizations usually give compensation for work in excess of the regular workday. Individuals are either paid time and a half for overtime or given compensatory time off.

7. *Bonuses.* Bonuses have been given by many profit-making organizations for many years. There are two common types. The first, profit-sharing bonuses, allows employees to share in the profits of the organization. Each employee receives a certain percentage of the profits. The second, stock bonuses, allows individuals to purchase stock at a cost below the current market price. In this way, individual employees can participate in the ownership of the corporation. Government institutions are also giving bonuses. They usually take the form of merit pay, with which an individual is rewarded for exceptional service. If the bonus becomes part of an individual's salary, it is not considered a fringe benefit. But if it is above and beyond his or her wage and does not become part of his or her annual earnings, it is considered a bonus.

8. *Pension and Insurance Plans.* An organization's retirement plan can be considered a fringe benefit, as can health, accident, and life insurance programs. These types of programs can be subsidized either fully or partially by the organization.

9. *Other Benefits.* There are a variety of other fringe benefits that an organization can provide its employees. Among these are recreation and leisure facilities and programs, legal advice and assistance, reduction in the cost of services provided by the organization, payment of educational fees, child care facilities and on-the-job health care, including counseling services.

Disciplinary Action and Grievances

Occasionally, employees' work behaviors violate the rules and harmony of the work place. If corrective measures are not taken, these actions can seriously impact the efficiency and effectiveness of the total organization. According to Culkin and Kirsh (1986: 241) disciplinary action is the process that addresses employee misconduct by administering corrective action and thereby serves to maintain a safe, harmonious and productive working environment.

There are four basic areas in which disciplinary action might be taken:

1. Unsatisfactory job attendance;

2. Unsatisfactory safety practices;

3. Unsatisfactory performance; and

4. Unsatisfactory job behaviors or conduct.

For specific reasons for disciplinary action in the four areas, see Figure 10.4.

In order to address these areas, leisure service organizations need to establish an effective and progressive disciplinary program. The focus of the program should be on early intervention and prevention, not punitive punishment. The idea is to bring the employee back into the fold of acceptable behavior and productivity.

Most individuals will conform to rules and procedures that they believe are reasonable, established in the best interest of the organization and the employee, and are fairly enforced. Thus, at the heart of any disciplinary program should be the following ten guidelines:

1. *Necessary.* Are the rules that are being enforced necessary to the efficiency and effectiveness of the workplace?

2. *Reasonable.* Can every employee abide by every rule, even with different job requirements, abilities, and needs?

3. *Enforceable.* Can the rule be enforced, or is it outside the jurisdiction of the supervisor and the agency?

4. *Communicated.* Have all rules for which infractions can trigger disciplinary action been communicated to the employees through written and oral forms?

5. *Consistent.* Are all supervisors consistent in their interpretation and applications of rules?

Figure 10.4
Reasons for Disciplinary Actions

Unsatisfactory job attendance
—Excessive absences
—Failure to give notice of absence
—Failure to report/remain at work without notice
—Excessive tardiness

Unsatisfactory Safety Practices
—Failure to report an accident
—Failure to maintain security procedures
—Endangering self or others
—Failure to use protective equipment

Unsatisfactory Performance
—Poor quality
—Poor productivity
—Incompetence
—Neglecting work
—Excessive time on assignment
—Waste of supplies or materials
—Improper or careless use of property or equipment
—Unauthorized disclosure of privileged information or materials
—Misuse of position

Unsatisfactory job behaviors or conduct
—Possession, sale, distribution, or use of illegal substances on the job
—Use of computer facilities or equipment for nonbusiness related purposes
—Possession, use, or threaten to use weapons
—Sexual harassment
—Immoral or indecent conduct
—Smoking in nonsmoking area
—Threatening or abusive language or gestures
—Insubordination
—Unauthorized use of telephone
—Unauthorized parking
—Sleeping during work time
—Gambling during work time
—Assault, fighting, or horseplay
—Loafing
—Falsification of records or statements
—Willful violation of rules, regulations or policies
—Unauthorized solicitation
—Conviction of a crime
—Interference with other's work
—Unfit condition for work

6. *Flexible.* Do violations proscribed by rule allow for mitigating circumstances?

7. *Timely Due Process.* When rules are violated, is corrective action taken immediately?

8. *Proof.* What substantial reasons must be present for the supervisor to initiate corrective action?

9. *Penalties.* What is an appropriate penalty for breaking a rule?

10. *Progressive.* Are employees given the chance to reform?

A progressive disciplinary program is sequential in terms of actions that may be taken for each instance of a particular offense. On rare occasions, where the behavior of the employee is illegal or so outside the bounds of ethical conduct as to damage the image of the organization, the immediate disciplinary action that may be taken is either suspension or dismissal. Fortunately, these types of actions on the part of employees are few and far between. Therefore, under normal circumstances, the following order of corrective actions are taken:

1. *Informal counseling.* This would involve the supervisor meeting with the employee to make the employee aware of the breach of conduct and how the action affected the organization, by offering guidance as to the appropriate and desired behavior expected and counseling as to ways that the employee can take corrective action. This should be a short nonconfrontational discussion. An example of this would be when an employee begins to show

up late to work. If the problem persists, then the second step would be a formal oral warning.

2. *Oral warning.* Unlike the informal counseling session, the oral warning is a documented notice that the supervisor has met with the employee and formally notified the employee that his or her actions are unacceptable. A copy of the oral warning is then placed in the employee's personnel file.

3. *Written warning.* This formal document is the third stage of a progressive disciplinary program. A memo or written warning form, which details what the offense is, the attempts that have been made to bring the offense to the notice of the employee (informal counseling and oral warning), the corrective actions asked of the employee and their response, and future penalties that will be imposed if action is not corrective, is placed in the employee's personnel file. Both the supervisor and the employee should sign this document, and the employee should receive a copy of the signed document.

If further offenses occur, the employee may face a combination of penalties, including:

1. Reduction of pay;

2. Demotion; and

3. Dismissal.

As outlined above, disciplinary actions cannot be arbitrary and should follow accepted practices of due process. Following a structured procedure protects both the agency and the employee rights.

Grievances

Although disciplinary action is usually a top-down process, a grievance is a bottom-up procedure that provides a due-process avenue for the employee who feels that he or she has been unfairly treated. Although an employee-initiated process, having a formal grievance procedure helps management in four ways:

1. It helps to fulfill the employer's need for recognition and belonging by giving the person an avenue to have someone "upstairs" listen;

2. It establishes an orderly process to ventilate pent-up emotions which, left unchecked, might be turned into negative behavior in the workplace (e.g,. work stoppage);

3. It reduces abusive supervisory practices; and

4. It is used to evaluate and revise labor contracts during the negotiation process.

Leisure service managers need to understand that even under the best of circumstances, there will sometimes be tension and disagreement in the workplace. Many times, these feelings are expressed as *gripes*, in which the employee is simply letting off steam. Employees do not expect anyone to take griping seriously and change things, its just part of the process of relating with one another. However, when gripes become *complaints*, managers need to take notice. Complaints may be real or

imagined. Either way, they usually express an employee's dissatisfaction over a perceived injustice. In one instance in a midwestern city, a constant complaint about the lack of toilet paper in the employees' restroom eventually led to a work stoppage and intense negotiations between the labor union representing the employees and management. For the employees, the lack of response to their restroom needs came to represent a general feeling of noncaring on behalf of management. This incident points out why even supposedly trivial complaints should not be ignored. Usually if not dealt with, complaints can result in a formal *grievance* being filed. Grievances are formal complaints put in writing, which contain the following:

1. What are the circumstances, situations, events that have caused the dissatisfaction?

• Who was involved?
• Where did the situation occur?
• When did the situation occur?

2. Why have the circumstances, situation, or events constituted a grievance?

• What needs to be rectified as a result of the incident?

3. How should the situation be addressed?

• What specific action(s) does the grievant think should be done about the matter?

Similar to a formal discipline procedure, the grievance process is generally seen as being multistep in nature (See Figure 10.5). To work, this procedure must guarantee employees the right to air their grievances and appeal to successively higher levels of management

Figure 10.5
Formal Grievance Procedure

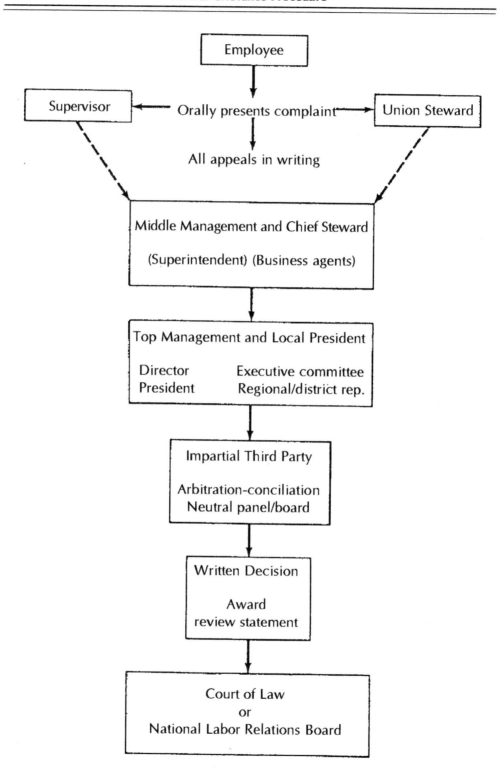

Source: Culkin & Kirsch (1986:264)

without fear of reprisal. When employees view the formal grievance procedure as a sham, leisure service organizations open themselves up to union organizers who offer employees a better balance of power between the employer and the worker.

The steps in a formal grievance procedure are as follows:

1. *Oral presentation to an immediate supervisor or union steward.* Whether union or nonunion, the step is the same. That is, the employee with a complaint talks first to the immediate supervisor. In cases in which a labor union is in place, the employee may go to the union steward, who determines if there is a cause for a grievance (usually a violation of the contract). The union steward may be the person who then presents the complaint to the supervisor. According to Caulkin and Kirsch, (1986:265), 75 percent of grievances are solved at this level.

2. *Written grievance submitted to middle management.* If the supervisor and employee cannot solve the complaint, then a formal grievance is filed at the next level of management. Once the grievance is put in writing, its destiny is out of the hands of the employee, the supervisor, or the union steward. Both management and union officials will determine how far the grievance will be pursued.

3. *Written grievance submitted to top management.* The final step in nonunion leisure organizations is the submission of the grievance to management executives at the top of the organization. If the employee is still unsatisfied with the result, he or she may seek legal redress outside the organization. In those organizations that operate under a union contract, an arbitrator or neutral third party may be called in to try to settle the dispute. Depending on the outcome of this action, the employee may finally seek redress in the legal system. Again, this is a rare occurrence, but can happen, especially in cases in which the employee feels he or she has been legally discriminated against by employment practices.

It should be evident that the key to avoiding grievances is to try to settle complaints before they become formal grievances. In order to do this, leisure service managers must practice the following:

1. *Early detection.* Be sensitive to sudden changes in employee attitudes, enthusiasm, and interest in the job, and in relationships with coworkers.

2. *Understand causes of complaints.* Disciplinary actions, salaries, promotions, and work schedules are all potential sources for complaints. A sensitive manager will know that actions in these areas may cause unpleasant reactions by employees.

3. *Listen and observe.* Understanding doesn't mean agreement. When an employee comes in with a complaint, ask the employee to suggest a solution but don't offer one "off the cuff."

4. *Gather the facts.* Make sure that you know all that is involved in the complaint before trying to take action.

5. *Document.* All discussions and investigations should be recorded. You never know when you will have to defend your actions to others.

6. *Make a decision.* Don't leave a disgruntled employee dangling. Decisions should be made as soon as possible and based on all the facts that have been gathered.

7. *Take action.* If the decision goes against the employee, outline what steps or options are available for the employee to pursue. If the decision is in favor of the employee, try to implement corrective action as soon as possible.

8. *Follow through.* Don't assume the situation has been rectified until you have proof that action has been taken. This means getting back in touch with the employee in a timely manner.

9. *Don't be offended.* Should the employee choose to go up to another level with a grievance, don't take it personally. Some grievances may only be able to be settled at another level. One needs to maintain a positive working relationship with the employee despite the grievance action.

In-service Staff Training and Development

Training is essentially the responsibility of the employee's immediate superior. Although many managers recognize that training within their organization is an important component, little time is invested, proportionately, in this area. For one reason or another, training has taken on an unfavorable image. For a great number of people, training has been thought of as an unpleasant task to organize and a process to be endured.

Leisure service managers recognize that training is a valuable organizational tool. They know that training can increase performance and create opportunities for individual employees' growth. The productive manager will set aside organizational resources that can be invested in the training process. Essentially, organizational inputs in terms of the training process will increase employee output. Training is a process by which organizations can enable their employees to operate more effectively and efficiently. It can and should be viewed as a positive force within an organization, a mechanism that can be beneficial in meeting the individual needs of employees as well as the goals of the organization.

What Is Training?

Training should not be viewed as an end in itself. It is a process that enables an organization to reach certain ends or goals. The formal procedures used in a training program can facilitate employee development. Training is undertaken to produce behavior that will contribute to the attainment of an organization's goals and objectives. Therefore, we define training as a process that organizations use to change employee behavior, which contributes to the overall mission of the organization and the personal and professional growth of the persons involved.

Training helps organizations in many ways. It reduces organizational costs by reducing the amount of time necessary to orient a new employee to the job environment. Training helps an organization deal with its inexperienced employees by providing them with knowledge and skills that enable them to perform at an optimum level within a short period of time. It also reduces the losses that occur because of waste in the production of services; training helps an organization make better use of its resources by minimizing wasted human energy, materials, and supplies. Training programs are generally viewed by employees as supportive in nature. Finally, training helps improve the creation, management, and distribution of activities, facilities, and information offered during training sessions. Therefore, not only do employees benefit from the training process, but so do those who consume services.

Training programs can fail for a number of reasons. Among the more significant is the refusal of managers to accept the responsibility for developing and implementing training activities. The process of training cannot be undertaken on an ad hoc basis. It must be thoroughly planned and well thought out because it represents an investment of an organization's resources. Failure by a manager to develop clear guidelines that are well-integrated with an organization's goals results in chaos.

Determining Training Needs

To determine what training procedures are required, an organization must undergo an analysis of itself and its subcomponents. First, it must determine what it is trying to do. The content of any training program must be linked to the tasks that are to be completed by an organization. There should be an understanding of the relationship that can potentially exist between a given training program and the tasks or assignments within an organization. Next, the organization must determine exactly what skills, knowledge, or attitudes an individual employee must have in the performance of a given job. In other words, both the operations of an organization (i.e., the tasks that are to be performed) and the individuals within the organization must be analyzed. In this way, the organization is able to fuse together the jobs as it has designed them and the individual skills of employees. Determining needs simply involves fitting these two components together.

Once an organization has analyzed its operation and its employee needs, it must determine who within the organization is going to be responsible for developing a training program. Large organizations have formal training departments. In smaller organizations, the training function is the responsibility of various staff members. In either situation, an organization must assign to someone the authority to carry out training activities. Again, many training efforts fail because there is not a well-thought-out plan that provides for training activities.

An important factor in the concept of training involves educating employees to recognize the benefit of training. Individuals learn much more effectively if they are motivated toward goals that they feel are attainable and meaningful. In Chapter Five, we discussed the theoretical concepts involved in motivating people. These concepts obviously apply to the training process. The question centers on how to get individuals moving toward the achievement of training goals and have them recognize the benefits of an organizational training program. The leisure service manager can take a number of positive steps in this area. First, he or she can spell out the goals of the training program by documenting its specific objectives and identifying the procedures necessary to carry them out. Next, the manager can show employees how they can directly benefit from a training program. It might be demonstrated that jobs are made easier, that employees may grow within the system by taking advanced training that will lead to higher-level jobs, that consumers are better served if employees increase their technological competence, and so on. Finally, the manager can demonstrate to individuals that a training program can contribute to their needs and goals. By developing a new skill or improving an existing one, individuals will feel a sense of achievement and, as a result, increase their job satisfaction.

Types of Training

There are three types of training: orientation or preservice training; in-service training; and developmental training.

Orientation or Preservice Training

As mentioned earlier in this chapter, orientation training is directed toward providing a new employee with the necessary knowledge, skills, and attitudes to perform a function with an organization prior to actual placement in the work environment. This may involve instructing a new person in the specific requirements of the job. The training may simulate the actual work experience. A person who will be required to operate a riding lawn mower on the job may be instructed in the operation of a nonrunning mower—a dry run, so to speak.

Orientation training may also involve indoctrination of a new staff member in the philosophy of the organization. A person may be required to discuss the policies of an organization with an appropriate staff member. Discussion may also involve employee benefits, work hours, uniform requirements, payroll distribution, and other related matters. Indoctrination is perhaps one of the most important areas of employee training and also often one of the most neglected.

Finally, orientation usually involves introduction of the new staff member to the work environment and co-workers. Basic to the experience of being a new employee is the element of uncertainty. She or he is faced with unfamiliar surroundings and people. The point of this type of orientation training is to allow the person to become comfortable in the environment. In many cases, this can involve even the trivial elements of a new job (e.g., where to obtain office supplies, how to use the phone). This training takes the edge off the employee's impending uncertainty about his or her new job.

Why is orientation (preservice) training important? Primarily, this type of training represents the employee's first contact with, thus his or her first impression of, the organization. This impression will most likely be a lasting one, and it is to an organization's advantage to make it a favorable one. Certainly, the attitudes that are developed during this initial period of time will be pronounced and will affect, to a certain extent, the long-term success of an individual within an organization. Each new person should be viewed as part of the team of the organization. After all, everyone in an organization was a new staff member at one time. People should be made to feel comfortable and should be encouraged to become active and productive members within the mainstream of the organization. Orientation training facilitates these activities.

In-Service Training

Once a person joins an organization, his or her need for training continues. It cannot be assumed that a person has been given all the information he or she needs during the initial training period, or that he or she has ceased to grow professionally. There are three types of in-service training. The first type revolves around the mandatory training required with new technological advances, the second type concerns the reinforcement and expansion of the initial training, and the third type is developmental training to enable individuals to expand their knowledge and abilities.

Technological advancements in society have a dramatic effect on the delivery of leisure services. Companies with new products and services that change or modify the nature of professional practice are continually approaching leisure service organizations. To keep up with these technological advancements, staff members must receive training. When a new product is introduced, members of an organization must acquire corresponding knowledge and skills to use it effectively. The new advancement may require proficiency in a technical skill (e.g., conversion from hand shears to an electric hedge trimmer), or it may involve the acquisition of new cognitive information (e.g., the use of network analysis in construction projects).

The second type of in-service training is the reinforcement and expansion of the initial training. It is extremely difficult for a manager to cover all the areas necessary in the orientation of a new employee. As a result, training must be spread out over a period of time. It is shortsighted to think that an individual will have the ability to cover and retain, during the orientation period, all the material relating to his or her job. Further, the manager may lack sufficiently large blocks of time to give proper orientation training.

Initial training should be reinforced for two reasons. First, individuals will not retain all the information presented during the initial orientation training; it may be necessary to reiterate some of this information. Second, training is undertaken to elicit certain types of behavior or responses. To ensure that employees exhibit certain kinds of behavior, the manager uses in-service training to reinforce organizational ideals. In other words, employees can stray from the goals of the organization. By continually discussing the direction of the organization in light of the employee's needs, an organization becomes more productive.

Leisure service organizations are dynamic institutions, responding to the changes that occur in society. These changes may be reflected in the adoption of new organizational policies and procedures. In-service training in this area is crucial. As organizations assume new directions, their human resources should be brought in line with the changes. Primarily, this type of training revolves around the discussion of new programs and the mechanisms that are to be used to provide them. For example, one of the more dramatic changes in the provision of public leisure services has been the expansion of sports programs for women. Such a change affects policy within a given leisure organization, necessitating the acquisition of new skills, knowledge, and attitudes on the part of the staff.

Developmental Training

Developmental training is a long-range program that helps individuals realize their potential for growth. It is directed toward improving work performance by providing individuals with an opportunity to expand their personal knowledge, skills, and ability. It emphasizes individual growth by allowing individuals to fully realize as much of their own potential as a given learning environment will allow. Edginton and Eldredge (1975: 12–13) write that developmental training allows people to expand their individual abilities and capacities and helps them satisfy their needs for growth. They state:

Individuals have a need to satisfy intrinsic and extrinsic values. Intrinsic aspects of work relate to the need for personal fulfillment, recognition, self-enhancement, responsibility, and self-esteem. Extrinsic needs include financial remuneration and work conditions. People are motivated by each of these elements, and if they are provided with an opportunity to take advantage of either set, job satisfaction should result. This is especially true when extrinsic needs are met and an individual can move toward satisfying his or her intrinsic needs. Opportunities for individual growth and development obviously go hand in hand with both sets. A developmental training program that allows an individual to realize potential will contribute to the growth and development of one's abilities and capabilities, adding to the satisfaction of intrinsic and extrinsic values.

Concerning the key concepts of a developmental training program, they also write:

Developmental training is a long range training program, whereas orientation and in-service training programs usually satisfy short-term or immediate objectives. Commitment to the development of an individual takes place over an extended period and should be viewed as a cyclic process that is continuous. Short-term objectives are continuously recycled until the broader goals (maximizing human potential) are realized. As this process essentially has no end, developmental goals are achieved rather than the actual ultimate maximization of an individual's potential for growth.

Developmental training rests upon the assumption that management, on the whole, is responsible for providing a noncoercive supportive work atmosphere. This involves giving "active support" to employees. Active support, and its resulting climate, is distinguishable from acceptance or approval, in that it leads to the development of trust, loyalty, and confidence between a manager and his subordinates. This relationship is necessary to allow an individual to expose his or her weaknesses, in order that the growth process can take place.

As mentioned, developmental training must focus on the needs and concerns of each individual. Since no two people are alike, the same training procedures, methods, and techniques cannot be employed to develop any two individuals.

It is important to recognize that external forces do not necessarily modify behavior. An individual's behavior is internally modified. Developmental training only provides an opportunity that may, or may not, facilitate behavior modifications in an individual. As the modification of behavior is an individual matter, the ability of a manager to perceive individual differences and capabilities, and accordingly plan, is essential. Further, when an individual recognizes a need for development, it may be self-induced and self-sustained. Although a program may result from external forces . . . . development can be carried through a person's own efforts informally or formally.

Developmental training focuses on an individual's ability to perform a given a task or assignment, rather than on his or her personality. Too often, employees . . . [are] . . . provided . . . [with] . . . opportunities for growth because their particular personality traits are complementary to those of their superior. Many competent individuals have been summarily sacrificed because a park and recreation director was more interested in promoting a social relationship than a professional one.

As all individuals within an organization have the ability to contribute or detract from organizational goals, developmental training should be universal. Staff and line positions, full time and part-time personnel, can all be given the opportunity to achieve their growth potential. It seems critically important that leisure service organizations focus training efforts on those individuals actually delivering services. The essence of any leisure service organization recreation department is found in the services that it delivers to the public. Hence, the public's impression of a leisure service organization results, in part, from those individuals actually offering services. The majority of these people are part-time people who are fortunate to have orientation training, let alone de-

velopmental training. These individuals, who have a major impact on the success or failure of organizational goals, are forgotten when it comes to training. Although many employees are with an organization only a short period of time, it seems essential to create opportunities that allow for individual growth and hence contribute to the achievement of organizational goals.

Developmental training should . . . [enhance] . . . an individual's current work assignment, rather than focusing primarily upon training a person for promotion. The immediate thrust of a developmental program should be directed toward improvement of current work performance. Directing a person's attention away from his or her present job situation, in may cases, results in a erosion of work performance. It is desirable to continually broaden an individual's horizons, however not at the expense of his or her present work assignment.

Training and the Learning Process

Training activities are directed toward helping individuals change themselves. It is important to remember that only individuals themselves can initiate responsiveness to the learning or training process. Training creates the opportunity for people to change themselves by providing certain types of experiences that facilitate growth. As such, training should be viewed as an individualized process that helps an employee acquire the skills, knowledge, and attitudes necessary for him or her to be more productive on the job.

Learning may be defined as a relatively permanent change in behavior. This infers that there will be an observable change in a person's behavior as he or she gains, acquires, or modifies his or her knowledge, skills, and attitudes. A number of factors determine the amount an individual will learn and the rate at which he or she will learn. The environment is one of these. It consists of a variety of stimuli—sounds, objects, people, and so on. There are two types of stimuli within the environment that affect learning: nominal stimuli and functional stimuli. Nominal stimuli are the many factors scattered within the environment that an individual *could* be experiencing (i.e., has the potential to experience), but because there is a lack of focus on these stimuli, they are not necessarily attended to. In other words, it is happenstance if the individual notices and/or gains information from these stimuli. Functional stimuli are the stimuli that the individual is *in fact* experiencing.

The role of the manager is to structure the environment to ensure that a person focuses on certain stimuli. The training process is used as a method of drawing on an individual's attention to a given set of circumstances within the environment in order to bring about a change in that individual's behavior. The manager provides training to ensure that an individual focuses on a particular set of information (functional stimuli). Learning, then, occurs within the individual during the training process. Productive training results in individual behavior changes that the process has been structured to achieve.

Calvin Otto and Rollin Glaser (1970:), who integrated the concept of learning with the process of training, identify nine principles that can be used as guidelines in the training process. The following is a list of their nine principles, each accompanied by our discussion of it:

1. *People learn by what they do.* This principle suggests that individuals are influenced greatly by their own actions. Therefore, it is extremely important for individuals to learn proper methods and procedures. Once an individual has learned an incorrect method or procedure, he or she is likely to retain this skill as taught, even though it may be in error. It is wrong to assume that a person will learn a correct response simply by the process of discovery. It is not effective and efficient to perpetuate the trial and error philosophy of learning to continue over an extended period of time.

2. *People learn more effectively when they are reinforced immediately.* Training sessions often fail because they do not provide adequate mechanisms for feedback from employees. We all have endured unimaginative training activities that were essentially one-way processes of communication. This is not an effective way of having people learn. There must be opportunities for immediate feedback and reinforcement if effective learning is to take place. We recommend that positive rewards of reinforcement, rather than negative ones of coercion, be used. Training programs should be arranged in such a manner that feedback and immediate reinforcement become integral parts of the training process.

3. *People learn more effectively when correct responses are rewarded frequently.* Not only should reinforcement be immediate, but it should also be frequent. Reinforcement can increase the retention of material.

Feedback should initially be fairly continuous, scaling down to intermittent reinforcement. Eventually, the individual being trained should develop his or her own internally generated reward system for performance. At this point, the manager needs only to act as a resource person and provide reinforcement to the individual occasionally, as indicated by the individual's performance.

4. *Training an individual in a variety of settings will increase the range of situations in which the individual may function with the learned skills.* One of the goals of training is the transfer of knowledge from the training session to the work environment. Training programs that provide an opportunity for an individual to experience a range of different settings and experiences are more successful in terms of equipping an individual to cope professionally in a variety of situations. It is hoped that, by equipping individuals with certain skills in the training program, they will be able to apply this general knowledge to unique problems that might occur in their jobs.

5. *The climate generated by a manager's motivational efforts will affect the acquisition of desired behaviors.* In this book, we have stressed motivation as a key to managerial responsibility by devoting Chapter Five to it. The training environment represents a setting wherein the principles of motivation outlined in Chapter Five can be applied. The critical element to recognize is that the type of motivational techniques used by a man-

ager can have a great impact on a person's ability to learn. For example, individuals can be motivated primarily by reward, in the form of approval from their superiors. This approach can result in a positive motivational climate. On the other hand, individuals can be motivated by threat or punishment. This approach may result in a negative motivational climate. Another way to motivate people includes the creation of a climate that allows for curiosity, stressing the opportunity for individuals to explore their own abilities and environment. It is important for the manager to recognize that both positive and negative forms of motivation will reinforce learning.

6. *Learning with understanding is more permanent and can be transferred more effectively than rote learning.* This suggest that learning has more impact and is more easily retained when an individual understands the broad concepts as opposed to fragmented bits of information. Frequently, maintenance personnel are trained in specific aspects of their job (e.g., tree trimming, grass cutting, etc.) without knowledge of the reason behind their functions or an appreciation or understanding of the relationship of these functions to a department's entire operations. For example, teaching an individual how to prune a tree can be accomplished in two ways. The first procedure, by rote, is to suggest that there are three necessary steps: (1) Make a cut in the limb from the bottom six inches from the trunk of the tree; (2) cut the limb from the top two inches from the first cut; finally, (3)

cut the limb off. On the other hand, it is more appropriate to explain to a maintenance worker the *reason* that the three cuts are made in a tree: to take the weight off the limb to avoid stripping the bark from other parts of the tree. In addition, it might be important to further explain why a park and recreation department would be involved in tree trimming. By explaining the reasons for tree pruning (e.g., to control the shape and beauty of the plant), a maintenance person is in a better position to understand why he is doing what he is doing, and learning should have a greater impact.

7. *Individuals' perceptions of what they are learning will determine how completely and rapidly this information is absorbed.* It is important to remember that the way in which material is received is greatly dependent on individual discrimination. If a person feels that the information being transmitted has little value, he or she will have a more difficult time learning it *unless* the manager is able to change or modify this perception in the presentation of material. It is extremely important to bear this in mind when selecting a strategy for presenting material.

8. *Individuals learn better at their own pace.* The rate of learning varies as people vary. Although in principal this concept is sound, it is difficult to establish self-paced learning programs. Much of the training that takes place in leisure delivery systems is undertaken within a fixed time frame. This is especially true in the training of part-time personnel in activity leadership positions. It might be appropriate to take this factor into consideration when selecting employees for a job and establishing a training program. For example, one way to present the rules and regulations of an organization is to have a person lecture to a group of people, responding to questions as they arise during the discourse. Another way would be to provide individuals with the rules and regulations and a question-and-answer study guide for home use. In this way, individuals can learn the rules at their own pace.

9. *Different types of learning require different training processes.* The basic principle underlying this concept is that the acquisition of certain kinds of knowledge, skills, and attitudes requires different training methods. Learning how to dribble a basketball cannot be accomplished without demonstration by the trainer and active physical participation on the part of the person being trained. Attitudes and values may require an experiential approach to training that allows the person being trained to engage in meaningful discussions and to have an opportunity for values clarification. Again, different types of learning require the manager to select different training processes. But there is a common thread that binds all these approaches together. Trainees must have an opportunity for verbal and physical participation for the experience to be meaningful to them.

Summary

Human resource management is a staff function concerned with the acquisition, working relationships, retention, and development of individuals in the organization. All leisure service organizations, to one extent or another, are involved with personnel functions. There are a number of specific activities in which the leisure service manager may be active, including the development of a personnel plan, the recruitment and hiring of staff, the assignment and promotion of employees, the administration of a compensation package, the appraisal of employee performance, and the training of employees. The development of a personnel plan includes forecasting future employee needs and developing job description for recruitment purposes. Recruiting and hiring involve finding qualified individuals and then screening and interviewing potential candidates. Promoting individuals within an organization is based on two factors: merit and seniority. Merit is based on an employee's work performance, whereas seniority refers to an employee's length of service. Compensation is used to help organizations remain competitive with other systems while rewarding excellent performance. Benefits paid beyond an individual's normal wage are known as fringe benefits. Sick leave, holidays, and vacations are examples of these types of employee benefits. Performance appraisals are used to audit the work of an organization's employees.

In the latter part of this chapter, we discussed the training of employees. Training is directed toward changing employee behavior. Unfortunately, the necessity of training has been neglected by many leisure service delivery managers. There are three types of training. Orientation, or preservice, training is directed toward providing new employees with the skills they need for successful placement in the working environment. In-service training helps employees learn new job-related skills and reinforces previously learned material. Developmental training attempts to help individuals develop their capabilities while supporting the work of the organization.

Human resource management, unlike other organizational functions, is concerned with the management of people within the organization. Its primary function is not to produce services for public consumption, but to ensure that the individuals working within the organization are dealt with fairly and equitably. In turn, it is assumed that satisfied employees will be productive employees and that the services offered to a given constituency will be delivered optimally.

Discussion Questions

1. What is human resource management?

2. Discuss the personnel function of position analysis and classification. What is a civil service system? What are its advantages and disadvantages?

3. Identify and discuss laws pertaining to employment that have an impact on leisure service organizations.

4. Discuss the concept of a Personnel Assessment Center. What do you think are its advantages and disadvantages?

5. Identify and define different types of appraisal techniques.

6. What elements constitute a compensation package for an employee? What is the difference between a wage and a salary employee?

7. Identify four basic areas in which disciplinary action of employees may be required in a leisure service organization.

8. What is a grievance?

9. Identify and discuss different types of staff training.

10. What is the relationship between training and the learning process?

References

Archer, M. (1974). *An introduction to Canadian business.* Toronto: McGraw-Hill Ryerson.

Beeler, C. (1999). *Human resources employment in management of park and recreation agencies.* van der Smissen, Moiseichilc, B., Hartenburg, V. & Twardzik, L., (Eds.) Arlington, VA: NRPA, 489–533.

Busser, J. (1999). *Human resource management in management of park and recreation agencies.* van der Smissen, Moiseichilc, B., Hartenburg, V., and Twardzik, L., (Eds.) Arlington, VA: NRPA, 489–533.

Chruden, H. J., & Sherman, A. W., Jr. (1968). *Personnel management.* Cincinnati, OH: Southwestern.

Culkin, D., & Kirsch, S. (1986). *Managing human resources in recreation, parks, and leisure services.* NY: Macmillan.

Edginton, C. R., & Eldredge, R. E. (1975, August). Developmental training: Methods and procedures for your department—Part 1. *Park Maintenance, 28* 12–13.

McKinney, W., & Tsu-Hong, Y. (1989). Personnel Management in large U.S. park and recreation organizations. *Journal of Park and Recreation Administration, 8,*(2) 1-25.

Otto, C. P., & Glaser, R. O. (1970). *The Management of training* (Reading, MA: Addison-Wesley.

Strauss, G., & Sayles, L. R., (1972). *Personnel: The human problems of management.* Englewood Cliffs, NJ: Prentice-Hall.

Chapter

11

Managing Legal Issues

Photo courtesy of the Battle Creek (MI) Parks and Recreation Department.

Managing risk is an important feature of the work of today's leisure service manager.

Introduction

North Americans pride themselves on being a place that is governed by the rule of law. This means that any group of individuals has access to rights, privileges, power, and authority that allows them to operate within society. This is also the case with leisure service organizations. In many cases, these rights and so on are derived from formal legal codes. Legal considerations fall within the political environmental subsystem. Knowledge of the legal parameters will enable leisure service managers to concentrate their efforts on areas that they know will serve their clients most productively.

In recent years, leisure service managers have had to face yet another consequence of the legal system–that of liability. With the increase of litigation in the country, leisure service organizations have had to pay serious attention to risk management issues. Risk management is a process by which an agency attempts to protect the customer from injury and the organization from financial loss.

This chapter will examine the legal environment that now faces the leisure service manager in society. We will review basic concepts of laws and regulations that govern the delivery of leisure services as well as their ability to function as independent entities. Risk management and aspects of legal liability will also be examined, as well as other safety issues that relate to providing the optimal leisure environments for individuals.

Legal Aspects of Leisure Services

Laws enable leisure service organizations to exist and operate. Generally speaking, the law is thought of as a code that governs or regulates people's behavior and lives. It defines, in the simplest sense, what is good or acceptable and what is bad or unacceptable. Laws enable or ensure people's right to engage in activities that society defines as being acceptable; conversely, laws regulate or prohibit those activities that society maintains are unacceptable. The law is a formal code of behavior that exists to maintain the welfare of the culture. Laws enable individuals and organizations to prioritize the needs of organizations in relation to society as a whole. Thus, by having a uniform set of legal codes, people are able to live together harmoniously, contributing to the general welfare of all society.

Although most societies have judicial and law enforcement systems that control the behavior of individuals and organizations to see that they conform to the law, these mechanisms in and of themselves are not sufficient to make the application of and compliance with the law successful (at least not in North America). Efforts must be made within leisure service organizations to educate their members and those they serve about the importance of the law as it applies to service delivery if they are to operate productively. Thus, we will examine legal matters as they pertain to the delivery of leisure services.

Types of Law

A number of types of law affect leisure service organizations. Each type governs different relationships and has a different source of power. Five more common types of law that affect leisure service organizations are as follows:

1. *Public law* consists of laws that come into existence by government formulation. Public law serves to regulate the relationships that exist between government and individuals at the federal, state or provincial, and local levels.

2. *Civil law* basically governs relationships between individuals and affects such matters as contracts, personal liability, and transfer of property.

3. *Common law* establishes relationships between individuals. This type of law occurs as a result of judicial rulings, which are based on the norms and customs of society.

4. *Statutory law* is derived from legislative bodies. At the federal level, in the United States, senators and representatives establish the law. In Canada, members elected to Parliament make the law. At the state or provincial level, elected individuals are also engaged in establishing statutory law.

5. *Administrative law* is that set of laws established by various public agencies to enable or regulate their work activities. These laws may govern such activities as collecting revenues and dispensing licenses and permits.

There are many other types of law, including admiralty, case, citation, martial, probate, penal, military, and international, to name a few. Each of these types of law is written and enacted for a specific purpose and to govern particular relationships. All the types of law mentioned, and still others, may have an impact on leisure service organizations. But public, civil, common, statutory, and administrative laws are those with which the leisure service manager should be familiar. Although it is important for a manager to have an understanding of various types of laws, an attorney should handle their actual interpretation and application. Most agencies have a lawyer as part of their staff or contract for a lawyer's services when needed.

Powers of Government

Government at the federal, state or provincial, or local level is endowed with certain powers by virtue of its sovereignty. Sovereignty may be viewed as the legitimacy that a government body maintains in its jurisdiction. A government's sovereignty enables it to exercise certain powers. Among these are the powers to levy and collect taxes; provide services for the general welfare of citizens; establish and enforce certain laws, rules, and regulations; and exercise eminent domain.

Federal Authority

The initial authority for providing leisure services in Canada and the United States rests at the federal level of government. Two important documents, the U.S. Constitution and the British North American Act, serve as instruments that provide for the establishment of sovereignty and serve as the legal basis for government. Both documents spell out the relationship of the federal government to its subdivisions. They provide an orderly division of power, functions of government, and responsibilities between the federal government and the state or provincial governments.

The U.S. Constitution establishes a federal system whereby the federal government shares power with state governments. Listed in the Constitution are powers that are delegated to the states and those that are implied or explicitly held by the federal government. The expressed powers listed in the Constitution include the right of the federal government to collect taxes, declare war, and regulate trade. The implied powers exist to enable the federal government to be responsible for the welfare of its citizens in an ever-changing environment. It is under the jurisdiction of implied powers that the federal government is enabled to address itself to the leisure needs of the nation.

The Constitution provides that certain powers are reserved exclusively for state governments and that, in some cases, the federal and state governments may concurrently provide services. It is under this provision of the Constitution that states have the power to address their efforts to the leisure needs of their constituents. These relationships between the federal government and individual states have provided a framework whereby the aims of government and the steps in achieving them are facilitated.

Canada was established as a federal state in 1867 by an act of the British Parliament. However, it wasn't until the Constitution Act of 1982 that Canada developed its own legal document. Previously, legal authority was provided through the British North American Act, 1867. These acts have provided the legal mandate for internal self-government. The Constitution Act, 1982, contains the Canadian Charter of Rights and Freedom and other provisions, such as mechanisms for amending the Constitution of Canada. In 1999, the Constitution Acts from 1867 to 1982 were consolidated. The Act gives the Canadian Parliament the power to "make law for peace, order, and good government." It specifically establishes the relationship that is to exist between the provinces and the federal government. The federal government is assigned general powers that are not assigned exclusively to the provinces. The Canadian legislation comprises a framework of government and provides for the orderly exercise of its power. These Acts provide the legal and moral basis for the federal government to meet the social needs of Canada's citizenry. It is within this general mandate that the leisure needs of Canadians are officially addressed by government. However, unlike a majority of countries whose basic law derives from one document, Canada's basic law comes not only from a set of documents known as Constitution Acts, but also a set of unwritten laws and conventions. This comprises all of the acts passed since 1867, up to and including 1993. As a result, all constitutional documents during that time period have the force of law. This is analogous to laying a foundation (Constitutional Act, 1867) and then building on it and modifying it as the need arises (the successive acts.)

State or Provincial Authority

The federal constitutions of the governments of both the United States and Canada reserve certain powers for state or provincial governments. In the United States, these powers are outlined in the Tenth Amendment of the Constitution, sometimes called the "States Rights Amendment." Specifically, the Amendment states that those powers not residing in the federal government are reserved for the states. As such, state and provincial governments engage in a variety of activities that result in either the provision or the regulation of leisure services. State or provincial governments maintain law and order, regulate business, and operate a number of public service programs, including state and provincial park and recreation systems. Further, state and provincial governments have direct authority over local governments, including municipalities, townships, and counties. The relationship between state or provincial governments and local forms of government is somewhat similar to that which exists between the federal government and its states or provinces; that is, certain activities are reserved by the state or provincial government, and other powers are delegated to the local subdivisions of government.

Local Authority

Local authority is granted to local jurisdictions by the state or province and is usually established in the form of city or county charters. These documents, and the authority they grant, form the basis on which the local agency offers leisure services; these documents also establish the laws and ordinances that regulate the use of these leisure services. Local laws and ordinances also affect profit-making leisure service organizations. For example, local laws may affect hours of operation, location of facilities, and other factors. Local laws or ordinances must not be in conflict with federal, state, or provincial laws. In many states and provinces, the basis for establishing public leisure services is very specific. According to Reynolds and Hormachea (1976), there are five types of legislation that grant legal powers to local subdivisions of government to provide parks and recreation services: enabling acts, special purpose laws, regulatory laws, special districts, and provisions for home rule.

1. *Enabling Acts.* An enabling act is a statutory law that authorizes a local subdivision of government to establish parks and recreation services within its area of jurisdiction. This type of permissive legislation does not necessarily require local subdivisions of government to establish parks and recreation services. Broad enabling legislation usually provides a local subdivision of government with the power to:

. . . Authorize a board or agency or a means of administering, staffing, and financing a recreation service; specify the powers, conditions and restrictions; authorize the organization and conducting of recreation activities and programs; permit two or more public agencies or jurisdictions to operate recreation programs jointly; and authorize the acquisition, ownership, development, and maintenance of recreation areas and facilities, and the accepting of gifts (Reynolds & Hormachea, 1976:42).

2. *Special Purpose Laws.* State governments can also establish special purpose laws, which authorize a specific type of leisure service to be established within a specific locality. For example, special legislation may be enacted to allow an individual community to establish park services with a unique type of governing body. Park and recreation services in Clinton, Iowa, were established through a specific act of the state legislature. This act provided a separate, independent government agency to operate the community's park and recreation services. No other community in the state of Iowa has the specific type of governing arrangement that is found with this jurisdiction.

Another example is the "Niagara Parks Act" in the province of Ontario, which was enacted to preserve the beauty surrounding Niagara Falls. This act, legislated by the provincial parliament in Ontario, has enabled this particular system to acquire and maintain a large number of park areas and to operate a number of unique services, including its own educational institution. The important thing to remember about special laws is that they apply only to the specific locality for which the law is written.

3. *Regulatory Laws.* Regulatory laws are established to inhibit or regulate certain types of behavior for the health, safety, and protection of the public. These state or provincial laws are directed toward ensuring that uniform standards or codes of behavior are maintained in certain types of operations. Perhaps the best example affecting park and recreation agencies is that law which regulates the operation of aquatic facilities. Throughout Canada and the United States, swimming pool managers are required by law to maintain certain levels of sanitation. Other regulatory laws that affect leisure service managers in both public and private agencies are those governing the handling of food.

A number of federal laws affect both public and private leisure service organizations. Perhaps the most significant are those that deal with civil rights. The federal governments in Canada and the United States prohibit discrimination in the provision of services and the employment of individuals based on race, color, or national origin. The Fourteenth Amendment to the U.S. Constitution prohibits racial discrimination and guarantees equal protection of the law to all citizens of the United States. This amendment also infers that the "separate but equal" doctrine is not valid in the provision of leisure services. Another example of federal legislation that may affect public and private leisure organizations is that dealing with employment practices such as child labor laws, minimum wage standards, safety of employees, and others, some of which have already been discussed in Chapter Ten. State authority usually regulates laws governing business activities and those jointly regulated by state and federal government.

Another form of government regulation occurs when federal agencies establish guidelines that must be adhered to when accepting federal funds. For example, state agencies in the United States receiving money from the Land and Water Conservation Fund Act must accept the provisions established by the federal government, specifically those of the Department of the Interior. All other applicable Federal statutory law and federal administrative regulations must also be adhered to by the grantee. This results in a complementary relationship whereby the federal government uses its vast resources to influence the operation of state and local governments. Still another source of governmental regulations is through the rulings made in federal courts.

Many statutory laws, administrative regulations, and court decisions have an effect on the provision of leisure services. Further, there has been a strengthening of the federal government in the past several decades. This has resulted in a lack of clarity in the boundaries between federal and state, or provincial jurisdiction. For example, many states have specific legislation regarding discrimination. It would, however, be difficult to determine what role the federal government has played in the creation and enforcement of this type of law. Obviously, it would be extremely difficult to document all the federal and state or provincial laws that affect the provision of leisure services in either the public or the private sector.

4. *Special Districts.* Numerous states have established provisions that allow for the establishment of special parks and recreation districts. This type of legislation allows for the provision of specific types of governmental services that have independent and autonomous governing boards with taxing powers. Originally, special districts were established to ensure that parks and recreation services had an independent and continuous flow of tax revenues and that those individuals on governing boards, in their role as board members, were dedicated solely to the provision of leisure services. Also, special districts have enabled the establishment of agencies having broader areas of jurisdiction than traditionally defined by a given local subdivision of government.

Thus, park districts and other types of special districts, such as water and sanitation, have allowed for a more effective and efficient way of meeting the needs of a given constituency. Perhaps the two states most dominated by this method of organization of public park and recreation services are Illinois and California. Figure 11.1 shows steps that the Park District Code in the State of Illinois outlines for the establishment of a park district. There are numerous reasons why the park district form of organization has been suggested as an excellent mechanism for the provision of commu-

nity leisure services. On the other hand, many individuals have suggested that establishing a separate, independent unit of government leads to chaos, lack of cooperation, and increased governmental fragmentation. Rodney (1964:82) outlines the pros of the argument.

a. A recreation district provides for fiscal independence and thus better continuity of services.

b. District boards and their professional staff are free from political influences.

c. District boards can devote all their time and energy to recreation and park problems.

d. Greater flexibility in establishing and changing programs is possible under an organizational pattern that is focused on one basic function.

e. District operation makes it easier to interpret needs directly to the people.

f. Unified long-range planning for programs and facilities can be given to a geographical area encompassing all the people, rather than being restricted to artificial political boundaries of a city.

g. Larger districts that encompass a number of urban areas make for economy of operation and less duplication of service.

On the other hand, opponents to district organization stress the points following:

Figure 11.1
Illinois Park District Code

(1) A territory having a population of less than 500,000 legal voters and so lying as to form one connected area, no portion of which lies in an incorporated park district, may be incorporated as a park district.

(2) A petition bearing the signatures of not less than 100 legal voters resident within the limits of the proposed district is filed with the Clerk of the Circuit Court of the county in which the greatest portion of the district lies requesting that the Circuit Judge call an election to submit the proposition of organizing a park district to the voters.

(3) Upon the filing of the petition the Judge is required to set a date, time and place for a hearing upon the subject of the petition.

(4) If the Circuit Judge finds, upon the hearing, that the petition as filed meets the requirements of The Park District Code, and that the boundaries a set forth in the petition are reasonable boundaries, the Circuit Judge is required to order an election. In the order the Circuit Judge also fixes the time and place or places within the proposed district at which an election may be held to determine the question and to elect five commissioners as the governing body of the park district. The order also names the persons to act as election judges.

(5) The form of ballot is specified in the Code and in addition to the names of nominees must contain five blank lines for write-in votes.

(6) The Park District Code requires the signing of an affidavit in all elections, which affidavit shall contain the following: (a) the name and address of the voter, (b) statement that the voter resides within the particular district and (c) statement that the person desiring to vote is a registered voter.

(7) Each person desiring to run for commissioner must file his nominating petition, bearing the signatures of at least 25 qualified voters, with the County Clerk not less than 15 days prior to the date of the election.

(8) The return of the election is made to the Circuit Judge who conducts the canvass of the returns and enters an order determining and declaring the results. If the district lies in two or more counties, a copy of the order must be filed with the County Clerk of each county other than that in which the order was entered. The cost of the election on the proposition to organize a park district is paid by the county or counties in which the district is located.

(9) Within 30 days after the declaration by the court of the result of the election, the five commissioners elected are required to meet and determine by lot the term for which each shall hold office. Two shall serve for six years; two shall serve for four years; and one shall serve for two years, respectively, from the date of the next odd year an election would otherwise be held.

(10) At this meeting of the commissioners, the Board also elects one member as President, and one member as Vice-President, who hold their office for a term of one year. The Board also shall then appoint a secretary and a treasurer, who need not be members of the board, and prescribe their duties and fix their compensation. If the secretary and treasurer are selected from the members of the board, they must serve without compensation. The board may also appoint an attorney, a director of parks, and recreation superintendent, fix their salaries and define their duties. One person may serve as director of parks and recreation.

(11) At the first meeting of the commissioners of a newly formed park district, or as soon as possible thereafter, the board should adopt (a) an ordinance prescribing the rules for the conduct of the business of the park district; (b) an ordinance setting forth the regulations and restrictions for the use of the park system; and eventually (c) a traffic ordinance. Appropriations and Tax Levy Ordinances will also be needed.

(12) Following the adoption of the administrative ordinance, the following committees from the membership of the board may be appointed by the President: (A) Finance; (B) Buildings and Grounds; (C) Police; (D) Recreation; and (E) such other special committees as may be desired, i.e., concessionaires, etc.

a. Establishment of a recreation district only aggravates government problems by adding another overlapping taxing jurisdiction.

b. Independent-district organization fragments government services and creates problems for unified planning.

c. It is more economical to have one governing body provide for all services, rather than have independent boards plan separately for single functions.

d. A multiplicity of small recreation districts can neither plan effectively nor enlarge their services, owing to their limited tax base. (Rodney, 1964:82)

5. *Home Rule.* What is home rule legislation? Enabling legislation sets forth specific guidelines that local subdivisions of government follow in the establishment of their services. Enabling legislation covers such items as the type of government the local subdivision may form (e.g., council manager, strong mayor), how much it may levy in taxes, and what specific types of services it may provide. Home rule legislation is permissive legislation in that it allows a local subdivision of government to determine what specific type of government it would like and how that government is to be arranged internally. It further allows local communities to determine at what rate they are to be taxed.

Why is this important for parks and recreation services? We live in a period of time dominated by one factor: change. Even though much enabling legislation has been written in a general manner, it has not met the specific needs of some communities that have occurred as a result of change. Enabling legislation, for some communities, is restrictive legislation. As government in the United States and Canada has grown, there has been, in general, a need to find mechanisms that allow individual communities to create and group services in ways that are specific to the needs of a particular community. Further, certain communities rely more heavily on their governmental services than others and therefore have need for a broader tax base. In other words, home rule legislation allows the type of governmental structure that best meets the needs of individual communities to be tailor-made.

Eminent Domain

One controversial power that the federal, state, and local governments have that is worth noting here is the right of eminent domain. This right means that government has the power to take property it deems necessary for public use. Eminent domain is based on the notion that all property is subject to the control of the state and is under its sovereign power. The right of eminent domain gives government agencies the right to take the property of an individual if that individual has refused to sell it to the governmental agency for an equitable sum. The process used by government to facilitate this maneuver is known as "condemnation." If an individual refuses to sell his or her property to the government, the government can bring court proceedings to acquire the land.

The use of eminent domain is generally thought to be the last resort to which a public park and recreation agency should turn in order to acquire land. Government agencies may be required to show the necessity of this action. There are some limitations to the use of eminent domain: In certain cases, it is unconstitutional. For example, not all leisure resources are considered within the auspices of eminent domain. As Leighty (1973:90) suggests, public beaches have been regarded as a legitimate resource that can be acquired through the use of eminent domain, but public theaters have not.

Risk and the Legal Environment

Whether large or small, employing a multitude of employees or few, having many facilities or none, all leisure service agencies have one thing in common. They all face potential loss from an unknown risk. Kasier (1986:) defines risk as "a specified contingency or peril," whereas Webster's defines it as "the chance of injury, damage or loss; a hazard." According to Dorfman (1998), pure risk is a loss exposure in which there are only two outcomes: no change in condition or a loss.

Risk management is defined as the process of determining what risks an organization faces, considering ways to deal with those risks, and implementing the decisions (Lai, Chapman, & Steinbock, 1992). Recently, for instance, parts of the northeastern United States and Canada were without electricity for over two weeks due to an ice storm (Nature deals another blow to northwest, 1998). The storm was so severe that people could not remember how long it had been since they had an ice

storm that severe. Without electricity, homes and businesses alike were without heat. Without heat in the buildings, water pipes froze and burst. Additional expenses resulted for building owners, because cleaning and repairs had to be made before buildings could be occupied again. This is an example of a weather-related loss that has both direct and indirect costs to a leisure service agency. The direct cost is the cost of cleaning and repairs that must be completed before the building can be occupied again. The indirect cost is the loss of income to the agency because the agency cannot fulfill its mission while the building is being repaired.

Other natural elements may also cause property damage. Snow, wind, hail, lightning, rain, tornadoes, and floods are examples of acts of nature that may damage property, interrupt the delivery of services the agency provides, and cause a loss of income. A car accidentally running into a building, riots or civil disturbances, vandalism, malicious mischief, and glass breakage may also damage agency property. All of these types of property damage are potential sources of interruption of service delivery for an agency. Leisure service organizations need to protect themselves from loss due to these types of interruptions.

However, loss of property is not the only potential source of loss facing leisure service agencies. Lawsuits pose a second potential source of loss. Lawsuits may be filed against the leisure service agency by customers because of real or imagined acts done by agency employees or volunteers while they were carrying out the agency's mission. Lawsuits may also be filed because a participant perceives that an employee or volunteer didn't do something he or she should have done. Leisure service agencies need to protect themselves in the event a lawsuit occurs as a result of employees' and volunteers' actions in carrying out the agency's mission.

Leisure service agencies also face the potential for loss from lawsuits based on acts that are unrelated to the agency's mission statement, but which are necessary in the day-to-day operation of the agency. These acts include performing building and facilities maintenance, supervising programs, clearing sidewalks, and operating the agency's motor vehicles. Loss may also occur due to an error or an omission of a required act on the part of a staff member or director of the organization, embezzlement and dishonesty of employees, and failure of a contracted service provider to properly maintain the agency's computer or other key pieces of equipment. All of these named events represent the potential for loss to occur to the agency. It is obvious from this list that the leisure service manager needs to pay attention to the potential risks facing the agency and institute a plan to try to minimize an agency from potential losses.

Civil Law and Leisure Services

In our society, people have a fundamental right to be free from the wrongful acts of others. As such, we have laws that serve to regulate the conduct of persons who are in close contact with one another. Filing a lawsuit is one method that may be used to ensure that laws are obeyed. According to Baley and Matthews (1989), lawsuits also serve other purposes. They establish liability and serve to return the victim to the condition he or she was in prior to an incident occurring. They also serve to deter negligent conduct by holding people and organizations accountable for their actions.

In the United States, there are two broad divisions of law: civil and criminal. As mentioned, civil law defines the rights individuals have in protecting themselves and their property from wrongful acts committed by other persons, whereas criminal law has to do with crimes against society. Under both types of law, the person or organization bringing the charge is the plaintiff, and the person accused of wrongdoing is the defendant.

Judgment standards are different between civil and criminal law. In civil lawsuits, the judgment standard is based on the preponderance of evidence. In a criminal trial, the standard is that the defendant must be proven guilty beyond a reasonable doubt (Peterson & Hronek, 1997).

Although the United States has less than six percent of the world's population, it has 51 percent of the world's practicing attorneys. In 1885, there were less than 2,400 combined criminal and civil cases being tried in U.S. District Courts. By 1980, there were 112,734 civil cases alone. That number rose in 1990 to 241,992 civil cases, with an additional 36,886 criminal cases; in 1996, the number of civil cases amounted to 269,132 with 47,889 criminal cases. Likewise, the number of cases appealed has grown from less than 200 combined criminal and civil cases in 1885 to over 51,991 in 1996 (Peterson & Hronek, 1997).

There are at least four reasons for the increase in lawsuits:

1. Fault for injuries has shifted from the participant to the sponsoring agency and staff.

2. Attorneys receive payment according to the contingent fee system. Under this practice, payment

to the attorney is contingent on the plaintiff receiving money from the claim.

3. Insurance companies have liberalized their practice of paying small claims. It is less expensive for insurance companies to pay small claims than to incur large expenses to defend themselves in litigation.

4. A comparative negligence standard has been adopted by the legal profession. We will discuss negligence in greater detail later in this section.

Torts

Civil wrongs are known in the legal profession as torts. According to Peterson and Hronek (1997:3) tort law governs noncriminal relationships among people, businesses, and govern-

mental entities. To consider a given act a tort, three elements must be present:

1. A breach of a legal duty that requires a person to conform to a certain standard to prevent injury or damages

2. Some direct connection between the legal duty and the resulting injury or damage

3. Actual loss or damage to the person or property of another

Figure 11.2 outlines the six general categories of torts in the United States. If the plaintiff wins a tort lawsuit, he or she may receive compensation from the defendant for the wrongs that were done. There are four types of damages that may be awarded by the court in a tort lawsuit (Dolan, 1972).

1. General compensatory damages, to pay for pain, suffering, injury and the upset caused by the wrongdoing

Figure 11.2
Six General Catagories of Torts in the United States

1. **Negligence:** Covers premises, program supervision and facilities supervision. Most common tort claim against leisure service entities.

2. **Strict Liability:** Encompasses animals, product liability, food service and drinking water quality.

3. **Nuisance:** Deals with user injuries, land use, and controls.

4. **Intentional Torts:** Involved with personal wrongs including: Battery (unwanted touching) Assaults (threats), false imprisonment (confinement without arrest) defamation (Lies about one's character) libel (written lies), and slander (spoken lies).

5. **Property:** Revolves around trespass to land (going upon another's land without permission), trespass to Chattels (property other than real estate), and conversation (dealing with property of another without right).

6. **Constitution Torts:** Covers those wrongs based on constitutional laws including: Invasion of privacy (right to be left alone), due process (requirements of a search warrant, summons, etc. related to regulations and economic interests), liberty (right to freedom of movement), property (right to own property or be compensated for governmental taking), speech (right to say what one believes), religion (right to worship as one wishes, equal protection (right of all citizens to be equally treated regardless of race, ethnic origin, gender or age) and civil rights (rights guaranteed by constitution and other laws.

2. Special damages, to reimburse the plaintiff for financial loss from medical expenses and lost earnings

3. Punitive damages intended to punish the wrongdoer—these are imposed when malice or maliciousness is involved

4. Nominal damages, which are awarded when the injury is only slight and the responsibility of the party at fault must be recognized

Governmental Immunity

In the United States, the legal system is based on English common law. One privilege granted to English kings was sovereign immunity from lawsuits. The concept was carried over to government at all levels in this country. Early in our nation's history, however, it was recognized that a court was needed to hear tort claims against governmental entities. According to Peterson and Hronek (1997) the Court of Claims was then established and remained until it was deemed inadequate due to increased caseload. Cases formerly tried by the Court of Claims were referred to the state court in the state where an alleged wrong occurred, under the Federal Tort Claims Act passed by Congress in 1946. This act made the United States liable for torts filed because of the negligence, wrongful acts, or omissions of federal employees or agencies, with some exceptions. One exception does not allow for punitive damages; another specifies that the suit must be filed within two years; and another provides that the government will not be liable for actions done with due care while executing a statute or regulation, even though the statute or regulation may be invalid.

Individual states have implemented state statutes that contain essentially the same concepts as the Federal Tort Claims Act, and in all of the states, consent has been granted to sue state and local agencies under tort. However, at the same time, most states also have laws that limit the amount of claims or eliminate claims in certain categories of administration, usually referred to as discretionary functions. For example, the government is usually immune from suits regarding personnel actions, budget distribution, decisions made at the planning and policy levels, legislative actions, and administrative processes.

Doctrine of Respondeat Superior

Private corporations, such as racquetball or tennis clubs, or agencies, such as the YMCA or Boy Scouts, are not governmental in nature and are not offered immunity from liability. However, because of their "public service" status, they are offered some limited immunity from liability (Peterson & Hronek, 1997).

This limited liability comes in the form of protecting employees and volunteers of public entities, as well as private corporations, from liability as long as they are performing within the scope of their assigned responsibilities. This doctrine of *respondeat superior*, or "let the master answer," is an important concept. The result is that the corporation, not the individual board or commissioner member, coach, or leader, may be liable for the negligent acts of its administrators, trustees, and board officers in the carrying out of a board policy or direction. The employee would face liability, however, if he or she engaged in an illegal act, or in the carrying out of a policy or direction, did not follow the rules and generally accepted standards of care. Thus, it is important that all members of the leisure service organization understand their duties and responsibilities and act within the limits imposed by their job descriptions and prescribed duties. As long as they do this, they will enjoy certain protection under the law.

Contract Liability

As more and more leisure service agencies contract for services, it is important for the leisure service manager to understand the elements of contract liability. Many organizations, especially private ones, enter into cooperative arrangements that are mutually beneficial. This exchange, known as a "transaction" or "contract," involves the transfer of goods and services from one party to another. Contracts permit organizations to enter into agreements in order to provide or receive certain products or services. In the case of the latter, organizations contract for services that they are not equipped to provide for themselves for reasons of practicality, flexibility, or specialization.

Contracts are created by mutual agreement between two or more parties and are enforceable by law. For a contract to exist, there must be mutual agreement between the parties. The contract must be between two parties that are capable of binding themselves to such an agreement. Contracts must also stipulate the consideration (i.e., money) that is to be exchanged between parties. Lastly, a contract must conform to other laws in order to be legal. In other words, an organization cannot sign a legal contract to do something illegal. If an organization cannot meet its contractual obligations, state or provincial laws governing contract performance may be brought into effect. Contracts that are subject to interpretation and disputes are settled in the courts.

Why is contract law important? Contract law covers the entire field of business law. Therefore, it affects sales, property, partnerships, and other factors that affect private and public leisure service organizations. Some general guidelines relating to the legality of contracts are the following:

1. Illegal contracts are not enforceable;

2. Contracts that give one party an unfair advantage over another are not enforceable;

3. Incompetent individuals are not responsible for obligations stemming from their involvement in contractual agreements;

4. In general, contracts may be verbal or written, but certain transactions must be made in writing (e.g., the selling of real estate);

5. Once one party has accepted the offer of another, the contract becomes legal;

6. Most contracts must guarantee that both parties receive some consideration; and

7. When an organization violates an agreement, the matter may be taken to court and damages may be awarded the wronged party.

Generally speaking, individuals within leisure service organizations are not liable as individuals (in terms of their personal assets) for any damages resulting from a breach of contract. It is important to remember that illegal contracts are not binding contracts. So if a representative of a leisure service organization has made a contract outside the jurisdictional limitations of the organization, the contract is void. On the other hand, if the disputed contract is within the authority of the organization and resulted simply as an exercise of poor judgment, the contract can be enforced. An individual in an organization or corporation who acts as an agent of the organization or corporation is not personally liable for disputed contracts; that is, an individual is viewed as an agent of the organization, and the organization, as the principal, is responsible for the actions of its agents.

Some of the more common contracts entered into by leisure service organizations include those made for the construction of facilities: operation of special facilities, such as golf courses, restaurants, and amusement parks; joint use of facilities; and special services, such as custodial and janitorial services.

Contracts should be executed with the help of an attorney. However, Peterson and Hronek, (1997:3) list four points that the leisure service manager should be aware of:

1. *Authorization.* Check with legal counsel to ascertain statutory authorization for the contract contemplated.

2. *Contract Terms.* Prior to entering into contract negotiations, the leisure service manager should compile a list of nonnegotiable contract requirements. These requirements, along with compensation, contract time periods, and contract parties should be clearly identified. Contracts that are ambiguous and lack details are invitations to a breach and litigation. The leisure service manager should be guided by the rule that the contract must be of sufficient detail to guarantee the level of service contemplated within a reasonable time period and for adequate consideration. Unrealistic terms and criteria lead to problems. Incorporate all terms into the document.

3. *Bidding.* Public agencies generally are required to seek bids on certain types of contracts or on contracts above certain dollar values. This procedure is governed by state statute as well as local procedures and ordinances. A good leisure service manager should determine bid requirements and specifications prior to negotiating any contract.

Private organizations will also find that bidding reduces costs. Frequently, commercial recreation agencies, as a matter of corporate policy, seek bids on selected purchases. These procedures may not be as elaborate as the public bid process.

4. *Contract Review.* A leisure service manager should develop policies and procedures for reviewing contracts with legal counsel. The key to successful contract reviews is in establishing and adhering to policy and procedure.

As mentioned before, contracts can be very complex, and the advice of legal counsel should be part of contract development. Attorneys should not make management and budget-related decisions on contracts, but should assist the manager in preparing a contract document that is unambiguous and meets the goals sought by the parties.

Recreation Land Use Statutes

Before turning our attention to specific elements of liability, one more area needs to be discussed—that of land use liability statutes. All states, with the exception of Alaska and North Carolina, have enacted Recreation Land Use Liability Statutes. North Carolina has laws that limit landowner liability only in regard to their State Trails System, and Alaska has legislation pending. In the other 48 states, recreation use liability statues generally protect landowners, both public and private, from suit by non-fee-paying recreationists who use their property. As a general rule, the claimant must prove at least gross negligence in order to establish a basis for suit under the Recreation Use Liability Statutes. One level of negligence above gross negligence is called "Willful and Wanton Negligence."

Unlike mere carelessness constituting negligence, willful or wanton misconduct is more outrageous behavior, demonstrating an utter disregard for the physical well-being of others. Willful and Wanton Negligence has a strong element of being an intentional action by a defendant that is so obvious that he or she must be aware of it. It is usually accompanied by conscious indifference to the consequences, amounting almost to willingness. An example would be to string a steel rope barrier four feet high across a pathway in an area open to motorcycle enthusiasts. This type of barrier is an invitation to disaster, especially if the landowner did not forewarn invitees about the area.

Under a recreation land use liability statute, the landowner owes no duty to care for recreational users or to guard or warn against known or discoverable hazards on the premises. The protection from suit found under this statute is lost when a fee is charged for the use of the premises or, as previously mentioned, the landowner is guilty of either gross or willful and wanton misconduct.

It is important for leisure service managers who have outdoor areas under their jurisdiction to carefully analyze their state's Recreation Land Use Statutes. At this time, most of the Recreation Use Liability Statutes apply to all public lands (local, county, state, and federal) within a state.

Elements of Negligence

As indicated in the previous section, the primary basis for most lawsuits is negligence; that is, the lack of due diligence or care by the leisure service agency or its employees. Black's Law Dictionary defines negligence as "the omission to do something which a reasonable man guided by those ordinary considerations . . . would do, or the doing of something which a reasonable and prudent man would not do (1978: 930).

Hronek and Spengler cite one of the earliest examples of a negligence tort in their book, *Legal Liability in Recreation and Sports* (1997) as occurring in 13th century England. The case goes like this:

"A very angry husband caught another man with his wife and was chasing the man down the street with an axe. The angry husband threw the axe at the man, missed, and struck a bystander. The bystander sued the man and was awarded a judgment from the court because of the injury. The husband certainly did not intend to injure the bystander, but his negligent act in fact caused the injury." (15)

Whether negligence exists depends on the particular circumstances related to each case. The laws and court decisions are very complex, so few generalities can be applied. However, in all cases where negligence is alleged to have occurred, the same four elements must be proved:

1. It must be proved that the defendant has a legal duty of care, that is, to be legally responsible to the plaintiff;

2. The plaintiff must prove there was either a failure to perform a required task or a breach of duty;

3. There must be some direct connection between the damages and the actions or lack of actions by the defendant. Simply stated, the plaintiff must prove that the breach of duty was the cause of the injury. This is commonly called "proximate cause;" and

4. A plaintiff must prove that he or she suffered damages, e.g., a physical injury, mental anguish, or financial loss.

The concept of negligence may presuppose there is some standard of conduct or behavior out there by which negligent behavior can be judged. Yet no fixed rules govern negligence—only those set by society, which establishes some kind of standard expected for that product or activity. For instance, since 1981 the Consumer Product Safety Commission (CPSC) has published recommended guidelines for playground safety in public venues. Although no leisure service agency can guarantee that a child will not get hurt falling from equipment, it can be held liable if it allows an unreasonable risk to occur through the lack of proper maintenance, surfacing, and design. Thus, if the playground is found not to conform to the accepted guidelines as designated by CPSC, it may be assumed that the agency, which has a legal duty to provide a safe playground, is negligent in that duty.

The courts determine the standard of care required of recreation and sport activities. "The standard of care is usually based upon the 'normal or established practice' common throughout a state or nation under similar circumstances," according to Hronek and Spengler (1997:17). Thus in the playground example, although CPSC guidelines are voluntary, they do serve as the basis for the standard of care in providing safe playgrounds. This is one reason why the National Recreation and Park Association has sponsored the National Playground Safety Institute to certify playground safety inspectors.

Another aspect of legal duty has to do with the doctrine of unforeseeable consequences. Although a serious accident or property loss may have occurred with strong elements of negligence, it may not have been foreseeable in the specific circumstances or situation. There are many interpretations of and opinions on what is foreseeable and what is not foreseeable. The ability of a person to foresee a danger depends on the individual's training and experience. "Foreseeability" is the ability to see or know in advance what is a reasonable anticipation that harm or injury may result because of certain acts or omissions—"as a means that the wrongdoer is not responsible for consequences which are merely possible, but is responsible only for consequences which are probable according to ordinary and usual experience" (Black's Law Dictionary, 1978, 524). In other words, the courts don't demand that the leisure service manager possess "mind-reading" skill; but they do expect reasonable anticipation of risk and good common sense. Thus, if the manager allows a playground to fall into disrepair, it is foreseeable that an injury to a child may occur.

Whether a legal duty exists is a question of law to be determined by the court. Once the court has established the duty, it is the jury's responsibility to determine whether the defendant conformed to a standard of care of reasonable prudence and foresight sufficient to protect the plaintiff against unreasonable risk.

Once a standard of care is established, the second element of negligence comes into play—that of failure to conform to the duty. Negligent conduct may occur because a person did something that was dangerous, or the same negligent conduct could occur because a person failed to do something. Implied in this is the fact that the defendant was somehow involved in the activity that resulted in the loss or injury. There are three ways this involvement is viewed as a breach of duty:

1. *Nonfeasance.* The defendant did not perform some act that ought to be performed, omitted performing a required duty at all, or totally neglected his or her duty.

2. *Misfeasance.* Misfeasance is improper performance of some act, which a person may lawfully do.

3. *Malfeasance.* Evil doing or ill conduct occurred. This is the commission of some act which is positively unlawful.

Returning to the playground case, nonfeasance may be the improper maintenance of the playground environment. Misfeasance may be installing the playground equipment improperly. Malfeasance may be deliberately failing to tighten the bolts that hold the playground equipment together.

In order to prove negligence, the plaintiff must prove that there was a relationship between the plaintiff's injury or damage and the act or omission by the defendant. Again, using the playground as an example, when parents make a claim of injury on behalf of their child as a result of an injury on a playground, the plaintiff's parents must prove that the incident occurred on the defendant's playground as the result of the defendant's negligence. This infers a causal factor. In other words, the plaintiff must show that the defendant, by doing or not doing something, was the proximate cause of the injury or damage. In a playground case, the parents may charge that the failure to keep the surfacing material at the proper depth as outlined in the CPSC guidelines, was the direct cause of the severity of their child's injury.

Proximate cause is not a simple element, rather, it is a very complex problem made up of a number of different problems that are not distinguished clearly by the law (Peterson & Hronek,

1997). A defendant can always point to someone or something else as the actual cause of the incident. It is up to the plaintiff to make the connection between the defendant and the cause.

The final element in negligence that must be proven is that there was an actual loss or damage to the plaintiff. There can be no negligence without injury to person or property. The word "damage" refers to loss, injury, or deterioration caused by negligence. Damage can involve physical or mental harm or damage to property. A plaintiff may be awarded three types of damages:

1. Compensatory damages are awarded to a person as compensation, indemnity, or restitution for harm sustained.

2. Punitive damages are awarded to a person to punish the other litigants because of their outrageous conduct.

3. Consequential damages are awarded a person for suffering because of the act of another event, even though the act was not directed toward the first person specifically and the damages did not occur immediately.

Defenses in Negligence

When negligence is alleged, there are several defenses that can be employed by leisure service agencies (see Figure 11.3). A brief description of these defenses follows.

Assumption of Risk

A person may not recover damages for an injury received when he or she voluntarily subjected himself or herself to a known and appreciated danger. This assumption of risk is predicated on the following requirements: (1) The plaintiff has knowledge that the activity

Figure 11.3
Defenses Against Negligence

- Assumption of Risk
- Comparative Negligence
- Contributory Negligence
- Governmental Immunity
- Failure of Proof
- Notice of Claim
- Statute of Limitations
- Release or Waiver or Agreement to Participate

engaged in has dangerous elements, (2) the plaintiff appreciates the nature and extent of the danger, and (3) the plaintiff subjects himself or herself to the danger. Participants in recreation and sports cannot assume risk for something when they do not know the inherent danger of the activity, do not comprehend the risk in relation to their physical and mental capabilities, or do not appreciate the magnitude of possible injury.

Participants only assume the risk for aspects inherent in the activity. They may properly assume that it is the duty of the sponsoring agency to provide appropriate facilities, equipment, instruction, and supervision.

It should be noted that young children, especially those under the age of seven, do not appreciate the nature and extent of dangerous situations. Therefore, an "assumption of risk" defense is not an option when the plaintiff is a young child.

Comparative Negligence

This defense places on either the defendant or the plaintiff the entire burden of the loss for which both the defendant and plaintiff are, in fact, responsible to some degree (Comparative Negligence). There are four different ways that states approach the concept of comparative negligence (see Figure 11.4):

1. *Pure Comparative Negligence,* which allows the plaintiff to sue regardless of the level of his or her own contribution to the injury or damage, unless the plaintiff is 100 percent at fault. For example, if a plaintiff was deemed 80 percent at fault and the defendant was 20 percent at fault and the plaintiff's damages were $10,000, the plaintiff would receive $2,000.

2. *Fifty Percent (50%) Rule,* which bars recovery if the plaintiff's negligence is greater than that of the defendant. Thus, in the above case, the plaintiff would not be able to recover even $2,000.

3. *Forty-Nine Percent (49%) Rule,* which bars recovery unless the plaintiff's negligence is less than that of the defendant. In this case, if the plaintiff and defendant were each 50 percent at fault, the plaintiff could not recover.

4. *Slight/Gross Rule,* which bars recovery unless the plaintiff's negligence was slight and the defendant's negligence was gross by comparison.

Contributory Negligence

This defense has basically been replaced by the concept of comparative negligence; however, it still helps to outline a negligence defense. This defense is used when a plaintiff contributes to his or her injury or damage to such an extent that the plaintiff breached an expected standard of conduct. Only in Alabama, Maryland, North Carolina, and Virginia would this form of defense be effective, as was shown in Figure 11.4.

Failure of Proof

This defense means that it is incumbent upon the plaintiff to prove all four elements of negligence (duty, breach of duty, proximate cause, and damages) in order for negligence to be found. Failure to prove will result in dismissal in the prepleading stage of litigation.

Figure 11.4
Comparative Negligence Laws by State

States with Pure Comparative Negligence: Alaska, Arizona, California, Florida, Illinois, Lousiana, Iowa, Kentucky, Michigan, Missouri, Mississippi, New Mexico, New York, Rhode Island, Washinton, and Puerto Rico.

States with Fifty Percent (50%) Rule: Connecticut, Delaware, Hawaii, Indiana, Massachusetts, Minnesota, Montana, Nevada, New Hampshire, New Jersey, Ohio, Oklahoma, Oregon, Pennsylvania, Texas, Vermont, Wisconsin, and the Virgin Islands.

States with Forty-Nine (49%) Rule: Arkansas, Colorado, Georgia, Idaho, Kansas, Maine, North Dakota, Utah, West Virginia, and Wyoming.

States with Slight-Gross Rule: Nebraska, South Dakota, and Tennessee.

States without Comparative Negligence Principles: (Note: These states have some judicial adoption of the principle, but the principle is interpreted on a case by case basis). Alabama, Maryland, North Carolina, South Carolina and Virginia.

Notice of Claim

These statutes and ordinances require an injured or damaged person to file a notice of claim within a certain time period, usually 30 to 120 days. The notice of claim allows the agency to conduct an investigation into the validity of each claim and settle legitimate claims without litigation. Some courts hold that failure to provide a notice is a valid reason for denying the opportunity to file a legal claim against governmental agencies.

It should be noted that a minor normally has until the time he or she reaches majority to file a claim. Likewise, a person who is incapacitated due to illness or some other legitimate reason can rightfully wait to file a claim until he or she gains the mental or physical capability to proceed with the filing.

Statute of Limitation

Statutes of limitations vary from state to state. This is the time period allowed between the time of the alleged negligent incident and when a suit must be filed. In most simple claims, this time period is two to three years; however, there are variations in time periods by state. Also, certain categories of claims, such as property damage, have longer statutes of limitations than do personal injuries, wrongful death, or libel.

Waivers, Releases, and Agreements to Participate

These are not normally considered a part of tort doctrine; rather they are documents that tend to justify, excuse, or clear the defendant from fault or guilt arising from the incident. These documents must be written to be effective. Waivers and releases are contracts. As with other defenses, the court's response to waivers and releases has varied with individual judges and jurisdictions.

It should be noted that waivers and releases have a higher likelihood of being validated by the courts if they are specific and are related to high-risk activities such as whitewater rafting, mountain climbing, spelunking, and so on. Thus, the leisure service manager should use these instruments with adult participants to help establish an "assumption of risk" defense if needed.

Because minors are unable to contract, the use of waivers and releases to wave the rights to use would be considered improper. The best legal instrument to limit the liability for minors is therefore the "Agreement to Participate." This document must be specifically worded to cover the risks and dangers involved in the activity in detail. It must include all the rules of conduct required for safety and organization purposes so that the minors and their parents or guardians understand what is expected of them. The Agreement to Participate documents the fact that the legal guardians understand the dangers involved and have allowed their minor children to participate in the activity. Further, it is an agreement to inform their children about the rules and safety aspects of the activity.

Risk Management

It should be clear from the discussion concerning negligence that the best defense is one that is preventive in nature. That is, the leisure service manager needs to be proactive in understanding what conditions or situations can constitute a risk, and then take steps to minimize those risks. Thus, every leisure service agency should have a risk management plan in place. This section will discuss a six-step process to employ in developing a risk management plan for a leisure service agency (see Figure 11.5).

Step 1—Identification of Potential Sources of Risk

Because each leisure service agency is unique, potential sources of risk vary by agency. For example, a nonprofit museum may have little risk exposure from its program in contrast to an outdoor adventure program for youth run by the local parks and recreation department. Whatever the agency, however, the need to identify each potential risk

that the agency might face is crucial. It is not possible to plan or manage risks prior to a loss occurring unless they have been identified. The leisure service manager should be aware of three main categories of risk that the agency faces: property damage, public liability, and business operations.

Property Damage

As previously mentioned, natural elements such as snow, wind, hail, lightning, rain, tornadoes, and floods may damage property, interrupt the agency's delivery of services, and cause a loss of income to the agency. In addition to the damage caused by the elements, there are additional costs for cleaning that must be completed before the building can be occupied again.

A car accidentally running into a building, riots or civil disturbances, van-

Figure 11.5
Six-Step Process to Developing a Risk Management Plan

Step 1: Identify potential sources of risk

Step 2: Creation and adoption of philosophical statements

Step 3: Risk Analysis and evaluation

Step 4: Risk control and reduction of loss exposure

Step 5: Plan implementation

Step 6: Periodic plan review

dalism, malicious mischief, and glass breakage may also damage agency property. All of these acts damage property and are potential sources of interruption of service delivery for a leisure service agency.

Public Liability

As outlined in the previous section, lawsuits pose a second potential source of loss. Lawsuits may be filed by agency customers against agency employees or volunteers, including board members. Leisure service agencies need to protect themselves in the event a lawsuit occurs as a result of employees' and volunteers' actions in carrying out the agency's mission statement.

Leisure service agencies are also faced with the potential for loss from lawsuits based on acts that are unrelated to the agency's mission statement, but which are necessary in the day-to-day operation of the agency. These acts include performing building and facility maintenance, clearing sidewalks and pathways, and operating the agency's motor vehicles.

Business Operations

Loss may occur due to an error or an omission of a required act on the part of an officer or director of the organization, or due to embezzlement and dishonest employees. Loss may also occur because a contracted service provider fails to perform according to the contract, as in the example mentioned previously of the failure to properly maintain an agency's computer system, resulting in equipment failure and the loss of important information. Indirectly, the agency may lose income because it cannot fulfill its mission while the problem that caused the interruption of business operations is being remedied. All of these named events represent potential sources of loss to the agency. Therefore, leisure service agencies have a need to protect themselves by identifying risks in these categories.

A designated agency risk manager can help in this identification process. The risk manager may begin the process of risk identification by inviting professionals from outside the agency and employees inside the agency to join in the project. Outside individuals to consider include the agency's legal counsel, the insurance broker, the director of a similar organization, a building safety engineer, and a risk manager from a local business or government office. Inside the organization, the manager may begin by setting aside time to educate all employees, from the top of the organization down, about risk management. This helps to foster a culture that supports risk management throughout the organization. Education may be done in a regular staff meeting or in a special meeting. The goal is to create awareness about the importance of risk management and make it everyone's responsibility. All employees should be asked to identify risks inherent in the nature of the work they perform. Each list of identified risks is then submitted to the risk manager for inclusion in the comprehensive plan.

One of the items that the agency's insurance broker may be able to provide is a preprinted checklist to audit the agency's risk exposure. There are various checklists available. By comparing the checklist with the list that has been compiled by agency personnel, the risk manager should be able to identify all foreseeable risk areas of the agency.

Step 2—Creation and Adoption of Philosophical Statements

The second step in the process is to develop philosophical statements that are in keeping with the agency's mission and that provide the framework for the risk management plan. For example, an agency that serves teenage youth by providing adventure activities to them may have in its mission statement a sentence that reads: "Our purpose is to facilitate mental development in teenage boys through their participation in adventure programs." A philosophical statement that incorporates risk management might read: *"The (name of the agency) believes in risk management. Our aim is to use qualified leaders and reasonable care to provide the highest quality of adventure program services."*

From the above example, it can be seen that philosophical statements do not provide minute detail. Their purpose, along with the agency's mission statement, is to provide the framework on which the risk management plan is built. Philosophical statements should state, in general terms, the agency's belief in developing a risk management program. They should identify the importance of risk management to the agency. They should also state who in the agency is responsible for risk management, namely, the director, the controller, or the risk management officer. The statements should also describe the limits of authority the person in that position has.

The statements should list the acceptable approaches to be used to manage risk. The statements should also note the extent to which the agency is willing to assume financial responsibility for certain risks and when it is appropriate to transfer the risks by insurance. For example, with its building insurance, the philosophical statements may state that a $500 deductible clause is acceptable. This means that the agency would be responsible for the first $500 of expenses should any damage occur to the building.

Last, the statements should also include the agency's program scope and the required credentials for agency personnel. For example, the philosophical statements may state that insurance coverage is required for all adventure activities and that only certified instructors will conduct all such activities.

Without a guide, it can be a difficult task to create philosophical statements for an agency. Peterson and Hronek (1992) indicate that a place to start is with the agency's existing ordinances, charters, master plans, and administrative manuals. A review of these documents may show that they are out of date for the agency; however, parts of the statements or phrases they contain may still be valid. The appropriate phrases may be copied or combined to create new statements. Peterson and Hronek (1997) suggest that "action words such as aim, purpose, qualified leaders, services, commitment, and reasonable care" be used to convey the message. Figure 11.6 is an example of a risk management philosophy that includes the elements discussed in the preceding paragraphs.

The proposed philosophical statements should receive approval from the agency's board before work is started on the detailed risk management plan. Approval by the agency's board or city council ensures their support of both the process and the plan. Successful lawsuits against volunteers, directors, and officers of leisure service agencies are rare in tort liability cases (Roha, 1994). As mentioned earlier, individual board members and the agency's manager or administrator have immunity from prosecution for acting within the scope of their authority.

Creating statements based on the agency's mission statement is more likely to result in an agency continuing to fulfill its mission in the event of loss. An example is a Boys & Girls Club, which

Figure 11.6
Sample Risk Management Philosophy

It is the basic purpose of the (agency name) to establish, improve, manage, and finance (purpose). We are committed to a philosophy that will provide these services at the highest level possible. We pledge our support to using only qualified and trained leaders in accord with the best and most reasonable standard of care possible. To that end, we endorse the establishment and maintenance of an extensive program to manage risk safety within the organization.

Source: Peterson and Hronek (1992) *Risk management for park, recreation and leisure services,* 33.

provides services to disadvantaged youth in an inner city. Often those youth in the greatest need cannot afford even a small membership fee. In addition, the fee itself does not cover the actual expenses incurred by the agency in servicing the youth. In those situations where youth cannot pay, there is no difference in the level of service provided. Services are not denied. This position represents a programmatic risk to the agency, but it is one the board of directors has chosen to accept.

Step 3—Risk Analysis and Evaluation

Once the risks are identified and the philosophy of risk management is adopted, the next step is to evaluate the extent of the loss exposure. Leisure service agencies need to keep in mind

that risk evaluation extends beyond the financial costs of a harmful act. Agencies stand to lose public goodwill and volunteer resources if they cause a serious accident. Whether or not a leisure service agency is ultimately held liable for a harmful act, the public's perception of an agency's having caused harm detracts from the agency's primary mission. Based on the philosophy adopted by its board, each agency has its own set of risks and level of risk aversion. Each agency's risk evaluation process is thus individually shaped by that agency's unique set of risks and level of risk aversion.

Identifying and evaluating potential sources of risk is an ongoing process due to the rapidly changing legal, physical, and interpersonal environments that comprise the leisure service agency. The factors shown in Figure 11.7 should be considered when evaluating risk. How these factors are evaluated depends on whether tort or loss of property is involved. Insurance professionals using computer calculations usually perform the first two items shown in Figure 11.7. Items three and four are usually estimates of agency personnel. The agency's mission statement and philosophical statements should be relied on during this exercise because they contain guidelines about the levels of risk the agency is willing to retain and those that must be managed by transferring to another organization. Evaluating risks in this manner allows for conscious decisions about which risks can be tolerated by the organization, which require insurance coverage, which can be reduced or controlled without sacrificing the program being offered, and which are too large for the agency to bear.

Van der Smissen (1990) classifies severity of risk in two ways. The first

Figure 11.7
Factors to Consider When Evaluating Risk

1. How well the risk may be evaluated.

2. The probability of loss occurring.

3. The severity of the risk.

4. The frequency with which the risk may occur.

5. The agency's mission statement.

way is financially, or the impact on the agency being able to continue to provide services. From a financial perspective, degrees of severity are considered to be vital, significant, or insignificant. Vital losses are catastrophic and would cause bankruptcy in private agencies or an increase in taxes for government agencies. Significant losses would require a reduction in either services or expenditures or both. Insignificant losses are losses that may be covered by current operating revenues.

The second way in which van der Smissen (1992) classified severity is in relation to programming and participant bodily injury. In this context, seriousness is also classified as high, medium, or low. The more serious the injury, the higher the liability for the agency. Two examples of high injuries are those that are fatal or result in quadriplegia. Injuries considered to be medium may also be disabling, but to a lesser degree. Although they may linger for an extended period of time, they are

not permanent. Low injuries are either temporary or a minor permanent disablement.

For any injury, the likelihood of its occurring is known as frequency of occurrence. The likelihood of injury or sickness occurring depends on the nature of the risk being evaluated. Weekly might be considered often for some risks, such as minor cuts and bruises, whereas yearly may be considered often for other risks. Risks of medium frequency occur occasionally, whereas risks of low frequency rarely occur. Figure 11.8 is a model of a matrix that may be used as a guide to decide the proper method for dealing with risk.

Step 4—Risk Control and Reduction of Loss Exposure

Once each potential risk has been identified and evaluated, a decision must be made on the best way to minimize potential losses to the agency. If the severity or extent of the risk has not been correctly evaluated, the best measure for controlling the risk will not be chosen. If the most appropriate approach for the agency's resources is not chosen, the risk management plan will not reach its goals.

According to the literature, there are four general approaches used to control risk. Available agency resources will determine which option is chosen. The options are: (1) eliminate the risk, (2) transfer the risk to others by contract, (3) retain the risk, and (4) reduce the risk.

Risk Elimination

Option number one, risk elimination, is further subdivided into two categories: avoidance and discontinuance. Avoidance may be chosen when the agency is making a decision about whether or not to enter into an activity. An activity may be discontinued when it is deemed to be too great a risk for the agency. This type of decision may be appropriate when an organization is unable to meet the standard of care required to offer an activity in an appropriate and safe manner. Whether or not a risk is avoided or discontinued depends on the agency's mission statement.

Risk Transfer

The second option for dealing with risk is to transfer it to a third party. This is a financial method for handling risk, and there are several ways to use it. Included are purchase order agreements where the merchandise is shipped free on board (FOB). Under this method,

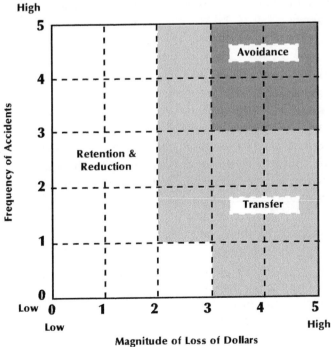

Figure 11.8
Risk Decision-Matrix

Source: Kaiser (1986), p. 231.

the seller retains responsibility for the goods in transit until they are delivered. Lease agreements, contracts for services, clientele agreements, and appropriate insurance coverage may also be used.

Risk Retention

Retention is the third method for dealing with risk. It also is a financial method. Retention occurs when the agency chooses to pay for all or part of a given risk. Retention may be active or passive. Active retention occurs when the risk has been identified, evaluated, and a conscious decision made to pay any loss incurred out of current operating income. Passive retention occurs when the risk is retained through error or oversight.

Risk retention may be financed through the use of deductibles in insurance policies or by setting up a reserve fund. This method may be the preferred method for handling risks that occur infrequently or that have a low impact on the agency.

Risk Reduction

Risk reduction is an operational method of controlling risk. This means that agency personnel carefully look at all areas of the agency's operations to determine what can be done to limit the agency's exposure to risk. This method is used in conjunction with the financial methods previously discussed. Its purpose is to lessen the frequency and severity of loss suffered by the agency and to allow the agency to continue to fulfill its mission in the event of loss. Figure 11.9 lists those areas in which documented policies and procedures are key components of reduction. The

person in charge of risk management may want to consult with an insurance professional, the agency's attorney, or a professional from a similar agency to gain knowledge about customary professional practices of those providing similar services. Lack of knowledge about standards does not excuse an agency from failing to comply with them (van der Smissen, 1989).

Step 5—Plan Implementation

Implementing the plan is a two-step process. First, the best management approach must be chosen for the identified risks. Then policies and procedures need to be developed for each of the following areas: program development, staff and volunteer development, management of agency clientele, site and facility development, and public relations.

Program Development

If risk management goals and objectives were not developed at the time the agency's program offerings were initiated, they will need to be developed now. The risk management plan should include the operational practices and procedures that will be implemented to manage the potential risks of each program offered. These practices and procedures should address the following elements of program development:

1. Using qualified personnel;

2. Requiring instructors to teach progressively while considering the principles of human development and the participants' skill and experience levels;

**Figure 11.9
Key Areas for Policies and Procedures**

1. Administration of programs and services

2. Standards of competence for personnel

3. Management of agency clientele: their characteristics, how they are to be supervised, and emergency procedures for their safety

4. Management and maintenance of the agency' physical facilities

5. Public relations

3. Requiring the appropriate number of instructors for the program, participants, equipment, and areas used;

4. Pointing out potential dangers to the participants; and

5 Being certain each program has been authorized by the agency's administration and governing body.

Staff and Volunteer Development

Both Corbett (1995) and Baley and Matthews (1989) cite common sense as the most effective and inexpensive risk management technique. Use of common sense to hire well-qualified professionals and to recruit good volunteers decreases the number of situations that may lead to lawsuits. In addition to recruiting appropriate personnel, it is necessary to screen driving records of potential employees and volunteers before hiring them and to check with the carrier of the agency's automobile insurance for suggestions on risk management for vehicles and the volunteers who are frontline service providers. It is also necessary to write clear job descriptions, to provide a thorough orientation program for newly hired personnel, and to provide feedback on a timely basis by regular monitoring and evaluation of paid staff and volunteers. Check to be sure they have the ability to perform their assigned tasks, taking into account both their skills and judgement. Also, require continuing education for both employees and volunteers. This atmosphere fosters thinking about risk management on a daily basis.

Management of Agency Clientele

In addition to providing programs at progressively difficult levels, it is necessary for agency program providers to have an understanding of human growth and development. This is necessary because people of different ages have different abilities. It will facilitate providing age-appropriate programs for the clientele.

Management of clientele also pertains to establishing safety rules and procedures for the facility and the programs being offered, including emergency procedures and accident reporting and analysis. It involves consistently enforcing the rules and, if necessary, requiring proof that the participant is physically able to participate in the activity.

Site and Facility Development

To minimize potential loss from the facility and site, it is necessary to have a site plan and to use it. First, walk around the premises of the agency. Specifically, look for hazards, both inside and outside. Envision the premises in an emergency and from the viewpoint of persons who have physical or mental disabilities. According to Peterson and Hronek (1992), the standard of reasonableness is used to judge a provider of services. An individual provider and the agency are responsible to use ordinary and reasonable care to keep the premises reasonably safe for visitors and to warn visitors of any dangers.

Public Relations

In this context, public relations means having informed staff and a well-maintained facility. It also means treating people as you would like to be treated, enforcing the rules consistently among all agency clientele, and informing the public about the agency's stand on risk management. This can be accomplished through program brochures, news releases, staff meetings, speeches, and in-service training. All of these things convey a positive message about the agency.

Public relations also means having a designated spokesperson for the agency in the event of a disaster or incident. All agency personnel are to refer requests for interviews or statements to the designated person. This individual should be the only person to provide information to the press.

Step 6—Periodic Plan Review

We live in a constantly changing environment. Because of this, it is necessary to review the risk management plan periodically. Decisions and assumptions that were used to create the plan need to be reviewed to see if they are still valid. Outcomes from the plan must be weighed against the assumptions that were made when the plan was created. If necessary, changes must be made to reflect the current environment in which the agency operates. Changes should also reflect any change in the agency's mission statement and any operational practices that have changed since the plan was last updated. The plan should also reflect changes in procedures that are used to manage the potential risks to meet the agency's objectives.

The agency's risk manager should participate in the following tasks to facilitate plan evaluation.

1. Maintain an efficient incident reporting and claim handling system.

2. Maintain and periodically revise an accurate record of the location and current replacement value of all physical properties.

3. Routinely review job descriptions for employees and volunteers to ensure that the descriptions accurately reflect the tasks being performed. Provide additional training that may be needed for employees and volunteers to perform their required tasks.

4. Obtain information on changes in operating procedures.

5. Be involved in planning new programs or activities to be sure that they do not increase the organization's risks.

6. Provide written communication to various personnel who need to know the extent of each insurance coverage that is purchased, and the procedures to be followed with respect to that insurance.

7. Ensure that protective devices such as burglar and fire alarms are properly installed and periodically maintained.

8. Provide continuing counsel and evaluation of problems as they arise. In conjunction with outside specialists, review loss prevention activities.

9. Establish formal and informal information systems to gather and integrate data into a computer program for loss analysis.

10. Review the organization's philosophical and policy statements and its procedure manuals for the suitability of required procedures and for legal compliance.

11. Review financial statements and contracts the agency has executed with outside vendors.

12. Review safety records provided by Occupational Safety and Health Administration (OSHA) and by providers of workers' compensation. (Lai et al.; 1992: 220)

If an agency fails to manage the risks associated with its operation, the agency may suffer damage to its public image and financial loss. It may also be forced to stop providing services. Because risk management is an inherent part of day-to-day agency operations, it is imperative that the leisure service manager understand the elements of risk and implement a risk management plan that protects the organization from loss.

Summary

Leisure service managers need to have a basic understanding of the laws that affect the operation of their agency. These laws provide the foundation for the operation of programs, services, and facilities of the agency. Laws at the federal, state, and local levels all have an impact on what an agency can and cannot do in carrying out the mission statement.

Complementing an understanding of laws is knowledge about risk and how risk management affects the operation of an agency. No agency operates in a risk-free environment. Thus, a leisure service manager must identify potential risks that can result in liability for an agency.

If a lawsuit occurs, the leisure service agency will be charged with negligence, that is, that either the employees or some officer of the agency did something in such a way as to cause injury or damage to the customer. Four elements of negligence must be proved in order for the plaintiff to successfully win a civil liability case against an agency. Thus, the leisure service manager must understand the concepts surrounding negligence and the possible defenses to use against a negligence charge.

Finally, it needs to be understood that the best way to avoid lawsuits is to adopt a risk management plan. Such a plan is preventive in nature and helps to protect customers, employees and the agency from an unsafe environment. A six-step risk management plan was presented to help the leisure service manager protect his or her agency from loss due to lawsuits.

Discussion Questions

1. Identify and define different types of laws that are pertinent to leisure service organizations.

2. How do the U.S. Constitution and the Canadian Constitutional Act have an impact on the delivery of leisure services in each of these two countries?

3. Identify and define different types of laws that play a role in the delivery of leisure service at the local level of government.

4. What is eminent domain?

5. What are torts?

6. The legal system in the United States is based on what type of common law?

7. Why is contract law important?

8. What are some of the defenses that can be used when negligence is alleged?

9. Outline steps that can be used in developing a risk management plan.

10. Identify four ways in which risk can be controlled.

References

Baley, J. A., & Matthews, D. L. (1989). *Law and liability in athletics, physical education and recreation* (2nd ed.). Dubuque, IA: William C. Brown.

Black's law dictionary (1979). (5th ed.). St. Paul, MN: West Publishing Co.

Dorfman, M. A. (1998). *Introduction to risk management and insurance* (6th ed.). Englewood Cliffs, NJ: Prentice-Hall.

Dolan, E. F. Jr. (1972). *Legal action.* Chicago: Contemporary Books, Inc.

Hronek, B., & Spengler. A. (1997). *Legal liability in recreation and sports.* Champaign, IL: Sagamore Publishing .

Kaiser, D. A. (1986). *Liability and law in recreation, parks and sports.* Englewood Cliffs, NJ: Prentice-Hall.

Lai, M. L., Chapman, T. & Steinbock, E. L. (1992). *Am I covered for . . .* (2nd ed.). San Jose: Consortium for Human Services, Inc.

Leighty, L., (1973). *Legal considerations in Managing municipal leisure services.* Lutzin, S. & Storey, E. (eds.) Washington DC: International City Management Association. 90-98.

Nature deals another blow to northeast. January (1988). *Des Moines Register,* p. 5A.

Peterson, J. A., & Hronek, B. B. (1992). *Risk Management for park, recreation, and leisure services* (2nd ed.). Champaign, IL: Sagamore Publishing .

Peterson, J. A., & Hroneck, B. B. (1997). *Risk management for park, recreation and leisure services* (3rd ed.). Champaign, IL: Sagamore Publishing.

Reynolds & Hormachea (1976). *Public recreation administration.* Englwood Cliffs, NJ: Prentice-Hall.

Roha, R. R. (1994). If volunteer work leads to a lawsuit, who pays? *Kiplinger's Personal Finance Magazine, 48,* 132-134.

Rodney, L. (1964). *Administration of public recreation.* New York: Ronald Press Co.

van der Smissen, B. (1990). *Legal liability and risk management for public and private entities.* Cincinnati, OH: Anderson.

Webster's new twentieth century dictionary of the English language. (2nd ed.). (1980). Boston: Riverside.

Chapter

12

Interagency Cooperation and Collaboration

Photo courtesy of the Montgomery County Department of Park & Planning Commission.

Leisure service managers must work with the entire community and promote interagency cooperation as a necessary element of their management strategy.

Introduction

This chapter discusses collaboration and cooperation arrangements in the delivery of leisure services. Specific examples are given relative to leisure and human service delivery. Of particular importance is the identification of strategies to assist leisure service managers in the development of cooperative arrangements. These strategies include collaboration models, partnering, contracting, outsourcing, and privatization.

Many leisure service managers might say: "We have been outsourcing for decades!" Yet what has occurred is a mixture of terminology, definition and perception. Keene (1998) notes that there has been an imprecision historically in the use of terms surrounding privatization, outsourcing and related activities. These differences and similarities will be discussed in this chapter.

This chapter is designed to assist the leisure service manager in the formulation of cooperative agreements that involve schools, as well as non-profit, military leisure service organizations. Particular attention to process, guidelines, and management is given. It should be noted that cooperative arrangements have been in existence for many years in leisure services. Importantly, these arrangements are in a constant state of change due to social, political, cultural and environmental influences that have an impact on the leisure organization.

The Need for Collaboration in Leisure Service Delivery

The need for collaboration and partnering in leisure services has been growing over the past 20 years. There have always been voluntary affiliations with parks, recreation, and youth services, one form of which is the cooperative arrangement. Tindell (1984) noted that citizen involvement in parks and recreation services is one form of partnership. In many communities, this involvement takes the forms of advocacy, appointed committees, volunteering, political appointments or elections (to various boards and commissions), and direct financial support.

Kraus and Curtis (1990) point out that leisure agencies of all types must coordinate their efforts and cooperate in identifying and meeting public needs for recreation programs and services. Benest, Foley, and Welton (1984) have emphasized that due to budget cuts,

reductions in government support for leisure services, and growing trends in privatization, leisure organizations need to create partnerships to develop new resources. Havitz, in *Models of Change in Municipal Parks and Recreation: A Book of Innovative Case Studies,* (1995) observed that many innovative program and service models were a result of input from public, private, and non-profit corporations. These model case studies reflected cooperative ventures, partnerships and facilitative philosophies, rather than the "go-it-alone" solution to leisure service delivery.

The need for cooperation in the delivery of youth services is prevalent in the literature. Larnes, Zippiroli, and Behrman (1999) noted that in order to have effective youth development programs, there must be efforts to establish strategic parrnterships between public and private institutions to maximize the resources and facilities. They further recommended that the creation of coalitions, councils, or coordinating bodies is needed to serve as a network and support system for youth serving agencies. Indeed, experience has shown that the planning of programs for youth that involve the school and community agencies is fundamental to their success (Dryfoos, 1999). Pittman (1991) may have stated the need for collaboration best when he wrote that youth serving organizations need to make a concerted effort to work more collaboratively with each other and with other organizations (especially public sector agencies) to do following:

1. Draw national attention to positive youth development and the needs that these organizations have been attempting to meet for years;

2. Develop common goals and strategies; and

3. Ensure programs complement rather than duplicate or compete against each other.

The third item is of critical importance because it affects many agencies. Maximizing limited fiscal-, human-, and facility-based resources is of growing importance and will continue to be so. Lankford (1991a, 1991b) conducted a series of futures research in Oregon and Washington among park, recreation and youth-serving agencies. It was reported that collaboration and partnering among public, private, and nonprofit leisure organizations were needed not only to address the complexity of community problems, but to improve the quality of services, and to maximize resources. Similarly, Lankford and DeGraaf (1992) reported that U. S. Navy and U. S. Army Morale, Welfare, and Recreation organizations identified collaboration and partnering as critical needs of the future, and that strategies needed to be developed to implement such arrangements. The managers who took part in the research stated that they were competing with other leisure organizations unnecessarily, and that they could have a more positive impact on the community by creating collaborative arrangements. Cooperation among leisure service providers has taken on various forms (Kraus, 1997):

1. Planning, development and management of recreation facilities as a joint venture between public, private, or nonprofit entities;

2. Privatization of parks, facilities and programs through sub-contracting;

3. Corporate assistance for programs and projects; and

4. Cooperative sponsorship of varied programs by public, voluntary, and business organizations.

McLean, Bannon, and Gray (1999) note that examples of outsourcing in the provision of leisure services are plentiful, ranging from contracting with individual instructors for various classes and activities to alliances with other organizations, such as school districts or youth-serving organizations. They also point out that some leisure organizations have outsourced all of their operations, retaining only administrative functions within the agency (to monitor quality of services and the contracts). It is common among leisure service organizations to contract for maintenance services, street tree management, parking and security services at special events, and at times, facility management (such as golf courses).

Examples of Partnerships, Cooperation, and Collaboration

Levin (1999) notes that there are effective means to address teenage crime by partnering with various agencies and experts. Many U.S. cities have implemented programs aimed at curbing youth violence and crime. Local officials are partnering with parents, business and religious leaders, teachers, social workers, and psychologists to provide constructive activities for young people. These partnerships offer adult-supervised programs for after-school hours, such as programs in conflict resolution; community projects; and athletics.

Society's conventional response to the problems of young people is to target the problem and develop intervention or prevention programs for individuals who manifest the problem or are at high risk of it.

However, the problems are often more complex and overlapping. Some research shows that overlapping risk and protective factors affect the occurrence of all youth-related problems, and that prevention strategies aimed at enhancing the development of these youths, reducing specific risks to communities, and strengthening protective factors are likely to be more successful than programs addressing the problem behaviors themselves. Barton, Watkins, and Jarjoura (1997) note that strategies deserving wider consideration for addressing youth issues should be "comprehensive community initiatives" that create collaborative partnerships among public officials, service providers, primary institutions, and citizens to promote the well-being of children, youths, and families.

Werth (1997) reported on a partnership between the staff of a General Accounting Office (GAO) and an inner-city school. The staff adopted an Adopt-a-School Project to provide volunteers for both academic and after-school clubs and programs. A staff coordinator was appointed to help spread the leadership opportunities. The program offers young people another adult to communicate with and to turn to when needed.

Efficiency in service delivery has been noted as one motivation for developing working relationships with and among associated organizations. Economic development projects offer many opportunities for public, private, and nonprofit organizations to work together. Cooperation between govern-

ment agencies and the private sector in developing countries toward the promotion of efficient public service is crucial to sustainable economic development (Bennet, 1998). The public–private sector partnership may come in different forms, such as active involvement of private companies in economic development projects or their participation in planning and establishing economic guidelines. Furthermore, sustainable development policies must be enforced in both nonprofit and for-profit companies.

Although part of the youth-serving type of partnership, the school-to-work programs are good examples of what can be accomplished. State, community, and private sector programs can help the U.S. educational system graduate students with employable skills. These school-to-work initiatives incorporate mentoring, work-based learning, job shadowing, internships, and youth apprenticeships. These programs can also decrease student drop-out rates by generating renewed interest and relevance to real-life circumstances. Leisure service organizations can and do play a significant role in these types of arrangements. The school-to-work movement both integrates work-related skills into the classroom through school reform and teacher training, and gives students real working experiences through internships, apprenticeships, and mentor relationships. Leisure service organizations provide many opportunities for young people to work within the system, and to develop appropriate social and learning skills. A vice president of the New York City-based Segal Company notes that she and the students, tutors, and mentors usually devote more time each month because they also organize group activities with the students, such as skating parties, museum visits, and picnics (Dolainski, 1997).

In the City and County of Honolulu (Hawaii) Department of Parks and Recreation, an extensive system of volunteering exists for the care of parks. There are over 300 parks on Oahu. The program, encouraged and motivated by Malama Aina ("care or love of the land") traditions, almost works by itself. In the smaller parks, one or more individuals take responsibility for cutting grass, grooming the ball field, picking up litter and trash, and so on. As Walter Ozawa (1994), past Director of Parks and Recreation, noted, these are the heroes behind the scenes.

Brooks (2000) has contracted with the Lassen National Forest to operate and maintain campgrounds over a 10-year period. This contract uses university students from California State University at Chico and other professionals. The students gain experience, the Forest Service gains a trained labor force, and the users of the campgrounds experience a better camping service.

The Maui (Hawaii) County Parks and Recreation Department has formed important collaboration and cooperative arrangements with the public (Buck, 2000). These arrangements take the form of community volunteer advisory groups to recommend programs, services, and management of the leisure services. Each community has an advisory board, while the county Department of Housing and Human Concerns provides grant-writing services to fund youth programs and support services such as transportation. The Parks and Recreation Department facilitates and enables the programs through staff support.

Arts and crafts fairs provide a way to generate funds for many organizations. The Hawaii Recreation and Park Association (HRPA) sponsors an arts and crafts fair every year, and has instructional programs as well as vendors (Wong, 2000). The proceeds go to support HRPA, with a significant amount of money going to the Kapiolani Community College (KCC) Scholarship program. KCC provides the space on campus, HRPA organizes the event, and the event is staffed by public, private, and nonprofit recreation professionals and University of Hawaii recreation students. The event is the single most important fund raiser for HRPA, and it provides a community service relative to art appreciation through instruction.

Kauai (Hawaii) Department of Recreation (Carvalho, 2000) uses the support of the HPRA, private business donors, the University of Hawaii, and nonprofit youth agencies to develop sports and social recreation summer programs for youth. Training, mentoring, and implementation of programs is facilitated by Carvalho's staff.

The HRPA has teamed with the University of Hawaii's Program for Recreation Research and Service to conduct professional training programs on all the Hawaiian islands (Spoehr & Lankford, 2000). In addition, the partnership program provides research services to the county parks and recreation organizations. This research is used to influence policy, improve programs, and assist in community planning and program development. The work requires a fee, yet is far below what staff or consultants would require. The quality is high, and is therefore a service to the community.

The University of Northern Iowa has a unique and effective partnership providing services to children and youth. The university has created a partnership with the U. S. Army, U. S. Navy, U. S. Air Force, U. S. Marine Corps and U.S. Embassies to plan, operate, and manage youth services worldwide. The program, *Camp Adventure™ Youth Services* has been recognized as an innovative and effective way to partner with youth service organizations to offer high-quality programs. Students gain experience; the professional staff at the site gain training, ideas and quality programming assistance; and the youth experience great programs.

On Maui in Hawaii, two cooperative ventures were implemented in 2000. First, an in-line hockey rink opened at a beach park. The rink was built and is managed by a nonprofit hockey club. The club carries the insurance and liability risk. Secondly, adjacent to the hockey rink is a skateboard park. The park is operated (insurance and liability as well) by the YMCA. In a high-use area, with demands from tourists and residents, the county was able to diversify facilities and activities without adding significantly to its budget (Buck, 2000).

The U.S. Army of Hawaii has formed a youth and community partnership to address leisure service issues. This partnership consists of nonprofit organizations (Ys, Boys & Girls Clubs); the Honolulu Police Activities League; the City and County of Honolulu Department of Parks and Recreation; and the U. S. Army, U. S. Air Force, U. S. Navy, and U. S. Marine Corps' Moral, Welfare, and Recreation services programs. There are regular meetings to determine needs, issues, and service delivery strategies.

The University of Oregon's Department of Planning, Public Policy, and Management has created the "Community Services Center." This program is directed at identifying organizational staffing, research, and service needs in Oregon. The staff prioritize the needs of organizations, develop a contract, recruit students from any Oregon college campus, and conduct the work. This is a win–win situation for all (Povey, 2000).

Finally, on the Island of Hawaii, the Kona (Hawaii) District Department of Parks and Recreation facilitated the development of a playground near Captain Cook. The playground was developed with over 300 volunteers over a two-and-a-half-year period. There are painted murals, wood carvings, and ornate woodworkings. Interestingly, there has not been any vandalism; this is truly a community park, built, managed, and cared for by the community (Patowski, 1998).

It should be obvious by now that leisure organizations must be prepared to work with many organizations, leisure and human services alike. Second, a varied mix of groups and individuals are willing, ready, and interested in our leisure service systems. It is to the benefit not only of the community, but the leisure organization as well to develop practical and effective cooperative agreements. The following section details the characteristics of these agreements.

Principles and Practices of Cooperation and Collaboration

The foundations of cooperation, collaboration, and partnering are built on the incentives and information exchanged between parties in some form of a contractual relationship.

Partnering refers to a form of contracting, but is not binding as a contractual agreement. It is a self-enforcing agreement because the parties involved realize the importance and strength of working together to solve more complex problems or deliver services. Contracting services refers to the act of paying a fee for a specified service. Outsourcing refers to contracting for services, granting franchises to public and private firms, and the use of volunteers to deliver public services (U.S. Government Accounting Office, 1997).

Cooperative agreements among local governments usually have the following characteristics:

1. They are generally agreements between two governmental or non-profit units concerning a single activity;

2. They pertain to services, rather than facilities;

3. They are not permanent and contain provisions for future renegotiations or termination by either party;

4. They have stand-by provisions that come into effect only when certain conditions arise; and

5. They are permitted by state legislation that authorizes cooperation among government entities in specific areas. (Cooper et al., 1998:)

It should be noted that leisure service organizations do create agreements to operate facilities. Furthermore, leisure organizations may contract for more than a single activity. In the 1980s and 1990s, government organizations were encouraged to contract services, due primarily to budget pressures. This period saw a proliferation of service agreements among governmental organizations. Specifically, a number of councils of governments (COGs) and special service districts were organized to provide fire, safety, transportation, and leisure services for metropolitan areas (for example, Portland, Oregon's Metropolitan Service District). In fact, some places have seen the county and city merge to become one unit (Nashville, Tennessee, for example). In Hawaii, each main island is a county, and is governed by a mayor and council. Therefore, one parks and recreation department on each island is responsible for leisure services (however, Maui County includes Molokai and Lanai).

Collaboration and Partnering

Selin and Chavez (1995) suggest that collaboration is needed because of the complexity of society and interdependence of economies. They note that collaboration implies a joint decision-making approach to problem resolution, where power is shared and stakeholders take collective responsibility for their actions and subsequent outcomes from those actions. Selin and Chavez identified the model for collaboration shown in Figure 12.1. It should be noted that they reported the use of this model within the context of recreation, parks, and leisure service management, however, the model is based on collaborative processes within social and political systems. Therefore, it is likely to be useful within many other situations, given slight modifications to the contextual framework within which the leisure manager must operate. They identify the following collaborative model concepts.

Figure 12.1
Collaborative Models

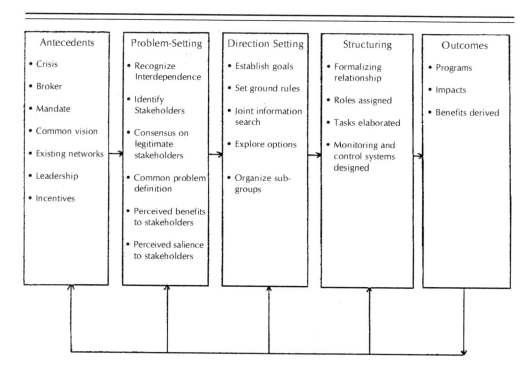

Source: Selin, S., & Chavez, D., (1995). Developing collaborative model for environmental planning and management. *Environmental Management, 19*(2), 189–195.

1. *Antecedents* are those that motivate an organization to adopt a collaborative or partnering approach to service delivery, such as legal mandates, incentives (possibly budgetary or political), common values, or vision.

2. *Problem situations and contextual frameworks*—Leisure organizations can and do form ventures with other organizations to solve common problems and work with stakeholders (those with an interest or claim to the issue or service in question).

3. *Direction setting* occurs as participants (organization and stakeholders) realize a common purpose and need to work together. This phase allows those involved to work toward a common purpose.

4. *Structuring of the arrangement* provides a sense of responsibility and purpose, and assigns tasks and roles. This phase also sets up a means to evaluate and monitor progress of the collaborative arrangement.

5. *Outcomes* are the realization of the programs and solutions agreed upon, and an understanding of the impacts and benefits of the collaboration.

The term "partnering" has been used to describe many such cooperative and collaborative arrangements. Partnering refers to a working relationship with a high level of trust and close cooperation between two parties that contract with each other to accomplish mutually beneficial outcomes (Domberger, Farago, & Fernandez, 1997). A partnership is a mix of activities between public service agents, citizens, the private profit-making sector, and the nonprofit sector (Benest, Foley, & Welton, 1984). Benest et al., further suggest that a partnership is an effort to work together to form a collaboration or combined operation.

Kraus and Curtis (1990) suggest the term "synergy" to describe such arrangements. The results of partnering can lead to reduced conflicts between organizations, fewer chances for litigation, financial benefits due to time savings and the sharing of expertise, and a better work environment (Cole, 1993). However, Edginton and Neal (1982) and Edginton, Madrigal, Lankford and Wheeler (1990) have reported that recreation and park executives and managers do not give high priorities to partnership activities within the framework of organizational goals. This may have implications for the extent and quality of various partnership agreements.

In the mid 1980s, the U.S. Army Corps of Engineers in the Pacific Northwest was expending considerable amounts of money and effort in dispute resolution. By the end of the decade, they had shifted their focus to avoiding disputes. The process was called "partnering" and has since become a model for business, government, and industry (Cole, 1993). The partnering approach to service delivery allows all parties to agree in the beginning on a formal process and structure in order to focus on creative cooperation and work that avoids adversarial confrontations. There are four basic assumptions of partnering, according to Cole (1993):

1. *Trust.* This is the foundation for a partnership and is viewed as a basic assumption of the relationship. Agreements are deemed reliable and maintained throughout the process.

2. *Collaboration.* Partners work to understand each other's interests and satisfy each other's concerns. They work out win–win solutions. Collaboration goes beyond coordination; it means that the parties do not take advantage of one another.

3. *Commitment.* The partners commit to mutual success. Partners let things happen, help them happen and make them happen for the benefit of the partnership.

4. *Communication.* Partnering requires management of conflict and misunderstanding. Open communication is necessary, in an honest and candid manner.

Partnership Strategies

Partnering requires that all stakeholders be involved in the process of developing the agreement, goals, implementation, and evaluation of the service delivery program. This ensures that a teamwork approach is used to enhance the quality of the services produced. Cole (1993) suggests implementing a partnering workshop with stakeholders to develop a better relationship. This workshop would provide an overview of the partnership, principles of team building, communication and conflict-resolution exercises, development of a mission and goal statement, adoption of a process to resolve future difficulties, and creation of a charter. Cole further notes that four general phases exist in partnering: planning, implementation, evaluation, and adjustment. In planning, the stakeholders meet to develop a plan for the partnership in terms of purpose, process, and implementation. Domberger, Farago and Fernandez (1997) provide the several steps for developing partnerships.

1. Conduct a search process by all parties based on the needs of the community and organizations.

2. Identify expected partnering outcomes, products, or programs based on needs.

3. Hold a workshop on how to achieve the outcomes, products, or programs.

4. Develop contractual agreements or a "partnering charter."

5. Hold regular meetings between partners.

6. Conduct an evaluation and review of the outcomes, products, or programs.

Benest, Foley, and Welton (1984) suggest the following strategies for developing partnerships in leisure services. These strategies are similar to the steps mentioned above, but include aspects that have an impact on the leisure manager and the duties of a manager. They include:

1. Exerting leadership by recognizing common interests between organizations. The leisure manager must focus on the vision of how the community could be improved by these joint ventures. Recognition

of a preferred future would be acknowledged by all organizations involved.

2. Networking by the leisure service manager in order to become more aware of all the organizations involved and how they can complement each other. Participation in task forces, committees, and community meetings by staff and management will assist in this process.

3. Sensitizing the partnership group to the needs of the clients or target group. Forums, workshops and meetings are used to enhance sensitivity to each other's needs within the context of the group to be served.

4. Becoming a resource for the partnership and community is also of importance. The lead agency (often the public organization) identifies the needs of the groups involved and determines how best to provide necessary resources for the program.

5. Providing a structure is important to establishing a formal relationship. Often contracts provide this structure. These contracts are signed by the policymaking bodies of each organization to provide a definition and expectation of services provided and responsibilities.

6. Development and adoption of a work program and process is needed. This process formalizes how to dialogue, resolve conflict, and interact, and it establishes procedures.

7. Structuring pressures and incentives to form the partnership motivates organizations to change and respond to community needs. These pressures are the recognition of unmet needs, duplication of services, media attention, and formal requests for partnerships. Incentives include inclusion in grant writing or funding of programs, and political and community support and influence.

8. Generating momentum is the last strategy. The leisure service manager must identify the successes and gains, and promote and support the partnership. This will create a sense of purpose and excitement for those involved.

Leisure service organizations contemplating partnerships and cooperative ventures should make sure that formal agreements exist. The formal agreement lists the legal responsibilities, liabilities, maintenance, and supervision details of the venture. This agreement helps to resolve disputes as well. There should be a system in place for interagency communication on the status and evaluation of the project, a method to conduct a cooperative needs assessment and analysis, and a means of community involvement in the venture. Furthermore, adequate and detailed record keeping of the costs and benefits of the venture is necessary. This information can be used to justify continued operation or dissolution of the joint venture. Consequently, the leisure service manager must work with the partners to develop a common fiscal reporting process. Additionally, the risk management and insurance procedures must be solidified and agreed upon.

Outsourcing and Privatizing

Privatizing government services have become common place. Cooper and colleagues (1998) noted that privatization is one of the most widely discussed trends in contemporary public management. They do note that there is no true privatization, because the basic authority and responsibility for delivery of services is retained by the public sector. Privatization occurs when private for-profit organizations assume responsibility for providing leisure and human services normally supplied by public agencies (Benest, Foley & Welton, 1984).

Outsourcing provides an opportunity to foster economic development through employment in the private sector. These ventures provide a mechanism for working more effectively with nonprofit organizations that can bring experience and expertise to complex service delivery problems on a temporary basis, rather than by setting up more or less permanent government programs.

There is every reason to believe that outsourcing and continued privatization of some leisure programs and services will continue and deepen in the future. Outsourcing is a tool and must be managed. Therefore, it is important to recruit and train public managers with strong negotiation skills. They must be educated in contract administration skills.

McLean, Bannon, and Gray (1999) identify outsourcing as the provision of some leisure services through contractual relationships in order to provide cost-effective programs and services. However, not all outsourcing is conducted to address societal issues and needs. Rifkin (1995) is highly critical of outsourcing because many people can be discarded from the employment rolls. This drives wages down, not to mention benefits, for full-time employees. Rifkin further identifies that companies cut costs on labor by contracting with outside suppliers for goods and services, who pay low wages to their employees and virtually no benefits.

To consider outsourcing, a government agency needs to determine what is inherently a governmental task. The GAO (1997) notes that governmental functions fall into two categories: (1) the act of governing, that is, the discretionary exercise of governmental authority; or (2) monetary transactions and entitlements. Outsourcing candidates hold the belief that the government should retain responsibility for the activity, but that it can be done by someone other than the government's own employees (Keene, 1998). Keene suggests three questions that help to determine if a service should be outsourced.

1. Do we need to keep doing this work?

2. If the work needs to be done, could another agency or contractor do the work better?

3. Is the work being performed in the most efficient manner, or does it need to be fundamentally reengineered?

Summary

The long-term success of an entrepreneurial government (outsourcing, franchising, privatizing) depends on effective leadership, not just management. The management and decision-making bodies of the leisure service organization need to be committed to adopting a facilitating and enabling approach to service delivery. There is no doubt that governmental units have moved a long way from the original constitutional design of national, state, and local governments (Cooper et al., 1998). There is a complex web of intergovernmental and governmental agreements with private and nonprofit sectors for the delivery of leisure services.

These trends suggest that leisure managers must be adaptable and capable of understanding that the delivery of services is a complex collection of different kinds of organizations performing a variety of functions in a number of ways. This complexity requires planning and coordination of effort. Along with these cooperative arrangements and ventures, more complex fiscal, risk management, and accountability pressures have emerged.

Many constraints exist to the creation of partnerships, some of which include governing boards and commissions that are suspicious of the motives of other organizations, leisure managers unaware of or unwilling to collaborate based on a lack of awareness of community needs, and the complexities (legal, fiscal) of working with another organization. However, it appears that the trend toward partnering with and joint ventures among other leisure and human service providers is healthy and effective.

Discussion Questions

1. What is collaboration?

2. Define partnering, and give an example of how it is used in leisure services in your community.

3. Define outsourcing and how it is used for leisure services.

4. Describe an example of privatization of leisure services in your community.

5. What are the necessary skills that a manager needs to be able to facilitate joint ventures?

6. Identify three youth services in your community that appear to be duplicative.

7. Design a process to have these three youth services create a partnership.

8. Call your local parks and recreation organization and ask for a list of private contracts for park operations and programs.

9. What are the benefits of partnering?

10. What are the limitations of privatization?

References

Barton, W. H., Watkins, M., & Jarjoura, R. (1997). Youths and communities: Toward comprehensive strategies for youth development *Social Work, 42*(5), 483–494.

Benest, F., Foley, J., & Welton, G. (1984). *Organizing leisure and human services.* Dubuque, IA: Kendall/Hunt.

Bennet, A. (1998). Sustainable public/private partnerships for public service delivery. *Natural Resources Forum, 22*(3), 193–197.

Brooks, F. A. (2000). *Lassen National Forest campground operations and maintenance program.* Chico, CA: California State University.

Buck, J. (2000, March 29). *Facility scheduling, management and cost savings* [Interview]. Maui County Department of Parks and Recreation, Kihei Aquatics and Community Center Complex, the Hawaiian Recreation and Park Association. Kihei, Maui.

Carvalho, B. (2000, January). *Partnering in Kauai County.* Presentation to Hawaiian Recreation and Park Association Board of Directors. Makiki Recreation Center.

Cole, E. (1993). Partnering: A quality model for contract relations. *The Public Manager, 22*(2), 39–42.

Committee for Recreation/Education Cooperation. (1979). *Let's cooperate: A handbook for recreation/park and education agencies.* Sacramento, CA: California Park and Recreation Society.

Cooper, P. J., Brady, L. P., Hidalgo-Hardeman, O., Hyde, A., Naff, K. C., Ott, J. S., & White, H. (1998). *Public administration for the twenty-first century.* Fort Worth, TX: Harcourt Brace College.

Dolainski, S. (1997, May). Partnering with the (school) board. *Workforce, 76*(5), 28–35.

Domberger, S., Farago, S., & Fernandez, P. (1997). Public and private sector partnering: A re-appraisal. *Public Administration. 75* (4), 777-787.

Dryfoos, J. G. (1999). The Role of the School in Children's Out of School Time. *The Future of Our Children, 9*(2), 117-134.

Edginton, C. R., Madrigal, B., Lankford, S., & Wheeler, D. (1990) Perceptions of organizational goals: A study of Oregon park and recreation directors and board/advisory perceptions. *Journal of Park and Recreation Administration, 8*(2), 70-84.

Edginton, C. R., & Neal, L. L. (1982). Ordering organizational goals. *California Park and Recreation,* 12-14.

GAO. (1997, July). *Comptroller general, terms related to privatization activities and processes.* GAO/GGD-97-121. Washington, D.C.: U.S. General Accounting Office.

Havitz, M. (ed.) (1995). *Models of change in municipal parks and recreation: A book of innovative case studies.* State College, PA: Venture Publishing.

Keene, W. O. (1998). Federal outsourcing: Part 1. *The Public Manager. 27*(1), 16.

Kraus, R., (1997). *Recreation programming: A benefits-driven approach.* Boston: Allyn and Bacon.

Kraus, R., & Curtis, J. E. (1990). *Creative management in recreation, parks, & leisure services,* (5th ed.). St. Louis, MO: Times Mirror/Mosby College Publishing.

Lankford, S. (1991a). Challenges of the 1990s. *Leisure watch, 6*(1), 4-5.

Lankford, S. (1991b, January/February). Future issues in parks & recreation. *Oregon Park & Recreation Society Newsletter,* 8–9.

Lankford, S. V., & DeGraaf, D. (1992). Strengths, weaknesses, opportunities, and threats in morale, welfare, and recreation organizations: Challenges of the 1990s. *Journal of Park and Recreation Administration, 10*(1), 31–45.

Larnes, M. B., Zippiroli, L., & Behrman, R. E. (1999). When school is out. *The Future of our children. 9*(2), 4–20.

Levin, L. (1999). A effective response to teenage crime is possible—and cities are showing the way. *The chronicle of higher education, 45,* (35) B10–12.

McLean, D. D., Bannon, J. J., & Gray, H. R. (1999). Leisure resources: Its comprehensive planning (2nd ed.). Champaign, IL: Sagamore Publishing .

Ozawa, W. (1994). *We add quality to life. Presentation to Hawaii Recreation and Parks Association, Annual Conference.* Honolulu.

Palowski, R. (1998). *Personal interview on playground development and the captain cook community.* Hawaii County Department of Parks and Recreation, Kona District. Kailua-Kona, Hawaii.

Pittman, J. (1991). *Promoting youth development strengthening the role of youth serving and community organizations.* USDA Extension Service, National Initiative Task Force on Youth At Risk. Washington DC.

Rifkin, G. (1995). *End of work.* New York: Tarcher, Putnam.

Selin, S., & Chavez, D. (1995). Developing a collaborative model for environmental planning and management. *Environmental Management. 19*(2). 189-195.

Spoehr, J., & Lankford, S. (2000). Innovative programs. *NRPA's APRS Newsletter, 3.*

Tindell, J. (1984). Expanding citizen-professional partnerships: Grass roots community development in leisure services. *Journal of Park and Recreation Administration.* p. 65.

Werth, J. B. (1997). Partnering the easy way. *The Public Manager. 26*(2), 57–58.

Wong, A. (2000). *Diamond Head arts and crafts festival. Hawaii Recreation and Park Association.* Presentation at California Parks and Recreation Society Conference, Sacramento, CA.

Chapter 13

Information Systems and Computers

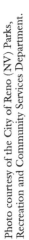

Computer knowledge and skills are essential for the contemporary leisure services manager.

Introduction

This chapter describes the types of information systems that leisure service managers need for decision-making purposes. The chapter also presents information on technology, computers, and the management of the flow of decision-making information and support systems. We examine issues related to the effective management of computing in organizations, the impacts of computing on organizations and work, and the diffusion of computing innovations within and among organizations.

Computers are affecting organizations through their impact on decision making, employment, structure, orga nizational politics, and work life. Computers aid managers in the decision-making process by helping in monitoring organizational activities. Instant access to information translates to control and coordination of organizational activity. Rifkin (1996) notes that computer technology allows information to be processed horizontally rather than vertically, in effect collapsing the traditional corporate pyramid in favor of networks operating along a common plane. This new structure allows information to be processed quicker and more efficiently. Importantly, understanding how information enters, exits, and moves through organizations will define the organizational structure of the future (McLean, Bannon, & Gray, 1999). As organizations grow in complexity, managers will depend more heavily on various internal and external sources of information. This complexity increases the numbers of points at which decisions must be made, ranging from the individual decision makers at the line level to the strategic decision makers at the top. The better the information, the better the resulting decision, because there is less risk and uncertainty in the expected outcomes.

Evans (2000) points out that innovation is exploding all around us in every industry, every market, every business—and the only thing that's certain is that what the world looks like today is not at all what it will look like six months from now. Evans further points out that the real challenge in the future is how to extract the necessary combination of information and knowledge from the technology.

This explosion of communication-based technology will require specialization in the area of information and technology management within leisure service management. A variety of new terminology and acronyms have surfaced as a response to the growth of technology in the workplace. Management information systems (MIS) are designed to provide information to decision makers and the organization. Although MIS is not new, the information technology (IT), information systems (IS), and information resource management (IRM) are constantly evolving and facilitating change in organizational communication, structure, and service delivery. The need for comprehensive MIS has resulted from three basic factors: (1) the importance of information in decision making; (2) mismanagement of current information; and (3) the increased use of personal computers by individual decision makers (Donnelly, Gibson, & Ivancevich, 1990).

Growth of Computers and Information Technology

Computer technology has realized a significant and rapid growth in power, speed, and versatility, let alone size. To provide an idea of the growth rate of technology and computers, Rifkin (1995), Griesemer (1985), and Zientara (1981) provide the following summary of major technological innovations. In 1941, Konrad Zuse invented the first programmable computer. In 1944, scientists from Harvard and MIT invented the Mark I, which was 50 feet in length and 8 feet high. A few years later, scientists at the University of Pennsylvania unveiled a computer with 18,000 radio tubes, 70,000 resistors, 10,000 capacitators, 6,000 switches, 40 feet long, 20 feet high, and weighing more than 30 tons. In 1947, the transistor was developed to replace the vacuum tube. This machine was eventually named the Universal Automatic Computer (UNIVAC) and was used by the U.S. Census Bureau in 1950. It was this computer that helped to predict Eisenhower's victory over Stevenson, which then created a great interest in computers (Rifkin, 1995). In 1959, the integrated circuit was discovered, which was a transistor that could put chip switches on a silicon chip. This invention lead to a generation of computers that were smaller and less expensive. In 1973, Intel developed the 8080 computer chip, setting the stage for small and powerful computers. In 1975, Tandy introduced the first home computer, TRS-80. Apple introduced the Apple and MacIntosh computers in the early 1980s, which revolutionized home and office computing. Gradually, desktop computers have become as powerful and fast as central processing units. In the mid 1980s, a 60-megahertz computer was fast and became the standard by the end of the decade. In March of 2000, Intel and AMD began selling a 1,000 gigahertz chip, with an announcement that a 1,500 gigahertz was to follow. A gigahertz PC is double the speed of higher-end computers on the market, and 10 times more powerful than the top end unit just four years earlier (Maney, 2000).

The use of computers and information systems has both deepened and widened in organizations over the past decade. The availability of ever cheaper and more powerful personal computers has put increasing computing power into the hands of greater numbers of people throughout organizations. Changes in computer use continue to accelerate as networks within and between organizations and other people link users. Bertot (1999) noted that this constant increase in technological capability has created an environment for public organizations to:

1. Innovate and find new ways to reach government service users;

2. Adopt a customer service model for users;

3. Achieve and measure attainment of goals and objectives through the strategic use of information technology;

4. Measure outcomes and effects of services;

5. Reengineer organizational practices to better meet the needs of internal and external users;

6. Collaborate with other service providers by sharing information; and

7. Adopt new management structures due to IT use.

Expenditures for workplace technology have undergone a dramatic increase, and are expected to continue. Caudle, Marchand, Bretschneider, Fletcher, and Thurmaier (1989) estimated that states were spending more than 3 percent of their executive branch operating budgets on information resource management (IRM) ($19.9 billion for all fifty states). Fletcher and Foy (1994) estimated that this total had reached $52.6 billion by 1993. Fletcher, Bretschneider, Marchand, Rosenbaum, and Bertot (1992) estimated that county governments in the United States were spending $23.38 billion on IRM, or 17.06 percent of their annual operating budgets. Kraemer and Norris (1994) indicated city governments spent 3 percent of their operating budgets on computing in 1993. Finally, the General Services Administration places spending by federal executive agencies at $25 billion in 1993, or two and one-half times more than in 1983 (GAO, 1995). The U.S. General Accounting Office (GAO) estimates federal obligations at $26.5 billion for 1996, but notes that this number may underestimate the total due to reporting requirements. The rapid evolution of computing and communications technology offers unprecedented opportunities, but it also presents many challenges for the management of computing in public, nonprofit, and private organizations.

Management of Computing and Information Technology

Managers continually search for, acquire, and assimilate new technologies to affect the functioning of their organizations. Under the best of circumstances, organizations will manage the process of diffusion as part of an overall strategy for using computing technologies to achieve the organization's goals. Fraser (1993) noted that organizations need to balance conflicting objectives with regard to timing and pacing of IT investment. There is a need to balance conflicting objectives where:

- End users seek user-friendly, fast, and reliable information technology tools and applications;

- IT staff seek standard and uniform installations for each member of administration; and

- Managers seek to keep costs down while still fulfilling the mission and providing high levels of service to customers.

Bugler and Bretschneider (1993) examined how interest in new information technology (IT) develops and where the technology acquisition process is likely to be initiated in public organizations. Their findings suggest the following: (1) public organization managers seek new information technologies to overcome barriers to outside communication and to improve their reporting ability to outside agencies; (2) organizations with higher levels of outside contacts are more likely to become aware of new technologies that might be applied to those problems; and (3) innovation diffusion is driven largely by end users trying to solve specific problems rather than by technical elites with greater knowledge of the new technologies. Studies of the private sector show that MIS managers usually rate the value of IT more highly than do other executives (Kraemer, Gurbaxani, Mooney, Dunkle, and Vitalari, 1994).

Caudle (1990) found that strategies for developing information technologies in the federal government tended to come from middle management rather than from top managers, who are often political appointees. These users are often referred to as "end users." Unlike top managers or MIS managers, they are the ones who understand the problems and challenges faced by the organization. They also have long-term relationships with people in external organizations, developed over years of interaction. The combination of knowledge of organizational needs and sources of external information appears to put these managers in the best position to pull technology into the organization. (Kraemer & Dedrick, 1997)

Suppliers of new technologies often promote those technologies through channels that only reach their fellow technologists, such as MIS managers, who are often unfamiliar with the problems and needs of end users or how to present the capabilities of products to those users. A MIS manager who understands the needs of end users should be able to make the translation that is necessary to relate technological capabilities to organizational needs, but these findings suggest that this is often not the case. Therefore, it is vital that the leisure service manager insist that the MIS manager work closely with staff and management of the organization to ensure that the products purchased and the eventual information generated is useful for decision making.

The Standish Group, which researches IT project management, reports that only 26 percent of corporate IT projects in 1998 were successful—completed on time, on budget, and with all the features originally specified. That number was a big improvement over the 16 percent success rate in 1994 (Raths, 2000). Guidelines for improving the success rate of IT projects include involving end users from beginning of the project's design and inception, choosing team members who are empowered to make decisions concerning process and design, keeping project-related information in a central place, and managing meetings so that both the team members and upper managers are well-informed about the project's development. Other important management factors include the avoidance of mission inflation, the maintenance of quality standards, and the deployment of a reliable project tracking system. Raths (2000) interviewed information management specialists about how to keep IT projects on track. The following were noted.

1. *Get users involved from the start.* IT managers don't see business in the same way as users and line managers. IT managers will create the best technical system, but perhaps not the best system from a business standpoint.

2. *Choose your project team carefully.* Look for good communicators with an interest in technology — people who really understood the way information flowed through their departments, people who were the informal leaders in their areas.

3. *Keep project information in one place.* With all the shared-media products available today, there's really no excuse not to have a central repository for all the data and "to do" items attached to a project. It can be as simple as a server directory where people can find meeting notes and a database containing all the different open issues of the project. This is especially important for geographically dispersed teams (such as dispersed parks, recreation centers, etc.).

4. *Meetings, meetings, meetings!* Although meetings can become tedious, they are essential to keeping everyone on the same page, as well as to build team spirit. It's also important to meet regularly with upper management on important projects.

5. *Earn the Nobel Prize for diplomacy.* Project managers must understand the pressures felt by both managers and IT people and help bridge the gap.

6. *Watch out for scope creep.* The biggest single cause of project overruns is changes in scope. If you do not manage the scope of the project,

your budget and schedule will be destroyed before you recognize that anything has happened. Make the scope visible to everyone on the team. Team meetings should include a regular, separate roundtable to discuss scope change requests. Often organizations make the mistake of waiting until a project is completed to do any sort of review- or audit.

7. *Maintain quality standards.* If the needs driving the project require a change in scope, ensure that the resources for the project change as well.

8. *Don't be afraid to call a time-out.* IT project managers get into trouble for a variety of reasons. Sometimes the project didn't have a senior-level management buy-in to begin with, or the team working on it had ulterior motives. Managers should not be afraid to take a hiatus and resolve whatever major issue is hindering progress before going any further.

9. *Use a proven tracking system.* Several products exist to help you keep track of IT projects via status reports. You can use spreadsheets and word processors to track projects and communicate progress.

10. *Roll with the punches.* Change is inevitable in a long, complex project. Often people get into scheduling trouble for believing vendors' promises, either about functionality or timing. Factors beyond the project manager's control are bound to emerge, for example, changes in project leadership, a change in project scope, or changes in funding or policy.

Effective Management of Organizational Computing Systems

Northrop, Dunkle, Kraemer, and King (1994) have investigated three factors that are commonly thought to effect computer use in organizations: training, friendliness of software, and users' background with computers. Using data from over three thousand public employees in 46 U.S. cities, they found that training is important but lacking. Northrop and colleagues found that users' computer literacy and prior training are more important than the number of years employees have used computers.

Several studies in the 1980s (Baily, 1986; Loveman, 1988; Roach, 1987) argued that there was little evidence of increased productivity in the American economy in general, and the service sector in particular, from the billions of dollars that had been spent on IT. However, Brynjolfsson and Hitt (1993), Lichtenberg (1993), and Kraemer and Dedrick (1994) have shown strong correlations between IT investment and productivity gains at the corporate and national levels. Kraemer and Dedrick (1997) note that it is difficult enough to try to measure the return on IT investment in the private sector, where output can be valued in revenue dollars. It is more difficult to calculate the return in public organizations, which provide public services, not services for sale. In any case, IT is equally important to all leisure service organizations.

Information Technology, Organizational Goals, and Work

Probably the most extensive research on computing in public organizations in recent years has dealt with how to manage information systems to achieve organizational goals. One of the most common arguments has been that MIS research, training, and practice has been too centered on technology rather than on the application of information systems (IS) to improve organizational functioning (Kraemer & Dedrick, 1997). Other studies (Davenport, 1993; Drucker, 1995; Hammer & Champy, 1993:162) suggest that the application of IT in itself does not result in productivity gains. Yet IT makes possible the rethinking of organizational processes and systems.

Part of the problem in justifying the expense of IT might lie in the training given in colleges. Caudle (1987) puts much of the blame on training programs and graduate school curricula that concentrate too much on technology management and not enough on information resource management (IRM). The IRM movement argues that organizations should focus on managing information resources rather than on technology per se (Kraemer & Dedrick, 1997). Caudle also argues that managers in public organizations are increasingly concerned with managing IT to improve organizational functions, but that management schools focus mostly on technical skills. Essentially, the issue is related to the need to have program staff involved in the adoption and use of technologies. Chisholm (1988) argues that active employee involvement is a crucial part of the work process as advanced information technology is employed in the organization.

Martin and Overman (1988) note that the failure of IT to transform organizations is due to the failure of managers to integrate information needs and cognitive expectations with the management activities of organizations.

Wildavsky (1983) blames MISs for generating raw data rather than useful information that can be incorporated into the decision-making process of organizations. The lessons here are central to successful leisure service organizations. Basically, the value of IT depends on the way it is integrated into the management processes of planning, organizing, decision making, implementation, and evaluation. Therefore, new technologies will not mitigate the impacts of a poorly performing organization. The management must be sufficiently organized to develop IT systems that provide real and relevant decision-making information.

Danziger, Kraemer, Dunkle, & King (1993) surveyed 1846 end users in 46 U.S. cities about organizational structure and the quality of the information system. Their findings suggest that three factors are related to quality and effectiveness: technology, people, and the state of computing development. To improve the technical performance of the computing function, managers should provide incentives to computing units "on the basis of explicit, measurable performance criteria such as the timeliness of response to users' requests for computing products, the reduction of down time, and the minimization of disruptions due to technical changes in systems and procedures" (Danziger et al. 1993:). It is increasingly clear that the key determinant of computing quality and value is likely to be the ability of organizations to tailor IT to their needs and characteristics. Kraemer, King, Dunkle, and Lane (1989) identified effectiveness of computing within an organization as the following: (1) the skill state—IS management controls computerization and applies computing resources to technical interests; (2) the service state, departmental management controls computing, and the operational interests of these departments are served; (3) the control state—senior management controls computerization, and its broad managerial interests are served; and (4) a mixed state exists in the absence of any of the three pure states. There is no consistent link between the control over means and the particular ends sought in the mixed state. Management action (and need), whether direct or indirect, is the controllable driver of computing development and change.

Computing technology has had a major impact on how work is done, how decisions are made, how organizations are structured, and how people interact. Some impacts are obvious: (1) documents are typed and stored on computers rather than on typewriters; (2) spreadsheets are used for financial planning; (3) records are kept in electronic databases; and (4) memos are distributed via electronic mail. Other changes are less obvious, but they are possibly more significant in their impact. Access to information can change the location and nature of decision making, entire job classifications disappear while new ones are created, layers of management are eliminated, organizational politics take on new dimensions, and jobs can become more or less satisfying to workers (Kraemer & Dedrick, 1997).

Much of the debate about computing and organizational structure has focused on whether computing causes the centralizing or decentralizing of decision making in the organization. In the days of centralized, mainframe computing functions, it was thought that computing systems would tend to centralize the decision-making process. However, it appears that the access to

desktop PCs has tended to decentralize access to information and has led to predictions that decision making will likewise be decentralized as lower-level managers take advantage of the opportunities offered by that access to information (Kraemer & Dedrick, 1997).

Computing and Work Life

Most research indicates that computing increases the level of stress and pressure on workers (Attewell, 1987; Danziger & Kraemer, 1986; Kraemer & Danziger, 1990; Perolle, 1987). However, many studies have found that computers have had a positive effect on workers' job satisfaction and interest in their work. For example, the ability and access to manipulate information gave them a greater sense of control over their work (Kraemer & Danziger, 1990). Most empirical research has concluded that computing generally has expanded the number of tasks expected of workers and the array of skills needed to perform those tasks.

The impact of computing on social interaction in organizations has increased noticeably with the widespread use of computers made possible by the introduction of personal computers. Peer-to-peer relations have been affected most by information systems that cross departmental boundaries. The interdependence between individuals and work groups has increased as such systems allow and even require sharing of information and coordination of activities (Kling, 1992; Kling & Jewett, 1991). Communication among peers also has increased; in particular, the use of e-mail and PC networks has increased communication among geographically dispersed peers (Snizek, 1987). In terms of interactions between supervisors and staff, computers have had mixed effects on the quality of social interaction. The use of e-mail can lower the barriers to communication caused by different status levels, resulting in more uninhibited communications between supervisor and subordinates (Sproull & Kiesler, 1986).

The Manager and Information

The purpose of gathering, organizing, and analyzing information for the management of leisure service organizations is to provide data that will help achieve objectives. The budget is one of the primary ways of defining such objectives and determining the organization's future activities. The budget is central to the strategic plan. An example of quantifying program tasks is the number of person-days required to complete tasks. Specifically, current youth services of an organization may include six separate, yet interrelated services to which time is assigned for each task and action by a staff member. Identification of person-days and associated costs allows the leisure manager to plan for future budgets and make reallocations. Buck (2000) notes that implementing a facility scheduling software package at the new Maui Kihei Aquatics Complex will save about 400 person-hours over the first phase of the project. The software costs are significant, yet will be paid for within the first year of operation. Not only will there be yearly savings, but the accuracy of scheduling will be significantly improved.

Management indicators and monitoring may consist of efforts to control time, set work targets, estimate staffing levels, measure employee performance, measure program effectiveness, and produce periodic reports for the decision makers. Lane County Council of Government in Eugene, Oregon, tracks staffing related to research needs in order to project hires for the coming year. Kansas City, Missouri, uses an MIS system to improve productivity that compares information on actual and expected levels of achievement.

The importance of strategic alignment with or linkage to the mission of the organization via the MIS is critical. However, Fraser and Sibley (1998:) note that some barriers exist in creating this alignment:

1. Proper training of the management team, who are usually too heavily trained in either technology or management, but not both;

2. Poor communication among management and IT personnel;

3. Understanding of non-information technology staff and management of the difficulties of providing good computer service;

4. Not having a well-written and understood strategic plan;

5. Not ensuring that all divisions have strategic plans consistent with the overall strategic plan; and

6. Allowing interacting divisions to have separate and uncoordinated strategic plans.

Fraser and Sibley also identified the following strategic alignment issues relative to information technology: (1) the need for coordination of the strategic plan with the budget and resource requests; and (2) modifying the operating budget requests without proper notification of other departmental units. It is essential that the management of the leisure service organization communicate regularly about intentions, data needs, and strategies in order for the IT personnel to provide appropriate databases.

Computers, Technology, and Decision Making

Information is really the fuel that drives organizations (Donnelly et al. 1990). Managers convert information into action through decision making. Therefore, generating only information that is useful for decision making is crucial. More information is not better; it clouds the usefulness and management of relevant information. Most manager's complaints about information and technology are as follows: (Donnelly et al., 1990:566)

1. There is too much of the wrong kind of information and not enough of the right kind;

2. Information is so scattered throughout the organization that it is difficult to locate answers to simple questions;

3. Vital information is sometimes suppressed by subordinates or by managers in other functional areas; and

4. Vital information often arrives long after it is needed.

The contribution of computing to decision making stems from two factors: (1) the enhancement of the ability to organize, maintain, and retrieve information needed to make a decision; and (2) the modeling power of computers, which allows large amounts of information to be reduced to key indicators that are understandable and usable by decision makers. (Kraemer & Dedrick, 1997)

Decision support systems (DSSs) have one purpose, that is, to provide the manager with necessary information for making intelligent decisions. DSSs are differentiated from management information systems (MIS) by having a direct objective of supporting decision making. A computerized database is not a DSS. A DSS is a support to decision making via the steps of problem identification, choosing relevant data, selecting a problem-solving approach, and evaluating options. Thus, a DSS is part of the MIS. Normally, a DSS helps make comparisons using system-wide data, whereas an MIS helps to track records and so on. An MIS provides information; a DSS shapes information (Donnelly et al., 1990). MISs capture and retrieve information for the entire organization, whereas DSSs capture and retrieve information for managers for specific purposes.

DSSs provide decision makers access to powerful models and all the data necessary to run those models under different assumptions and conditions. DSSs do not provide the answers to complex questions, but the process of modeling can facilitate decision making by clarifying the issues under consideration, requiring decision makers to specify the assumptions they are making, and focusing attention on areas of disagreement that require compromise. (Andersen & Dutton, 1995; Kraemer & King, 1995) This process of stating assumptions allows the leisure service manager the opportunity to better understand the political realm in which they operate. At more sophisticated levels of decision making, the value and role of computer-based models are more indirect. DDSs generally do not provide the answers to complex questions, but the process of modeling can facilitate and improve the decision-making process.

The types of information needed by managers for decision making using a DSS and MIS are: planning, control, and operations. Planning decisions involve formulating objectives for the organization, the amounts and kinds of resources necessary to attain these objectives, and the policies that govern the use of the resources. Planning information comes from external sources and relates to present and future scenarios. Requirements for data gathering increase the technical capabilities of agencies, which improve the analytical quality of the planning process. Data requirements also increase opportunities for citizens to use data to participate in the planning and policy-making process. The availability of data empowers new participants, allowing them to call attention to issues and more effectively influence the decision-making process. In this case, the simple act of gathering, managing, and providing access to data helps to democratize the decision-making process, an interesting outcome not often considered by champions of decision support systems (Dandekar, 1988; Innes, 1988; Slater, 1984).

Managers make control decisions to ensure that the organization's performance is consistent with its objectives. Control information comes mainly from internal sources (often interdepartmental) and involves developing budgets and measuring the performance of staff.

At the operational level, computers are useful for setting the stage for decision making and for monitoring the organization's activities in order to alert managers to the need to make a decision. These decisions focus on the day-to-day activities of the organization and how efficiently its resources are being used. These tasks are accounting, inventory, and scheduling. This information is usually internal and comes from a designated department. First-line staff and supervisors are the primary users.

Designing a Decision Support System

Leisure service organizations operate within a complicated context of clients, regulations, community values, expectations and user behaviors. Leisure service organizations, like any organization, must deal with two broad types of information flows: external and internal (adapted from Donnelly et al., 1990; see Figure 13.1).

External information flows proceed from the organization to the environment or from the environment to the organization. The inward flow of information is referred to as intelligence information, and the outward flow as organizational communication. Basically, these are the conduits for connecting the organization to the external environment. Intelligence information includes data on the various elements of the organization's operating environment (community, clients, policies, regulations, mandates, programs, services, and competition) for use in evaluating strategic and long-range planning information on the economic (consumer trends), social, and cultural environments in which the organization operates. This information informs decision making and is part of the DSS.

Organizational communication flows outward from the organization to the various components of the external operating environment. Promotion, public relations, advertising, pricing, long-range and strategic plans, and policies are forms of organizational communication. It is obvious that the content of the flow of information is mostly controlled by the organization.

Figure 13.1
Information Flow and Information Types for Leisure Organizations

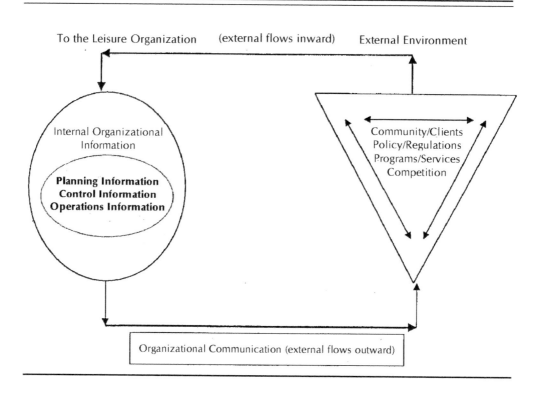

Within Figure 13.1, one can see that the planning, control, and operations information flows vertical and horizontal within the leisure organization. This flow is titled intraorganizational information. The important aspect is that all information flows should be part of the plan and not allowed to function without a direction, hopefully one coordinated by the IT manager and leisure service manager. The objective is not to withhold information, but to make sure the information reaches the proper staff person or division in a timely manner.

Donnelly and colleagues (1990:575) suggest the following functions of a decision support system.

1. Determination of management and organizational needs. Leisure managers should be involved in the development of the information system that they intend to use. Kotler (1986) offers the following starting points from which to begin the development of the system.

a. What types of decisions do you make regularly?

b. What types of information do you need to make these decisions?

c. What types of information do you receive regularly?

d. What types of information would you like to get that you are not now getting?

e. What information would you want daily? Weekly? Monthly? Yearly?

f. What types of data analysis programs would you like to see made available?

2. Information gathering and processing. There are five components to processing data.

   a. Evaluating the confidence you have in the data, such as its reliability.

   b. Indexing provides classification for storage and retrieval once the data have been gathered.

   c. Abstracting, that is editing and reducing the data in a way that only the relevant data for the task are produced and presented.

   d. Dissemination, or getting the information to the staff in a timely and useable format.

   e. Storing the information in a way that it is accessible in the future.

3. Information use in decision making. If the right questions were asked in step one above, then the information is likely to be effective in decision making. Timeliness and accuracy of information is crucial.

Figure 13.2 presents the model of how these functions operate within the context of decision making and orga-

Figure 13.2
Functions of a Decision Support System for Leisure Organizations

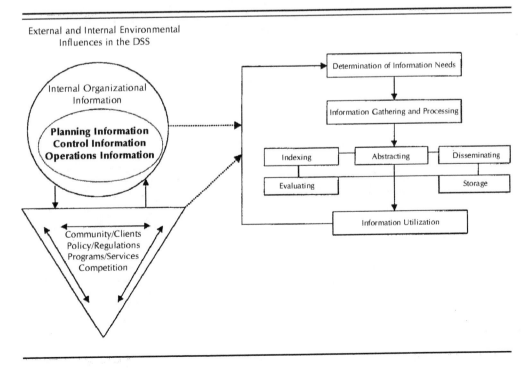

nizing information. It can be seen that the organization's external and internal flow and control of information influences use and evaluation in determining information needs. This point is critical, in that the determination of information needs must be related to the context in which the leisure organization functions.

Organizing a Decision Support System

Leisure service organizations are faced with many issues that have an impact on the information needs of each organization. However, no matter what the size or sector (private, public, or nonprofit), they all have in common a need to organize information. Some rely on only a simple word processor, spreadsheet, and database. Some larger organizations use a central system operated within the city or county government. In any system, one would find marketing, financial, accounting, logistics or operations, planning, and personnel systems (divisions or departments). Figure 13.3 presents a model for organizing the DSS for leisure managers that shows centralized data banks and two subsystems. This system allows for managers of other units to access information from a variety of departments. Therefore, designing such a sys-

Figure 13.3
The Central Data Bank in a Decision Support System for Leisure Organizations

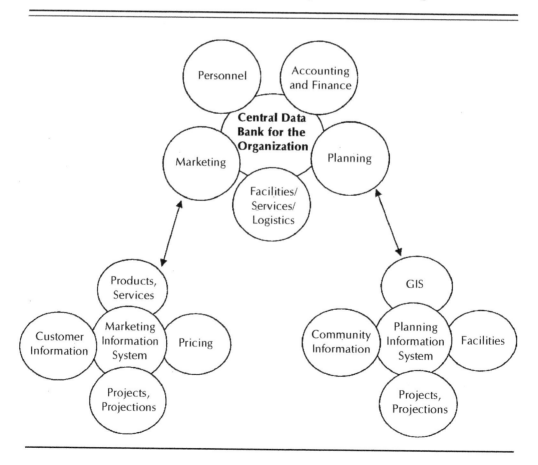

tem requires a "system-wide perspective" (Necco, Gordon, & Tsai, 1987). This perspective implies building a central data bank and information center, and viewing the information as an important organizational resource.

The central data bank is the core of the DSS. Centralizing information means that critical information does not have to be duplicated; it is housed within one area and accessible to managers for decision making. White and Christy (1987) caution that the information center must be able to justify its existence through improved information in terms of quality, access, and timeliness. Donnelly and colleagues (1990:578) note that a basic weakness in most organizations is the absence of a central information center for gathering and processing information. They note that three steps are necessary for developing an information center:

1. Dispersed information activities must be identified throughout the organization;

2. These activities must be viewed as parts of a whole; and

3. These activities must be brought under the management of a separate centralized information center.

Information should be regarded as a basic resource, just like funding and staffing. Information is vital to success when it is timely and accurate. Donnelly and colleagues (1990) note that one of the major reasons DSSs have increased within organizations is due to the growth in information technology. It is important for the leisure service manager to realize that the development and implementation of a DSS is only to facilitate more effective management decision making.

Challenges and Issues for Leisure Service Managers in the Information Age

Purchasing and Investments

Leisure service managers are continually faced with the challenge of purchasing computer and information technology that is up-to-date and powerful enough to operate newer software systems. The following objectives should be realized or used as a guide in purchasing new equipment (based on Andrus & Lane, 1989; Horine, 1995):

1. Improved efficiency and accuracy;

2. Elimination of redundancy of activities and tasks;

3. Improved reaction time, quicker generation of data and reports;

4. Production of accurate and timely financial and budget statements;

5. Reduction of expenses by using staff more efficiently; and

6. Ability to generate additional revenues by more effective pricing, fund-raising, and marketing.

Cagle (1993) suggests that to begin developing an information system, an organization should obtain the advice of professionals, have a goal for the end product or process, and keep it simple.

The system, if properly designed, can grow with organizational needs. Other suggestions are to have vendor support in place for troubleshooting. Examine what other comparable leisure organizations use and determine the successes, failures, and likelihood of these with a similar system for your organization. Finally, Bay (1993:12) suggests that managers should do the following:

1. Establish commitment from all using units, departments, administrators and decision makers;

2. Establish communication links between users, departments, administrators, and decision makers;

3. Establish control to ensure that individuals and groups maintain their focus on the goals and objectives of the data-processing system; and

4. Establish reasonable and affordable costs.

Fraser (1998) recommends that managers not only provide basic service to staff, but ensure that small or specialized groups obtain necessary software and hardware, for example, graphics programs for budget and policy analysis, statistical packages for analyzing community and user data, geographic information system (GIS) for the planning staff, and so on.

Policy Issues and Information Technology

Kraemer and Dedrick (1997) suggest there is reason to believe that current developments in computers and technology might be upsetting the delicate balance struck by the Constitution among the branches of government in the separation of powers doctrine, among the levels of government in federalism, between government and the people in the amendments, and between various factions in the political system in the electoral process. These public management issues might include the following:

1. The government's own use of information technology in the delivery of services to citizens;

2. The provision of easy access to government information for individuals, groups, and corporations, and the pricing of such information; and

3. The performance impacts of information technology in terms of quality and cost of service delivery.

Bertot (1999) was quoted earlier in the chapter with regard to the innovations in service delivery and management due to technology. These innovations have also led to policy questions. Information technology provides users with more access to information, and allows the government to provide more, in the following areas: (1) better dissemination methods (Library of Congress Web site reporting on Congress and legislation), (2) virtual government (24-hour services on-line, for example the University of Hawaii's library access system); (3) interactive on-line services (see Arizona's on-line driver's license renewal program as an example); (4) public relations (see for example the U.S. Department of Agriculture's Web site); (5) promotion of open government (on-line or televised hearings and meetings); and (6) mandated Web sites for services (the least intensive with mere organizational charts, mission statements, and photographs).

Figure 13.4 presents the major types of electronic or digital government services in use today and their potential policy implications (Bertot, 1999). As a result of the services listed above, Bertot notes four areas of concern: (1) privacy, (2) authentication and security, (3) records management, and (4) benchmarking. Privacy issues center around the access log, which captures a user's Internet protocol (IP) address. Of concern here is the fact that a user leaves a trail of Web site use, thereby allowing service providers a way to build user profiles. In terms of government service, this issue is of greatest concern within the area of interactive services. There have been a number of court cases involving this issue.

Authentication and security issues are of concern in nearly all digital and information technologies. Authentication is a process of user verification (users are who they say they are). Service providers need to know who they are working with in order to provide the correct services, and service users need to know they are getting the correct service. This area is of crucial importance when working with sensitive documents and files. For background information, see http://wwe.cdt.org/digsig/index.html.

Records management issues are prevalent within all the services listed in Figure 13.4. Governments are obligated to disseminate written records, in gen-

Figure 13.4
Types of Electronic or Digital Government Services and Their Policy Implications

Types of Electronic/Digital Government Services and Policy Implications				
	Issue Area Implications			
Type of Electronic/ Digital Service	Privacy	Authentication/ Security	Records Management	Bench- marking
Dissemination	X	X+	X+	X
Virtual Government	X	X	X	X+
Interactive Services	X+	X+	X+	X+
Public Relations			X+	X-
Promotion of Democratic Principals		X-	X	X-
Mandate Fulfillment			X-	

X+ - of greater concern
X - of concern
X- - of lesser concern

Source: Bertot, J. C. (1999). Challenges and issues for public managers in the digital era. *The Public Manager, 27*(4), 27–31.

eral. Yet the issue of electronic media is in flux, as more and more agencies release media via the Web. Therefore, record management issues become more complex: There is a need to define what a government publication is, and there is a need to consider ways to preserve electronic records. A Web site to consult on this matter is: http://istweb.syr.edu/~mcclure/guidelines.html.

Benchmarking is an attempt by government agencies to determine the efficiency, effectiveness, and overall effect of agency activities as a means to improve. Web traffic (as measured by Web log files) provides one way of establishing efficiency. These provide data on users: what sites they visit, and what needs they may have. However, these data have privacy implications.

The leisure service manager and the decision-making body of an organization need to be aware of these issues and be prepared to spend adequate resources on information technology. Offering electronic services begs larger policy questions. Leisure service organizations would do well to follow these guidelines.

1.   Consider the implications for services, not only technically, but the legal and policy implications as well.

2.   Manage the potential privacy, authentication, and records management issues.

3.   Coordinate and consult with other public organizations to ensure that similar standards and procedures are in place.

4.   Realize technology will challenge existing policies more rapidly than expected (modified from Bertot, 1999).

Summary

Computers are affecting organizations through their impact on decision making, employment, structure, organizational politics, and work life. Computers aid managers in the decision-making process by helping to monitor organizational activities. Instant access to information translates to control and coordination of organizational activity, and improves service.

As organizations grow in complexity, managers will depend more heavily on various internal and external sources of information. The better the information, the better the resulting decisions, because there is less risk and uncertainty in the expected outcomes.

This explosion of communication-based technology will require jobs that specialize in information and technology management in the leisure service organization. A variety of new terminology and acronyms have surfaced as a response to the growth of technology in the workplace. Leisure service managers must remain involved with the MIS of the organization in order to ensure that it meets the needs of staff, managers, decision makers, and the client base. The use of computers and information systems has both deepened and widened in organizations over the past decade and has a profound impact on organizational structures, primarily due to rapid communication and dissemination of data. The rapid evolution of computing and communication technology offers unprecedented opportunities, but it also presents many challenges for the management of computing in public, nonprofit, and private organizations.

Discussion Questions

1. Why are more comprehensive deci-sion support systems necessary?

2. Describe IT, IS, DSS, and MIS.

3. When viewing the history of computing and information management, what trends are there in information management?

4. What is the key difference between MIS and DSS?

5. Describe the external and internal flow of information for a leisure service organization.

6. Describe a model to best develop a DSS in a leisure organization. What role does the internal and external flow of information play?

7. Explain the importance of a central data bank. How would this help the leisure service manager?

8. Why is it important to examine the role of information in decision making? Why not study computers?

9. What policy challenges will leisure managers face in the digital or information age?

10. What should leisure managers be aware of relative to purchasing technology?

References

Andersen, K. V., & Dutton, W. H. (1995). The future of economic modeling in political decision making processes. In K. V. Andersen (Ed.), *Information systems in the political world*. Amsterdam: IOS Press.

Andrus, S., & Lane, S. A. (1989, March). Computerizing the athletic department. *College Athletic Management, 1,* 30–34.

Attewell, P. (1987). The deskilling controversy. *Work and Occupations 14*(3), 323–46.

Baily, M. N. (1986). What has happened to productivity growth? *Science, 234,* 443–451.

Bay, R. (1993, May). The four Cs for computer success. *School Business Affairs,* 10–13.

Bertot, J. C. (1999). Challenges and issues for public managers in the digital era. *The Public Manager, 27*(4). 27–31.

Brynjolfsson, E., & Hitt, L. (1993, December). *Is information systems spending productive? New evidence and new results.* Proceedings of the 14th International Conference on Information Systems, Orlando, Florida.

Buck, J. (2000, March 29). *Facility scheduling and cost savings* [Interview]. Maui County Department of Parks and Recreation, Kihei Aquatics and Community Center Complex, Kihei, Maui.

Bugler, D. T., & Bretschneider, S. (1993). Technology push or program pull: Interest in new information technologies within public organizations. In B. Bozeman (ed.) *Public Management: The State of the Art.* San Francisco: Jossey-Bass.

Cagle, R. (1993, March). Learning computers. *Fitness Management, 1,* 48–51.

Caudle, S. L. (1987, Spring). High tech to better effect. *The Bureaucrat,* 47–52.

Caudle, S. L. (1990). "Managing information resources in state government. *Public Administration Review, 50*(5),515–524.

Caudle, S. L., Marchand, D. A., Bretschneider, S. I., Fletcher, P. T., & Thurmaier, K. M. (1989). *Managing information resources: New directions in state government—A national study of state government information resources management.* Syracuse, NY: Syracuse University, School of Information Studies.

Chisholm, R. F. (1988). Introducing advanced information technology into public organizations. *Public Productivity Review 11*(4),39–55.

Dandekar, H. C. (1988). *The planner's use of information: Techniques for collection, organization, and communication.* Chicago, IL: American Planning Association.

Danziger, J. N., & Kraemer, K. L. (1986). *People and computers: The impacts of computing on end users in organizations.* New York: Columbia University Press.

Danziger, J. N., Kraemer, K. L., Dunkle, D. E., & King, J. L. (1993). Enhancing the quality of computing service: Technology, structure, and people. *Public Administration Review, 53*(2) 161–169.

Davenport, T. H. (1993): *Process innovation: Reengineering work through information technology.* Boston: Harvard Business School Press.

Donnelly, J. H., Gibson, J. L., & Ivancevich, J. M. (1990). *Fundamentals of management* (7th ed). Homewood, IL: BPI/Irwin.

Drucker, P. F. (1995). Really reinventing government. *Atlantic monthly 275*(2), 49–61.

Evans, B. (2000, March 13). The innovation explosion. *Information Week, 22,* 174–175.

Fletcher, P. T., Bretschneider, S. I., Marchand, D. A., Rosenbaum, H., & Bertot, J. C. (1992). *Managing information technology: transforming county governments in the 1990s.* Syracuse, N Y: Syracuse University, School of Information Studies.

Fletcher, P. T., & Foy, D. O. (1994). Managing information systems in state and local government. In M. E. Williams (Ed.), *Annual review, of information science and technology 29.* Medford, NJ: Learned Information.

Fraser, M. B. (1998). Strategies for timing and pacing of IT investments. *The Public Manager 26*(4), 41–44.

Fraser, M. B., & Sibley, E. H. (1998). Strategic IT alignment and managing the use of very large databases. *The Public Manager 27*(1), 39–42.

Griesemer, J. R. (1985). *Microcomputers in local government.* Washington, DC: International City/County Management Association.

Hammer, M., & Champy, J. (1993). *Reengineering the corporation: A manifesto for business revolution.* New York: Harper Business.

Horine, L. (1995). *Administration of physical education and sport programs.* Madison, WI: Brown & Benchmark.

Innes, J. (1988). Effects of data requirements on planning: Case studies of environmental impact assessment and community development block grants. *Computer, Environmental, and Urban Systems, 12,* 77–88.

Kling, R. (1992): Behind the terminal. In W. Cotterman & J. Senn (Eds.), *Challenges and strategies for Research in Systems Development* New York: Wiley & Sons.

Kling, R., & Jewett, T. (1991): The dynamics of computerization in a social science research team. *Social Science Computer Review, 9*(2) 246–275.

Kotler, P. (1986). *Principles of marketing.* (3rd ed.). Prentice-Hall: Englewood Cliffs, NJ.

Kraemer, K. L., & Danziger, J. N. (1990) The impacts of computer technology on the worklife of information workers. *Social Science Computer Review, 8*(4) 592–613.

Kraemer, K. L., & Dedrick, J. (1994). The payoffs from investment in information technology: Findings from Asia-Pacific countries. *World Development, 22*(12) 1921–1931.

Kraemer, K. L., & Dedrick, J. (1997). Computing and public organizations. *Journal of Public Administration Research and Theory, 7*(1), 89–124.

Kraemer, K. L., Gurbaxani, V., Mooney, J., Dunkle, D., & Vitalari, N. (1994). *Business value of information technology in corporations.* Irvine: University of California, Irvine Center for Research on Information Technology and Organizations.

Kraemer, K. L., & King, J. L. (1995). Computer-based models for policy-making: Uses and impacts in the U.S. federal government." In K. V. Andersen (Ed.) *Information systems in the political world* (pp. 129–146). Amsterdam: IOS Press.

Kraemer, K. L., King, J. L., Dunkle, D. E., & Lane, J. P. (1989). *Managing information systems: Change and control in organizational computing.* San Francisco: Jossey-Bass.

Kraemer, K. L., & Norris, D. F. (1994). *Leading edge computer use in U.S. municipalities* [Special data issue]. Washington, DC: International City/County Management Association.

Lichtenberg, F. R. (1993). *The output contributions of computer equipment and personnel: A firm level analysis* (Working Paper No. 4540). Cambridge MA: National Bureau of Economic Research.

Loveman, G. W. (1988). An assessment of the productivity impact of information technologies (Working Paper No. 88-054). Cambridge, MA: MIT, Management in the 1990s Project. .

Maney, K. (2000, March 30). The 1-gigahertz PCs have power to . . . what? *USA Today,* p. C1.

Martin, J. A., & Overman, S. (1988). Management and cognitive hierarchies: What is the role of management information systems? *Public Productivity Review, 11*(4), 69–84.

McLean, D. D., Bannon, J. J., Gray, H. R. (1999). *Leisure resources: Its comprehensive planning* (2nd, ed.). Champaign, IL: Sagamore Publishing .

Necco, C. R., Gordon, C. L., & Tsai, N. W. (1987, December). Systems analysis and design: Current practices. *MIS Quarterly,* 461–478.

Northrop, A., Dunkle, D., Kraemer, K. L., & King, J. L. (1994). Computers, police, and the fight against crime: An ecology of technology, training, and use. *Information and the Public Sector, 3,* 21–45.

Perolle, J. A. (1987). *Computers and social change.* Belmont, CA: Wadsworth.

Raths, D. (2000, March 13). Managing your three-ring circus. *Information Week, 22,* 93–95.

Rifkin, J. (1996). *The end of work.* New York: Putnam.

Roach, S. (1987). *America's technology dilemma: A profile of the information economy.* New York: Morgan Stanley.

Slater, D. C. (1984). *Management of local planning.* Washington DC: International City/County Management.

Snizek, W. (1987). Some observations on the effects of microcomputers on the productivity of university scientists. *Knowledge, 8,* 612–24.

Sproull, L. S., & Kiesler, S. (1986). Reducing social context-cues: Electronic mail in organizational communication. *Management Science, 32*(11), 1492–1512.

U.S. General Accounting Office (GAO). (1992, September). *Perceived barriers to effective information resources management: Results of GAO panel discussions.* Washington, DC: U.S. General Accounting Offices, Information Management and Technology Division.

U.S. General Accounting Office (GAO). (1995, July) *Information technology investment: A government-wide overview.* Washington, DC: U.S. General Accounting Office, Accounting and Information Management Division.

White, C. E., & Christy, D. P. (1987, December). The information center concept: A normative model and a study of six installations. *MIS Quarterly,* 451–460.

Wildavsky, A. (1983). Information as an organizational problem. *Journal of Management Studies. 20*(1), 29-40.

Zientara, M. (1981). *The history of computing.* Farmingham, MA: CW Communications.

Chapter

14

Monitoring, Evaluation, and Research

Photo courtesy of the City of Phoenix (AZ) Parks, Recreation and Library Department.

Evaluation insures greater accountability in the leisure service organizations.

Introduction

The monitoring, evaluation, and research task for leisure service is the focus of this chapter. This chapter is written to provide the leisure services manager with basic information in which to initiate an evaluation, and to judge the quality of the evaluation effort. Effective leisure service organizations con-duct evaluation and marketing research (needs assessments) to determine needs and market opportunities within their communities. Specifically, the leisure service organization attempts to better understand its constituencies in order to provide needed services and develop effective marketing and promotion pro grams. Effective leisure service managers monitor the organization's progress of programs and services in order to align organizational philosophy (goals, vision, and policy) with the community values and needs. Similarly, leisure service managers evaluate programs and services in order to determine effectiveness and impact of various services and programs. We will explore the monitoring, evaluation, and research functions of the leisure service manager. As noted above, this chapter will not attempt to address all aspects of evaluation and research. For more detailed information on research and evaluation methods, it is recommended that the leisure service manager refer to Mitra and Lankford (1999), Henderson and Bialeschki (1995), and McLean, Bannon, & Gray (1999).

The field of leisure services is diverse and complicated in terms of the issues and trends that have an impact on the policies, programs, professional needs, and community support for leisure services. In such a diverse field, where do we find answers to our problems? Henderson and O'Neill (1995) note that most of the foundation of our knowledge comes from allied fields such as psychology, sociology, forestry, and business, as well as from criminal justice, urban affairs, and health. Therefore, as a profession, we rely on concepts, models, and theories grounded in the physical sciences (e.g., exercise science and physiology), behavioral sciences (e.g., psychology), and social sciences (e.g., sociology, geography and urban planning) for the provision, management, and evaluation of our services.

Why Conduct Evaluation and Research Projects?

Practitioners conduct research in the pursuit of resolving leisure service problems and issues. Leisure service managers come from a wide array of disciplines; likewise, they are responsible for a wide range of programs and services. Mitra and Lankford (1999) recognize that many practitioners need to monitor and evaluate programs and services, yet do not appreciate the full extent to which systematic research may be of value in this management task. The authors provide some examples of the types of scenerios that can be addressed through evaluation and research.

- The superintendent is concerned with identifying the factors that are promoting decay of urban parks and recommending appropriate policy actions to the policymaking board.

- A sports management specialist employed by the university athletic department is attempting to conduct ad conversion studies to determine the effectiveness of local advertising.

- A marketing director for the local convention and visitors bureau is concerned about the image of the community and how it compares with other competing destinations.

- A program manager is attempting to understand what type of recreation and social programs in which youth-at-risk would be attracted to participate.

• An open space planner is helping a community conduct long-range land use plans that address parks, bike lanes, and river access acquisition and management.

• A youth worker is trying to determine how to operationalize the concepts of motivation, leisure participation, and subsequent satisfaction levels to address at-risk populations.

• A parks planner and policy analyst is charged with identifying the social, economic, environmental, and personal benefits of recreation in the community to justify a budget request.

• A district superintendent is concerned with identifying factors that may help to motivate full-time, part-time, and seasonal recreation and park staff.

• A community center manager is working with the board of directors of the community association to determine the optimal administrative structure.

• A manager is working with the board of directors to determine voter attitudes toward a proposed bond issue for an aquatics facility.

• A program director is concerned about the lack of participation from women, seniors, and people with disabilities.

Why Do Evaluation Research for Leisure Services?

Anyone whose job depends on information about what people do or want should know how to obtain that information in a valid and systematic manner (Sommer & Sommer, 1986). This is especially true in leisure services, where managers and staff, on a daily basis, must be concerned with "what people do during their leisure time," "what people want to do during leisure time," and "what people experience during their leisure time." Specifically, leisure professionals must know how to interview, construct questionnaires, observe behavior, evaluate programs, and conduct various kinds of experimental research projects.

Kraus and Allen (1997) note a number of specific needs in leisure services that can be met through systematic, carefully designed research and evaluation studies. They identified: (1) the need to improve, test, or apply new practices to upgrade leadership and management operations; (2) the need to understand the leisure experience (motivations, structure, and consequences) and needs of clients; (3) and the need to measure outcomes of experiences to provide documentation and support for what we do as a profession. Henderson and Bialeschki (1995) believe there are eight reasons to evaluate leisure services: (1) determine accountability of services; (2) assess or establish baseline data on programs; (3) assess the attainment of goals and objectives; (4) ascertain outcomes and impacts of programs; (5) determine keys to success and failure; (6) improve quality control; (7) set future directions; and (8) comply with complex external standards. Murphy, Niepoth, Jamieson, and Williams (1991) also note that evaluation should consider the organizational goals, personnel, facilities, and programs.

Of particular concern and importance is the ability of leisure service personnel to conduct a systematic evaluation. Lankford and Privatsky (1989) conducted a study of randomly selected leisure service organizations (city, county, and special districts) in Oregon, Washington, and Northern California to determine how evaluation is used, and to what extent their staff could conduct the necessary evaluations. They reported:

- The majority of organizations (94 percent) indicated evaluation costs were part of each program budget.

- The majority of organizations (83 percent) reported they needed more training in evaluation.

- Only 30 percent of the organizations indicated they had someone on staff who could "conduct" a valid and reliable evaluation of a program or service!

- The organizations indicated that the following areas of the leisure service system were evaluated at some time in the past: goals and objectives, fiscal resources, areas and facilities, personnel, and programs.

It should be of major concern to leisure service managers that there are not enough professionals with adequate skills to conduct a monitoring, evaluation, or policy research project. It is assumed that consultants are hired to fill the void, yet how can leisure managers know how to evaluate the work of the consultant, not to mention the method, budget, and overall proposal submitted to the organization? Murphy and colleagues (1991) note that in the leisure field, evaluation has undoubtedly been the weakest and the most disregarded of all the management functions.

This is not only a problem in the field; it is a problem in academics as well. A number of weaknesses and inadequacies have been noted within the leisure research being produced. In the area of therapeutic recreation, Bedini and Wu (1994), found in a review of articles ($n = 46$) published in the *Therapeutic Recreation Journal,* that the use of theory, sophistication of designs, strength of measurement, and application continue to be problems in the field. Additionally, in the publication *A Literature Review: The President's Commission on Americans Outdoors* (1986), almost all of the authors mentioned inadequacies in leisure research. The papers consisted of literature reviews of trends and demands, values and benefits, natural resources management, special populations, motivations and barriers, activity participation trends, urban recreation, tourism, financing, and information and communication. What was noted in almost every paper, and certainly in each of the above-mentioned areas, is that the theories, methods, and analysis and statistical treatments are substandard and in need of improvement. These reviews were meant to have an impact on application in the field. The points here are that as leisure managers: we need to (1) better acquaint ourselves and our staff with evaluation methods and applications; and (2) to influence decisions, we need to have better data to justify our needs, proposals, and programs.

Evaluation and Research as Management Decision Making

The leisure service manager's role in evaluation and research is difficult. The manager has a dual responsibility to accurately specify the problem of interest, then evaluate the output to make sure it is of the proper type and quality to make decisions. Therefore, the leisure service manager must have an understanding of research processes and methodologies used by the organization's evaluators. If this understanding is lacking, then the leisure service manager, and the leisure service organization, is reliant on the evaluator to generate useful decision-making data. Similarly, managers must rely on other research to help make decisions. One cannot judge the worth of the data and report without knowing some basic information about evaluation and research.

Systematic research can lead to improved decisions and problem solving, as well as provide documentation of the worth and value of our services. Leisure services include, but are not limited to, parks planning and design, parks and facilities maintenance, recreation programming, natural resource management, and tourism services. What ties these professionals together at a decision-making and research level? Primarily, there are four common functions that facilitate dialogue and decision making: (1) the recognition that a problem exists or an opportunity for improvement of services exists; (2) the collection and synthesis of information; (3) the generation of alternatives to address the problem or opportunity; and (4) the communication of the observations and findings (Mitra & Lankford, 1999). The above four points are merely key tasks in systematically making informed decisions using the research process. In leisure services, we often work in group decision-making situations. Therefore, it is necessary to develop a range of alternative decisions that will influence leisure service delivery and decision making. Consequently, collective decision making becomes an important part of the research design

and planning process. Ewert (1990) suggests that collective decision making can produce a research agenda that takes into account a broader spectrum of "customers" and more perspectives than generally is the case with any one individual or small group of in-house specialists. Leisure service professionals need to be aware of and be able to use a range of methods to engage the "public" or "client" in the decision- making process through the use of research. These methods can be of critical importance in determining community values, and in translating those values into the organization's vision, goals, and objectives, as well as its policy.

Importantly, research that documents the effectiveness of our programs and activities can help increase our visibility and credibility (Bialeschki, 1994). Unfortunately, a rational and scientific sequence of inquiry is often not followed in the documentation of our services, or in the recognition and resolution of leisure service delivery problems. Why is this so? Normally, we find that the current political climate is not conducive to the systematic study of service delivery problems. For example, a special interest group may be pressuring "Recreation and Park Commission" to preserve an open space parcel. Rather than recommend a study to identify whether such a parcel is needed, is worthy, and is financially acceptable, the Commission may recommend approval rather than face the angry special interest group. Lack of time or deadlines also may affect an organization's ability to conduct appropriate research. Additionally, budget constraints may hinder the implementation of appropriate research studies to solve problems. Finally, staff may not have the expertise to conduct the research, as noted earlier in this chapter. In any case, given the above

constraints, leisure service professionals, working collectively, can at a minimum make note of the following questions in order to make more informed
decisions by using a systematic means of
analyzing and addressing issues of concern (Mitra & Lankford, 1999:5):

1. What is being studied?

2. Why is it a problem, or opportunity, for the organization?

3. What concepts or models are
available to adequately justify the
use of various problem-solving approaches?

4. What accepted studies, theories,
or assumptions are these concepts
or models based on?

5. Finally, what will be the expected results from the research endeavor?

Leisure service managers need to
answer or understand some preliminary
concerns before conducting an evaluation. Leisure service managers need to
determine the potential uses of and
reasons for conducting the evaluation.
The answers will help them in determining the level of detail, budget, staffing, data collection, statistical procedures, and presentation. Some of the
basic questions to be answered prior to
evaluating use:

• Who needs the evaluation information?

• What specific purposes will the
evaluation serve, that is, how will
the information be used?

• What specific questions must
the evaluation answer in order to
serve these purposes?

• What kind of information is
needed to answer these questions?

• When must the survey be completed so that the results will get
maximum use?

• What resources are there for
carrying out the evaluation?

• How are the results to be reported and to whom?

• Who should do the evaluation
and under what conditions?

• What methods or techniques
(e.g., mail survey, telephone interviews, face-to-face interview, etc.)
should be employed?

• Who—and how many—should
be queried? (Modified from Lankford
& Neal, 1999; Murphy et al., 1991)

What are the objectives of the decision-making process in leisure services?
In leisure service practice, often the
objectives are to improve the quality of
life and the human condition. Consider
the following diagram that portrays possible planning, management, and policy
issues faced by a local leisure service
agency manager and the subsequent
proposals that might be considered.
The process of leisure services in contemporary society encompasses many
political, economic and sociocultural
externalities that have an impact on or
influence the type of services delivered
at the local level (see Figure 14.1 and
Lankford, 1990). How is the process of
leisure research related to this model of
the delivery system? In the provision of
services, the policy, planning (and design), evaluation (and research), and
service implementation are reliant on

Figure 14.1
The Political, Economic, and Sociocultural Environment
of the Leisure Service Delivery System

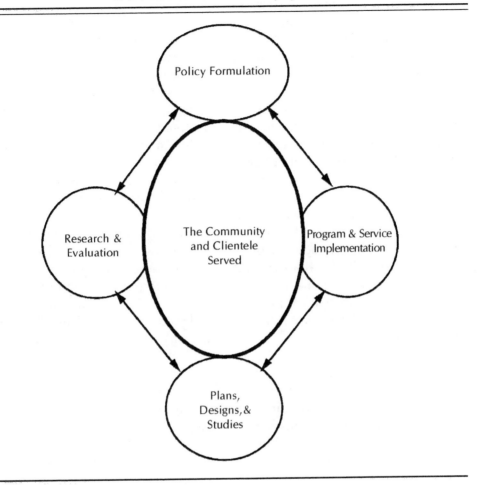

each other to address the needs of the community. Furthermore, in order for the evaluator or policy analyst to successfully design and implement a study, he or she must be able to understand and consider the nature and scope (influence) of all the above components of the system.

Evaluation and monitoring are important in the implementation and management of successful and meaningful programs. Evaluation research helps professionals understand leisure and recreation behavior better, which may help to justify programs and lead to the development of new and better programs (Henderson, 1994). Interestingly, Henderson and O'Neill (1995) noted that a recent study suggests that 41 percent of the respondents regularly read the research update, which surpassed other columns such as the Washington Scene and Product Round Up in NRPA's *Parks and Recreation* magazine. Yet many (practitioners) criticize the type of research that is conducted in leisure services in that it is of little use or relevance to practice. Practitioners are usually disinterested in theoretical research studies, and tend to view them as "ivory tower" preoccupations that do not address the concrete issues or real problems that need to be solved (Kraus & Allen, 1987). Consequently, Henderson & O'Neill (1995) explored the question of whether or not research has contributed to the advancement of professional practice. They noted that practitioners and academicians need to participate in the activity of research and to communicate what needs to be researched. Specifically, if what needs to be researched is agreed upon by both groups, there is a greater chance that the research will help to advance practice. Conversely, if the research and subsequent dialogue are not transmitted through our professional publications then research may have little impact on practice.

In order to influence practice, improve services, and address the critical issues of today, leisure evaluators must become more proactive and action oriented. Many have suggested that unless we as individuals are embedded in the world out there, our understanding of what is relevant can itself be archaic (Allison, 1995). As Ewert (1990) noted, research, whether conducted formally or informally, is an integral part of a park and recreation organization. Research is how every agency gleans information regarding how it should use its resources or what problems are being encountered. It is important, then, to develop a closer working relationship between practitioners and evaluators.

Characteristics and Areas of Importance in Evaluation Research

The following section presents some basic information to enable the leisure service manager to view the evaluation process from a systematic point of view. Additionally, a number of key concerns are presented to allow the leisure manager to become better acquainted with characteristics of quality research. Research (and evaluation) is careful, patient, and methodical inquiry done according to certain rules, guidelines, or accepted practices (Sommer & Sommer, 1986), and implies a careful and systematic means of solving or addressing problems (Mitra & Lankford, 1999). Research implies a planned, systematic approach to solving problems or discovering the answers to complex issues.

The two most common reasons for doing leisure research are: (1) to obtain answers to pressing questions or problems, and (2) to contribute to theories of leisure behavior. Generally, providing answers to pressing questions or problems has been referred to as *applied research*. It is usually conducted to solve some immediate problem or take advantage of opportunities in the market. Applied research uses the scientific method to answer a specific question for a specific group at a given point in time and is less concerned with the discovery of new knowledge (Chadwick, Bahr, & Albrecht, 1984). Examples would include conducting a study to determine why some teenagers are not participating in after-school programs, or what programs certain age groups desire in the way of leisure programs. One type of research that is receiving increasing attention is program evaluation. For the most part, this involves determining the effectiveness of a leisure service or program. Rossman (1995) defines evaluation as "judging the worth of program services on the basis of an analysis of systematically collected evidence." Evaluation is valuable in that it can guide legislative action (Sommer & Sommer, 1986), and that it can help make judgments of worth in three ways: (1) in program development, (2) in organizational management, and (3) in establishing accountability (Rossman, 1995). Additionally, a recent and emerging concept, quality assurance, is related to the assessment and evaluation process (Edginton, Hanson, & Edginton, 1992).

Investigations designed to answer general long-range questions about leisure behavior are considered *basic research,* and are generally motivated by the evaluator's curiosity. In practice, the division between applied and basic research studies is far from clear (Sommer & Sommer, 1986). However, basic research is typically directed toward advancing scientific knowledge for its own sake (Rossi, Wright, & Wright, 1978). Thomas and Nelson (1990) note that considerable controversy exists in the psychology, education, and physical education literature about whether research should be more applied or basic. Some see the distinctions between them as a reflection of the attitudes and objectives of the evaluator rather than the research activity, per se (Rossi, et al., 1978). Others (Leedy, 1985) argue that the basic difference between applied research and basic research lies in the depth to which basic research probes the underlying causes and meanings of observed phenomena, and in the sophistication with which it demands that the collected data for observation be interpreted. However, Henderson and Bialeschki (1995) noted that evaluation (applied) and other forms of research only differ in their objectives or purposes, rather than in their designs or methods of execution. Many times, the two types of research are indistinguishable (Rossi, Freeman, &

Wright, 1979), whereas most research incorporates some degree of both applied and basic methods (Thomas & Nelson, 1990). In terms of comparing paradigms between research and evaluation, we can generalize and note that research normally uses experimental and correlation methods, whereas evaluation-type research relies on a systems approach (input, processing, and output) and an objectives approach (objectives, means, and measures). For comparative purposes, it is useful to examine the characteristics of basic, applied, and evaluation research as presented in Table 14.1 (from McMillan & Schumacher, 1984).

Much has been said about the distinctions between what are referred to as basic or pure research and applied or action research. In our estimation, these distinctions are vague and rather meaningless in the resolution of problems or confirmation of knowledge, unless of course fundamental and systematic research procedures are not followed or are loosely followed. In fact, all research types are a form of inquiry. Inquiry can take as many forms as necessary, as long as they are systematic and consistent (Short, 1991). What would constitute a systematic and quality research effort? The following guidelines can be used to determine what constitutes a quality research effort that is, one having the characteristics of all or some of the following (modified from Nachmias & Nachmias 1987; Stoddard, 1982; Thomas & Nelson, 1990). For the purposes of delineating steps to the research process, the following is presented:

1. Identification and delimitation of a problem and the subproblem, stating the relationships;

2. A thorough review and analysis of relevant literature to include other studies, plans, and documents;

Table 14.1
The Leisure Service Organization Holistic Management Model

	Basic	**Applied**	**Evaluation**
Description of Research Type	Physical, behavioral and social sciences	Applied fields such as medicine, social work, engineering, and education	Practice at a given site or sites, in specific programs, or for specific policies
Purpose	• Test theories and discover scientific laws, basic principles • Determine empirical relationships between natural and social field • Determine analytical relationships among events	• Test the usefulness of scientific theories within a given field • Determine empirical relationships within a given phenomena • Determine analytical relationships among events within a field	• Assess the merit or worthiness of a specific practice or program • Assess the worth of a specific practice
Typical Role of	Scientist given field	Evaluator within a practitioner at a site(s)	Evaluator or investigator
Level of discourse	Abstract, general within science	Abstract, general within a given field	Concrete, specific to a particular practice
Generalizability of explanations	Relate to physical, behavioral, and social sciences	Apply to a given field	Apply to a specific practice at a given site(s)
Functions	• Add to scientific knowledge of basic laws and principles • Advance further practice or program inquiry and methodology	• Add to research-based knowledge in a given field • Advance research and methodology in a given field	• Add to research-based knowledge and method of a specific practice • Aid in decision-making at a given site(s)
Intended ultimate outcomes	Accepted body of scientific knowledge in physical, behavioral, and social sciences	Accepted body of research-based knowledge in a given field	Change of practice at site(s) and knowledge in field of application

Source: Adapted from McMillan, J. H., Schumacher, S., Mitra, A., & Lankford, S. V. (1984). *Research in education.* Boston: Little, Brown.

3. Specifying and defining research questions to be analyzed to help make decisions;

4. Designing a research study and method to address the research questions; developing a research plan;

5. Choosing the subjects, administering the tests or questionnaires, or conducting observations;

6. Analyzing and reporting the results; and

7. Discussing implications of the findings and making any necessary adjustments in programs, or recommending further research.

Quality research, whether basic or applied, involves much more than designing and implementing an appropriate methodological plan or analysis of data. Some of the most important activities or tasks occur prior to designing the technical methodology or analysis (Majchrzak, 1984). Importantly, the evaluator must focus on selecting and defining the problem. The following section delineates the steps in defining the problem, collecting the data, and reporting the data.

Review and Analysis of Relevant Studies, Policies, and Reports

The goal of the literature review is to develop a knowledge and understanding of previous work or activity on the topic being researched. Use of the literature to identify possible variables related to the problem or opportunity is crucial at this stage. Examining previous studies, or obtaining advice and opinions from local experts, provides the evaluator some level of assurance that the project is on the right track. The task of the literature review is intricately intertwined with the research problem and formulation task. The task is to work toward specifying the problem so that it becomes manageable in the course of the research project. As a word of caution, Isaac and Michael (1985) note some common errors in conducting reviews of other studies. These include hurriedly conducting the review and proceeding to do research before having a thorough understanding of the problem; relying too heavily on secondary sources; concentrating on research findings, and overlooking methods and measures; and faulty copying of citations and notes.

Evaluation Research Questions and Subproblems

Sometimes it is difficult to identify or separate the problem from the subproblems. Use of experts and literature often helps define the issue under question and leads to the identification of the proper components to examine. An example of problems and subproblems may be viewed as follows. Today leisure service professionals cite problems with youth-at-risk, and use them as a justification for additional taxpayer support. Leisure service professionals profess that providing recreation programs will have a positive impact on the youth and will reduce crime and gang activity. A number of variables may have some influence on the findings and outcomes. The problem, then, is that we need to justify the influence that recreation programs have on youth-at-risk. Subproblems or related variables that need to be defined, measured, and controlled for could include the facilities used (adequacy, equipment, lighting, location, etc.); leadership presence (style, personality, knowledge, etc.); type of program (sports, social); number, age, and gender of participants; self-concept of participants; local police support attitude or presence; parental involvement and awareness; gang activity or influence; drug and alcohol use and abuse; and school-related programs and support. Table 14.2 provides examples of research questions and associated subordinate questions as an example of the considerations the evaluator must be attentive to and be prepared to address (adapted from Hedrick, Bickman, & Rog, 1993).

Assume we conducted research on a particular community and concluded that recreation programs had a positive impact on youth and lowered crime rates. However, given the nature of the variables listed above, we must question whether or not the increased police activity and involvement had anything to do with lowering the crime rates in the area. Did the school institute drug, alcohol, and gang awareness programs? How did this influence perceptions and rates of leisure involvement? Did the

Table 14.2
Examples of Primary and Secondary Questions

Primary	How prevalent is drug use among high school students?
Secondary	What percentage use cocaine at least weekly?
	What percentage use marijuana daily?
	What percentage sell drugs to other students?
Primary	How many homeless children are there in town?
Secondary	How many are below age 12?
	What percentage are black, white, Hispanic, and Asian?
	What percentage are living in parks?
Primary	Is the park district making optimum use of its staffing?
Secondary	What are the qualifications of staff and their expertise?
	How much time is consumed by maintenance and administrative tasks?
Primary	Did the after-school study hall and play program increase graduation rates for seventh and eighth graders?
Secondary	Were there different rates for male and female students?
Secondary	What kinds of subsequent after-school opportunities did the students pursue?
Secondary	What was the cost per student?

new program make parents more aware of their children's activities? Did the parents make more of an effort to become directly involved with their children's leisure-time involvement? As you can see, the issue becomes quite complex; consequently, we must identify the components (subproblems) of the topic in question in order to better understand the issue, design appropriate methods, and interpret the findings.

Developing a Study Design and Deciding on Data-Collection Method(s)

In terms of choosing methods, the problem must come first. The problem should drive the data collection and analysis procedures. Specifically, the

evaluator must ask: "What questions must be answered?" and "How will they be approached?" The next issue involves the time and resources available. Considerations include the evaluators' time and budget, subjects' time limitations, the setting, or ethical questions.

The evaluator constructs a research design to maximize internal and external validity (see Chapter Three). Attention should be paid to the control and manipulation of variables, establishment of criteria to evaluate the data, and instrumentation (whether to develop an instrument or adapt an existing instrument). As can be seen in the research plan described previously, the evaluator paid particular attention to variables of interest and influence, controlled them through statistical methods, and indicated the development of an instrument.

Choosing Subjects, Conducting the Study, and Collecting the Data

Generalizability is related to the problem of external validity and data collection (sample size). Essentially, the evaluator attempts to determine to what other situations the results apply, other than the sample on which the results are based. The results obtained in one study are limited to the population from which the sample was drawn, if simple random sampling methods are employed (sampling is described later). Evaluators can enlarge the study to include subjects from other areas in order to generalize. If studies repeatedly turn up the same differences or similarities, then the results can be considered generalizable and not simply a characteristic of a single situation.

Although some sample designs, such as nonprobability and simple random designs, are limited in generalizability, steps can be taken to increase the validity of a study. Specifically, purposive or quota samples should employ random selection of subjects. Observational studies should employ random selection of days, times, events, and sites, to reduce bias. Interviews conducted as intercept surveys should be made of every *n*th person entering the interview site. The point is to try to approximate randomness in the technical sense (to provide as equal an opportunity for selection as is possible), and to devise ways of reducing or eliminating sources of error (Sommer & Sommer, 1986).

Beyond sampling technique, the next obvious question is what would be the sample size requirements? Larger samples generally provide more reliable and representative data than small samples. Specifically, larger samples have smaller sampling errors, and greater reliability, and they increase the power of statistical tests applied to the data. However, the reduction in sampling error may not be worth the time, money, and resources. There are arguments that favor small sample sizes, such as that small samples of subjects cost less to administer tests and to conduct the analysis of the findings; and small samples are sometimes more manageable and convenient, especially in exploratory work. In any case, the following should be considered when deciding on the sample size.

1. *Statistical probability level desired.* How accurate do you want the findings to be?

2. *Available resources and time constraints.* Small samples are easier to manage than large ones.

3. *Number of subsets to compare or differentiate.* The sample must contain large enough subsamples for comparison purposes, such as age, and gender, in order to make meaningful comparisons.

4. *Refusals and bad addresses.* Samples sometimes must be increased to allow for unusable data or rejections. For example, if the survey is given to employees, we can generally expect higher return rates than would occur with the general population. The evaluator must consider the topic, its potential interest to the sample, and the length and convenience of the instrument when determining sample sizes.

Finally, a clear description of the sampling method and return rate should be developed for the written report. This allows readers an opportunity to evaluate the generalizability of the data. Perfectly representative samples are difficult to obtain due to out-of-date or incomplete listings of potential respondents. Many evaluators often settle for a less than perfect sampling procedure in order to obtain respondents that are accessible and cooperative (Sommer & Sommer, 1986). However, the evaluator should strive for a comprehensive sample method and report the procedures fully. Once the data are collected, the evaluator is ready to begin the data analysis and reporting phase of the project.

Sampling Information for the Leisure Manager

Leisure service managers must understand some basic sampling terminology in order to evaluate the best method available for their own work, to evaluate other studies, or to guide the development of a request for proposal and subsequent contract with a consultant. Lankford and Neal (1999) offer the following.

Sampling. We could conduct a study of an entire population (sometimes referred to as a complete canvass of a population). The advantages are that we can assume consensus or a count of the target population on some issue or need. An obvious disadvantage is the time, money, and difficulty of controlling the quality of the project. Therefore, we normally take a sample of the target population. The advantages are that there are lower costs, less time, and improved quality control.

Target Population. The target population is the group to be studied, for example, all participants of the soccer program with telephones.

Sampling Frame. Lists, registers, and maps are used to determine the sampling frame, either singly or combined. It is necessary to have all people represented in these lists (to exclude no-one), avoid duplication in the lists (to include no one twice), and be current and accessible to the evaluator. There are two types of sampling frames: (1) those with telephone numbers listed in the directory covering the study area—this type consists of lists of actual elements to be sampled; and (2) those that do not involve using lists of elements to be sampled, but that provide a systematic description of those elements, for example a map of an area within which the target population resides.

Sampling Unit. The sampling unit is the single element of the target population from which the sample is to be selected. This could be the head of the household, a child in the home, and so on.

Random. A random process is one that ensures that every sampling unit has an equal chance of being selected.

Probability Sampling. This means that any individual has the chance to be included in the survey.

Sampling Error (Bias). This refers to discrepancies between the distribution of characters in the sample population and the population as a whole. For example, you are doing a study to find out if people are willing to support a new serial levy to build a new community center and your sample drew too many nontaxpayers.

Sampling Error and Confidence Levels. Quantity is not a substitute for quality. Sampling does not gain in accuracy when the numbers are increased if procedures are biased. Statistical theory identifies the level of error in a sample. At a 95 percent confidence level, the probability of being whole is 5 times out of 100.

Simple Random Sample. To get a random sample a random number is selected to start and used until the size needed is complete. Randomly selected units are chosen from the sampling frame without regard for the demographic or social characteristics of the target population.

Stratified Random Sample. A population is divided into subpopulations, ones stratified by census tracts, income, age, and so on, and every *n*th person is sampled. The procedure for selecting a stratified random sample is first to divide the population into groups which in themselves are relatively homogeneous but differ by selected characteristics. The key is to select a variable that may influence the ability of one group to participate in or use a service. Families with children and without is one such variable, the assumption being that those with children are markets for specific kinds of recreational facilities and services. You can further stratify a sample by subdividing groups according to rural and urban families, for a two-stage stratified random sample. It is important that the sample selected in the first stage be proportionate to the sector or the target population they represent.

Systematic Sample. The strategy used here is to pick every *n*th person (fifth, eighth, etc.), with the first selected at random. You will need to determine the size of the sample desired, and divide the sample size needed for research. First, select a number from 1 to 9000 from a table of random four digit numbers. Assume number 1,622 was selected; next divide 9000 by 400, which

is 22. Take the client roster (sampling frame) and start with number 1,622 as the first unit chosen, then add 22 and select number 1,644 and so on until 400 have been chosen.

Cluster Sample. This sampling technique is used to survey all units in a census tract or other division. Cluster samples save time and money. Select sample units by dividing the sample frame into clusters equal to the size of the total sample. Then select one cluster at random. This method works when population characteristics are distributed throughout the sampling frame. This technique is especially valuable when looking at parks or open space areas.

Sample Size. Questions will arise with regard to what sample size should be used for a study for both budgetary reasons, representativeness of the community, and decision making. Table 14.3 describes the variability due to sampling. Errors due to nonresponse or reporting errors are not reflected in this table. In addition, this table assumes at least a simple random sample. Estimates may be subject to more variability than this table indicates, due to the sample design or the influence of interviewers on the answers obtained; stratification might reduce the sampling error below those figures indicated.

As shown in Table 14.3 chances are 95 in 100 cases that the real population characteristic lies in the range defined by $\pm$ the number indicated in the table, given the percentage of the sample reporting the characteristic and the number of sample cases on which the percentage is based. To use the tables, find your population size on the left side of the table. Then decide how much variation ($\pm$ in percentage points) you want in your findings. For example, if your town is 2,500 in population, you decide

Table 14.3
Sampling Size for Specific Confidence Limits and Precision 95% Confidence Interval (=0.5)

POPULATION

SIZE	+/-1%	+/-2%	+/-3%	+/-4%	+/-5%	+/-10%
500	b	b	b	b	222	83
1,000	b	b	b	385	286	91
1,500	b	b	638	441	316	94
2,000	b	b	714	476	333	95
2,500	b	1,250	769	500	345	96
3,000	b	1,364	811	517	353	97
3,500	b	1,458	843	530	359	97
4,000	b	1,538	870	541	364	98
4,500	b	1,607	891	549	367	98
5,000	b	1,667	909	556	370	98
6,000	b	1,765	938	566	375	98
7,000	b	1,842	959	574	378	99
8,000	b	1,905	976	580	381	99
9,000	b	1,957	989	584	383	99
10,000	5,000	2,000	1,000	588	385	99
15,000	6,000	2,143	1,034	600	390	99
20,000	6,667	2,222	1,053	606	392	100
25,000	7,143	2,273	1,064	610	394	100
50,000	8,333	2,381	1,087	617	397	100
100,000	9,091	2,439	1,099	621	398	100
—	10,000	2,500	1,111	625	400	100

95 percent confidence interval (=0.5).
b = Those cases where 50 percent of the universe in the sample will give more than the required accuracy.

Source: Modified from Yamane, T. (1967). *Elementary sampling theory.* Englewood Cliffs; NJ: Prentice-Hall; and Sudman, S. (1976). *Applied sampling.* New York:Academic Press.

that ± in 5 percent is sufficient, so 345 people need to be surveyed (assuming a large return rate). Assume your findings indicate that 62 percent of the respondents support the new swimming pool. This percentage could vary from 57 percent to 67 percent.

Conduct Data Analysis and Report Findings and Results

As a guide for analysis and writing, the evaluator should consider three questions: (1) how much? (2) how many? and (3) compared to what

(Schmerl, 1988)? The "how much" and "how many" are easily communicated and analyzed in most studies. However, the "compared to what" question is really at the heart of what we are trying to do in research, because it specifically guides us in the collection, analysis and compilation of data. Schmerl notes that it is an organizing principle, beginning with the tentative idea of how the data might be usefully compiled (displayed) for comparison and discussion. Specifically, the evaluator needs to focus on the hypothesis and raw data, then determine the most efficient and comprehensive means of designing tables and graphs to present the important pieces of data.

Systematic Procedures for an Evaluation

When the leisure service organization decides to conduct an evaluation of services, surveys (mail, telephone, intercept, and interviews) are most often the choice of the evaluators (Mitra & Lankford, 1999). In fact, it has been suggested that surveys may be the only efficient means of obtaining information (Elmquist, 1988; Stipak, 1980; Watson, Juster, & Johnson, 1991; Webb & Hatry, 1973) for community needs assessments, attitudes and evaluation of programs and services.

When conducting an evaluation for a leisure organization, the evaluator must work with the leisure service manager to determine, agree upon, and execute the following tasks. Figure 14.2 presents the flowchart for conducting an evaluation of a major program (Lankford & Neal, 1999). Figure 14.3 presents another version of this flowchart. This process was used to develop a major needs assessment for the U.S. Army Hawaii's Morale, Welfare, and Recreation program (Lankford, 1994). You can see that the process is divided into a draft and approval phase; a data collection and analysis phase; and data interpretation, solution, and questionnaire design. It is important to note that this process used focus groups, both intercept surveys (at random facilities and times) and mail-out surveys, and a trend analysis survey (comparative survey of worldwide successful programs and services). Another unique feature of Figure 14.3 is that the final steps included staff meetings to discuss program implications with the evaluator. This feature allows the staff to better understand the findings, and ideally leads to use of the findings and further recommendations.

Obviously, a minor program evaluation would not go through all of these steps. It is also important to note that although there is a progression of steps, they are not purely sequential. In any case, the steps are as follows:

Preliminary Steps

1. Determine objectives (the problem(s) or question) of the study and obtain approval to conduct the evaluation.

2. Select the most appropriate survey method (mail, interview, telephone, observation, or a combination of methods).

3. List necessary resources (people, money, and materials).

4. Establish the accuracy level desired (usually 95 percent confidence interval, ± 5 percent).

Make a budget estimate and secure the necessary financial support.

Figure 14.2
Flowchart of the Research Process

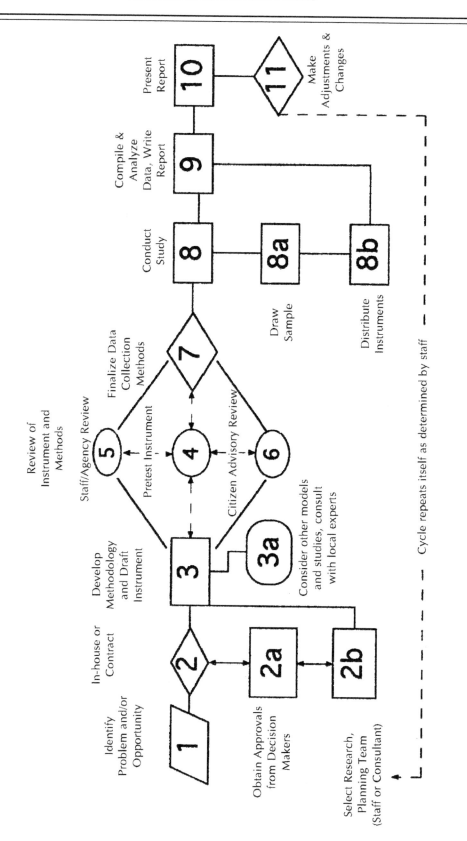

Figure 14.3
Needs Assessment Process of
U.S. Army Hawaii's Morale, Welfare, and Recreation Program

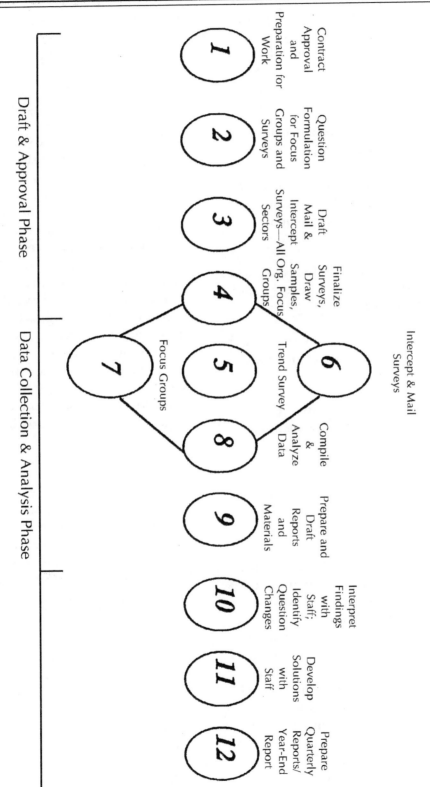

Develop a timeline for the project (with exact tasks for each person and due dates)

Operational steps are implemented after the evaluator, manager, staff, and others (possibly the community and decision-making groups) agree upon the preliminary steps. These are as follows:

Operational Steps to the Evaluation

1. Draw a sample (choose the people or units to be interviewed or questioned) from a comprehensive list.

2. Develop an initial questionnaire (determine appropriate techniques and proper order).

3. Pretest the questionnaire and make the final changes; develop the final questionnaire.

4. Distribute the survey via mail, intercept, or interview method.

5. Collect the data (it should be noted that a response rate of 50 to 60 percent or better usually provides data from respondents that is not statistically different from those people who did not respond to the study. Therefore, the leisure manager must insist on high response rates from the evaluator, or else the decisions made using the data may be flawed from the beginning. Dillman (1978) notes that to get a response from the survey being used, it may take from 5 to 15 phone calls (in the case of telephone surveys), two to three mailings (for a mail-out survey), or three to five visits to a home or business (in the case of personal interviews).

6. Edit and code the questionnaire for analysis, checking for errors. Use of a spreadsheet to enter the data is sufficient for generating tables and graphs, as well as to provide descriptive statistics.

7. Analyze the data using descriptive statistics and cross-tabulations of male/female, age, user/nonuser, and occupation. The leisure manager must know beforehand which variables need to be cross-tabulated with other variables. This is based on the research questions in the beginning of the study. Do not allow the consultant to charge excessive rates for each cross-tabulation. It happens too often that some consultants build into the work plan a clause that each cross-tabulation (for example, percentages of male and female responses on Question 1, etc.) would cost the leisure organization upwards of $35 or more. This does not sound like much, but when you have a survey with 25 to 40 questions, it limits what can be accomplished with the data.

8. Report the results (e.g., summary, findings, conclusions, and recommendations) to the staff and the community. Discuss the findings, revise the report, and revise the analysis, if needed. Use the findings; otherwise, the effort and data are not useable, and are a waste of money and time.

Some possible areas for evaluation of programs and needs assessments include, but are not limited to, the following.

Demographic. Demographics aren't needed in every study but may be used for comparison with other data to indicate the representatives of the sample or for cross-tabulations with other data collected. It is recommended that any data be compared with the U.S. Census for the community being studied.

Leisure Behavior. This refers to frequency of use of areas, facilities and programs, barriers and constraints, ceasing participation, what prompts participation, and variations (e.g., seasonal changes).

Leisure Needs. These refer to the preferences, wishes, desires, etc. of participants.

Opinions, Attitudes, and Facility Attributes. The adequacy of facilities and parks, the need for new facilities, the location of a facility, the safety of an area, and design issues in terms of access and safety might also be explored.

Opinions, Attitudes and Program Attributes. These include program location and hours of operation, level or quality of leadership of front-line staff, the quality of staff (competence, courtesy, etc.), the quality of a program (customer service), leisure motivations, program effectiveness, the reputation and image of a program and its instructor, specific proposed policies, and adequacy of public information or promotional materials.

Strategies for Getting What You Want from Your Survey

Leisure service managers need to have some idea of what they want from the research and evaluation effort in order to guide the project. Additionally, they need to be able to make the most of the findings to have the greatest impact. What follow are general guidelines to help leisure service managers make sure the effort has the maximum impact on decision makers, the community, and staff (Lankford & Neal, 1999).

1. Make the investment of time and effort to contact policymakers. Informed policymakers will be more likely to support the project and its eventual recommendations.

2. Have a willingness to sacrifice your own research agenda or direction; be willing to adjust and be flexible. When the community, policymakers, or staff have ideas, be flexible. This allows ownership in the project.

3. Involve policymakers in the research process. Many successful projects involve people who have a possible say in the eventual project and its outcomes. These people will be less likely to criticize the effort if they have been involved with the study. Their involvement shows how carefully you have structured the study and data collection.

   a. Design the research instrument.

   b. Select the variables to be studied.

   c. Determine the scope of the study.

   d. Collect data in the field.

4. Have a work session or seminar with key policymakers and officials or citizens to involve them in drafting the final document.

   a. This creates a situation in which they are supportive of findings and hesitant to criticize.

   b. The work session helps to internalize the findings; there fore, the study becomes part of their mind-set, and they will support the final document.

5. Cultivate the media–get the media involved in research effort.

    a. If the public is aware, they will most likely support your efforts. You will need a contact person for the media.

6. Regarding language choice; speak human language to policymakers and members of the community. Do not use jargon in the presentation of the report or in the text of the report. Presentation should not be more than about 15 minutes long. Break-out sessions and follow-up meetings are necessary to allow people time to digest the material and its recommendations.

7. Avoid research that treats research findings as reality. Use soft, conservative language, such as, "The results appear to suggest that . . . " rather than, "The study proves what we have known all along. The program needs to be eliminated."

8. Be rigorous in the research approach. Using systematic methods is your best ally and proves you were concerned with a quality approach.

9. Be aware of and knowledgeable about political processes and the political situation before, during, and after the study process.

10. Importantly, the leisure manager must get out in the trenches when the data-collection process is underway. Be seen! This shows that you are supportive, involved, and concerned about the issue being studied.

Summary

In the first part of the chapter, we explored what constitutes systematic research, evaluation research, and applied research. Systematic research suggests specific, purposive steps to ensure that the findings are representative and reliable and that the methodology is valid. Evaluation research is commonly referred to as applied in nature. Evaluation research is conducted when we need to answer immediate problems and to suggest changes in programs, policies, goals, and objectives.

The latter part of the chapter discussed procedural issues that the leisure service manager must be aware of relative to evaluation, needs assessment, and research. Often the leisure service organization contracts for this type of research for a variety of reasons, such as lack of expertise, need for an outside perspective, or lack of resources (staffing, funding, etc.). It is important for the leisure service manager to understand basic terminology in order to develop requests for proposals or internal work plans for evaluative work, and to successfully evaluate a consultant's work plan and final product.

It was noted in this chapter that the leisure service manager can learn more about evaluation methodology through training and other related books. It was also noted that the manager and staff should be concerned with the quality of the approach being taken, regardless of whether it is undertaken in-house or with a consultant. Simply because a consultant does the evaluation and research does not imply that it is necessarily of adequate quality.

Discussion Questions

1. Discuss what is meant by basic, applied, and evaluation research.

2. What is the role of the leisure service manager in initiating evaluation studies?

3. What is meant by "systematic" research?

4. What steps are involved in an evaluation study?

5. What does the manager need to be aware of in terms of sampling?

6. What is an adequate response rate for a study?

7. What is nonresponse bias, and how does it affect findings of the study?

8. What size sample should you use for your community?

9. What strategies would you use to position the study effort to have the longest impact on the community?

10. Discuss what types of services need to be evaluated in your community?

References

Allison, M. T. (1995). The question of relevance: Introductory comments. *Leisure Science*, 17(2), 121–124.

Bedini, L. A., & Wu, Y. (1994). A Methodological of Review Research in *Therapeutic Recreation Journal* from 1986 to 1990. *Therapeutic Recreation Journal* (Second Quarter). 87–97.

Bialeschki, D. (1994, May). What's happening in our curriculum in recreation, parks resources, leisure sciences. *Parks and Recreation*, 27.

Chadwick, B. A., Bahr, H. M., & Albrecht, S. C. (1984). *Social science research methods*. Englewood Cliffs, N J: Prentice-Hall.

Dillman, D. A. (1978). *Mail and telephone surveys: The total design method*. New York: Wiley & Sons.

Edginton, C. R., Hanson, C. J., & Edginton, S. R. (1992). *Leisure programming: Concepts, trends, and professional practice* (2nd ed.). Dubuque, IA: Brown & Benchmark.

Elmquist, M. (1988, June). Hitting the jackpot with citizen surveys. *Planning*, 20–22.

Ewert, A. (1990). Decision-making techniques for establishing research agendas in park and recreation systems. *Journal of Park and Recreation Administration*. 8(2), 1–13.

Hedrick, T. E., Bickman, L., & Rog, D. J. (1993). *Applied research design: A practical guide*. Newbury Park, CA: Sage.

Henderson, K. A. (1994, July). Not for researchers only. *Parks and Recreation*, 14–17.

Henderson, K. A., & Bedini, L. A. (1994, January). Emerging cultural paradigms and changes in leisure sciences. *Parks and Recreation*. 24–28.

Henderson, K. A., & Bialeschki, M. D. (1995). *Evaluating leisure services: Making enlightened decisions*. State College, PA; Venture.

Henderson, K. A., & O'Neill, J. (1995, January). Has research contributed to the advancement of professional practice? *Parks and Recreation*, 17.

Isaac, S., & Michael, M. B. (1985). *Handbook in research and evaluation*. San Diego, CA: Ed.

Krauss, R., & Allen, L. (1987). *Research and evaluation in recreation, parks, and leisure studies*. Columbus, OH: Publishing Horizons.

Lankford, S.V. (1990). *A research method for community surveys*. Unpublished monograph, Department of Planning, Public Policy, and Management, University of Oregon, Eugene.

Lankford, S.V. (1994). *Market research strategies and methods* (U.S. Army Hawaii, MWR Department, Marketing Division). Honolulu, HI: University of Hawaii, Department of Kinesiology and Leisure Science.

Lankford, S.V., & Neal, L. L. (1999). *Survey research for communities in the Northwest Territories of Canada* (Workshop Manual for Municipal and Community Affairs, Sport North and Aboriginal Sports Federation). Professional Services, World Leisure and Recreation Association.

Lankford, S.V., & Privatsky, L. (1989). *A study of evaluation competencies of park and recreation personnel in the Pacific Northwest*. Unpublished monograph, Department of Leisure Studies and Services, University of Oregon, Eugene.

Leedy, P. D. (1985). *Practical research: Planning and design.* New York: Macmillan.

Majchrzak, A. M. (1984). *Methods for policy research.* Newbury Park, CA. Sage.

McLean, D., Bannon, J. J., & Gray, H. R. (1999). *Leisure resources: Its comprehensive planning* (2nd Ed.). Champaign, IL: Sagamore Publishing .

McMillan, J. H., & Schumacher, S. (1984). *Research in education: A conceptual introduction.* Boston: Little, Brown.

Mitra, A., & Lankford, S. V. (1999). *Research methods in parks, recreation, and leisure services.* Champaign, IL: Sagamore Publishing .

Murphy, J. F., Niepoth, E. W., Jamieson, L. M., & Williams, J. G. (1991). *Leisure systems: Critical concepts and applications.* Champaign, IL: Sagamore Publishing .

Nachmias, D., & Nachmias, C. (1987). *Research methods in the social sciences.* New York: St. Martin's Press.

President's Commission on Americans Outdoor (1998.) *A literature's review.* Washington, DC: Government Printing Office.

Rossi, P. H., Freeman, H. E., & Wright, S. R. (1980). *Evaluation: A systematic approach.* Beverly Hills, CA: Sage.

Rossi, P. H., Wright, J. D., & Wright, P. H. (1978). The theory and practice of applied social research. *Evaluation Quarterly, 2,* 171–191.

Rossman, R. J. (1995). *Recreation programming: Designing leisure experiences.* (2nd Ed.). Champaign, IL: Sagamore Publishing .

Schmerl, R. B. (1988). Written communication. In H. C. Dandekar (Ed.), *The planner's use of information: Techniques for collection, organization, and communication.* Chicago: American Planning Association.

Short, E. C. (1991). *Forms of curriculum inquiry.* Albany: State University of New York Press.

Sommer, R. S., & Sommer, B. B. (1986). *A practical guide to behavioral research: Tools and techniques.* New York: Oxford University Press.

Stipak, B. (1980, Sept./Oct.). Local government's use of citizen surveys. *American Society of Public Administration.* 521–525.

Stoddard, R. H. (1982). *Field techniques and research methods in geography.* Dubuque, IA: Kendall/Hunt.

Sudman, S. (1976). *Applied sampling.* New York: Academic Press.

Thomas, J. R., & French, K. E. (1986). The use of meta-analysis in exercise and sport: A tutorial. *Research Quarterly for Exercise and Sport, 57,* 196–204.

Thomas, J. R., & Nelson, J. K. (1990). *Research methods in physical activity.* Champaign, IL: Human Kinetics.

Watson, D. J., Juster, R. J., & Johnson, G. W. (1991). Institutionalized use of citizen surveys in budgetary and policy-making processes: A small city case study. *Public Administration Review, 51* (3), 232–239.

Webb, K., & Hatry, H. P. (1973). *Obtaining citizen feedback: The application of citizen surveys to local governments.* Washington, DC: The Urban Land Institute.

Yamane, T. (1967). *Elementary sampling theory.* Englewood Cliffs, NJ: Prentice-Hall.

Index